*Professional Gentlemen:
The Professions in Nineteenth-Century
Ontario*

R.D. GIDNEY AND W.P.J. MILLAR

*Professional Gentlemen:
The Professions in Nineteenth-
Century Ontario*

A publication of the
Ontario Historical Studies Series
for the Government of Ontario
Published by the University of Toronto Press
Toronto Buffalo London

© Her Majesty the Queen in right of the Province of Ontario 1994

Printed in Canada

ISBN 0-8020-0619-1 (cloth)
ISBN 0-8020-7580-0 (paper)

Printed on acid-free paper

Canadian Cataloguing in Publication Data

Gidney, R.D. (Robert Douglas), 1940–
 Professional gentlemen : the professions in
 nineteenth-century Ontario

 (Ontario historical studies series)
 Includes index.
 ISBN 0-8020-0619-1 (bound) ISBN 0-8020-7580-0 (pbk.)

 1. Professions – Ontario – History – 19th century.
 I. Millar, W. P. J. (Winnifred Phoebe Joyce),
 1942–   . II. Title. III. Series.

 HD8038.C32O54 1994   331.7'12'09713   C94-931189-8

This book has been published with the assistance of funds
provided by the Government of Ontario through the Ministry
of Culture, Tourism and Recreation.

For the past and the future

Frederick Gourlay Millar (1876–1972)

and

Catherine Anne Gidney (b. 1969)

Contents

The Ontario Historical Studies Series
  Goldwin French, Peter Oliver, Jeanne Beck, and Maurice Careless *ix*

Preface *xi*

Part One: The Making of Professions in a New Society

  1 Images and Transcripts *3*

  2 Compromises and Competitors *26*

  3 The Moment of Mid-Century Radicalism *49*

  4 The Placid Progress of the Law *70*

  5 Doctors and the Price of Occupational Closure *85*

  6 The Ministry: Coming to Terms with Disestablishment *106*

  7 Professional Work *125*

  8 Professional Education *152*

  9 Making Careers, Making Money, Making a Place *180*

Part Two: Reconstructing Profession

Reconstructing Profession: An Introduction *203*

10 Parvenus *212*

11 Professions 'Overcrowded' *248*

12 Clergymen and the Ascendancy of the Laity *268*

13 Professional Organizations at Bay *283*

14 The Impact of a Changing Political Culture *303*

15 'Who Was Then a Gentleman?' *322*

16 Portents Bleak, and Promising *335*

17 The Universities and Professional Education *354*

18 Retrospect *377*

Appendix: Procedures and Sources for Quantitative Analysis *393*

Notes *407*

Index *497*

The Ontario Historical Studies Series

For many years the principal theme in English-Canadian historical writing has been the emergence and the consolidation of the Canadian nation. This theme has been developed in uneasy awareness of the persistence and importance of regional interests and identities, but because of the central role of Ontario in the growth of Canada, Ontario has not been seen as a region. Almost unconsciously, historians have equated the history of the province with that of the nation and have often depicted the interests of other regions as obstacles to the unity and welfare of Canada.

The creation of the province of Ontario in 1867 was the visible embodiment of a formidable reality, the existence at the core of the new nation of a powerful if disjointed society whose traditions and characteristics differed in many respects from those of the other British North American colonies. The intervening century has not witnessed the assimilation of Ontario to the other regions in Canada; on the contrary, it has become a more clearly articulated entity. Within the formal geographical and institutional framework defined so assiduously by Ontario's political leaders, an increasingly intricate web of economic and social interests has been woven and shaped by the dynamic interplay between Toronto and its hinterland. The character of this regional community has been formed in the tension between a rapid adaptation to the processes of modernization and industrialization in modern Western society and a reluctance to modify or discard traditional attitudes and values. Not surprisingly, the Ontario outlook has been, and in some measure still is, a compound of aggressiveness, conservatism, and the conviction that its values should be the model for the rest of Canada.

From the outset the objective of the Series' Board of Trustees was to describe and analyse the historical development of Ontario as a distinct region within Canada. The Series includes biographies of several premiers, and thematic studies on the growth of the provincial economy, educational institutions, labour, welfare, the Franco-Ontarians, the Native Peoples, and the arts.

Professional Gentlemen is an account of the development of the professions in nineteenth-century Ontario. The authors begin by 'considering what Upper Canadians themselves meant' by the term 'profession' and their conception of the 'place of the professions' in their society. In practice, they recognized three professions – lawyers, doctors, and clergy, who shared broadly a complex set of assumptions about the relationship among liberal education, specialized knowledge, status, and income. Despite the efforts of these groups to define and protect their status, the notion of 'profession' began to change in the latter half of the century, and other groups such as engineers and teachers sought recognition as 'professions.' By 1900 the clergy had become ministers dependent on their congregations for their salaries, and the privileges of law and medicine were under attack. An 'uninstructed' but powerful public had emerged as the serious threat to the place of professional men in Ontario society.

R.D. Gidney and W.P.J. Millar have written a scholarly, thorough, and thoughtful work on a subject hitherto largely unexplored in its Ontario context. It will be an indispensable source for all those interested in the past and present roles of the professions in Ontario's social and political order. We hope that it will stimulate new research and writing on this significant subject.

The editors and the Board of Trustees are grateful to R.D. Gidney and W.P.J. Millar for undertaking this task.

GOLDWIN FRENCH
PETER OLIVER
JEANNE BECK
J.M.S. CARELESS

Toronto
August 1993

* The corporation known as the Ontario Historical Studies Series ceased to exist 31 August 1993. This volume was completed and approved for publication before 31 August 1993.

Preface

As its title indicates, this is a book about the professions in nineteenth-century Ontario. But what do we mean when we speak of a profession? For centuries the word has carried two parallel meanings in English.¹ Used in one sense, it is simply a synonym, or a polite euphemism, for any occupation or job. 'And what,' a person might ask a stranger at a cocktail party, 'is your profession?' But the word has always had a more restricted meaning as well, referring to some kinds of occupations and not others. In this sense, the practice of medicine is described as a profession, and factory work is not. Our study focuses on those occupations which are commonly thought to constitute professions in this second, more restrictive, meaning of the word.

There is now an enormous literature devoted to elucidating the special character of the professions in the modern world. While some of it has helped to inform our work in various ways, it is generally of limited use in understanding the past.² For one thing, the traits often used to identify a profession provide an uncertain or even misleading historical guide. In the eighteenth and early nineteenth centuries, for example, the English barrister was indubitably a member of a profession; yet the bar lacked any formal requirements for professional training and had no professional association.³ Far into the nineteenth century, moreover, leading members of the bar remained profoundly sceptical about the necessity or usefulness of an academic education in the law.⁴ Similarly, much recent literature excludes the clergyman or the military officer because neither fits tidily into modern conceptions of what constitutes a profession. Yet in the past both were pre-eminent professions compared, say, with medicine. As the American historian Gerald Geison argues,

> there is, in fact, good reason to suspect that all of the existing models of professions and professionalization are inadequate to some degree and in some

respects. Whether they conceive of professionalization as the emergence of benign, apolitical, 'non-economic,' and homogeneous 'communities of the competent,' or whether they see it as a conspiratorial, stratifying, and exploitative process in tune with the needs of capitalism, the existing models are simply unable to account for the richly diverse forms and distribution of professional groups as we meet them in actual historical experience.[5]

Some sociologists have come around to that viewpoint as well. After more than a decade's work exploring its meaning, Eliot Freidson, the foremost American theorist of the professions, concluded that the concept is not generic but rather historical and parochial, with ambiguous, contradictory, and varied meanings arising from a particular time and place. Identifying traits is a useful and even necessary task, Freidson acknowledges, for without them we cannot describe or define the phenomenon we propose to study. But they must be treated as historically contingent, and understood in that context.[6]

What, then, do we mean when we speak of a profession? Because it is a historically grounded concept, its meaning must emerge from a close study of the ways in which people understood it in the past, rather than by ahistorical theorizing. Ontario was born in the transitional decades between the eighteenth and nineteenth centuries. It was a product of the Anglo-American world of the Georgian era. The social and political assumptions shared by Upper Canadians were rooted in that context. Those assumptions were, in many respects, profoundly different from ours, and sometimes uncongenial to the modern mind. Yet, as is true for Ontario's larger history, the ways in which the colony's founders construed the professions would play a large part in shaping what the professions were to become in modern society.

Thus our study begins by considering what Upper Canadians themselves meant by the term, and how they conceived of the place of the professions in their own society. Throughout the rest of Part One, we will explore the world of the professional gentleman in Upper Canada, focusing first on the transfer of assumptions and institutions from Great Britain, and then on the constraints and modifications a new environment imposed upon them. Though we speak here of Upper Canada, and will generally retain that nomenclature in this section of the book, we will pursue these themes far into the third quarter of the nineteenth century, and after the colony had become the new province of Ontario. Part One concludes with three chapters which attempt to portray aspects of professional lives – work, education, and careers – primarily in the middle decades of the century. In Part Two, which begins with its own introduction, we will cross-cut back across the century, picking up the larger political, economic, and social forces which, by the late nineteenth century, would gradually transform the congeries of occupations included among the professions, and begin the reconstruction of the meaning of profession itself.

WHILE WE WILL deal with a considerable range of occupations in the chapters that follow, we have also been selective. Cumulatively the surviving sources are very extensive, and limits of space, as well as time, constrained our efforts to broaden our occupational base. In any case, it was never our intent to present a comprehensive catalogue of all forms of work which might be considered as 'professional,' however loosely the term is construed. This book is as much about an idea as it is about varieties of work, and our aim has been to use a few exemplary cases, and to use them in a comparative way, to illustrate our overarching themes. Thus the Christian ministry is represented by Anglicans, Presbyterians, and Wesleyan Methodists; we have not, however, attempted to integrate the histories of other Protestant denominations or of Roman Catholics. Similarly dentists and teachers receive a good deal of attention; others, such as military officers, pharmacists, or nurses, are hardly more than mentioned in passing. Even then we do not pretend to present a full-scale history of any occupation. In the main, the task of writing comprehensive 'occupational biographies' remains to be done by other historians and in other books. We hope, nonetheless, that a selective approach, set in a comparative context, offers insights about the political, social, and economic history of professional work that studies of individual occupations do not, and indeed cannot, accomplish.

In the name of stylistic felicity, we have taken some liberties with our terminology. Often enough we use 'clergyman' and 'minister' interchangeably, though, strictly speaking, that kind of usage was not common before mid-century. Similarly we sometimes refer to the Churches of England or Scotland as 'Anglican' or 'Presbyterian,' and to both as 'established' or as 'the national churches,' though such phraseology is also technically incorrect. There are other examples besides. In all cases, we should add, 'clerical' refers to ministers and not clerks. Throughout the chapters that follow, moreover, the reader will frequently find the word 'laity,' or one of its variants, juxtaposed against 'professional.' We speak, for example, of the lay or secular press in contrast to the various professional journals, of lay as against professional opinion. But this means that a professional in one chapter can turn into a member of the laity in the next – that is, someone who does not belong to the occupation we happen to be dealing with.

Any generic use of a term like the 'laity' has its own problems. We recognize that it does not represent a homogeneous entity but rather a profoundly segmented one, divided along lines of gender, class, race, geography, and other things besides. Where appropriate, we try to take account of these differences. But in a book such as this, it is essential to have some literary fiction which enables us to contrast and compare, primarily and without undue verbiage, those who were 'insiders,' members of a particular occupation or professionals as a group, and those who were 'outsiders.' For the same reason we also use the term in order to distinguish between *expressed* public opinion and the views of professionals themselves.

DURING THE RESEARCH and writing of this book we have accumulated many intellectual debts. First and foremost, we want to express our appreciation to the three editors of the Ontario Historical Studies Series (OHSS), Goldwin French, Peter Oliver, and Jeanne Beck, who were unfailingly supportive, offered us good advice and sound criticism from beginning to end, and at critical moments did their best to save us from ourselves. Despite their own busy schedules, a number of friends and colleagues have volunteered to read drafts of chapters, or indeed large portions of the manuscript, and we have benefited greatly from their thoughtful commentary and encouragement. Thus our special thanks to Jennifer and J.T.H. Connor, Rebecca Coulter, Gordon Darroch, Alison Prentice, S.E.D. Shortt, Marguerite Van Die, John Harley Warner, and William Westfall. Jacalyn Duffin kindly allowed us to read an early draft of her book on James Langstaff. Others provided us with their unpublished research papers or directed us to material we would not have discovered ourselves; we hope their generosity is adequately acknowledged in the text or the notes. All sins of commission and omission remain our own.

The financial assistance provided by the Board of Trustees of the OHSS was indispensable to the completion of this project. So was the support, financial and otherwise, of successive deans of the Faculty of Education, The University of Western Ontario, from Paul Park to B.B. Kymlicka. Confronted by our demands for more information than they could reasonably be expected to provide, and more boxes than they could reasonably be expected to cart, archivists across the province have managed to remain gracious and helpful: all of the staff of the Archives of Ontario, and especially Karen Bergsteinsson; the United Church of Canada Archives; the Anglican Church of Canada General Synod Archives; the Baldwin Room of the Metropolitan Toronto Reference Library; the Queen's University Archives; the University of Western Ontario Regional Collection; the Law Society of Upper Canada

Archives; the now defunct Toronto Academy of Medicine Archives; and the Faculty of Dentistry Library, University of Toronto.

Our daughter Catherine worked interminable hours over several summers as a research assistant and girl Friday. Indexing the *Globe* taught her fortitude; cutting the lawns taught her character. Or we, at least, like to think so. During the course of this project, moreover, she transformed herself, against our best advice and probably her own best interests, from a high-school student to an apprentice historian. We hope this book is a modest exemplar for her. Finally, to Frederick Gourlay Millar, an archetypal nineteenth-century professional gentleman, and his daughter Helen Millar Becker, our fond remembrance and our gratitude respectively, for providing us with the perfect place to write and, probably more important, to think.

R. D. GIDNEY and W. P. J. MILLAR
Smokehouse Island
Oliphant, Ontario
July 1993

*Part One:
The Making of Professions
in a New Society*

1
Images and Transcripts

Like their contemporaries elsewhere, Upper Canadians sometimes used the word 'profession' in its inclusive sense, to refer to a wide variety of ways in which individuals earned their living. But in its more restrictive meaning, they applied it almost exclusively to divinity, medicine, and the law – the three quintessentially 'learned' or 'liberal' professions, whose origins dated back to the medieval universities and beyond. In 1810, for example, an anonymous correspondent to the *Kingston Gazette* wrote, in passing, that 'a small part of the community need to prepare themselves for the learned professions, for a small proportion only will be useful as divines, lawyers, or physicians.'[1] In a speech in the Assembly in 1825, one politician objected to any monopoly of the professions, which included 'gentlemen of the law, church and physic.'[2] And such definitions were still conventional well past mid-century. Indeed, any more inclusive list was as likely as not to name another occupation traditionally defined as a profession, that of military officer. 'When a parent was thinking of occupations for his sons,' said one legislator in 1854, 'he looked round on the professions which would secure their positions in society, and said one would enter the army, another the bar, or [the] medical and another the church.'[3]

But what did people mean by the term '*learned*' profession? It did not refer primarily to training in the skills of a particular craft. Obviously no professional man who wanted to make a living could expect to succeed without mastering a certain amount of technical knowledge. But to be learned required something else besides – and something more highly valued in the Georgian and early Victorian world than expertise itself.[4] That was the acquisition of a liberal education. Physicians, barristers, and clergymen had, ideally at least, attended one of the ancient British universities and studied the languages and literature of ancient Greece and Rome. If they had had no opportunity or time to attend a university, they had been introduced to Latin at a grammar school. At a time when familiarity with the classical languages was a *sine qua non* of the educated man, entrance to a learned profession, even on the rudest frontier, demanded proof of classical attainments.[5] When Charles Duncombe and John Rolph attempted to open the first medical school in Upper Canada, at St Thomas in 1824, their advertisement included the warning that 'every student before admission is expected to have a complete knowledge of the LATIN language, or to give satisfactory assurances of immediately acquiring it; for which purposes a competent teacher will be resident in the village.'[6] Applicants were frequently refused licences to practise medicine in the colony, as were two in 1825, because they were 'deficient in Pharmaceutical Chymistry and classical education.'[7] And in 1820 the Law Society introduced a rule requiring students 'to give a written translation in the presence of the Society of a portion of one of Cicero's Orations or perform such other exercise as may satisfy the Society of his acquaintance with Latin and English composition and ... no person who cannot give proofs of a liberal education shall hereafter be admitted upon their books.'[8]

Since the point is sometimes misunderstood, it is perhaps worth reiterating that classics were not required primarily because they gave access to the technical knowledge of a craft. It might indeed be the case that the clergyman needed a knowledge of koine Greek to rightly interpret the New Testament, though classical Greek alone unlocked no keys in that respect. A modicum of Latin might be necessary if doctors were to understand the formulas necessary to prepare their own prescriptions. But an acquaintance with the classics was prized for other reasons entirely. When, in 1832, three Niagara doctors complained about the low state of the medical profession, they focused not upon medical skills but upon 'the want of liberal information and of those respectable attainments that should characterize members of a learned body, and which are absolutely essential to inspire the people with confidence in the healing art.'[9] Or consider the comment of a schoolboy friend of the young Robert Baldwin, written in 1819 – a juvenile effusion but telling nonetheless:

My dear Baldwin you cannot think how much I feel for the want ... of a classical education. The Law is like many things else it requires a good scholar; those who are not so, are bound to act in an inferior degree: this I cannot bear; my mind aspires to the acme of my profession, which I never can attain, understanding nothing with facility but English authors. Do not blame me when I say I envy you in the knowledge of Latin & Greek ... When in company should a subject be started in which latin is necessarily introduced I redden, avert my head, and feel as if people were looking at me and ready to say translate that.[10]

What both these quotations point to is the social role that classics played in nineteenth-century society. They conferred authority upon expertise. And they could do this because they were hallmarks of a liberal education – that education possessed by, and requisite to the status of, a gentleman. They were not the only requisites, it is true; but they were a critical component, for they bestowed upon the recipient the qualities of character and culture which constituted one of the badges of his social authority, and which legitimized his right to be recognized as a gentleman before his peers and the world at large.[11]

The education of a professional man, however, extended beyond an acquaintance with the classical languages, and there was no sharp distinction between this first or preliminary stage of a liberal education, obtained in a grammar school or through more advanced studies in classics, mathematics, and philosophy in a university, and the content of professional education itself. What made the professions 'learned' was the embedding of their specialist knowledge or technical expertise in the science of law, medicine, or theology. And here we are using 'science' in the way it was used until late in the nineteenth century to refer to any body of logically coherent, rational, systematized knowledge. In this sense professional education was conceived to be a part of, or an extension of, a liberal education comprising both general and specialist components. All educated men would learn something of the law and its principles from their study of ancient politics and jurisprudence and from modern history or philosophy, just as they would have passing familiarity with the science of theology.[12] But such subjects would also enrich and inform, in an especially pertinent way, the specialist studies pursued by the student-at-law. Theologues would learn the ancient tongues or immerse themselves in mental or moral philosophy not only as part of their general education but as a necessary scaffolding for interpreting scripture or understanding theology. A preliminary education was, in other words, both preparatory to and part of professional education, while the latter built upon but also encompassed the ground of the liberal arts and sciences. To practise a learned profession was to apply the liberal sciences to the most central concerns of society – to make manifest the accumulated knowledge and wisdom of the past in the arts of government and the cure of bodies and souls. In a telling phrase, one medical practitioner could speak of each of the three learned professions as one leg in the 'tripod of a country's erudition.'[13]

To have a profession, then, was to have more than an occupation. It was to lay claim to full membership in that group which was to guide the destinies of Upper Canada by providing it with its political leadership, its central social values, its ruling ideas, its erudition. Before the 1840s, Robert Fraser persuasively argues, Upper Canada's dominant élite believed that their society must be ordered by hierarchy, stability, and agrarianism, and led by gentlemen rooted in the land. Borrowed from an idealized model of the Georgian social structure in Britain, such convictions assumed the existence of an aristocracy and a landed gentry. In Upper Canada, however, an aristocracy proved hard to establish, and thus, according to its self-proclaimed gentry at least, 'social leadership devolved upon those who most nearly approximated the attributes of an aristocracy.'[14] It consisted of the few, in John Beverley Robinson's words, who had 'the advantages of education, of superior intelligence, and of wealth, and of respectable stations in society, whether arising from public employment or from the exercise of the liberal professions.'[15] These, then, were to be Upper Canada's gentlemen. While it conferred a status upon them that might have been contested in Britain, it was not entirely incongruent with the ethos at home; even there, the meaning of 'gentleman' had long been somewhat ambiguous and, especially from the late eighteenth century onwards, the ideal of the 'professional gentleman' was increasingly pervasive.[16] Indeed, by the Victorian period, writes Arthur Engel,

> high social position was a crucial element in people's conception of professional work. Anthony Trollope expressed succinctly this popular understanding in his definition of a profession as 'a calling by which a gentleman, not born to the inheritance of a gentleman's allowance of good things, might ingeniously obtain the same by some exercise of his abilities.' To the middle and upper classes, the idea of the 'gentleman' was the most important of status distinctions. It embodied the ideal of ruling-class egalitarianism: all men were certainly not socially equal, but all gentlemen were. Fundamentally, a profession was an occupation which a gentleman could follow without losing his claim to this coveted social position.[17]

Upper Canada, then, was to be led by gentlemen, including 'professional gentlemen,' who held respectable positions in society, even if they owned no great estates, and who, by their education and character, would, as John Beverley Robinson put it, 'exercise a salutary influence in society.'[18]

Still, in early nineteenth-century Upper Canada, as in England, not all those engaged in preaching, doctoring, or lawyering were automatically deemed to be 'professional gentlemen.' Without doubt, barristers – those constituting the upper branch of the legal profession and qualified to plead before the superior courts – could lay claim to that status. Even when their social antecedents were doubtful, they had at least been touched by a liberal education, and once the Law Society enrolled them on its books as students, it declared them gentlemen.[19] Attorneys, who constituted the lower and separate branch of lawyers in England and the colony, were more suspect: they began not as 'students-at-law' but as articled clerks, their apprenticeships focused on the more technical, illiberal aspects of law; their work, encompassing most of the 'paperwork' of the law – the drafting of wills, deeds, and other legal instruments – was considered to be routine and pettifogging; their ethics were sometimes viewed as questionable; their social origins might be dubious, and as practising attorneys they were more likely to be, as Peter Russell points out, only marginally respectable.[20] Should English attorneys be admitted to the Law Society of Upper Canada? Be cautious, one member of the Assembly warned in 1825: 'In England attorneys were far from being respectable; they would have recourse to any expedient to advance their interests.'[21]

Similar distinctions existed in medicine. In England, physicians – those who diagnosed and prescribed for internal medicine – could claim to be gentlemen, liberally educated and belonging to an élite gentleman's club known as the Royal College of Physicians. Some surgeons, members of the various royal colleges of surgeons or those holding military commissions, might acquire respectability. But the surgeon-apothecary – the general practitioner of the eighteenth and early nineteenth centuries – had a more ambiguous status, linked as he was to trade through his sale of drugs, and with more humble antecedents and educational background.[22] The practice of an occupation, in other words, did not necessarily confer a high social status, and that was especially true for medical practitioners. What did confer it was not skills or technical knowledge *per se*, but reputability, connections, and an appropriate general education. Thus some surgeon-apothecaries might have it and others might not. In 1821 a bill to license American-trained doctors who could not pass the examinations of the Upper Canada Medical Board was opposed by W.W. Baldwin because competition from such doctors 'would have the effect of excluding from the Province gentlemen of the profession.' Christopher Hagerman, in supporting the bill, nonetheless recognized the same distinction: 'If the country were sufficiently supplied with medical gentlemen he would oppose this bill, but there were but few inhabitants in many parts, and they could not afford to pay professional gentlemen ... he feared if this bill were thrown out it would injure these persons.'[23]

No less than barristers or physicians, clergymen of the Church of England were deemed to be gentlemen, and so, generally speaking, were the educated ministers of the Church of Scotland. Baptist, Congregationalist, or Methodist ministers were not. 'Made another attempt to get to church on a fine frosty morning,' Mary O'Brien wrote in her diary in the late 1820s. 'We had, however, our drive only for our pains, for on our arrival we found instead of our clergyman a Methodist preacher.'[24] Even while John Beverley Robinson praised Methodist ministers for spreading the gospel to wilderness communities 'where a clergyman of the Church of England has never been heard,' he described the former as 'dissenting preachers.'[25] However admirable their efforts, they were not gentlemen.

Nor, it almost goes without saying, were women. In Upper Canada there were dissenting sects which allowed or encouraged them to preach, but women were not to be found in the pulpits of the Anglican or Presbyterian churches.[26] They might provide various kinds of health care and even sell their services for a fee, but they were not recognized, legally or otherwise, as 'physicians' or 'surgeons,' and, among the prosperous at least, a preference for trained doctors in midwifery was already beginning to establish itself.[27] But more is at issue here, in any case, than simply the tasks women might or might not do or the skills they might exhibit. A classical education, as David Noble has pointed out, was critical to one particular form of masculine identity, something that helped differentiate males of a certain class not only from other men but from women besides.[28] When Robert Baldwin's young friend 'reddened' at the thought of being asked to translate from an ancient tongue, his anxiety, we suggest, arose from something other than just his ignorance of a particular sort of academic knowledge. It was also rooted in the sense that he had not attained the full measure of manhood that the social authority of the learned professions rested upon. The meaning of 'profession,' moreover, incorporated the notion of 'skill' within a larger matrix of abstract knowledge and formal training. And the world of 'scientia,' of the systematic bodies of knowledge that comprised the sciences of theology, medicine, and the law, was the exclusive preserve of males. Upper Canada might have its gentlewomen, and its women, genteel or not, who ministered to the care of bodies and souls. But the ideal of the professional gentleman was gendered through and through.

Yet another defining characteristic of a learned profession was the assumption that professional men must have some secure source of income to lift them above mere pecuniary concerns and maintain them in independent circumstances.[29] On the one hand, they had a right to this because they were, *ipso facto*, gentlemen. But equally, professional men dealt with the most intimate and vital affairs of humanity: their souls, their health, their rights, their property. Just as an independent maintenance assured in the political sphere a disinterested concern for the public good,[30] so disinterested judgment and advice on theology, civil and property rights, and therapeutics depended on pecuniary independence from the client. As Adam Smith had put it in *The Wealth of Nations*,

> We trust our health to the physician, our fortune and sometimes our life and reputation to the lawyer and attorney. Such confidence could not safely be reposed in people of a very mean or low condition. Their reward must be such, therefore, as may give them that rank in society which so important a trust requires. The long time and great expense which must be laid out in their education, when combined with this circumstance, necessarily enhance still further the price of their labour.[31]

Thus could professional men claim that monopolies, sinecures, and special economic privileges of other kinds were not only indispensable but in the public interest. Petitioning for a new bill to regulate medicine in 1846, a group of doctors informed the legislature

> that the majority of the public cannot reasonably be expected to justly establish the qualifications of those who tender them Medical Services; consequently, most civilized nations have endeavoured to establish such regulations as will secure to the afflicted, the services of educated men, worthy of confidence, and protect them from ignorant pretenders to Medical skill.[32]

'A Clergyman whose subsistence arises from the Voluntary contributions of his hearers,' the magistrates of the Home District wrote in 1797, 'must often Bow to the caprice of the Crowd, must always be dependent, can never be respectable.'[33] Barristers, for their part, might have clients, but they did not have employers. Barristers, indeed, could not be 'paid' at all; rather, they received an 'honorarium' for their services. As one sixteenth-century English jurist described it, in a passage quoted in Upper Canada as late as 1861,

> The fees or rewards which they [barristers] receive are not in the nature of wages or pay, or that which we call salary or hire, ... but that which is given a learned counsellor is called *honorarium*, and not *merces*, being indeed a gift which giveth honour as well to the taker as to the giver; neither is it certain nor contracted for; no price or rate can be set upon counsel, which is invaluable and inestimable; so it is more or less according to circumstances – namely, the ability of the citizen, the worthiness of the counsellor, the weightiness of the

cause, and the custom of the country. Briefly, it is a gift of such a nature, and given and taken on such terms, as albeit the able client may not neglect to give it without note of ingratitude (for it is but a gratuity – a token of thankfulness) yet the worthy counsellor may not demand it without doing wrong to his reputation.[34]

The income of a professional man, then, was like the income received from land. Metaphorically at least, it was not earned by labour but akin to the rents produced by ownership. A profession was a form of property and, like land itself, freed the gentleman from dependence on the will of others.[35] Attorney General H.J. Boulton put the argument for an independent maintenance when, in 1830, he told the Select Committee on the Administration of Justice that 'the profession of the Law is a learned and honourable one ... To this body is confined the almost exclusive knowledge of those rules, which guide society in the several relations of life, and bind it together for mutual benefit and advantage; and the way to make them respectable is to afford them the means openly and without disguise, of reaping those emoluments from their labours which will place them above suspicion.'[36]

Boulton's comment also points to another characteristic feature embedded in the meaning of 'profession.' To have a profession was to have a 'vocation' – a calling, a sacred duty, a commitment not only to the service of others but to the larger social good. Doctors not only cared for the sick but, as men of science, searched out the causes of the diseases that plagued humankind. Clergymen not only saved souls but propounded those moral and religious doctrines that shaped the good society. Lawyers, as Boulton said, practised a craft which '[guides] society in the several relations of life, and bind[s] it together for mutual benefit and advantage.' Thus professional men, in Donald Scott's phrase, 'inhabited a moral domain beyond the marketplace,' carrying responsibilities not only important to individuals but vital to the public weal.[37] This too gave them a claim to an independent maintenance and a respectable station in society.

To be a professional gentleman, moreover, entitled one to membership in the collegial bodies which, formally or informally, ruled the profession itself – the various colleges of physicians or surgeons, for example, the Inns of Court, or the synods and assemblies of the churches. Used in this context the word 'college' did not refer to a teaching institution but to a body, often holding the legal status of a corporation, engaged in collegial self-rule. Though in eighteenth-century Britain some of these institutions, like the Inns of Court, were somnolent, they remained potent symbols of the long-established right of professional men to govern themselves by means which encapsulated the idea, as Arthur Engel put it in a passage quoted earlier, of 'ruling-class egalitarianism.' Not surprisingly, colonial professional men unselfconsciously sought to establish similar institutions in Upper Canada: the Law Society is one example; the College of Physicians and Surgeons is another. We will return to these developments later in this chapter. The point here is simply that independent gentlemen, by ancient tradition, held the right to determine their own rules for governing their occupations.[38]

But more important than any formal set of rules were the shared assumptions about the proper conduct of the professional gentleman which applied broadly to lawyers, doctors, and clergymen alike. On the one hand, there was what was commonly referred to as 'professional etiquette,' the relations among practitioners themselves, and, on the other, the rules that should govern their relations with the public. Professional men, for example, showed courtesy by not poaching each other's clients, patients, or parishioners, by not underbidding fees or defaming the reputation of a fellow practitioner. They did not advertise or hire themselves out to others. They received honoraria or stipends, not wages. Drawn originally from the customary traditions of gentlemanly behaviour, such expectations had gradually been transformed into occupational norms, and though only beginning to be codified in any formal way in the early nineteenth century, they constituted the ethical prescriptions designed to maintain the tone and character of the profession and to distinguish it from the occupations of those engaged in the ordinary pursuits of life.[39]

Finally, one other recurring phrase deserves notice. Just as, in the wider world, people could be divided into those who were respectable and those who were not, in religion, medicine, and law a key dichotomy was structured around the word 'regular.' Professional gentlemen, like other gentlemen, were 'regularly bred,' 'regularly taught,' 'regularly educated.' One of the two pillars of Christianity, according to John Strachan, was 'a regular ministry.' Norwich Township, according to a local report submitted to Robert Gourlay, contained 'one regularly bred practitioner of physic and surgery.'[40] What Upper Canadians needed most, Thomas Radcliff told his English readers, was 'a resident and regular clergy.'[41] In rejecting the applications of two attorneys to be allowed to practise in Upper Canada, 'nothing appeared to satisfy' the Legislative Assembly, said one MLA in 1825, 'that they were regularly bred to the law.'[42] Nowhere do we find any explicit definition of the meaning of 'regular,' but it clearly bore important connotations for contemporaries. A regular was a man who was respectable; who had the right educational and social credentials; who could be trusted to exercise sound judgment, hold sound values, and practise his craft according to the canons of reputable authorities and precedents. Dissenting ministers were not illegal in Upper Canada, but, as Strachan phrased it, they were, nonetheless, 'unauthorized teachers.'[43] To be regularly bred was to be 'authorized'; it was to have absorbed, by socialization as much as formal education, the conventions and values which acted as a safeguard against the propounding of strange or unauthorized doctrine in law, medicine, and divinity alike. To put it another way, a regular was what a 'quack' was not. Though that latter word was most frequently used in medicine, it was also applied by clergymen and lawyers to those who encroached on their own prerogatives. And it was used not so much to indicate a differential level of skill as to distinguish between those who were 'authorized,' who were regular and respectable, and those who were deemed not to be.

Obviously such language is redolent with assumptions about the structure of society and the sources of social authority. But that is just the point. Especially in the late eighteenth or early nineteenth century, a profession was not to be defined simply by its technical knowledge or expertise, nor were 'expert' and 'professional' synonymous terms. Rather, the title 'profession' was an indication of the social ranking of particular occupations, or even of similar distinctions among those who might practise the same craft skills. What conferred privilege upon barristers, physicians, and clergymen was not simply the nature of the work and the conditions under which it was carried out, but the fact that these occupations were taken up by gentlemen, by those who had acquired a liberal education, by those who had claims to belong to the respectable classes. To study the professions, in sum, whether in early Upper Canada or in some later period, is to study not just the world of work and occupations but also Weber's triad of status, class, and power – and, one might add, gender as well.

There is, of course, always a substantial gap between the mental maps of the social order held by contemporaries and the buzzing confusion of the real social world. Distinctions were never as sharp or as clear as we have just tried to delineate them. In Britain most professional men were urbanites and had long been so. They are perhaps best classified as members of the urban middle class rather than as gentlemen in the more traditional sense.[44] By the early nineteenth century, the status of the attorney and the general practitioner was rising, so that it was no longer easy to dismiss their claims to respectability, especially in the more inchoate social environment of Upper Canada. Quacks and irregulars could sometimes be respectable. The pretensions to gentility of backwoods doctors or clergymen could be mocked. The very elements constitutive of the definition of a profession helped blur its meaning, as they always had.[45] Common-school teachers might be beyond the pale, but what about those teachers who were also clergymen or other university graduates and who taught in grammar or private schools?[46] What about gentlemen who were architects, or the sons of professional gentlemen who became civil engineers?[47] All of these ambiguities and more would prove fruitful sources of change. As William Westfall remarks, nonetheless, Upper Canada before 1840 was 'a curiously eighteenth-century world,' and that was true not only of its ruling doctrines of church and state but of its more mundane habits of thought and institutions, including its forms of local government and even the way it regulated its town markets.[48] If there were ambiguities and disjunctions, there was also a certain clarity about who constituted a professional man. Drawing on the conventions and assumptions of a Georgian world-view, the professions consisted, in the main, of barristers, physicians, and clergymen, learned gentlemen all and thus fit to take their place among the other leading citizens of early Upper Canada.

The mental maps which structured this conception of the social world and rendered it intelligible were imported by emigrants from Britain. If the vast majority of Upper Canada's settlers consisted of small farmers, mechanics, and labourers, there were, nonetheless, a few who by any standards of the time were highly cultivated individuals, products of the best educational and professional institutions in Britain. The lawyers who initially shaped Upper Canada's legal institutions, men like W.D. Powell, William Osgoode, John White, and John Elmsley, were products of the English Inns of Court.[49] Indeed, a significant number of the early lawyers had attended Oxford, Cambridge, or Trinity College, Dublin, and had practised in British courts before coming to Upper Canada. Though the law rapidly came to be dominated by native sons, they were the children of American Loyalists or British emigrants and were educated by grammar-school masters who were themselves mostly products of British universities. J.J. Talman estimates that more than 70 per cent of all Anglican clergymen before 1840 were born in the British Isles, and that nearly half, and probably nearly 60 per cent, of the total number were educated at Oxford, Cambridge, and Trinity College, Dublin, alone.[50] Of the fourteen Presbyterian ministers in the colony in 1831, twelve had been born in the United Kingdom.[51] A majority of the doctors licensed during the 1830s held qualifications from either a British university or one of the colleges of physicians and surgeons in England, Scotland, or Ireland.[52] In 1836 five of sixteen members of the Medical Board of Upper Canada held degrees in medicine from the University of Edinburgh, which was still one of the premier medical schools in the English-speaking world, while six more were licentiates of the Royal College of Surgeons (London).[53] Given this influx of British professional men along with other middle- and upper-middle-class emigrants forced to leave home, it should not surprise us that their notions should be so powerful a force in shaping perceptions of what constituted a professional gentleman or how professional institutions were to be rightly ordered.[54]

THE WAY IN WHICH the colonial élite attempted to re-establish in the wilderness the full panoply of British institutions is a familiar story in Upper Canadian history. The balanced constitution, including an aristocratic element based on land ownership, administrative appointments, and the profession of law; the provision of an established church; the maintenance of a hierarchical social order based on traditional bonds of deference; the role of patronage, sinecure, and monopoly in securing loyalty and ensuring economic security; the social codes of gentlemanly behaviour; the fierce determination to reassert the boundaries that separated those who were respectable from those who were not: all of this has been sensitively portrayed by past and present scholarship. The production of regularly bred professional men and the re-establishment of professional institutions played a key part in this vision of Upper Canada's future. The church and the law, above all, were to be bulwarks of constitutionalism and loyalty. But colonial leaders also expected that the services of professional men would be available to minister to their own spiritual and material needs, and they took it for granted that the new colony would have facilities for turning their sons, nephews, brothers, and friends into the next generation of professional gentlemen.

The first prerequisite for the creation of the learned professions in Upper Canada was the establishment of suitable educational institutions – a system of grammar schools spread across the province and, above all, a provincial university.[55] While the project had engaged the interest of colonial administrators virtually from the beginning of settlement, its chief proponent and tireless promoter was John Strachan. For Strachan, the university was to serve as a great instrument of church and state, as indeed the professions themselves did, ensuring sound religion and sound politics. Its role was especially vital in law and divinity. Because the colony lacked great landed proprietors or privileged orders, the law would become 'the most powerful profession' in Upper Canada. It was, therefore, 'of the utmost importance' that law students 'should be collected together at the University, become acquainted with each other ... and acquire similar views and modes of thinking, and be taught by precept and example to love and venerate our parent state. It is surely of great consequence that a class of intelligent men belonging to a profession which offers the highest inducements of reputation, wealth, influence, authority and power, should be actuated by sentiments and feelings of attachment to the British Empire.'[56]

Strachan was also increasingly concerned by the desperate shortage of Anglican clergymen. Unless clergy could be found to minister to the wants of the people, the sects, with their republican origins, would win large numbers of followers, and thus 'the mass of the population will be nurtured and instructed in hostility to all our institutions, both civil and religious.' An Upper Canadian university would educate local boys for the ministry in an environment which would encourage 'that deep theological and literary inquiry' necessary to produce a regularly bred colonial clergy.[57] By the mid-1820s the lieutenant-governor concurred with these arguments, as did some key members of the colonial élite, and thus by 1827 Strachan had his royal charter establishing the University of King's College, with power to grant degrees in all faculties. It would, of course, take another fifteen years actually to get it open, but that is not the issue here. What is pertinent is that the establishment of the university was believed to be *integral* to the project for re-creating the ethos and institutions of the learned professions.

Indeed, whatever might be their objections to the exclusive control of King's College, or to the more general pretensions of the Church of England in Upper Canada, when the Church of Scotland and the Methodists came to establish their own institutions of higher education in the late 1830s and early 1840s the same rationale was pre-eminent in their minds. Both Queen's and Victoria sought and received charters which allowed them to offer professional as well as arts degrees. As Egerton Ryerson explained in his inaugural address as principal of Victoria College in 1842, the college would have both a preparatory department offering 'the various branches of an English Education,' and a collegiate or undergraduate course embracing 'the several branches of a Classical and Scientific Education. The former is requisite to the ordinary duties of life; the latter is requisite to *professional* pursuits; and I may add, necessary to extensive and permanent success in any of the higher employments to which one may be called by the authorities or voice of his country.'[58]

There were other essential steps to be taken, however, if British institutions were to be preserved in Upper Canada. Above all, a resident and regular clergy had to be not only educated but *maintained*. Upper Canada had neither the plenitude of ancient endowments nor the compulsory tithes or land taxes which served to underwrite the stipends of clergymen in England, Ireland, or Scotland, and which assured them – or many of them at least – a comfortable competence without the need to rely on the financial support of their congregations.[59] But a substitute for these traditional means of support was provided by the Constitution Act of 1791, which set aside an enormous endowment of nearly seven and a half million acres of prime agricultural land for 'the maintenance and support of a Protestant Clergy.' The phraseology was unfortunate to say the least, for the meaning of the word 'Protestant' would be contested throughout Upper Canadian history.[60] But the intent of the Constitution Act was clear: Upper Canada was to have a religious establishment sustained by the material assistance of the state. The principle behind such support was straightforward. For Anglicans, and for nearly all Presbyterians, it was the fundamental duty of government to promote religion, and to that end, to provide for the maintenance of the servants of God.[61] 'The voluntary contributions of the people,' John Strachan insisted, 'as the experience of the various dissenting denominations sufficiently proves, being a source too precarious, and a dependence upon it at variance with the nature of an establishment – inconsistent with the respectability and independence of the clergy, and likely to disturb the harmony which ought to exist between them and their flocks.'[62]

Rectors appointed by the Crown, serving parishes in the settled countryside endowed with glebe lands; missionaries in newly opened townships supported by their portion of the Clergy Reserves; bishops and archdeacons representing a national church in the councils of the province – seen through the hindsight of history it seems an absurd and hopeless vision. And yet as John Webster Grant has remarked, 'to its advocates the concept of a church establishment was logically compelling.'[63] Moreover, it had the sanctification of centuries of history, not only in England but elsewhere as well; indeed, as William Dummer Powell had said in 1797, the principle was admitted everywhere 'but in France and the American States,'[64] the twin founts of all the evil genies that needed to be put back in bottles. And similarly with the conception of the early nineteenth-century clergyman himself. Viewed from our own perspective, it is hard to envision a time when clergymen stood, along with lawyers, as professionals *par excellence*. But for most members of respectable society, and especially those from England or Scotland, the idea of a learned clergy drawing authority not only from their calling but from the social authority they gained as gentlemen, with a right to an independent maintenance and a secure place among the leaders of local and even national society, captured the very essence of the professional ideal.

AS JOHN STRACHAN had recognized in his call for the establishment of a colonial university, the other key profession in making Upper Canada the image and transcript of Great Britain was the law. But here again he was only echoing sentiments expressed by Simcoe and other senior administrators of the 1790s. Barristers were to form part of the aristocracy of the infant colony and thus were declared eligible, along with magistrates, for the maximum land grants made to individuals – 1,200 acres apiece. Even their wives were to receive 600 acres, making them the equivalent of 'old' merchants and members of Parliament.[65] But of far more importance, during the 1790s the conditions for the growth of the professional bar were established in two other ways.

First, there was the reform of the courts. During the 1780s and early 1790s, the court system of the old province of Quebec had been extended willy-nilly to the Loyalist settlements, and the civil courts in each district operated not only with unlimited jurisdiction within their districts but in a relatively informal fashion. In all but the Western District, the judges were laymen; litigants either participated directly in their own cases or used lay advocates; and the court procedures were simple and non-technical in nature.[66] In many respects it was a system ideally suited to a frontier colony where settlements were isolated, distances between them great, levels of education relatively low, lawyers few, and neither individuals nor governments had the cash to pay for lawyers, judges, and other court officials.

To Simcoe, Chief Justice William Osgoode, and John White, Upper Canada's first attorney general, however, the court system was entirely unsatisfactory. As English barristers, Osgoode and, even more so, White were highly critical of the quality of lay judgments and lay advocacy. Moreover, there were clear inconsistencies in the decisions handed down in the different districts. More pertinent still was the conviction that the administration of justice had to be assimilated to British models. The need for cheap and easy access to justice in small claims was acknowledged, and thus in 1792 the Courts of Requests were established, placing the resolution of disputes in minor matters in the hands of local justices of the peace, a substantial decentralization in the administration of justice. These courts remained in the hands of lay judges and lay advocates. Major legislation introduced in 1794 pointed, however, in the opposite direction. The Judicature Act of that year established district courts with jurisdiction limited in monetary matters to £15 or less, and a Court of King's Bench to be located at the capital and in possession of major judicial responsibilities. Common-law procedures were introduced in both courts. District court judges were to be paid by fees only and were to be appointed by the lieutenant-governor. Without salaries attached to the post, it was assumed that these judges would mostly be laymen. But salaries adequate to attract English barristers were established for the Court of King's Bench. In order to provide an initial cache of lawyers to meet the demands of the act, the lieutenant-governor was given power to grant a licence to practise to a maximum of sixteen individuals who could best act as lawyers, even if they were not fully qualified, though they were not allowed to train students.[67]

Both the intent and the effect of the Judicature Act were to make a place in the infant province for the regularly bred. Lay judges there might well be in the district courts, and lay advocates or litigants themselves might still appear at the bar, but the sheer technical complexities of the common law – a body of law and procedures accumulated over centuries, involving a plethora of archaic or Latin phraseology and demanding high levels of precision in the fine detail of a case – made lawyers more necessary than before. In the major cases coming before the Court of King's Bench, they were essential. And the salaries attached to that court ensured that there would be a small cadre, at least, of judges regularly trained to the law.

In 1797 Attorney General White brought forward a second, no-less-pathbreaking piece of legislation which created the Law Society of Upper Canada. Consisting of all those already admitted to the bar, the Law Society was intended to promote 'the establishment of order amongst themselves, as for the purpose of securing to the Province and to the profession a learned and honourable body, to assist their fellow subjects as occasion may require, and to support and maintain the Constitution of said province.' The members of the Society were given a monopoly over the right to practise 'at the bar of any of His Majesty's Courts, though the Judges themselves could admit barristers qualified to practise in Britain or her other North American colonies.'[68]

There are at least two things about the act especially worthy of note. First, the phrase 'to support and maintain the Constitution of said province' was no throw-away line. A professional bar was intended to be more than a set of technical experts administering a complex legal machine. Most of the men admitted to the bar before 1797 by lieutenant-governor's licence had been hand-picked for their loyalty to Simcoe's dream of re-establishing, without blemish, British institutions in Upper Canada. Moreover, the Convocation of Benchers (that is, the governors of the Law Society) would, from the beginning, conceive of their task as the building of a socially conservative legal élite.[69] Monopoly over practice, in turn, would provide the economic base for political and social leadership. Before the legislation of 1794 and 1797, there had been little need for lawyers. Together the two acts ensured that there would be a shortage. Delays in the administration of justice, especially in the Court of King's Bench, became a matter of loud complaint in the years before 1812 as a handful of lawyers tried to cope with a growing number of cases from all parts of the province. The number of law students that any lawyer was allowed to train in his office had to be increased twice before 1810, and in 1803 the legislature gave the lieutenant-governor power to create a second batch of laymen licensed by the government to practise law even though they were not fully trained – a group of men thereafter dubbed, by the irreverent at least, as 'heaven-born lawyers.'[70]

So long as the shortage was severe, such measures were tolerated by the Law Society, but as the law increasingly became a vital means by which the colonial élite provided for its sons, and as the rising tide of British emigrants after 1815 began to wash up English and Irish lawyers on Upper Canadian shores, the Society concluded that better dykes were necessary. In 1822 an act to incorporate the Society also contained a clause which transferred control over the licensing of emigrant British lawyers from the judges to the Law Society itself, making it much more difficult for non–Upper Canadian lawyers to practise in the colony.[71]

To the cynical, the clause may appear a case of naked self-interest. Yet, as Blaine Baker remarks, human motives are always mixed, and it is, in any case, more important to read in their defence of the clause the ways in which Upper Canada's 'legal-administrative aristocracy ... conceived of themselves, how they understood the roles they were fulfilling, what theories of order they embraced.'[72] And those theories of order were nicely illustrated during debates, in 1823 and 1825, over private members' bills to admit to practice particular lawyers who had been rejected by the Law Society. When Robert Nichol pointed out in 1823 that W.W. Baldwin himself had been 'heaven born' to the law, Baldwin replied that at that time there had been a real shortage of lawyers in the province. 'But at the present time,' he continued,

there was no deficiency. Lawyers were to be found in every district; independent of which the number of young gentlemen that were now articled to the profession would be sufficient to answer the demands of the country. It must be well known to honourable members, that parents were educating their sons at a great expense for the profession of the Law, and, it would be great injustice to the parents of these children to admit gentlemen coming from other countries. *If the present bill pass, other gentlemen would apply, and they would be breaking in upon the establishment.*[73]

Similar arguments were heard again in 1825, but John Beverley Robinson, the attorney general, warned of more ominous consequences.

'He thought it highly impolitic and dangerous to society to admit strangers to the profession without knowing them well.' They would inevitably be entrusted with important responsibilities and references from abroad were not adequate securities in such matters. 'He had known men of character coming from England with the strongest recommendations, who, in a very short period, turned out infamous. The young men brought up here,' Robinson continued, 'are known from their infancy, their habits and mode of education were securities for their honourable proceedings, and he thought it would be not only unjust to them, but dangerous to the community to admit applicants who are unknown to them.'[74] These two passages provide a revealing glimpse of the nexus of eighteenth-century assumptions about the nature and organization of society. On the one hand, there is the settled conviction about an 'establishment' in which a small élite have a right and a duty to rule, and to be maintained for doing so. On the other, there are the securities for good conduct: the importance of personal knowledge as an assurance of competence and character, the intimacy of a small tightly knit community as the best guarantor of integrity and honour among those who ruled.

However we assess the motives behind such restrictive legislation, by the 1820s lawyers had secured for themselves a firm place among Upper Canada's leading citizens. Some, like Baldwin, had actually become akin to the landed aristocracy; for those less fortunate, the reform of the courts, the monopoly of the Law Society, and their collective influence in the legislature ensured them a maintenance which gave them both independence and respectability. And that process of consolidation would continue through the 1830s and into the early 1840s.

The shortage of professional men in the early decades of the colony's history and the need to decentralize the administration of justice had meant, as we have already suggested, that many of the district court judges were laymen rather than lawyers. This was especially true of the more isolated or undeveloped parts of the country. In the Home District, which included Toronto, where lawyers were thick on the ground from the beginning, the appointees had all been professionals. But, particularly before 1820, many of the judges in other districts were laymen, and in a few, like the Western District, lay judges were being appointed well into the 1830s.[75] For most of the early period, these appointments occasioned few complaints since the fees in the district courts, especially those in outlying regions, were not large enough to provide an adequate living.[76] There was, nonetheless, the sense among lawyers that such a situation was unsatisfactory or irregular. When Christopher Hagerman, the solicitor general, was asked in 1830 by the

Select Committee on the Administration of Justice how these courts might be improved, he replied that they needed to be made more 'respectable' by changes which would 'ensure the acceptance by professional men of the appointment of Judges of the District Courts. This could, I think, be best accomplished by providing for these Officers a stated salary, rather than allow them to derive their income from fees as at present.'[77]

To the lawyers, the situation with respect to the Courts of Requests was even more unsatisfactory. These courts were in the hands of local JPs, virtually none of whom were lawyers. As local institutions, the courts were numerous, and the justices numbered more than a thousand.[78] Inevitably many were ill educated or unfamiliar with the forms and substance of the law, and, according to one lawyer at least, looking back at the past from the vantage point of 1861, 'the great majority ... were in a high degree ignorant, and as presumptuous as they were ignorant.'[79] The remedy for this state of affairs was obvious: oust the laity from any role in the administration of justice in the lower courts.

In the legislative session of 1841, a bill was introduced to abolish the Courts of Requests and replace them with division courts, far fewer in number, at which the district court judge was to preside. All new judges, however, were to be required to be Upper Canadian barristers, and they were to be paid fixed salaries. The judges were also to serve as chairmen of the Courts of Quarter Sessions.[80] Speaking in support of the bill, Robert Baldwin argued that anywhere upwards of two-thirds of the commissioners 'are altogether unfit for the responsible situation in which they are placed. Whether it is attributable to improper appointments or not, persons have no confidence in these courts; they will not go to them because they cannot expect to receive justice.'[81] The bill had been introduced by William Draper, but he had the unqualified support not only of Baldwin but of such men as Sir Allan MacNab, Colonel Prince, and Sandfield Macdonald.[82] What brought such ill-assorted politicians together on this particular issue? They were, of course, all lawyers. The laity may indeed have been incompetent in too many cases, and the common law was undoubtedly technical and complicated. But the tenor of the argument is one that will recur throughout the rest of this volume; professionals know best and should therefore be placed in positions of special privilege and sustained by monopolies and sinecures. Laymen, moreover, had no place in debates about the administration of justice. When J.P. Roblin a few years later had the temerity to criticize a particular change in the courts, he was promptly put in his place by Colonel Prince in terms which would echo through the decades to come: the colonel 'always listened with great pleasure to his honourable friend ... because there was a great deal of good sense in his remarks; he was quite happy to be enlightened by them on every other subject, but he (Col. Prince) did not think he was quite the man to instruct the House on matters of law – (laughter); he was a good farmer, and a well-informed man, but no lawyer.'[83]

The bill of 1841, in any case, passed without difficulty and thus created one more solid prop upon which the monopoly of lawyers over the law would be built. In 1845 a further step was taken when the practice of the district courts was assimilated to the procedures of the Court of Queen's Bench. As Solicitor General, arch-Tory Henry Sherwood introduced the bill; sitting on the other side of the House, Robert Baldwin was one of its most vigorous proponents. 'With regard to the alteration in the manner of pleading,' Baldwin told the legislature,

he knew of nothing more objectionable than having two different systems of pleading in two tribunals which imposed a burthen on the lawyer in the inferior court, which could scarcely be sustained (hear, hear), involving the necessity of examining thousands of documents. In this, as in all other matters, the more simple the practice is made the better for the clients and for the profession also. He knew it was a vulgar error that lawyers wished to have a cumbrous system of obtaining justice. (Hear, hear.) He denied it in the name of the profession, and believed that the majority of lawyers in the house would coincide with him. (Hear.) The system laid down in the bill, he was well aware, had received the approbation of the greatest lawyers in England, and he believed it to be the cheapest and easiest way of disposing of causes.[84]

Vulgar error or not, the procedures of the superior courts were complex and formal; to introduce them in the lower courts was to make lawyers all but indispensable there as well.

WHEREAS THERE ARE relatively rich sources on the early history of lawyers and clergymen, the resources for doctors are much thinner. Indeed, there is little more than the barebones records in the legislative journals of failed or successful bills.[85] Though initiatives to regulate the practice of medicine date back to 1792, and over the next twenty-five years several acts would be put in place and then repealed, the first enduring piece of legislation was passed in 1818; it established the Medical Board of Upper Canada and gave it the power to examine candidates who wished to practise in Upper Canada. If the board was satisfied with the candidate's professional qualifications, it recommended him to the lieutenant-governor, who, after being 'satisfied of the loyalty, integrity and good morals of such applicant,' issued a licence to practise.[86] The penalty for illegal practice was set at £100. Military officers, graduates of any university in the empire, and female midwives did not, however, need a licence. A number of administrative improvements were made in an amended act in 1819, and meanwhile the Medical Board was constituted and began its work that same year. In 1827 the law was modified to widen somewhat the Medical Board's control over practice, to lower the penalty to £25, and to require graduates of any university in the empire to produce appropriate proofs of qualification and to obtain a licence from the governor before beginning practice, though they still did not need to pass the Medical Board examinations.[87]

In terms of their social status, doctors in Upper Canada could hardly compete with the clergy or the bar. The undisputed gentlemen of the profession, the members of the Royal College of Physicians (London) and the other élite corps of physicians, rarely settled in the colony, leaving the field to the less prestigious surgeon-apothecaries from Britain, to the home-grown, and to American immigrants. The best of these, however, were respectable enough. There were ex–military officers and well-qualified surgeons like Christopher Widmer, of gentry background, a member of the Royal College of Surgeons (London), a half-pay officer, and a man who by the 1830s moved in the highest social circles of the colony. There was Lucius O'Brien, eldest son of an army officer, a graduate of the University of Edinburgh, and member of the RCS (London). W.C. Gwynne, the son of an Irish clergyman, was a graduate of Trinity College, Dublin, with further training in London and Edinburgh. John Rolph was a Cambridge graduate, a member of the RCS (London), and a barrister to boot.[88] Along with others like them, they could not help but maintain the image of medicine as a learned and respectable profession. And the Medical Board, if less prepossessing than the Law Society, could at least ensure minimum levels of competency.

They had ambitions beyond the Medical Board in any case. It was, at best, an examining board appointed by the government, with no powers over medical education beyond its examination requirements and no influence over the character of the profession itself. Using their links to other members of the Toronto élite, and their institutional bases such as the Medical Board or the local medical society, leading doctors like Widmer and Gwynne pressed during the 1830s for the establishment of a medical school and stronger legislation to regulate the profession and suppress quackery. Their efforts were crowned with success in 1839 when the legislature chartered the College of Physicians and Surgeons, which incorporated the medical profession; gave it full powers of self-government, including control over the education and licensing of doctors; and strengthened the penalties against illegal practice.[89] It was a major (if short-lived) victory. It gave doctors the kind of professional organization lawyers had had since 1797 and assimilated Upper Canadian medicine, in a rough way at least, to British institutions. Indeed, it went farther. Upper Canada now had a single college and a unified profession; British doctors were governed by some twenty or more corporations, which left the profession divided and warring against itself.

There is no surviving record to explain just why the doctors were so successful in 1839, but a plausible explanation lies in the political situation at the time. The toryism of the conservative assembly elected in 1836 was powerfully reinforced by the Rebellion of 1837, and the colonial political élite was determined to take the opportunity not only to root out all things democratic and American but to reinforce the 'Britishness' of Upper Canada. There were a surprising number of doctors 'caught up in the revolt, perhaps a dozen or so.'[90] And in both private and public, conservative voices saw dissident professional men as dangerous agitators. As one member of the Medical Board expressed it, Upper Canada was a 'country overrun with Yankee pretenders' to the science of medicine, who exercised a political influence 'more extensive than the itinerant religious professors from the same country.' Their pupils, he added, were of the same principles.[91]

The act foundered on a technicality.[92] The Royal College of Surgeons (London) took exception to it on the grounds that it trespassed on their own privileged position, and consequently the legislation was disallowed. The Medical Board was automatically restored, its membership consisting mainly of the same men who had headed the College, and thus nothing changed so far as policy was concerned. They continued to be active in plans for founding the medical faculty of the University of King's College, which finally opened in 1843. And there was no reason for doctors to be anything less than optimistic about obtaining additional measures to regulate the practice of medicine in Upper Canada. In 1843 a select committee of the assembly firmly rejected a petition to repeal existing medical legislation, on the grounds that, 'in all civilized countries, the Science of Medicine is only intrusted ... to those who have received a liberal education, are obliged to go through certain prescribed studies ... and undergo a severe examination.'[93] Indeed, in a second report the committee advocated a new medical bill which would have substantially extended the powers of the profession to regulate itself, to set the course of studies required for a licence, and to strengthen the provisions against quackery.[94]

OVER THE COURSE of the four or five decades since first settlement, colonial institutions did not, in any literal sense, become the 'image and transcript' of those at home. There was no precise parallel in England, Scotland, or Ireland to the Law Society of Upper Canada or to the Medical Board. And by that point, the religious ascendancy of Anglicanism had been compromised by the loss of exclusive control over its land endowment, for the Clergy Reserves Act of 1840 had given the Church of Scotland access to a share in its profits and appeared to substantiate the Kirk's claims that it was a coestablished church in Upper Canada. On the other hand, institutions for providing the elements of a classical education were increasingly accessible, and King's and Queen's colleges, providing both undergraduate and theological education, were about to open. A maintenance for the churches seemed secure, and the powers of the Law Society ensured that loyal and learned gentlemen of respectable connections would dominate the bar. If doctors had lost their self-governing college, it seemed a temporary setback, and they had reason to be optimistic about the future. Though in some respects attenuated, and differing in detail from the British exemplar, the outlines of a Georgian establishment appeared to have been put in place.

Lawyers got pro status in 1797
Doctors got pro status in 1839

2
Compromises and Competitors

The preceding chapter, the disconcerted reader may already have noted, constitutes an oddly lopsided reading of Upper Canadian history. Professional gentlemen are well represented, but the colony has no other cast of characters. There are clergymen unburdened by dissent, and doctors but no quacks. Equally, we have had much to say about transplanting a professional ideal but nothing about the forces that might modify or undermine it. This chapter attempts to redress the balance. The dilemmas of providing professional services in the colony, we shall argue, would begin to reshape some traditional ideas about the organization and social role of the professions. Competitors put down deep roots, fracturing the market for their services and challenging the efficacy of their knowledge. And Georgian assumptions would increasingly be confronted by new ideas hostile to special privilege.

THE EFFECTS of these forces weighed most heavily on the Anglican and Presbyterian ministry. And they first made themselves felt through the corrosive impact of economic circumstance on the notion of an independent maintenance. If the colony was to be evangelized and secured for the two national churches, the countryside had to be supplied with clergymen. But how were they to be supported? The Clergy Reserves had been set aside by the founders of the colony to underwrite the costs of maintaining a religious establishment, but for decades after 1791 land was cheap and the reserves failed to fulfil their promise. In the meantime the churches depended for their very survival on financial aid from Britain. In the two decades after 1815, the Church of England in Upper Canada was sustained almost entirely by the mission work of the Society for the Propagation of the Gospel in Foreign Parts (SPG). Aided by large annual grants from the imperial government, the SPG was able to recruit English clergymen for the colony and offer them stipends of

£200 a year. Together with small gifts from their congregations, pew rents, and their own personal resources, that amount allowed for a comfortable, if modest, standard of living well within the range gauged necessary to maintain respectability.[1]

From the early 1830s, however, the British government began to cut its grants to the SPG, and the Society's own priorities began to shift to other parts of the empire. As a result its stipends fell steadily during the 1830s and 1840s, especially those offered to new or prospective recruits. Clergymen already established in Upper Canada before 1833 saw their annual allotment drop from £200 to £170, and new clergymen were guaranteed only £100, figures which remained fixed until the late 1840s despite the fact that £200 continued to be considered the absolute minimum necessary to support a clergyman and his family in a respectable manner.[2] Contributions from funds controlled by the Executive Council, moreover, were cut off in 1840–1 when those funds were surrendered and replaced by a civil list. And in 1840 the Church of England lost its exclusive right to the Clergy Reserves Fund. Though its contributions continued to be substantial, the overall amounts allocated to Upper Canada by the SPG failed to keep pace with population growth, and revenues from the reserves were never sufficient to narrow the gap between needs and resources. The result was that the church was hard hit on three fronts. Established clergymen experienced declining incomes, prospective recruits could be offered meagre stipends at best, and the church itself lacked the resources to meet the needs of a growing population. There were, John Strachan complained bitterly in 1837, 'very few men in the Colony looking forward to the Clerical profession. Parents are debarred by the great poverty of the Church, from directing the attention of their children to the sacred profession.'[3]

For its part the Church of Scotland confronted the same dilemmas in even more extreme form. It received proportionately less in government grants. Until the mid-1820s no systematic financial aid was forthcoming from Scotland, and even after the Glasgow Colonial Society had been established, it never had the kind of resources available to the SPG. Like that of the Church of England, the growth of the Kirk was stunted by the lack of resources to sustain its ministers adequately or to multiply their numbers.[4]

Neither church, on the other hand, was prepared to stake its future on the exclusive support of the laity. In part that was because of the conviction, especially before the 1830s, that much of the population was too poor to provide adequately for their ministers.[5] But for many clergymen it was also impossible to reconcile received notions of respectability and independence with the modest income and lowered status that voluntarism might entail. 'Their education,' said one Presbyterian in the late 1820s, 'and the decorum that is expected from them, prevent them from freely using the means which frequently ingratiate religious teachers not belonging to any establishment, with the people generally; yet they have hardly any other dependence for subsistence and keeping together a congregation, than their being agreeable in everything to the people.'[6] Another prominent Scot, the Rev. Mark Stark, commented in the same vein: 'Unless there is some effectual provision made for the support of religion in this country I certainly contemplate that all the respectable clergy of all denominations who will not submit to methods of extracting a livelihood from the people which would bring them into the contempt of the people themselves will be obliged to seek other professions for their maintenance.'[7]

An anonymous Anglican pamphleteer was even more forceful: the Clergy Reserves must never be given up, he insisted, for the sake of those clergy who had struggled so hard 'to support their families and to maintain that decency of appearance which their education and their status requires.' If the reserves were lost the clergyman would soon

find himself on a level with the other Christian sects, soon would he have to look to the 'voluntary system' for his main support. And then would he find ... that unless possessed of income arising from other sources, he would scarcely have a seemly garment to put on; with difficulty find wherewith to spread his homely table; soon would he be compelled to put his daughters out to service, or to trade; and see his struggling partner obliged to dress his food, to clean his house, and perform the meanest of the menial acts of servants.[8]

Despite clerical antipathies the churches had no choice but to face up to the fact that congregational support must constitute at least one cornerstone of church finance. Before the late 1830s the SPG did not *require* local contributions to salary, and it is probable that many congregations contributed little or nothing to the clergyman's stipend.[9] From early in that decade, however, as the SPG began to face other and more pressing demands, it increasingly insisted that the Upper Canadian church stand on its own feet.[10] One step towards making the church independent was taken in 1842 with the founding of the Church Society. The intent was to mobilize lay financial support through an organization which would collect funds from local parishes and use the money, in part at least, to supplement clerical stipends. The laity were necessarily involved in the Church Society, playing a major role in policy making and managing its affairs. But Strachan and his supporters were especially careful to preserve the independence of the clergy by requiring that salary supplements would come from the central organization and not its local branches. 'It was,' says Curtis Fahey, 'an attempt to reap the benefits of the "voluntary system" while simultaneously avoiding the consequences which so often ensued when individual congregations were directly responsible for the maintenance of their ministers.'[11] The Church Society could not, however, finance the whole cost of clerical stipends by itself, and thus Strachan's second response was to push his local communicants harder. As the decade wore on, his letterbooks filled with demands that local congregations do more, with rebukes to local laymen about their niggardly support for their minister, and with flat refusals to provide clergymen when local effort was not forthcoming.

By the late 1840s the situation was critical. The SPG was now insisting that all its stipendiary grants be matched by local contributions, and though the Clergy Reserves had just begun to produce substantial revenues, it was clear that the reserves fund would never meet more than a small part of the financial needs of the church. In a crucial pastoral letter of 1851, Strachan confronted these hard facts directly. He did not despise, he said, the contribution made by the Clergy Reserves, but in itself it was inadequate to sustain the church. Thus there was 'nothing of moment left to us but the Voluntary principle; and although it has never succeeded in any place or country, in bringing the Gospel to every creature ... it is all that is left to us to work upon.' He was not, he insisted, advocating the voluntary system in itself,

for I consider it open to the gravest objections; and I believe it to be the duty of every Christian Government to provide for the religious instruction of its people, as it is for the father of a family to train up his children in the ways of Gospel truth and holiness.

But the necessity is upon us: there is now no alternative; and, because it is a necessity, I am convinced that God will bless it, and from this I take comfort and encouragement.[12]

As this passage makes clear, Strachan was not reconciled to voluntarism; he and other church leaders continued to consider it both economically ineffective and a 'degrading influence' on the clergy, reducing the minister 'more [to] the servant of his congregation than of his God.'[13] The pressures towards voluntarism had been inexorable nonetheless.

In principle the Kirk was as resolutely anti-voluntarist as the Anglicans.[14] Yet, there was a stronger tradition within the colony of congregational support, and even when the assistance of the Glasgow Colonial Society became available in the mid-1820s, congregations were required to match its grant before it would provide a resident clergyman. This mix of congregational and external support would continue, in one form or another, past mid-century. From the 1830s direct government grants were an important source of clerical incomes, and from 1840 so was the Kirk's share of the Clergy Reserves Fund. Indeed, the disruption of the Canadian church in 1843–4 had the paradoxical effect of enriching those ministers who remained loyal to the Church of Scotland. Secessionist Free Church ministers were ruled ineligible to receive funds from the Clergy Reserves, and thus the Presbyterian share went to a smaller number of clergy. Such subsidies were considered to be vital to the welfare of the Kirk. Complaining about the indifference of the laity to inadequate ministerial salaries, the editor of *The Presbyterian* remarked in 1848 that, 'happily, our Clergy Reserves Fund will supplement in some measure the niggardliness or poverty of particular congregations.'[15] Issue after issue of that journal nonetheless reveals the same dilemma facing the Anglicans: by itself the fund could not underwrite adequate ministerial stipends or sustain the expansion of the church; but voluntarism corrupted the relationship between a congregation and its minister, compromising his ability to reprove the wicked and proclaim the path to righteousness.[16] And yet, there seemed no alternative. As one minister put it, 'to the Voluntary principle, we conceive, all Protestant bodies in the Province must principally look for the means of maintaining and extending their usefulness.'[17]

The Free Church, for its part, was divided on the matter. Many leading laymen, including Peter and George Brown, were resolute voluntarists, and so were some of the clergy. But until the late 1840s, a majority of the clergy continued to uphold the principle of government support for religious establishments. The moment of truth, as John Moir suggests, came in January 1848, when, because of an accumulating surplus in the Clergy Reserves Fund, additional denominations gained access to it. Some congregations of the Free Church applied for funding, others opposed it, and in the ensuing struggle at Synod a compromise position was hammered out.[18] The doctrine of establishmentarianism was reaffirmed, but the issue of government grants was declared 'of subordinate importance'; people might disagree about it and it might or might not be legitimate, depending on the circumstances. No government had the right to endow error, however, and since the Canadian government was funding churches teaching erroneous doctrines – presumably the Roman Catholic Church – the Free Church declared against accepting government funds.[19] Thus, however reluctantly, the Free Church committed itself to voluntarism. Its early success in attracting a number of wealthy congregations and rich laymen may have made the decision easier, but initially at least voluntarism was hardly a boon to the ministry. At mid-century most Free Church ministers received salaries between £100 and £150, a good deal less than their state-aided brethren in the Kirk, who received £150 each from the Clergy Reserves Fund alone.[20]

Whether driven by the dictates of doctrine or by economic necessity, in any case, by 1850 both the Anglican and Presbyterian churches had embraced voluntarism as at least one component of church finance. Economic and political realities within the colony and developments outside it had begun to challenge traditional expectations about an independent maintenance and about the appropriate relationship between clergymen and laity.

THERE WERE IMPORTANT, if less dramatic, adaptations in medicine and law as well. Above all, the internal divisions which separated physicians, surgeons, and apothecaries in England, each group with its own corporation and descending ranks of social prestige, broke down in the colony. These distinctions were already blurring in early nineteenth-century Britain; outside of the large cities, the majority of practitioners were 'surgeon-apothecaries,' the progenitors of the general practitioner.[21] But members of the Royal College of Physicians, who constituted the undisputed élite of the profession, rarely emigrated to the colony and thus were not numerous enough to reassert their social and professional pre-eminence, while the surgeons and other practitioners who made up the bulk of Upper Canadian doctors had no stake in re-establishing a system that stigmatized them as inferior. No less important, and even more so than in provincial England, the specialization implicit in the distinction between physician, surgeon, and apothecary could not be maintained in an environment where paying customers were in short supply. If a doctor were to make a living, he needed to be all three at the same time. Thus, while the Medical Board had the power to license men solely as physicians or surgeons, it virtually never did so, turning the colony's regular doctors into general practitioners certified to practise all of the various branches of medicine.[22]

A similar 'declension' took place among lawyers. In England there were clear social and professional distinctions between the barrister, on the one hand, and the attorney or solicitor, on the other. The spirit which animated those distinctions was present in the colony as well: in 1797 the Law Society Act introduced different rules for the training of each branch of the profession. But, except in a few cases, lawyers could not make a living as barristers alone and thus they routinely qualified and practised as both barristers and attorneys, so that the two branches of the profession were in effect united.²³ At least among York's legal élite, however, there was always the conviction that the respectability of the bar was compromised by that union, and there is a long, if sporadic, record of attempts to reintroduce the distinction, preserved in England, of a bar entirely separated from the lower branches of the law. One critical step in that direction occurred in 1822 when the Benchers sponsored legislation which eliminated all powers of supervision by the Law Society over attorneys or their articled clerks.²⁴ From that point onwards, a clerk who had articled for the required five years received a certificate from his master and presented it to one of the judges of the superior courts. If the latter was satisfied, the clerk was admitted to practise as an attorney or solicitor. From 1822, in other words, those who were attorneys only were banished from the charmed circle of barristers constituting the membership of the Law Society. For the next thirty-five years, there were no entry or educational standards for articled clerks beyond those imposed by their individual masters, and the only guarantee of their competence came from the judges who issued their certificates to practise.

The act of 1822 was but one of several attempts before mid-century to sharpen the distinction between barrister and attorney. In 1830 the Benchers passed resolutions which would have made it impossible for any new barrister to practise as an attorney, and the same goal was sought by legislative action in 1840. Neither initiative succeeded, the first having been rejected by the superior court judges who were the Law Society's Visitors, and the second by the legislature itself.²⁵ The separation of the bar, however, remained an ideal for at least some leading lawyers throughout the period. As William Draper remarked in 1830, 'I think that the moral character of the profession is lowered by the combination, for ... I am somewhat disposed to think that there is much in the business of an Attorney which ... is foreign to that high tone of feeling which cannot be too much cultivated at the bar.'²⁶

The legislation of 1822 did not put an end to the union of barrister and attorney *per se*. Whatever people like Draper might have preferred, barristers did not stop qualifying as attorneys. If the bar stamped a lawyer with the mark of respectability, it was his practice as an attorney which made him a living. Thus throughout the entire period the vast majority of lawyers qualified in both branches of the law. Indeed, this was true of even the most socially and professionally distinguished barristers in the province. However routine, pettifogging, or socially suspect the work of the mere attorney might be, it was, as one leading lawyer put it in the early 1820s, 'the most lucrative part of the profession' and for that reason alone could not be dispensed with in a successful practice.²⁷

OTHER COMPROMISES were necessary as well. Emigrant professionals might themselves be well educated, but, as local boys entered law, medicine, or the church, there was an inevitable decline in the levels of both preliminary and professional education. Before the 1840s especially, a preliminary general education consisted at best of the elements of Latin, mathematics, and English subjects, obtained at one of the public or private grammar schools or through some form of private tuition. If a student's parents had the financial means, he might receive a much more sophisticated education, but since the vast majority of boys destined for the professions left school and began apprenticeships in their early or mid-teens, the preliminary education they received was markedly restricted, compared at least with the expansive ideals prevalent in England at the time.[28] A declension in the standard of professional training was no less apparent. The emigrant surgeon was almost certain to have attended lectures at a medical school and walked the wards of a hospital. Until the 1830s neither opportunity was possible for Upper Canadian medical students unless they went beyond the confines of the colony.[29] Ministerial candidates were likely to study their theology under the supervision of a hard-pressed country clergyman, living in his house and with access to nothing more than his personal library. Even in Britain most doctors and many lawyers never darkened the door of a university. But a university education was of great symbolic importance nonetheless, and contemporaries were well aware of that.[30] Without the presence of a local university to provide both preliminary and professional education, the identity of professional men as members of the *learned* professions was at risk of being increasingly attenuated.

Finally, there was the threat to respectability posed by the demands of making a living. Visitors from Britain were particularly struck by the mutations in the professional ideal they encountered in the colonies. 'The system here is very different,' J.R. Godley wrote of Upper Canada in 1844, 'and the tendency of it is to lower very much the dignity of the learned professions. When the doctor is in the habit of attending upon a resident family, he sends in his accounts at the end of the year, like the tailor or shoemaker.' Similarly with lawyers: 'It is very difficult for men brought up with high and mighty notions of professional dignity, "honoraria" etc., to reconcile themselves to the mode of practice which prevails,' Godley continued. 'Lawyers here are both barristers and attorneys ... but business is managed much more after the fashion of the latter branch of the profession than after that of the former. In the first place, they send in their bills regularly for work and labour done, and a cause pleaded in court, or an opinion upon title, is charged in the same way as the drawing of a brief.'[31]

Before 1840 the respectability of the Church of England had been enhanced by the number of its clergymen with degrees from Oxford, Cambridge, or Dublin and with connections to the gentry, the military, or the imperial government.[32] Church leaders, however, had long recognized that they needed to train up a local ministry.[33] Yet this in turn raised fears that it would be accompanied by a decline in the social status of the clergy. The most respectable members of the community, 'from which candidates for the ministry are usually derived,' were failing to encourage their sons to enter the church, wrote A.N. Bethune in 1846. 'In this case it becomes the more necessary to encourage what, in the colonies, may be termed the middle class of society – that is, the sons of farmers and respectable tradesmen.'[34] The same fears stalked the Kirk. 'Young men of respectable connections and good education are everywhere crowding into the professions of law and medicine,' one minister wrote in 1848, 'because these are supposed to offer a fair chance of that competence and honour which are legitimate objects of human pursuit.' But without improved salaries the church 'will neither be able to obtain from Scotland, nor to educate in Canada, an adequate supply of ministers. The standard of Ministerial qualification will be lowered; and the whole aspect of our Church will be changed in those characteristics in which, in our native land, we have been most wont to admire it.'[35] Altogether, then, social conditions and economic constraints not only imposed changes in the organizational as well as the educational standards of each of the professions but also posed the threat, especially for the clergy of the two national churches, of a substantial decline in their social standing.

WHETHER IN BRITAIN or its colonies, professional men were not the only individuals in the early nineteenth century who drafted legal documents, cured the sick, or offered the promise of salvation to sinful humanity. Even as the three learned professions established themselves in Upper Canada, there was the parallel growth of alternative ways of providing these services. And that reality was also a part of the environment within which the professions took shape. The rise of religious diversity and denominational conflict is a well-known story, and for that reason we will deal with it only briefly. Our treatment of the growth of quasi-legal services offered by the laity is also brief, but primarily because we know so little about it. We will have more to say on medicine not only because the evidence is richer but because the content may be less familiar than is the case with religion.

It hardly needs saying that in Upper Canada the clergy of the two national churches never had a clear field to themselves. One consequence of the growth of dissent, however, was to fracture the market for clerical services. The established church, whether in Scotland or England, was organized geographically, with a single minister assigned to each parish. A parish was, among other things, an economic unit which in one way or another provided a clergyman with his living. But in Upper Canada the competition for souls was such that a variety of ministers could be found everywhere. At the beginning of the nineteenth century, one Scottish minister warned his colleagues that 'unless the presbyterian settlers of Upper Canada receive an immediate supply of new ministers they will be rent into so many sects that they will be unable to support a minister of any denomination.'[36] More than thirty years later, William Proudfoot made exactly the same point. 'Scattered as the population is,' he wrote of southwestern Ontario, 'the people are rendered more destitute of religious institutions, in consequence of their being split into so many sects, whereby no sect is able to support a teacher by itself. There seems no way of remedying this evil. The people could not bear an established church which might go far to cure it; and there is no class of society, which possesses such influence as to draw the rest after it.'[37]

In the battle for lay support, moreover, dissent had an edge which the two national churches could not match. Baptists, Congregationalists, above all Methodists, were not opposed or even indifferent to an educated ministry; but an advanced education was not a prerequisite for a preacher, and all of them assumed that ministers would live off the voluntary support of their congregations, cutting their coats to fit the cloth their adherents could afford. Dissenting ministers, in other words, were not required to be gentlemen. This gave them great advantages over their brethren in the two national churches.[38] Congregations could be more easily organized, a larger pool of recruits to the ministry tapped, and sources of support more widely spread. The Methodist system of itinerancy in particular enabled that denomination to entrench itself in rural Upper Canada and appeared to pose the greatest threat to the hegemony of the national churches. The enthusiasm inherent in camp-meetings, instant conversions, and shouting preachers; sermonizing by uneducated parsons and laymen; the structure of itinerancy itself – the very keys to Methodist success represented for respectable divines the antithesis of sound religion. Reactions ranged from uneasy tolerance or grudging admiration for their methods to unqualified condemnation. 'They are in one view useful and calculated to succeed among the lower order of society,' wrote the Rev. Romaine Rolph in 1827; 'but they are also a very dangerous set of missionaries not only on account of many doctrinal errors which they propagate but also on account of their antipathy against the Established Church.'[39]

On the latter point at least, Rolph was quite right. By the late 1820s the attack on the special privileges of the Church of England, and above all on its university and the Clergy Reserves, was in full swing. But dissent was also a menace for another reason. Voluntarism made a minister wholly dependent on his congregation and thus robbed him of the independent maintenance which was a crucial conceptual link to his status as a gentleman. Even if he was generously supported, voluntarism implied a different notion of what constituted a professional man. Its advocates rarely conceded that the shift was of consequence; indeed, they commonly pointed to the success of voluntarism in the United States as an example of the fact that it posed no fundamental threat to the status of the clergy.[40] Egerton Ryerson was more forthright on the matter. 'As the voluntary system is the only one that the state of society will admit of being established in this province,' he wrote in 1839,

... so it is the most efficient agency of promoting the general ends of religion in this country ... In reference to the Clergy, I admit that their support may not be always sure, or even adequate; as I admit that they may sometimes suffer want, on account of which their labours and usefulness may be circumscribed; I admit that their temporal circumstances are not in general as comfortable, and what is generally termed respectable, as when they derive their support from the state; as I admit that they may sometimes be compelled to work with their hands in order to supply the lack of voluntary liberality on the part of others; but each of these circumstances was associated with the respectable, the efficient, the divinely constituted ministry of the Apostles themselves.[41]

Ryerson's claim to the contrary notwithstanding, the apostles were tentmakers and fishermen, not gentlemen, and his formulation explicitly challenged nearly all of the Georgian presuppositions about the clergy as professional men. Thus it is not surprising that the clergy remained profoundly unsettled by the steady progress of Methodism, which, despite massive British immigration, had established itself by 1841 as the third-largest denomination in the province, barely outnumbered by the Anglicans and Presbyterians themselves.[42] Dissent not only posed a political threat to the aspirations of clergymen, but offered an alternative conception of the ministry which struck at the core of their identity as professional men.

LAWYERS FACED NO such challenge. On the one hand, their numbers, before the 1840s at least, remained small: only sixty-four lawyers had been called to the bar between 1797 and 1820, and before 1835 the number of new barristers rarely exceeded ten or fifteen annually.[43] On the other, they had always had the exclusive right to practise in the superior courts, and would gradually lay claim as well to the same right in the district (or county) courts. Settling almost exclusively in Toronto or the 'district towns,' where the courts and registry offices were located, they could make their livings from their monopoly over the higher courts and from that part of the lawyer's work which belonged primarily to the attorney and was commonly referred to as 'conveyancing' – services that involved proffering advice and drafting the pertinent documents for a large number of transactions relating to the business of everyday life, including wills; deeds; the sale, lease, and purchase of land; affidavits; assignments and bonds of various kinds; contracts; mortgages; powers of attorney; and many other routine documents.[44]

Lawyers, however, had absolutely no monopoly over conveyancing as such. Across huge tracts of the countryside, moreover, they were thin on the ground; indeed, there had been recurring complaints about the shortage of lawyers throughout the colony's early history.[45] Thus conveyancing was carried out by the laity as well. The custom in Tecumseth Township, the Rev. Featherstone Osler tells us, was that, when the father died intestate,

all property went to the eldest son, leaving the rest of the family destitute. To remedy this I generally advised the making of wills. There being no lawyer nearer than Barrie and even had there been the people would not have gone to him on account of time and expense and the dread of letting him know their intentions and circumstances, and the strong Irish prejudices against making a will, I became general will drawer and by doing so gave comfort to many a family.[46]

Before mid-century the evidence of lay conveyancing is scanty, but if Osler engaged in such activities, it is plausible to assume that other educated men who were not licensed lawyers did so as well.

As the evidence multiplies after mid-century, in any case, it came to be taken for granted that lay conveyancing was already widespread. 'At present,' as one lawyer put it in 1860, 'the conveyancing in the country parts is chiefly done by Registrars and Schoolmasters.'[47] 'In Canada,' said another in 1858, 'the conveyancer is the nearest schoolmaster, some broken-down tradesman, or a grocer's clerk with an hour or two unemployed.'[48] As that phraseology suggests, lawyers viewed lay conveyancers as ignorant pretenders, and found them as objectionable as irregular medical practitioners were to doctors.[49] But whether they approved or not, they agreed that lay conveyancing was well established by the third quarter of the nineteenth century, and there is no reason to think that it originated after mid-century. More plausibly, it was already widespread before 1850, sinking deep roots especially in country places where trained lawyers were rarely met with. Until mid-century, it is true, there are no recorded complaints about it, but we suspect this is attributable to the fact that the small number of lawyers in practice had enough work to keep them busy without worrying overmuch about lay conveyancers in the backwoods. When, in later decades, it did become an issue, they found themselves fighting a rearguard action in occupied territory, a story we will return to in another chapter.

WE ARE ON MUCH BETTER ground when we turn to medicine, in part because of the ritual condemnation of quackery by regular doctors throughout the colony's history, and in part because the 'quacks' and their allies fought back. Thus both parties left a paper trail for the historian to follow. And there is, indeed, no reason to doubt that irregular practice was widespread in Upper Canada. In the debates over new medical legislation in the early 1820s, it was widely agreed that in the countryside particularly, unlicensed medical practice was common, and that would remain the case well into the middle decades of the nineteenth century.[50] Like lawyers, licensed doctors remained relatively few in number until the 1840s and they tended to settle in urban communities where there were enough prosperous people to afford their services and pay their fees.[51] As Robert Gourlay put it on one occasion, 'A country surgeon at home has hard work of it; what may he be supposed to have where the population does not amount to seven *bodies* to the square mile and where fees must be received per the barrel, or the bushel; perhaps in lumber.' The fact was, he added, 'few men who could stand the examination of such as were regularly bred and well educated, and fewer still who had received a degree in a university, *would* practise. Nobody above the rank of a common cowleech would travel round a circle of forty or fifty miles, in the wilderness, for the pittance which could be collected ... and save in the larger villages, Kingston, Niagara and York, nothing like a genteel subsistence could be obtained.'[52]

One of the rare systematic analyses of a doctor's account books goes a long way to sustain Gourlay's view – or at least to explain why so many doctors and clergymen owned farms or sought other sources of income beyond their professional services. In their assessment of the medical practice of Harmaunus Smith in Wentworth County between 1826 and 1867, Charles Roland and Bohodar Rubashewsky conclude that, even in his busiest years, Smith never made a full-time living from his practice and depended on a variety of other activities for the substantial wealth he gradually accumulated. Smith, moreover, was no marginal member of the profession; the authors point out that by the 1850s he was far wealthier than most of his Ancaster medical colleagues.[53] The problem was that, with some exceptions, a country medical practice was not only exceedingly hard work but simply didn't generate enough income to provide a respectable living and thus to attract large numbers of highly qualified practitioners.

That professional services were uncertain in the countryside is clear from the record of public and private complaints. 'The doctors from Europe,' reads a petition of 1821 to the legislature from the Midland District, 'plant themselves in Towns; Country Practice is too fatiguing for them. They cannot expose themselves to the severe Canadian winter, and we cannot pay their exorbitant charges; in them we can place no dependence.'[54] The memoirs of Susanna Moodie and Anne Langton confirm the claims of the petition. In three recorded instances, when one or the other woman feared for the life of a family member, she sent for the village doctor; in all three cases he failed to come. 'Perhaps he did not like to incur the expense of a fatiguing journey,' wrote Moodie, 'with small chance of obtaining a sufficient remuneration.'[55] But even the promise of ten dollars from Anne Langton failed to tempt the doctor out to the bush farm where she lived.[56]

It is important, however, not to interpret the existence of unlicensed practice as merely a bad second choice, something thrown up by the unique conditions of a frontier community short of 'properly trained' doctors, or simply the exclusive resort of the poor or the isolated. As any number of historians have shown, irregular practice flourished in pre-industrial societies everywhere, and its clientele cut across the social spectrum. Moreover, the line between regular and irregular was not always firmly drawn. In the early nineteenth century, British and American medical practitioners were a varied lot, and the habit of turning to irregulars for medical assistance was part of the cultural baggage carried to Upper Canada by generations of immigrants.[57]

Just who constituted the unlicensed medical practitioners of Upper Canada? In the first place there were perfectly competent British or Upper Canadian doctors who simply never bothered to apply for an Upper Canadian licence.[58] Some had trained through apprenticeships in Upper Canada, while others had attended American medical schools but lacked either the preliminary education or professional knowledge demanded by the Medical Board. 'I have been practising like many other quacks for five years,' one unlicensed doctor explained at mid-century in an application to a Toronto medical school; 'my father not being able to help me I have never been able to attend the Lectures. I studied with a Doctor from Edinburgh College for two years and have been practising since.'[59]

A reasonable level of literacy, moreover, gave the laity access to medical texts and guides which enabled anyone to diagnose symptoms and prescribe drugs. Country shopkeepers routinely did both; so indeed did druggists or chemists, diagnosing an illness over the counter and selling their wares as cures.[60] Blacksmiths were also traditionally called upon to treat people, since they were expected to know something about medicine from working with animals.[61] And it was widely assumed that educated laymen, especially clergymen, would know something of medicine. Consider again that jack-of-all-professional-trades, the Rev. Featherstone Osler. 'For many years,' he wrote in an autobiographical sketch, 'there was no medical man nearer than the Holland Landing. I was compelled to act as such. Confidence and a few simple medicines often did wonders.'[62] He recorded an example in a letter home in 1837: 'I was riding out not long since when a poor woman stopped me to say that she had a sick infant in her arms which she wished me to see and prescribe for ... another woman came to me with a bad leg, another with his arm, two women came to have their teeth drawn etc. – 'tis of no use for me to plead ignorance – they shake their heads and say "Oh you know very well, Sir," so that I am obliged to think of something, always taking care to give nothing but what I am sure will do no hurt, should it do no good.'[63] On another occasion, 'a very respectable man in his appearance came to be bled.' Osler, however, referred him to the doctor: 'The poor I rejoice to assist in every way in my power, but if I continue to give medicine to all, gratis, my practice will increase to an extent which will be troublesome.'[64] While similar recorded examples are rare, it is reasonable to suppose that many other clergymen did as Osler did. The pastoral theologians of the eighteenth and early nineteenth centuries considered medical care to be part of the duty of Anglican clergymen, especially where doctors were not available. And the same was true of the Church of Scotland.[65] Nor was lay practice restricted to clergymen alone. In his chronicle of medicine in early southwestern Ontario, Edwin Seaborn notes examples of immigrants who came with well-stocked medical chests and became instant doctors. One such individual described his experience to Seaborn in this way:

In medicine, *nolens volens*, I had to practise. It was brought about in this way. My good mother was the possessor of a large and valuable medicine chest, prepared and fitted up with common and ordinary drugs in use in that day, by a celebrated chemist in Old London (a Dr. Reese) who also published with it a most useful work, describing uses and usual dosages, which, if well studied, would almost make a doctor of you at once ... when it became known that such an apothecary's shop was in our settlement, how it was resorted to by our suffering humanity.[66]

It also appears that much of the unlicensed practice in Upper Canada was carried on by women. Doctors who disapproved of 'ignorant females' practising midwifery sometimes labelled them quacks, but female midwifery was perfectly legal in Upper Canada and it was taken for granted that those engaged in it were 'generally employed' throughout the countryside.[67] In the larger towns they even advertised their services in the newspapers, which suggests that some at least had substantial, if not full-time, practices, and that they were competing with local doctors for the same sort of clientele.[68] Though it is tantalizingly thin, some evidence exists to suggest that the services of female practitioners extended well beyond midwifery. We have, for example, a complaint by a doctor in 1851 about 'a number of female quacks who practise all over the country, and are a great nuisance, I do not mean by attending obstetric patients, but by attending common cases of disease.'[69] While Featherstone Osler doctored the men, his 'good wife attended to the women and children.'[70] Anne Langton routinely distributed small phials of quinine to neighbours suffering from the fevers common in the bush.[71] Undoubtedly much of women's medical practice was part-time or occasional, and some of it was probably unpaid; but then so was the practice of men like Featherstone Osler.

These various forms of unlicensed practice are best described as traditional in nature. Regular doctors might condemn itinerant bone-setters or 'ignorant' midwives, but the latter were part of the culture of the early nineteenth century, and the regulars were in any case unlikely to criticize the likes of Featherstone Osler, who probably adhered to the same sort of therapeutic doctrines as licensed doctors themselves. But, in the 1830s and 1840s, a new phenomenon appeared – the 'medical sect.' The sectarians not only offered licensed doctors economic competition but openly challenged the efficacy of regular therapeutics as well.

WHAT WAS IT THAT differentiated regular medicine from the 'sects'?[72] Most licensed doctors in Upper Canada shared a common set of therapeutic doctrines. Disease, in their view, was a state of physical disequilibrium manifested in various generalized symptoms. It was the duty of the doctor to intervene actively when illness occurred, and to bring to bear an armoury of practices designed to cure the disease by attacking its symptoms. For example, bleeding relieved agitation or fever, and blistering acted as a counterirritant to draw off the sources of disequilibrium. Strong purges aided the body in a similar way, the favourite cathartic being large doses of 'calomel' (or chloride of mercury).

By mid-century some of the most extreme forms of regular therapeutics were being abandoned, but it is important not to understate the 'heroic' nature of some of these practices lest the 'quacks' be dismissed as merely a bizarre fringe. Consider some examples. In 1835 a southwestern Ontario doctor penned this well-regarded passage on treating the cholera:

If the treatment be begun very early ... 20 or 30 grains of Calomel, with half a pint of hot ginger tea and rendered more diffusible by adding a small quantity of brandy or whiskey, and keeping the body warm, will be all that is necessary ... fulness at the pit of the stomach ... is a pretty sure indication for the necessity of bleeding ... draw three half pints or more ... if you fail of getting blood first, try again, and be sure to make a large opening in the vein, even make an orifice in each arm ... if you succeed in bleeding ... the danger is greatly diminished.[73]

When, after a long journey across the Atlantic, Catharine Parr Traill fell ill on her arrival at Cobourg, the remedies prescribed by the doctor were 'bleeding, a portion of opium, blue pill, and some sort of salts – not the common Epsom.'[74] In 1821 Anne Powell reported to her daughter that a neighbour was very ill with pleurisy and was 'much weakened by bleeding and had yesterday a large Blister applied.'[75] In 1848 the young Robert Baldwin, Jr, reported to his father that Dr Widmer had diagnosed his ailment as 'Neuralgia. I don't know whether I ought to put a capital N in Neuralgia but I know that there was capital hurting in the blister he put behind my ear to cure it.'[76]

In nineteenth-century Upper Canada there were three important alternatives to the system of therapeutics pursued by regular doctors. In the main they had spread northwards from the United States. One group, known as the botanics, emerged out of the numerous and unorganized 'root doctors' common in rural North America in the early nineteenth century. As one of their Canadian leaders explained in 1851, they went by 'various names, Botanics, Thomsonians, Hydropathists etc. many of whom had been studying and practising in Canada West, with general success, for 15 or twenty years.' They practised a 'reformed system of medicine' which depended upon herbs and other 'natural' medicines, and rejected 'bleeding, minerals and poisonous substances.'[77] The botanics tended to confine themselves to rural areas, and most lacked any formal training in a medical school. Not all of them were Thomsonians, but the latter group had constituted something like an organized movement in the United States since the 1820s, and by the 1840s the same was true in Upper Canada.

There was, as well, a second group, known as 'eclectics,' who borrowed therapeutic principles from both the regulars and the botanics, 'in attempting to employ all that was perceived to be beneficial while rejecting what they considered to be unsatisfactory' – especially the mineral purgatives and bleeding characteristic of heroic therapy.[78] Before mid-century the eclectics and botanics were relatively undifferentiated; after that, the former began to lay stress upon more systematic training at 'some Eclectic Medical College, that thus we may become equally qualified, as to learning and other attainments, with the other branches of the medical profession.'[79] Taken together, the botanics and eclectics were not a peripheral element in Upper Canadian medicine. Though perhaps predominantly rural, they could be found in the towns and cities as well, and they were not only numerous enough at mid-century to form their own association but, when threatened by an extension of the penal laws against illegal practice, were able to mobilize a substantial lay constituency, including some influential members of the political community.[80]

The third alternative therapeutic system was homeopathy. The homeopathic approach to therapy was based on two principles: the treatment and cure of disease by dosing the patient with drugs which, in a healthy person, caused the same symptoms exhibited by the sick person; and the doctrine that extremely small doses of drugs were sufficient, and desirable, for treatment. The homeopaths were new to Upper Canada in the late 1840s and differed from the botanics or early eclectics in two important respects. Unlike them, the homeopaths established their practices in the larger towns and cities and were both well educated and well trained, often indeed beginning as regular doctors and then converting to homeopathy.[81]

How, one might ask, did the patient fare under the care of these various sorts of doctors? We do not know how many people suffered or died from the ministrations of the fraudulent or the ignorant. But we do know that homeopaths and regulars were likely to be equally competent in such skills as surgery or obstetrics, and the same is true of the schooled eclectic. Where widely accepted therapies existed, such as smallpox vaccine, all three types of practitioners might make use of them. Otherwise, they all pursued therapeutic methods which, when not actually dangerous, were generally ineffective. There was, indeed, sometimes good reason for the patient to prefer an irregular practitioner. At the very least, herbal medicine and small doses promised a less ferocious attack on the patient's system than massive blood-letting or violent purging with mercury. By mid-century, in any case, Upper Canada's medicine resembled its religion. It had three or four 'sects,' of which regular medicine, or so at least its opponents claimed, was just one.

Having said that, however, it is important to avoid condescending to the past. In the main, mid-century medical practitioners were not charlatans, and the laity were not fools. Catharine Traill was not only bled and dosed with salts at Cobourg, but she also *believed* it cured her: 'the remedies proved effectual,' she wrote, 'though I suffered much from sickness and headaches for some days.' The younger Robert Baldwin may have suffered from his blister but he added, 'at any rate it cured it.' Seized by an agonizing pain in his side, the Rev. Mark Stark sent for a doctor who 'bled me and afterwards sent me a blister to put on. The pain soon subsided.'[82] There are many other examples besides. In this sense regular therapeutics legitimized itself because it was seen to work, and though we know far less about the alternative therapies, the same is probably true for them as well.[83] At mid-century, in any case, medicine was accepted as 'the uncertain art' and, in the words of one contemporary, 'I laugh at those grave personages [doctors] when in health, but am I unwell, I submit to murderous prescriptions.'[84] We forget too easily, moreover, that in the mid-nineteenth century there was a competing explanation for illness and death that was far more compelling than any medical theory. The knowledge and skills of doctors were undoubtedly valuable, the editor of the *Christian Guardian* intoned in 1834, but in any understanding of illness or death it was a paramount error to exclude the agency of God: 'Because in the Divine Administration "it is appointed unto all men to die." Diseases of the body and disorders of the physical world, such as tempests, earthquakes, lightning, etc., are the appointed means to this determined end. Within certain though undefined limits, human skill or agency can no more control the means than it can defeat the end.'[85] At mid-century, in sum, people acknowledged the existence of medical knowledge and skill, and at the same time acknowledged its limits. Though the efficacy of modern medicine is infinitely greater, we do no differently today, submitting ourselves to therapies that don't always work, and refusing to lapse into therapeutic nihilism just because doctors can't always cure cancer, heart disease, or the common cold.

There is, however, a fundamental difference between past and present: the moral legitimacy of medical practice was not confined to licensed practitioners. From family papers, diaries, and other pertinent records of the time, it seems fairly certain that, among the middle classes at least, regular medicine was conventionally preferred; but it is no less true that it was not recognized as a form of therapeutics which definitionally or exclusively produced superior results, and even the more prosperous were frequently to be found exploring alternative therapies.[86] Homeopathy proved to have particular attractions for the upper and middle classes. Its practitioners were trained, its therapy was gentler, and its claims to efficacy appeared at least as legitimate as those of regular medicine.[87]

Regular medicine had another chink in its armour as well. John Harley Warner has pointed out that one crucial element in the professional identity of regular medicine was informed judgment arising from prolonged experience in observing and treating illness and disease, a factor rated more important than extensive training in medical science. He has also noted the central role of the doctrine of specificity – the importance placed on understanding the particular circumstances which governed the interplay of patients and diseases.[88] But both of these doctrines were two-edged swords: 'untrained' midwives and unlicensed 'quacks' might claim legitimacy on the same grounds. There were some men in the countryside, said Barnabus Bidwell in 1822 in defence of unlicensed practitioners, 'who, by their long course of practise had acquired that skill and knowledge which were derived from experience ... They were practically acquainted with the diseases of this climate and country, and the most successful modes of treating them; and yet were less capable of passing a satisfactory examination before the medical board, than students recently from their studies, but destitute of experience. Some of these experienced Physicians and Surgeons,' Bidwell continued, 'would their neighbours trust with their health and lives sooner than they would other scientific Physicians of elementary learning without the benefit of experience. And such would be his own choice in case of sickness.'[89]

Upper Canadians, in any case, had considerable choice as to the kind of medical practitioner they employed and the kind of therapeutic regime they might experience. However imperfect it might be, there was a market for medical services which provided work for different kinds of practitioners. And regardless of the law, the Medical Board, or the laments of regular doctors, the unlicensed or irregular practitioners had, by mid-century, sunk deep roots in Upper Canada, especially in those parts of the colony beyond the reach of the cities and larger towns.

AT THE SAME TIME as various forms of irregular or lay practice in religion, law, or medicine were establishing themselves in the colony, a menacing strain of anti-professional sentiment was growing which challenged the pretensions of the professions and sought the abolition of their privileges. Such views were part of a complex of ideas which together constituted what E.P. Thompson has called 'small producer ideology' or 'popular radicalism' and which condemned 'Old Corruption' in both Britain and the colonies, demanding an end to all establishments, special privileges, and monopolies in church, state, and civil society generally.[90] Criticism of the professions was a recurring subtheme in the writings of men of international influence like Tom Paine or William Cobbett, and in Upper Canada, of William Lyon Mackenzie. Professional monopolies were, in their eyes, simply one part of a larger system of rule by which the unproductive classes lived off the producers of society's wealth, extracting income from the farmer, the artisan, the merchant, and the manufacturer, through the tithes, fees, and taxes they could sequester by virtue of their control over patronage, the administration of government, and monopolies of office. Part of the reform program throughout Upper Canadian history, and especially of radical reform, was the destruction of the *ancien régime*, and that included traditional professionalism.

Perhaps no issue galvanized Upper Canadians as did the future of the Clergy Reserves. In a colony characterized by religious pluralism, indeed where the majority of the population was non-Anglican, the special privileges of the Church of England and its claims to be the established church were seen as a profound affront to the principles of religious liberty and religious equality. The attack on the Clergy Reserves cut across the political spectrum and was rooted in religious as well as political ideologies. Regardless of their politics, Methodists, Baptists, Congregationalists, Presbyterians, and even some Anglicans found common ground in opposition to the enormous land endowment set aside for the Church of England, and between 1828 and 1836 alone, seven bills for the sale of the Clergy Reserves were passed by Reform and Conservative majorities in the assembly, only to be rejected by the Legislative Council.[91]

Before 1850 neither medicine nor law suffered anything like the sustained attack that the Anglican clergy experienced. But they were not immune from the radical rhetoric of the day. William Riddell, Ontario's pioneer legal historian, recorded the recurring outbreaks of complaints about the Law Society's monopoly, excessive court fees, and the shortage of practitioners; more recently, Paul Romney has drawn attention to the same phenomenon.[92] The special privileges of the Law Society were also a repeated subject of criticism in the reform press throughout the 1820s and 1830s.[93] Nor was such criticism merely a hobby-horse of men like Mackenzie who could be dismissed by the respectable as extremists. Neither W.H. Merritt nor David Thorburn, to take but two examples, could be described as a wild-eyed radical, and both condemned, in unqualified terms, the abolition of the Courts of Requests. They flatly rejected the charges of lay incompetence, Thorburn describing these institutions as 'emphatically' the 'poor man's court' because justice in matters of small claims was cheap and close to home.[94] And Merritt called attention to the fact that 'there [are] upwards of thirty lawyers in this house (a laugh) and it affords an excellent opportunity for them to provide Judgeships for members of their profession (Hear, Hear).'[95] Merritt, moreover, was among a handful of MLAs who unsuccessfully tried to derail the 1839 act creating a college of physicians and surgeons through a wildly contrary amendment which would have virtually set the rest of the act at naught:

Provided always, that nothing in this Act shall prevent, or be construed to prevent the inhabitants living in the country or remote parts of the Province, (in the event of sickness in their families, and there not being within a convenient distance a physician authorised to practice under the provisions of this Act, or from inability to procure the services of such physician, or a probability of not being able to procure the services of such in time, and that serious consequences would be likely to occur from delay) to procure the medical assistance of any skilful person they may think most likely to render essential service, and that no such skilful person who shall judiciously render such services, shall be liable to any of the penalties imposed by the Act.[96]

Merritt's dissent on both the law and medical bills also reminds us that we are not dealing with unrelated attacks on particular occupations, but with something more like a coherent outlook suspicious of inherited institutions apparently designed to enrich a colonial gentry at the expense of the productive and even the poor members of society. To Mackenzie it was the government's 'offensive and defensive alliance with the chartered banks, Canada Company, "Lawyers Trade Union" and bribed clergy.'[97] The same conviction informed the arguments put forward by James Wilson, a Reform member of the legislature. Speaking in 1821 about a medical bill, he warned that 'if no person were allowed to practice but regular practitioners, they would charge so high, that the poor could obtain no benefit from them. A poor man might come fifty miles from the wilderness for their assistance; he might be in the greatest distress, but he was not well able to pay and there was no relief for him. The Physician, *like the Lawyer who is always fond of a high charge*, would attend a rich man, within a few miles of him; but the poor, in remote parts, might perish for want of assistance.'[98] The problem, said Wilson a few years later, was that 'we have too many lawyers already; the growth of these, and Established Clergymen and Doctors was oppressive to the country, and there appeared to be no end to the troubles and afflictions they brought upon people.'[99] Similarly, Jennifer and J.T.H. Connor have drawn attention to the way in which Thomsonian medical doctrine was enmeshed in a larger political program designed to end the tyranny of the old regime.[100] Not surprisingly, two of the Upper Canadian editions of Thomson's *New Guide to Health* were published in the early 1830s by outspoken reformers, one of them being William Buell. And Thomson's language, political as well as medical, would soon become an integral part of Upper Canadian radical rhetoric. The attempt to restrict medical practice, said one correspondent to the *Brockville Recorder* in 1844, was like the attempt to maintain religious monopolies. It merely promoted 'ignorance, arrogance, and Doctorcraft amongst a few Medical Monopolists.' Knowledge of one or many languages, liberal or little education, was really irrelevant to medical practice. For illness 'is universally observed by attentive men, and our native Vegetable Medicines that we are defending the right to use and sell without restraint, are far better known to persons of rural habits, and best applied ... by unlearned empirics, so called in contradistinction to those who have learned to clothe these plain matters with mysterious and unmeaning technicalities.'[101]

THE PROFESSIONAL GENTLEMEN of Upper Canada, in sum, had never had things all their own way at any time in the colony's history. There were always competitors, and critics who contested their view of the world. The two national churches were surrounded by dissent. Quacks 'infested' the countryside, and medical sects rose up to challenge the legitimacy of regular therapeutics. The privileges of all three learned professions came under attack in the legislature and the press. By the early 1840s, nonetheless, the institutions and assumptions of Georgian professionalism were still largely intact. Whether either could survive the political and economic forces that were changing the face of Upper Canada during the middle decades of the nineteenth century remained to be seen.

3
The Moment of Mid-Century Radicalism

Though the critics of the professions continued to make their voices heard throughout the 1840s, a sustained attack on professional privilege was deflected for most of the decade as even the most radical elements in the Reform Party remained united behind social conservatives like Robert Baldwin in order to secure responsible government. After 1848, however, there was room on the political agenda for other issues, and the rising tide of political radicalism ensured that professional men would bear their full share of its brunt.

The mid-century assault on the professions was carried out by an unstable political coalition and motivated by a variety of economic and social aims which reflected the complex and sometimes conflicting cross-currents of Upper Canadian liberalism.[1] There were business and commercial interests eager to remake the world in their own image by sweeping away all the accumulated debris of the past. There were those who, often without any other common ground, joined in the attack on the Church of England in the name of religious liberty. There were the old radicals and newly minted Clear Grits whose aim, as William McDougall once put it, was 'to roll the country down to a commonsense democracy.'[2] Perhaps Francis Hincks caught the spirit of the era best when he wrote to Robert Baldwin that 'we are now fighting the battle of the *middle* classes against the aristocracy.'[3] The meaning of either term may have been amorphous in the relatively inchoate social world of the 1840s, but his phrase reflects the widely shared conviction that Upper Canada's old regime had to be replaced by institutions and assumptions more congruent with an age of economic expansion and political reform. Inevitably the entire edifice of Georgian professionalism, so tightly woven into the social and intellectual fabric of the past, would come under attack as well.

EACH OF THE PROFESSIONS has its own history in the years around mid-century and, as each came under scrutiny, the focus of attention might shift from one set of issues to another. Yet throughout the period two underlying principles gave some coherence to the attacks on all three professions. First, in an era increasingly informed by the doctrines of free trade, the professions represented, especially to liberal and radical critics, prime examples of the evils and follies of monopoly. To one extent or another, old reformers like William Lyon Mackenzie, more cautious liberal moderates like George Brown, or the young turks of the Clear Grit movement such as William McDougall, all agreed that free trade was a force for the liberation of humanity not only in commerce but in religion, medicine, and law as well. Monopoly bred inefficiency and corruption, masked incompetence, and pitted the private interest of a class against the public good. In a passage resonant with the broader attack on the presuppositions of Georgian professionalism, Brown condemned the whole tendency of the state-church system:

It raises the pastor above his flock, makes him independent of them – independent for life; clothes him in purple and fine linen, and separates him effectually from the great mass of society ... Place a man in any situation, with a provision for life secured to him whether he does his work well or does it ill, and as soon as you do so, you will make him lazy and inefficient ... But very different is it under the voluntary principle. A man who commences studying for the pulpit must weigh well his qualifications; he must consider if he can obtain a Church by his ability, and keep it filled by his energy and zeal.[4]

A monopoly in medicine, wrote the editor of the *Examiner*, was 'an insidious and crafty project. Art and industry and skill want no "protection," but it is often enough sought by those who seek only for professional influence and personal aggrandizement.'[5] In Upper Canada 'men are allowed to select their own ministers,' William Lyon Mackenzie told the legislature in 1851, 'and why not be allowed to select their own lawyers. The country wished to get rid of this principle of monopoly because it was contrary to the genius of the age ... He desired any man who chose to do so, to stick up his shingle, and call himself a lawyer, just as he could do if he were a watchmaker. The ablest man would always get the greatest practice.'[6]

The corollary principle was that of equal rights for all and special privilege for none. It was applied vigorously by the likes of George Brown against religious establishments, which in his view were dangerous to civil liberty. Men had the fundamental right to choose their faith, Brown had always argued: the alternative was tyranny and persecution.⁷ But the same principle applied to other professions as well. The people of Upper Canada, wrote the editor of the *North American* in 1852, 'maintain the right ... to employ their Doctors as they do their Ministers, or blacksmiths, or carpenters, or Members of Parliament themselves. They claim the right to employ those in whom *they* – not Parliament – have most confidence ... we have a decided objection to giving any one class of the community *peculiar* privileges, for this single and sufficient reason that they have no *right* to them.'⁸

'Peculiar privileges,' then, fettered the economic, social, and moral progress of humankind, stunted the growth of knowledge and science, and constrained the individual's civil liberties. These were hardly new themes in the political discourse of nineteenth-century Upper Canada, but they had acquired powerful protagonists in the years around mid-century and would be more persuasive to a larger constituency than at any other time except, perhaps, in the last two decades of the century.

FOR THE TWO NATIONAL churches, the first fruit of these doctrines was the renewed conflict over the Clergy Reserves which convulsed the colony between 1848 and 1854. The central issues at stake were always those of church–state relations, the meaning of civil liberties, the correct interpretation of scriptural prescriptions, and the best means of sustaining the work of the churches in a new era. But the role and status of the minister of religion also continued to constitute an important subtheme, and inevitably became a part of the larger argument whenever the future of the Clergy Reserves was debated.

In 1851, for example, a two-day public debate took place at Simcoe in which a bevy of distinguished ministers of several denominations participated. Benjamin Cronyn, the rector of St Paul's, London, spoke for the Anglicans, defending state aid on the grounds that it was a tithe sanctioned by scripture, essential to provide an independent and respectable maintenance to the clergy, and the only effective means by which the evangelization of society could be carried out. Ministers could hardly be recruited if no provision was made for their support. 'The inheritance which God has bestowed on me are my talents ... and the education which brought these talents into the market.'⁹ But that inheritance, to be put to best use, required material support. Thus, Cronyn concluded, it was a divine duty imposed on governments 'to see that ministers of the gospel be provided in every part of the country – [to] the poor as well as the rich – especially [to] the poor in order that those who cannot pay on the voluntary system ... who cannot themselves support a minister' would have one nonetheless.¹⁰

The voluntarists at Simcoe agreed with Cronyn that the tithe in support of the churches was a 'Divine Command.' But they insisted it must be obeyed out of individual conscience and not enforced by the state on all citizens, which constituted a violation of religious liberty. They also interpreted the meaning of ministerial independence differently. Anglicans had always worried about subjection to the whims of a congregation and the tides of popular passion. To the voluntarists it was not dependence on a congregation that was to be feared but rather government grants themselves, which would result in ministers 'degraded to mere hirelings and servants of any state government.'[11] As to the necessity for grants to sustain the work of the church among the poor, the Rev. William Gilmore, a Baptist minister, quoted St Paul on the rapid growth of the early church and added that, 'in the course of all their itinerancy, never do we hear the apostles complain of want of funds to keep them in any locality. Never I say; yet we know that at that time the state afforded no relief.'[12]

The apostles, indeed, became a favourite stalking-horse, the voluntarist press pointing to their efficacy despite the lack of any state support, and the Anglican and Presbyterian journals replying that they were efficient *despite* often being in poverty.[13] Similarly, during the legislative debates on the Clergy Reserves, one MPP, Arthur Rankin, struck at the entire nexus of assumptions underpinning the views of men like Cronyn. Some people believed 'that it was absolutely necessary to provide for the maintenance of clergymen in a proper station. It was argued that a clergyman was a gentleman, whose education was costly, and that his position in society was what was commonly known as the position of a gentleman. Did Jesus Christ come into this world as a gentleman? Were his immediate followers gentlemen?' The essential problem with the Church of England ministry, Rankin went on, was that parents treated it like any other profession – as a means of securing their sons a fixed income and a position in society; but these were entirely wrong motives to 'prompt a man to devote himself to the service of God.'[14]

The long and passionate debate over the Clergy Reserves has been described by many historians and we do not intend to review it in any detail here. It ended with the secularization of the reserves in 1854. Both the Church of England and the Kirk fought bitter rearguard actions, petitioning the Crown, sending representatives to oppose it before the imperial Parliament, and lobbying hard among those Canadian MPPs who might rally to their cause.[15] For Strachan the implications seemed appalling, and *The Church* echoed his worst fears. The incomes of nearly all clergymen would fall precipitously, its editor warned early in 1854, but even more ominous, it would become impossible to attract new candidates for the ministry. 'So long as there is a prospect of something fixed, trifling though it may be – something to shield them in a slight degree from entire dependence, young men of talent qualified to adorn any profession will ... be found to come forward.' But there would be far fewer without some form of fixed stipend. 'Parents will rarely give any encouragement to their children to enter such a poor profession.'[16] The Kirk reacted no differently, the editor of *The Presbyterian* describing it as 'a calamity' for all of the same reasons.[17]

There were, indeed, grounds for such pessimism about the future. The settlement of 1854, as J.L.H. Henderson writes, was 'clearly a defeat of the first magnitude for the idea of a national church.'[18] And it was also a symbolic turning-point in the development of the clerical profession itself. Anglicans and Presbyterians had become but two denominations among several others, and their ministers had to learn to live in an environment which exalted the virtues of voluntarism and pluralism. If they were not to be part of a civil establishment responsible for the good order and direction of their society, in command of an independent income which would secure their dignity as professional gentlemen, what were they to become?

BY THE EARLY 1850s, the medical profession was in crisis as well. Initially at least, the loss of the College of Physicians and Surgeons in 1841 was seen as nothing more than a temporary set-back. Almost immediately, prominent doctors in Toronto and Montreal set about organizing petitions and drafting bills which would strengthen the Medical Board or replace it with something akin to the failed legislation of 1839. In 1845 a bill covering both Upper and Lower Canada was proposed; in 1846 there was one for Upper Canada alone.[19] Neither got beyond first reading, but in the next year the legislature approved a medical incorporation act for Lower Canada.[20] Buoyed with the hope that a similar measure would quickly be forthcoming,[21] Upper Canadian medical men put their own bills before the legislature, first in 1849 and then again in 1850 and 1851.

What was it that provoked this thirst for new legislation? According to their own accounts, medical men were motivated by two overriding considerations. One was their belief that quackery was a growing menace.[22] The other was the conviction that standards of general and professional education needed to be raised and entry to the profession more closely regulated. Legislation which encapsulated these objectives, the petitions of the mid-1840s had maintained, 'would confer upon the practitioners of medicine, the independence, respectability, and advantages, which the incorporation of the Law Society has obtained for its members, and thus ultimately raise the medical profession to that position in public regard to which it is, by its utility and importance, so justly entitled.'[23]

The surviving medical record of the 1840s is not rich. There is no Upper Canadian medical journal before mid-century and we must rely on a Montreal-based journal which focused mainly on Lower Canadian interests. Few other sources exist to help elucidate practitioners' views or the divisions among them. The two issues of quackery and education nonetheless constituted the core of the concerns they articulated and deserve to be taken seriously. But they need interpretation too. As the population grew it is perfectly plausible to think that so too did the incidence of 'quackery': more midwives, more counter-prescribing druggists, more botanics and others who were not regularly bred. But was it simply this which provoked the growing volume of complaint? Throughout Upper Canadian history most regulars treated quacks as their natural enemies, but they were not necessarily economic competitors. Careful work on rural practice in early modern England suggests that the community itself played a vital role in lending sanction to different types of practitioners, all operating in close proximity to one another. 'The situation tended to create a "system of competencies" with the scope of practice defined largely by what the practitioners' skills were perceived to be.'[24] Something rather similar existed in late eighteenth-century America, as Laurel Ulrich's penetrating analysis of one midwife's diary makes clear: doctors had their place and their role, but much of routine medical practice fell to others.[25] That such patterns might also have existed in Upper Canada is at least a plausible explanation for the coexistence of midwives, root doctors, bone-setters, itinerant tooth-pullers, and licensed practitioners in the same community: the midwife practising her particular skills, except perhaps in cases of unusual risk; the root doctor and the regular having equal legitimacy in those cases bearing on internal medicine, where the efficacy of the regular was most uncertain; and the trained regular prized for his ability to deal with difficult births, for his surgical skills in lancing boils or removing growths, or for repairing fractures beyond the skills of the local bone-setter.

This, we concede, is pure surmise on our part, but there is one element which gives it plausibility. While the regulars had always routinely condemned the dangers of quackery, it is only around mid-century that the chorus of complaints rises to a crescendo. This may be nothing more than an artefact of the surviving medical record. But it may, on the other hand, reflect the fact that so long as there were relatively few licensed doctors, irregular practice did not constitute an economic threat, and a system of overlapping competencies could be tolerated. After 1840, however, the number of regular practitioners began to multiply. According to J.T.H. Connor's estimates, the number of licentiates in Upper Canada more than tripled, from 160 to 520 between 1840 and 1851, and the ratio of doctors to population dropped, from 1:3,000 to 1:1,830.[26] Almost certainly the bite of competition among regulars themselves grew keener. Thus they began to train their guns on all forms of irregular practice in order to lay claim to the work hitherto done by the midwife, the druggist, or the bone-setter. The cry of excessive competition, in other words, may well have arisen because of changes within regular medicine itself *rather* than from the multiplication of irregular practitioners, or, perhaps, *along with* their multiplication. We will never know for certain because we have no means of estimating the quantitative dimensions of unlicensed practice in the nineteenth century. It fits, nonetheless, a wider pattern the reader will encounter in other chapters of this book. It also fits the experience elsewhere. In his careful analysis of overcrowding among general practitioners in early nineteenth-century England, Irvine Loudon suggests that the outcry against quackery coincided with periodic surges of overcrowding within regular medicine.[27] Under such circumstances it would certainly make sense to pursue both the suppression of quackery and the reduction of new entrants through higher educational standards.

But there may have been a second important reason for seeking such measures. What was new about quackery in the 1830s and 1840s was the appearance of medical sects or movements which directly challenged both regular therapeutic doctrines and the nature of medicine as a learned profession. In a fruitful essay on regular medicine in antebellum America, John Harley Warner has argued that this development was of critical importance for it compelled regulars 'to reflect upon their relationship to those who were assailing them. The rise of medical sectarianism,' Warner continues,

heightened regular practitioners' awareness of their group identity and its rooting in allegiance to a shared tradition. At the same time, those who chose to bind themselves to established tradition self-consciously began to consider who among their brethren shared their beliefs and who dissented from them, a distinction that could not be reduced to education or skill alone. *For the first time in American medicine, heresy – not ignorance – became a crucial issue.* With the strengthening concept of orthodoxy, regular physicians looked for ways of setting themselves apart from heterodox healers and purifying their own ranks.[28]

Warner has evidence for his hypothesis; for the 1840s at least, we have almost none. Yet, on the face of it, the notion looks eminently plausible. The condemnation of quackery, which would grow in volume into the 1850s, along with the call for improved education and corporate control over the regulation of entry and internal discipline, would help to sharpen the distinction between regular and heterodox medicine. And certainly in the 1860s and 1870s, this was a pre-eminent concern of the medical leadership in Upper Canada. Stiffer penal laws and a corporate identity would build a level of professional solidarity not only by reducing competition but by reinforcing the claims to exclusive therapeutic legitimacy and to regular medicine's continuing place among Upper Canada's learned professions.

WHATEVER THE INTENT of the regulars, in any case, all three of the mid-century medical bills went down to defeat.[29] Factionalism among Toronto doctors and indifference or dissent among their country colleagues made it easy for politicians to conclude that doctors themselves disagreed on the best course to pursue. The irregulars, moreover, mounted a vigorous campaign, burying the legislature with petitions opposing the medical bills and calling for 'the untrammelled right of choice in relation to the *philosophy and means of health.*'[30] If the Baldwin papers are any indication, the politicians were also alerted privately to the opposition which existed at the grass-roots level. Eli Gorham was only one of several of Baldwin's supporters in his own riding who wrote to protest the incorporation bills. 'There is many in this part,' said Gorham, who

> feel grived at the part you take in the Medical Bill there is such a large majority in favor of root Doctors as some of the members are pleased to term the Bottanac Doctors, if the Medical Bill should pass and become a law it is my settled Belief it could [not] be put in force in this part, so determined are the people to have the privilege of choosing their own doctors ... for my own part I had much rather be cured by a quack than killed according to Law. There is three Doctors of the old School in Newmarket and one Thompsonian and he gits more to do than all the other three and no act of parliament can prevent the people from judging who they will have to cure them, I hope if you git this letter before the Bill is past or disposed of you will Reconsider the Bill and oppose its passing.[31]

But the defeat of the various medical bills was not due simply to internal divisions or to effective lobbying by the 'root doctors' and their supporters. By the early 1850s there was also an unmistakable crisis of confidence among the middle and upper classes about the efficacy of regular medicine. The spread of botanic and homeopathic doctrines, the doubts about heroic therapeutics expressed in Britain and America by a small but growing phalanx of regular doctors, the failure to cure or control the recurring outbreaks of cholera, the personal horrors of bleeding, blistering, and dosing with mercury, and the 'conversions' of some doctors to alternative therapeutics had created a market in medical ideas among the educated laity. And that in turn bred deep reservations about the *monopolistic* privileges of regular medicine. From the late 1840s onwards, a growing number of influential voices expressed the view that certification by a medical board controlled by regular practitioners was no longer an essential prerequisite for competence. In the House, in 1850, J.S. Macdonald could point to doctors 'who had not qualified themselves according to the provision of the bill by a course of study, but still they were men of skill and talent.'[32] To the editor of the *Christian Guardian*, it was an 'outrage' to 'prevent experienced and intelligent men from attending a patient or taking a fee, merely because they have not regularly graduated, although they may have been the only means of saving life.'[33] The editors of reform papers like the *North American* concurred and said so repeatedly; but so did the editor of the more conservative *Leader*.[34]

It was at this point that shifting perceptions about therapeutic doctrine began to mesh with the larger currents of mid-century Upper Canadian political thought. Leading doctors were occasionally wont to blame their plight on 'the levelling spirit of the age,' or the 'democratic elements of our communities,' and they were not entirely wrong to do so.[35] 'If carpenters or masons came before the House to demand such privileges as to exclude competition,' said W.H. Merritt, 'it would be thought monstrous; why should the learned professions have a monopoly?'[36] For one Grit, Peter Perry, the issue was not incorporation, which he was not opposed to, but monopoly. 'He would ask the members of the House if they did not consider themselves capable to judge what physician was best able to satisfy their wants. He was sure they did, and yet they endeavoured to deprive the people of a similar privilege.'[37] The following year, indeed, Perry would act on his convictions in resorting to 'a botanical physician' to save his life, after regular medicine failed him.[38] Here then was the voice, not only of irregular medicine, but of political radicalism as well, seeking to put an end to all manner of sinecures, monopolies, and closed corporations, and thus to 'roll the country down to a common-sense democracy.' Such views were echoed by many others in the Assembly and in the press. Indeed, had it not been for Lower Canadian votes, it is entirely possible that the whole system of licensing might have been abolished. W.B. Richards proposed a bill to do just that in 1851, and on second reading his Upper Canadian colleagues split their votes almost evenly – fourteen for it and fifteen against.[39]

To those influential Toronto doctors who had promoted them, the rejection of the medical incorporation bills was a humiliating defeat. They were especially galled when their 'sister professions' deserted them – when clergymen signed petitions in support of the quacks, or when lawyers, secure behind the ramparts of the Law Society, voted for free trade in medicine.[40] 'The clerical and legal professions of Canada have the benefit of acts of incorporation by which means they are permitted to regulate all matters appertaining to their particular class,' wrote the editor of the *Upper Canada Journal of Medical ... Science*, 'and it is unjust that the medical profession of Canada West should alone be excluded from a similar benefit.'[41] The outcome, in any case, was conceived to be a disaster. Surrounded by quackery, and unable to control their own numbers, discipline their own members, or raise their own educational standards, doctors increasingly perceived themselves, as one regular bleated in another medical journal, burdened with 'blighted hopes, empty pockets, and a degraded position'; unless something was done immediately, they would inevitably 'sink step by step, until we arrive at the last rung of the social ladder.'[42]

THE FACT OF THE MATTER was, nonetheless, that regular medicine remained privileged under the law. The Medical Board of Upper Canada, consisting solely of regulars, retained its legal powers to examine all practitioners except those with a degree from a British or colonial university, and the licence to practise depended upon a candidate's success in the examination. But if no single system of therapeutics could claim exclusive legitimacy, how could the existing law be justified? Some replied, unequivocally, that it could not, and turned to the model that lay at Upper Canada's doorstep. In the United States, most eighteenth-century licensing laws had already been repealed, and medical free trade reigned supreme.[43] This was the policy proposed by the Upper Canadian eclectics when they demanded 'the untrammelled right of choice' in medicine, and if their petitions are any indication, the policy had broad popular appeal. It had, as we have already seen, support from influential laymen as well. For example, William Buell and James Lesslie, as editors of the *Recorder* and *Examiner*, and W.H. Merritt, W.B. Richards, and Billa Flint in the legislature, all at one time or another advocated repeal of the existing legislation and the introduction of American-style *laissez-faire*.[44]

The tide of support for unrestricted free trade in medicine, however, began to ebb in the years following 1852, paralleling the decline in political radicalism itself. By the second half of the 1850s, one rarely finds an influential voice in either the press or the legislature calling for the repeal of all restrictions on the practice of medicine. There was, on the other hand, no support for the *status quo*. Instead, a middle position gradually emerged which favoured neither unqualified free trade nor monopoly.[45] The law needed to be changed, in other words, but not simply repealed. Sound training had to be ensured, and competence certified by some public authority. The diversity of medical systems needed to be preserved, yet the health and the pocketbooks of the public needed protection against ignorance and charlatanism. Supported by petitions from across the province, a bill to legalize homeopathy was introduced in the Assembly in 1859. According to the *Leader*, the regulars lobbied vigorously against it,[46] but despite their protests the bill passed easily. The new act established a board of homeopathic doctors to examine and license their own practitioners. It specified the standards of education required of students and provided for the election of future board members by the practitioners licensed under it. Two years later, in 1861, and again accompanied by bundles of petitions, another bill passed swiftly through the legislature, giving eclectic practitioners their own board with the same structure and responsibilities as that of the homeopaths.[47]

The settlement of 1859–61 resolved the policy dilemmas of the 1840s and 1850s. In principle at least, the public could now distinguish between trained and untrained, competent and incompetent practitioners, and the latter were legally excluded from practising for hire. But the legislature had refrained from legalizing one particular form of training or system of medicine. There were now three boards to supervise medical education and certify competence, and the laity retained powers of choice in the realm of medical systems: they could be bled or poisoned, steamed or blistered, doped with small doses or large, as they saw fit and according to their own lights.

To most regulars it must have seemed a stinging rebuff.[48] For sixty years they had been recognized as the only legal practitioners in the colony; however meaningless the distinction might have been in reality, it was a potent symbol of their special claims. Now, like the Churches of England and Scotland, regular medicine had, in effect, been disestablished. The same sort of attenuated voluntarism which characterized Upper Canadian denominationalism, making all sects more or less equal and eligible for government aid or recognition, now reigned in Upper Canadian medicine as well.

NO LESS THAN DOCTORS or clergymen, lawyers were also under fire in the years around mid-century. In public meetings, in the press, and in the legislature, critics called for a wide variety of changes to make the law cheaper and more accessible to ordinary Upper Canadians. Criticism of the legal system, however, took two quite distinct forms. One of these was a narrowly focused attack on the Court of Chancery, an institution which drew the particular ire of Upper Canadians, laity and lawyers alike. The other constituted a much more wide-ranging assault on the entire edifice of the law, including the special privileges of the legal profession itself.

First established in the colony in 1837, Chancery was an 'equity court' which had developed in England as a means of affording relief in certain cases where the application of the common law might have, by itself, led to injustice. Unlike the common law, 'where the strict rule of precedent sometimes led to injustice in individual situations,' writes one historian, 'in equity, the precepts of fairness and conscience allowed the Chancellor [or judge] greater freedom to determine each case on its own merits.' The court developed its own procedure and rules of evidence, and its jurisdiction was especially related to such areas as 'the supervision of trusts, the guardianship of infants and lunatics, the administration of estates of deceased persons, ... mortgages, ... bankruptcy cases, and the drawing up of accounts for commercial partnerships in which disputes arose.'[49]

'Precepts of fairness' indeed. By the early nineteenth century the English court was already notorious for its tortuous procedures, expense, and delay, so much so that it would provide Charles Dickens with one of his bleakest portraits of any of his society's institutions.[50] Imported to Upper Canada it proved no different. Chancery had provoked widespread hostility from the time it was founded and, in the early years, a desperate shortage of trained Chancery lawyers (known as solicitors) didn't help matters.[51] The court sat only in Toronto, and thus, as the *North American* put it, the unfortunate country suitor had to retain 'solicitors accustomed to high fees and to whom he was an utter stranger ... The proceedings were carried on far from the *locus in quo*, and every step was necessarily attended with great expense. Ruinous delay could hardly be avoided, and at last the vexed plaintiff found his "decree" had cost him infinitely more than it was worth.'[52] The lawyers themselves were cynical: said Skeffington Connor in a letter to W.H. Blake, 'I was all Saturday in Chancery, that's the business I like ... the speaking colloquial, the pace slow and dignified, the pay handsome, and a gentlemanly understanding among practitioners to make it handsomer.'[53]

Almost from the beginning of its history there were attempts to reform the court, and by mid-century it had become a favourite target of ultra-reformers – abolition bills or resolutions were introduced by radicals in each of the sessions between 1850 and 1853. Among lawyers in the legislature, the court had its defenders, including such senior members of the profession as Robert Baldwin and William Draper.[54] A large number of lawyers, nonetheless, tended to be as critical as the laity, and as energetic in supporting abolition. Opposition cut across party lines as well. Sir Allan MacNab, no Grit radical, declared in 1850 that 'at that moment there could be no more popular measure in the country than the destruction of the Court of Chancery,' and in the same debate the ministerialist J.C. Morrison conceded that complaints were widespread about 'the delays, the expense, and the useless forms and proceedings tolerated there.'[55]

Such was the antagonism of Upper Canadian lawyers to the Court of Chancery that it occasioned one of the rare incidents when law reform provoked a major political crisis. In 1851 William Lyon Mackenzie introduced a motion in the legislature to abolish the court. The motion was defeated, but a majority of Upper Canadian politicians voted in favour of it, and as a consequence, Baldwin, the leader of the Reform Party for a decade, resigned from office. His resignation over this apparently minor matter has puzzled historians and they have tended to assume that it was provoked by his fellow Reformers voting against him.[56] In fact, a majority of Reformers actually stood by Baldwin, and his resignation speech points the finger in another direction altogether. The Upper Canadian *lawyers* in the House had voted thirteen to six in favour of Mackenzie's motion, and it was this want of confidence which pained Baldwin most deeply.[57] For years, he said, he had seen it as 'his duty to pay particular attention to all matters referring to the judicial condition of the country,' and since at least 1841 he had endeavoured to put the colony's courts on the best possible footing. Indeed, he had played a key role in formulating plans for the reform of Chancery during the 1840s and in ensuring that these plans were implemented in 1849. Nearly all the lawyers in the old Upper Canadian Assembly, he argued, had supported the creation of the Court of Chancery, he had closely consulted the leading members of the bar before proposing changes, and in 1849 virtually all the lawyer-politicians, regardless of party, had supported the reform legislation. Yet 'upon this purely professional question' they had now voted to abolish the reformed court, only two years after it had been established, and despite the fact that the relevant legislation had been 'supported out of the House by the opinions of gentlemen of the bar, and opposed in the House by five solitary members, only one of whom belonged to the profession.'[58]

Baldwin resigned, then, not because a majority of his own party voted against him but because his professional colleagues had deserted him on 'a purely professional question,' one on which he had fashioned his policies to conform not only to his own best judgment but to those of other 'gentlemen of the bar.' The episode is, perhaps, an unusually poignant insight into the conception of a profession held by Baldwin and others of his generation, a conception in which the mutual obligations of professional men, the solidarity of the profession, the understandings shared among gentlemen, and the responsibilities which fell to a distinctive rank in society took precedence over the duties and loyalties of politics. With the help of Lower Canadian votes, Mackenzie's motion had been defeated, and a majority of Baldwin's own supporters had stood with him. Twelve of the thirteen lawyers who voted for the motion were Tories or non-ministerialists; they were, in other words, not even his political allies. Baldwin resigned nonetheless.

HOSTILITY TO THE COURT of Chancery transcended politics or profession, and was nearly as widespread among conservatives and moderates as it was among radical reformers. The latter, however, were not prepared to limit their own critique of the legal system to one particular institution. Drawing on the long-standing antipathies to special privilege embedded in the popular radicalism of the day, the Clear Grits called not only for the abolition of Chancery but for the codification of the law, for the simplification of law and judiciary alike, and for 'depriving the profession of law of all monopoly.'[59] William Lyon Mackenzie added his own voice on these issues when he re-entered the House in 1851. The demand for the reform of the legal system, moreover, was not confined to Parliament. A number of apparently short-lived but vociferous local law-reform societies established themselves at mid-century to promote the introduction of 'arbitration' or 'conciliation' courts – courts which would do away with lawyers altogether and allow 'the producing parts of the community, viz., the farmers and mechanics' to 'settle matters of dispute among themselves instead of the present expensive and sometimes ruinous system.'[60]

In radical eyes at least, the chief impediment to all schemes for law reform was the lawyers themselves. Speaking at a meeting in Niagara, a local farmer remarked that 'lawyers like leeches are very good in their place (laughter) but they were getting so numerous now that they often obtruded themselves where they were quite out of place, as for instance in parliament (loud cheers).'[61] And there was at least a kernel of truth in the *North American*'s version of the course of law reform in Upper Canada: '"Law Courts, law costs and lawyers are the curse of the country," say the people. "Our system is complicated and expensive, we must reform," say the newspapers. "Oh yes," echo the lawyers *in the House*, "we must have law reform" and forthwith a new court is created and two new judges added to an old one that was condemned as a nuisance even with one judge.'[62]

The political success of radicalism at mid-century inevitably brought such sentiments directly into the legislature. Aside from the attempts to abolish the Court of Chancery, there were at least six other bills or resolutions to reform the legal system introduced between 1850 and 1853.[63] In 1850, for example, William Notman proposed a sweeping measure to reduce court costs, streamline procedures, and throw open the profession 'to all the world; any person should be allowed to conduct his own cause, or to authorize anyone to appear for him.'[64] In 1851 and 1852 William Lyon Mackenzie introduced a bill to establish conciliation courts, explaining that their object 'was to establish legal machinery by which lawyers would be paid to prevent law suits, not to encourage them.'[65] In 1851 he also brought in a bill to open the courts to anyone who wished to practise in them.[66]

And how did the lawyers react to such schemes? On most of the recorded votes, lawyers were divided. Moreover, two of the six radical measures were introduced by lawyers themselves – William Notman and H.J. Boulton. There was, in other words, no unanimity on these matters any more than on many others. Not surprisingly, however, most lawyers were opposed to the radical platform on law reform and especially to the idea of abolishing their monopoly over the courts. The reaction to Notman's bill, for example, was sweeping condemnation. To J.H. Cameron, Notman 'proposed to destroy the profession.' To Henry Sherwood, it was 'a revolution in the whole system of jurisprudence.' Notman's plan 'to make everything simple and plain in the practice of the courts' was so extreme, said Robert Baldwin,

as to reduce us to a state of barbarism ... As to throwing open the profession to all, it was impossible by doing so to do away with lawyers; call them what they will there must be lawyers, who devote their time to the study of the subject. You could no more do without them than without merchants ... He thought however that it would have a tendency to lower the character of the profession, which by its respectability in education and standing assisted in maintaining respect for the law and gave the public confidence in the power they possessed of obtaining justice.[67]

None of the radical law-reform bills got very far in the House. Some were withdrawn and others defeated on first or second reading by large majorities. But that does not mean they were not taken seriously. Unlike doctors or clergymen, lawyers were both numerous and influential in the Assembly, and when these issues arose, senior politicians from both sides of the House – men who were also leading lawyers – were there to speak their minds. To hear both John A. and Sandfield Macdonald, Henry Sherwood and Robert Baldwin, Henry Smith and W.B. Richards speak with a common voice in condemnation of Mackenzie's conciliation bill of 1851 is to be reminded that Mackenzie too had a constituency, which, however mute it may appear a century later, was taken seriously by contemporary politicians.

Taken very seriously. Even as he spoke in opposition to one of Mackenzie's bills, Sandfield Macdonald admitted that 'it is a very popular measure; it reads well and county constituencies would like to have a bill of this kind which at first sight proposes to do away with lawyers altogether.'[68] When the same proposal was introduced the following year, John A. Macdonald's response was no less telling. He would vote, he said, 'for a reference to a Committee in order to prevent the member for Haldimand [Mackenzie] from getting up an agitation on the subject.'[69] The handful of recorded divisions on Mackenzie's bills provide additional evidence for the popularity of his proposals. In 1851 the Upper Canadian vote to give his conciliation bill the six-month hoist was a narrow fifteen to fourteen in favour, and a third of the lawyers in the House voted with Mackenzie, not against him.[70] Later in the same session Mackenzie moved second reading of his bill to authorize 'Her Majesty's Subjects to plead and reason for themselves or others in all Her Majesty's courts.' This time the Upper Canadian vote on the six-month hoist was carried by a relatively narrow margin of five votes.[71]

The radical tide ebbed quickly however. In 1850, even before Mackenzie's voice was added to others in the legislature, there had been four proposals for radical law reform which together would have abolished the Court of Chancery, ended the lawyers' monopoly, simplified procedure, and lowered costs. By the session of 1852–3, Mackenzie stood alone as the sole advocate for radical measures, and the initiative had already shifted to the moderates in the House, including those lawyers who wanted substantive but not fundamental changes in the legal system. Whatever innovations moderates might favour, in any case, there was no more talk of throwing the courts open to all Her Majesty's subjects. The Law Society was not to be 'disestablished' as the national churches were about to be, nor was there to be the kind of qualified free trade in law that would emerge in medicine.

One reason for this lies in the priorities the various issues had on the political agenda of the early 1850s. It was political radicalism that constituted the lawyers' chief enemy, and even at its peak it was, at best, a potent but never a dominant force. Religious voluntarism, on the other hand, could mobilize both voters and politicians to an extent that political radicalism could not hope to match. With the exception, perhaps, of responsible government, the secularization of the Clergy Reserves was the most urgent issue in Upper Canadian politics and one that no government or party could ignore. Support for secularization, moreover, spanned the political spectrum. When the Reformers failed to settle the question between 1850 and 1853, the Liberal–Conservative coalition did so, even if the measure was unpalatable to the old Tories in the House. Free trade in medicine was never remotely as important an issue as the Clergy Reserves, but it had something of the same appeal. In the early 1850s both Reformers and Conservative politicians could be found voting against the medical incorporation acts, and it was under a Conservative regime that the homeopathic and eclectic incorporation acts were passed. All of the initiatives which threatened the Law Society or the lawyers' monopoly over the courts, on the other hand, came from either the Grits or independent radicals like Mackenzie, and whatever the degree of support those initiatives might have had among the voters, they had relatively limited appeal to other members of the House.

The disproportionate presence of lawyers in the legislature undoubtedly mattered as well. Though they had sometimes been accused of exercising undue influence in the old Upper Canadian legislature before 1841, their actual numbers had never been especially large. In the 8th Parliament (1820–4), for example, only eight of forty-three MLAs were lawyers, and in the 13th Parliament (1836–40) the figure was only nineteen of seventy. But after 1841 it was a different matter. Not only were there many Lower Canadian lawyers in the House but the number of Upper Canadian lawyers rose steadily throughout the 1840s; by 1848 they constituted twenty-two, or more than half, of the forty-three Upper Canadian members of the legislature, and, following the elections of 1857, just under 40 per cent.[72] Like other people, lawyers differed in their political views, and they were to be found among the Clear Grits as they were among Conservatives and moderate Reformers. The overhaul of parts of the court system was of genuine interest to many lawyers, and attempts to lessen costs or streamline procedures would be pursued throughout the 1850s. But most lawyers did not favour measures designed to dismantle their profession. Their influence in cabinet, moreover, and in the legislature generally could not help but work against any 'root and branch' reform of the law. Mackenzie's comment on the situation, though probably unfair and *ad hominem*, is surely not without some pertinence: 'He feared ... that in a house of 47 lawyers any attempt to mitigate burthens pressing more heavily on those least able to bear them would meet no favour.'[73]

ALTOGETHER, the mid-century assault on the learned professions provoked a good deal of lamentation about the decline of civilization as Georgian professionals knew it. The degradation of the professions was seen by the editor of the *Upper Canada Journal of Medical ... Science* in 1853 as proof of the 'downward tendency of the Anglo-Saxon race.'[74] Two years earlier *The Church* had carried an editorial, entitled 'Free Trade in Law, Physic and Divinity,' which identified the attack on the professions in the legislature as but one more attempt 'to reduce all things to one common level and to elevate presumption and ignorance into the places of education and experience.' The attempt to throw open the courts to all was 'to substitute impudence for learning and ignorance for knowledge. In Divinity they made a bold effort to destroy the possibility of any man of education penetrating the bush, where his services are most wanted, by withholding from him any means of subsistence. In Physic they have unremittingly attempted to destroy the regularly educated practitioner, and elevate into his place any pretender who chose to conceive that he had the ability, without a knowledge of the human frame, to cure human infirmities. All in all,' the editor concluded, the colony was being asked to 'submit to a system which is the first step to generate Socialist Doctrines in Canada, and to introduce that levelling spirit which never will be contented till experience is overborne by pretensions – education by ignorance – and the truths of the gospel by the doctrines of the atheist.'[75]

Despite the hysteria embedded in such rhetoric, the fact of the matter was that change was far less dramatic than it might have been had the full force of religious voluntarism and political radicalism been allowed free play. Lawyers, after all, escaped entirely unscathed, and while regular medicine was in some respects 'disestablished,' first by the weight of public opinion and then, at the end of the 1850s, by law, still there was to be no unrestricted free trade in medical practice. The principle of *licensed* practice and the distinction between those who were qualified and those who were not survived intact.

Not even the churches experienced the full-scale disaster that many clergymen had predicted. While the bulk of potential revenue from the Clergy Reserves was lost, the clergy were not stripped of their stipends nor were the rectory lands confiscated. Confronted by the need to settle the Clergy Reserves question once and for all, the imperial government had imposed on the local legislature one non-negotiable term: those clergy already receiving stipends from the fund must continue to receive them for life. At the request of the two churches the Liberal–Conservative administration agreed to an arrangement of even greater advantage to the churches and one that its Reform predecessor would almost certainly have rejected. A formula was worked out, and written into law in 1854, which provided an estimate of the total amount each clergyman was likely to earn over the rest of his working life, and upon the consent of each individual involved, the government agreed to allocate that amount to a 'commutation fund' for each church. That fund, in turn, could be used not only to pay existing salaries but to generate revenues which might be applied to the larger purposes of the church for years to come.[76] 'But for the spirited admission by the Ministry of the Commutation clause,' said Strachan thankfully, 'the destruction of the church by a lingering death was in all human probability inevitable.'[77] At the synod of 1855, the Kirk's moderator, though less apocalyptic, expressed similar sentiments.[78] The commutation settlement was, in sum, a significant defeat for extreme voluntarism and political radicalism for it preserved, in however attenuated a form, endowments for the maintenance of religion.

DEVELOPMENTS IN UPPER CANADA, then, did not parallel those in the United States, where religious voluntarism had been gaining ground for decades and where, by mid-century, most states had abandoned traditional licensing requirements for both medicine and law. In Upper Canada the settlement of the 1850s was much more moderate, and the continuities with the past more apparent. The reasons for this outcome deserve consideration.

One was the very fact of the union of the Canadas itself. As was the case with so many other important issues during the union, Lower Canadian votes on measures affecting the professions frequently moderated or blocked proposals which attracted powerful support in Upper Canada. On such diverse issues as the conciliation courts' bills, the abolition of Chancery, an end to the lawyers' monopoly over the courts, or the elimination of medical licensing, recorded divisions, which were sometimes very close if one counts only the Upper Canadian members, were lost by large margins if one includes Lower Canadian votes as well. In a few cases, such as the Chancery resolution that led Baldwin to resign, Lower Canadian votes actually altered the results of the vote among Upper Canadian members. Defensive about attacks on their own incorporated institutions and professional privileges, Lower Canadians were reluctant allies of any Upper Canadian faction which proposed to repeal similar arrangements in Upper Canada. Indeed, a medical incorporation act for Lower Canada had passed in 1847 and some of the most vigorous proponents of an equivalent measure for Upper Canada were Lower Canadian medical doctors who were members of the legislature.[79]

The sheer 'Britishness' of Upper Canada presumably played its part as well. At mid-century a near-majority of the entire population was British-born; but among adults the figure was substantially higher than that, and thus British precedents exercised a large influence on Canadian institutions.[80] Though the exact arrangements varied in the different parts of the United Kingdom, law, medicine, and the national churches had special privileges and protected status, and many British emigrants, especially middle-class emigrants, took it for granted that this was, in some sense, the natural order of things.

Far more than other professional men, Upper Canada's lawyers tended to be born and educated in the colony itself.[81] But, as R.C.B. Risk notes, 'the traditional education and associations of the legal profession, and the powerful appeal of being part of the massive traditions of the English legal system' bred a reverence for English precedents and more general ways of doing things.[82] Thus while there were lawyers who consistently voted for free trade in medicine, and even one or two who advocated it for law, a significant majority of lawyers voted in favour of the medical incorporation bills of the early 1850s, and opposed the one bill which would have abolished the legal privileges held by regular doctors. Lawyers, in other words, tended to be a conservative force in their defence not only of their own institutions but of the established medical institutions as well. They may have been willing to support therapeutic diversity, but they were not prepared to abandon the notion that education, training, and licensing were signals of competence – signals they believed to be in the public interest.

Finally, there was the reconstruction of Canadian politics between 1852 and 1854, which immeasurably strengthened the impulse towards conservatism. As the Grits made their peace with the Hincksites and then George Brown failed to rally all of the forces of liberalism behind him, the range of the political agenda narrowed down until it excluded nearly all radical departures in social policy. With the relative decline of the Grits, and except for the redoubtable Mackenzie, who clung on until 1857, the ideology of the small producer lost its voice in a legislature increasingly dominated by the lawyer-entrepreneur.[83] Even Brown, the emerging leader of the Reform Party, who called for free trade in medicine often enough throughout the 1850s, and on occasion criticized the monopoly of the Law Society, spoke in a different tenor than the Grits. In his election platform of 1851, for example, he had this to say about the reform of the legal system: 'The system of Law and Equity administered in Canada has of late attracted much attention, and a loud demand for Reform of the exorbitant law costs hitherto exacted has been heard throughout the Province. If a Commission were appointed, as in England and the United States, composed partly of lawyers and partly of practical businessmen, to enquire and report on the whole question, I am convinced the end would be highly beneficial.'[84] The young turks and old radicals who had launched the Clear Grit movement at mid-century had stood for root and branch reforms, implemented immediately. George Brown proposed to appoint a commission, made up of sound men with moderate views, to study the question.

IN THE YEARS immediately around mid-century, then, professional men experienced a sustained attack on their traditional institutions and assumptions. Some changes were an inevitable result. The secularization of the Clergy Reserves, which for six decades had been the most potent symbol of an established church, signalled the final transition to religious pluralism. Public toleration of 'quackery' and the legalization of the 'sects' dethroned regular medicine. But the principle of licensed practice survived intact not only for law but for medicine as well. There was to be no free trade in either occupation. The fabric of Georgian professionalism had been compromised but not torn asunder, and it remained for forces other than political radicalism to continue the work of remaking the meaning of profession in nineteenth-century Upper Canada.

4
The Placid Progress of the Law

For the legal profession the moment of mid-century radicalism was succeeded by a much more conservative era during which anti-professional sentiment was largely muted. Motions introduced in the legislature in 1856 and 1857, the latter by William Lyon Mackenzie, to throw open practice in the courts to all citizens were defeated by overwhelming majorities, and after that the voice of early Upper Canadian radicalism appeared to be stilled.[1] There was sporadic grumbling in the press about the monopoly powers of the Law Society.[2] And there was, as well, a continuing thread of criticism about excessive legal fees.[3] Such sentiments were common enough to prickle the sensibilities of the editor of the *Upper Canada Law Journal* and provoke him now and then to oracular denunciations: 'Cheap law, like cheap whisky,' he wrote on one occasion, 'is a curse to the people.' It would only multiply litigation and encourage 'ill-feeling, malice and hatred. What so much discourages the litigious as a wholesome dread of law costs?'[4] That aside, however, outcries against the lawyers were uncommon in the quarter-century after 1850. Insulated by this benign political atmosphere, the development of the profession took place almost entirely outside the public eye. These were, nonetheless, critical years for lawyers as they attempted to increase their role in the administration of justice, secure expanded powers of occupational self-regulation, and exercise greater control over the market for legal services.

Throughout the middle decades of the nineteenth century, leading lawyers carried out a substantial reorganization of the judicial system in Upper Canada, and these changes were accompanied by others which enlarged both the influence and the role of lawyers in the courts, as well as creating a variety of new jobs reserved for lawyers alone. The superior courts had always been the preserve of qualified lawyers, and the only significant change in that situation took place in 1849 when a new court of final appeal was created, removing all judicial functions from the executive and thus ending a practice whereby laymen could sit on an appeal court.[5] The professionalization of the lower courts, however, had hardly begun before the middle decades of the nineteenth century. The first major step, as we have already noted, took place in 1841. From that point on, all district (from 1849, county) court judges were required to be barristers, and they, in turn, constituted the judges of the new division (or small-claims) courts, replacing the lay judges of the old Courts of Requests. The division court judges were also appointed chairmen of the Courts of Quarter Sessions. For the first time, then, the presence of men trained to the law was required in the lower civil and criminal courts. The assimilation of procedure in the superior and county courts, moreover, introduced a new level of formality and technical complexity to the latter, made their procedures more opaque for the laity, and increased the necessity of employing attorneys and barristers.[6]

In the cities, by mid-century, the role of the lay magistracy acting in Quarter Sessions had been partially replaced by recorders courts in which the judge was a professional man. In 1857 the legislature passed the County Attorneys Act, which established for the County Assizes and Quarter Sessions a local public prosecutor whose duty it was to conduct cases in these courts and, more generally, to give advice to local magistrates. And the county attorney was required to be a barrister. At the Quarter Sessions he gradually supplanted the traditional private and lay prosecutors, and at the county level the job was amalgamated with that of clerk of the peace.[7] England, so the argument went, might still rely on an ancient system of lay magistrates, but in Upper Canada professionalism was essential if justice was to be served. Introducing his motion for second reading of the County Attorneys bill, the attorney general, John A. Macdonald, 'urged the necessity of the appointment of the officers in question as legal advisers to the magistrates who, although a respectable body of men, were in a different class from the Magistrates in England, all of whom were highly, many of them legally-educated men.'[8]

The County Attorneys Act is no isolated instance of the diminishing role of the laity during the middle decades of the nineteenth century. Paul Romney has described the extraordinary rise of the attorney general from a functionary of government to the leading member within the Ontario cabinet. The critical task of shaping the law or reforming its institutions, including the powers of the Law Society itself, would fall to a series of lawyers who were also premiers of the province.[9] Romney has also written persuasively, and at times eloquently, about the gradual reduction in the role of the jury in both criminal and civil cases, and there are other more mundane examples besides.[10] In the name of justice, competence, or efficiency, professional men steadily expanded their role in the administration of justice, displacing or reducing the influence of the laity in some cases, and creating new jobs for themselves in others.

Not only did they take charge of the commanding heights of the legal system, but they occupied, where they could, its nooks and crannies as well. Consider, for example, the office of notary public. A commission as a notary generated modest but steady income from fees and was coveted by a variety of local office-holders and other educated men, lay and professional alike. In the early years most notaries were necessarily laymen, but at least from mid-century the appointment increasingly became a lawyer's preserve. As Macdonald explained to one lay applicant in 1855, it had become government policy to grant a commission only to 'legal practitioners, who from their professional education are most qualified to perform the duties of a Notary. In some parts of Upper Canada, the rule has been waived from the circumstance of no lawyer residing in the vicinity.'[11] That, moreover, was to remain the policy of successive governments, ensuring that the revenues of the office would accrue to lawyers as they began to infiltrate the villages and hamlets of rural Upper Canada.[12]

We are not suggesting that the increasing professionalization of the legal system was due to cynical self-aggrandizement, nor do we believe this to be the case. The common law was a highly technical body of rules, and minute accuracy as to details and the correct use of often obscurantist phraseology could be decisive in the outcome of a case.[13] There were undoubtedly ill-educated magistrates as well as clerks of the peace unable to cope with the procedures they were obligated to execute. Lay notaries, no matter how well educated, routinely dealt with property and other matters that lawyers believed required expert handling. The complexities of the law, moreover, increased as economic and social life itself became more complex. Lawyers, in other words, could make a good case that training, expertise, and experience were to be prized in such matters, and often did so.[14]

Before mid-century, nonetheless, there were sceptics and critics who opposed the further professionalization of the legal system, and some who even dared to propose alternatives to it. Nor were such ideas confined to a coterie of radicals. Political moderates like W.H. Merritt or David Thorburn had taken exception to the expanding role of professional men in the lower courts, and there were others as well: in 1849 the Toronto City Council objected to the professionalization of the police magistrates on the grounds that there were, 'as is very well known, many unprofessional men in the Country who are at least equally qualified to discharge the duties.'[15] But it was the lawyers who carried the day, and after mid-century they appeared to have near-unanimous support in the legislature and little opposition in the press. In the debate over the County Attorneys Act, for example, only the lone and now isolated voice of William Lyon Mackenzie questioned the need for county attorneys to be barristers.[16] The rest of the debate and the discussion in the press focused on other issues. In the main, that would continue to be the case until the late 1870s.

Nor is it hard to understand why this was so. Lawyers exerted a powerful influence in the legislature, especially in the cabinet, and they tended to arrogate to themselves the right to define the direction and character of law reform, and to treat knowledge of the law as their own private preserve. Someone like George Brown might continue to assert the primacy of the laity over the professional in these matters, to insist, for example, that while medicine was an esoteric field of knowledge 'little understood by most, any man of good education can read and understand Blackstone. The statutes of the land are not made by lawyers for lawyers. They are intended for the public and may be understood without a knowledge of Horace or Euclid.'[17] And such convictions might still carry weight in Britain, where the lawyers' custodianship of the law was contested by the existence of a powerful tradition of aristocratic lay leadership both at the local level and in Parliament. But in Upper Canada there was no equivalent counterbalance. As Macdonald himself had put it, the colony's magistracy was of 'a different class' and needed the counsel of professional men. Indeed in Upper Canada leading lawyers saw themselves as the best approximation to aristocratic leadership in the colony, and thus their influence ensured that their vision of things would prevail.[18]

WHO WERE THESE 'aristocrats' of Upper Canadian society? The governing body of the Law Society did not include all prominent or successful lawyers, but its composition is indicative of the power and prestige that the law could command. Nor does one need a finely tuned prosopographical study to analyse its membership, for most of their names are familiar to any student of nineteenth-century Ontario. Until 1871 the Convocation of Benchers held office for life and they themselves selected each new Bencher. To take a metaphorical snapshot of the Benchers in the late 1850s is to reveal a group of men who had come of age between the 1820s and the early 1840s, shaped by the institutions and assumptions of Georgian Britain or Upper Canada, scions of its best families or young men who had been able to make their way among them.[19] The 'Visitors' of the Society – those who exercised a supervisory role over it – were the nine senior judges of the highest courts, and included John Beverley Robinson, William Hume Blake, William Draper, Archibald McLean, and W.B. Richards. The treasurer (or chief officer) was Robert Baldwin. Among the Benchers were such men as S.B. Harrison, J.H. Cameron, Sir Allan MacNab, John A. Macdonald, Sandfield Macdonald, A.J. Fergusson, J.C. Morrison, Philip M.M.S. Vankoughnet, John Ross, Oliver Mowat, Henry Smith, Lewis Wallbridge, and Edward Murney. Half of the men appointed between 1846 and 1856 could list QC after their names. Eleven had served as either attorney general or solicitor general. Some, like Vankoughnet, were members of the Legislative Council; others, like Mowat, were established legal stars who would become influential politicians. Many had played prominent roles in Upper Canada's political life at some point since the early 1840s. Some, though less well-known historical figures, were nearly as familiar to contemporaries: Adam Wilson was Robert Baldwin's junior partner throughout the 1840s and, in the next decade, would be elected mayor of Toronto; others, like Skeffington Connor or Alexander Campbell, were close allies or partners of leading political figures. Most were Toronto men, but the Benchers included those, like Wallbridge, Campbell, or Charles Baby, who were among the leading figures in other communities. In many cases these men were also 'lawyer-entrepreneurs,' deeply involved in the economic growth of their communities and ranking among their social élite as well. The Visitors and Benchers, in other words, were not simply well connected to the levers of power and influence in Upper Canadian society, they *were* some of its principal levers.

As for the Law Society itself, it functioned much like a gentlemen's club. 'Public meetings [of the Benchers] were reserved for self-affirmation, rhetoric, and other forms of self-justifying public statements,' writes Blaine Baker. 'Convocation provided a private setting in which the Benchers did things informally, confident that their proceedings would remain *in camera*. Convocation Chamber might just as well have been John Beverley Robinson's drawing room.'[20] Osgoode Hall, the Law Society's spacious and imposing quarters, provided temporary accommodation for students and barristers from other parts of the province, contained an impressive library, and housed the superior courts as well. The Benchers met regularly to examine candidates for admission to the bar, but aside from that they engaged in remarkably little other regulatory activity. The rules and regulations that governed the bar were relatively few. As late as 1859, when the Benchers published the second consolidated set of 'rules' of the Law Society, the text contained some fifty-five printed pages. Twenty of these pages and about half the total number of rules refer to educational or examination standards and admissions policies or procedures. Most of the rest is housekeeping relating to the internal organization of the Convocation of Benchers or the regulation of Osgoode Hall itself.[21] The job of the Benchers, in other words, was primarily to maintain the bar as a learned and honourable profession, and until the late 1850s at least that entailed little more than the judicious regulation of education. Most new candidates were known quantities, their reputability guaranteed by one or other of the Benchers or by other barristers known to them. Examination standards had traditionally tended to be lax, or so it was claimed in the late 1850s – a natural enough situation when the Benchers would know the educational and social backgrounds of the candidates in any case.[22] Beyond that there was little need for much formal regulatory activity. In a profession that had no more than 500 members at mid-century and where face-to-face contact in the superior and county courts was a frequent occurrence, the gentlemen of the bar could govern themselves according to a common code of honour arising not so much from the occupation itself as from their shared social experience and expectations.

DURING THE 1850s, nonetheless, new pressures began to impinge upon that small and comfortable world. The law, as any number of historians have noted, was pre-eminently the profession of choice for the sons of Upper Canada's establishment, and was as well a powerful magnet for other young men who had to make their way in the world without a large inheritance or an 'interest' which would obtain them a government sinecure.[23] The law offered the promise of financial security, comfortable respectability, and, to those with extraordinary talent and ambition, the lure of financial fortune or political fame. Not surprisingly, then, a growing number of young men sought entry to the occupation. According to the Law Society's own records, between 1840 and 1858 the number of barristers and attorneys in Upper Canada doubled, from 267 to 530. By 1870 their numbers had increased by more than half again, to 893.[24] Despite the patent success of many individual lawyers, and the security the occupation offered to most others, these growth rates provoked a deepening sense of unease. Even in the early 1840s, Oliver Mowat, then a law student and junior Chancery lawyer, watched nervously as term by term the trickle of young men came up for call to the bar. 'I have heard it calculated,' he told his brother in 1840, 'that about 300 have been admitted into the Law Society within the last four years as students. Verily, at this rate every man, woman and child will soon become their own lawyer.'[25] Two decades later, in 1859, a young Torontonian's diary recorded a visit by friends: 'Osler's two brothers here with him for a few days going to pass at Osgoode Hall like everyone else. Upper Canada will be flooded with lawyers I am afraid.'[26] The fear of overcrowding was expressed in the legislature and in the pages of the *Law Journal*.[27] It found its way into public and private advice to potential emigrants.[28] Nor was it merely the protective reflex of lawyers or their student-clerks. The secular press agreed that a problem seemed to be looming. 'The extraordinary rush of young men into the profession of the law ... has startled the community,' the editor of the *Globe* noted in 1863; 'we will find it very difficult to believe that the legal profession is not numerically fast outstripping the rest of the population, and far more than supplying its wants.'[29] Law, it seemed, was becoming the victim of its own success.

The threat posed by growing numbers, moreover, was not interpreted as a narrowly economic problem. The prosperous and successful editor of the *Law Journal* and his correspondents may not have worried unduly about their own incomes, but they were clearly exercised about the consequences for the respectability of the profession. Eager advocates of the doctrine that 'more means worse,' they fretted over the social tone of new recruits and the possibility that 'briefless barristers' would be tempted to ungentlemanly behaviour and shoddy practices. Too many entrants, said one lawyer, 'without ability to ensure an honourable practice,' would inevitably drive some 'to various devices to earn a livelihood, which not only bring their own names into discredit, but also reflect disparagingly upon the profession to which they belong.'[30]

As the fears of overcrowding increased in the two decades after 1850, leading lawyers began to formulate strategies designed to bring the profession under tighter control. To cope with the growing numbers in the profession, the Law Society proposed to raise entry standards and to make its examinations more difficult. Attempts would be made to limit the deleterious effects of competition by imposing more effective internal discipline on members of the Law Society. Central to all of this, however, was one critical initiative: the reassertion by the Law Society of control over those attorneys and solicitors who were not also barristers – over those who practised only 'the minor branch of the profession.'

DURING THE 1820s and 1830s, the reader will remember, some leading barristers had favoured the sharp separation of the role of barrister from that of attorney or solicitor.[31] Though full-scale segregation proved too extreme a measure for most lawyers to swallow, in 1822 the Law

Society had wiped its hands of anything to do with the education or regulation of attorneys, leaving such matters entirely to the discretion of individual lawyers who took on students as clerks and to the judges who admitted them to practice. That legislation, however, backfired on the Society in an entirely unexpected way. Without any stipulated entry or certification standards, it was much easier to become an attorney than a barrister, and from the 1830s onwards a growing number of young men became articled clerks without, at the same time, becoming students-at-law. The result was the growth of a large number of attorneys (and after 1837, solicitors) who were not barristers. By 1840, 40 per cent of the legal practitioners in Upper Canada were attorneys only. And though that proportion declined to just under 30 per cent over the next twenty years, the actual number of attorneys and solicitors who were not barristers continued to climb, rising from 119 to 147, an increase of about 24 per cent.[32]

Over the same period, from 1840 to 1858, the number of barristers grew even faster, more than doubling, from 183 to 383. Inevitably, they found themselves competing for the routine business of a legal practice against 'mere attorneys.' In some cases, moreover, attorneys were even acting as advocates in the county courts. That was one of the prerogatives which was supposed to distinguish the barrister from the attorney, and in 1847 the Law Society challenged the right of attorneys to act as advocates, hoping that King's Bench would rule definitively that only barristers could plead in the county courts. Overruling the views of the two puisne (or junior) judges, however, the Chief Justice decided that the county court judges were the appropriate authorities to determine who could act as advocates in their own courts, and while some judges refused to allow attorneys at the bar, others, especially in the more remote districts, were more lenient.[33] By the 1850s, then, attorneys and solicitors were posing a double threat to the bar: not only were they economic competitors but they challenged its exclusive prerogatives as well.

In the newly established *Upper Canada Law Journal*, editor and correspondents alike called for action to protect the incomes and reputability of the educated and learned branch of the profession. Typically, a correspondent in 1855 pointed out that, unlike the barrister, who was under the discipline of the Law Society, the attorney could offer no sureties to the public of his fitness to practise. 'A young man whose only qualification for entering on the study of law is the ability to read and write, may be articled to an Attorney.' At the end of his five years he might be admitted to practice, and yet 'may know nothing whatever of professional duties, may in fact be grossly illiterate and deficient in every acquirement that would enable him to act with safety and advantage for a client.' The solution, the author continued, was to apply an educational test to attorneys, as was done with barristers, 'and there is more need for it. The former are infinitely more in the way of inflicting injury by ignorance or turpitude than the latter.' And because they operated in the privacy of their offices instead of in open court, incompetence or worse was unlikely to be exposed.[34] The editor of the *Law Journal* agreed entirely. The education of attorneys needed to be more closely assimilated to that of barristers, he argued, by imposing a preliminary examination designed to test candidates' general accomplishments before articles were begun, as well as a final admissions examination to evaluate a clerk's professional knowledge.[35]

Sentiments such as these lay behind the passage of the Attorneys' Admission Act of 1857, which required all articled clerks to pass a Law Society examination before they could apply to the judges for permission to practise.[36] That innovation was not accompanied by the introduction of a parallel preliminary examination, and thus the measure was more modest than that proposed in the pages of the *Law Journal*. The act, nonetheless, marks the point at which the Law Society began to re-establish its authority, willingly relinquished in 1822, over the 'minor branch of the profession.' It also began the process of making admission as an attorney more difficult, by denying clerks the opportunity to supplement their meagre salaries by periods of employment in some other occupation.[37]

During the 1850s, the Law Society also began to tackle the problem of the growing number of barristers by restricting the number of students-at-law. Here the Benchers had no need of new legislation, for they had always had the power to control entry to the bar. Nor did they even need to change the formal admissions standards. They simply increased the difficulty of the examinations. Between the 1840s and the early 1870s, there were no substantive changes in matriculation requirements for students, but from at least the middle 1850s it is clear that the Law Society examiners demanded higher standards for a pass and failed significantly more candidates than they had before.[38]

Neither tougher examination standards nor the Attorneys' Admission Act of 1857 served to stem the flow of young men into law, however. By the middle 1860s complaints about overcrowding were more vociferous and more common than ever before. In the *Law Journal*, correspondents and editor agreed that examination standards for law students needed to be stiffened and other hurdles introduced as well, but the main villains of the piece were, once again, the attorneys. The act of 1857 allowed the Law Society to examine clerks at the end of their articles, but the Society had no other means to control numbers. It could not impose a preliminary examination on clerks as it did on students-at-law, nor could it limit the number of articled clerks per attorney to fewer than the four allowed by law. Given the uses to which articled clerks could be put in any law office, most barristers were probably no more fastidious in their choice of clerks than were most attorneys. But in the pages of the *Law Journal*, it was the latter who were castigated not only for pumping out the largest number of new attorneys possible but for indiscriminately allowing anyone, regardless of education or social background, to become an articled clerk. 'As a general rule,' wrote one barrister,

an attorney will enter into articles with anyone who applies be he gentleman or vulgarian, black or white, educated or ignorant, intelligent or stupid, the rector's son or a stable boy, it makes no difference. The result is that the ranks of the profession are constantly receiving not very desirable recruits. I am no advocate for exclusiveness or caste, according to merit its due wherever found, but the gradations of society are as necessary a result of our existence as a race as is the alternation of day or night to the existence of the earth as part of the solar system.

His solution was Draconian: require all clerks to serve their full five years without salary or any other monetary reward, and substantially increase the examination fees charged by the Law Society.[39] Another correspondent went further, urging that stiff premiums be charged all articled clerks as the price of their apprenticeships. Simply making access to law much more expensive would result in fewer and more respectable entrants.[40]

Excessively high examination or apprenticeship fees, however, trespassed upon some fundamental mid-nineteenth-century political convictions. Above all, they challenged the belief that careers must be open to talent, and that industry and intellectual merit must count for more than wealth alone. Thus most observers rejected the idea of applying explicitly monetary solutions to the problem of overcrowding; they turned instead to what might now be called 'standards of educational excellence.' Monetary schemes, said *Vox Populi*, would 'only open a wide door to the sons of the wealthy, while the hard-reading sons of the poor would be excluded from the profession.' A more suitable approach was to establish 'a high degree of literary attainment.' If the Benchers 'wish to exclude the stupid and the ignorant, they must make the course of study severe ... They must make the profession a *learned* one not in name alone but *in deed*.'[41]

The Benchers apparently agreed. Between 1868 and 1872 two major initiatives were taken to raise educational standards for both students and clerks. Early in 1868, presumably at the request of the Benchers, Edward Blake introduced a bill in the legislature which gave the Law Society the right to establish two new examinations, to be written during a clerk's period of articles. The Society had the requirements for these examinations in place within the year and took the opportunity, at the same time, to introduce similar examinations for students-at-law.[42] Then in 1871 the Benchers agreed to ask the government for even wider powers over the education of attorneys.[43] The pertinent legislation was passed early in 1872 and, among other things, gave the Society permission to introduce a preliminary examination for articled clerks. Convocation then approved a series of changes which saw a substantial rise in the matriculation standard for students-at-law, and for the first time, an entrance examination for articled clerks.[44] To become a student-at-law still required higher educational attainments than those demanded of articled clerks, but in other ways the pattern of education for both students and clerks began to be assimilated: both now faced entrance examinations, two sets of very similar intermediate examinations, and a final one for either the call to the bar or admission as an attorney. As educational standards rose, moreover, the incentive to train only as an attorney was substantially reduced.

The effects of these various initiatives, and especially of the new legislation of 1868 and 1872, can be read in the pages of the *Law Journal*. From 1855 until 1872 overcrowding within the ranks of the law was *the* issue of professional interest; for the rest of the 1870s it virtually disappeared from view. The statistics of growth confirm the shift as well. According to the *Law Lists*, between 1858 and 1870 the rate of increase for all lawyers was about 68 per cent; between 1870 and 1879 it dropped to 24 per cent. The census returns show a similar pattern: rates of increase running at over 100 per cent in the 1850s and over 80 per cent in the 1860s, and then plummeting to 21 per cent during the decade of the 1870s. The new regulations, in other words, did not put anything like a full stop to the growth of the profession. But, for the first time since mid-century, they substantially reduced the rate of increase to about the same as that for the total population of the province, and to a rate well below that for the workforce.[45]

The reintegration of the attorneys was completed in 1876 when amendments to the Law Society Act gave the Society the power to make rules governing all aspects of 'the interior discipline and practice' of both branches of the law.[46] The act may have been intended, in part at least, to clarify the powers of the Law Society to discipline barristers, but in general terms those powers had existed since 1797. The real innovation, however, lay in its effects on attorneys and solicitors. Since 1822 attorneys had been subjected only to the discipline of the judges; now, they too were to be placed under the authority of the Law Society.

In the years following 1876, there remained a large gap between the formal power of the Law Society and its actual ability, or willingness, to impose discipline on Ontario lawyers. Moreover, the Law Society still lacked exclusive jurisdiction over its members, for the courts retained their traditional powers over barristers and solicitors alike. Curtis Cole has offered a persuasive account of the disciplinary role of both the Society and courts after 1876 and there is no need to reiterate that history here.[47] But the act of 1876 remains an important benchmark, for it was the last major step in bringing the attorneys back into the Law Society's fold and in fusing together the two branches of the profession. In 1870, 30 per cent of all lawyers were attorneys or solicitors who were not barristers. By 1878 that had already declined to 25 per cent, and by 1891 to 15 per cent.[48]

THE INTERNAL HISTORY of the legal profession in the third quarter of the nineteenth century is a relatively peaceable one, soporific indeed, if compared with the internal dissension that wracked either the Anglican Church or the medical profession. Nor was there much outside interference: it was the rarest occasion when anyone went so far as to demand the abolition of lawyers' closed shops. As the radical 'root and branch' critique of professionalism faded away in the early 1850s, the legitimacy of lawyers' professional privileges came to be taken for granted, at least by those who were thought to matter in Upper Canadian society. Moreover, leading lawyers found it relatively easy to extend the power of the Law Society in any of those areas defined as within the prerogatives of the profession. The Benchers moved resolutions and consulted with professional men in the cabinet, and laws were passed raising educational standards, or circumscribing attorneys, or extending lawyers' roles in the courts, all without public debate, without a public outcry, without, indeed, apparent public interest. Secure behind the bulwarks of the Law Society Act, controlling many of the levers of power in society, constituting a key element of the economic and social élite, the law, as an organized profession, had little difficulty obtaining the objectives it set for itself. It may not in fact have been that easy, but certainly the surviving public record makes it look that way.

In attempting to come to grips with growing competition, however, the Law Society had also embarked, almost certainly unselfconsciously, on a course which would change the configuration of the occupation itself. A number of students of the professions have pointed to the tensions which exist within the world of professional occupations between exclusiveness and market control. 'In order to control the market, the occupational body must include anyone with a reasonable claim to expertise, but such inclusion brings in marginal practitioners, who lower the standing of the high-class members.'[49] In law that tension was apparent from the 1820s to the 1870s as élite barristers first tried to distance themselves from the attorneys and then attempted to bring them back within the fold. In England the bar chose to remain a distinct and separate branch of the law and thus sustain its exclusivity, but that also provoked much public conflict and intraprofessional rivalry.[50] In Ontario that kind of exclusivity was not an option since most barristers were also attorneys in any case; still, by re-establishing control over those who were attorneys only, the Law Society absorbed those who hitherto had been defined as less respectable. Inclusivity, in other words, brought with it an inevitable dilution of the traditional view of the law as a small, cohesive group of gentlemen-barristers. It also completed the homogenization of the occupation itself. Though assumptions underpinning the traditional distinctions between the higher and lower branches of the law had been transferred to the colony, differentiation had begun to decline from early on. For economic reasons alone, barristers usually qualified as attorneys or solicitors, as we have already seen. And now the attorneys were gathered in as well. The end result was that in common parlance, if not formally, practitioners all became 'lawyers.' The occupation, in effect, became more generic in nature. And that development was undoubtedly reinforced by the decision, taken in 1881, to abolish outright the term 'attorney.' Henceforth in Ontario there would be only barristers and solicitors, and most would be both.[51]

Increased inclusivity and greater homogeneity, it must be said, did not necessarily ensure internal unity or unanimity. Even as old divisions declined, new sources of diversity, discord, and differentiation were being spawned, issues we will return to in other chapters. These too would contribute to the transformation of the Law Society from a gentleman's club to something more like a modern occupational organization. Perhaps the first step in that direction, however, occurred in 1871, when the Benchers ceased to be a self-perpetuating oligarchy, and became a body elected by the occupation as a whole.

The details of this change are murky. It may have begun in 1866, when Adam Crooks resigned as a Bencher because his colleagues had failed to elect Edward Blake to a vacant seat. 'The Benchers ... are the representatives of the profession at large,' Crooks wrote in his letter of resignation, 'yet they are self-elective and the other members of the

Society have no voice in or control over, the election of a Bencher. In no way are the Benchers answerable to the opinion of the rest of the Profession. I have always felt that this was anomalous and should be remedied. So long, however, as this Constitution worked reasonably well, I was not one of those who desired a change on merely theoretical grounds.' Crooks charged, however, that the system had revealed its weakness by failing to recognize Blake's pre-eminent claim, and he could 'no longer consent to being considered as submitting to it.'[52]

Crooks's resignation may have been motivated by purely personal pique – certainly the editor of the *Law Journal*, who opposed the change and had as little to say about its merits as possible, suggested that it was. Yet Matthew Crooks Cameron, another prominent member of the bar, had also refused an appointment as Bencher because he objected to the Society's oligarchic constitution,[53] and reform clearly had a broader appeal as well. Even the *Law Journal* had to concede that a petition in favour of elected Benchers, forwarded to the legislature in 1869, had been signed by a large number of lawyers. After a private member's bill had been thrown out on a technicality, the pertinent legislation was adopted as a government measure and became law in 1871.[54]

YET ANOTHER departure from the Georgian past is recorded in the preceding pages. During the first half of the nineteenth century, the Law Society had introduced a variety of requirements for those who wished to become barristers. But what mattered most was sponsorship, not 'academic achievement.' Candidates had to be recommended by some member of the profession and appear before the assembled Benchers to demonstrate that they had acquired the appropriate manners, morals, and intellectual qualities suitable to a professional gentleman. It had seemed perfectly reasonable, moreover, to exclude strangers from 'breaking in upon the establishment'; what needed to be ascertained, as John Beverley Robinson had said in 1825, was that potential candidates were 'known from their infancy' so that 'their habits and mode of education' would serve as 'securities for their honourable proceedings.'[55] Character and reputability were the key benchmarks, and rigorous, formal examinations were unnecessary because a candidate was either a known quantity himself or was sponsored by those who were.

During the middle decades of the nineteenth century, however, such selection criteria as 'known from infancy' and the exclusion of 'strangers' ceased to be acceptable. Indeed, the latter was replaced by the notion that strangers had an inalienable right to break in upon the establishment according to the principle of 'a career open to talent,' while 'merit,' something Robinson thought he could discern through either personal intimacy or its surrogate, sponsorship, came to mean something measured by success on examinations. These changes are, of course, familar ones, marking the shift from ascription to equality of opportunity, from sponsored to contest mobility. But they are no less important for that. As the Benchers and other leading lawyers became exercised about growing numbers they turned unselfconsciously to such meritocratic devices as formal, written examinations, or more exacting academic standards, as means of selecting qualified applicants. They did so not only because they wished a more effective means of restricting entry but because they believed it was fairer. In the process, nonetheless, and in relatively short order, entry to law became inextricably linked to paper credentials – examination results and educational certificates. Once again, an invisible line had been crossed, from a Georgian to a Victorian world, and from a world we have lost to one which contained the intimations, at least, of our present.

5
Doctors and the Price of Occupational Closure

Like lawyers, medical practitioners in Upper Canada increased rapidly in number during the middle decades of the nineteenth century.[1] Between 1851 and 1871 the proportion of doctors in the colony more than doubled, rising from 4.0 to 9.7 per 10,000 people. During the single decade of the 1860s, the population grew by 16 per cent, but the number of 'physicians and surgeons' recorded in the census grew four or five times as fast.[2] Like the lawyers before them, doctors watched with a growing sense of unease as the tide of new practitioners flooded onto the market. But there were two critical differences in the ability of each profession to cope with the problem. First, the growth in the number of lawyers had been accompanied by a marked expansion in the occupational terrain they controlled, creating new jobs and more secure ground for lawyers as a group. Second, the threat of oversupply could be contained by measures designed to make it more difficult to become either a barrister or an attorney. Before the mid-1860s, however, regular medicine was entirely bereft of either of these means to control its own destiny.

The courts, for example, offered a variety of full-time, salaried appointments for some lawyers, and a steady volume of work for many others. Doctors had no such institutional base. There were fewer than a dozen hospitals in the colony, they were exclusively the resort of the poor, they provided only a handful of appointments, most of them part-time, and even then a resident doctor was the servant of the lay trustees. Leading doctors may have vied among themselves for hospital appointments, but these were hardly the equivalent of a position as, say, a superior court judge or a county attorney. Nor did the hospitals provide the volume of part-time work for large numbers of doctors that the administration of justice did for lawyers. The municipal boards of health, on the relatively few occasions they were established, consisted of laymen, not doctors. Though from time to time some temporary positions as civic sanitation or health officers became available, not even Toronto had a salaried medical officer of health until 1883, and for many municipalities such appointments were not made until well after that.[3] The municipal and county jails provided a handful of positions as jail surgeons or other similar roles, and there were militia appointments as well, but none of them was a full-time job. There was no poor law requiring the employment of local practitioners as there was in Britain. The only part-time appointments available in large numbers were as local coroners. In the two decades after 1850, it does appear as though this role was gradually professionalized. In the 1850s only a minority of coroners – and in some counties a small minority – were doctors; by the late 1860s and early 1870s, in many counties a majority of them were medical men.[4] Even then, however, a significant number of laymen were appointed as well.

Doctors, in sum, had neither a core institutional base which they could build upon, as the lawyers had in the courts, nor as many, or as profitable, nooks and crannies to make their own. Most lawyers, it is true, had to earn their livelihood in competition with each other, but they also had occupational preserves sheltered from the full force of the marketplace. Most regular doctors had no such protection, competing for fees in an unrestricted market not only against each other but against the homeopaths, the eclectics, the druggists, the midwives, and various other practitioners.

The regulars, moreover, had no institutional equivalent to the Law Society which would allow them to control the number of entrants to the profession. In principle that was the job of the Medical Board, which had broad powers to establish the criteria for obtaining a licence to practise medicine in Upper Canada. By the 1850s, however, the powers of the board had been fatally compromised by loopholes in the legislation establishing it. The most important was the exemption from examination granted to anyone holding a medical degree from a British or colonial university. As local medical schools were founded, they normally affiliated with one of the colonial universities, and in the two decades after mid-century most of Upper Canada's new doctors came from these schools. Without the power to examine medical graduates for a licence to practise or to impose a standardized curriculum on the schools themselves, the Medical Board was rendered largely irrelevant to the medical profession at the very time when the Law Society was becoming more assertive in regulating the legal profession. In some respects, indeed, regular doctors were even worse off than the homeopaths or eclectics. The latter two groups had, at least, a single portal through which all potential practitioners had to pass, and thus could determine the quantity and quality of candidates for a licence from their boards.

AS SO MANY medical men had argued all along, what regular medicine needed was something like the traditional medical guilds of Britain; something like the abortive College of Physicians and Surgeons of 1839; something, indeed, like the Law Society itself. Galvanized by the threat of rising numbers, by the patent ineffectiveness of the old Medical Board, and probably above all by the humiliation of 1859-61, leading regulars began in the 1860s to put aside their differences in order to work towards that goal. Initially, they proceeded cautiously. Rather than the unlimited powers encapsulated in the act of 1839 or those in the bills proffered in the years around mid-century, the draft legislation they put before the legislature in early 1865 was no more than a 'registration' act, almost certainly modelled on the British Medical Act of 1858. No one except licensed doctors could use such titles as 'Physician' or 'Doctor of Medicine,' but there was to be no ban on unlicensed practice, nor was there to be any interference with the existing homeopathic or eclectic boards.

It was clauses such as these, in turn, which probably explain why the House was prepared to look kindly upon the bill. No claim was made to monopoly over either therapeutic doctrine or the right to practise. As a result, doctors obtained, in September 1865, what they had coveted for so long, a self-governing organization which could control entry and educational standards and the other conditions of a licence to practise. Policy was to be set by a Medical Council comprised, on the one hand, of a mix of those representing the interests of the medical schools and the various universities which had powers to grant medical degrees (whom we will refer to as the 'schoolmen') and, on the other, of 'territorial representatives' elected every five years by practitioners residing in twelve provincial ridings. The bill took effect in January 1866, the first elections were held in the spring, and the first meeting of the new Medical Council convened in May of that year.

The act of 1865, however, constituted a delicate compromise between the interests of practitioners and schoolmen, and, in the years that followed, the terms of that compromise came unglued. The territorials found they had far less power to control the schools than they had thought, and they quickly became so disenchanted with the outcome that they decided to go back to the legislature in search of a stronger hand. Thus, at its meeting in 1868, the council appointed a committee composed of five territorial representatives, including Drs Clarke, and

Brouse, to draft a new bill which would better suit the majority of its members.

AND JUST WHO were Drs Clarke and Brouse? Who, indeed, constituted the leadership of regular medicine during the critical decade of the 1860s and beyond? When we examined the influential members of the Law Society in the late 1850s, we met a bevy of outstanding contemporary figures. With one or two exceptions, such as John Rolph, the leading medical men are far less well known, and yet they were as important in shaping the profession of medicine as the Benchers were to the future of law. Using a variety of biographical sources, we have attempted to construct a group profile of those who might be considered to belong to the medical élite: the editors of the medical journals, the members of the Medical Council during the late 1860s and 1870s, the MPPs who could claim to represent their profession in the legislature, and the leading schoolmen who influenced a generation of medical students.[5]

Of some eighty biographies in all, forty produced usable information about the occupations of fathers. Thirteen doctors were the sons of doctors, Anglican clergymen, or lawyers. Another nine were the sons of non-medical military officers. Among the other occupations, there were nine farmers and five businessmen; in some cases at least we know that these fathers were very prosperous indeed. One 'farmer,' for example, had been a lieutenant-colonel in the Loyalist military, with all the land-grant implications that entailed, while another father was Angus Bethune, one of Montreal's leading fur-traders, later a director of the Bank of Upper Canada. The medical élite, in other words, was drawn disproportionately from the professional classes, the military, and prominent businessmen, the very group that constituted the core of Upper Canada's gentry class.

About half of these eighty doctors were either born in the colony or raised there from such a young age that they can be considered natives. A very high proportion had educational records which sharply distinguish them from the vast majority of their contemporaries. A remarkable number attended Upper Canada College or the preparatory department of Victoria College, and most of the rest had been exposed to the elements of a liberal education at one of the local grammar schools. Something like two-thirds of the entire group had received some or all of their professional training in the leading centres of medical education in Britain or the eastern United States – Edinburgh, London, Dublin, New York, or Philadelphia. This is, perhaps, not surprising for those who emigrated to the province. What is far more remarkable is that nearly two-thirds of the Upper Canadians also received or completed their medical training abroad. Many had gained experience in the great London teaching hospitals and had acquired a qualification from the Royal College of Surgeons (London) as well. This alone set them apart from most of their medical contemporaries. A comparative analysis of the Medical Register for 1872 tells us that only 16 per cent of all Ontario-registered doctors held British qualifications or a degree from one of the prestigious American medical schools. Our biographies, in other words, describe a leadership group drawn from some of the most respectable elements in early nineteenth-century society, who had received a general education superior to that of the vast majority of their contemporaries, and who had benefited from some of the best professional training offered in the English-speaking world.

A handful of biographical sketches helps to flesh out the generalizations of the last few paragraphs. William Aikins, a key figure behind the legislation of 1865, was the son of a wealthy Toronto Township farmer and had gone to Victoria College; he then pursued his medical education under John Rolph, following that up with studies at a leading American medical school in Philadelphia. Upon his return he joined the staff of Rolph's Toronto School of Medicine, was a founding member of the reorganized Toronto School of Medicine when most of its faculty rebelled against Rolph's leadership, and went on to become the first dean of the University of Toronto Faculty of Medicine. Business investments made him a wealthy man, he himself was a leading Methodist layman, and his brother James was an important Upper Canadian politician from the mid-1850s onwards. A member of the Medical Council from 1866 to 1880, Aikins was perhaps the most influential schoolman on the council. Though he was never one of its editors, his active support was probably critical in the establishment of the *Canadian Journal of Medical Science* in 1876, which served as the house organ of the Toronto School of Medicine.

John Fulton was born on a farm near Fingal, Ontario. He too was a product of Rolph's school and completed his professional training in New York and London, returning with qualifications from both the Royal College of Physicians and the Royal College of Surgeons. Though he was a professor at Victoria in the 1860s and at Trinity College medical school from 1871, Fulton's greatest contribution was made through the columns of the *Canada Lancet*, which he owned and edited from the early 1870s until his death in 1887. Throughout the entire period, his was the premier voice upholding the highest ideals of medicine as a learned profession and the doctor as a professional gentleman.

There were other influential schoolmen as well: in Toronto, Edward

Hodder, James Henry Richardson, and Norman Bethune, to take but three more examples. The first two were, respectively, the sons of a captain in the Royal navy and an Episcopal Methodist bishop. Bethune came from a distinguished Upper Canadian family of professionals and businessmen and was the nephew of A.N. Bethune, an Anglican bishop of Toronto. All three held British qualifications and helped found Toronto's various medical schools, taught in them, and played active roles in the medical politics of the day. Outside Toronto there were men like John R. Dickson and Michael Sullivan, both professors at Queen's who at one time or another represented the Kingston medical school on the Medical Council and who played prominent roles in that community. Dickson, who was the first president of the council in 1866, was a close friend of John A. Macdonald, one of the founders of the Kingston hospital, and superintendent of the Rockwood Asylum during the 1870s. Sullivan, a surgeon, was elected as an MPP in 1876 and appointed to the Senate in 1884.

The territorial representatives on the Medical Council, especially those from outside York County, tended to be a somewhat different breed. They were far less likely to have British or American qualifications unless they themselves were emigrants, and their power base rested not just upon their standing with the local medical men who elected them to Council but on their wider reputations in the communities where they lived. One good example is William Clarke, one of the first doctors in Guelph, who had made himself a wealthy man through a variety of business ventures, had turned his hand to local politics, served as a mayor of Guelph and as an MLA in the 1850s and mid-1860s, and was reputed to have played an important role in the passage of the 1865 act. Though retired from politics by the late 1860s, he was a member of the Medical Council in 1868, and his political savvy was put to use in helping to shepherd the new medical bill through the legislature. His teammate for this task was William McGill, an Oshawa practitioner who was both an MLA and a member of the Medical Council. William Brouse was cut from the same cloth – a successful practitioner in Prescott, an active business and community leader, a long-time member of the Medical Board and then of the Medical Council, a federal MP from 1872 to 1878, and eventually a senator. The list could be extended, but the pattern in the other biographies is much the same. The territorial representatives on the Medical Council were, above all, local 'notables,' not just doctors but leading businessmen and local politicians who had a rich network of connections to the larger political and economic élite in Ontario society.

THE NEW MEDICAL BILL which was brought before the legislature in the autumn of 1868 resembled the act of 1865 in many ways. It continued the General Council, with the same mix of territorial and institutional representatives. The council, moreover, remained responsible for maintaining a register of licensed practitioners, setting matriculation standards, and fixing the program of medical studies. But there were also three innovations. One was of largely symbolic significance: the corporate body of licensed practitioners was to be known as the College of Physicians and Surgeons of Ontario (CPSO). The bill also included clauses that would strengthen the hand of the territorials over the schoolmen, and, more ambitious yet, it proposed the reintroduction of a penal clause against unlicensed practice, something the regulars had not even dared to hope for in 1865.

The politicians, on the whole, were willing to support these innovations, but only at a price which appalled large numbers of doctors and badly split their leadership. An amendment, introduced in Committee of the Whole, abolished the homeopathic and eclectic licensing boards and made those who held their qualifications full members of the college. The governing council was expanded to give them ten seats out of a total of twenty-eight, far greater representation than their numbers warranted. They were, moreover, guaranteed the right to appoint their own examiners for their special subjects.[6] The amendment took by surprise all but those doctors closest to the proceedings in the House. Yet it met no significant opposition from the laity and, indeed, received widespread approbation from both politicians and the press.[7]

The origins of this remarkable amendment lay, in part at least, in the cross-currents of medical politics over the preceding decade. In 1869 there were, as there had always been, doctors who were adamantly opposed to any compromises with the homeopaths or eclectics. There were also those among the latter groups who were convinced that medical differences and personal animosities ran so deep as to make cooperation impossible.[8] But since at least 1865 there had been other men in both camps who, mostly for tactical reasons, supported a unified profession. The very existence of a register of doctors from which they were excluded made it easier for their enemies, as one eclectic complained, 'to stigmatize Eclectics and Homeopaths as quacks.'[9] Moreover, all licensed doctors, regardless of their therapeutic doctrines, had a stake in controlling the numbers of new doctors entering the marketplace: as the editor of Ontario's new medical journal put it late in 1868, all of the effort since 1865 to raise educational standards at the medical schools 'remains practically useless because it cannot be applied to the

Homeopathic and Eclectic Schools of Medicine. Persons who are not able to pass the examinations in the regular colleges are notoriously in the habit of going before the so-called Eclectic Medical Board and obtaining a certificate which entitles them to practise ... We wish such laws to be passed and enforced as will ensure the competency of all who practise Medicine.'[10] Thus, as the bill passed through the House, both regulars and irregulars lobbied the politicians to support unification.[11]

More important to the outcome, however, was the attitude of the laity itself. As they had since the 1850s, both the *Globe* and the *Leader* continued to support the principles of therapeutic diversity and high standards of education. A sense of unease about the continuance of three distinct licensing authorities, each with somewhat different standards, is also evident in the debates on the bill.[12] But the crucial factor was the reluctance of a few key members of the House to put the irregulars at any disadvantage. During the debate several members spoke in favour of the homeopathic system, but the most influential was Matthew Cameron, a member of the cabinet. He said in defence of the amendment:

It was time that these professions which had hitherto been at daggers drawn, should hereafter be in a position to recognize each other, as having the same *status*. He had seen an allopathic practitioner go into the witness-box and swear deliberately that homeopathy was a humbug. He had himself, though a layman, seen those practical evidences of the benefit of homeopathy, which had made him feel that it was very rash ... for any one to declare on his oath that that was a humbug, which a number of highly respectable persons were following as a profession.[13]

To Cameron and other influential politicians, in other words, the irregulars were as much 'real' doctors as the regulars, and integration was the political price exacted for a new medical act. As one doctor reported to council afterwards, the objectionable clauses 'had been forced upon them. Mr. M.C. Cameron had said that "he would not let the bill pass without the clauses."' The choice, as William Clarke saw it, was either to accept the amendment or 'to see the bill defeated as a whole, and their scheme of a Central Board broken up.'[14]

The politicians went even farther. Clauses were added which gave *anyone* the right to register who had been 'actually practising' in Ontario before 1850 so long as he could produce proof of having attended one course of lectures at any 'recognized medical school' anywhere. The price of obtaining the new medical act, in other words, was inclusivity. If there was to be a medical monopoly in Ontario, it was to include all those who had the remotest claim to being trained practitioners, however marginal that claim might be, or however dubious their reputations among the regularly bred.

THOUGH THEY WOULD HAVE second thoughts within the year, for the newly regularized irregulars, integration caused little immediate concern. The new act seemed to protect their doctrinal peculiarities, and it gave both homeopaths and eclectics access to the public register of licensed physicians.[15] The reaction among many regular physicians, however, was consternation. The act provoked a vociferous outcry, especially from leading doctors in Toronto, Hamilton, and Ottawa. It was, in their view, a 'calamity' which forced them to amalgamate with 'pretentious humbugs' and 'deluded simpletons.'[16] It was also a public embarrassment, bringing condemnation upon them from the august voice of the *Lancet* (London) and from medical leaders in the rest of Canada.[17] In April the medical section of the Canadian Institute in Toronto organized a 'large' meeting where speaker after speaker condemned the act 'in very energetic Saxon.' The meeting ended with a resolution demanding that the Medical Council take 'prompt and energetic steps to secure our release from associations so repugnant.'[18] When the resolution was presented to Council, Drs McGill and Clarke stoutly defended their part in securing the act for the profession, and attacked the resolution as merely the work of a clique of Toronto doctors. A vote on the resolution was, nevertheless, a close one – nine to six in favour of the act.[19]

The Toronto dissidents then decided to go to the profession as a whole. At the Canadian Institute meeting, they had urged the territorial divisions across the province to elect repeal candidates in the forthcoming council elections.[20] J.N. Agnew, the secretary of the medical section, agreed to stand in Toronto on a repeal platform, as did candidates in some of the other divisions. Toronto doctors also organized a petition for circulation throughout the province, protesting against being forced 'into a degrading and hitherto unheard of association with persons styling themselves homeopaths and eclectics.' Among the first to sign their names were many of the most distinguished Toronto schoolmen and practitioners, and as the petition went the rounds it collected the signatures of leading doctors in Hamilton and Ottawa as well.[21] It is impossible at this remove to assess with any accuracy the full extent of the opposition. But it is clear that it ran deep and that many of the doctors most prominent in professional affairs in both the past and the future were 'irreconcilables' in 1869 and 1870. Edward Hodder, James

Richardson, W.R. Beaumont, William Canniff, James Bovell, the two Rosebrughs, Norman Bethune, and C.B. Hall were only some of those who signed the Canadian Institute petition.

Given the fact that only 13 per cent of all the registered doctors in Ontario were either homeopaths or eclectics, and that no more than a handful of previously unlicensed doctors ever applied for registration, one must ask why so many of Ontario's most prominent practitioners took such extreme exception to the act.[22] One answer is that the homeopaths in particular were far more influential than their numbers alone would indicate. We suggested, in an earlier chapter, that by mid-century the middle and upper classes were experiencing something of a crisis of confidence in the therapeutic efficacy of regular medicine. And these doubts seem to have gathered strength over the two decades that followed. If many families continued to rely exclusively on regular doctors, others were willing to turn to alternative therapies, and that included homeopathy. Indeed, a leading regular would declare in 1869 that 'half the members of the Legislature were Homeopathists' and 'it was a well-known fact that the heads of Law, the heads of Divinity, and the leading men of the City [of Toronto] identified themselves with the Homeopathic system.'[23] This may have been exaggeration for effect, but there is also some independent evidence to sustain it. During the second half of the 1860s, for example, the diaries of a future Chief Justice of Ontario and a leading Brantford minister both refer to consultations with homeopaths.[24] Matthew Cameron's vigorous defence of homeopaths and eclectics in the House suggests similar loyalties. When they needed political clout, as they would in the mid-1870s, the homeopaths could count on a number of very prominent Torontonians to attend a public meeting in support of their cause.[25] Throughout the late 1860s and 1870s, the voice of the *Globe* was solidly in favour of preserving therapeutic diversity, and Gordon Brown, who was running the editorial pages at the time, was almost certainly sympathetic to homeopathy itself.[26] Homeopathy constituted a particular threat to regular medicine's élite, then, because it had been successful in capturing the loyalties of some of Ontario's most influential citizens. Regulars might dismiss other sorts of 'quacks' as the resort only of the ignorant and deluded. In this case, 'heresy' had gained a degree of legitimacy that rivalled their own.

But there was also a second reason why leading regulars opposed the act so vehemently. Consorting with 'quacks' was not merely a question of tolerating differences that might arise between men of science, but an attack on the very notion of regular medicine as a liberal profession. 'Our diplomas,' said the Canadian Institute resolution, 'even though conferred by the universities of the old World, have thus lost their value, and our standing is levelled down to that of men ignorant of their own language and of every other; unacquainted with the natural sciences, even those most closely connected with the healing art.'[27] To J.N. Agnew it was 'as wrong in principle, if not in degree, to coerce the different "schools" in medicine into a distasteful union, as it would be for the Legislature to attempt to compel religious bodies ... to meet together in a common Synod, for united ecclesiastical legislation for the spread or propagation of diverse religious systems.'[28]

These were the voices, however, of successful city doctors who saw the issues in terms of their professional reputations and their social standing. Those more precariously situated, and especially those in the smaller towns and villages, saw things differently. To them the act represented the promise of an effective voice for country doctors in their professional affairs, a renewed attack on quackery, and a cap on the flood of competitors pouring out of the schools. The council elections held in the spring of 1869 revealed that a majority of the regulars were prepared to celebrate the act's virtues and live with its flaws. Even Dr McGill, who had voted in the legislature in favour of the integration clauses, was returned.[29] The main item on the agenda for the first meeting of Council was a repeal motion, sponsored by Agnew. The debate was long, furious, and, towards the end, acrimonious and *ad hominem*. The depth of division among the regulars can be gauged by the fact that the eight new territorial representatives split their votes, and thus the regular doctors on Council supported the act by a narrow margin of ten to seven.[30] However close the decision, nonetheless, the fact of the matter was that a majority voted to sustain the act.

THE GUERRILLA WARFARE against the act continued for many months. At the second annual meeting of the fledgling Canadian Medical Association, held in Toronto in 1869, those who supported the bill were denied committee positions, while William Clarke was investigated by the Ethics Committee on a charge of consulting with homeopaths.[31] Over the next two years, moreover, leading opponents of the act would throw their weight behind the CMA's initiatives to obtain a dominion registration act which would supersede the Ontario legislation and which would also exclude the 'quacks.'[32] Protests continued to be heard at the Medical Council meeting in April 1870, and in May the Hamilton Medical and Surgical Society amended its constitution to exclude homeopaths and eclectics, reiterating at the same time its determination to abide by the CMA code of ethics by refusing to hold consultations with either.[33] A year later, in the spring of 1871, a group of Toronto doctors organized themselves to lobby their politicians about repeal during the forthcoming provincial election.[34]

Despite these initiatives, however, organized opposition to the act declined steadily throughout 1870 and 1871, while its supporters became ever more vocal and more widely representative of the profession. As the act began to make itself felt indeed, even some of its most ardent critics became converts.[35] Initially, the most common defence of the act was that given the political circumstances it was the best that could be obtained. But as the months passed, two other arguments gained prominence. One directed attention to the impact of the first set of central examinations in 1870. The year before, 196 doctors had been licensed to practise in Ontario; in 1870 there were only 42.[36] The declining number of new doctors was in itself a forceful defence of the act. What was the alternative? asked the editor of the *Dominion Medical Journal*. It was American-style free trade in medicine:

Now we wish this alternative to be well considered in all its bearings, and we doubt not that every young medical man knows what that would lead to. We have the statement ... from the leading practitioners in the United States, that the profession there is in a deplorable state. Men of education and abilities are driven from the field, finding that they cannot make a respectable living. The ignorant and uneducated, and even those in a good position in society, are so easily imposed upon by designing scoundrels ... that [respectable doctors] becoming disgusted, relinquish a profession which brings them neither honour nor remuneration in any shape.[37]

A more Machiavellian defence was directed at those who most objected to amalgamation with the quacks. As one southwestern Ontario doctor put it, 'the Ontario Act was serving a good purpose in hugging Homeopathy and Eclecticism to death.'"[38] Dr Clarke expressed a similar view: 'One thing he desired to see, and that was the extinction of the Homeopathists and Eclectics; and if they [the regulars] gave the Bill fair play, before ten years, such would be the force of intelligence, not one of them would be found in the Province.'[39]

As the virtues of the act were recognized, moreover, the only available alternative – the CMA's dominion registration bill – lost almost all its Ontario support. The CMA bill, its critics pointed out, excluded the homeopaths and the eclectics; to support it would only invite the legislature to re-establish their separate licensing boards. John Fulton, the editor of the new *Canada Lancet*, threw his whole weight against the bill. On the one hand, he argued in 1871, it would be a disaster to tamper with an act which had already gone a long way towards 'eliminating ... from our ranks a vast horde of illiterate or incompetent persons ... It has materially lessened the numbers entering the regular profession and now at the close of the second annual examination ... we find that *not one* single candidate has entered for examination or registration as a homeopath or eclectic.' That by itself was reason enough to reject the CMA initiative. But he also laced his arguments with a familiar dose of Upper Canadian nationalism. The bill gave massive overrepresentation to Quebec, he pointed out: 'The old sentiment of the superiority of the east [is] as strongly asserted as it ever was ... We know it used to be said that the codfish of the Gulf were counted against Upper Canadians in the discussions on Rep. by Pop. – but we did not expect to have that absurdity perpetuated in the constitution of a new Medical Council.'[40] When it came time to vote on the issue, the majority of the members of the Medical Council agreed. In both 1870 and 1871, the council rejected motions to support the CMA bill on the grounds that it would interfere with Ontario's own medical legislation.[41] With that, the issue died, at least as far as Ontario was concerned, and while individual irreconcilables continued to make their voices heard, there ceased to be any concerted opposition by regular doctors to the Medical Act of 1869.

THE DECLINE OF organized opposition, however, was not accompanied by growing goodwill towards the homeopaths and eclectics. Antipathies continued to run deep, and throughout the early 1870s the regulars on the Medical Council did what they could to make life miserable, especially for the homeopaths, excluding them from key committees or making it difficult for their students to meet Ontario's medical or licensing regulations. Indeed, the sheer level of harassment finally led the homeopathic representatives to resign and prepare legislation which would reconstitute the homeopathic board as an independent licensing agency.[42] That bill came before the legislature early in 1874 along with another from the Medical Council itself, seeking among other changes a reduction in the number of homeopathic seats.

The politicians, however, were having none of it. In 1869 they had chosen to preserve therapeutic diversity within a unified profession. Five years later, in 1874, they were unwilling to abandon that principle, and thus they imposed a settlement on both parties. The homeopathic bill was rejected as unnecessary and 'undesirable,' while the council's bill was amended to maintain the same homeopathic representation and to further protect the access of homeopathic students to a licence to practise. With that, the majority of regulars subsided into acquiescence, and in ensuing years even began to work cooperatively, as occasion demanded at least, with their homeopathic colleagues.[43]

Their *homeopathic* colleagues, the reader will note. As we remarked in an earlier chapter, the eclectics relied on the therapies of both regular and alternative medicine; by the early 1870s fully a third of registered eclectics were themselves graduates of regular medical schools, and without a college of their own, most of their students were attending local medical schools run by the regulars.[44] Given all this, and the pressures exerted by the regulars within the council, the eclectics began to contemplate a merger with regular medicine. There were mixed feelings, but by late 1873 a majority of them concluded that their interests would be best served by a union with the regulars, and thus the Medical Act of 1874 included a clause arranging for their council seats to disappear five years after the new act became law.[45]

SUMMARIZING SOME OF the recent international literature on the sources of professional identity among nineteenth-century doctors, J.T.H. Connor remarks that the very fact that the amalgamation of regulars, homeopaths, and eclectics

could be contemplated let alone actually implemented, is ... suggestive that a different professional ethos or identity existed in American and Ontarian physicians ... As John Harley Warner has argued, American physicians appear to have centred their professional identity upon the notion of therapeutic practice, rather than on formal corporate structures such as licensing, educational and other regulatory bodies as was the case in Europe and the United Kingdom. Ontario physicians, too, reflecting more the British model of medico-corporate identity seem to have placed a greater emphasis upon regulatory agencies to define their profession, with actual therapeutic practice appearing to be placed in a secondary position. That is, despite the animosity displayed by some regular physicians towards eclectics and homeopaths, when all is said and done the latter were licensed practitioners and therefore were due recognition; it appears that a consensus evolved whereby it was thought better and more prudent to nurture professional affinities rather than accentuate therapeutic differences.[46]

Both 'better *and* more prudent'? While we think there is some truth in this interpretation, we also have our reservations. Certainly the British influence, the indigenous tradition of licensing doctors, and the repeated attempts to establish a self-governing organization point to the importance of formal corporate structures in the self-image maintained by Upper Canadian regulars. But a distinction needs to be between that and what happened between 1869 and 1874. A corporate identity was one thing; 'amalgamation' with the quacks was quite another. On the latter point British regulars had the same antipathies as their American counterparts, while some of the most influential Upper Canadian regulars condemned amalgamation without qualification and, indeed, organized a campaign to repeal it. Our own impression is more in accord with a passage by Warner we quoted in an earlier chapter.[47] Sectarianism was not just ignorance but heresy, a threat to the good name of medicine, and thus it was all the more urgent that good men stand together against it. The rise of rival systems encouraged an emphasis on orthodoxy, and helped unite regulars behind the attempt to establish their own organization. It was no accident, we suggest, that compromise and consensus among regulars themselves emerged so quickly after the medical legislation of 1859–61. That legislation had legitimized the quacks, so far as the public was concerned at least, and, equally, had 'disestablished' regular medicine. Heresy, in other words, had won a major victory. With disestablishment, the regulars had lost an identity, much like their professional counterparts in the Church of England, and it became more urgent to create institutions around which some sense of occupational coherence could be rebuilt. Some eminent doctors were prepared to make their peace with the eclectics and homeopaths, but on the whole there were few regulars, especially among the élite, who thought the quacks deserved 'due recognition' or that it would be 'better ... to nurture professional affinities.'

But 'more prudent,' yes. And here we return to the critical role of the laity in determining the course of events from the 1850s onwards. What distinguished the Ontario case from the American was the contingencies of local politics and the differences in the political culture. Whereas the Americans had opted for free trade in medicine, Upper Canadians had, in 1859–61, retained the principle of qualified practice but extended it to the eclectics and homeopaths. Whatever the regulars might think, the laity had defined the latter groups as 'real doctors,' and between 1869 and 1874 had made that definition stick. The former could either learn to live with it or put at risk the benefits of an organization they had coveted for so long and achieved in 1865.

The majority of regulars swallowed their pride and chose to live with amalgamation. The traditional basis for professional identity, however, died more slowly. Even in 1881 William Canniff, no obscure member of Ontario's medical fraternity, could tell a Canadian Medical Association audience that 'if two mariners, one of whom believed the earth to be a flat disc, while the other held the commonly-received hypothesis of its spheroidal form, were asked to act together in navigating the same ship around the world, how could they co-operate? We do not wilfully refuse to meet homeopaths; we simply decline because it would be a grim farce ... The result must be a failure of justice to the patient, which may jeopardize his prospect of recovery.'[48] Such views, and such anchors for professional identity, would not be discarded until medical men were able to formulate a new self-image rooted in the laboratory and in the sceptical empiricism of 'the scientific method.'

Having said all that, we also want to distance ourselves somewhat from Warner's emphasis on 'therapeutic practice' as the prime source of professional identity. For Upper Canadian doctors at least, more nuance is needed. It was neither therapeutic doctrine nor practice alone which fostered professional identity but something else, of equal importance, besides. Consider again the angry protest of the irreconcilables of 1869: by forced amalgamation 'our diplomas, even though conferred by the universities of the old World, have thus lost their value, and our standing is levelled down to that of men ignorant of their own language and of every other; unacquainted with the natural sciences, even those most closely connected with the healing art.' The quacks, the protest asserts, didn't even know the collateral sciences, let alone the broader world of literature and science. The emphasis here falls not so much on medical doctrine or practice as on the notion of the regularly bred doctor as a member of a learned profession, including all that entailed, from the right to self-governance possessed by gentlemen to the liberal education and the social standing they had a right to claim because of it. That too would change as new doctors began to acquire similar medical and preliminary qualifications, and as the meaning of a liberal education itself began to undergo reconstruction. But as late as the 1880s, the traditional symbols of professionalism could still evoke powerful loyalties.

WHILE LAW CONSOLIDATED an already well-established position during the third quarter of the nineteenth century, the position of regular medicine had virtually been revolutionized. At a nadir in 1859–61, its fortunes had risen spectacularly in the decade after 1865. Whatever the compromises that had to be made along the way, by 1875 the College of Physicians and Surgeons was a firmly established institution with powers, much like those of the Law Society, to control entry standards, license practitioners, and drive out unqualified practice. The scope of the achievement raises an issue of some importance: how are we to account for that success?

Over the last two decades or so, a number of 'revisionist' historians of the rise of the medical profession have fastened upon the limits of the therapeutic arsenal in the nineteenth century, as well as the narrow confines of 'valid' medical knowledge, and have consequently concluded that better explanations lie elsewhere, above all in the manipulation of public opinion and of the political arena. While in some respects our own explanations parallel this interpretation, we want firmly to reject its excesses. It is now beyond debate that most of the great victories of modern medicine took place after the turn of the twentieth century and that even the major breakthroughs of the 1880s and 1890s, in germ theory above all, had no immediate clinical impact.[49] In Ontario, moreover, the critical legislation which allowed the profession to consolidate its control was introduced at a time when 'valid' medical knowledge was all the more fragile. Thus to link the rising fortunes of the medical profession with a quantum leap in medical skills or therapeutic effectiveness is quite simply wrong, and on this point the revisionists have rightly rejected more traditionalist accounts of nineteenth-century developments.

Viewed from the late twentieth century, nevertheless, it is easy to underestimate the more modest but substantial progress that had been made in instrumentation, in the use and extent of the pharmacopoeia, in the understanding of the course of disease generally, and above all in surgical techniques, where the impact of anaesthetics and antisepsis was already beginning to work a revolution.[50] In Toronto and other cities, patients benefited from the work of skilled surgeons, indubitably at the cutting edge of these new developments, and from a small but growing number of specialists equipped with new ophthalmological and other instruments.[51] And if general practitioners employed such skills more uncertainly or erratically, there is at least a modest amount of evidence that they too adapted their practices to conform with surgical advances or with the retreat to a kinder, gentler use of the physician's pharmacopoeia.[52]

As Kenneth Ludmerer remarks, moreover, 'equating the effectiveness of medicine with therapeutic cures represents a very narrow view of what doctors do and ignores the other important functions of medicine, such as alleviating suffering, prolonging life, and providing reliable diagnosis and prognosis.'[53] Knowing how to use the limited pharmacopoeia that did exist, being able to extract painful teeth with some skill, dressing wounds and lancing boils using safer and less painful techniques, being able to tell a patient the difference between a life-threatening and less fatal tumour, are skills not to be denigrated just because nineteenth-century doctors lacked an arsenal of 'magic bullets' to cure all of humankind's great plagues. As we have tried to argue throughout this chapter, the success of the profession depended on the support of the laity – the politicians and the influential voices among public opinion. One element, though not the only one, in winning that support was the modest but steady expansion of informed medical practice. While the *Globe* might mount a sturdy defence of therapeutic diversity throughout the period, it rarely belittled the knowledge and skills of the intelligent, trained, physician; what it objected to was a *monopoly* over practice, and when he was ill, or dying of a gunshot wound, George Brown like others turned to a trusted physician for comfort and relief.[54] That medical care didn't save him, as it might have now, is really beside the point. With far less prestige or knowledge than in the modern world, doctors could hardly impose a professional *coup* upon the laity without their consent. Sharing a common world-view, which included explanations about illness and disease, patient and doctor built the bonds of trust, in Charles Rosenberg's words, on 'a conspiracy to believe.'[55]

But to believe what? The growing influence of the medical profession could also draw on the changes taking place within the wider cultural arena. During the nineteenth century, science in all its forms acquired enormous cultural authority, and the 'theatre of science,' in Christopher Armstrong and H.V. Nelles's felicitous phrase, promoted the conviction that it held the key to every form of material and intellectual progress.[56] In a penetrating review of the literature in 1983, S.E.D. Shortt pointed to the significance of this shift for the fortunes of the medical profession. It was, he writes,

a cultural context in which scientific innovation and the aspirations of medicine coincided ... medicine gained prestige not through enhanced therapeutic efficacy, but as a result of an increasing public faith in the value of science. Certainly, on a personal level, some individual patients owed much to the refinements in medical techniques and their perception of the profession doubtless reflected these experiences. Beyond such encounters, however, literate inhabitants of the nineteenth century appear to have internalized first the authenticity and then the utility of science as a mode of perceiving and responding to the external world. In this cultural climate, medicine's time had come.[57]

For much the same reason, doctors were also gradually wresting obstetrics out of the hands of female midwives, first among upper-class women who could afford their services, and then increasingly among the urban middle class. There were a variety of reasons for this transition, as other historians have pointed out, but what seems clear is that women themselves played a critical role in it by actively seeking the assistance of a licensed doctor, and they did so because of their conviction that he had superior skills and training. That conviction may have been misguided, in part at least; but, as Wendy Mitchinson has put it, 'the increasing prestige of science' gave the advantage to the physicians: 'Because physicians were able to align medicine with science in the popular mind' they could argue 'that they could provide better care than midwives, especially midwives who were untrained.'[58]

The argument presented by Shortt and Mitchinson, nonetheless, sweeps across the entire nineteenth century; when it is applied more narrowly to the 1860s and early 1870s, it needs to be tempered. Medical knowledge was accumulating but was still limited compared even with three or four decades later. As a way of understanding the world, 'science' was ascending but far from ascendant. Scepticism about the superior expertise of doctors, especially in areas like normal childbirth and therapeutics, was widespread, and alternative forms of medical care remained popular long after the legislation of 1865–74. Indeed, the penal clauses of the Medical Act of 1869, directed against all forms of unlicensed practice, including midwifery, proved far less efficacious in stamping it out than doctors had either expected or hoped. These are all issues we will return to. Still, the generalized impact of science should not be discounted; rather, it was one part of the matrix of reasons why medical men were able to convince at least a portion of public opinion that restrictive legislation was in the public interest.

There were, as well, potent intellectual counterweights to moderate and even deflect the ingrained resistance of the more radical strand of mid-nineteenth-century liberalism to any form of occupational privilege. One came from the mainstream of Protestant social philosophy, whether Anglican, evangelical, or the Scottish 'common sense' philosophers of the late eighteenth century. Individuals were not free to pursue their own selfish interests or appetites without restraint; they were hedged in by their duties to God, and they lived in communities where they had duties to others. Under certain circumstances, then, it was perfectly legitimate for the civil authority, itself ordained of God, to restrain individuals from hurting themselves or others. Thus, for example, when individuals succumbed to the temptations of alcohol, or exploited man's depravity by selling it, government was fully justified in intervening to protect or restrain them. And so, it might be argued, with 'quacks' and 'charlatans.' What constituted 'legitimate' medical practice might be disputed in the two decades after 1850; but those who made policy in the era were not prepared to countenance what they considered to be unqualified practice. The second counterweight could be found in the common law itself. The exercise of the 'police power' had deep roots in Anglo-American law, writes one British historian. 'From time out of mind, markets had been controlled, obligations had been imposed on common carriers, entry into some occupations had been restricted, while others required applicants to obtain licences ... and when health and safety was at risk summary action without prior application to the courts was justified.'[59] Thus, even aside from questions of medical knowledge or the influence of science, there were aspects of the intellectual environment which might predispose influential members of the laity to support intervention on behalf of those they considered qualified to practise medicine.

Beyond that, there is one other contextual factor as well. Doctors could not help but gain an advantage from the broadly based 'protective impulse' which animated so many other groups in the society as they sought, in Thomas Haskell's phrase, to protect those vital interests 'that were endangered by the utopian principle of laissez-faire.'[60] Moulders, grocers and druggists, manufacturers, dairymen and coopers, and many other occupational groups besides, all attempted to combine, in the decades after 1860 especially, in order to defend skills, preserve conditions of work, or exploit the new opportunities that social and technological change seemed to offer.[61] In their clash with competitors and their search for legislative sanction, doctors were doing no more than others in attempting to build protective barriers around their skills and their conditions of work. Indeed, in their own view they were not so much seeking to obtain new forms of control as to restore old ones.

As both business and labour historians have demonstrated, nevertheless, some of these groups were successful and some were not. What gave success to the doctors? However one assesses their special skills or the validity of their therapeutic practices in the 1860s or 1870s, these were not, in themselves, enough. As any number of social scientists and historians have pointed out, technical knowledge and skills must be transmuted into a form of property before they can be made to pay off.[62] Moulders were able to defend themselves when coopers could not, Gregory Kealey remarks, because they were able to maintain control of the shop floor. Out of that they could build an effective organization to control the conditions of their work.[63] For doctors, it was access to the political arena that counted. The leaders of Ontario medicine were highly educated and eminently respectable members of Victorian society. They not only considered themselves but were widely recognized by others as constituting one of the three 'learned professions.' Their social authority was anchored not only in an occupation but in their class position. They were mayors, MPPs, leading members of voluntary associations, active in the life of their churches and of

Ontario's universities; they married lawyers' sisters and gave their daughters in marriage to clergymen's sons. Eminent physicians ministered to the physical ailments of powerful men and their families. In the legislature they could make their case to a houseful of lawyers and ask no more than what their brother professionals already had. Thus, what *also* mattered to their success was their access to the levers of power in the parochial political world of Victorian Ontario.

6
The Ministry: Coming to Terms with Disestablishment

It was the clergy of the two 'national' churches who had borne the brunt of political conflict from the 1820s onwards, and who had experienced the most dramatic changes in their circumstances. Coming to terms with disestablishment meant that they had to rebuild many of their institutions and reorient their assumptions. New forms of governance had to be created and the relationship between clergy and laity redefined. Financial affairs needed to be reordered. And the churches had to learn to live with those who were recognized as legitimate competitors by large parts of the population. Though the Kirk and the Free Church also had to confront them, some of these challenges hit hardest at the Church of England. With the secularization of King's College and the Clergy Reserves, virtually all the ties which linked the Church of England to the colonial state had been cut. The loss to the church was more than financial. Cast adrift from its traditional ideological moorings, no longer an ecclesiastical establishment, the Church of England had to redefine its relationship to civil society and the nature of its mission in the secular world.

A number of historians in recent years have outlined the broad contours of this search for a new identity. They have drawn particular attention to the growth of self-government and the new emphasis on 'the church as a sacred institution' separated from the secular world and focused more exclusively on its pastoral duties to its own flock.[1] They have also described the economic impact of voluntarism and the bitter conflicts over doctrine which divided the church during the middle decades of the nineteenth century. Inevitably all of these developments affected the role and self-image of the individual clergyman. If, as we put it in a previous chapter, he was not to be part of a civil establishment responsible for the good order and direction of his society, and in receipt of an income which would secure his dignity as a professional gentleman, what then was he to become?

THE GROWTH OF SELF-GOVERNMENT was an inevitable outcome of the course of Upper Canadian politics in the 1840s and early 1850s. The separation of church and state meant that the colonial church had to learn to survive on its own resources and to create the machinery which made that possible. A variety of legal restrictions and established conventions retarded that development, however, and it was only the crisis of 1850-4 which provoked a concerted effort to obtain it. The relevant negotiations with both the imperial and colonial governments have been detailed elsewhere and need not be reiterated here.[2] But, by 1857, the colonial church had obtained the right to establish its own synods and to pass legislation affecting its own affairs. In effect, the Church of England had established its spiritual and temporal independence from the state.

Self-government meant more than independence from the state, however. It also gave ordinary clergymen their first opportunity to express themselves in the councils of their church. Until mid-century they had had no direct influence except when, and if, the bishop chose to seek their advice. In 1857 Upper Canadian clergymen acquired full powers of self-regulation within the larger framework of the Church of England. All clergymen were entitled to attend their diocesan synod and to vote on the business before it. The synod was not, it is true, a straightforward example of majoritarian democracy; the clergy were but one estate or 'house' within Synod, and the bishop held veto powers over all new legislation. Out of the struggle between church and state, nonetheless, had come a form of organization which allowed clergymen a significant degree of control over their own professional affairs, including such vital matters as ecclesiastical discipline, the terms of appointment for bishops and priests, and the selection of their own bishops.[3]

The organizational structure of the church changed modestly over succeeding years. The Diocese of Toronto, at one time encompassing most of modern Ontario, was gradually subdivided. During the third quarter of the century, for example, Huron was carved out of the western part of the diocese, Ontario out of the east, and Algoma from a portion stretching from Muskoka to the Ontario-Manitoba border. Except for Algoma, a 'missionary diocese' dependent for its financial survival on external support, each diocese had its own synod, which met annually.[4] From the early 1860s Anglicans had also established a 'provincial synod' which brought together, every three years, representatives from all of the dioceses in eastern British North America and which was the predecessor to a national organization established in the 1890s.

DURING THE MIDDLE DECADES of the nineteenth century, a majority of Anglican clergymen, and in central and eastern Upper Canada a large majority, were adherents of high church doctrine, which was in turn infused and revivified by tractarianism.[5] That the coming of self-government was accompanied by the growth of this powerful ideology of clerical independence was, we suggest, no coincidence. The tractarian movement had re-emphasized the Anglo-Catholic traditions of the church as the intermediary between God and man, its role as a guide to the laity in the interpretation of scripture, and the place of the sacraments as the instruments and not just the symbols of divine grace. Concomitantly it provided a theological justification for the necessity of an independent church, for the clergy as a distinct and indispensable order in society, and for a claim to social authority resting exclusively on their role as the ordained priests of a sacred institution.[6] Ideas such as these gave clergymen a new understanding of their place at the very moment when it was most needed. The 'counterworld of the sacred,'[7] and above all the tractarian ordering of the relationship between priesthood and laity, church and state, legitimized a separate sphere for both the church and its clergy at that point in history when the more traditional civil and social roles were being stripped from them in any case.

But tractarianism served other purposes as well. Perhaps because of its origins at unreformed Oxford, in an intellectual environment irreconcilably antagonistic to some of the most dynamic political and social forces at work in the nineteenth century, tractarian doctrine tended to be remarkably congruent with the more traditional ideal of the professional gentleman – in its emphasis, for example, on independence from the laity, on belonging to a distinct order in a society organized by rank and station, on collegial authority versus submission to the state. From this perspective the commitment of so many Anglican clergy to high church doctrine may be interpreted as an attempt to rework the presuppositions of the old regime during an age when that social order was crumbling.

The same revolution which had created an independent, self-governing church, however, also gave birth to a new role for the laity within it. In principle the laity had always been represented within the Church of England through the ecclesiastical supremacy of the monarch and Parliament. But synods and convocations had long consisted of the clergy alone. The American episcopal church, on the other hand, had brought laymen into its councils since the 1780s as a means of mobilizing their support behind the principle of episcopalianism in the new republic.[8] Before the late 1840s John Strachan had been of two minds about the matter, and so indeed had his clergy. On the one hand, lay participation was essential in order to persuade congregations to contribute generously to the church's coffers. On the other, there were deep reservations about admitting the laity to the councils of the church for fear that they would demand a voice not only in its temporal but in its spiritual affairs as well.[9]

As financial conditions worsened, nonetheless, and as the church's enemies grew ever more aggressive, Strachan became convinced that there was no alternative but to call upon the voice of the laity. Thus, in 1851, he invited each congregation to elect two delegates to attend a three-day 'visitation' designed to express the united opposition of the church to the secularization of the reserves and to petition the imperial government against it. The meeting was an enormous success and an effective demonstration of solidarity in the face of adversity.[10] With that happy precedent as a guide, Strachan continued to invite the laity to be present at the other proto-synods held before 1857, and in that year non-clerical representation was incorporated into the constitutions of the new diocesan synods of both Toronto and Huron. The influence of the laity was carefully hedged, however. There was to be no 'Rep. by Pop.' in the Church of England: clerical and non-clerical representation was to be roughly equal, and each group was to vote as a separate 'order' so that legislation could be passed only by means of concurrent majorities. Despite these safeguards, many clergymen remained nervous. As the editor of *The Church* said, following one meeting in 1856, 'The spirit of encroachment on the part of the laity, in functions which angels uncalled would fear to touch, was what alarmed us. The particular matter under discussion, we considered as comparatively unimportant; the feeling, however, was too evidently, as a quiet brother ... whispered to us, "Religion made easy – every man his own priest!"'[11]

THE CLERGY HAD GOOD cause to fret. Just as most of them adhered to high church doctrines, so indeed the vast majority of laymen were evangelical in temper,[12] and on a wide variety of issues tractarianism and evangelicalism represented polar extremes. To the claims made by the former about the role of the episcopacy or the distinctive sacred office of the ordained priest, the latter juxtaposed the supremacy and sufficiency of scripture, justification by faith alone, and the priesthood of all believers. Typically, the evangelical *Echo* denounced the notion that the ministry was 'a priesthood in any sacrificial sense of the term,' a doctrine which was 'one of the fundamental errors of Popery and its humble follower Tractarianism.'[13] For the high church, then, the clergy constituted a distinct and authoritative order of men; for evangelicals the distance between laity and clergy was much less, the latter being distinctive because they performed a specialized occupational role rather than because they represented a conduit linking God to the world.[14]

To the modern reader the issues at stake here may seem both archaic and arcane. In the middle decades of the last century, nonetheless, they had the power to divide families and friends, to polarize congregations and whole dioceses, in Upper Canada as elsewhere. In some dioceses the conflicts were muted or infrequent.[15] But in the Diocese of Toronto, warfare was almost the norm throughout the middle decades of the nineteenth century, above all in the 1870s when an inept bishop and bitter party divisions threatened to rend the Anglican communion asunder. At various times in the two decades after 1850, for example, the lay representatives on Synod fought to eliminate the episcopal veto, to obtain a stronger voice in the election of bishops, to play a role in the discipline of the clergy or in regulating clerical garb and liturgical practices.[16] Whatever the particular issue, the underlying implication was that, within Synod, the laity had an equal say in the management, not just of the temporal affairs of the church, but of its spiritual affairs as well.

Nor were the evangelical laity of the Diocese of Toronto to be easily dismissed. When, in 1873, the high church clergy managed to exclude every evangelical, lay or clerical, from the synod executive committee and the provincial synod, the evangelicals formed the 'Church Association' as a pressure group. Its membership included a large number of powerful laymen, among whom were W.H. Draper, S.H. and Edward Blake, Daniel Wilson, Sir Casimir Gzowski, J.G. Hodgins, Hon. James Patton, Henry and William Gooderham, and many others of similar standing. As H.E. Turner remarks, the list was 'rich with representatives of commerce, industry and the professions (judges and queen's counsels, reeves and mayors, majors and colonels, civil servants and merchants); indeed, the roll-call reads like the Anglican contingent at the tip of Ontario's pyramidal class structure.'[17] Still, to the early 1870s at least, the laity lost most of their battles: episcopal authority was sustained, and the laity kept at arm's length on matters of clerical discipline and liturgical practices. Given the episcopal veto and the requirement for concurrent majorities in the two Houses, lay incursions were generally resisted, though not without a high cost in terms of morale and the church's public image.[18]

AMONG THE MANY ISSUES which divided clergy and laity in the two or three decades after mid-century was one of particular importance to the clergyman's sense of identity. This was what was commonly referred to as 'the patronage question' – who was to control the appointment of ministers to congregations or parishes. Though the majority of clerical appointments in England continued to be made by individual laymen or by the Crown, nearly all the traditional forms of lay patronage had disappeared in Upper Canada by the mid-1850s.[19] Most appointments, indeed, had always been made by clerical authorities, and even the patronage of the rectories, originally in the gift of the governor, had been transferred at mid-century to the Church Society, which chose to lodge it in the hands of the bishop. This arrangement suited the clergy admirably for it accorded well with the high church doctrine that the clergy constituted a separate and distinct social order which must maintain its spiritual independence despite the growing financial clout of the laity in church affairs. 'It has been an essential rule in God's church,' said Bishop Bethune in 1870, 'that ministers should be sent to the people and not called by them.'[20] Or as high church spokesmen were frequently wont to put it, the sheep could not be allowed to choose their shepherd.

That clergymen were 'sent' and not called was not only a divine injunction, but integral to the ability of the clergyman to do his job properly. The clergy, 'like other men, are open to temptation,' the Rev. Adam Townley wrote in 1858,

and if their flocks are not only *their voluntary paymasters but also their patrons*, how difficult must it be for them, especially if they have wives and children dependent upon their salary, faithfully to rebuke the secretly cherished sins, or the more popular worldliness of, it may be, the very chief of their parishioners ...?

Indeed, it is further equally evident that by such parochial elections the official position of the pastor is so lowered that it can scarcely be expected that his flock, especially the richer members of it, for wealth is naturally self-sufficient, will look up to him with that holy reverence and sweet confidence with which the Ambassador of Christ should ever be regarded both for the honour of his Lord, and the good of his charges themselves.[21]

Evangelicals, not surprisingly, and especially the evangelical laity, took a dim view of such sentiments. The laity were also inclined to give short shrift to arguments about the need for a maintenance to ensure a minister's independence. 'A clergyman was sent to a parish to do Christian work, not to obtain a livelihood,' said one lay member of the Toronto synod, 'and he could not do any valuable service as long as he was not in harmony with the members of his congregation.'[22] And the financial arguments were often bluntly put. It was the laity, said Daniel Wilson at another synod meeting, who built the churches and contributed to clerical salaries, 'and they would more readily maintain the church if this right [to a voice in appointments] was admitted.' Such an innovation, replied one clergyman, would 'break the Bishop's pastoral staff before his eyes.' To another, it would 'lower the tone and character of the clergy – the social, moral, and religious status of the clergy should be carefully preserved.'[23]

The intensity of feeling on both sides made the patronage issue a fruitful source of conflict in the synods of all dioceses, but especially in those where clergy and laity were most divided by doctrinal differences. When, in the late 1860s, the Synod of the Diocese of Toronto was incorporated, for example, the patronage formally lodged in the Church Society was transferred to the diocese and a fierce debate ensued about how it was to be exercised. The majority of laymen fought hard to secure a voice for the congregations, but their motions were soundly defeated by a solid phalanx of clergymen. The latter, on the other hand, were no less soundly defeated in their attempts to lodge appointments solely in the hands of the bishop. In the end a compromise was struck. In a canon of 1871, the power of appointment was given to the bishop, but no vacancy was to be filled until he had consulted the representatives of the congregation in question.[24] Except in the Diocese of Ontario, where the bishop had unqualified powers of appointment, some variation of the Toronto formula was put in place in other dioceses as well.[25] A compromise it was, but one in which the clergy won the greater victory, formally at least. The bishop was obliged to 'consult' but not required to follow the advice he might be given. Thus, to the early 1870s, the clergy appeared to have been successful in containing the claims of the laity to expand their authority at the expense of the clerical order.

THE UPHEAVALS which convulsed the Church of England in the three decades after mid-century had few reverberations among Upper Canadian Presbyterians, in large part due to the fact that many of the issues dividing Anglicans had already been resolved in Scotland by the Reformation settlement or by subsequent developments within the Presbyterian polity in both Scotland and the colonies. As they established their Kirk sessions, presbyteries, and synods, for example, colonial Presbyterians were simply re-creating a traditional organizational structure which provided for a full measure of self-government within the church. This system of 'church courts' (or governing bodies) gave all ministers an equal voice in such matters as internal self-discipline and the spiritual affairs of the church generally. Nor did the role of the laity pose fundamental problems: it too was represented, both in Synod and in the presbyteries (the regional units), each congregation appointing one of its elders to attend these senior church courts, where the voices of the clergy and laity were coequal. Presbyterian forms of government were no more majoritarian democracies than those of the Church of England; with only one lay elder representing each congregation, the weight of the ministry in church affairs remained disproportionate to their numbers. Even so, church policy reflected the views not only of the clergy but of representatives of the laity as well.[26]

Congregations also retained an unequivocal right to 'call' their own minister. In Upper Canada, at least, there was no parallel among Presbyterians to the struggles of Anglicans over patronage. Nor did a minister belong to a separate and distinctive order within the church; he was simply one of the ordained officers of a congregation, albeit with specialized duties, a prolonged education, and a unique public authority to interpret the word of God. Presbyterians, on the other hand, were not 'congregationalists.'[27] The presbyteries retained the power to approve each call and to intervene in disputed cases. Thus Presbyterian forms of government attempted to strike a balance between the powers of shepherd and flock, and between the ministry and the laity as a whole.

By mid-century, moreover, even the fraught question of church–state relations had been largely resolved, though at great cost to the church itself. After a decade of bitter party warfare between moderates and evangelicals, the Scottish church had split apart in 1843 over lay patronage, an issue which encapsulated a broader struggle about the spiritual independence of the church from state interference. The question had little relevance in Upper Canada, but loyalties to the homeland were intense, and Scotsmen overseas found themselves embroiled in conflict as well. The result was the splintering of the colonial church in 1844 and the formation of the Free Church of Canada.[28] The disruption did not lead to a significant breach over doctrine or forms of governance, both branches of Presbyterianism remaining loyal to their common heritage in this respect. Ironically, it also pre-empted the kind of internal dissension between evangelicals and those of other views which was to wrack the Anglican communion, by creating two distinct denominations: the Free Church, overwhelmingly evangelical in temper, and the 'moderates' who remained in the 'old Kirk.' Thus each party acquired its own institutional vessel, making possible a degree of consensus unimaginable among contemporary Anglicans.

IN COMING TO TERMS with disestablishment, nonetheless, the Church of England and the Kirk shared one piece of common ground – a shelter against the full impact of voluntarism provided by the commutation clauses of the Clergy Reserves settlement. The government of the Canadas, the reader will remember, had been forced by the imperial authorities, as part of the settlement of the Clergy Reserves question, to guarantee the stipend of any clergyman already receiving one. It could have opted to make payments directly from its own funds; instead it agreed, with the consent of the individual clergymen involved, to transfer the equivalent of their lifetime stipends to the churches themselves. In a few cases church leaders had to engage in a certain amount of arm-twisting, but in the end all of the clergymen, without exception, agreed to 'commute' their stipends to their churches. Though the payment of these stipends constituted a first claim on the newly created 'commutation fund' of the Kirk and the Church of England respectively, the result was to produce a substantial pool of capital, one that would gradually produce revenues that could be used to promote the general welfare of both churches.

The settlement meant, in the first place, that all those ministers on the commutation list would remain, for life, independent of the vagaries of voluntarism. Congregational financial support might supplement their salaries, but in the main their income would come from the commutation fund. To those already ensconced in the more prosperous parishes of Upper Canada's towns and cities, the commutation fund assured them a comfortable living; to others it made the difference between straitened circumstances and modest prosperity. And since some of the commuted ministers were young men in 1854, the fund continued to support them far into the nineteenth century, and in a few cases into the next.[29]

In the first decade or so, there was little left over in either fund after the stipends of commuting ministers had been paid. But as older ministers died off, capital began to accrue and interest mounted.[30] The churches used this money in a variety of ways, but mainly it was allocated to salaries. One or two Anglican dioceses used the fund to supplement the incomes of its poorest ministers, usually those assigned to mission stations, but in most cases a set share of the total annual interest was allocated to all non-commuting ministers – those who entered the ministry after 1854 – in order of seniority, a method of rewarding those with long records of service in the church and ensuring that they had incomes adequate to their family responsibilities and advancing years. In most cases as well, the sums were used to reduce the disparities among senior ministers by distributing the surplus revenues only to those whose total income fell below a certain figure. Whatever the exact arrangement, the impact was substantial. In the early 1880s, for example, 40 per cent of the clergy in the Diocese of Toronto were receiving income from the commutation fund, either as commuting ministers or as non-commuting senior clergy. Most of the latter received $400, no trivial supplement to the amounts raised by congregations or drawn from other sources of parochial income.[31]

The legacy of the commutation settlement, in sum, was to cushion the churches substantially against the full shock of secularization, and indeed to cushion them for decades to come. It sheltered all commuting ministers from the full impact of the transition to voluntarism, generated surpluses which were used to supplement the salaries of some non-commuting ministers throughout the second half of the nineteenth century, contributed to the other financial needs of the churches, and preserved, for Anglicans especially, the symbolic link to a maintenance independent of the laity. In this latter respect, indeed, the commutation fund constituted a materialist base for the superstructure of tractarian doctrine that animated so many Anglican clergymen throughout the latter half of the century. But it also shielded them from the need to face up to the full implications of voluntarism, making it more difficult, even as the century wore on, for high churchmen especially to come to terms with their new circumstances.

IN SOME RESPECTS, indeed, the real trauma of disestablishment in the two or three decades after mid-century arose from another source altogether: the fundamental cultural shift which legitimized religious pluralism and made dissent respectable. There had, of course, always been ministers of religion who did not belong to either of the two national churches – those who, especially before 1850, were habitually identified, by leading Anglicans at least, as 'dissenters,' whose congregations were 'conventicles,' whose churches were 'meeting Houses,' whose sacraments 'lacked efficacy,' whose ministers were 'self-constituted, self-authorized teachers.'[32] High Churchmen clung to such shibboleths far into the century. During the three or four decades around mid-century, nonetheless, the term 'clergyman' gradually came to be used generically, and the ministers of most of Upper Canada's major denominations were accorded recognition as professional men. Though we propose to explore this shift by focusing on the Wesleyan Methodists alone, not only because of their importance in nineteenth-century Ontario history but because they made the transition first and most decisively, we suggest that our arguments might be equally applied to the ministry of other denominations as well. A word of warning to the reader, however: for the sake of stylistic felicity we will generally use, without qualification, the word 'Methodist' in the pages that follow; but, unless otherwise noted, we are referring exclusively to its Wesleyan branch.[33]

How then were Methodist ministers able to make the transition from saddle-bag preachers to respectable members of Ontario's professional class? What matters most to that story is the growth of religious pluralism and its political impact between the late 1820s and the 1850s. Methodists, along with other dissenting sects, might have begun their history in Upper Canada on the fringes of respectable society; certainly, they remained outside the privileged ranks of those who ruled the colony. But, by the 1830s, Methodism in particular had become a potent political force. Not only had it consolidated its hold on the countryside but it had made significant inroads in the towns and cities. It had, moreover, attracted a substantial number of respectable adherents, including prosperous farmers, merchants, and a sprinkling of professional men – men who voted, who served as JPs, who sat in the legislature.[34] Throughout the period, these men of property and influence would be among the shock troops in the assault on religious privilege. The ministry itself was active in colonial politics, during the 1830s especially, and above all in articulating an alternative to Anglican, Tory conceptions of the good society and the loyal citizen. Ideological and social respectability, in turn, contributed to what David Mills has described as the integration of Methodism 'within the social structures of the province,' making it ever more difficult for their enemies to dismiss Methodist ministers as ignorant fanatics and itinerant pedlars of sedition.[35]

Though a gradual process, the steady progress of disestablishment between the 1830s and the mid-1850s had the effect of levelling the distinctions between church and dissent, clergymen and 'unauthorized teachers.' The Marriage Act of 1831, for example, was hailed in the *Christian Guardian* as 'a fair legalization of the clerical character of all the clergy of all the denominations in the province.'[36] The chartering of denominational colleges like Victoria and Queen's, and the eventual secularization of the University of King's College, effectively undermined John Strachan's dream of a single national university under Church of England control and forced him to establish his own denominational college, which was increasingly viewed as simply one among the others. During the 1840s government patronage was, as a matter of policy, extended to include representatives of all denominations on such local institutions as the grammar-school boards.[37] The appointment of Egerton Ryerson as superintendent of education was hailed, by Methodists at least, as a powerful symbol of religious equality and of the respectability and influence of their ministry.[38] Above all there was the secularization of the Clergy Reserves. Such changes as these could not help but diminish invidious distinctions between the ministers of the different churches and, in the public mind at least, create a more inclusive conception of the ministry as a homogeneous occupational category.

The combined effects of disestablishment and the prosperity of its membership, moreover, laid the groundwork for a growing parity in clerical incomes between Wesleyan ministers and those of the Church of England and the Kirk. In the 1820s and 1830s, Methodist salaries were far below the standard set for Anglican clergymen. At a time when the latter could expect a stipend of £170 or even £200, married Methodist itinerants received only £50 plus some modest additional allowances from their congregations.[39] And if, as the clergy of the Church of England claimed, £150 to £200 was the absolute minimum required to maintain respectability, then Methodist ministers, on the grounds of income alone, were to be classed among the unrespectable. In 1855 the basic Methodist stipend was raised, and while unmarried preachers might get much less, a married man with two children could expect to receive £75 plus rent and other allowances;[40] still, this was probably less than the incomes of the commuted clergy of the two national churches, who could count on anywhere from £112 to £150 in addition to whatever their congregations might agree to give them.

During the 1860s, however, these differences began to dwindle. As the number of non-commuted clergymen began to multiply, their salaries were increasingly tied to the variable limits set by congregational benevolence. With growing wealth and numbers, and congregations long-inured to voluntary giving, Methodism had little difficulty in matching the kind of stipends received by the average Anglican or Presbyterian minister.[41] By 1868, indeed, one spokesman for the Free Church declared that the Wesleyans were 'the best paid ministry in the country. Their system of finance and ministerial support is such, that no minister within their ranks, if at all efficient, has less than $600; and while their nominal salary is small, the ... [perquisites] and extra allowances are so allocated as to swell that amount up to the sum we have indicated.'[42] The previous year a clerical correspondent to the *Christian Guardian* had remarked, in similar fashion, that 'in all fairness it is right to say that Wesleyan ministers, as a whole, are as well-supported as ministers of other denominations.'[43] Professional status was, among other things, firmly rooted in a material base. Modest though the sums might be, the salaries earned by Methodist ministers increasingly enabled them to assimilate their lifestyles and their expectations to those of other professional men in their communities.

HISTORIANS like Neil Semple and William Westfall have drawn attention to other lines of convergence between Methodism, Anglicanism, and Presbyterianism during the middle decades of the nineteenth century. It was in these years, for example, that Methodism developed an institutional structure designed to sustain the continuing loyalties of its individual members and its effectiveness as an established organization. Special-purpose buildings for religious services, built in styles that contemporaries recognized as churches, became the norm. A complex committee structure took shape to administer the business of Conference.[44] There was, as well, 'the tempering of revivalism' that both Semple and Westfall have described so well – the more moderate interpretation of the meaning of religious experience, the greater emphasis on the ordinary means of grace, on gradualism, and on a life of holiness.[45] Associated with these changes, however, was yet another development which might be described as the growth of a 'regular' ministry – regular at least as Anglicans or Presbyterians might recognize it. Exhortations to more sober modes of pulpit demeanour and dress found their way into the pages of the *Christian Guardian*.[46] A 'settled' ministry became more common as ministers were stationed to a single congregation in the larger towns or cities, or assigned to a circuit centred on a village parsonage. Though Conference resolutely clung to the principle that ministers should be reassigned to new circuits every three years, the very existence of churches, parsonages, smaller circuits, and assignments to particular congregations could not help but diminish the image of the Methodist parson as a rootless saddle-bag preacher.[47] As other historians have pointed out, that image was largely illusory – Methodism had always been a highly structured, hierarchical *organization*;[48] but it had been powerful among respectable folk in the first half of the nineteenth century, and its decline made it that much easier to assimilate Methodists to more conventional notions of what a clergyman should be. Much the same might be said of the declining role of local (or lay) preachers, which, said Methodism's enemies, not only 'secularized' the ministry but confounded clerical and lay roles.[49] Long considered an essential adjunct to the ordained ministry within the Methodist polity, by the 1860s and 1870s laymen were increasingly considered inappropriate occupants of the pulpit.[50] Thus in yet another way Methodism was assimilated to the assumptions of other denominations and to the traditional model of a regular ministry.

At the same time as these changes were taking place, there was a shift in the ministry's own self-image, away from the ideal of the selfless saddle-bag itinerant and towards more conventional notions of middle-class respectability. It was expected that parsonages would not only be built but properly furnished. Salaries must be generous enough to enable ministers to buy libraries, and preaching schedules reduced to allow time for study. The use of a buggy was increasingly preferred to travel by horseback. The necessity of servants was bruited, along with the resources to send a boy to college. Rarely expressed before midcentury, such expectations became common coinage in the pages of the *Christian Guardian* after that.[51] These expectations were hardly exceptionable; they were routinely heard in the Anglican and Presbyterian press. But the very fact that they were heard among Methodists too is telling testimony to the distance the Wesleyan ministry had come since its heroic age in early Upper Canada.

ABOVE ALL, there was the growing importance of formal education, both preliminary and professional. Though never opposed in principle to an educated ministry, Upper Canadian Methodism put relatively little weight on education, in the early years especially. As Neil Semple puts it, 'the essential criteria for the early itinerant were a basic level of literacy, supplemented by as sound a grounding as possible in the Bible and Wesley's works, experience in preaching, and, most important, a conversion experience that regenerated his fallen state.'[52] Before the mid-1860s the only preliminary education required for a preacher on trial was a knowledge of English grammar and the ability 'to write a good hand.'[53] Beyond that, probationers underwent a four-year program of self-directed study, reading a relative handful of texts assigned by Conference, with their progress evaluated each year by a senior minister. For many Methodists, moreover, there was an embedded suspicion about any innovation giving priority to learning over piety, and that applied to both higher standards of preliminary education and formal schooling in theology. Learning was, at best, a tool in forwarding God's work rather than an end in itself; indeed, learning could even cripple the work of evangelism by promoting a coldly rational form of religiosity which many Methodists identified with the learned ministries of the Church of England or Scotland.[54]

Though they had always to work within the constraints this intellectual context imposed, there had always been some leading Methodists who were eager advocates of the ideal of an educated ministry, and their numbers grew decade by decade. Successive editors of the *Christian Guardian*, for example, were consistent proponents of higher educational standards even if the warmth of their enthusiasm might wax or wane according to their own predispositions.[55] Their argument had two central threads: the need to appeal to an increasingly educated and respectable laity who sought more intellectual sustenance than backwoods fire and brimstone, and the need to direct the new currents of literary criticism and scientific discovery into channels that would sustain rather than undermine Christian belief. Expressed as early as the middle 1830s in the pages of the *Christian Guardian*, these convictions would remain the staples of the case for an educated ministry for decades to come.[56]

Sceptics there were, and their voices continued to be raised far into the late nineteenth century.[57] Indeed, the frequency and forcefulness of the appeals for higher standards of education made by E.H. Dewart and other Methodist leaders throughout the 1870s and 1880s are themselves proof of the doubts many Methodists entertained about transforming their ministry into a learned profession. Still, despite all the reservations, there was a steady drift towards higher educational standards and more formal schooling. There was sporadic talk from the 1840s onwards of establishing a theology class at Victoria College. Its arts program, which included theological subjects for those intending to become ministers, and especially its preparatory department, provided a large number of ministerial candidates with the elements of a literary education. By the 1850s, moreover, Conference was giving material encouragement to the pursuit of such studies by providing some probationers with financial subsidies to attend Victoria.[58]

In 1865 the minimum preliminary standards for preachers on trial were raised to the equivalent of a good common-school education, and those probationers who attended college were rewarded by a shorter period of circuit work while on trial.[59] A few years later a Chair in theology and a course leading to the degree of Bachelor of Divinity were established.[60] The vast majority of ministerial candidates attending Victoria, it is true, took only a partial arts program or a modified, and much shortened, theological course which did not require such high entry standards. But the creation of the BD program was a potent symbol, indicating a new level of commitment to the importance of a learned ministry. A far more radical departure occurred in the early 1880s when the entry standard for *all* probationers was raised to university matriculation or the equivalent.[61] The intent, in other words, was to require a full high-school education, including several years of Latin, for admission to ministerial ranks. The new standard was, in fact, one of the casualties of the Methodist union of 1884 and would not become a rule of the church for another decade.[62] It is indicative of the Wesleyan outlook nonetheless. In the debate over the matter at the General Conference of 1882, there were even those who wanted to insist on Greek, though that proved too much for the majority to swallow.[63] But Greek or no Greek, the debate revealed the presuppositions which underpinned the proposed matriculation standard. As one lay delegate from Guelph put it, high schools were now located everywhere and matriculation was easy to achieve. 'Lawyers, doctors and others in secular professions were obliged to reach it, and he saw no reason why ministers should not have as good an education as men in *other* professions.'[64]

GIVEN THE TRADITIONAL Methodist emphasis on piety over learning, it is perhaps worth pausing to consider just why educational standards rose so rapidly in the years after 1865. The yearning of ministers themselves for recognition as respectable members of middle-class society undoubtedly played its part, as did the sense that Methodism, often seen by its adherents as the new 'national church,' deserved to occupy a place in society equivalent to that claimed by those of the discredited establishment. But the critical factor was that the call to the ministry proved irresistible to several generations of devoted young men who, after mid-century, flooded the church with more candidates than it could easily accommodate.[65] On the one hand, that enabled the Methodists to meet the demands of both rural and urban communities better perhaps than any other denomination. But it also led to the division of circuits and the multiplication of stations, straining to the breaking-point the purses of local congregations and the funds of the church itself. Neither the scarcity of ministers nor the needs of the church could thus be used as arguments to justify the maintenance of easy access or low educational standards. As E.H. Dewart would state the case in 1881,

We think the time has fully come when the literary qualifications demanded of all the candidates of our ministry should not be lower than university matriculation. We can see no danger whatever of excluding men called of God by such a requirement. All our Conferences feel the need of a rigid sifting of candidates. But how are they to be sifted? Every thoughtful man will see the difficulty of doing this in Conference, or even at District Meeting. We would be very far from recommending the substituting of literary examinations for the more practical tests employed in the past. But the energy, and patient, persevering labour, necessary for the attainment of a thorough education, are a very practical proof that a man possesses at least some of the qualities necessary for success in the work of God.[66]

Higher educational standards, in other words, would jeopardize neither an adequate supply of ministers nor the primacy of the test of piety, and they would be a more efficient selection mechanism to boot. The very success of Methodism in attracting young men as candidates to the ministry, in sum, also made it possible to move towards a learned ministry without apparently compromising one of its most fundamental tenets.

By the early 1880s, it is true, Methodism still had few graduates in either arts or theology, and its claim to a learned ministry could still be dismissed by those who derived satisfaction from doing so, as was the case with one Anglican clergyman who calculated in the pages of the *Dominion Churchman* that, while half of all Anglican clergymen were university graduates, only one-eighth of Methodist ministers held university degrees.[67] Even a few years later, his estimate wasn't very far off. By 1890 only about 10 per cent of all Methodist ministers held arts degrees, and barely 1 per cent had completed a BD.[68] But the fact of the matter was that Methodism had a growing number of graduates, and in any case many more had attended Victoria for some period of time in either arts or divinity without actually graduating.[69] By the 1890s, moreover, the church's matriculation requirement for all its probationers was equal to that of law or medicine, and thus Methodists could now claim to have as high a standard of general education as two of the three traditional learned professions.

THE TRANSFORMATION of Wesleyan Methodism during the middle decades of the nineteenth century did not go unnoticed by those who experienced it, nor by those outside the denomination. Commenting in 1865 on the latest set of statistics for the Kirk – figures revealing a depressing level of stagnation – the editor of *The Presbyterian* asked his readers to glance for a moment

at the position of the Methodist Church in Canada. See how it stands now in the columns of the census, and then look back through a vista of thirty-seven years, and see it as Dr. Strachan saw it – a handful of itinerants, without a single settled minister in the whole province. O Presbyter! would you know the position of the Methodist Church in Canada to-day, divest yourself of the idea that it is confined to the poorest and most illiterate class of the community, and that the Methodist parson is always the wearer of a thread-bare coat and a 'shocking bad hat.' Discard, too, the idea that Methodism is a hole and corner affair, and that its ministers preach only in tumble-down school-houses in the backwoods, or in mean brick buildings in the back streets and alleys of great cities. That is not the case. Look into the Methodist church in Great St.

James' Street, Montreal, and say if it is second to any Protestant church in the city. In the country parts neat and commodious churches are everywhere springing up; their number is legion.[70]

He might well have added that its congregations included not only wealthy merchants and manufacturers but prominent professional men as well.[71] Among the other reasons for the changing character of the Methodist ministry was the fact that men such as these demanded a ministry that they could meet on equal terms. 'It was not very pleasant,' said one leading Methodist in 1882, 'to have men – lawyers and doctors – sitting in the pews with the consciousness that they knew far more than the man who was teaching them from the pulpit.'[72]

CLERGYMEN OF THE TWO 'national' churches had based their claim to special status – what made them professional gentlemen and distinguished them from dissent – not only on their education but on their right to an independent maintenance and their role as servants of both church and state. Once disestablishment was accomplished, however, there was less to mark them off except their education. Increasingly, if not entirely, dependent upon voluntarism, they made much the same income as their Methodist or other competitors; once the latter began to acquire an advanced education, they increasingly lost their edge in learning as well. And if ministers of any respectable congregation could claim to be professional gentlemen on account of their influence, income, and education, it could not help but have a levelling influence, reducing the Anglican or Presbyterian divine to an unwelcome equality with his dissenting colleagues. It might well be that social distinctions remained, and that, in the cities and towns especially, the best-paid Anglican clergymen might still have a considerable advantage; but, compared with a few decades earlier, the clarity of the distinction had been smudged. In a culture prizing religious equality, the term 'clergyman' tended to become generic, and the characteristics appropriate to a clergyman were applied to all. On one occasion in the late 1860s, George Brown had penned an editorial bemoaning the inadequate remuneration offered to ministers and, in the process, describing them as 'expected to be gentlemen in education, and feeling and taste,' expected to 'maintain themselves and their families in something like outward gentility,' expected to give their boys and girls 'a respectable education.'[73] Brown, however, was editorializing not about Anglicans or Presbyterians alone, but about Toronto clergymen generally; and, for the secular press at least, such usage was an embedded part of the notion of a clergyman from the 1850s on.

For the Wesleyan Methodists there was less and less incongruity in such terminology. Their message attracted not only the poor but the wealthy and respectable, and the latter in turn provided the financial wherewithal to underwrite the increasing respectability of their ministers. The ministry, for its part, refused to turn its back on the world, choosing instead to engage the intellectual currents of the age, and as a result it committed itself not only to piety but to learning. It was the cry of the church militant and not the protective impulse which transformed the Methodist ministry from saddle-bag preachers and 'unauthorized teachers' into respectable members of the learned professions. But that in turn was possible only because of larger transformations at work, above all the profound cultural shift which delegitimized the claims of the two 'national churches' to hold a privileged place in Upper Canadian society.

7
Professional Work

Throughout the preceding chapters we have had much to say about professional ideals and traditions, organizations, and the politics of professionalism in nineteenth-century Ontario. But what did professional men actually do? What activities constituted professional work? In the pages that follow we turn to these questions. First, however, a disclaimer about our definition of 'work.' Many, perhaps most, clergymen, lawyers, and doctors were leading members of their communities. They were involved in a variety of voluntary associations, in municipal and provincial politics, and in the province's economic life.[1] But rather than attempting to describe the broad range of these activities, we will focus on the core tasks which professional men were licensed and trained to do, a focus that is of some importance since too many studies lay primary emphasis on other aspects of professional lives, while the lawyer *qua* lawyer, for example, is lost in the story of lawyers as political figures or entrepreneurs.

Surprisingly enough, the professional journals, which we rely on so much in other chapters, have relatively little to say about the patterns and experiences of daily work. Thus the sources for this chapter are primarily business and financial records, personal correspondence, and, above all, diaries. To prevent an excessive amount of biographical detail cluttering up the text, we will introduce some of our diarists here. Among the ministers are Nathanael Burwash, Henry Flesher Bland, Donald McKerracher, William Cochrane, and J.F. Lundy. Burwash hardly needs an introduction, but the reader should understand that we have used his early diaries, written during his initiation into the work of the Methodist Church, rather than those which chronicle his leadership role at Victoria College.[2] Henry Flesher Bland was the father of a much more famous figure, Salem. The elder Bland, born in England and ordained as a Methodist minister, emigrated to Canada in the 1850s.

Between the 1860s and 1880s, he was assigned to a variety of circuits in Ontario, including Kingston and Belleville in the 1870s and Renfrew in the early 1880s.[3] Donald McKerracher was a missionary to, and then first minister of, the Presbyterian congregation in Port Arthur from 1875 to 1881, dying prematurely shortly after accepting a call to Wallaceburg in 1881.[4] William Cochrane was another Presbyterian. Born in Scotland, he received much of his education in the United States, latterly at Princeton Theological Seminary, and was called first to an urban church in New Jersey and then in 1862 to Zion Presbyterian Church, Brantford, where he remained until his death at the end of the century. Almost from the beginning of his Canadian career, he assumed a prominent role in Presbyterian affairs, serving as convenor (or chairman) of the Home Mission Committee of the Canadian Presbyterian Church during the 1870s, and later as church moderator.[5] By the time of his death in 1898, indeed, he was not only prominent within his denomination but was described as one of the 'leading men' of Brantford.[6] (And, to the best of our knowledge, he is the only person in this book immortalized in fiction, providing the model for Dr Drummond, the estimable Presbyterian minister in Sara Jeannette Duncan's *The Imperialist*.)[7] Our Anglican is J.F. Lundy, the son of a Yorkshire clergyman and a graduate of University College, Oxford, who emigrated to Quebec, taught there, and was ordained in the 1830s. In 1848 he settled in Niagara, and from 1849 to 1867 served as rector of Grimsby. Well educated and well connected – he had served as vice-principal of McGill College in the 1840s and had married Eliza Sewell, daughter of the Chief Justice of Quebec – he came to Upper Canada in the wake of her death and began his diary at least in part to console himself.[8]

Finally, there are two lawyers. George Duck, Jr, of Chatham, the son of a Kent County farmer, was a successful young lawyer when he began his diary in the 1850s. Already the county's clerk of the peace, he would later be appointed county attorney and would die prematurely in 1859.[9] Robert A. Harrison, who also died young at the age of forty-five, cut a much grander figure. Born of an English family and educated at Upper Canada and Trinity colleges, he articled with two of Toronto's leading law firms, was called to the bar in 1855, served as chief clerk in the Crown Law Department, then entered an extremely successful partnership where he made his name as one of Upper Canada's best courtroom lawyers, and was appointed chief justice in 1875. He was also a prolific author of legal works and one of the editors of the *Canada Law Journal*.[10]

WHILE THE GEOGRAPHICAL setting for work might vary enormously, ranging from the edge of settlement to thriving market-towns and cities,

Ontario's professional men shared the common ground of the worksite and the work process – the micro-environments where particular skills were exercised and the actual tasks performed. Worksites can be crudely divided into public and private places, and throughout the nineteenth century the two outstanding examples of the former were the pulpit and the courtroom. Here ministers and lawyers exhibited their skills in institutional settings, and before an audience. Clergymen preached the word of God, enunciating the individual and collective spiritual goals for their congregations and society at large. In the courts, justice was not only done, but *seen* to be done, in matters of concern to individuals and in those where the collective good was maintained against breaches of the criminal law. 'The importance of the occasion and the number of participants,' Paul Romney has written, 'made the assizes the great public event of the year, at least when there was no parliamentary election.'[11] Two of our clerical diarists routinely attended the assizes, while lawyers sometimes noted the large crowds attending spectacular trials, or a more modest congregation of spectators at the county and division courts.[12]

The physical setting for these public performances might be impressive: a cathedral church or the growing number of aesthetically pleasing parish churches described by William Westfall; Osgoode Hall, where the superior courts were convened, or the jewels of civic architecture – the complex of court-house, jail, and registry office in many county towns – documented and illustrated with such loving care by Marion MacRae and Anthony Adamson.[13] 'Twas not always thus however. Ministers also preached in barns, schoolhouses, and the plainest of country churches. Nor were the courts always grand, especially before mid-century in either Toronto or most county towns, and the division courts were something else again. 'In Townships where a Town Hall has been erected by the Municipalities, the use of it is commonly given; and it is the same with respect to Common School Houses and Temperance Halls,' wrote the editor of the *Upper Canada Law Journal* in 1856. 'In the back country,' he continued, 'it is almost impossible to procure a suitable room for holding a court' and the result was that defendants and suitors had to force their way through densely crowded rooms, 'to be pushed and crushed' at the very time 'when they should have all their wits about them.' Lacking any other accommodation, the last resort was the local tavern.

No doubt Tavern keepers will be very ready to offer the best room they have for holding a Court; but why? because they expect to sell their liquors. That is the plain reason. They wish to draw custom to the bar ... Just let our readers picture to themselves a small low room, crowded to suffocation, with no desk for the Judge, – no railed compartment for the Officers of the Court – the witnesses, the immediate parties to a suit or their professional agents, but all huddled together – the place redolent of tobacco and whiskey – not a few of the suitors dividing their attention between the proceedings in the Court and the doings in the bar-room – preparing themselves to 'fight out their cases.' This, it must be admitted, is not a place where the Judge could be expected to preserve order and decorum.[14]

Be it ever so humble, nevertheless, both the minister and the lawyer or judge performed part of their work in an institution that was public in nature, where the play of their talents was on public view, and where the social authority of the servants of God and of Justice was displayed. What is missing from this congeries of public institutions, however, is the hospital. For most of the nineteenth century, hospitals were not only few but charitable institutions for those who could not afford to obtain help elsewhere. Until the rise of the general community hospital, a movement that began only in the 1870s, doctors, with but few exceptions, did not work there.[15]

Where, then, did they work? That question brings us to the private or non-institutional worksites of professional men. When not in church or on pastoral visits, clergymen worked at home, in a 'study' if they were fortunate enough to possess a good parsonage, or, if not, wherever room could be found. When not in court, lawyers worked in offices, usually separate from their residence, where they did the paperwork that constituted the bulk of a lawyer's business, met their clients, and stored the substantial records and files they accumulated. Doctors' work, on the other hand, was carried out primarily in other people's homes. Though virtually all of them maintained offices or 'surgeries' – the British term was still conventional usage in nineteenth-century Ontario – most of their work entailed travel to the place where people were ill, injured, or about to give birth. Jacalyn Duffin estimates that, throughout James Langstaff's practice, something like 80 per cent of his work consisted of 'visits,' and our own less systematic forays into the account books and other records of nineteenth-century doctors suggest that this was typical.[16] As to the location of their surgeries, in the middle decades of the century at least, these were likely to be in their homes. Peter Goheen has mapped the 'trip to work' for several occupations in Toronto in 1860, including physicians; of some forty doctors only two kept offices separate from their residences.[17] While some doctors in Brantford between 1851 and 1881 always maintained separate offices, it seems to have been less common than among lawyers.[18]

WHAT DID PROFESSIONAL MEN actually do to earn their livings?[19] And what were the rhythms of professional work in mid-nineteenth-century Ontario? For the clergy there were four core tasks, and these were near-universal regardless of locale or denomination. Of first importance was conducting the services of the church, which included administering the sacraments – communion, baptism, and the like – and delivering the related sermon. Here we meet a good example of the disjunction between the task as formally defined and as perceived by the individual doing it. Since the order of service in the various churches was highly structured and largely routinized by the combined weight of doctrine and tradition, what stands out in the diaries is the central role of the sermon. For the clergyman, it formed the focus of the task. Preparing the sermon – meditating upon it, reading around its theme, and writing it out either in sketch notes or in detail – occupied a substantial portion of the work week. Some did a little every day. After morning devotions, Henry Flesher Bland began each weekday with 'prep.' Others began in mid-week and reserved most of Saturday to complete it.

For all ministers the culmination of the work week, and its most demanding day, was Sunday, when they routinely conducted a minimum of two, and usually more, services, and in addition supervised the Sunday school, held confirmation classes, administered holy communion or baptism, or engaged in like activities. In the large Anglican or Presbyterian churches, such as Cochrane's in Brantford, ministers normally preached twice, once in the morning and again in the evening. For clergymen stationed in the smaller urban areas, Sunday tended to be more arduous. As assistant to the ailing rector of Niagara in 1849, J.F. Lundy routinely assisted with services at St Mark's, Niagara, but he also preached weekly at Queenston and Eight Mile Creek. On Sunday, 28 January, for example, Lundy rose at eight and was 'at the Sunday School in good time – a very good attendance ... A small congregation. I preached ... a sermon from Isaiah ... At two I left for Queenston, where was an excellent congregation ... I then rode on to the 8 mile creek – roads very bad, frozen mud all the way and I was 15 minutes past time after 2 hours on the road. Here too was a full gathering ... I rode home and arrived at $8^1/_2$ – self and horse very tired.'

The 'Preachers' Plans' that directed the work of Methodist ministers and lay preachers each week throughout the year reveal similar contrasts. As early as the mid-1850s, for example, London already constituted a city circuit with two ministers almost exclusively assigned to the three town congregations and only occasionally venturing out to one of the nearby stations. A few years later, on the Port Hope Circuit, its three ministers were primarily responsible for the town congregations but also made regular stops at all the country stations over the course of a month of Sunday services. The Muskoka Circuit plan for 1871, however, shows quite another pattern. Here we are no longer dealing with a town and the stations in a nearby township or two. In March, the senior preacher held services during the first week in Draper, Smith's Falls, and Gravenhurst; during the second, at Severn Bridge, 'Morrison's House,' and Port Severn; the third, at Bracebridge, 'Taylor's,' and 'Zimmerman's'; and the fourth week, at 3 Mile Lake and Port Carling. Only Bracebridge and Port Carling had congregations large enough to warrant two services on a Sunday, and the circuit included the Huntsville area as well.[20]

Ministers also normally presided at one or more devotional services, such as a prayer meeting, each week; during the holy seasons, especially Lent and Easter, their daily responsibilities could be much heavier. For Methodists there were also a variety of other special meetings, from love-feasts to camp meetings. Nathanael Burwash spent two full weeks at one of the latter during September 1861, recording it in illuminating detail, but returned to town on the intervening Sunday to conduct his scheduled services there. Beyond that, there were the unpredictable demands occasioned by the rituals of marriage and burial. After preaching at his three stations one Sunday in March 1849, Lundy noted, he 'struggled through the mud to Mr. McNab's house' near Eight Mile Creek, 'and married him to Eliza Brooker with whom he has cohabited for years. He gave me a dollar and a half.' During February and March 1875, Donald McKerracher officiated at three funerals and, reads one other entry in March, 'to the Mattawa station on the Dawson Road, 25 miles from here ... Snow very deep. Reached about 7 p.m. About 10 p.m. united in marriage Mr. Emery Lalonde and Miss May Aitkens. This is the first couple I have married. May they be happy. Home next day.'[21]

A second and closely related part of a clergyman's work was study and reading. While our impression is that most professional men did some of this, keeping up with their journals or reading other material pertinent to their work, it seems that only in the case of the clergy was it a systematic, almost daily, part of their routine. *All* of our clerical diaries, indeed, indicate that a large part of each weekday morning was reserved for this purpose. Most immediately it was part of the process of preparing for the Sunday sermon. But study and reading reached beyond the exigencies of the next sermon to broader purposes. It was also designed to frame the intellectual context of exegesis and apologetics which provided the continuities of understanding and interpretation embedded in successive sermons, Sunday after Sunday, and which gave coherence to the whole. Thus we find young Burwash in December 1861 devoting much of his mornings to 'reading Wesley and Fletcher on Christian Perfection,' or Flesher Bland working his way systematically through a series of books, the entries sometimes cryptic and sometimes not: 'Talents,' 'Dox,' 'Froude,' 'Gibbon,' 'Athens' – the latter two appearing daily for some months in 1880–1; he was apparently reading, conjointly, Gibbon's Rome and Bulwer's Athens. Finishing Bulwer, he noted that it 'scarcely fulfils its title "Rise and Fall" – closes with a critique of Sophocles – elegantly written.'[22] What's important about these and similar entries in other clerical diaries is the reminder that their reading was not confined to theology alone. The clergy were expected to provide intellectual as well as moral leadership for their flocks, giving interpretive meaning to human history and contemporary society, and they took that task seriously, drinking deeply from the springs of eighteenth- and nineteenth-century thought and opinion.

A third central task was pastoral work. This included what we might describe as individual counselling and group work: moments when a pastor guided an individual towards conversion, shored up a wavering faith, or made the ministerial presence felt at a young people's tea or a meeting of Sunday-school teachers. But above all it meant pastoral visiting. The first duty here was to visit the infirm, the sick, the aged, the dying, the grieving, bringing words of comfort and hope, or where pertinent performing the last rites.[23] Generally such ministrations meant a visit to the home, but not always. Still very much a neophyte, Nathanael Burwash was once asked by a woman who 'kept a low groggery' to visit a girl dying of consumption. 'For a day or two I shrank,' but finally he girded up his loins. The dwelling-house was reached by passing 'through the barroom. This is full of bloated loungers, some just commencing their career of sin, others old and greyheaded and looking like veteran soldiers of the devil.' He passed through nonetheless, ministered to the girl, and returned on three other occasions to see her as well.[24]

Beyond such special cases was the more routine work of regular visitations to all the members of the congregation. This activity, it is worth emphasizing, was not simply a neighbourly social call, though ministers paid many of those as well. Rather, it was the occasion when the institutional church, represented by its minister, made its presence felt in the home and reaffirmed its abiding concern for the spiritual welfare of individuals and families. 'My rule,' wrote one Anglican clergyman in 1887, 'is to visit everybody under my charge twice a year ... I generally read a portion of scripture, catechize the children, make a few remarks suitable to the occasion, and pray in accordance therewith.'[25]

Visiting, our diaries tell us, was an enormously time-consuming task. In the cities and towns, it could be incorporated into the daily routine. In Hamilton, during January 1866, for example, Burwash usually accomplished three to four visits every day. During the week beginning 17 December 1881, Bland, now in Pembroke, made a total of twenty-four visits. Daily visiting in the city was also part of William Cochrane's routine, but in addition he set aside special days, when the roads were good, to visit his country parishioners.[26] Such activities could be especially arduous in the back townships, as another Anglican clergyman pointed out in 1870: 'Very much time is consumed on these parochial visits, through so many concessions and sidelines still remaining unopened; not unfrequently, therefore, 4 miles have to be travelled to reach a family only a mile distant across a swamp, or through the forest ... These annoyances are not so frequent in the front townships, where the lines, generally, are opened and unobstructed.'[27]

Finally, there was the work of church governance and administration. At the local level this meant regular business meetings with those who governed the congregation – the vestrymen, the Kirk sessions, the stewards – seeing to everything from the payment of ministerial salaries and other vital aspects of local finance to matters relating to repairs and additions; the purchase of an organ; updating the membership or baptismal roll; preparing annual reports to the presbytery, synod, or conference; and a host of other details involving the management of a small organization. Beyond that there was also the moral discipline of the membership: expelling the fallen or reprimanding the wayward. In March 1870, 'Mr. G. Smith and his wife Jane,' according to a minute in one Presbyterian session book,

of their own accord came forward and confessed to a Breach of the Seventh Commandment committed previously to marriage ... they expressed their resolution to walk more humbly and circumspectly in the future and were restored to full standing in the church ...

... 3 July 1870. Miss Mary Smithers presented herself before the Session, confessed the crime of fornication and wished to be received in Church and have the child baptized ... promised in the future with the help of Almighty God to conduct herself with all propriety ... received into the Church.[28]

But ministers were not only engaged in managing small organizations; they were also participants in governing and administering much larger ones. Of all our occupations, indeed, it is the minister who stands pre-eminent as 'the organization man' of the nineteenth century. He was responsible for collecting funds for the enterprise, taking his part in the work and responsibilities of the presbytery or the quarterly meeting, and participating in the policy-making and administrative processes of Synod, General Assembly, or Conference. For a minority, this constituted a major commitment of time and effort, and a heavy burden of work additional to their other tasks. Consider William Cochrane's summary entry in his diary for the week of 19 to 26 November 1872. After the usual Sunday services on 19 November he spent all day Monday 'preparing for Presbytery.'

Left on Tuesday at 7 AM for Ayr and preached at 2 to a large congregation. Took part in the services of Ordination (Mr. Thomson) and presided in the evening at the same. Wed. went at 6 AM to Paris, thence Toronto, thence Uxbridge, where I preached at 7:30 in Mr. D's church. Thurs. attended Ontario Presbytery and pled the call from Woodstock to Mr. McTavish, but without success, as he declined both the calls presented. Returning to Toronto at 7 PM, went on to Hamilton at 10 PM and reached Paris by the midnight express at 1. Remained there till the Buffalo Express came at 3 and home.
Fri. morning. All day Friday very tired. Sat. at studies till 11 PM. A very hard week indeed.

The next day, nonetheless, he preached his usual two sermons and 'examined the Sunday School.' Not all of Cochrane's time was spent like this, but he was frequently overwhelmed by the sheer weight of his dual responsibilities as pastor and church administrator.[29] Beyond that he was also one of the founders and the president of the (Presbyterian) Brantford Ladies' College, and taught there for some years.[30]

EACH OF THE CORE TASKS that clergymen engaged in presented its own challenges. In an age infinitely less secular than our own, when most people, or at least most respectable people, routinely attended church on Sunday, at a time when oratory rather than overtime could glue people to their seats, the Sunday sermon was one of the week's highlights. And there were a *lot* of them. Toronto had some ninety places where religious services were held, one Anglican cleric estimated in 1882; in each there were 2 sermons a Sunday, for a total of 180, 50 more on weekdays for a total of 230 a week, or 920 monthly, or 11,040 a year.[31] That, the reader will note, was in Toronto alone. Put another way, if the ordinarily devout attended 3 sermons a week, he or she would hear 156 sermons a year, not counting those given on special occasions. If the average sermon lasted half or three-quarters of an hour each, the cumulative time is roughly equivalent to sitting through three full undergraduate courses annually (though without the examination at the end).[32]

Since sermons would normally be delivered by the same clergyman, there was considerable pressure to be original, different, and challenging every week. Good sermon preparation was a demanding art, and reputations stood or fell by it. Nor were judgments confined to the congregation alone. Before the age of movies and television, sermons were *reviewed* in the press. During the 1870s and 1880s, for example, the *Globe* routinely sent its scouts out on Sunday and printed their summaries the next morning – often occupying a full page or more.[33] Sermons and sermonizing, moreover, were the subject of editorials and controversy in the correspondence columns. 'The Feebleness of Modern Preaching' was one typical foray by the editor of the *Mail*; 'Politics in the Pulpit' one from the *Globe*.[34] Assessed in public, sermons and sermonizers were also weighed around Sunday dinners and at other gatherings where the laity gossiped, and were even the subject of running commentary in some of the diaries. 'Church – Strachan preached,' Robert Harrison scribbled one Sunday night. 'Much pleased with his strong common sense views as compared to the twaddle of some of his clergy.'[35] '5 Feb. 1860, Sun. Kendall – Sermon long and trashy, a great affliction.' '3rd Jan. 1858. Sun. Went to St. George's Church with Mason and Alicia. Dr. Lett read one of his rambling, careless, pointless, footless, and useless sermons. Most of the congregation asleep during delivery of it.'

To some extent, one couldn't win in any case. Should sermons be extempore or written? Shaped to grace and elegance or by the fire of spontaneity? This was a recurring issue among clergymen, but, said one Anglican, there was no satisfying everyone. 'I have asked lawyers and doctors concerning this matter, and their judgement is in favour of written sermons; I ask farmers and they declare they like extempore sermons.'[36] Young Burwash stewed over criticisms of his own style in 1861: 'I am thought to be too harsh in my sermons. Is it so? Would coaxing and love and comforting sermons do more good? Should not men feel their sins?'[37] Ministers even had to endure scrutiny from their peers: of one funeral service, William Cochrane noted that 'Rev. Mr. Hood was present and I asked him to take part. Some of our Brantford ministers have so little to do in their own congregations that they kindly attend all my funerals. I should be thankful for their kindness, but it shows a sad ignorance of ministerial etiquette.'[38]

Nor was pastoral work without its strains. Congregations or individuals could be excessively demanding, and there was much discussion in the clerical press about how much was too much, one exasperated Methodist declaring that 'THE EXPECTATIONS OF THE MAJORITY OF THE PEOPLE ON THE SCORE OF PASTORAL ATTENTION CANNOT BE MET.'[39] To enter a home and exhort or reprove, moreover, was always a delicate operation. The Rev. William Bell, on a visit to the family of J.G. Malloch, a county judge and one of Perth's leading citizens, had the temerity to lecture the household on strict temperance. Mrs Malloch and her daughter took umbrage, telling Malloch that Bell 'shall not take liberties and interfere with the management of household,' leaving the judge to deliver the bad news himself.[40] Of more consequence was the ever-present danger involved in visiting the sick. Wrote Cochrane in September 1870, 'Many cases of Typhoid fever some of a most malignant type but I have no fear. If the Lord intends me to catch such a disease by infection or otherwise, when in the discharge of duty, his will be done.' The process of church governance had its own tensions. Personality conflicts could tarnish the relationship with elders or trustees. Dissension might arise over salaries and subscriptions. Clergymen might have fancy ambitions about the kind of church architecture they wanted which outran the patience or pocketbooks of their parishioners.[41] Doctrinal disputes might be endemic, between a high church rector and his evangelical flock, for example, or suddenly arise at some flash-point, a new hymn-book or the installation of an organ.

Clergymen also faced two larger challenges and their attendant dangers. One was the issue of moral rectitude. Unlike most other occupations, the ministry was not expected merely to conform to community moral standards but to exemplify them. As G.M. Grant put it on one occasion,

A member of any other profession may be guilty of offences but no stigma is on that account attached to his profession. He is referred to in the newspapers as a man and a brother. The fact of his being a lawyer, doctor, engineer, merchant, or mechanic is of course mentioned, but without any significance attached to the fact. Should a hundred merchants fail or be guilty of immorality, it is not thought to reflect on those merchants who do not fail or who are not guilty. But should a clergyman fall into sin, it is telegraphed all over the world, particular stress being laid on the fact that he is a clergyman ... Or, should a weak brother make a silly speech on any subject, it is sure to be headed in the report as 'Clerical Folly' .... The world expects more of us – as far as morality at any rate is concerned – than it does of other professions.[42]

Our own impression is that Grant's assessment was an accurate one, and others shared it at the time. Cases of a fall from rectitude, through drink or lewd acts, for example, were more than personal tragedies for those involved. They could divide or even destroy congregations, set ministers of the same faith against each other, and cause turmoil and grief to those who had to mediate or attempt damage control.[43] But they also rippled out beyond the congregation and the denomination, eliciting sensational stories in the secular press, with headlines like 'Clerical Scandal' or 'Kissing Clergymen.'[44] In serious cases the denominational journals tended to be more circumspect, but they could descend to the trivial and the picayune, especially when it concerned the ministers of other denominations. Witness the occasional forays in the *Christian Guardian* condemning 'Dancing Divines,' Anglicans, needless to add. 'Dancing kept up for three hours! A dance in the house of a minister of Jesus, instead of prayer meeting and singing the praises of God, and edifying conversation. *O tempora! O mores!*'[45] Indeed.

The other danger was doubt, publicly expressed. In an age when religion was taken seriously by a large and influential portion of the public, and one in which theological speculation was rife, 'heresy' on the part of a minister could cause a public uproar. During the 1870s, for example, the Macdonnell case not only threatened to split the Presbyterian church but was closely followed for months in the editorial, news, and correspondence columns of the *Globe*.[46] The social and cultural role of the minister in nineteenth-century Ontario was a large one. Just because of that, the price for moral or intellectual deviance was high.

When clergymen reflected on their work, they occasionally referred to the 'enormous advantage' they had over other professional men 'in not being tied down to fixed hours, or chained to a desk or an office and being able to do his work how or when he likes.'[47] This too shows through in our sample of diaries. Within limits, clergymen had the power to vary their schedules to suit their own internal rhythms, to study when it suited them best, to visit in the afternoon or evening as they saw fit. By way of contrast, except when they were in court, Robert Harrison and George Duck reveal in their diaries a fairly monotonous routine: 'To office,' usually six days a week. But a flexible schedule also had its drawbacks. The office closed eventually, and the lawyer went home; clergymen found it difficult to find time they could call their own. And what seems to have suffered most was study time – the hours allotted for broader reading and meditation. It was on this point, at least, that diarists like William Cochrane complained most bitterly.[48] The other drawback was that much of the clergyman's work was invisible. In the same way as modern academics are popularly assumed to be on holiday for half the year and for most of any given teaching week, nineteenth-century clergymen were victims of the view that 'he only works on Sunday.'⁴⁹ In the countryside, moreover, there was the added difficulty of convincing those who toiled with their hands that reading, thinking, and writing constituted 'work.'⁵⁰ Or, as Sara Jeannette Duncan put it, in the eyes of the laity, the minister was 'supposed to be a person of undetermined leisure – what was writing two sermons a week to earn your living by? – and he was probably the more reverend, or the more revered, from the fact that he was in the house all day.'⁵¹

WORK IS NOT ONLY a process of production of goods or services but the terrain where sociability and occupational solidarity are engendered. Through many of the preceding paragraphs, it may appear that the minister worked in an environment largely isolated from his colleagues. In much of his daily work, this was true, but we have also pointed to the fact that clergymen belonged to organizations, and these provided critical counterweights. The district meeting, the presbytery, the annual synod or conference were occasions which brought ministers together, quarterly or annually, not only to do business but to socialize among themselves.⁵² The importance of such occasions, and the high levels of sociability they involved, are reflected in the diaries. A Methodist district meeting or the deliberations of a presbytery often took up most of a week.⁵³ It meant a break in the routines of daily life, travel to some other town, staying with friends, dinners with colleagues, mutual comfort and support. Annual meetings were even more of a highlight. Henry Flesher Bland, who could usually encompass the activities of a full week on one page of his diary, filled nine pages in June 1870 with his running commentary on the Annual Conference. As local travel improved and as the clusters of settlement thickened, moreover, 'ministerial associations' developed, which again brought clergymen together on a weekly, monthly, or quarterly basis.⁵⁴

Beyond these associational activities, however, there was also a great deal of more informal visiting – occasions when one clergyman took another's pulpit and thus the two spent much of the day together, stayed at each other's houses when travelling, or entertained each other before or after some formal meeting. J.F. Lundy, for example, had a close clerical friend across the border from Queenston and the two of them visited almost every month.⁵⁵ During 1849, moreover, Lundy journeyed to Toronto four times for various reasons, and one of these trips exemplifies the way business and sociability could be combined on such occasions. In January he set off to matriculate a student at King's

College and also to receive a Doctor of Civil Law for a thesis he had written on Mortmain. He arrived on a Tuesday. 'Saw Drs. McCaul and Beaven from whom I heard that I must be detained until Friday night ... Called upon Dr. Hodder and at 5:30 came up to the college where I was hospitably entertained by Dr. Beaven, and whence I now write. W. Bettridge [another Anglican clergyman] and daughter and Miss Cronyn came in during the evening. W.B. appears to be a conversible and well-informed man – we had much chat until 12.' The rest of the week was much the same, a mix of college and personal business but also a full round of socializing, especially with clerical colleagues. Other diaries tell a similar tale.[56]

In the backwoods, on the other hand, maintaining contact with professional colleagues must have been much more difficult. Writing to his wife from 'Southampton–Saugeen' in 1856, a doctor recounted that 'six miles from here we came across the clergyman of the parish, returning from Toronto via Owen Sound, on foot and carrying his valise, umbrella and a greatcoat. His parish includes the whole country and he has not a church in it, though one is in course of erection.'[57] Now here was a clergyman walking from the railhead at Owen Sound through what was still hardly more than bush, a distance of some thirty miles, and we suspect his opportunities for professional sociability were substantially more limited than those of people like Lundy who lived in settled parts of the country. The same might be said of a Presbyterian minister in Osgoode Township in 1860 who had to call off a pulpit exchange with a colleague because 'I am afraid ... the wretched state of the roads would prevent our intended exchange [and] I suspect that the River Castor which overflows its banks on the way between [us] will be bursting its rotten covering and heaving upon its bosom so as to prevent passengers from going that way.'[58]

WHAT DID LAWYERS DO in nineteenth-century Ontario? Using the surviving account books, business records, correspondence, and diaries, we can draw a collective portrait of their work which would hardly surprise the reader. In the courts lawyers appeared as judges or as advocates in criminal cases and civil suits. Beyond that they played a key role in the regulation of property: drafting and arranging for wills, deeds, mortgages, leases, and bankruptcy. They conducted arbitrations or negotiated settlements in disputes. They collected debts or threatened to do so on behalf of a client. They managed property for absentee owners. They gave advice to clients. They worked for individuals and companies – railways, banks, insurance and land companies, and other commercial enterprises. Obviously not all of them did all of these things all the time. Once a lawyer was appointed to the judiciary, he became a salaried civil servant, and after mid-century could not pursue a private practice on the side. A few lawyers made most of their living by practising in the courts: Oliver Mowat and Robert Harrison are good examples. Large numbers of Toronto lawyers acted as agents for country lawyers, conducting cases in the superior courts on their behalf, doing the paperwork that could be done only in the city, making the necessary contacts with government offices or Toronto businesses, taking instructions or offering advice to their country colleagues in this or that particular case.[59] Lawyers in county towns performed a similar service for those living elsewhere in the county, and once Ottawa became the federal capital a firm could specialize in agency work there.[60]

Judging by the surviving record, nonetheless, most lawyers earned their living from the routine personal and business affairs of their neighbours: transferring land or facilitating its conversion to other purposes, dealing with the relationship between creditors and debtors, and, when necessary, appearing in the division or county courts in minor civil or criminal cases. Though he would later move on to greater things, the young Thomas M. Benson kept an account book outlining just such a practice. In the two or three years after 1857, when he opened an office in Port Hope, his clients included Dr A.O. Kellogg, for whom he drafted a mortgage, attended to a suit, paid registry fees, sent a letter, and drafted a landlord's warrant. For a local butcher he collected a claim and drafted a birth certificate. He 'attended the magistrates' on behalf of a labourer, drafted mortgages for a millwright and a dentist, and for the latter also attended a suit. He carried out much the same sort of tasks for a chairmaker, a barber, a painter, and a carpenter. Most of his clients were local, though a scattering of entries tell of work for clients in Lindsay, Peterborough, and Omemee, and nearly all were individuals; the Omemee Land Company is the sole exception.[61]

Accounts and legal files tell us something about the nature of the lawyer's work; diaries tell us something about its rhythms. During the first four months of 1854, George Duck was engaged in various activities, but nearly all of his time was spent in the office. He drafted wills; devoted whole days to conveyancing; worked at preparing papers and accounts for the Great Western Railway, which had engaged him to look after their local affairs; brought two parties together to settle an unidentified dispute; acted as arbitrator in a commercial case and one involving the railway; gave advice to a client on a Chancery matter; wrote large numbers of letters to or on behalf of clients and other lawyers, and, after George Brown had 'called in re land in Zone,' settled the titles and the transfer of property for Brown's Bothwell estate. Duck's schedule during these four months, however, was punctuated by court appearances – a day or two at Quarter Sessions in early January, a two-day trip to Toronto to appear before the Court of Queen's Bench in early February, following which he took a day to travel to Hamilton where he hired a team of horses and went off to inspect some lots for a Chatham client. One day in March was spent in the Chatham Division Court, two days in early April at Quarter Sessions and the County Court, and most of the last week of that month at the spring assizes in Chatham.[62]

George Duck's work routines were, we think, roughly typical of those pursued by most lawyers. But there was also a small group of barristers who, in comparison, spent a disproportionate amount of time as advocates in the courts. During the 1860s Robert Harrison was in partnership with James Patterson, and together they built a notably successful practice which included a number of large corporate accounts. Harrison was engaged in some conveyancing work and, like Duck, spent a good deal of time in the office. But, in the main, that time was spent preparing court cases; and much of the rest of his time, day in day out, was spent in the courtroom – on the assize circuits and in the superior courts, the county courts, the Toronto division court, and even occasionally in the local police court.[63] Virtually from the beginning of the partnership, litigation became his main, if not exclusive, activity. Our clerical diaries suggest a good deal of commonality in the cycle of work, whether country or city and across denominations; our lawyers' diaries and the other records we have seen suggest some substantial degree of differentiation in the kinds of work lawyers engaged in, and in its rhythms.

WHILE THE COURTS were an important worksite for lawyers, they also played another role as well, and one that had no parallel among our other professional groups. The courts not only were places where work got done but served as fundamental institutions for legal sociability and solidarity. To explain why this was the case, we need first to describe what might be termed the 'seasons' of the judicial calendar. Though individual judges of the superior courts might meet with lawyers 'in chambers' at any time of the year to weigh arguments about procedures or the disposition of particular cases, they also sat as a group in Toronto to hear cases argued during the four annual 'judicial terms,' periods of about two weeks each. As well, each judge was assigned a 'circuit' of five or six counties where he would preside over the disposition of both criminal and civil cases, in what were known as the spring and fall assizes. In the 1850s and 1860s, for example, there were five circuits outside Toronto, and individual judges would spend a week or ten days in each county town, so that they would be 'on the road' for a period of six weeks or two months, twice a year.[64] Beyond that, each county had its own system of courts, presided over by a resident county judge. The County Court and the Court of General Quarter Sessions convened in the county town four times a year. The (county) Division Courts, again presided over by the county judge, met a variable number of times, depending on the size of the locality and the business generated. At mid-century, for example, Middlesex County was carved up into eight portions: the London Division Court met eight times during the year, but the second division (consisting of Bayham, Malahide, and South Dorchester) met five times, and the fourth division (Dunwich and part of Aldboro) met only twice.[65]

In the way they operated, this assemblage of courts was rather like a railway network. Sittings were staggered throughout the year, scheduled in advance annually,[66] and each court, like a station, was linked to all the others by an invisible set of rails devoted to transporting lawyers to and fro across the province with tidal regularity. Lawyers went up to Toronto in large numbers during the judicial terms to work with their agents in superior court cases. Toronto barristers descended on the county towns to present their own briefs or argue cases on behalf of local lawyers. Country lawyers attended their own county courts, visited those in other counties, or worked the circuits of the division courts. At the semi-annual assizes, lawyers from Toronto and from all over the countryside would congregate in successive county towns.

Court sessions were periods of intense, prolonged hard work, with judges and lawyers sometimes engaged for ten or twelve hours a day. Dockets could be incredibly crowded. At the Cornwall Spring Assizes of 1856, there were seventy cases to be disposed of; one local lawyer, J.F. Pringle, was listed as attorney in nineteen of them, and Sandfield Macdonald was scheduled to appear in forty-five.[67] Two years later, Henry O'Brien noted that the fall assizes at Guelph had seventy-four cases entered: 'This is owing to suits being brought here from outer Counties. Never saw so many strange lawyers here before. The place is actually swarming with them.'[68] Still a student-at-law, O'Brien dreaded the 'horrid assizes ... They unsettle everything and prevent one setting to regular study work, if they were to last a week longer I think I should forget all the office work I ever learned.'[69]

The sessions of the various courts could also be chaotic. On the division circuits, county judges turned up late, didn't turn up at all, or announced they had to catch the 11:30 a.m. train just as a lawyer was about to present his case.[70] Before the telegraph or the telephone, slow communications could derail the order of business as well. 'Started for Arnprior and Ross,' J.G. Malloch noted of one of his first circuits as judge in the division courts of the Bathurst District, 'reaching Carleton Place, and found a letter from the Clerk at Arnprior ... that the business was all settled. There was also a letter at home...that there was only one suit at Ross, and that would likely be settled – Consequently I did not go to either of the places, but returned home. I learned afterwards that the Clerk and Bailiff attended the Court at Olmstead, the suit not having been settled, but the plaintiff did not attend.'[71]

Amid all the hard work and the pressure of events, nonetheless, there was also a remarkable round of socializing, where lawyers made new business contacts, consolidated old ones, dined and travelled with the august among the profession, entertained each other in their homes, stayed at the same hotels, and even slept together: 'Memorable trip to Goderich assizes with Hagerty J., his first circuit,' Henry Becher noted in March 1856; 'Snowdrifts terrible. We had to give up and sleep at Mr. Cooney's, the J[ustice] and I in one bed, Mr. and Mrs. C. and baby in the other.'[72] At least in the middle decades of the century, most lawyers, the obscure and the élite, those on the make and those who had made it, seem to have experienced this mix of business and social activities. Travelling as clerk to Archibald McLean on the latter's first assize circuit in 1837, the young Sandfield Macdonald hobnobbed with the local élites in the Western and Gore districts, dined repeatedly with Allan MacNab, Crown counsel on the circuit, and played cards with William Draper on the steamboat trip back to Toronto.[73] Nearly four decades later, in Almonte, a young attorney, still not a barrister, noted in a letter to his father, 'I had the new [County] Judge – Senkler – staying with me Wednesday, Thursday and Friday last. He is a very nice man and is giving unusual satisfaction as a Judge.'[74]

The assize was a particularly important occasion for it was marked by the 'Bar Dinner' hosted by the visiting judge and attended by the local bar along with those lawyers present from Toronto or elsewhere. During the Perth Assizes of May 1842, J.G. Malloch noted tersely that he had been 'invited to dine with the Judge [Chief Justice John Beverley Robinson]. All the Bar with Dr. Christie and another doctor from Bytown.'[75] Commencing his first circuit as chief justice in October 1875, Robert Harrison travelled to Owen Sound, staying there from Tuesday to Saturday and wading through a heavy docket of civil and criminal cases, the latter including indecent exposure, common assault, rape, and forgery. But, on the Tuesday night, he held table for eighteen lawyers and local court officers at a hotel, his dinner and bar bill for the occasion substantially exceeding the costs of his accommodation for the entire week. The ritual was repeated the following Tuesday when the assizes opened in Stratford, and again the next week in Woodstock. The bar dinner, indeed, was so much associated with the assizes that George Duck took special note of one judge, who 'seems never to give dinners like many of his predecessors and does not make the landlord's fortunes.'[76] These formal occasions were accompanied by a round of more informal socializing as well. On Saturday night in Owen Sound, the local bar had returned the honour by entertaining Harrison at another dinner. In between, Harrison had dined with legal acquaintances; he had then gone with others to two church services the following Sunday and, in Stratford, had a meal with 'the members of the bar staying at the hotel.'[77]

We are not dealing here, we want to emphasize, with the idiosyncratic social propensities of one senior judge. Perhaps our sources are not representative, but it does appear that such activities were pervasive. 'I've been busy all the week till tonight at our assizes,' William Douglas, a Chatham lawyer, wrote to his wife in 1861; 'As usual we had a great deal of fun one way or another and although the labour is hard and wearisome it's very pleasant and repays one for most of the annoyances generally credited to the profession.'[78] Though he was always glad when it was over because of the press of business, George Duck routinely recorded the round of dining and visiting which accompanied the assizes, and usually had guests staying with him, including the circuit judge and very often Henry Becher from London.[79] Or consider Robert Harrison's activities at the Kingston Assizes in 1859 when he was still a rising member of the profession. On Monday, 9 May, he made the trip from Toronto by railway, noting the number of other lawyers aboard for the same purpose. Arriving in Kingston, he went 'to Smith and Henderson's office' and they 'recommended to go to City Hotel as Judge Burns was there.' Later that day he attended court, where he received a 'hearty welcome from Kingston Bar,' and in the evening took a stroll with Sheriff Corbett. The next day, having no cases, he visited the penitentiary and dined with the judge. Wednesday and Thursday he was in court, but dined again with the judge and was introduced to C.S. Ross, cashier of the Commercial Bank, who told him how anxious 'he and Archibald J are to have me as solicitor.' On Friday he and Adam Wilson, another prominent Toronto lawyer, found themselves on opposite sides in court but dined together afterwards along with Judge Cummins. Saturday, Harrison ate breakfast with Burns, attended court, and then returned to Toronto by train, meeting J.H. Cameron on the way. For country lawyers the trip to Toronto for term offered a like experience. During one typical week-long excursion to the city, made in June 1854, Duck met several times with his agents and spent three days in court, but he also socialized every evening with lawyer friends, both from Toronto and from other parts of the province, and met some new colleagues besides.

Other professional men had their own occasions when 'doing business' was also a time for conviviality with friends old and new. But lawyers, we suggest, were a unique case. Of their two main worksites, one in particular provided them with a remarkable web of professional contacts which were cemented not only through doing business together but through the social occasions which surrounded it. The sheer frequency of these occasions, moreover, made them powerful tools both in promoting solidarity and in socializing the young into the mores of the craft.

DOCTORS WERE NOT DIARISTS, or so at least it appears to us, though for the sake of future research we hope to be proven wrong. Thus we have little sense of the daily rhythms of work we have attempted to convey in the case of lawyers and clergymen. On the other hand, doctors did write letters, keep records of patients and financial accounts, and occasionally leave helpful memoirs. There is, as well, Jacalyn Duffin's systematic quantitative analysis of James Langstaff's practice in Richmond Hill between 1849 and 1875. In a landmark article published in 1988, and in a full-scale monograph which is richer still, Duffin has drawn a detailed, fascinating portrait of the work of a general practitioner and of the range of illnesses and injuries that beset Upper Canadians in mid-nineteenth-century Ontario.[80]

Until at least the last quarter of the nineteenth century, almost all doctors were general practitioners. In Toronto a handful of physicians or surgeons could make their living as specialists, but it was rare elsewhere. Even in London, in the 1870s, one local doctor remarked, 'a surgeon could not make a living by his surgery alone at that time, since it was so limited.'[81] Thus the practice of nearly all doctors included medicine, surgery, and midwifery, though not in equal parts. Medicine was the main preoccupation, constituting in Langstaff's case something like 80 per cent of his work. Doctors examined patients and diagnosed the various fevers and other maladies of the sick as best they could with the limited knowledge and tools at their disposal. Duffin describes Langstaff's procedure as follows:

The pulse was the most frequently recorded piece of information. He followed its rate, rhythm, and quality and used it and, to a lesser extent, the respiratory rate, as a day-to-day indicator of the patient's condition. He examined the diameter of the pupils in cases of coma and noted the state of the fontanelle in small children with severe febrile [feverish] illness. From the earliest days of his practice, he made use of percussion and auscultation [tapping the body and listening to its internal sounds] ... True to his century's preoccupation with bowel function, Langstaff was increasingly concerned about the state of the intestines.

He rarely used a body thermometer, Duffin continues, but based his assessment on his own sense of touch, 'and the presence of flushing, chills, and tachycardia [a rapid heartbeat]. Sometimes he inspected blood, urine or sputum' for abnormal colouration and odour. The examination completed, Langstaff would make his diagnosis and prescribe a remedy. In some cases he might bleed the patient; more commonly he would dispense drugs for comfort and cure. In the 1850s these included quinine (for malaria), opium, antimony, mercury, Spanish fly plasters, ipecac, and jalap, though as Duffin points out, the list broadened and changed by the 1870s.[82]

Dispense medicines, the reader will note. In early Upper Canada even such august members of the craft as Christopher Widmer did so,[83] and though the practice probably declined in the cities and towns as druggists' shops increased, it remained common in the countryside throughout the century. The travelling doctor with a saddle-bag of medicines was a stock nineteenth-century figure of fun, Dr Dulcemara hawking his elixir of love being only one of the more egregious examples. But caricature was rooted in reality. Compounding skills were required of all medical students, accounts rendered 'for services and medicines' survive by the score, and when, in 1885, one *Lancet* reader enquired about how to reconcile a well-stocked medicine chest with the need for compactness on long journeys, the editor referred him to an advertisement for 'A.A. Mellier's medical saddlebags.'[84]

Surgery constituted something like 5 to 10 per cent of Langstaff's practice, but most of this consisted of what were termed minor operative procedures such as lancing boils, removing small tumours and tonsils, bone-setting, applying dressings to injuries and burns, and extracting teeth.[85] Given the risks and the difficulties, 'capital operations,' such as amputations, lithotomies, or the removal of large tumours, were few, especially before the last quarter of the nineteenth century when anaesthetics and antisepsis began to reduce the horror of major surgery.[86] Until then it was a measure of last resort and was 'heroic' for all concerned. Robert Petch, a country doctor living north of Toronto, offered this dispassionate description of one case in a letter to William Aikins in 1852. A young man

had the misfortune to have his leg pass through the cog wheels of the horsepower of a Thrashing Machine grinding the Tibia and Fibula into very small pieces, a very profuse hemorrhage took place from the Anterior and Posterior

Tibial Arteries. The patient was of a very Plethoric habit and bore both the shock and loss of blood remarkably well. After applying the Tourniquet I determined upon an amputation above the knee and not having the opportunity of a consultation [i.e. the help and advice of another doctor] I had to be satisfied with the assistance of Countrymen who were in the house at the time and they certainly deserved credit for the able manner in which they assisted me. The ligatures came away on the 9th day and in 6 weeks the stump was nearly well, not a single disagreeable symptom supervened.[87]

All this, the reader is reminded, without anaesthetics. Of the four other cases Petch describes, moreover, three also involved accidents with farm machinery, and Henry Orton of Guelph noted that most of his major surgery arose from the same cause, adding that it was the result of exposed machinery and free-flowing liquor at bees.[88]

The third part of general practice was midwifery. Other historians, in particular J.T.H. Connor and Wendy Mitchinson, have described the growing role of the doctor in childbirth during the nineteenth century, supplanting the midwife and the neighbour, and we will not reiterate their accounts here.[89] But midwifery constituted an important part of the doctor's work, year in year out, and, in Langstaff's experience at least, increased during his practice from about 6 per cent of his cases at mid-century to something like 12 per cent in the 1870s. Langstaff, Duffin notes, rarely saw an obstetrical patient before confinement, 'attended the delivery for no more than an hour, and usually saw the new mother again only once postpartem, if at all,' unless there were serious complications.[90] This pattern of attendance only at the point of crisis was typical of practice generally. Doctors were almost exclusively engaged in ministering to those already ill, injured, or in labour. With the exception of life insurance examinations, a growing business in the later nineteenth century, doctors did not see those who were well.[91]

Because he dealt in crises, one part of the rhythm of a doctor's work was singularly different from that of other professional men. Virtually all the contemporary accounts and reminiscences note the burden of night calls, the difficulties of travel in the black of night, and the long trip home. Henry Orton remarked that he 'always came home in my midwifery cases, or night visits, if concluded in the night, wherever it was practicable. None then had spare beds in the country. If I was detained and wanted to lie down, I lay down on the floor with my clothes on and feet to fire when cold, but however dark, if once I started home and got the horse on the right track, he would go back by the road he came.'[92] Richard Bucke complained bitterly on one occasion, 'I have had one full night's sleep in the last seven nights, three of these nights I did not have my clothes off at all.'⁹³ And though we have defined the domestic visit as a private worksite, one needs to understand this in its mid-nineteenth-century context. Doctors routinely pursued their work in the presence of relatives and friends. Petch, as we have already seen, carried out an amputation surrounded, and assisted, by the patient's co-workers. Susanna Moodie noted how 'Canadians flock in crowds to visit the dying,' and recounted a doctor's story of saving a man by chasing friends and neighbours out of the sickroom, thus giving him the peace and quiet he most needed.⁹⁴ In describing one difficult obstetrics case, a mid-century Wardsville doctor remarked in passing that he arrived to find 'the house, as usual, filled with women, all eagerly on the *qui viva*, to know whether the patient was to live or die.'⁹⁵ In such circumstances, and especially when treatment was less sophisticated and procedures less arcane than now, reputations could hang on success or failure adjudicated by the laity. Complained one Whitby doctor in the pages of the *Globe*, funeral gossip was especially damaging. 'A doctor's position is at times a very trying one ... He must weigh possibilities and do the best he can. Is it fair, or generous or christian' to blame a doctor's treatment when commiserating at the graveside?'⁹⁶

Doctors had none of the formal, organizational forms of professional sociability that characterized the ministry. Nor, before the days of the general hospital, was there a worksite which routinely brought them into contact with each other, as the courts did for lawyers. For most of the nineteenth century, local medical societies appear to have been few, ephemeral, and, where established at all, limited to the towns and cities.⁹⁷ There was, however, one form of professional sociability which was organized around doctors' worksites and routines – the consultation. A rural practice, as Duffin points out, did not mean professional isolation, especially in the older, more settled parts of the country. Doctors were surrounded by colleagues, and they called upon each other frequently for advice in a difficult case or for assistance in an operation; sometimes they were invited in as well by patients seeking a second opinion. During the period 1849–54, for example, Langstaff consulted 52 times with some 20 different doctors, and over the 40 years of his practice, some 200 times with more than 150 different colleagues. In the early years, Duffin notes, Langstaff sought advice; in later years his own experience was called upon.⁹⁸ There was, moreover, nothing unique in the Langstaff record: descriptions of cases printed in the medical journals are full of references to consultations, occasionally involving three doctors or more. Doctors were not only colleagues but competitors, and sometimes such consultations could be fraught with antagonism and with charges of patient-stealing or slanders against the reputation of one or another of the attending doctors. That reality, we suggest, helps to explain the disproportionate emphasis in the various codes of ethics on the etiquette of consultations. But that aside, at the level of day-to-day routine, the consultation appears as an important source of sociability and solidarity for medical men and especially for those outside the larger cities and towns.

ONE OTHER ASPECT of the work process deserves attention here and that is the role of the partnership. Though not unknown among doctors, partnerships appear to have been uncommon. In all of his biographies of early doctors, for example, Canniff records but a single case,[99] and we have found only a handful of examples in the later nineteenth century. Nor did the medical journals ever take the matter up to discuss either its pros or its cons. In law, on the other hand, it was a common arrangement, especially in Toronto. 'In 1870,' Elizabeth Bloomfield notes, 'Toronto had 55 firms with at least two partners,' twenty of which had three or more. Outside Toronto there were 128 partnerships, though only 16 of them had three members and none was larger. 'Two of every three of Toronto's lawyers ... worked in partnerships, while only two of every five of the non-metropolitan lawyers had a partner.' These latter figures remained constant to 1920, while the proportion of lawyers in partnership in Toronto rose to three-quarters by that year.[100] Compared with other professional occupations, lawyers tended to work in groups.

Partnerships might be established for purely contingent reasons – such as ageing, illness, or interests outside the office, and above all business and politics. Here we find both doctors and lawyers forming partnerships.[101] But aside from such special circumstances, lawyers commonly did so for other reasons as well. Given a certain critical mass of business, the work of the barrister and the attorney or solicitor could be split between partners and, by their combined activities, each generating work for the other, profits could be attained which equalled more than the sum of their individual contributions. For the attorney it meant, as one lawyer put it, that there would be no need 'of your giving your briefs to strangers,'[102] and for someone like George Duck, it meant that he could afford to be away from home regularly – in court or on other business – without the routine of the office falling hopelessly behind. For those who sought to establish pre-eminent reputations in the law, it allowed them to specialize. 'I would not give up the common law,' William Hume Blake advised his son Edward in 1856; 'I do not mean that you should drudge as an *attorney*. I would try to throw that sort of business on my partner, failing that on my clerks ... But I would appear in Queen's Bench and at Nisi Prius *wherein I could find opportunity* and I would appear, always, with a determination to win, *and having bestowed upon my case that ... consideration* which alone deserves success, and if you can do that I think I can promise with almost perfect confidence that under God's Blessing you will succeed.'[103] Alternatively, a new partner could bring his own specialist strengths to complement those of others. Robert Harrison could offer James Patterson not just his rising courtroom reputation as a prosecutor while still employed in the Crown law office, but substantial crown agency fees which John A. Macdonald had promised to throw his way.[104] Harrison and Patterson were joined a little later by the Chancery lawyer Thomas Hodgins: they would give him their Chancery cases while he would pass on to them 'all his common law, conveyancing, etc.'[105]

DID CLERGYMEN WORK in partnerships? One might point to the occasional cases where they had assistants or curates, or to the Methodist circuit, which was, in some respects, a joint enterprise. But we want to draw attention to a different form of partnership: that of the minister and his wife. Here, however, an important distinction needs to be made. The domestic economy of professionals and other members of the middle class, and its relationship to sustaining male careers, deserves further study, and a model already exists in the distinguished work of Leonore Davidoff and Catherine Hall.[106] It is clear, indeed, from our own sample of nineteenth-century diaries and correspondence that professional men and their wives were partners in a wide variety of ways: wives provided emotional support, gave advice and acted as sounding boards when a critical career decision had to be made,[107] managed the household, and in many cases contributed directly to the economic survival of the family through teaching and other activities. We want to distinguish, however, between these roles and a wife's engagement in the core tasks of professional work identified in the preceding pages. We do not find wives in lawyers' or doctors' offices or in court, though we have located a few rare references to doctors' wives doing such things as driving through the night while the husband slept in the back of the sleigh, and we suspect some of them kept an eye on the office while the doctor was making his round of visits.[108] Nor do we find any commentary on the subject in either the medical or law journals.

In the case of the clergy, it is different. In the clerical journals the role of the wife was a subject of recurring interest. The tone is mostly one of complaint about the unfair burdens imposed on the minister's wife, but there is much to be learned from the assumption that the wife was a part of the team. Consider, for example, an article in the *Canadian Churchman* of 1869:

Such wives sustain a semi-official relation to the parish, and the parish has some sort of claim upon their time and strength. The wife of a physician owes no duties to her husband's patients, but a minister's wife is to be one who, by virtue of her position, is bound to discharge innumerable duties to the congregation. She may be young and inexperienced (some wives are) but she is expected to be the president of all the benevolent societies; she may have a large family of her own largely dependent on her own labour, for her husband's salary is not enough to allow her to live at ease, but she is expected to visit the sick and the poor; she is likely to have her particular friends, to find one house pleasanter than another, for she is human, but she must treat all alike ... These and similar arrangements are absurd. The husband receives an income for acknowledgement of his services, she receives none.[109]

A decade later, a Methodist minister remarked in passing that 'most ministers with a small pittance are expected to give the time of their wives as well as their own to the work of pastoral visitation.'[110] And in the mid-1890s, an Anglican journal fell upon what it labelled 'A Church Tragedy,' a Chicago incident in which a woman had drowned herself, her mind having given way under the strain of trying to meet the organizational expectations of the congregation. 'There are hundreds of parsonages,' the editor intoned, 'where her escape from the burdens of a minister's wife will excite envy.'[111]

There is a good deal of confirmation in our diaries that ministers' wives participated in the work, and that wives bore 'the same relationship to female parishioners as the husband to the males.'[112] Obviously, they were not to be found in the pulpit. But they were active in the societies associated with the congregation – taking leading roles in organizing and sustaining sewing circles, prayer meetings, benevolent societies, and in fund-raising for church improvements. J.F. Lundy's second wife played the organ at Sunday services.[113] William Cochrane's second wife spent a great deal of time assisting him with his large volume of correspondence, addresses, and newspaper articles.[114] 'Preached at Prince Arthur's Landing in AM then drove to the Fort,' Donald McKerracher noted one Sunday. 'Attendance good. Mrs. McK visited the Sabbath School and was pleased at the attention, attendance and teaching.'[115] Above all there was pastoral visiting, sometimes done alone and sometimes with their husbands. 'Seven Visits with Emma,' Flesher Bland recorded in his diary one day.[116] Wrote Jennie Cochrane one day in 1874, 'After dinner I went over to the Widow's home to see a sick woman there, read to her for a while.'[117] Ministers' wives also seem to have accompanied their husbands on circuit, to Synod or Conference, and on other sorts of 'business' trips, something that does not appear to have occurred among doctors or lawyers. All in all then, wives appear to have taken an active part in 'the business of ministering' in a way that has no parallel among our other occupations. They bore the burden of managing the domestic economy as well; but they were also partners in the enterprise ministers were engaged in. If George Duck and James Langstaff had mused on their expectations of a wife they might have agreed with Nathanael Burwash that she should be 'pious, amiable, clever, strong, and healthy.' But they would hardly have asked that she be able to draw up a will or lance a boil. Added Burwash, 'and feel herself as much called to and interested in the work of soul saving as her husband.'[118]

8
Professional Education

How did ministers, doctors, or lawyers *learn* to do the tasks we have just described? By one means or another, neophytes must be socialized into occupational roles and identities, and learn the array of skills required to practise an occupation successfully. Only part of this can be accomplished in classrooms or by reading books. Ministers must not only study theology but learn to deliver an effective sermon. Doctors must not only study medicine but acquire experience in diagnosis, where skill is a matter of judgment as well as knowledge. Professional education, in other words, is not just a matter of 'learning about' but of 'learning how.' While we will necessarily have something to say about both in this chapter, our main emphasis falls upon the ways in which students actually learned to practise a craft.

We begin with a straightforward description of the process of professional training, focusing mainly on the three or four decades after 1850, and will treat, successively, medicine, theology, and law, Then, in a more analytical vein, we will try to account for the marked differences that existed between medicine and theology, on the one hand, and law, on the other. That, in turn, will engage us in an assessment of the efficacy of the various modes of 'learning how,' and an attempt to identify the characteristics which distinguish nineteenth-century professional education from its modern counterpart. A preliminary comment with respect to the clergy, however. We have already considered the growth of an educated Methodist ministry and we will not return to that subject here. In general outline, Anglican and Presbyterian theological education had many things in common, but in order to avoid excessive complexity – too many institutions and too many sets of academic regulations – we will use the professional education of Presbyterian ministers as a case-study in our comparison of learning to lawyer, doctor, and minister in nineteenth-century Ontario.

IN EARLY UPPER CANADA most forms of professional training were carried out by some method of formal or informal apprenticeship. Students attached themselves to an established practitioner, read the recommended texts in his library, followed him on his round of daily activities, practised the simpler tasks under his eye, and were gradually given more responsibility as they learned to work on their own. It was a model of 'learning how' that had deep historical roots, and it was, in any case, a practical necessity in a new colony that lacked the institutional infrastructure to sustain alternatives. But there were also other models available, either well established or emergent in the early nineteenth century. The Scottish Church had long required a period of study in a university divinity faculty, normally for three or four years following an arts degree, or the equivalent.[1] Anglican theological education at Oxford and Cambridge was at a nadir in the period, but pressures were mounting to establish a more rigorous program of studies, and some dioceses, at least, were already creating alternative institutions to provide formal instruction in theology.[2] And medical education, in England especially, was undergoing a revolution as experience in one or another of the great London hospitals, along with attendance at the anatomy schools increasingly attached to them, began to supplement and then supplant learning through apprenticeship.[3]

Not surprisingly, these various models of learning formed part of the cultural baggage of emigrant professional men and, as the colony began to mature, were re-established in Upper Canada. In the two decades around mid-century, universities were founded with charters to grant degrees not only in arts but in medicine, theology, and law as well. Theological instruction began at King's and Queen's colleges in the early 1840s. When King's was threatened by secularization, Strachan organized his own theological seminary at Cobourg and later established Trinity College in large part for the same purpose. Following the disruption among Presbyterians, the Free Church almost immediately set about establishing Knox College. Medical schools were organized as well. Throughout the middle decades of the nineteenth century, Toronto always had at least two and sometimes three, and a permanent school in Kingston was founded in 1854. These schools are sometimes described as 'proprietorial,' meaning that they were owned and operated by instructors who were also practitioners, and that they were financed as any other business might be. They were, nonetheless, almost always affiliated with one of the local universities, which awarded degrees to their students and established the regulations for those degrees. No less important, both cities acquired general hospitals which could be used by the schools for teaching purposes. By the 1850s, then, professional education in theology and medicine was increasingly institutionalized, and increasingly approximated the range of experience available in Britain.[4]

Though both accommodation and faculty might be makeshift in the early years, by 1860 or so the medical schools in Toronto and Kingston each had seven or eight instructors drawn from the two cities' leading practitioners. Lectures were delivered during terms which lasted five or six months a year. Until the last quarter of the century, when timetables grew ever more crowded and complex, classes typically began early in the morning, broke off at noon or 1:00 p.m. so students could attend the hospital during visiting hours, resumed late in the afternoon, and continued into the evening – a schedule designed so that each instructor could lecture either in the morning or late in the day in order to accommodate the imperatives of maintaining a private practice. Clinical lectures at the hospital were delivered by those who also held hospital appointments.[5]

The curriculum was organized around the ancient tripartite division of medical practice itself: medicine or 'physic,' which dealt with disease and therapeutics; surgery; and midwifery. The exact titles of courses offered by the schools or demanded for a degree at the universities varied from year to year and from one school to another, but students were expected to attend lectures on the principles and practice of medicine and in the related area of *materia medica* – the study of pharmacy and the therapeutic effects of drugs; the principles and practice of surgery; midwifery and the diseases of women and children; chemistry and sometimes botany; the 'Institutes of Medicine,' or physiology; and anatomy, pathology, and medical jurisprudence. The program of studies listed in the university calendars normally required three years of courses at a recognized medical school; twelve months of concurrent attendance at a general hospital, including clinical lectures and demonstrations in both medicine and surgery; and one year of study with a doctor learning such things as the compounding of medicines and the routines of the office.

In the pedagogy of medical education, it is perhaps worth emphasizing, the place of the hospital rivalled that of the school. Whatever its role as a charitable enterprise ministering to the poor and the destitute, there was never any doubt that a critical subsidiary purpose was to train medical students. As one doctor put it in a speech given at the opening of Trinity Medical College in 1850, students must take every opportunity to attend hospitals and dispensaries

> as it was only by familiarizing themselves with the appearance of disease in all its stages, and under all combinations of external circumstances that they could

acquire a proper faculty of surgical diagnosis; nor should this acquaintance be derived solely from visual inspection — the touch should be educated as well as the sight. They should accustom themselves to the *feel* of the injured part ... under examination ... clinical instruction is the foundation of medical education ... at the bedside of the patient, around the operating table, and by autopsial investigation, a thorough practical knowledge of disease is alone to be obtained.[6]

Indeed, so important was hospital attendance that it was required for all medical degrees in Upper Canada from the time the universities began to award them.

In 1865 the Medical Council acquired authority to regulate medical education through its examinations and curricular prescriptions. Almost immediately it adopted a rule that it would not recognize the certificate of instruction 'of any lecturer who lectures on more than one branch of medical science; nor must he deliver more than one lecture daily.'[7] The result was to force the schools to increase the number of these instructors from the seven or eight typical around 1860, to twelve or fifteen by 1870.[8] The regulations of the council also brought a degree of standardization and uniformity hitherto lacking among the various schools. But it did not substantially change the fundamental character of the curriculum already put in place by the schools themselves.[9] Thus in the 1870s and 1880s, the regulations of the College of Physicians and Surgeons of Ontario remained much like those introduced by the medical schools during the previous two decades: four years of professional study, including three (and after 1880, four) winter sessions of six months each at a recognized medical school; a year or more 'attending the practice of a general hospital'; and a period of study with a qualified practitioner. The number of required courses multiplied, but this was largely due to the subdivision of old ones. The most notable shift was the steady increase in the amount of clinical instruction carried out in the hospital at the bedside, and the concomitant decline in apprenticeship to an individual doctor. The length of the apprenticeship term was reduced from twelve to six months in 1870, and by 1884–5 not even this part of medical training had to be acquired in a doctor's office but could be obtained in a dispensary or hospital instead.

FOR THE MEDICAL SCHOOLS it was relatively easy to sustain courses of didactic lectures, and to add new subjects as the schoolmen or the Medical Council saw fit. Practical training proved to be a more recalcitrant problem. For most of the nineteenth century, in Ontario as elsewhere, the study of anatomy lay at the heart of medical education. Until the great breakthroughs in physiology and biology late in the century, anatomy constituted the chief means of gaining understanding about the structure and function of the body and its various organs, and it was an essential prerequisite to surgery. Though students might begin with a textbook like Gray's *Anatomy*, attend lectures on the subject, and learn from watching a demonstration in the dissecting room of a medical school or the 'dead-house' of a hospital, sooner or later they had to perform dissections themselves. The schools, however, were faced with a perpetual shortage of bodies. The hospital mortuaries were one source; Queen's also had the advantage of laying hold of the bodies of inmates who died in the provincial penitentiary.[10] The Anatomy Act of 1843 had allowed 'the body of any person' unclaimed by friends or relatives, and 'found publicly exposed, or who immediately before death had been supported in and by any Public Institution receiving pecuniary aid from the Provincial Government,' to be delivered up for dissection, and in any community with a medical school an Inspector of Anatomy could be appointed to allocate unclaimed bodies to the school, keep records, ensure decent burials, and the like.[11]

Upper Canada, however, had no large pauper population, few hospitals, and fewer workhouses, and thus, as the number of medical students rose, shortages persisted. Before the 1870s, not even Toronto could provide enough material to meet the needs of its medical schools. Some of the demand was met by students themselves through grave-robbing, with the none-too-well-concealed connivance of their instructors. Remarking in 1854 on the fact that the Trinity faculty had been able to sequester bodies from the hospital through the favouritism of the hospital doctors, a younger colleague informed Rolph that 'our [dissecting] room has been plentifully supplied chiefly through the aid of students.'[12] Two years later a country doctor recommended two of his students to the head of the Toronto School of Medicine, assuring him of their studious habits and competence in anatomy, and adding that they 'both seem fond of the *odour* of a *graveyard* and I assure you will be among the most expert in obtaining dissecting material.'[13] There is evidence indeed that students were engaged in grave-robbing in both Kingston and Toronto into the 1870s and early 1880s.[14] It may have been relatively rare, an act of last resort by those to whom training in practical anatomy was an indispensable prerequisite; but what is clear from the editorials in both the medical and the secular press is that a perennial shortage of anatomical materials limited practical experience throughout much of the middle decades of the nineteenth century and remained a problem even in its closing decades.[15]

Until the 1880s, at least, the quality of clinical training remained a source of even greater concern and was the subject of endless editorials and correspondence in the medical press. There were far too many didactic lectures required by the College of Physicians and Surgeons, said editors and correspondents alike, and too little time spent at the bedside. The CPSO examinations emphasized book-learning rather than tests of practical competence, with the inevitable result that students were lax in their attendance at the hospital, and too idiosyncratic in the cases they observed. 'As a rule,' said the editor of the *Canadian Journal of Medical Science*, 'all who happen to live between Parkdale and Lesslieville will rush to the hospital to see a major amputation, while but a small proportion of them will spend 15 minutes in examining a case of pneumonia or measles.' He had recently been amazed, he added, 'to see a class of 15 students, who had followed the physician somewhat hurriedly through a couple of wards, leave in a body, while a simple fracture of the leg was being dressed, and a few weeks later we had the opportunity of discovering at an examination that not three of them knew how to bandage an ankle.'[16]

But fewer lectures and a more practical emphasis in examinations would be of little use if clinical instruction itself was not improved. In a typical editorial in the *Lancet*, John Fulton complained that

> the ordinary method of clinical teaching pursued in most hospitals is to allot the clinical clerks [senior students] the duty of taking down the cases which are read aloud at the bedside by the physician, and then the interrogatories, remarks and treatment are given in a voice sufficiently loud for the crowd of students to hear, though they may possibly not be able to see the case. Those most worthy of note are subsequently made the theme of a clinical lecture in the class-room of the school or hospital.

The chief defect of this mode of instruction, Fulton continued, was that the student was never obliged to exercise his judgment and had no opportunity for trying his own skill, and thus, despite even the best academic training, he was upon graduation 'a practitioner who has never practised.' The solution, once again, was more extensive 'hands-on' training at the bedside, and more rigorous and frequent evaluation of the student's skills at diagnosis and treatment.[17] Among other things, said the editor of the *Canadian Practitioner*, this required decreasing the size of classes in the wards by breaking up the crowd of students following a single physician into groups of ten or more, each with its own instructor/examiner.[18]

Yet the improvement of clinical education was easier said than done. In the two decades after mid-century, the relationship between the Toronto schools and the Toronto General Hospital was especially problematic, rivalries between the former making arrangements for clinical instruction a recurring source of friction.[19] Then in 1868 the government cut off its grants to the medical schools along with those given to the denominational colleges. That left the schools solely dependent on student fees to cover running costs and adequate remuneration for their instructors. Thus the expense of innovations always had to be weighed against their income. Didactic lectures to large groups of students were relatively cheap; increased clinical instruction, a reduction in the size of clinical classes, and the costs associated with more anatomical study, which meant keeping dissecting rooms open longer and hiring more assistant demonstrators to supervise the work, all involved substantial increased expenditure. There were also opportunity costs. The more time the schoolmen had to give to their schools and to hospital instruction, the less they had for private practice. Given such considerations, it is perhaps not surprising that change came slowly in the first half of the 1870s, when fewer students were entering medical school as a result of the impact of the new CPSO regulations, and then increased dramatically as student numbers rose from the mid-1870s onwards.

TO TAKE BUT ONE example, consider the development of the Toronto School of Medicine (TSM).[20] In 1870 it had a staff of twelve physicians, half of whom held hospital or similar appointments in the city's charitable institutions. Five were either educated in Britain or had acquired British qualifications following their initial training in Upper Canada. During the first half of the 1870s, the TSM was located near University College, while Toronto General Hospital stood some distance away, on Gerrard Street, east of Parliament. After Victoria College's medical department closed in the early 1870s, however, the TSM acquired its medical school building,[21] located directly across the street from the hospital, while at the same time the hospital itself had expanded to include a new fever wing, the Eye and Ear Infirmary, and the Burnside Lying-in Hospital. Thus clinical and teaching facilities were centralized and expanded; in the years that followed, the TSM added more lecture and library rooms, a pathological museum, and laboratories for the study of chemistry and physiology equipped 'with all the apparatus required in teaching these important subjects.' In its announcement for the 1883–4 session, students were promised 'a thorough and systematic course of bedside instruction where they would be encouraged to examine patients carefully, and make their diagnoses and keep notes of cases.' Two years later the calendar added that 'bedside instruction [will be] systematically given in the medical and surgical wards to a limited number of students in each class.'

Along with these advances in clinical instruction, the TSM had been changing in other ways as well. By 1885 it listed sixteen physician-educators; two other instructors responsible for chemistry, botany, and zoology; and an assistant demonstrator in anatomy – a total of nineteen in all. Nine of the sixteen physicians were involved in clinical teaching at the hospital. Throughout the 1880s the courses offered during winter sessions expanded steadily to include toxicology, normal histology, pathology, chemistry, botany and zoology, and even medical psychology, a 'clinical course offered at the Asylum and illustrated by cases at the Toronto General Hospital.' As well as lectures in anatomy, the 'demonstrator attends daily at the Dissecting Room for the purposes of directing students in their dissections and examining them on dissected parts ... At least 3 examinations will be given upon each part before granting a certificate.' The dissecting room was open nine hours each weekday and additional assistants were appointed to help out when the demonstrator could not be present.

By the mid-1880s, in sum, the proprietary medical schools had been notably successful in extending the range of clinical instruction, in adding laboratory work in physiology and pathology, and in seeing that all students received more practical instruction in basic and surgical anatomy. The number of students had increased rapidly over the same decade – in the session of 1886–7, one observer noted, the two Toronto schools had more than 500 students between them, and the combined annual revenues from student fees amounted to something like $40,000 a year.[22] It was figures like these which underwrote the schools' capacities to secure adequate physical facilities, increase their staffs, and update their program of studies. Their success, moreover, was widely recognized at home and abroad. Their certificates, or the university degrees they prepared students for, were accepted by British authorities as equivalent qualifications, and their achievements were acknowledged at home as well: remarked the editor of the *Globe* early in 1887 of the Toronto schools, 'both of them are thriving lustily and both are doing excellent work.'[23]

PRESBYTERIAN THEOLOGICAL EDUCATION had something of the same mix as medical education: classroom instruction, combined with the kind of practical training which paralleled clinical education in medicine. Though the precise location of subjects within the curriculum at Queen's or Knox varied slightly, as did the course titles, the program of study at both institutions was essentially the same. The arts subjects included Greek and Latin; mathematics and natural philosophy; and logic, mental, and moral philosophy. Theological studies comprised systematic theology, biblical criticism and interpretation, church history, and pastoral theology. Hebrew was a required subject for both churches, and the Kirk demanded Chaldee as well.[24]

With Presbyterian union accomplished in the mid-1870s, the General Assembly struck a committee to review the program of theological studies, but its report in 1879 recommended few changes in traditional practices. The matriculation standard for theology was to remain either a BA or an alternative course of three years of study in Latin, Greek, English, Hebrew, mathematics, history, philosophy, and science. Theology was to consist of three terms of six months each, and, as E.R. Schwarz has summarized it, to include courses in

'Apologetics' (the intellectual defense of Christianity), 'Systematic Theology' (a thorough examination of Christian ideas), 'Exegetics' (the techniques of deriving the meaning of Scripture; such studies used the Greek and Hebrew texts); 'Biblical Criticism' (the study of Scripture as literature); 'Church History' (the study of the history of the Church, usually beginning with the work of Paul of Tarsus), 'Homiletics' (the techniques of sermon preparation and preaching), and 'Pastoral Theology' (the application of theology to the work of a pastor, but in practice frequently used as an opportunity to give instruction in important practical matters neglected elsewhere).

Compared with the curriculum at mid-century, this meant the subdivision of some subjects into separate courses but, other than that, little substantive change. The committee's recommendations were adopted without controversy, and 'the theological programme itself remained unchanged till 1910.'[25] As George Rawlyk and Kevin Quinn have demonstrated, indeed that was to be the case at Queen's far into the twentieth century.[26]

Classroom instruction was organized around a combination of lectures and exercises. Though the exact meaning of 'exercises' is not clear, a Queen's report of 1852–3 describes them as follows. In mental and moral philosophy and logic, and in theology, 'a pretty full course of lectures' was delivered in the mornings, and then in the afternoon 'the students were regularly examined on the lectures of the morning. They were also required to do a weekly essay of considerable length on some subject unfolded in the lectures.'[27] Practical training took a variety of forms, some of it closely supervised and some of it not. Along with classes in pastoral theology, students were instructed in homiletics and expected to give practice sermons before the professors and their peers.[28] There were also special classes created to link knowledge and practice. In 1855 at Knox, for example, Principal Willis noted that he had added to his regular load 'the superintendence, weekly, of a class of entrants, whom he has initiated in the first principles of written composition and public speaking.' During the same year, George Paxton Young reported that he 'had a Bible class, which met every Sabbath morning in the Divinity class-room, at which all students, not otherwise engaged, were invited to attend. The object of the class was practical, rather than exegetical; but while practical ends were mainly kept in view, the attainment of these was aimed at through a strictly (and even minutely) correct exposition of what was read.' Again, 'once a month, all the College classes rallied at the hour, when both the Professors were present, and the Students were addressed on the more practical subjects of clerical manners and experimental piety.'[29]

Students also had extensive opportunities to observe exemplary practice. They visited the city churches two and even three times on a Sunday to watch some of the best preachers in the province, whether of their own churches or others. Beyond that there was the work of the college missionary societies, which, though student-run, were almost certainly initiated or encouraged by the professors themselves, and which were important arenas for gaining practical experience. In 1848, for example, the Knox Missionary Society met monthly to organize student activities,

at which meeting an essay was read on some subject connected with missionary operations; ... in Toronto 17 prayer-meetings were held weekly by the students, and 600 tracts distributed once a fortnight; ... 10 preaching stations were regularly, and 7 partially supplied every Sabbath, besides the General Hospital; and though these labours necessarily occupied much time, still the students found themselves benefited thereby. They had more strongly pressed upon them the great value of time; they saw more the need of every proper preparation for the great work of the ministry, and especially they learned the close connection that existed between these exercises and the salvation of souls.[30]

While these activities were important training grounds, there is good evidence to think that the churches would have liked to have had something much more systematic as well. At mid-century the Kirk Synod had attempted to introduce its own apprenticeship system, passing a resolution that required its probationers to spend one full year as assistants to experienced ministers 'for the purpose of being trained to the practical part of the Pastoral work.' The shortage of ministers, however, led the presbyteries to reject the proposal: as the Hamilton Presbytery put it, 'in the present circumstances ... it would be highly injudicious to delay unnecessarily the settlement of our young Licentiates.'[31] Thus the church was forced to fall back upon more *ad hoc* expedients. As the report of the Knox Missionary Society suggests, one was the extensive use of students to fill vacant preaching stations on Sundays. But more important, senior students were increasingly assigned to the home-mission field, spending four or five months each summer in full-time pastoral work.

We can flesh out the experience of learning to minister by turning to the record left by Donald McKerracher, whom we have already met as a young Presbyterian minister at Prince Arthur's Landing (Port Arthur). In the early 1870s McKerracher kept a diary of his student days at Knox.[32] It reveals a cycle of learning that filled every day of the week. Lectures and exercises, observation, practice, and social activities formed a seamless web of formal and informal initiation into his occupation. The first two weeks of January 1874 were typical. Weekdays were spent attending classes, studying, and preparing essays. On the first Friday evening, McKerracher participated in a debate at the Literary Society: 'Question. Do men ever perform disinterested actions? Should have prepared better but hope that in my life work I shall not have to argue against my conscience.' He spent most of Saturday 'preparing a Sermon for Dr. Proudfoot' and then in the evening attended a prayer meeting conducted by one of the other students. On Sunday morning 'heard Mr. Alexander Stewart at College St. Church ... In the evening heard Rev. Mr. Anderson preach in Knox Church ... The matter of both sermons was good but lacked vigor in delivery.' The following Wednesday he had to read his own sermon before Dr Proudfoot and the other students. 'Criticism,' he noted, was 'not nearly so severe as last year.' Almost every evening that week, he attended a 'Sunday School Institute' – meetings about how to organize and run Sunday schools – conducted by a Dr Randolph of Philadelphia, though there was also an address by 'Mr. Jas. Hughes of the Model School on Errors in Sunday School Teaching.' Saturday morning was spent reading and then he was off to Aurora, where he was to preach the next day. 'Had the pleasure of Principal Caven's company, also Mrs. Caven, who were going out to Richmond Hill ... Kindly received by Mr. & Mrs. McGilvray,' his hosts for the next two nights. 'Went with them to Mr. Oliver's to the singing practice.' Sunday was no day of rest. 'Bible class at 9:30. Lesson the call of Moses. Preached to a good congregation at 11 a.m. After dinner with Mr. D. Fotheringham at Mr. Doane's drove with Mr. F. to Newmarket. Bible Class & Sabbath School. Preached in the evening to about 55 or 60.' Early the next day he was back on the train, again with the Cavens, and arrived in Toronto in time for lectures, which on Mondays began in the afternoon in order to accommodate the large number of students travelling back from preaching stations during the morning.

The summer before, McKerracher had been sent as a home missionary to Prince Arthur's Landing. Much of his time was spent reading, for like most Presbyterian theologues, he would have been expected by both his presbytery and the college to continue his academic progress during the summer. But at the same time he was learning through practice. 'Sunday, May 18. Preached in the morning to a congregation of about fifty in the basement of the Methodist church kindly given by Mr. Halstead [the local Methodist minister]. After dinner went in the tug "Mills" to the Fort and preached a sermon to about twenty.' From Tuesday to Saturday he read in the mornings, paid pastoral visits to local Presbyterians, and investigated the possibility of obtaining land for a church.

Sunday, May 25. Preached in the morning at the Landing. Attendance about sixty. Would probably have been larger were it not that the steamer 'Manitoba' was in sight. She was in the dock when we came out. The Captain had the good sense not to whistle, consequently the Congregations were not disturbed. Was rowed over to the fort by two young men ... and preached to about twenty. There is not that interest taken there that we would expect. Several absent who should be there. Went in the evening to hear Mr. Halstead, who preached from Ps.68.18.

Having himself preached two sermons that Sunday, the reader will notice, McKerracher then went off to the Methodist church to hear a third! Monday it was back to his usual weekday routine: 'Read as usual. Visited some in the afternoon ... Joined the Temperance League ... Temperance is very much needed in this place.'

Summer work as a missionary was a hard taskmaster. As one theologue noted, 'Students going into the mission field are often placed in the most trying circumstances. Generally they are perfect strangers to the places to which they are sent; as a rule these places have had no regular services, perhaps none at all, for a long time previous. The people have become careless, and it will require much ingenuity and skill to arouse them.'[33] The inexperienced, in other words, were sent to what was one of the most difficult ministerial tasks of all – organizing a new congregation, or resuscitating one that had been without a minister for months or even years – and often without experienced counsel within reach.

IN CONTRAST TO either medicine or the ministry, the education of the student-at-law was carried out almost entirely through apprenticeship and self-directed study, and this was true during virtually the whole of the nineteenth century.[34] From 1797 students served a term of five years, the only exception being a reduction to three years for graduates in arts. But beyond that, and especially before mid-century, the Law Society's educational regulations were minimal indeed. A student appeared before the Benchers to pass his matriculation examination, and, five years later, to pass his bar admission examination. The only other requirement, introduced in the late 1820s, was that students must keep four 'judicial terms' observing the superior courts in Toronto. Each term comprised a period of approximately two weeks coinciding with the quarterly sittings of the Court of King's Bench. For a minority of students, there were opportunities to supplement these requirements. Beginning in 1832 those resident in Toronto could attend the 'Trinity Class,' a cross between a student club and a more formal educational venture which may have survived a decade or so but no longer. Between the 1820s and mid-century, there were other student clubs in the city, as well as the various law lectures offered by King's College, Trinity College, and the University of Toronto in the years before 1854. But for the majority of students, those articling outside Toronto especially, the requirements consisted of the matriculation examination, the bar admission examination, and a total of two months or so observing the superior courts.[35]

During the mid-1850s the Law Society began to take a more activist approach. In 1854 and 1855 the Benchers approved a series of resolutions which set out a list of specific textbooks on which the bar admission examination would be based, and made the examination itself more rigorous.[36] But, more important, they established a series of compulsory law lectures during the two-week judicial terms.[37] The lectures began in 1855 and consisted of twelve presentations, one hour a day, six days a week. There were four different courses offered, one in each successive term.[38] Thus the Law Society had now made a limited commitment to formal instruction. Noting the various changes that had been made, and especially the introduction of compulsory lectures, the editor of the *Globe* remarked that the aim was 'to render the education of students, so far as the Society is concerned, less a matter of form and more a matter of substance than it has hitherto been.'[39] The term lectures continued through the rest of the decade, and in the early 1860s were increased from one to two a day.[40]

They did not survive very long, however. Between 1868 and 1872 the Law Society overhauled its entire apparatus for legal education.[41]

On the one hand, the academic rigour of a student's program of studies was substantially augmented. Two 'intermediate' examinations were introduced, so that students now wrote three professional examinations beyond matriculation: the two intermediates and the bar admission examination. At the same time the amount of reading required for all three examinations expanded dramatically.[42] On the other hand, the Society abolished both term-keeping *and* the lectures associated with it. No other form of compulsory classroom instruction was put in place until 1889. Between 1854 and 1868, then, students received, out of five full years of training, a modicum of formal instruction – something like a total of 48, later 96, hours of lectures, delivered over a timespan of about two months. Before 1854, and for two decades after 1868, most of them received no formal instruction at all. In the main, learning to lawyer in nineteenth-century Ontario took place outside classrooms. In this respect it was a profoundly different form of professional education than that experienced by theologues or medical students.

This does not mean that students-at-law were not expected to study. In preparing for admission to the bar, students were always engaged in a program of self-directed reading, and from the mid-1850s onwards that program became increasingly rigorous. Simultaneously, however, they also learned through an apprenticeship in a law office. Contemporary accounts of this experience are not plentiful, but as in the case of student ministers, they do survive, and we propose to illustrate the process by focusing on three diaries, those written by Larratt Smith, William Elliott, and Henry O'Brien.[43] The first two date from the 1840s. Larratt Smith was a product of Upper Canada College and in 1839 obtained a place in the law office of William Draper, surely one of the highest prizes any law student in the colony could hope for. Elliott was raised on the family farm in Middlesex County and, though well connected enough, lacked the advantage of a good grammar-school education, and, probably for lack of resources to pay the premium demanded for an apprenticeship by one of the more prestigious law firms, had to settle for a small office in London, still hardly more than a thriving village.

Both worked a six-day week copying documents; learning to draw up wills, deeds, and declarations; serving subpoenas; drafting briefs; keeping accounts; delivering papers to other offices and to Crown agencies; appearing in court on minor matters; and studying on their own whenever they found the time. Typical entries in Smith's diary for October 1839 include 'writing hard in office'; 'in office arranging papers'; 'went to Court House to compute interest in witness box, arranged papers in office, registered assignment in Commission Crown

Lands Department'; though on at least one Saturday he 'read all morning Stephens on Pleading.' Elliott did much the same, noting landmarks in his own progress by recording the first time he 'filed pleas in District office,' 'made up a brief,' 'passed three records.' Both would keep their required terms in Toronto observing the higher courts, but each of them visited the courts at other times as well. They clearly found this a valuable experience, Elliott taking special pleasure in attending the assizes when Draper presided as judge, and making copious notes on the cases.

Smith, on the other hand, had important advantages Elliott lacked. First, Smith went into a prominent Toronto office with a large and varied practice, including much government business – an ideal training ground. Indeed, when Draper became attorney general, Smith became his clerk. Draper was, as well, apparently a conscientious principal, quizzing his student orally and later giving him written examinations. Living in Toronto, law students also had ready access to the substantial law library at Osgoode Hall, including the court reports. With a good classical education, moreover, Smith didn't have to invest any time in preparing for the Law Society matriculation examinations; he could focus exclusively on his law studies. In 1843, while still a law student, he also entered the University of King's College to study law (and later took the law degrees of BCL and DCL).

Elliott, with a more uncertain educational background, had to spend several months during the first year of his articles boning up on his Latin and Euclid for the matriculation examination, which slowed his progress in reading law.[44] Initially he also appears to have found his texts harder to master because he was not trained in adequate study habits, though that came with time and discipline: in his 'reflections' upon the preceding months written on New Year's Eve, 1848, he noted that he had been 'getting into a more profitable way of reading carefully taking notes and looking them over at intervals.' Over the past year, he continued, he had worked his way through Blackstone, the whole of Stephens on Pleading, Chitty on Contracts, Cameron's rules, etc.; 'reading Stephens again and carefully taking notes, putting it in the form of question and answers.'

Without the family resources available to Smith, and married while still a student, Elliott had to hold a part-time job as local superintendent of schools. This helped finance his legal education, but also constrained it. Anxious to transfer to Toronto with all its advantages, he had to turn down an offer from W.H. Blake because it would have meant giving up his job.[45] It was a matter of great regret as Blake 'gives me poor hopes of being able to obtain a good knowledge of the higher walks of the profession without having access to the reports and that I cannot have in London where there are few or I may almost say no books at all that I can have access to.' Though Elliott never voiced any overt criticism of his principal, he rarely noted receiving much in the way of help with his studies. But, more important, and this is a recurring refrain, business was often slack and covered a narrow range of problems. While this left time for his job as local superintendent and for his legal reading, it limited the breadth of his experience, and he was acutely conscious of it.

Henry O'Brien, the third of our diarists, was an articled clerk and student-at-law during the second half of the 1850s. Born at Shanty Bay, he was the well-educated son of a prosperous gentry family, began his articles with a prominent Barrie lawyer, and then transferred to the firm of Fergusson and Kingsmill in Guelph. His diary at this point in his career illustrates the later stages of a lawyer's education. In Guelph, O'Brien was 'managing clerk' of the firm; between October and December 1858, he routinely spent six days a week in the office, studying on his own in the evening and recording so many pages covered a day. '25 Oct. 1858: Passed as the generality of days here, plenty to do in the office till dinner at 4:30 after that reading till the train came in where I went for letters.' But O'Brien also dealt on his own with clients and spent a substantial amount of time in court. On 19 October, for example, he appeared in Division Court at Allansville, afterwards going off with the judge to make some social calls. On 23 October he was at Puslinch for the same reason and won his suit there. On 2 November it was Division Court in Guelph, followed by a dinner in the evening with 'the Sheriff, Col. Hewat' and other guests. The Guelph Assizes opened the next Tuesday and engaged him fully for the rest of the week. Following that, we find him back to the routines of the office, pursuing cases in the division courts and doing the firm's year-end accounting. In December there was also the round of county courts. '11 Dec., Sat. At office till nearly 10 getting records for the County Court. Tues. At office till 9:30 going over briefs with Kingsmill.' The next day he was off to oversee those cases in the county court at Milton.

As we have seen in Elliott's case, it was important for young lawyers to spend some time in Toronto, and many of those who began their apprenticeship elsewhere completed their articles with city firms. Despite the broad experience available in Guelph, O'Brien did the same, arranging to enter John Helliwell's office early in 1859. His work routines there were much as before, but he also attended his term lectures and did a lot of socializing, getting to know other Toronto students and a wide circle of established lawyers. Still, his reading had to be kept up as well. '20 Aug. 1859. Arranged my course of study for attorney somewhat as follows – 1. Finish Stovy's EI. 2. Finish 2nd Volume of Taylor on Ev. 3. Read and rotate – Smith's Mercantile Law; Williams on P.P; do. on Real Prop. 4. Take a grind at Smith's manual of EJ. Do. Blackstone's 1st Vol. 5. Get up the Statutes, some Chancery, and go over books again if possible.'

THE PRECEDING ACCOUNT of the professional education of doctors, ministers, and lawyers may appear to have been organized into a hierarchy of descending pedagogical sophistication. Medical students are 'taught,' in classrooms and in the hospital. Theologues too are taught, though they also learn their skills in less supervised environments. Lawyers are left with an apprenticeship, and self-directed reading guided only by an examination syllabus. To frame the question in that way, however, is to assume that modern arrangements, which give first priority to classroom instruction, constitute an appropriate standard for understanding the past. Increasingly in the nineteenth and twentieth centuries, whole portions of the population were put in school, and kept there for longer and longer periods. This is true not just in the case of elementary or secondary education but for vocational education as well: the learning of a wide variety of craft skills came to be organized around the school rather than the worksite. And professional education was, in many respects, in the vanguard of this movement. Yet in most cases the historical norm was not schooling but apprenticeship; not the classroom but the worksite. One of the central questions in any history of the professions, then, is why this transition took place, and why it proceeded rapidly in some occupations and more slowly in others.[46]

In medicine the transition occurred during the first half of the nineteenth century, and it was accompanied by the development of a sophisticated pedagogy of practice, one that was to be much admired and imitated in the modern world. The shift from apprenticeship to clinical instruction organized around the school and the hospital, however, took place because of some very specific, and in many respects unique, historical circumstances. Though the hospital was already an integral part of medical education in late eighteenth-century and early nineteenth-century Britain, it was still supplementary to apprenticeship. At the hospital students could witness demonstrations of anatomy and 'walk the wards,' listening to, and observing the work of, a consulting physician or surgeon. Except for the handful who could afford to apprentice themselves to a consultant, practical experience for most students was largely to be obtained through apprenticeship arrangements which didn't include access to the hospital. But as advances in surgery and new techniques of diagnosis increasingly made the dissecting room and bedside experience with a wide range of cases all but indispensable, students flocked to the large hospitals. And as prominent doctors and then hospital trustees began to recognize the economic rewards of offering instruction in anatomy and in other subjects, they organized classes and then whole schools. The consequence was that a new pedagogy emerged which included lectures, observation and demonstration, and supervised individual and small-group instruction. Apprenticeship in medicine, in other words, did not decline because it was simply 'an idea whose time had passed' but because medical students began to learn *in crowds*, and increasingly at a relatively few large metropolitan hospitals. In effect, technical change and economic opportunity combined to reconstitute the virtues of apprenticeship on new terrain.

The special character of that new terrain, however, played its own role in fostering pedagogical innovation. One cannot, generally speaking, conduct experiments or learn by trial and error on the clientele of a lawyer's office, or on one's parishioners. The laity has some tolerance for beginners' blunders, but it is limited; confidence dwindles and people go elsewhere. That is also true of a physician's paying patients. When you rush to a doctor's office with a broken arm, you don't expect that the first attempt to mend it will be made by an apprentice. If one falls into the clutches of the modern teaching hospital, the situation is somewhat different; still, everybody is in the same boat: patients are poked and probed by the rawest recruit, gawked at by a crowd of students following a physician through the wards, and operated upon by those still learning their craft, all in a suitably democratic manner, without regard to the patient's wealth and social standing. Dissections are carried out, in the main, upon those who have volunteered their bodies.

This is not, however, the social environment within which either anatomical or clinical education in medicine developed. For most of the nineteenth century, only the poor with no other recourse committed themselves to the hospital; only the friendless or the destitute died there; only the unclaimed were eligible to be turned over for dissection. The subjects which students practised upon at the bedside, exercised their growing surgical skills upon, and learned their basic anatomy from were not the sick or the dead indiscriminately, but the sick and dead *poor*. In a riveting study of the origins and subsequent history of the English Anatomy Acts, Ruth Richardson has lifted the veil on the social meaning entailed in this relationship, and we ourselves have explored elsewhere its significance in nineteenth-century Ontario, but neither study reaches beyond dissection to include the living hospital patient.⁴⁷ It is a subject which deserves further attention from some suitably dyspeptic historian. Here we simply want to draw attention to the fact that the critical learning laboratory for nineteenth-century doctors was of a profoundly different character than that for lawyers, ministers, or indeed most other professional men. Behind the walls of the hospital, the blanket of reticence and dignity could be turned back, and the patient's 'confidence' in a physician discounted. Demonstrations, experimental treatments, and learning by trial and error could go on without damage to reputations and without fear of suits for malpractice. We mean all this in no denigratory spirit; but we also believe it important to recognize that what is often considered a model pedagogy of practice developed within a unique social context. Had doctors had only paying patients, instead of the objects of charity, to learn on, the outcome might have been different.

STILL, THE GROWTH of clinical education is only one part of the story. Medical students, and theologues as well, also learned in classrooms. Candidates for the ministry of the Anglican and Presbyterian churches spent six months a year, five or six years in a row, attending lectures or writing essays and completing other assignments relating to their courses. While at mid-century many medical students still learned their craft partly through apprenticeship, they increasingly congregated in Toronto or Kingston, where they too spent large amounts of time in school. For students-at-law there was no parallel experience. Calling for the establishment of more formal educational provisions, a petition to the Law Society in 1849 from a group of Toronto students took note of this difference: 'Many efficient schools have been established for instruction in Theology and Medicine, while the sister profession [of Law] ... suffers in this respect a total neglect.'⁴⁸

Why was this the case? It was not simply the result of indifference on the part of the Benchers or other influential lawyers. Indeed, a series of initiatives from the 1830s onwards points to a continuing thread of interest in the introduction of more formal instruction for law students. Blaine Baker has drawn attention to Convocation's resolution of 1832 providing for the establishment of law classes throughout the province.⁴⁹ But nothing came of that resolution except Robert Baldwin's Trinity class for Toronto students, and it was relatively short-lived. The Law Society also actively promoted the creation of a faculty of law connected with King's College, but after the abolition of the professional faculties in 1853, it did not pursue the question of university instruction further. The only significant innovations before 1860 were the introduction of compulsory lectures during term and a detailed examination syllabus.

Then, in 1861, the Law Society founded its first Osgoode Hall Law School and thus embarked, it must be said, on one of the more bizarre trains of events in the history of professional education in the province.[50] Intended as a supplement to the compulsory lectures during term, classes were voluntary, though incentives were built in to encourage attendance. The school survived, however, only until 1868, when it was abolished along with term-keeping and the lectures which accompanied it. Almost immediately the Benchers had second thoughts and re-established it in 1872. Once again attendance was entirely voluntary, but this time students had more powerful incentives to attend: those who passed the school's examinations were to be allowed up to one full year's remission in their terms of service.[51] Though the school drew a hundred or so students in its first year, numbers then declined, and in 1878 the Benchers once more shut it down. Following that, the Benchers attempted to encourage local law associations to initiate lectures throughout the province, and then in 1881 resuscitated the school yet once again, but this time without any incentives for students to attend. Not surprisingly, few did. The classes survived precariously over the next few years, with near-annual threats of abolition, until 1889. Over the course of some thirty-five years, in other words, from 1854 until the late 1880s, the Law Society had required compulsory lectures during term and then abandoned them, established a law school, abolished it, re-established it, abolished it once more, and then put it back in place to struggle on with few students and little enthusiasm.

How is one to explain this extraordinary tale of muddle and confusion? Other historians of legal education have pointed to the importance of the regional factionalism which increasingly gripped the profession in the years after mid-century and we agree that this provides part of the answer. Centralizing legal education in Toronto and forcing all law clerks to attend a school located there substantially interfered with the business of the law office throughout the rest of the province and was opposed for that reason alone. Yet questions remain. If everything can be explained by the politics of regionalism and the economics of the law office, why the resolution of 1832 or the experiment with compulsory term lectures at all? Why, indeed, the three attempts to maintain a law school on the basis of voluntary attendance? The answer, we suggest, lies in the uncertain relationship which existed between the science of the law and the art of practice. And it is that uncertainty which also helps explain differences in the patterns of professional education between medicine and theology, on the one hand, and law, on the other.

Among lawyers in all common-law jurisdictions, there was, and had long been, a deep-seated conviction that law was pre-eminently a practical activity and best learned by practice. Raymond Cocks, among others, has described how pervasively that view was held by the English bar throughout the nineteenth century,[52] and, given the influence of the English example, it is perhaps not surprising that it was dominant in Upper Canada as well. Lecturing to a group of law students in 1855, Adam Wilson, a leading Toronto barrister, had this to say about learning court procedures, or what he termed 'the practice of the courts': 'The reason I say it is practically the most difficult part of the law to acquire a knowledge of, is because much of it depends upon no other rule than that it is so, and no kind of reasoning would assist one in determining *a priori* what the particular rule should be upon any part of the practice.' Wilson went on to give an example, and then concluded with a more general point.

It is impossible that anyone should understand all this but he who has learned it – and I may say with great propriety – it is impossible for anyone to learn this, but he who has practised it. Practice can only be learned by practice, and therefore it is a tedious part of the law. Practice depends in great part on certain arbitrary rules which rest rather upon the memory than upon the mind, and it is therefore a difficult part of the law. Although tedious and difficult, and in many respects uninteresting, it is an essential part of our profession and therefore must be learned.[53]

Yet there were counterweights to this emphasis on learning by practice.[54] On the continent there was a long tradition of teaching law in the universities, and though, like theology and medicine, legal education had atrophied at Oxford and Cambridge, law was taught at Edinburgh as well. From the 1830s there were also attempts to sustain law lectures at the University of London. And in Upper Canada all of the new universities were chartered to establish law faculties, along with those of arts, medicine, and theology. There were, in other words, assumptions built into the culture that law would be taught in classrooms as well as learned in offices. Traditionally, 'academic law' dealt with principles, not practice, focusing on civil (or canon) law, the principles of jurisprudence, legal history, constitutional law, comparative and international law – areas peripheral to the making of livings in common-law countries but studies, nonetheless, which constituted a critical part of what people meant when they spoke of the law as a 'science' and a 'learned profession.' From at least the eighteenth century, moreover, there had been attempts to rescue the common law from its reputation as a body of capricious and arbitrary rules and cases, impose order on it, and bring it within the purview of the university. Blackstone, among others, had argued that the common law could be reduced to principles and that training by apprenticeship was not, in itself, enough: 'If practice be the whole [the student] is taught, practice must be the whole he will ever know: if he be uninstructed in the elements and first principles upon which the rule of practice is founded, the least variation from established principles will totally distract and bewilder him.'[55] During the first half of the nineteenth century, a number of English legal reformers reiterated Blackstone's arguments: the reform of the law and the reform of legal education went hand in hand; law must not only be learned in an office but 'taught' from first principles.

This sense – that the law was something more than an accumulation of cases and arbitrary rules of procedure, that it was also a science, a rational and coherent discipline which spoke to the larger study of human relations and the good society – runs through the rhetoric of leading lawyers in Britain and Upper Canada during the nineteenth century, and encouraged the Law Society to look beyond the office to the classroom. And it is this, we suggest, that helps to explain all of the initiatives in that direction from the 1830s to the 1880s: the resolutions of 1832, Baldwin's Trinity class that followed from them, the lectures provided gratis by distinguished barristers during judicial terms, the founding and refounding of the voluntary law schools. For at least some leading lawyers, and that included two of the Law Society's most distinguished treasurers, Robert Baldwin and J.H. Cameron, learning the science of the law was an integral part of educating the gentlemen of the bar.

And yet it failed to take hold. The reason, we suggest, is that the gap between the science of the law and the art of practice was simply too wide to be bridged. The 'principles of jurisprudence,' constitutional law, the law of the academy, might be important, but they didn't direct practice. Theory, to put it another way, might be interesting and even ornamental, but that could hardly justify *requiring* students to go to school to learn things that were not pertinent to practice. As one lawyer would put it in 1888, the student who 'can floor' his principal on the principles of jurisprudence, 'but render him no assistance in the "opening of a suit," will not have the chance of deriving from his seniors those practical lessons which are so much more thoroughly taught and so much more easily learned by participation with a skilled practitioner in his actual work.'[56]

In medicine things were different. The 'principles' of medicine and surgery directed or prescribed therapies and operative procedures, and thus courses on those principles were an integral part of a student's education. This has nothing to do, however, with the relative efficacy of medicine. Medical theory was, at mid-century, mostly wrong and much of its therapeutic application positively dangerous to the patient. But it was a body of systematic knowledge deemed pertinent to practice. The same point might be made about the theological courses required of students for the ministry. Systematic theology and church history were not divorced from practice; rather, they defined and justified the commitments a minister made to a particular denomination and the truths he would deliver to his congregation over a lifetime of Sundays and holy days. Without the principles of theology as taught at Queen's, Knox, or Trinity, one was not a Presbyterian or Anglican minister but something else altogether. Medical men, in sum, prescribed according to doctrine, or 'science,' and so did clergymen. Thoughtful lawyers gave cognizance to the importance of the principles of jurisprudence, the science of the law, but they didn't think it was something every lawyer had to know. Thinking about the meaning of the law, going to school to learn how to think about it, was an honourable pursuit, but it did not a lawyer make.

THE RESULT WAS a system of education organized primarily around the worksite. Among historians of professional education, the value of apprenticeship has generally been viewed with suspicion or scepticism, and this is especially the case in law.[57] Why this should be so is not clear. In the previous chapter we reviewed the core tasks of the lawyer in some detail, and our student diaries reflect a thorough and systematic initiation into these tasks. Students learned in the office to do the paperwork of the profession by observation and imitation, then trying it on their own. They learned to work in the division and county courts. They travelled up to Toronto for terms, not just to observe the superior courts but to conduct some of their principal's business in those courts. As they matured they dealt with clients and conducted their own cases, under their principal's supervision. They spent whole weeks assisting at the assizes. They learned, moreover, in an environment marked by both intimacy and sociability – by the relationship between a principal and one or two students, on the one hand, and the professional sociability that surrounded the courts, on the other. When Archibald McLean was appointed a judge of the Court of King's Bench in 1837, he took Sandfield Macdonald, his student, with him on his first circuit. Wrote Macdonald of that experience, 'I am not aware of any advantage to a student surpassing that of going [on] the Circuit, for besides its general lucrativeness, it ... extends greatly the sphere of one's acquaintance, makes him familiar with the forms and customs of the Court, by observing the system pursued in conducting the variety of suits then tried and determined and enlarges his knowledge of the several Townships and districts through which he travels.'[58]

Few students were fortunate enough to have that kind of unique opportunity. But their work routinely took them into the courts and thus brought them into contact with the webs of sociability the courts entailed. One does more than simply make new acquaintances when one 'hangs around' worksites; one acquires knowledge, techniques, and values through listening to and watching professionals at work and play. Given the prevailing assumption that learning to lawyer was about the art of practice, in sum, there seems to have been a remarkable congruence between the skills students needed to acquire and the skills they actually learned. The challenge is not to make the case for apprenticeship but to explain what circumstances undermined the conviction that it was an efficacious form of professional education.

We also suspect that there was a good deal more close supervision of law students than some contemporaries were prepared to admit and some historians have recognized. Students may have been left on their own to read for examinations or figure out the 'whys and wheretofores' of legal doctrine, though not even that can be assumed to have been common. But mistakes in the office could be costly in time, money, or both. 'I do not know what I am to do with young Fitzgerald,' wrote Adam Wilson to Robert Baldwin in 1842, 'when he is here he either does so little that it is of no service to us or does that which is expensive to be undone – he knows nothing of the profession and requires in the simplest matter to be instructed.'[59] Whatever else it was, an apprenticeship was an economic relationship in which clerks were engaged in productive work. Because of that, there were inevitably areas of close supervision, even if more general guidance might be lacking.

The quality of the experience was certainly uneven – witness the different accounts of William Elliott and Larratt Smith. But equally clearly, apprenticeship was seen as an effective educational tool not only in law but in other occupations as well. Its virtues were obvious enough to the mid-century Kirk that Synod attempted to add a full year of it to the theological program, and failed only because of the shortage of ministers. In some respects, indeed, it might be argued that, of aspirants to our three professions, the Presbyterian theologue was at the greatest disadvantage. The law student worked under the guidance of his principal. The medical student learned to practise in an increasingly structured and supervised system of clinical education. Students in theology might be taught how to craft a sermon in a classroom, or come to imitate good examples through observation, but much of the rest came through unsupervised trial and error. One tried a sermon out in Aurora or Prince Arthur's Landing, and either it worked or it didn't; one made a pastoral visitation on one's own and said the wrong thing, or the right thing too earnestly, and learned the lesson or didn't. There was no one there to correct mistakes or counsel the student towards improved techniques.

Consider, in any case, the views of William Leitch, principal of Queen's and senior professor of divinity between 1860 and 1863. In his inaugural address at Queen's, he offered one of the rare extended commentaries that have survived from the mid-nineteenth century on the nature of professional training. And in doing so he demonstrates that he at least had no preconceptions about a hierarchy of esteem which placed 'science' above practice, and the classroom above learning by doing. He began by asking what were the objects of a Divinity Hall: 'First, to acquire theological knowledge, and second professional training.' But which had priority? 'I have no hesitation in giving it as a long-cherished conviction that our theological halls, to meet the wants of the Church, must be looked on mainly as training institutions ... I hold that the distinctive feature of our Halls ought to be a practical one, and that the teaching of the science should be only regarded as a means to an end.'

This did not mean that theology was in any sense dispensable. In an age of doubt and scepticism, Leitch continued, every individual needed to understand the basis of his faith, and the minister had a special responsibility in that regard. But 'theology, regarded merely as a science, is only a branch of a liberal education, and whether taught through the press or the divinity hall, should form a part of the training of every well educated man.' The minister, on the other hand, studied theology in order that he might apply it, 'and the grand aim of the hall is to train the student to the practice of this art. When this is overlooked, the scientific teaching of the hall may only encumber instead of aiding a minister when he enters on the pastorate.' Nor was it enough to learn the principles of homiletics or pastoral theology. 'Besides the art of preaching, skill is required in visiting the sick, dealing with cases of conscience, conducting prayer-meetings and managing Sabbath schools, missionary societies and other benevolent schemes ... students should, as far as possible, be trained to the performance of the actual duties.'

Leitch then turned to the example of medicine to illustrate his meaning.

Scientific lectures are delivered by the professors in the medical faculty, but they would be comparatively of little value if this were all. The science is given, only that a practical training may be based upon it. The hospital, the laboratory, the dissecting and operating rooms, are open to the student, that he may actually practise the science which is taught him in the lectures. The community would be justly alarmed were it announced, that the medical faculty gave only lectures, and that students were to be licensed to practice who never felt a pulse, mixed a prescription, or assisted at the amputation of a limb. And is it not a still more alarming consideration, that young men should be appointed to the cure of souls who have had no practical training whatever in the art?[60]

Such views, it must be said, were not Leitch's alone; G.M. Grant expressed similar opinions in his own inaugural address as principal of Queen's nearly twenty years later,[61] and they were reflected, less systematically, in the medical journals and the debates over the establishment of a law school. What is important here, however, is that Leitch's analysis leads us beyond the schooling/apprenticeship dichotomy and towards a grasp of the distinctive character of nineteenth-century professional education. The divinity hall is not a place for speculation or arcane research but a training ground for practice. Science is the handmaid of art. Learning how takes priority over learning why. Given this outlook it is not surprising that Leitch could deem not only medicine but law to be an exemplar, that he could see the relationship between a principal and his student-at-law as an educative environment, that he saw no need to draw invidious distinctions between schooling and apprenticeship. The task of a professional as opposed to a liberal education was pre-eminently about learning to practise and not about something else.

The emphasis on the centrality of practice existed in large part because the direction of professional education was lodged firmly in the hands of practitioners. While we consider Blaine Baker's interpretation of nineteenth-century legal education misleading in some respects, we agree with the central thrust of his argument that the Law Society saw itself as an educative institution, and we want to extend his insight to our other professional organizations as well. Clergymen, lawyers, and doctors considered themselves to be members of a *learned* profession, and they organized themselves into self-governing *communities* of the learned, in the same way that the learned men of literature and science presided over the colleges of the ancient universities. One part of their responsibility was the education and socialization of the young towards a common social and professional identity. Thus they set standards of preliminary education reflecting the contemporary ideal of moral and mental culture, established professional programs of study, examined their candidates at regular intervals, and pronounced them fit not only to practise a craft but to become full members of a learned profession.

In the twentieth century we have gradually become accustomed to the notion of schools and universities performing all these tasks. The role of the professional organization in education has receded, surrendering much of its influence, if not all of its formal powers, to the school. Though we will touch on the beginnings of that transition in a later chapter, the process by which the idea of a community of the learned has narrowed down from the profession as a whole to its schools and schoolmen is worth a book in itself. In the mid-nineteenth century, in any case, it was different.

Not even the Presbyterian ministry was prepared to abdicate its *academic* responsibilities to the colleges it had itself created. After six years of study in arts and theology at Queen's, the graduating class of 1885 'appeared before the examining committee of the Kingston Presbytery to be taken on trial for licence.' All of the candidates wrote 'six papers, one hour for each – no orals, on Latin, Greek, Hebrew, Church History, Philosophy and Theology.' People might reasonably ask, remarked the student editor of the *Queen's College Journal*, 'why it is that the church recommends an entrant for the ministry to take as full a literary course as possible, but after he has done so it gives him no credit for having passed such an examination in that course. Why not take his college certificates as sufficient evidence of his knowledge in literary subjects?'[62] The editor thought it a sensible argument, as indeed he did in the case of the dual set of examinations medical students faced – from both the university and the CPSO.[63]

The fact remained, however, that the presbytery was the arbiter and not the college. Even the purely literary elements of the theologue's curriculum were set by Synod: it was not an arts *or* theology degree that was required for matriculation into theology, but certain literary courses prescribed by Synod. For Presbyterians, in other words, the church and not the university made a minister, bestowing the recognition that an ordinand had won not just his spiritual but his academic spurs as well. For that very reason, large numbers of theology students never bothered to 'graduate' from arts, and that is true of *most* students in theology, at Queen's at least.[64] One presented a set of course 'tickets' or a testimonial statement from the college authorities to the synod as proof that their requirements had been met, and that is what counted rather than the degree.

The role of the professional community in nurturing its young was made palpable by the active engagement of its members in the task of education itself. Theological professors were clergymen who were also leading members of synods and presbyteries and who, in many cases, retained full or partial responsibility for local congregations. Medical instructors were engaged in private practice. Lectures during 'term' were offered by leading barristers. A law student's master was, first and foremost, a practitioner. The Benchers, the Medical Council, the presbytery or synod which regulated studies and examined students consisted of practitioners. The task of teaching, interpreting, or writing about law, theology, or medicine, in other words, was not relegated to a distinct caste of academics who had special credentials or whose chief distinguishing characteristic was their distance from the routines of professional life itself. The nineteenth-century model of professional education, then, was based on learning from the exemplary *practitioner*, in whatever particular context that learning took place.[65]

9
Making Careers, Making Money, Making a Place

Just as professional education is a preparation for work, so it is but one stage of a more extended career path shaped first within the confines of the family and then drawing its bearings from the cumulative impact of schooling, religion, and the other formative influences of youth. Beyond that, it stretches on into adulthood as young people embark on careers, meet success or failure, establish their place in society, and graduate from neophyte to seasoned practitioner. We would like to know a great deal more than we do about the nature of these career paths and the forces that influenced them.[1] In this chapter, however, we have limited ourselves to three aspects that are of special relevance to other themes we are pursuing in this book. One of these follows on directly from the preceding chapter, and focuses on a critical moment in an individual's future: once a young man had completed his education and received a licence to practise, how did he actually launch a professional career? How, in other words, did he obtain a job or attract enough clients to pay the rent? Second, we want to give some attention to income and wealth. What could professional men expect to receive by way of recompense for the jobs they did, and how did that compare with incomes of others in their communities? Finally, we will examine the social complexion of our three learned professions in order to situate the making of careers and incomes within the social structure of nineteenth-century Ontario.

FOR THE CLERGYMAN, the process of establishing himself was relatively unproblematic: the distinctive characteristic of the clerical career was sponsorship, from the outset, by his own denomination. Having met the intellectual and spiritual qualifications demanded by the churches, the young minister was assigned to a job by the Anglican bishop or the Methodist Conference. Presbyterians could accept a call from an individual congregation or take an assignment from the Home Mission Committee. In either case, there was the expectation of salaried employment from the beginning of their careers through the auspices of a sponsoring organization. The price of such security was that, in the main, the young took on the toughest jobs with the lowest salaries: organizing congregations in new communities or ministering to widely scattered communicants in the countryside. Here they tested their talents, honed their preaching and pastoral skills, and learned the intricacies of mobilizing the enthusiasm and loyalties of the laity. Some, through incapacity or inertia, would never escape their initial circumstances. But after this first posting, most could expect to find jobs in the more settled villages, towns, and cities.

Once again, Donald McKerracher provides a good example. After completing his studies at Knox in 1875, he received calls from three country congregations in southern Ontario. In at least two cases they came from churches where he had first proved his capacities as a Sunday preacher during his student days, a typical means of making contacts for a first job.[2] For his own reasons, however, he opted to return, at a lower salary, to the Lakehead, where he had spent two summers as a student missionary. By 1880 his congregation had become self-sustaining, had constructed its own building, and had transformed itself from the object of mission work to a contributor to it. McKerracher himself had also established his reputation in the community at large and was elected to the school board in 1879.[3] Despite his success at the Lakehead, he did not stay very long, accepting a call to Wallaceburg in 1881.[4] He was not offered much in the way of additional salary, but now, raising a family, he was undoubtedly attracted by the advantages of a more settled community, and release from the rigours of missionary work beyond the Lakehead as well. He died shortly after moving to Wallaceburg; had he survived, he might have looked forward to at least one more call, to a larger church with an improved salary.

In a rough way, then, clerical careers were organized around seniority: one began at the bottom, but experience and industry led gradually to promotion. There had always been something of this pattern – ministers moving from missionary work to a rectory, from a country congregation or circuit to a more settled urban community. But the constricted salaries imposed by dependence on small congregations made upward mobility a necessity. Only the single man could afford to live on $400 or $500 a year, and only the young and fit could sustain the rigours of a back-country pastorate. As ministers married, began families, and aged, they inevitably sought posts offering more congenial surroundings and working conditions.

Though this may have been the most common pattern for ministerial careers throughout the century, there was another which short-circuited the seniority principle. Some young men of special education or talent, the latter including unusual pizazz in the pulpit, were assigned or called, from the beginning of their careers, to large, wealthy congregations or to a leadership role in their church. Egerton Ryerson was still in his mid-twenties when he made his reputation among Methodists by taking on John Strachan, and was editor of the *Christian Guardian* before he turned thirty. William Cochrane was called at a relatively young age to Brantford by a congregation who not only wanted but could well afford a man with a more sophisticated theological education than Ontario had to offer at the time, and one who had won his spurs, not on the local missionary field or in a rural pastorate, but in a city church in New Jersey. Nathanael Burwash is another example. 'Newburgh, Belleville, Toronto and Hamilton,' writes Marguerite Van Die, 'were all unusually prestigious stations for a young man just entering the ministry, and undoubtedly they indicate both respect for the young Burwash's abilities and the care with which the Stationing Committee of the Wesleyan Methodist Church was placing her college-educated ministers, still a relatively scarce commodity at the time.'[5] Both kinds of career patterns, in any case, illustrate the special role of the organization as the setting within which young ministers began their work.

THE NEOPHYTE DOCTOR or lawyer had no such advantages. In these fee-for-service occupations, a practice had to be carved out in the marketplace, and building a successful one was an uncertain venture. There may well have been any number of ways this challenge was met in nineteenth-century Ontario, but various forms of sponsorship were of critical importance: they paralleled the role of the organization in clerical careers and helped to shield the young from the full and potentially crushing weight of the marketplace.

First, there was the role of family and kin, above all the professional partnership between father and son, elder and younger brother, uncle and nephew. George Duck made a place for his brother Henry in the former's Chatham law firm.[6] One future president of the Canadian Medical Association joined his father in a practice near Selkirk, Ontario, in the late 1830s and then inherited it when the latter died.[7] There are many similar examples in both occupations: most recently Elizabeth Bloomfield has chronicled the remarkable number of family law firms in Guelph and Berlin.[8] Even when they worked at different jobs, fathers and brothers could play critical roles in helping beginners establish themselves. One way was a straightforward gift or loan of money to see them through the early years. Writing to his father, a successful Carleton Place merchant, in 1869, John Gemmill informed him that 'law has been very dull since I last saw you, indeed I may say I have done nothing at all since then but sit in my office without having a single man to visit me. Had it not been for your allowance I should have been in an awkward fix for money.'[9] Family was useful in other ways as well. Contemplating practice in the village of Almonte, the younger Gemmill remarked that 'I suppose you will be able to put a good deal of business in my way now that I am going into the same County as yourself.'[10] W.H. Bowlby of Berlin noted in 1858 that though his office had been open only two months, 'I am doing extremely well here through introductions from my brother Dr. D.S. Bowlby and other friends but soon I shall be independent.'[11]

Beyond the family there were other forms of sponsorship. One could, for example, enter a partnership with some other established practitioner. As an articled clerk, Angus Cattanach had sufficiently impressed Adam Crooks that the latter offered him a junior partnership immediately after Cattanach's call to the bar in 1859; though tempted by better money in Hamilton, Cattanach, in turn, jumped at the opportunity because he thought that 'Hamilton is a doomed place since the completion of the Grand Trunk Railway.'[12] One young doctor, uncertain about the future of his country medical practice, was advised by W.T. Aikins to become a junior partner to the ailing Dr Morrison in Toronto: 'If you go to Dundas or Peterboro, you, unaided, have to work yourself up, here you obtain at once the nucleus of a practice; the good will and assistance of those connected with our school ... together with the other advantages necessarily connected with our city as it is and will be.'[13]

Established professional men could help younger colleagues in other ways as well. Thomas Benson concluded his articles with Adam Wilson, who, by the late 1850s, was not only one of Toronto's leading lawyers but the city's mayor, and when other prominent lawyers consulted Wilson about a junior partner he was quick to recommend Benson as a prime candidate.[14] In his reminiscences, James Richardson gives this account of his early experience in the late 1840s:

Business was, as it always is, slow in coming ... By good chance Dr. Rolph was called to attend a lady named Ritchie, out in the country beyond Mastquatah, the residence of Mr. William Baldwin. It was night and Dr. R. declining to go recommended me. It was a case of puerperal convulsion and very severe. I succeeded in saving her life, and made the acquaintance of Mr. Baldwin.

Dr. Widmer had been his medical attendant but was getting feeble, and I became Mrs. B's doctor. In a comparatively short time I secured a fair practice and was doing well indeed, when the Professorship of Anatomy became vacant.[15]

Nurturing the right political connections seems to have been of particular importance to young lawyers. John A. Macdonald, for example, gave Robert Harrison a powerful drawing card in negotiating his first partnership by offering him an agency for Crown business.[16] Wrote John Gemmill to his father about the nomination of the Hon. Malcolm Cameron as candidate for Lanark South in 1869, 'Although not a great admirer of the old gentleman I intend keeping on the right side of him with an eye to the future. He can always throw professional business in the way of a young fellow.'[17] Most young doctors might not have had the background to exploit such connections, nor was it as pertinent to their work. But a good marriage might open the door to a new social circle, and being closely identified with a particular denomination or fraternal organization helped as well.[18]

Not all young men had access to the kinds of patronage and sponsorship we have described thus far. And there was, in any case, always one other way to start a career: ride off into the sunset by horse or to the end of the track, find a new community, hang up your shingle, and wait for the clients to appear at your door. 'At the age of thirty-six I was now legally qualified to study my Profession upon living people,' wrote Dr Peter Macdonald of his experience in the early 1870s. 'I purchased a horse and buggy, on credit of course as I had no money, and drove off north [from London] to espy the land ... I made my way to a small hamlet ... upon the banks of a river that flowed into Lake Huron.' Initially the place looked unpromising but he

took a stroll to see and be seen ... I called at the only drug store and had a chat with the proprietor about my intention to locate. He gave me strong encouragement and held out fair prospects for me. While chatting with the druggist, a few village people dropped in and I was introduced as a prospective doctor ... Each dropped a word of encouragement and appeared kindly disposed to my coming. The following day being bright and sunny I made a tour of the village, meeting and conversing with not a few and making enquiries as to the prospects of growth of the hamlet for the future.

Assured that a railway was about to be built, 'I nailed my shingle above the door and thus announced to the public that a new doctor had come to spend his fortune among them.' In the first two months he had little success, but on 1 July he made a rousing patriotic speech at a community celebration. 'After this day my medical stock went up in the market very rapidly ... My third month's earnings was three times as much as the two former months together.'[19]

Now we quite like this account of how to succeed without really trying; still, it is autobiography written long after the event, and there are other surviving reminiscences which tell a very different story of the difficulties of carving out a practice when some reservoir of sponsorship could not be tapped.[20] Yet there were at least some other doctors who proceeded in a similar way. Thomas Walton, an experienced ship's surgeon, tired of languishing in British ports between jobs, emigrated to Upper Canada in the 1860s and also struck out into the bush, locating himself first at Trout Lake and then in Parry Sound, apparently without any help from anyone.[21]

We remain cautious, nonetheless, about how common such experiences actually were. Consider a counter-example. In 1879, T.S.T. Smellie arrived in Port Arthur and established himself as one of that community's early medical practitioners. If only his initial advertisements had survived, one might conclude that his story was much like Walton's or Macdonald's; in fact it was quite different. Smellie was the son of a prominent Presbyterian clergyman, his brother was a barrister, and his sister married the minister of one of Toronto's largest and most respectable congregations.[22] Thus he had no shortage of good connections, and they in turn had good connections of their own. Intent on improving his prospects in life, Smellie exploited that network, consulting a clerical acquaintance who in turn contacted Donald McKerracher in Port Arthur, and the latter not only encouraged Smellie to come but apparently ensured that his name would be known in the community when he arrived.[23] Smellie, then, did not simply ride off into the sunset to seek his fortune; indeed, his story has more in common with the literature on the 'chain-migration' of families and individuals in nineteenth-century Ontario. True, he took risks; he was prepared to rough it in a new place and grow up with the country. But he did not, in any literal sense, strike out into the unknown.

In emphasizing the importance of the various forms of sponsorship, we are not denigrating the role of competence or skill in the making of professional careers. James Richardson did not build a practice because he was sponsored by Rolph but because he was successful when Rolph offered him an opportunity. The same might be said of young lawyers, whatever their initial advantages.[24] Skill alone, however, also created its own opportunities. Faced with a medical 'muff' who lacked the confidence even to attempt 'the plainest and simplest operation' in midwifery, Thomas Walton was able to establish his reputation among the people of Parry Sound simply by his greater self-confidence in his own skills, while the muff eventually left town.[25] To establish a practice, then, young professionals needed their skills. But, in a fee-for-service occupation, technical accomplishments also had to be *marketed*, and the risks of failure for the neophyte were substantially mitigated if one or another kind of sponsorship could be drawn on to attract a clientele among whom a reputation for competence could be built.

Beyond sponsorship and competence there was one other important ingredient in success, and that was location. Though it was less important if one entered a partnership, even then it mattered: Cattanach, as we have seen, turned down a better starting salary in Hamilton because he could see no future in the place. For a solo practitioner, location was critical. One had to begin where the competition from established men was not so great as to absorb all the paying customers, or where, at least, the promise of a growing population allowed room for one more practitioner. John Gemmill initially rejected Almonte, for example, because an experienced lawyer had advised him 'that Almonte not being a County town the business to be done is not large, in fact would hardly pay two practicing.'[26] Henry Orton, finding the town practice in Guelph already sequestered by a successful forerunner, had to begin in the nearby countryside or leave for somewhere else.[27] Not only was Smellie reluctant to risk his fortune in one of the towns or cities 'waiting for practice which may never come,' he was also nervous about not getting to Port Arthur quickly enough. 'Shortly after writing you the last time,' he fretted to McKerracher, 'I heard that a Dr. Campbell of Stratford had been in Duluth on his way towards the Landing ... I have been somewhat anxious to hear more about him, because considering the limited population of the District and ... not being able to go to Prince Arthur's Landing at once, I am afraid that the ground may be fully occupied before I arrive.'[28]

Even with the right location, and other advantages besides, beginning practice could be difficult. Patients or clients came slowly. Doctors had to work hard making the night calls others would not take, while lawyers had to settle for the small business that better-established practitioners passed by. One could settle in a place where there was work enough for the young practitioner but no certain promise of growth.[29] One could enter the wrong partnership and find oneself saddled with a ne'er-do-well or a drunk.[30] Mobility rates are not simply a measure of failure in nineteenth-century Ontario, but they are that as well. Of the twenty-six doctors in Hamilton in 1851, fewer than a third remained a decade later;[31] and of fifty-five doctors we have located in the census records for Brantford between 1851 and 1891, only nineteen, or about a third, persisted a decade or more. Lawyers in Brantford did somewhat better; still, from one census year to the next, only about half remained.

BUT SUPPOSING some degree of success was achieved, what did that mean in terms of income or material prospects? Evaluating nineteenth-century incomes or wages is a difficult task because the sources are scattered, scarce, and problematic. All that is as true for professional men as others, and especially so for doctors and lawyers. With clergymen, however, the task is made easier: not only were salaries a subject of interminable debate in the clerical press, but they were also regulated to some degree by the churches themselves. Minimum stipends and congregational contributions were usually set by synods or conferences; 'allowances,' including such things as 'horse-keep' or house-rent, were often provided; and though far from complete before the last quarter of the nineteenth century, to one extent or another financial records were collected and in some cases published annually.

We have already touched upon Methodist salaries during the middle decades of the nineteenth century in an earlier chapter, suggesting that a married man with two children could expect to receive £75 ($300) plus rent and other allowances, and that by the late 1860s the figure had risen to something like $600.[32] (The Canadas adopted a dollar currency in the late 1850s, and for purposes of comparison the conventional multiplier is $4 to the pound.) Initially at least, the clergymen of the Kirk and the Church of England could expect to do better, but, over time, much of that difference began to wash out. In the early 1850s nearly all the ministers of the two 'established' churches received a minimum of £150 a year from the Clergy Reserves Fund, and at least one Anglican clergyman with a country congregation considered that to be a typical total income for those based in the smaller towns and the countryside.[33] With the secularization of the reserves, commuting Anglican ministers continued to receive £150, and their brethren in the Kirk £112, plus whatever they could extract from their own congregations. Where such clergymen served wealthy congregations in the larger towns or cities, this might mean double or triple that amount, but, overall, congregational supplements were not great, in the 1850s and early 1860s at least.[34]

New clergymen, however, had no vested rights to a share in the commutation fund, and as they were added to the churches' rolls, either as missionaries or as pastors of settled congregations, significant disparities of income began to emerge.[35] Thus, for both the Kirk and the Church of England, there were those who lived near the bottom of the stipend scale – the young, the country pastors, and the missionaries –

and those who were substantially better off – those senior enough to be eligible for commutation funds, and those especially who also served wealthy congregations. The average stipend for the Kirk, nonetheless, which had stood at £163 (or about $650) in 1856, had risen to only $850 by 1872.[36] Moreover, the minimum stipend remained at the 1860 figure of $400 until 1873, when it was finally raised to $600.[37] Over the same period the figures for Anglicans tend to be only a little higher, and for the Free Church a little lower.[38]

As the sources improve in the later nineteenth century, we can obtain a much better fix on clerical incomes, including the differences between denominations, but, more important, on the range of salaries and the disparities which existed between town and country, young and old. Even in the cities these disparities were marked. The Toronto *Telegram* reported in 1889 that the average clerical income in that city was, for Anglicans, $1,000; for Methodists, $1,500; and for Presbyterian clergymen, $1,750. The reason why the figure for Anglicans was lowest, it explained, was that there were so many rectory assistants, who made low salaries of $600 or $700 a year.[39] Still, at least in the cities, most clergymen could expect to achieve the minimum salary levels set by their denominations. For the province as a whole, it was a different matter. In the 1870s and early 1880s, the Presbyterians, for example, were supposed to receive a minimum stipend of $600, and that was raised to $750 plus a manse in 1883.[40] But even these minimum figures were commonly breached, and the annual statistics record large income differentials between ministers in different presbyteries, depending on whether the latter were predominantly urban or rural, northern or southern. Kingston Presbytery, for instance, included St Andrew's Church and other large city congregations, but it also incorporated 'Tweed and Fuller,' 'Stirling and West Huntington,' and the mission station of Maynooth. Thus stipends in 1879–80 ranged from $300 to $1,800; they improved slightly over the next two decades, but by 1900 over a third of the clergy still received only $750 from all sources – less than the minimum at that point, though most ministers now lived in a manse – while the top stipend was $3,000.[41]

Stipends of Methodist and Anglican clergymen are harder to calculate because the printed figures do not always include various supplements and allowances. For Methodists the minimum salary was raised in 1874 to $300 plus board, fuel, rent, horse-keep and incidental expenses, for married ministers ($250 for ordained single men);[42] the *Christian Guardian* estimated that this translated to a salary scale of $800 and $750 respectively.[43] This was comparable to Presbyterian expectations. But again, there was sometimes a substantial gap between what clergymen were supposed to get and what they actually received. Summing up the situation in 1898, the *Guardian* reported that nine-tenths of ministers in all conferences received less than $1,000, and added that those who made $1,000 to $2,000 in towns or prosperous country circuits lived 'very comfortably,' but, on less than $1,000, they had to 'live carefully to keep out of debt, and do reasonably by their families.'[44]

Though there is occasional anecdotal evidence in private papers and the press, we have located no comparable sources for doctors and lawyers. We know that some lawyers, for example, became wealthy men, and a few doctors did too.[45] It is also reasonably clear that even the 'stars' of the clerical profession made far, far less than their legal equivalents.[46] Still, that tells us little or nothing about two critical questions: what *representative* differences might exist among the three occupations, and, more important, how did professional men compare with others in their community? In an attempt to tackle these issues, we have collected the census and assessment records from 1861 to 1891 for one community, and have examined the relationship between the assessed wealth of our three professions and the rest of the population. The community is Brantford, a county seat and a rapidly growing commercial and industrial centre throughout the latter half of the nineteenth century.

This sort of analysis has its own defects, but we leave a discussion of these to the appendix; the general reader is warned, nevertheless, that some of what follows is technical in nature and, more important, that we are talking here only about ratepayers. Large numbers of people who lived and worked in Brantford were never placed on the assessment rolls, among other reasons, because they were too poor. Thus when we talk about differences among ratepayers, we are already dealing, in the main, with the more prosperous. Moreover, we are not describing incomes but assessed wealth, which is both cumulative and heavily weighted towards real estate. Nor can we separate income earned from professional work, narrowly defined, as opposed to other activities – an important distinction, especially for lawyers and doctors. James Langstaff earned a comfortable income from his medical practice; he made himself a wealthy man through real estate speculation and other entrepreneurial activities, as did so many other professional men.[47] Despite these reservations, however, we think the close study of one community is at least some help in understanding the economic standing of professional men in nineteenth-century Ontario.

In Brantford most doctors and lawyers were in comfortable or prosperous circumstances throughout the period, and generally better off than the average assessed ratepayer (who was already, because of the skewing effect of averaged wealth, in the wealthier part of the population). In 1861 doctors and lawyers accounted for 2 per cent of those assessed; they held 5 per cent of the wealth. This imbalance continued throughout the rest of the century; in 1891 they formed 1 per cent of the ratepayers and held 4 per cent of the wealth. In other words, they always had more than their share of prosperity. And that, moreover, did not change much over time, suggesting that Michael Katz's 'structure of inequality' which he identified in Hamilton in 1851–71 held true in Brantford right to the 1890s.[48]

Brantford's doctors and lawyers, indeed, appear to have surpassed its businessmen in maintaining more than their share of wealth right through the second half of the century. In his study of the town's business community, David Burley has found that in 1851 it held over 90 per cent of assessed personal property and income, and half the assessed real estate. Although businessmen continued to form exactly the same percentage of the labour force, by 1881 those proportions had dropped to 72 per cent and 36 per cent respectively. This indicates, Burley suggests, that more people were earning assessable incomes and were accumulating property, and that the increase in assessment of those employed 'probably reflected a significant increase in the incomes of working people.'[49] We will return to this point to examine the effect of increasing general wealth on the perceptions of individual doctors, lawyers, and clergy about their own economic standing. But, in the aggregate, no real decline in the share of economic returns seems to have occurred for doctors and lawyers. Though, like businessmen, they formed the same percentage of all ratepayers throughout the period, the proportion they claimed of both real estate and personal property remained virtually unchanged (from 1861 to 1891, 3–4 per cent and 5 per cent respectively). Thus, *as a group*, these practitioners did not experience any relative decline in their share of the town's wealth.

There were differences between the two occupations: lawyers generally, as one might expect, tended to be wealthier than doctors. As one might also expect, within each occupation, by and large, the older the practitioner, the greater his wealth.[50] Over time, however, and as their numbers increased, the *range* of wealth within the two occupations tended to become greater. This may have been in part the result of a natural correlation of increasing wealth with age, as a core of settled professionals built up their earnings and investments over their lifetimes. But the expanding number of new practitioners also accentuated that wealth differential. Over the period 1861-91, the average assessment for both occupational groups lagged behind the increase reported by the wealthiest.[51] Thus the average assessment for doctors rose some three thousand dollars, from $1,356 in 1861 to $4,335 in 1891; for lawyers it rose approximately four thousand dollars, from $1,800 in 1861 to $5,953 in 1891. But the *highest* assessment reported by any doctor jumped by about eight thousand dollars between 1861 and 1891; for lawyers by twice that figure. It seems clear, then, that more practitioners were enjoying greater wealth, but that the range for both doctors and lawyers increasingly grew wider.

Finally, here, what of the Brantford clergy? Once again there were considerable disparities, both within and between denominations. For example, in 1871, James Usher, a sixty-three-year-old Anglican minister, was assessed for $900, and two Methodist clergymen, one a Wesleyan Methodist and the other an Episcopal Methodist, for about the same amount, though both were twenty years younger than Usher. But a fifty-nine-year-old Primitive Methodist clergyman tallied only $500, while a forty-two-year-old Congregational minister had just $100 of assessed wealth. As a group, however, clerical assessments were consistently lower on average than those of doctors or lawyers, and that was true for each census year. In Brantford, then, the clergy appear to be the poor brothers among the learned professions.

But how poor compared with the rest of their contemporaries? In 1861 seven out of ten clergymen on the assessment rolls ranked as poor to middling, and like proportions persisted in 1871 and 1881.[52] In 1891, however, ten out of fourteen clergymen reported above-average wealth. A remarkable reversal, the reader muses, provoked perhaps by a laity suddenly ravished by the spirit? A change in the tax laws, we reply. By 1891 a major exemption on clerical incomes had been removed, one that had masked the full extent of their incomes in earlier years. Overall, our Brantford clergymen might remain far less well off than their peers in law or medicine; but compared with most of their contemporaries in the latter half of the nineteenth century, they were still a relatively prosperous lot. The same conclusions, moreover, emerge from a study we conducted using the 1861 census and assessment records of five southwestern Ontario towns (including Brantford) ranging in population from 700 to 6,200. While there were 'poor' doctors and lawyers and 'prosperous' clergymen in all five communities, clergymen as a group ranked far below doctors or lawyers in economic standing, though well above the bulk of all ratepayers. We reiterate, nonetheless, a point made earlier: in many urban areas, clergymen were relatively well remunerated; in the rural countryside or in hamlets or small villages, the record is very different indeed.

TO ASK HOW WELL professional men were recompensed for their work is one question; to ask how or when they were paid is another. For one thing, they received their incomes at infrequent intervals. The Society for the Propagation of the Gospel paid its missionaries annually, and after mid-century ministers' salaries tended to be paid semi-annually or quarterly. Doctors sometimes received immediate payment for a procedure, and they were likely to demand it from transients or 'strangers.'[53] James Langstaff most commonly received immediate payment in the case of dental extractions, Jacalyn Duffin notes, 'perhaps because of the excruciating nature of toothache, juxtaposed to its simple solution and low fee.'[54] But, in the main, doctors billed their patients annually. By the 1860s and 1870s, some city doctors rendered their accounts twice a year, but even as late as 1875 the editor of the *Lancet* took it for granted that annual billing was 'usually' the case, urban doctors rendering their accounts in January and February, and country doctors after the autumn harvest.[55]

There was good reason for this. Professional men, as much as farmers and merchants, were enmeshed in an economy built upon long lines of credit.[56] They rendered their accounts and got paid for their services at those intervals when farmers had sold their crops, and when grocers or wholesale merchants had settled their accounts with debtors or creditors. What that meant, in turn, was that professional men, with the exception of the eminently successful (and not even they were necessarily exempt), were either always in debt or scrambling to keep up appearances. And no less important, they were dependent on being paid what was owed them so they could meet their own credit deadlines.

In the later nineteenth century, there is evidence that quarterly or monthly billing was becoming the norm in urban areas, and clerical salaries were following a similar pattern. Yet traditional practices declined slowly, especially in the countryside.[57] Even as late as 1893, a Presbyterian committee could report that

in 25 of our congregations the people seem satisfied to make an annual settlement with their pastor, – long credit and partial payments prevailing. The number of such cases is rapidly decreasing, and many Presbyterians rejoice to say that the annual settlement is a thing of the past. In 146 congregations the people try to get square with their pastoral obligations twice a year. *Quarterly* payments, sometimes in advance, are made by 308 congregations. Payments in *monthly* instalments is the practice in 158 congregations, while in 5 congregations payment is made *weekly*.[58]

Even then, professional men could not assume that debts would get paid on time or in some cases at all. For the country clergy, 'deficiencies' – the gap between the salary promised and the amount actually paid – were a common occurrence. Sometimes there were legitimate reasons for deficiencies and sometimes not: a bad harvest or unexpectedly low crop prices, on the one hand, or negligence and niggardliness, on the other. But whatever the reason, and especially given their small salaries and constrained circumstances, the shortfall was a constant source of bitter complaint throughout the century from Anglican, Presbyterian, and Methodist clergymen alike.[59]

Virtually all the primary and secondary sources agree that doctors billed for far greater amounts than they ever collected. Over the course of Langstaff's practice, Duffin remarks, 'fewer than half the debts [accounts] were paid in full,' and Roland and Rubashewsky's careful analysis of Harmaunus Smith's medical accounts tells a similar story.[60] When they were paid, in full or in part, it was often years after the service had been rendered. 'You are aware that young practitioners cannot afford to lose accounts like these,' Thomas Benson wrote a client in 1861 regarding a debt of some £25–30, 'and I must proceed to collect ... The cases are now nearly five years old and I cannot wait any longer.'[61] Nor was it only a problem for the neophyte. By the 1870s Benson was well established: he had his share of corporate accounts, could demand advances before taking on a case, and could afford to be choosy about his clients. Still, accounts accumulated for months and years, with payments being made in instalments rather than in full.[62]

When doctors or lawyers didn't get paid, they could write off a debt, discount it, settling for much less than the full amount,[63] or they could sue. The last, however, was not a straightforward option. Aside from the costs involved, it left the question of what constituted a legitimate or reasonable fee in the hands of judges, who might or might not decide in favour of the defendant or so reduce the cost of the bill that a suit ceased to be worth the effort or money involved.[64] Indeed, one of the reasons doctors sought (and won) the right to set tariffs of fees in 1874 was in order to establish recognized benchmarks for judicial decisions. But suits carried other risks as well. Legal action against a local family could not only earn its enmity, and thus cost a professional man a patient or client, but also 'make an unfavorable impression on the community' and thus threaten the viability of the practice itself.[65]

In the second half of the century at least, we have found no instances of lawyers being paid in kind or services, and this may reflect the more prosperous and urban character of their clientele. Cash payments were probably the norm for the city doctor as well. But country clergymen and country doctors took it for granted that some of their income would be in kind. In his first few years in practice, Henry Orton remarked, he rarely received more than £30 or £40 a year in cash, the rest of it coming in kind.[66] Harmaunus Smith, too, was often paid in goods and services.[67] Before mid-century at least, payment in services could also work in reverse. Called upon to do his statutory labour, one southwestern Ontario doctor arrived at the site with his 'tooth instruments ... I offered, if any of the men had decayed teeth, to extract them, and that they should do my statute labour, and in that way pay me, which was at once agreed to. I operated on several men, put up my instruments and went home, all parties being satisfied with the exchange of work, and I was perfectly contented that my statute labour was to be done without any outlay of money, which was a very scarce commodity in those days.'[68]

Being paid in services or in kind was a satisfactory settlement of accounts so long as professional men could put these forms of remuneration to work in the shape of horse-feed or household consumables, or barter them to pay off a debt owed the grocer. Still, clergymen in particular complained that goods were too often overvalued, and that in any case most of their expenses had to be paid in cash, something that farm folk didn't understand. 'The people, at any rate, in country places,' wrote one Presbyterian minister in 1857,

are not in the habit of purchasing the necessaries of life. Almost everything they use in their families is the produce of their own farms. They are not in the habit of paying money, as their Ministers have to do for everything which is used in the family. They look upon a hundred pounds as an immensely large sum, and think that it should go a great way to support a family. They are surprised when you speak of a Minister with a hundred pounds as being very inadequately supported. But the truth is, if they estimated the price of every article consumed by themselves or their families, they would soon find that their own expenditure was far above that of the Pastor, whom they looked upon 'as passing rich' not with £40 a year but with eighty or a hundred.[69]

Beyond clerical salaries and patient or client fees, professional men commonly found other ways of making money. We are not speaking here of those who made big money as entrepreneurs or real estate speculators but of more modest income supplements. When doctors, for example, wrote a prescription to be filled by a particular druggist, it appears that they usually expected to receive back a percentage of the dispensing fee.[70] In the late nineteenth century, health examinations for life insurance policies became a substantial business: a doctor could make more per certificate than he charged for an ordinary visit, and carry out the examination in his office to boot.[71] Some doctors owned drugstores or shared their ownership with brothers or fathers.[72] Lawyers often held local agencies for life insurance companies.[73] There were also civil appointments which brought small salaries or fees: the township superintendent of schools before 1871, the coroner, or the jail surgeon. Clergymen, especially from mid-century onwards, were generally expected to be disengaged from any secular preoccupation, including their traditional role as teachers in the grant-aided schools. But Anglican and Presbyterian clergymen continued to teach private pupils in their homes, tutoring youngsters in the elements of a classical education or cramming them for the various university and professional matriculation examinations, and they could also count on wedding fees to add to their incomes.[74]

Clergymen were also the beneficiaries of a singular income supplement, the congregational gift or donation party. It is remarkable how often one comes across the former in diaries and the clerical press: gifts of 'a sleigh and robes,' 'fur coat and cap,' 'a well-filled purse of money,' 'a pulpit gown,' a sewing machine for the minister's wife, 'a handsome new cutter, two comfortable robes, and a pair of elegant doeskin gauntlet gloves for driving,' 'two pigs.'[75] Such free-will offerings were, so far as we can see, much appreciated; the donation party, as a means of supplementing an income or making up deficiencies in a salary, evoked more equivocal feelings. Our Anglican clergyman, J.F. Lundy, admired the institution, and left us a vivid description as well. He himself had been invited to one such affair, and 'took a few books as gifts – about 7 the people began to arrive with their presents and about 150 people came – we had music and conversation and some games. The donations to their pastor amounted in value to about $125, there being $52 in cash ... there were provisions of all sorts – Beef, Pork, Poultry, flour, Sugar, cakes, dresses, gloves, Cordwood, Books and a ring.'[76] But such events could also invite the condescension of charity, implying that a minister and his family were beholden to the good will and generosity of a congregation rather than the rightful recipients of a respectable salary. After attending one donation party for a Baptist colleague in Brantford, William Cochrane noted in his diary that 'the more I see of ... [them], the more I loathe them. It is a mean contemptible way of paying ministers what is their due.'[77]

In detailing the difficulties that professional men had in collecting their fees or earning their livings, we are not making a case that they were peculiarly hard done by. Many others faced the same kind of pressures as well. The economic sanctions that small communities could bring to bear on those who were thought to overcharge or who pursued legal actions in the courts affected grocers as well as doctors. To the farmer afflicted by low prices for his produce or strapped for cash himself, the claims of clergymen and their families might easily appear excessive. And all were trapped in the web of credit and debt which characterized the economy of nineteenth-century Ontario. Professional men, nonetheless, were *also* a part of that economy, and as subject to the constraints it imposed as others of their era and class.

THE PLACE OF professional men in their society can also be illuminated by a review of their social and cultural characteristics. From the *Dictionary of Canadian Biography*, we have gathered data on those professionals who lived in Ontario and who died between 1850 and 1899.[78] Except for clergymen, where it is tautological in any case, the biographical information on religious affiliation is too sporadic to be useful, but it is nearly complete for place of birth. Not surprisingly, of some 250 cases, half were born in Britain – about 55 per cent. There are, however, important differences between occupations. Sixty-six per cent of the clergy were British-born (though for Presbyterian ministers that figure was 90 per cent, whereas for Methodists it was 45 per cent). Virtually all the rest were born in Upper Canada. Sixty per cent of the doctors were born in Britain, 25 per cent in Upper Canada, and 10 per cent in the United States. For lawyers, however, the story is quite different: only 39 per cent were British-born, while 47 per cent came from Upper Canada. Such figures reveal two things: first, the very high percentage of British emigrants, which could not help but give a particular tone and complexion to Upper Canadian professional life throughout the nineteenth century, especially if one considers that many of the Upper Canadian-born would have been raised by British-born parents and thus would have imbibed that cultural ambience as well; and second, the exceptionalism of the law, where the long-standing prohibition against emigrant practitioners 'Canadianized' the occupation far more quickly than medicine or the ministry.

Because the *DCB* is organized by date of death, it presents us with a 'snapshot' of an early generation of professional men, nearly all born in the 1830s or before. Thus, though the Brantford census data tell a similar story in many respects, they also capture change in ways the *DCB* cannot. In 1851 we are still dealing with emigrants: 83 per cent of Brantford's clergy and nearly all its doctors. Only the law is distinctive:

already, more than half the town's lawyers were Canadian-born. Over the succeeding forty years, however, there were some dramatic changes. By 1891, 81 per cent of lawyers and 75 per cent of doctors had been born in this country; theology lagged behind at 59 per cent (and that held true for Anglicans, Presbyterians, and Methodists alike), but even here the same trend is apparent. These shifts were undoubtedly due to the establishment of the colonial universities and medical schools, and to the rapid expansion during the middle decades of the nineteenth century of the grammar (or high) schools, which made local educational facilities widely accessible. Still, they also reflect the effects of the professional equivalent of the protective tariff, first in law and then in medicine. Whatever their own merits, the native-born increasingly had the advantage of living in a society which made it difficult for emigrant professionals, whether from Britain or the United States, to become practitioners in Ontario. Throughout the latter half of the nineteenth century, in any case, the Canadianization of all three professions proceeded steadily, and while the more subtle changes in attitudes and outlook this entailed remain a mystery, one must assume that it would have its impact in a wide variety of ways by the late nineteenth or early twentieth century.

The changing religious affiliations of Brantford's doctors and lawyers are of interest as well. In both 1851 and 1861, they were predominantly Anglican; by 1891 there were as many Methodists among them as Anglicans, and a larger number of other denominations represented besides. While it still did not parallel the distribution to be found among the population as a whole, there was, in other words, a steady broadening out as Anglicanism ceased to be the surrogate for gentry status it had been before mid-century.

Thus far we have been dealing with *all* of Brantford's professional men, whether they stayed in the community for decades or only for a few years. But there are also significant differences between those professional men who did remain and those who did not. A higher proportion of persisters were Anglican; there were more British-born doctors among the persisters, and more Ontario-born lawyers. These cultural characteristics were not representative of either the community at large *or* of all doctors and lawyers. While diversity, in other words, was an increasing characteristic of Brantford doctors and lawyers as a whole, it was much less a characteristic of the persisters, who tended towards homogeneity in religion and birthplace, a form of homogeneity which most resembled the cultural characteristics of the old Upper Canadian gentry class. Though the evidence is not conclusive on this point, moreover, it indicates that our persisters were also wealthier. Thus, we suggest, the persisters constituted an inner circle of professional men, a kind of professional establishment of those with power and influence, who formed one part of an interlocking local élite which included, as well, similarly situated manufacturers and businessmen. Other professional men came and went, living off the pickings the élite passed over, or, having failed to establish a secure place in Brantford, moved on to try their luck elsewhere.

When we turn to social origins, the evidence is harder to get at or seriously compromised. In Brantford we can locate the fathers of just under a third of our professional men, and the former were overwhelmingly from the upper reaches of society – merchants, manufacturers, and professional men themselves. Where we have assessment figures, these reveal men almost uniformly comfortably off or wealthy. And that pattern remains in place to the end of the century: by 1881 or 1891 there was a wider range of occupations among the fathers of professional men, but no substantial change in wealth. Despite the broadening of religious affiliation in the later period, then, there is no evidence here that there was any parallel broadening of the social pool from which professional men were drawn. Too much cannot be made of that conclusion, however, for the evidence itself is biased in its favour. We are in fact counting 'dual persisters,' fathers and sons, and that in turn means we are locating families who remained in Brantford not for one generation but for two. What we suspect, then, is that we are simply recording one more characteristic of our 'professional establishment': sons who settled in Brantford because family and kin would assure them of the contacts and clientele out of which successful practices could be built. David Burley offers a similar conjecture for his persisting businessmen. In both cases cultural and social capital could be exploited that newcomers had no access to.[79]

Another way to approach the question of social background is to draw upon the evidence available in the *DCB*. A father's occupation can be identified for some 150 entries, and, taken as a whole, the fathers were employed in prosperous or prestigious occupations: merchants, manufacturers, and dealers account for a quarter of them; 26 per cent were professional men themselves; another 21 per cent were military officers. Farmer fathers constituted 12 per cent and artisans 5 per cent of the group; in both cases, however, their sons tended to enter the ministry rather than medicine and law. In the case of lawyers and doctors, 70 and 77 per cent, respectively, had fathers who were in professional occupations, merchants, or military officers. The number of farmer fathers falls to 5 and 15 per cent, and of artisans, to 1 per cent and zero. Not all professionals or merchants were wealthy; not all farmers or artisans were poor. But the social background of the professional men who made it into the *DCB* was wildly unrepresentative of the population as a whole.

Once again, however, the *DCB* figures mirror the social world of the Georgian era. Can anything be said about those who entered the professions in the middle or later nineteenth century? The answer is, only indirectly, and by means of a prior question: who was most likely to have access to the schools that prepared students for the professions? In a previous study we have pointed to the steady expansion of the grammar schools in the latter half of the nineteenth century, and suggested that their sheer accessibility throughout the province gave large numbers of boys the opportunity to achieve the matriculation standards required by the various professions. Still, it must be said that the high schools remained predominantly (though never exclusively) the preserve of the middle class.[80] There was probably some broadening of the social pool available for the professions compared with the years before mid-century, but it can hardly be described as equality of access for all of Ontario's young men.

Moreover, one also has to take account of both the opportunity and direct costs of entering a professional occupation. Law students often had to pay premiums for their apprenticeships, and in the case of prestigious firms these could be very large amounts indeed.[81] Beyond that, there were the prohibitions on outside employment during an apprenticeship, and a whole variety of fees to be paid to the Law Society as well.[82] Medical and theological students could work for five or six months between school terms, but they had tuition fees to pay.[83] Additionally, most of them would have to raise the money for boarding in Toronto or Kingston. In that one respect, perhaps, law students had the advantage: most of them could live at home during the period of their apprenticeships, and most of them apparently did, in Brantford at least.[84] Thus there were always substantial economic barriers to entering a professional career. Schools might be accessible and mostly tuition-free. There were scholarships and bursaries, the opportunity to live at home or work for half the year, and, indeed, ample byways routed through the school system itself which allowed a young man to teach for a few years and thus raise the funds necessary to continue his education. The gates were never, in other words, entirely closed to the humble. But cultural and economic capital made it easier, and more common, for those who possessed them to pass through.

IF THE PRECEDING commentary on social background seems murky at best, there is in any case one indisputable conclusion that stands out in all the sources. Doctors begat doctors, lawyers begat lawyers, and, generally, professional men begat sons who became professional men of one sort or another (and daughters who married them). As we have already argued elsewhere, schooling, like money, land, or interest, was one element of what E.P. Thompson has called 'the grid of inheritance' – one form of patrimony a father might bestow on a son or daughter to preserve or advance a family's security, status, or continuity.[85] Anglican and Presbyterian clergymen in Upper Canada, for example, were not by any means wealthy, but they provided many of their sons with a classical education which opened the doors to the professions. Indeed, professional occupations generally were massively overrepresented in the grammar schools and colleges of Upper Canada, as they were elsewhere in the same period.

Having completed their schooling, sons followed in their fathers' footsteps in remarkable numbers. Of our *DCB* entries, 26 per cent had fathers in one of the learned professions; for law it was 29 per cent and for medicine even higher than that. Sensitive, perhaps, to the financial constraints of a childhood spent in the manse, clerical sons followed their fathers' footsteps less frequently, but even here 24 per cent of Anglican and 21 per cent of Presbyterian ministers had fathers who were clergymen. Where we can trace father–son linkages in Brantford, we find figures like the following: six doctors produced five doctor and two lawyer sons; four lawyers produced five sons who became lawyers, plus one doctor. Collectively, of course, more professional men came from non-professional families than the other way round; but the level of occupational (as well as social) reproduction in nineteenth-century Ontario offers an important insight into the nature of the society itself.

Part Two:
Reconstructing Profession

Reconstructing Profession: An Introduction

While professional gentlemen pursued their organizational goals, established their educational institutions, learned how to practise their crafts, and engaged in the making of livings, the occupational structure itself was changing around them. As agricultural prosperity increased during the middle decades of the nineteenth century, it force-fed the growth of domestic manufacturing, commerce, and service industries alike, and thus threw up an expanding non-farm population, concentrated, to be sure, in the growing cities and towns, but also radiating outwards into a host of rising villages and hamlets. Long-established urban occupations grew in size as increasing numbers entered their ranks, and a host of new occupations appeared: wholesalers and importers in the cities, travelling salesmen and retailers in the countryside; real estate agents, surveyors, conveyancers, and auctioneers feeding off rising land values, commercial growth, and the consolidation of farms; bankers, their agents, and their clerks; engineers to build the railways and other great public works; bookkeepers and accountants; artists and musicians; teachers and photographers. More wealth, and a growing population, also encouraged specialization. 'Increasing volumes and the complexities of commerce,' writes Michael Bliss, 'caused general merchants, who had dealt in anything and everything, to start to sort themselves out as retailers or wholesalers, importers or exporters, forwarders, brokers or auctioneers, drygoods or hardware men, grocers or jewellers, or specialists in some other commodity or trade.'[1]

Changes such as these were too vast to be accommodated within traditional conceptions of the social order. Even by mid-century, and especially after that, Upper Canadian society could no longer be tidily divided into a gentry class consisting of a handful of office-holders, professional gentlemen, and wealthy merchants, the natural-born leaders of society, and a largely undifferentiated mass of men below them known throughout the Anglo-American world as 'men of the middling sort' – its artisans and mechanics, yeoman farmers, shopkeepers, dissenting ministers, clerks, and all those other individuals who were neither privileged by wealth and power nor reduced to the penury of wage labour. Some who had hitherto been known simply as artisans became 'manufacturers,' while others lost their independence, becoming skilled employees. Workshops grew larger, and, as they did so, management, clerical, and production functions became more distinct and hierarchically organized. Some farmers consolidated or expanded their holdings in land, becoming increasingly prosperous and respectable; others became tenants or were dispossessed. The children of both fled to the west or to the towns and cities, and if they had been fortunate enough to acquire a little more education than most of their peers, they entered the world of non-manual work in all its manifest varieties. New technologies, organizational changes, and the expansion of capitalist enterprise may have blighted the hopes of many. But the sheer growth of the non-farm, non-manual workforce, along with its increasing differentiation, provided others with new occupational identities and new opportunities to fulfil their economic and social aspirations. As they took advantage of these opportunities, they also became participants in the making of Victorian Ontario's urban middle class.[2] From the late 1840s onwards, it would not only increase its numbers but become steadily more fine-grained, differentiated both vertically and horizontally. Its very expansion would also undermine the certitudes held by an earlier generation of Upper Canadians about the natural ordering of society and about the distribution of prestige within the occupational hierarchy.

The ideal of the professional gentleman was an integral part of the old society and so was the privileged place of the three learned professions in the social order. Inevitably, then, they would be affected by the forces at work in the new society, challenged by an insurgent liberalism determined to pull down the pillars of the *ancien régime*, or eroded by the impersonal pressures of economic and social change. Indeed, we have already begun to chronicle such developments in earlier chapters. There was, for example, the limited but not inconsequential impact of mid-century radicalism, and the gradual shift towards a generic view of the clergyman. Similarly, as law and medicine became more inclusive and homogeneous, they also became different sorts of occupations than before.

But the reorientation of the occupational order under way in the second half of the nineteenth century made many other changes inevitable as well. Just as the power of the colonial gentry would be rivalled and then superseded by such parvenus as the entrepreneur, the promoter, and the manufacturer, so parvenu occupations would arise to vie for a share of the prestige traditionally accorded only to law, medicine, and theology. Competitors of various sorts would threaten the social and economic security of professional men, as would demographic change and the reorganization of commerce. Shifts in the public mood, as significant as those which had brought about disestablishment and the legitimization of the medical sects, would breed criticism of their legal prerogatives and scepticism about the collective esteem they believed was rightfully theirs. Cumulatively, these and other changes would modify the place of the professions in the occupational order, create a different configuration of professional occupations, and begin the process of reconstructing the meaning of 'profession' itself.

THESE, THEN, are the themes that will preoccupy us in the second part of the book. We begin, in the next chapter, with the stories of some 'men of the middling sort' who set out to acquire the legal prerogatives and other accoutrements that would turn them into professional gentlemen. Some were successful, while others failed, or, at least, wound up somewhere else than they intended. Those aspirations and ambitions, however, raise a prior question. How was it even conceivable that such a project might be possible? The skilled artisan who made artificial dentures or designed and built mills and bridges; the druggist, tainted by his association with trade; the common-school master who taught for little more than labourers' wages, boarded around, and hardly knew more than the 'ABCs' himself – how could such individuals, and others like them, aspire to become regularly bred professional men?

On the face of it, the answer was obvious enough: they could not. Yet it had never been as simple or as clear-cut as that. The ideology of Georgian professionalism had never constituted anything like a tightly woven, logically rigorous theory about the nature of the occupational and social structure. It consisted, rather, of a set of quasi-autonomous assumptions about social standing, educational attainments, appropriate economic rewards, and vocational roles, notions only loosely coupled together and admitting enough inconsistency and ambiguity to make the ideal of the professional gentleman much more open-ended than it might at first appear. And these characteristics were exacerbated by the political and social circumstances of a new colony. Thus, especially in Upper Canada, there were always niches of discontinuity embedded in the ideal where claims might be lodged by those eager to improve the reputability of their own occupations.

The ambiguities inherent in the phrase 'professional *gentleman*' provide one good example of how the process could operate. Even in

England, with its aristocracy and a lesser gentry firmly rooted in the land, the definition of a gentleman had long been somewhat ambiguous and was to become even more so during the nineteenth century. For centuries it had identified not only those with landed wealth but those as well who possessed a genteel education and social or political influence, even when they lacked a landed estate.[3] By the eighteenth and early nineteenth centuries, writes George Kitson Clark, 'men and women became less certain of the sufficiency of the simple ideas of a hierarchy of birth and began to supplement and confuse the conception of a gentleman with the attribution of mental and moral qualities.' Since such qualities were not easy to assess directly, however, the test of education came to be important, on the principle that 'the natural instincts of a born gentleman should have been fostered by an appropriately liberal education. Therefore it came to be increasingly assumed that a gentleman would have had the education of a gentleman, a proposition which in time might carry the convenient converse that someone who had the education of a gentleman was likely to be a gentleman. It was a conception,' Kitson Clark adds, 'that was going to be of very great importance in the nineteenth century.'[4]

In Upper Canada, the impact was to be greater still. From the very beginning the dream of establishing a landed aristocracy in the colony had been a chimera. Cut loose from its ties to *landed* wealth, however, the meaning of 'gentleman' was even more open to being 'supplemented and confused' than in England. If any sort of wealth mattered, then successful tradesmen and artisans might claim to be gentlemen.[5] Equally, if the advantages of education alone were to be counted, then so might anyone who had acquired a modicum of the classics in one of the local grammar schools or, better still, in the relatively accessible and cheap colonial colleges. Those who were touched by Methodism or other forms of evangelical religion added yet another ambiguity to its meaning. 'By the end of the late eighteenth century,' write Leonore Davidoff and Catherine Hall about England (and there is no reason to think it shouldn't be applicable to Upper Canada as well), 'the association of gentility with an income and style of life requiring neither mental or manual labour was no longer acceptable to many of the middling ranks. A new claim was asserted, that *salvation* was the mark of gentility, that an artisan's son from a rural backwater who managed to educate himself and become a minister, had as much right to that epithet as an aristocrat.'[6]

And precisely these sorts of connotations rapidly became common currency in mid-century Upper Canada. By the term 'gentleman,' as one piece of boilerplate in the *Upper Canada Law Journal* explained, 'we do not mean merely a gentleman by birth, a man who has ancestors, but a gentleman by *cultivation, in mind, manners and feelings*. A wide range of examination,' the author added, 'would go far to secure this.'[7] A half-century or more earlier, the idea that a scholastic examination could make a gentleman would have seemed risible. Or another example: some people believed, said John McCaul at the University College convocation in 1861, 'that the only object of the College was to educate men for the learned professions.' But that was not the case, he argued; rather the college 'gave instruction in those subjects which become not merely the members of those professions but also the merchant and the farmer. In other words they taught those things which it was essential that a gentleman should know.'[8] But with this kind of inclusiveness, the term gentleman could be expropriated by anyone who could persuade public opinion, or even a segment of it, that his educational or moral credentials warranted that distinction.

Given its own ambiguities, the term 'profession' was no less open to expropriation. It had always been a multifaceted notion, incorporating connotations which extended beyond occupational designations to social reputability and educational qualifications. Thus, under the right circumstances, it could be extended to those who practised occupations other than divinity, law, and medicine. For most of the nineteenth century, for example, engineering was not commonly considered to be a learned profession. But there were those who, because of their social standing, could claim to be engineers *and* professional gentlemen. T.C. Keefer is one good example.[9] Keefer belonged to an eminently respectable Upper Canadian family and had finished his education at Upper Canada College, where he completed the seventh form – the closest one could come to a university education in the colony during the 1830s. Only after that did he commence his engineering apprenticeship.[10] Thus when men like Keefer declared their occupation a profession and compared it to medicine or the law, they spoke with a degree of social authority which could lend such assertions a credibility they might not have had otherwise.[11] A similar case could be made for those teachers associated with Upper Canada's colleges and grammar schools. They normally held university degrees and, before 1850 at least, most of them were either clergymen or, as was often the case with grammar-school teachers, divinity students working to earn enough money to continue their collegiate studies. After mid-century both occupations began to be secularized; but because of their association with the universities and their traditional close links to the clerical role, grammar-school and college teachers constituted plausible candidates for inclusion in an expanded definition of the learned professions.

The use of the word 'profession' as a prescriptive term also contributed to blurring its meaning and expanding its inclusiveness. Increasingly during the nineteenth century, it not only identified particular occupations but was used to indicate a state of grace which other occupations might achieve if only they recognized and acted upon their own best interests. The rhetoric surrounding the farmer is one good example. Beginning in the 1860s there was a growing concern about the flood of young men out of farming and into white-collar city jobs, including the professions. Newspaper editors bewailed the number of rural lads crowding into these urban occupations, and, lauding the free and happy life of the farmer, urged them to stay home and take up the occupation of their forefathers. This commentary, however, was frequently phrased in traditional language. Farming was the most independent of professions; the farmer did not simply work with his hands but was a chemist, astronomer, and botanist, 'a man of intellect as well as of action.'[12] The question, said one MPP in 1873, 'was simply which was the best system to educate Farmers' Sons to make Farmers, and to make Farming a profession. He believed that Farmers should have Colleges established for the sole benefit of educating their sons to follow farming as well as others have Colleges to educate their sons for Doctors, Lawyers, Ministers ...'[13] To the modern reader such rhetoric may seem inflated. It was pervasive nonetheless. Occupying the apex of the occupational order, the learned professions carried great prestige in the middle decades of the nineteenth century, and thus it is not surprising that, when contemporaries formulated their notions about the appropriate place of other occupations in society, they looked to the model of law, divinity, and medicine. But in borrowing from that model selectively, or emphasizing one part of it over others – by linking those who tilled the soil by manual labour with the idea of abstract knowledge or classical learning, for example – it inevitably became more inchoate and more open to expropriation.

Even the need to group occupations into categories for census or other purposes contributed towards inclusiveness. Were provincial land surveyors members of a learned profession? Perhaps not, but they did have to pass examinations, and thus Thomas Hodgins announced in his *Educational Directory for 1857* that its contents would include 'THE PROFESSIONS – Subjects for Examinations of Law Students and Barristers; Regulations of Medical Boards, and Provincial Land Surveyors in Upper and Lower Canada.'[14] When in 1882 the registrar general published a list which gave average age of death by occupation, one of his categories was headed 'Professional Men.' Not surprisingly, it included clergymen, lawyers, and doctors; but it also referred to dentists, engineers, editors, musicians, public officials, teachers, and gentlemen.[15] Such lists were hardly definitive, nor did they indicate parity of esteem among the occupations included. But as these sorts of summary categories became more common in the second half of the nineteenth century, they could not help but accustom people to the idea that the term 'profession' covered more ground than it had a few decades earlier.

What, indeed, did *learned* profession' mean in the colonial environment? In principle a student was expected to have acquired a sound liberal and classical education before he began professional training. Even in England there was a substantial gap between ideal and reality on this score, especially for medical men. In Upper Canada it was more like an abyss. Lacking any university before the 1840s, nearly all native-born professional men had nothing but a grammar-school education and thus had been exposed to no more than the elements of the classics. Perhaps the only exception to this was the relative handful of boys who studied at Upper Canada College long enough to complete the seventh form. Among the native-born at least, the first two generations of professional men in Upper Canada could scarcely claim the full inheritance of a liberal education. No one expected the colony's medical men to demonstrate more than a passing acquaintance with Latin, clergymen were ordained without completing an undergraduate degree, and even such distinguished gentlemen of the law as J.A. or J.S. Macdonald, Oliver Mowat, J.H. Cameron, or Robert Baldwin were not university men; indeed, only a handful of the Benchers of the Law Society during the 1850s had ever darkened the door of a university. This did not necessarily compromise their conviction that a university education should constitute the ideal entry requirement for such occupations.[16] The fact was, however, that by actual example all three of Upper Canada's learned professions set a standard of preliminary education that was not beyond the reach of other occupational groups who aspired to a more elevated position in society.

The Upper Canadian colleges made their own contribution to broadening the definition of a profession. Throughout the middle decades of the century, it was simply assumed that, while a handful of others might take up a course of collegiate studies, the undergraduate curriculum existed mainly to provide a preliminary education for future lawyers, doctors, and clergymen. Partly in response to the utilitarian impulse of the age, however, and partly due to the desperate shortage of students and funds, university leaders also began to appeal to a wider clientele. On the one hand, this took the form of speeches and articles extolling the virtues of a liberal education, not just for doctors or divines but for merchants, farmers, and mechanics as well – the kind of pitch, for example, we have already heard from John McCaul. On the other hand, the universities began to broaden their curricular base as well. In the 1870s, for example, Victoria College justified its new 'scientific course' in the following terms:

> Heretofore, the college halls have been frequented chiefly by men who intended to enter the *learned professions*, strictly so-called. The Arts Course must still attract these men, and furnish the most suitable discipline and culture for clergymen, lawyers, physicians, teachers, etc. There are, however, many young men who look forward to the occupations of engineering, surveying, mining, navigation, architecture, etc., etc., occupations full of promise in our country's future. Men with such expectations have hitherto, very generally, shunned universities, and perhaps not without reason, when the course in Arts was the only one open to them. Now, however, will be found in the Scientific Course the most profitable preparatory discipline for these pursuits, and at the same time a wide and liberal culture, such as will qualify the Graduate in Science for the highest social and political stations.[17]

Those intending to become engineers, surveyors, or architects did not immediately begin to pour into such courses, but that is not our point in any case. Whatever else they were intended to achieve, such innovations as these had an important symbolic value. By providing a place within its walls for occupations like civil engineering, the university mediated between technical expertise and the cultural authority bestowed by a university education. It indicated that engineers or architects might be not just a higher order of skilled artisans but professional gentlemen, and in the nineteenth century it was still that cachet which bestowed social power and prestige, and not the building of bridges or railways. And if the university could do that for engineers, it could do it for other occupations as well.

Finally, there were some fundamental shifts in the nature of both the high-school and college curriculum which modified traditional notions about the content of a liberal education.[18] We have already noted in an earlier chapter the blossoming prestige of science during the second half of the nineteenth century, and that, in turn, gave it a greater role in the curriculum of both institutions. But the expansion of science education was only one part of a larger curricular revolution which involved the growing importance of other modern subjects as well – English, history, and modern languages, for example. As all of these subjects crowded into the traditional curriculum, the pre-eminence of Latin and Greek was diminished. As it became accepted, moreover, that any of these subjects could do as much to discipline and furnish the mind as a study of the classics, specialization became more legitimate and could be more easily reconciled with vocational goals.[19] The changes in the high-school program were especially critical since, whatever the rhetoric about the centrality of the university in the education of the learned professions, it was actually the high school that provided all the preliminary education most doctors or lawyers received. What the new program of studies in the high school signalled was the end of the Georgian dichotomy between a liberal (or primarily classical) and an ordinary (or English) education. And that dichotomy, in turn, was a fundamental pillar of the distinction between the Georgian notion of learned professions, on the one hand, and the ordinary occupations that engaged the rest of mankind, on the other. As these distinctions began to wither during the second half of the nineteenth century, as science and other modern subjects found an equal place in the curriculum, as specialization became more respectable academically and more necessary for vocational reasons, it became easier for the leaders of a wide variety of occupations to claim that, while a superior education remained the *sine qua non* of a true profession, such an education did not necessarily consist of an arts degree or an acquaintance with the classics, and that knowledge of science, mathematics, and English might be an equally legitimate qualification.

There was, then, no monolithic theory which underpinned the ideology of Georgian professionalism and excluded, *a priori*, all occupations but divinity, law, and medicine. Rather, there were simply sets of loosely related and overlapping assumptions about the social standing associated with particular occupations, the relationship between education and reputability, and the privileges which appertained to gentlemen's work as much as to other aspects of their lives. All of these assumptions were porous enough to allow change to take place. Political and social conditions in the colony promoted that possibility, as did some of the larger forces at work in nineteenth-century society generally. It remained to be seen, nonetheless, which occupations could effectively exploit the opportunities thrown up by the ambiguities and inconsistencies embedded in the ideal of the professional gentleman. Equally, it remained to be seen how these ambiguities might themselves contribute to the transmutation of that ideal.

10
Parvenus

Consider the case of the dentists. In 1868 the Ontario legislature gave a fledgling dental association powers equal to those of the Law Society of Upper Canada, and greater than those possessed by the Ontario Medical Council under the Medical Act of 1865. To this day our dental historians believe the achievement to be a world first, and they are probably right, though it must be added that dentists in both New York and Ohio achieved similar goals within a few weeks of the passage of the Ontario act.[1] It remains a remarkable, not to say an anomalous, feat. Thus we propose to begin our account of the changing face of the professions in nineteenth-century Ontario with an attempt to explain how dentists, of all people, became one of the first of the new occupational groups to achieve, in law at least, the status of a 'learned profession.'

Before mid-century Upper Canada had few individuals who worked full-time at dentistry. Most dental services available were provided by itinerants based in the United States. Even as late as the 1830s, Toronto still had no resident dentist, and according to *Smith's Canadian Gazetteer* it had only two in 1846.[2] Over the next two decades, however, the number of dentists multiplied rapidly – from 36 in 1851 to 114 in 1861 and 230 in 1871.[3] The reasons for this substantial growth can best be understood by considering what they actually did and how their work was changed by the technical innovations that occurred during the middle decades of the nineteenth century.

DENTISTS, TO BEGIN WITH, did not make their living from pulling teeth. Extractions were probably one of the most common surgical operations in the nineteenth century, but they were also carried out by many different people besides dentists. Doctors routinely extracted teeth, but so indeed did all kinds of laymen, from blacksmiths to clergymen.[4] Inevitably in the latter category there was the omni-competent Featherstone

Osler, who recorded in 1838 that a man had come 'to say his wife was distracted with the toothache. She could not go out, and as the person who draws teeth was away, would I go? Though a job I much disliked, I went with him and extracted two of her teeth.'[5] There were as well itinerant tooth-pullers who worked the countryside, local residents who had acquired a knack for the task, and outright charlatans like 'Madam Manita, the Queen of Dentists,' who, according to an advertisement in a Hamilton newspaper in 1843, would, during a concert, 'extract teeth free of charge – no pain – by use of whips, swords, spoons and instruments invented by herself.'[6] When doctors or dentists did an extraction, the charges were rarely more than twenty-five cents a tooth, and the amount of competition meant that no one could carve out a living from that part of dentistry alone.

When dentists described their work, they commonly divided it into two parts: operative and mechanical dentistry.[7] The former included extractions, but, more important, restorative work such as filling cavities or making crowns, and the 'regulation of the teeth' – straightening children's teeth, for example, through the use of braces or other devices. Mechanical dentistry involved the making of partial or full sets of plates and teeth. Before 1860 especially, the bases for artificial teeth were made of gold or other metals, and the teeth themselves were either of human or animal origin, or made of some mineral compound.[8] One Upper Canadian dentist who began practice in the mid-1850s described the equipment necessary to carry out both the operative and mechanical aspects of his craft as follows: 'My equipment consisted of a charcoal furnace, anvil, sledgehammer, work bench, and a reasonable set of bench tools necessary for gold base plate work ... My instruments [for operating] consisted of a few long handled burs, rotated between thumb and finger, a little later a stud thimble with a cup in the palm of the hand for pressure. I had a fine set of forceps ... The filling material consisted of gold and tin foil made in ropes to be stuffed into the cavity prepared by the already described instruments.'[9]

It was restorative work, then, and the manufacture of artificial dentures which provided dentists with a living. These, it must be emphasized, were tasks that required substantial skills. Filling a cavity with gold or tin foil so that it adhered and was resistant to the pressures of mastication was no simple operation, while shaping artificial bases and securing teeth to them was work that could be done only by those who had acquired the skills of the fine moulder and metal worker. That said, however, it also needs to be understood that dentistry was an *artisanal* craft: except when actually filling teeth, dentists worked in 'the shop,' and their tools and training were those of the skilled craftsman.

Like some other types of specialized craftsmen in the nineteenth century, dentists largely catered to the carriage trade. The level of skill involved and the cost of gold and other material for fillings, bases, and teeth made dental services expensive. Writing to her son John in 1839, Ann Macaulay explained that she needed 'a half sett of teeth as I have not one tooth left on the lower jaw,' but the dentist she had engaged to do the work 'asks a terrible price for the best kind ... £30 for a half sett. I offered him £25 which I believe he will take but [he] is gone to the states and will not return till spring. I hope I shall be able to make the old ones last till then. I can do without the upper ones but lower ones are indispensable as I cannot speak but with difficulty. It is a shameful price, but I do not know how to do without.'[10] As a point of comparison, these prices were £5 to £10 higher than her son John was paying in 1839 to obtain a year's tuition for his young daughter in an exclusive Toronto private school.[11] In the two decades after mid-century, they may have declined somewhat; still, we find one dentist charging from one to three dollars for a gold filling, another anywhere from two dollars to six or eight; the price for '2 teeth on gold plate: $8' and for a full upper or lower set on gold, from $50 to $60.[12] Clearly only the relatively affluent could afford this kind of dental work in the decades around mid-century, a circumstance which helps to explain the small number of dentists resident in Upper Canada before the 1850s.

During these same years, nevertheless, there were a number of important technical innovations, some of which improved the quality of dental work while others substantially lessened its costs. Among the former were the 'continuous gum,' an invention which greatly improved the effectiveness and durability of artificial dentures; the rubber dam, which kept moisture at bay while the dentist worked at a gold filling; the 'dental foot engine' (the first mechanical drill); and a variety of improved hand tools.[13] Among those innovations which reduced the expense of dental work were two critical developments. One was the discovery of an effective amalgam – a mixture of silver, tin, and mercury – which was, like gold, tough enough to use as a filling on the working surfaces of the teeth. This new amalgam, which began to come into use before mid-century, had its problems, and because of these many dentists refused to use it: it was not as durable as gold; it was more prone to crack, shrink, and discolour, turning black a few months after insertion; and many doctors and dentists considered the amount of mercury involved to be highly poisonous. But amalgam filling had two great compensatory virtues: it was much easier to manipulate than gold, and it was much cheaper. Thus the costs of preserving teeth dropped substantially.[14]

The second innovation was even more significant. In 1844 Charles Goodyear patented his process for vulcanizing rubber. The new tough but malleable material produced by the process was put to many uses, and one of them was the manufacture of plates for artificial dentures.[15] Such plates were more comfortable than metal plates, produced as least as good a fit, and, most important, cost half as much. Even more than amalgam fillings, then, the use of plates made of vulcanized rubber meant that a much larger proportion of the population had access to prosthetic devices which increased their comfort, improved their appearance, and enabled them to digest their food more efficiently. Not surprisingly, the demand for dental services increased as well, and with it the number of men engaged in dentistry as a full-time occupation.

The introduction of amalgams and, above all, of vulcanite had another effect, however. It threatened to deskill dentistry and throw the craft open to all comers. Vulcanizers were relatively cheap to buy and fairly simple to operate, and could be carried around the countryside on a waggon. One dentist, for example, bought his first vulcanizer, weighing less than a hundred pounds, for $35.[16] Apprentices could be taught to make the new dentures within a few weeks – a profitable sideline for some established dentists – and could then set up in practice on their own. Amalgams made restorative work simpler, and with vulcanite there was no need to acquire the intricate craft skills of the metal worker. In the old days, one practitioner reminisced later, the dentist's workshop contained 'almost the full equipment of the jeweller and the moulder'; but the introduction of vulcanite brought 'degeneracy ... Competition for cheapness drove gold and platinum out ... and brought a lot of inferior men in.'[17]

Given such sentiments, it is probably no coincidence that the impetus to organize and seek an incorporation act followed almost immediately upon the introduction of vulcanite.[18] Though nothing came of the first initiative, in 1866 Barnabas Day, a Kingston dentist, sent out a circular announcing a meeting of Upper Canadian dentists, to be held early in 1867. That January nine dentists met in Toronto, formed themselves into the Ontario Dental Association (ODA), drafted a constitution, and called a second meeting to approve it. The following July some thirty-one dentists gathered in Cobourg to adopt the constitution; they also agreed to seek legislation to restrict the practice of dentistry to those who held a licence, to be awarded after an appropriate examination had been passed.[19]

In the process of recounting the story of his early career, Day himself left a record of his motives for calling the initial meeting of the Ontario Dental Association. 'Then rubber was introduced,' he reminisced in

1903, 'which afforded an opportunity for the itinerants which rapidly increased to that extent that I decided to make an effort to ask assistance of the other and older members of the profession to join me in such an undertaking, and accordingly I issued a circular to all the reliable members of the profession in Ontario from Ottawa to Hamilton.'[20] Day was no less forthright in his address to the ODA meeting of January 1868. The reason for organizing the profession was not 'for the purpose of monopoly and self aggrandizement, but to guard the public, as well as ourselves, against the pretentions of those illiterate empirics who swarm in almost every profession, and who prey upon the credulity or ignorance of a large portion of the community, and whose qualifications to take rank in the dental corps are about on par with those of a Hottentot.'[21] This is language we have, of course, heard before. There were yet other familiar themes: that of internal competition breeding degrading practices and unethical behaviour, and of established dentists taking large fees to grind out new practitioners who would only increase the difficulty of making a living for all.[22] As Andrew Abbott remarks of another occupation entirely, 'The elite have to move or get deskilled with the rest.'[23]

WHAT DO WE KNOW of Barnabas Day, the other founding fathers of the ODA, or indeed of those who came to sustain organized dentistry through its formative years?[24] Compared with our biographical knowledge of leading doctors or lawyers, the answer is, very little. Only a handful of them left a record of their lives, and even then the detail is often sparse. Most were native Canadians, though a few, like C.S. Chittenden, a long-time Hamilton practitioner, came from the United States. Several were the sons of farmers, though in all cases they seem to have come from prosperous families. Barnabas Day was born on a farm near Kingston; educated not only in local common schools but for several terms at the Newburgh Academy, a good grammar school at Napanee; and was then apprenticed, for a fee of $200, to Kingston's leading dentist, Dr J.P. Sutton. J.B. Willmott, born on a Halton County farm in 1837, spent at least a year at University College; apprenticed himself to a prominent Toronto dentist, W.C. Adams; and then attended one of the leading American dental colleges, graduating in 1871. Willmott was to become Ontario dentistry's leading schoolman throughout the late nineteenth century and beyond. In his early years of practice, he may well have trained another influential teacher, Luke Teskey. H.H. Nelles, raised in a prosperous Brant County farm family, was only one of several sons sent for their education to Victoria College; one brother was to become president of Victoria, and he himself became London's leading dentist. Charles A. Martin's father was a gunsmith and locksmith; Henry Robinson's father had studied medicine for two years in England and, after coming to Canada in 1832, had worked as a storekeeper, doctor, and tooth extractor.

They entered dentistry for a wide variety of reasons. Martin and his older brother had inherited from their father an unusual knack for fine metalwork and had become dentists because these were valued skills, even though they had no more than a common-school education. Nelles had begun medical studies in the office of a Simcoe doctor, but his health was not good enough to pursue medicine and thus, in his own words, he 'drifted into dentistry.' Robinson had run a sawmill for several years until 'the Reciprocity Treaty with the United States ended and Timber was very low, which made it necessary for me to make a living at something else as I had a wife and four children to support. And I concluded to take up Dentistry for at the age of 16 years I drew a tooth with the old fashioned Instrument called the Turnkey and by this time had become quite an Expert in using it.'

Nearly all these men learned their craft through an apprenticeship of no more than a year, and often less; Day set up in practice after only six months' training. The exceptions were those few – Nelles and Willmott, for example – who could afford the luxury of going to an American dental school for a year or two. But there is also a thread of evidence suggesting that some Ontario dentists, like Nelles, may have received a partial medical education,[25] while a handful went on to complete it. Barnabas Day graduated from Queen's College in 1862. After his apprenticeship in dentistry, Luke Teskey went on to qualify as both a physician and surgeon in London, and at least one other dentist prominent in the early affairs of the Ontario Dental Association, J.S. Scott, was also an MD.[26]

Taken as a whole, dentists were not regularly bred in the traditional sense. Their educational and social background was too variable for that. Among the founding members of the ODA there were, nonetheless, men of reputation and influence who knew how to work the levers of power. During the autumn of 1867, Day and Scott had secured the full support of the Medical Council, the medical schools, and several key members of the legislature, including Dr G.W. Boulter, an MPP who would shepherd the bill through the House. He was assisted by two other doctor-politicians, Drs Baxter and McGill, and the dentists could also count on the vocal support of William Aikins of the Toronto School of Medicine and of Dr Berryman of Victoria.[27] Petitions were organized across the province, but the centrepiece was one signed first by sixty-eight dentists and then by the mayor of Toronto and some twenty-eight MDs, including such luminaries as John Fulton, J.W. Rolph, William Aikins, James Richardson, and James Thorburn, George Brown's family doctor.[28] The third meeting of the ODA, held in late January 1868, coincided with the sitting of the House, and on the third day the membership rose to a man and marched to the legislature to be present when the petitions were presented and the bill introduced by Dr Boulter.[29]

The dentists did not get all they wanted. The bill had proposed to establish a closed corporation like the Law Society, with a board which appointed its own successors. At least one senior cabinet minister, Matthew Cameron, was having none of that; he had refused an appointment as a Bencher precisely because he objected to an oligarchic constitution, and he was not about to bestow it upon the dentists. The bill was amended to allow regular election of board members by all licensed dentists.[30] The original version, moreover, proposed that every dentist then practising would be required to submit to an examination.[31] This clause met predictable opposition from dentists outside the ODA and was also substantially modified. All dentists who could prove they had been practising for five years or more were to be automatically entitled to a licence; and all those in practice less than five years were exempted from any educational requirements beyond the examination for a licence. The legislature, in other words, was prepared to extend special privilege to expertise in the name of protecting the public, but not about to allow a clique to exclude established practitioners of recognized worth. Dentistry, like medicine, was organized on a broadly inclusive basis, gathering in all those, no matter what their qualifications, who could establish a claim to be practitioners. The closure of the occupation would be imposed only upon succeeding generations.

And what did the dentists win? The act, which became law in March 1868, created the Royal College of Dental Surgeons of Ontario (RCDSO), made up of all licensed dentists, and established a board of directors to be elected by the membership every two years. The directors were given powers to establish a dental college, to regulate the training of dental students, to examine them for their licence to practise, and to make rules and regulations for the government of the profession generally. Beginning in 1869 no person who lacked a licence was to be permitted to practise dentistry 'for hire, gain, or hope of reward' under pain of fine. Nothing in the act, however, was to interfere with the existing privileges of physicians and surgeons.[32]

COLLEGIAL SELF-GOVERNMENT, control over the conditions of work, the power to set educational standards, the exclusion of unlicensed practice

– what had begun as a straightforward manifestation of the protective impulse had ended with all the trappings of a learned profession. On the face of it the whole affair may seem like nothing so much as pretentious humbug. Only a handful possessed anything like a liberal education, while their training in dentistry was limited to a few months and consisted primarily of learning manual skills. At the age of twenty-one, C.S. Chittenden wrote of his own experience, he decided to 'study dentistry' under his older brother. 'I said "study" dentistry, but there was really so little to study that, practically, it meant watching him in the operating room and the laboratory, and receiving his oral instructions ... The only book he had for me to study was Harris' Practice, then about one fourth its present size. He was anxious to keep abreast of the times, but there was little to keep abreast of.'[33] To emphasize this feature of dentistry, we reiterate, is in no way to denigrate the craft skills a good dentist might have acquired. Skills equivalent to those needed for fine moulding of metal and jewellery work are not to be dismissed. The point is, however, that one did not 'study' dentistry; there was no elaborated body of knowledge, no curriculum to be pursued, no body of texts to be mastered. To give dignity to the profession, this had all to be invented in the years after 1868. Some dentists, indeed, were convinced the professionalization of their craft was unqualified humbug. In a letter to the *Globe*, written in 1874, 'Mechanic' decried the dental monopoly, arguing that no restriction should be put upon 'fair competition in any branch of labour.' The public, he continued, was perfectly capable of judging dentists' work,

just as it is of judging of the work of jewellers, carpenters, or blacksmiths, or any other tradesmen ... I have been engaged in dentistry for several years, and I have failed to discover that either chemistry or anatomy assist a dentist to fill, or pull, or make a tooth, or to do anything else within his legitimate business ... I don't wish to be called 'Doctor'... or to call myself a 'Professional' man, when I am no more one than any barber ... all sensible men would consider me either a knave or a fool.[34]

Men like Drs Day and Scott, like H.H. Nelles and J.B. Willmott, with their training acquired in American dental colleges, like the editor of the *Canada Journal of Dental Science*, founded in 1869, did not, however, see themselves as 'mechanics.' And that is apparent in the very language they used to explain dentists to themselves. They were not entirely indifferent to the technical knowledge which underpinned their craft; they could hardly make a living, after all, without it. But reputability could not yet be extracted from technical knowledge alone.

Thus in their speeches and articles they insistently evoked the language and images associated with the professional gentleman. Respectable dentists were resident, not itinerant: only those with 'established office practices' could join the Ontario Dental Association, while student membership was limited to those 'who shall have studied two years in a *regular* practitioner's office.'[35] 'In Dentistry as in Medicine,' John S. Scott remarked in an address thanking Dr Berryman for his assistance in obtaining the dental act, 'it will require the united efforts of regular physicians (and if you will allow me the expression) *of regular dentists* to keep the unprincipled from imposing upon an unsuspecting public.'[36] In its first set of rules for students, the RCDSO required them to provide proof that they had 'a liberal English education'[37] (which, to the contemporary purist, was a contradiction in terms).

The link between 'scientia' and dentistry had to be consolidated as well. Reviewing a new book on diseases and surgery of the mouth, the editor of the *Canada Journal of Dental Science* began with the phrase 'to those who love a scientific profession in which they are engaged, and who appreciate it as more than a mere mechanical craft.'[38] Indeed, the very 'mission' of the journal, he declared, was

> to elevate dentistry to the status of a useful and honourable profession. To this end he will not only aim at bringing it up to a higher standard, of scientific and practical attainment; but will endeavour to create a better professional sentiment – something which is very much needed, and a sense of the necessity of a higher standard of general intelligence and education. In a word, he will endeavour to inculcate the necessity of every practitioner being a gentleman, without which the profession cannot have that status which it is entitled to. Believing, as we do, that no Dental practitioner can properly perform his functions, who has barely a mechanical knowledge of his specialty, he will endeavour to show to students and practitioners the necessity of obtaining a respectable knowledge of the collateral sciences.[39]

In the pages of the *CJDS*, dentists were even coached in the new language they must learn to use: the proper terminology was 'profession, not trade; fees not prices; practitioner, operator or dentist, not workman; patients not customers; Instruments in the Surgery; Tools in the laboratory.'[40] As to the significance of that last term, dentists who, a decade or so earlier, had done their mechanical work in 'the shop,' or at 'the workbench,' now did it in the 'laboratory.'[41]

The phraseology found in the preceding paragraph, it must be emphasized, is not limited to an occasional rhetorical flourish; it is pervasive throughout the record of organized dentistry in the years immediately after 1868. And that record also testifies to the enormous influence of the ideal of the professional gentleman in nineteenth-century society. The leadership of organized dentistry wanted, no doubt, to improve the quality of dental practice *per se*; but, above all, they wanted to place technical knowledge and practice in a framework which would be acknowledged as *professional* work.

IN 1868, THEN, dentists had laid hands on those institutions which formed the legal structure of nineteenth-century professionalism – collegial self-government enshrined in law, the power to control practice, and the right to regulate entry to the occupation. Beyond that, they had a professional journal and had even founded a dental college, in 1869, where their licentiates were to be trained.[42] Confronted by technological breakthroughs offering both a threat and an opportunity, they had extracted victory from the jaws of defeat. What was it that made such an achievement possible? Though it was not the sum total of their business, dentists made much of their income from the manufacture and sale of plates. Craftsmen and tradesmen they indubitably were, then, but that was not quite the liability it might have been three or four decades earlier. They were fortunate in having a handful of leading practitioners who could be readily recognized as professional gentlemen – doctors like Day and Scott, or the dentist brother of Victoria College's president. They had the advantage of selling a highly valued product to the relatively affluent and thus moving in circles where they might command respect from the influential or powerful. Their first matriculation standard would be set no higher than 'a liberal English education,' but it was introduced at a time when the dichotomy between a liberal, or classical, and an ordinary English education was beginning to break down. The leadership of dentistry, in other words, was able to exploit the opportunities thrown up by the ambiguities and inconsistencies embedded in the ideal of the professional gentleman. And that, in turn, allowed them to lodge a successful claim to the legal privileges that professional status entailed.

But an equally important question arises here. What were the consequences for the meaning of 'profession' itself when it was hijacked in this manner? Already somewhat amorphous, it became more amorphous still. Another occupation, that of pharmacy, provides a useful illustration of what we mean by this. At almost exactly the time dentists were preoccupied with establishing their own professional organization, druggists were pursuing similar objectives and meeting with similar success. Indeed, they achieved their own closed shop three years later, in 1871. In a recent article describing that enterprise, R.J. Clark has provided a portrait of the development of pharmacy in Ontario that parallels our own account of dentists.[43] In the process, Clark has also drawn attention to the fact that, regardless of their legal entitlements, most druggists had never made a living from compounding or dispensing alone, and had thus long since branched out into the more general retail business. They sold paints and dyes, patent medicines and perfumes, medicine for animals, confectionery, photographic equipment and chemicals, fungicides and pesticides, soaps, spectacles, and by the late 1880s were just beginning to move into milkshakes. All of this made for good business. But it also carried the taint of trade. They required specialized training to obtain a licence to practise pharmacy *per se*, but they made most of their living much as grocers did. The result was an uncertain occupational status that was even reflected in the occupational columns of the published census statistics: from 1861 to 1881, druggists had been grouped with professional men; in 1891 they were moved to the retail category. And if the druggists could be either professional men or retailers, then why not the grocers and other storekeepers? We are, in other words, observing a kind of Gresham's Law at work. Untouched, in the main, by the virtues of a classical education, linked to the world of the artisan and tradesman rather than to that of the gentry, in command of undoubted skills but ones with tenuous ties to 'scientia,' druggists and dentists could hardly claim status equivalent to the gentlemen of the law, medicine, or the church. Yet they had acquired one of the distinguishing characteristics of the traditional 'learned professions.' If that, by itself, made them professional gentlemen, then the term meant less – and more – than it once did.

II

On the face of it at least, Ontario's land surveyors may seem unlikely candidates for inclusion in a book such as this. However respectable and useful an occupation, it is not usually considered to be among the leading professions of modern society. But land surveyors were the *only* other occupational group in the nineteenth century to acquire the kind of legal privilege attained by lawyers, doctors, dentists, and druggists. For that reason alone they merit our attention. A second reason is of equal importance. Any account of surveying in nineteenth-century Ontario constitutes an important and neglected chapter in the history of engineering as well.[44]

Throughout Upper Canadian history, the opening of the land and its settlement or exploitation by some other means was a primary function of colonial government and an important source of revenue for both government and private individuals. Estimating the extent of the land belonging to the Crown, reserving some of it, and alienating the rest for subsequent purchase and sale by individuals – all presumed that boundaries had been established to identify which portions were which and belonged to whom. Thus land surveying was a critically important activity, especially in early Upper Canada. The potential for endless confusion and disputes over title, moreover, put a premium upon competent work. As a result, surveying was a government-regulated occupation from the very beginning of British settlement. An ordinance of 1785 gave public authorities the power to examine surveyors before their appointment and required surveyors to preserve field notes and to post a £500 bond. The first Upper Canadian legislation to deal with surveyors, in 1818, provided that each be tested by the surveyor general or his deputy for 'fitness and capacity and competent knowledge of the theory and practice of surveying in all its branches'; upon posting his bond a successful candidate was issued a licence to practise.[45] In 1849 that act was supplemented by further legislation establishing a board of examiners composed of the commissioner of Crown lands and other government appointees, specifying the subjects of examination, and requiring a three-year period of training under a licensed surveyor. Successful candidates were entitled to identify themselves as Provincial Land Surveyors (PLS). Only those duly authorized under the act were to practise land surveying in the province.[46]

As an occupation, surveying had an ambiguous status. On the one hand, its educational qualifications were relatively high. One had always needed a fair acquaintance with mathematics and, by the 1850s, a grammar-school education or equivalent to meet the standards laid down for the preliminary and final examinations.[47] Especially in the early period, moreover, surveying was carried on by a number of members of the colonial élite, including John Bostwick, Mahlon Burwell, and Reuben Sherwood.[48] There was good reason for this. Surveyors often received a percentage of the land they surveyed as payment, and they were also in an ideal position to evaluate which portions of the public lands promised to repay handsomely a private investment. Indeed, for some of those involved it is not easy to know which came first: prominence, or surveying as the road to wealth and prominence.

Working conditions, on the other hand, could hardly be described as gentlemanly: month after month spent in the wilderness among mosquitoes and black flies or bitter cold, blazing lines through thick bush and swamps, with only an assistant or apprentice and a gang of labourers as company.[49] Surveying, moreover, was not usually a full-time job. It might be so, for a period of months or years, when, for example, large tracts of new lands were first being surveyed or extensive railway lines laid out. But eventually these jobs would be done, there would be no large-scale projects to replace them, and surveyors would have to turn their hand to other things. Alternatively they might be employed for a few months each year, or irregularly throughout the year. Thus it was common for them to engage in a range of related activities rather than to specialize exclusively in land surveying. One grouping, which frequently turns up in the business directories, focused on real estate: the valuation of property, auctioneering, surveying private lands or attesting under oath to boundaries, conveyancing, and the buying or selling of lands either as principal or as agent.[50]

The other set of activities spilled over into engineering, where the skills of laying out lines and marking off plots, of estimating costs and quantities of construction materials, of drafting plans and then supervising construction, all constituted something like a natural bundle of tasks applicable to a particular job. Individuals, firms, or public authorities always had the option of hiring specialists – a PLS to do the surveying, an architect to design, a civil engineer to supervise construction – but, in most cases, and especially for the common run of public or private work, they were more likely to hire one individual to do it all. Thus in the middle of the nineteenth century, and even later, the distinctions between surveyors and engineers (and even between those two titles and the 'architect' or the 'builder') were not sharply drawn; indeed, what one called oneself (or was designated by history) was largely an accident of personal preference, how one came to spend most of one's time, or the sort of projects which made one's reputation.[51] Most of those engaged in these crafts possessed the skills to do some or all of the others; the overlap between surveying and engineering was especially common, and where surviving diaries or other records indicate patterns of education, we find young men, primarily apprenticed as surveyors or engineers, seeking out opportunities to learn the skills of the related crafts.[52] Engineers had a special incentive to prepare themselves for the surveyors' examinations since without a licence as a PLS they could not do survey work, effectively losing one arrow in their occupational quiver.[53]

For much of the nineteenth century, surveyors spent a great deal of their time in the bush or at the edge of settlement. But by the 1870s and 1880s that began to change. Laying the survey lines across the prairies and mapping the route of the Canadian Pacific Railway were two of the great projects of the century; as they neared completion, however, scores of surveyors had to find alternative work.[54] Fortuitously, new opportunities appeared as the result of economic change in the long-settled parts of southern Ontario. Urban growth brought a construction boom. As town and city boundaries expanded, new tracts of countryside had to be subdivided; main thoroughfares and side streets surveyed and built or rebuilt; streetcar tracks, drainage, and water lines laid. Population growth and agricultural change, moreover, increased the incentive for farmers to clear what still remained of their waste lands. Some of it had simply never been brought into production, and some had hitherto been considered of marginal value. Though it is now commonly forgotten, huge tracts of Ontario, and especially the southwestern part of the province, once consisted of nothing but swamps and bogs, useless for farming or any other purpose and a major impediment to transportation and communication. During the last third of the nineteenth century, however, much of this land was drained, turned into highly productive farm land, and criss-crossed, for the first time, with township roads, drainage ditches, and bridges.[55] Drafting and implementing the legislation which provided funds and other incentives for these purposes, indeed, was one of the major accomplishments of the Mowat regime.[56] But the various ditches and watercourses, tile drainage, and municipal drainage acts also generated a large volume of work for those who surveyed the lots that had never been cleared, or resurveyed the boundary lines lost track of, who laid out the county and township roads and drainage ditches, and who supervised the construction of both. In town and country alike, then, economic change and legislative stimulus offered the promise of new opportunities for employment at the very moment when others were beginning to dry up.

As surveyors began to find steady work in the cities, towns, and rural countryside of old Ontario, they could also hope to settle and remain in one place. Though many would continue to free-lance, others would secure appointments as municipal engineers. Permanence, in turn, made associational activities possible; it is not surprising that the first successful attempt to organize a surveyors' association coincides with the changed economic circumstances of the last quarter of the nineteenth century.[57] The impetus for associationalism arose from the usual variety of motives. There was the hope, above all, that it would promote a sense of common identity which would, in turn, result in collective action to pursue common interests. There was unease about overcrowding,[58] and the fear that their educational standards were not keeping pace with progress in other occupations.[59] In the back settlements, it was asserted, unqualified 'quacks' were running lines on the cheap, cutting into their market;[60] and, in both town and country, those who were unlicensed but otherwise perfectly qualified, engineers or others who had acquired surveying skills, were doing the same. For that reason alone, licensed surveyors wanted new teeth in their legislation, above all the restoration of a penal clause which had been written into the act of 1849 and then omitted from revisions made in the mid-1850s.[61]

The single most pressing concern, however, arose out of the phraseology incorporated into the various drainage acts. According to the Municipal Drainage Aid Act, for example, if a majority of ratepayers petitioned for certain improvements, the council '*may* procure an examination' by an engineer or PLS to estimate the costs of the work and make assessments on each lot involved; the Ditches and Watercourses Act, 1883, required the appointment of 'a civil engineer, land surveyor, *or such person as any municipality may deem competent,*' at the request of any one owner.[62] Work, in other words, which the surveyor-engineers considered rightfully theirs could, without any breach of the law, be handed over without regard to formal qualifications to anyone whom the laymen on municipal councils deemed competent. That individual might be an engineer who was not also a PLS, but he might just as well be someone without recognized qualifications in either field. Thus economic change had opened up a new area of work, but occupational jurisdiction over it remained uncertain. If others could also do the new kinds of work available, the PLS, like the dentist before him, would face deskilling. More ominously, the work itself was not a full-time job; it had to be combined with other related tasks – surveying, laying out, and supervising the construction of drains and roads, for example, the work of either the surveyor or the engineer.

The surveyors, then, had plenty of incentives to organize, and, by the 1880s, the capacity to do so. After some preliminary correspondence among the more prominent, the founding meeting of a new association of surveyors convened in 1886.[63] High on the agenda was a concerted effort to lobby for amendments to the legislation governing their work. Though we know nothing of the details, negotiations between the officers of the association and senior cabinet ministers took place early in 1887, a new bill was drafted, and it passed into law later that year. Among its other provisions the act included the restoration of the penal clause, which gave the prerogatives of the licence some authority. Even more important, however, the educational qualifications specified in the act were extended to include a group of engineering subjects – something surveyors had never before been formally required to master.[64]

The act of 1887, then, represented a substantial gain for the PLSs. Their exclusive jurisdiction over the practice of surveying was strengthened against competition from the unlicensed. But, at the same time, the public was offered a guarantee that to hire a surveyor was also to hire someone with some qualifications in the area of engineering as well. A municipality had to employ a surveyor to lay out lines for roads, drainage ditches, and the like; since the surveyor could also supervise the construction of the roads and ditches, there was no need to hire anyone else.

Success was self-justifying. The new act had, almost immediately, proved to its members the value of the association, and made its leaders ambitious for something more. Their licence to practise was issued by the government, not by the association itself. The examining board was appointed by the government. Educational standards were fixed by the legislature and enshrined in the statute. However beneficent government may have been, and the surveyors hardly had cause to complain on that score, the symbol of having arrived at an appropriate station in society was self-governance after the manner of lawyers and doctors. Thus, with the achievements of 1886–7 behind them, the leaders of the association moved quickly to initiate plans for its incorporation. Proposals were debated in 1890 and 1891; a draft bill was approved; A.S. Hardy, the commissioner of Crown lands and one of Mowat's senior cabinet ministers, agreed to sponsor it; and it became law in 1892.[65] Compromises had to be made at various points,[66] but there were substantial gains as well. The incorporation act provided for a council of management and a board of examiners, both composed of a majority elected by the membership of the Association of Ontario Land Surveyors (AOLS), the permanent title the organization acquired. The council was authorized to establish the curriculum and examinations, and to discipline members. The prohibition on unlicensed practice was continued, and, rather than leaving it to individuals, as had been the case since 1887, the council was given the power to pursue unlicensed practitioners through the courts. Finally, the act also included a clause changing the occupational title from Provincial Land Surveyor to Ontario Land Surveyor; only those who were members of the organization could use that designation.

In 1892, in sum, the surveyors had acquired all of the legal prerogatives of the traditional learned professions: self-government, a restricted title, a monopoly over an area of work, and control over educational qualifications. And with their goal achieved, the association's president could declare, at the annual meeting of 1895, that they could now meet each other as 'professional gentlemen.'[67]

BUT WHY THE SURVEYORS, the reader may ask, and not the engineers? Engineering, after all, was to become one of the model professions of the mid-twentieth century[68] and even in the early nineteenth century there were eminently respectable men who were engineers, including military or ex–military officers and sons of people who could claim membership in Upper Canada's gentry class. As an occupation, however, engineering was, like surveying, and even more so than architecture, a pursuit which, for several reasons, bore an equivocal and uncertain status. In the first place it was stigmatized by its links to manual labour. Unlike those who ministered to body and soul or dealt in the principles and practice of jurisprudence, engineers were engaged in a world of *things*. They worked on construction sites alongside builders and contractors, artisans and labourers, and occupational distinctions could be blurred because of it. The very word 'engineer,' indeed, still tended to be redolent of grubby hands and tinkering with machines; in part this was because of its generic nature, applied as it was to everybody from boiler-tenders, steamboat mechanics, and threshing-machine operators, to locomotive drivers and heating and plumbing specialists. Should there be improved educational facilities for the training of civil and mechanical engineers in Ontario? James Loudon of the University of Toronto certainly thought so and was an early and vigorous proponent of the idea; but he was dismayed at the misconceived support it received from Sandfield Macdonald during a legislative debate on the subject in 1871. A school for engineers? Of course, said the redoubtable Macdonald; 'Was it not time that the drivers of our locomotives, who were entrusted with so many lives, should be thoroughly taught the business?'[69] Until sharper definitions than that pervaded the public mind, it was hard for those with occupational ambitions to convince people that engineering was a profession like the others.

Differences relating to education underscored the distinction as well. Like law students, fledgling engineers learned their craft primarily through apprenticeship to a practitioner, and learning took place on the job, in offices or worksites. Still there was a difference between the law office or the courts, and the construction project, the foundry, or the end of track. Nor could most engineers or their apprentices lay claim to a preliminary education in the liberal arts. There was also the sense that, while law, medicine, and divinity drew upon bodies of systematic knowledge, engineering was a practical activity, more like a business or a trade than a learned profession. As we have already seen, for example, when Canadian universities first began to offer courses for engineers and the like, they distinguished between those appropriate for the three learned professions and those for occupations where advanced technical instruction might be useful. Both might be offered within the walls of the university, but inevitably there could be no parity of esteem. This, it must be emphasized, was not some form of deliberate occupational snobbery; rather, it was part and parcel of the contemporary view of science in the larger order of things. 'Science' was still an amorphous entity, not yet unambiguously differentiated into higher- and lower-order activities, into academic and popular, pure and applied, what was appropriate to the university and to the technical school, the artisan and the savant. Even the occupational designation 'scientist' was brand-new. As Frank M. Turner remarks, William Whewell had coined it 'in 1834 and reasserted its usefulness in 1840, but the term enjoyed little currency until very late in the century.'[70] Over the long haul, and with the possible exception of medicine, no occupation would benefit more greatly than engineering from the nineteenth-century 'theatre of science';[71] but until it began to be organized into its modern social and academic hierarchies, engineering could not help but share in the ambiguities embedded in science itself.[72]

That process was already under way during the last quarter of the nineteenth century, and it was being actively promoted by prominent engineers and academics alike. James Loudon, determined to turn the new School of Practical Science (SPS) into a proper engineering school, is one good example. John Galbraith, professor of engineering at the SPS and later the first dean of engineering at the University of Toronto, is another. Still others, like Alan Macdougall, were among the founders of the Canadian Society of Civil Engineers (CSCE), organized in 1887 in the hope that it would become the voice of a united occupation and the engine for creating a new learned profession. To Macdougall, for example, the aim of the CSCE was 'to raise the tone of the profession to the standard it is entitled to, as the foremost of all the learned and scientific professions in the world.'[73] Macdougall, indeed, was the association's most ardent advocate in Ontario, instrumental in pressing the CSCE to support a series of bills brought before the Ontario legislature to make engineering a self-governing occupation. Making the case for that innovation on one occasion, Macdougall argued that

the time has come when the Profession of Civil Engineering should be placed on the same footing as those of Law, Medicine and Theology, that is to say, that no person should have the right to style himself a 'Civil Engineer', or to practise, or to be employed as such, unless he shall have been first duly and authoritatively admitted and declared to be a properly qualified member of the Profession by some regularly constituted Body or Corporation having powers corresponding to those enjoyed by the Barristers Societies, the Medical Societies and the Theological Schools of this country.[74]

It is this kind of rhetoric which accompanied and underpinned the view of the engineer as the 'master spirit of the age,' a view assiduously cultivated not only by Macdougall but by other leaders of the CSCE. Whether most engineers, let alone anyone else, would have taken such flamboyant claims seriously, even at the turn of the century, is open to question. But so is any explanation of the development of the occupation in late-nineteenth-century Ontario which focuses primarily on the program or activities of the CSCE. That association had national ambitions; was dominated by engineers in Montreal, where its headquarters was located; and drew the majority of its members, in the early years at least, from outside Ontario.[75] Thus it is not obvious that it represented either the voice or the interests of most Ontario engineers. We want to suggest, indeed, that it did not, and for a perfectly good reason. In Ontario a large number of engineers, and perhaps a majority of those who considered themselves civil engineers and who were permanently established in the province, were *already* organized, had already achieved a restricted title and at least a partial monopoly over their work. That is to say, they belonged to the Association of Ontario Land Surveyors.[76]

Undoubtedly there were both surveyors and engineers who dealt exclusively, or nearly exclusively, in surveying or engineering alone. But what strikes us as important is the extent of the overlap and the prevalence of the surveyor-engineer. Between 1886 and 1892, for example, half the membership of the AOLS listed themselves as engineers or with engineering qualifications.[77] Said one leading engineer in 1896, 'If we look at the engineers who are in practice in Ontario just now, we find that most of them are Land Surveyors – Land Surveyors first and Engineers afterwards.'[78] Said another the same year, 'In Ontario there are over 200 surveyors, a greater part of whom are already members of the [CSCE] ... They are probably better qualified to become civil engineers than half of the members we have in our Society ... *it has been well said that the Land Surveyors will soon be the Civil Engineers of Ontario.*'[79] This sort of overlap was characteristic not only of the rank and file, but of the leadership as well.[80]

There was, it must be said, a certain amount of antipathy between some engineers and surveyors. Among the stalwarts of the CSCE, there were those who tended to look down their noses at 'mere' surveyors, and beyond that there is some evidence to suggest that well-qualified engineers resented the fact that, while they were locked out of public surveying, the surveyors could trample all over their turf with impunity.[81] Equally there is good evidence to think that some leading members of the CSCE would happily have excluded land surveyors from membership in their association.[82] Whatever their preferences might have been, however, for most of the 1890s it was recognized that no legislation promoted by the CSCE would be successful unless it could win support, or at least acquiescence, from the AOLS. Macdougall's own forays were premised on integration of the two bodies.[83] The surveyors, however, were having none of that. As the president of the association noted in his review of the 1899 engineers' bill, 'Of course an amalgamation with our society would not do, as, while an Ontario Land Surveyor may readily prepare himself for a Civil Engineer, it would not be claimed that all members of the Canadian Society of Civil Engineers, made up, as it is, of such various classes, could qualify themselves for Ontario Land Surveyors.'[84] This, of course, was the nub of the matter: engineers were prohibited from practising in areas under AOLS jurisdiction, but surveyors could do engineering work with impunity and had nothing to gain (except the uncertain prestige of membership) by joining the CSCE. The civil engineers thus had to retreat from the notion of integration, and indeed, to make substantial concessions to the AOLS – concessions that would ensure the right of surveyors to continue to engage in engineering work – just to ensure that the AOLS would not oppose the CSCE bills in the legislature.[85]

Not that it mattered very much. For other reasons entirely, the CSCE was unable to persuade engineers to unite around it. Effective associationalism depends on continuity of contact, but engineers were a highly mobile group; many identified with the firms that employed them rather than with fellow engineers; others identified themselves with only their particular branch of engineering and were either indifferent or antagonistic to attempts by the CSCE to speak for them; yet others feared that provincial licensing would limit their ability to move and work freely throughout the Dominion. In the late 1890s, indeed, engineers were so deeply divided about the incorporation bills, and opposition from the mining engineers in particular so adamant, that a CSCE bill would probably have gone nowhere regardless of other circumstances.[86] By modern standards, in sum, there was no *organized* profession of engineering at the turn of the century, and no overriding sense of a common professional identity. If there is an exception to these generalizations, it lies in civil engineering, broadly construed. But in Ontario, if the civil engineers were organized at all, it was under the umbrella of the AOLS. The consequence was that most engineers saw little need to support the CSCE policy initiatives during the 1890s and certainly no need to abandon a legally entrenched organization for one that was not.[87] Eventually surveyors and engineers would go their separate ways and the latter would attain not only the legal prerogatives of professionalism but public recognition as one of Ontario's leading professions as well. At the turn of the century, however, that lay in the future; surveying and civil engineering remained, as they had been for some decades, the kindred spirits of the age.

III

The creation of the public-school system was one of the first, and perhaps the greatest, of all the experiments in social engineering undertaken in nineteenth-century Ontario. To its proponents, a universal system of education was one of the crucial levers for the elevation and enlightenment of humankind, the most potent force, next to religion, for good in the world. But like the spread of religion, the efficacy of public education depended upon the creation of a class of educational 'missionaries,' men of learning, of moral vision, of reputability in their communities, men who were worthy of the task set before them.[88] Transforming Upper Canada's schools, then, meant transforming its teachers as well.

At the forefront of this movement were the colony's professional men, and above all its ministers. John Strachan, Robert Murray, and Egerton Ryerson are only the most eminent examples. Though there were many medical men, some businessmen, and a few lawyers involved as well, the creation and administration of the system before 1871 was largely in the hands of the clergy; they contributed virtually all of its grammar-school inspectors, about 30 per cent of its county boards of instruction, and something like half of all local superintendents.[89] At a time when the apparatus of the modern state was only in its formative stages, there was as yet no predetermined conceptual slot in the occupational order where teachers might easily be filed. The notion of a civil service, of government or local bureaucracies employing large numbers of functionaries to perform the business of the state, was itself just emerging. All that those who created the school system knew for certain was that teaching had to be taken out of the hands of those they deemed ill-educated, ill-requited itinerants, and given to those more suited to fulfilling the high purposes of public education.

They turned, without much reflection, to the occupational image they knew best – to that of the teacher as a professional man, much as they saw themselves, or at least, wanted to be seen. The common-school act of 1850, said Ryerson, had made of teaching 'a public profession, recognized by law, and none but a teacher examined and licensed according to law, is permitted to receive a farthing of the School Fund, any more than a person not examined and admitted to the Law Society, is permitted to practice as a Barrister-at-Law.'[90] Financial security was to be gained as people came to recognize the value of employing the best-trained and educated men available. As salaries improved, the wandering schoolmasters of yore would be replaced by settled and respectable members of the community. Teachers' associations would be formed to create common bonds of occupational identity. 'While other professions – the clergy, the lawyers, the physicians, have long gained a certain position and influence in society, and have assumed the management of their own affairs,' George Brown wrote in 1850, 'teachers, as a class, have until lately stood alone, disregarded by the community.' But now this was to change, he added: teachers were to be trained like other professional men and would also form their own associations for mutual support and improvement.[91]

Nor were such notions far-fetched, to contemporaries at least. If some Upper Canadian teachers were ill-educated itinerants, others were respectable members of colonial society. Grammar-school masters had always made a respectable income and were, for their time, a cadre of highly educated men; so too were many of the early private-school teachers, and some, as well, of its common-school masters.[92] There were familiar models, moreover, elsewhere. The parochial-school masters of Scotland, for example, were as learned, in the words of a contemporary, as members 'of the other liberal professions,' and were by law appointed to their positions for life, guaranteed an annual stipend, and provided with a house and garden.[93] When not just Ryerson but men like George Brown, George Paxton Young, and Daniel Wilson called upon teachers to organize, to take their place as respectable professional men, it was more than an empty rhetorical flourish divorced from the realm of the possible.[94]

WRITING OF THE GROWTH of librarianship in the United States, Andrew Abbott notes that its origins lay in the prior founding, largely by lay initiative, of public and academic libraries, and he remarks that it was rather 'as if the medical profession was created to staff hospitals.'[95] Something similar might be said of the occupation of teaching in Ontario's state school system. Lay initiative created the system and the several thousand jobs that went with it. From the beginning, teachers had to work within a framework of law and regulation, and in a context which gave wide latitude to public opinion, whether it was local trustees and parents, or the legislature and the press. Until 1871, moreover, policy making and administration were largely in the hands of those who were not career teachers. Teachers themselves, in other words, played little part in either the making or the administration of the system. Yet the restrictions implicit in the licence to practise, the principle of professional training, explicitly acknowledged in the establishment of the Normal School in 1847, and above all the encouragement of the lay leadership also presented teachers with opportunities which might be exploited to raise their salaries, their social status, and their span of control over their work.

Some schoolmasters were aware from the beginning of these opportunities and eager to take advantage of them. At mid-century, for example, the Eastern District School Association forwarded to Ryerson a series of motions which, among other things, called for the privilege of self-government 'granted to other professions.'[96] From 1861, moreover, a province-wide organization was established, the Ontario Teachers' Association (OTA). Its membership was not remotely representative of the average teacher in Ontario. Rather it functioned as the voice of the occupational élite: the lay leadership and those schoolmasters who held the most secure and comfortable positions in the system – the grammar-school teachers, and heads and assistant masters of Upper Canada's urban common schools. The executive of the association for 1866/7 presents us with a typical profile. The president was the Rev. Dr Ormiston, a former grammar-school inspector and now minister of Hamilton's largest Presbyterian church. Of the twelve other members whose status can be identified, eleven were headmasters, either of union grammar and common schools or of large urban common schools, and eight had university degrees, in arts, divinity, or law.[97]

Not surprisingly, the issues they thought important reflected their backgrounds and situations.[98] They were not indifferent to such matters as salaries and working conditions, but they held that the key to progress on these sorts of concerns lay in the establishment of secure careers for all teachers, and in attaining the prerogatives of other professional men. That meant, above all, a well-educated and trained workforce, and an end to the powers exercised over teachers by the laymen appointed as superintendents and boards of examiners. Almost annually, from 1865 onwards, the OTA passed motions calling for their replacement by experienced teachers. 'Who,' asked one teacher in 1865, 'constituted the Board of Examiners of medical men, of clergymen, and of lawyers? Were they not the most eminent doctors, theologians and men trained in the law? Who, then, but the most eminent teachers in each locality should be examiners of teachers? If it was right in one case it was right in the other.'[99] Said one leading Ottawa teacher a year later, to appoint laymen as examiners was 'an infringement on the rights of teachers as professional gentlemen.'[100]

Such ambitions were nurtured by the lay leadership itself, both within the Education Department and among many of those who served as local superintendents and local examiners.[101] As a result, nearly all of the OTA's reform program was actually put in place. Through the

School Act of 1871, lay superintendents were replaced by county school inspectors, full-time officials guaranteed a respectable salary by the terms of the act itself. Though certain exceptions were made for those already in the job and for university graduates, newly appointed inspectors were required to hold a first-class public-school certificate of the highest grade.[102] County examining boards were left in place, but their membership was to be comprised of the inspectorate and those who held teaching certificates.[103] During the decade of the 1870s, moreover, both the preliminary and professional requirements for permanent teaching certificates were raised dramatically,[104] and the third-class certificate was consigned to beginners only. It allowed an individual to teach up to three years, but then the principle was 'up or out': either teachers achieved the academic and technical knowledge to obtain the second-class certificate, which now also required attendance at the Normal School, or they lost their licence to teach. And even those seeking the third-class certificate were required to obtain some preliminary professional training through attendance at the county model schools, established in 1877.[105] By the early 1880s, then, virtually the whole of the administrative apparatus had been professionalized, entry requirements had been rigorously tightened, and standards of preliminary education raised for all certification categories.

Reading the record as we have thus far, one might well discern a learned profession in the making. At times, teachers had exercised an effective influence in educational policy making. The impact they had on the shape of the legislation of 1871 was palpable.[106] For a short period in the early 1870s, they even had their own elected representatives in a reconstituted council of public instruction. And the consultations carried out by Adam Crooks, the first minister of education, were no less significant: when Ryerson wanted to test the waters, he organized 'county conventions' consisting primarily of local lay notables; Crooks consulted teachers themselves. As to the influence of the OTA, the editor of the *Globe* remarked in 1877, 'there is no other voluntary association, or even corporate body, in the community which has been able to exercise so direct and unmistakable an influence on the course of legislation during the past ten years.'[107]

The leading figures in Ontario education, moreover, were highly educated men. Principals of the public schools, who usually held first-class certificates, had attained an education equivalent to a partial undergraduate course in arts, even though they might have completed that education at the Normal School rather than a university. High-school principals had been required for years to have a university arts degree; high-school assistants were to have a degree or a first-class certificate.

Forty-five per cent of all those who qualified for a public-school inspector's certificate between 1871 and 1890 held degrees, nearly all of them in arts, though there were also a handful in medicine and law.[108] A luxury for most professionals, who had no need of it, the sheer number of arts degrees held by the professional élite in education gave them a legitimate claim to the prized encomium 'learned profession.' Even those people who held second-class certificates were required to have three years of high school and either obtain junior matriculation (or university entrance) or pass the equivalent non-professional examination for teachers. The standards they were required to meet, indeed, were either identical to, or virtually the equivalent of, the requirements for entry into one or another of the professions – medicine, divinity, and even law. Equally, while teaching hardly offered great financial rewards compared with the potential of medicine or law, it did at least offer male career teachers holding high-school appointments, or senior posts in urban public schools, secure salaries that would match those of most ministers of the Methodist or Presbyterian churches, if not the best of those enjoyed by Anglican clergymen.[109]

The cultural milieu of the wider world, moreover, remained supportive in many ways of teachers' aspirations. The pervasive Protestant moralism of the age made education the eleventh Commandment, and prominent teachers and clergymen could still speak of the common mission shared by teachers and ministers. In universities and colleges yet scarcely touched by the research ideal, university presidents and professors could still see teaching as a unified whole and reach out to their colleagues in the schools, offering moral support and experienced leadership. Beyond that there was the developing body of theory and practice which constituted the 'science of education.' A much-derided notion nowadays, it carried far more plausibility at a time when the social sciences were all relatively new and undifferentiated. Grounded in the mental and moral philosophy of the eighteenth and early nineteenth centuries, it held the promise of developing into a body of technical knowledge which would underpin and inform teachers' everyday practice. Advocating the establishment of a professorship in education at University College in 1876, Paxton Young, who was himself its professor of metaphysics, looked forward to the day when 'the science of education' with 'its foundations in the law of the mind shall be distinctly and practically understood.'[110]

A PROFESSION in the making, then? Viewed from another perspective, it all looked much less promising. Career teachers might have influence but, as they were gradually to discover, they could not assert control over their own conditions of work. They had campaigned successfully to professionalize both local and provincial levels of administration. But whom did these new professional experts serve? Was the Education Department an institution which could further the collective interests of teachers by promoting those interests as part of the more inclusive mission of public education? To put the question another way, was the department in some sense analogous to the Medical Council or the Law Society? Odd as the question may seem to the modern reader, it did not appear so to contemporaries. Three decades of rhetoric had insisted that the public-school system was the ground in which a profession of teaching was to be cultivated. The improvement of the schools and the elevation of the teacher's status were taken to be interwoven objectives. There was also the promising parallel with the law. Judges, drawn from the ranks of lawyers, presided over the courts of the land; the attorney general's office was in the hands of a lawyer; lawyer-politicians played a key role in making the laws, including those affecting lawyers themselves. After 1871 the administration of education was increasingly in the hands of experienced teachers, and it was the department, above all, which had the power to promote the interests of the occupation. Thus, though they might disagree on precisely how teachers' interests could best be represented, for leading members of the OTA at least the Department remained the focus of their hopes for collective advancement.

By the middle 1880s, however, a series of conflicts over administrative issues had gradually clarified the relationship between teachers and the state, effectively undermining the notion that the latter would adequately represent the interests of teachers themselves.[111] They were also being confronted by other inimical interpretations of their status. Responding in the correspondence columns of the *Globe* to a proposal for a government advisory council in which teachers would have an influential voice, 'A Citizen' of Toronto wrote that the school system was of vital concern to the public as well as to teachers. The latter 'are the paid servants of the people; the recipients of the people's money; that they should also have control of the whole educational machinery, including the taxing machinery, and be able at their own pleasure to direct affairs in their own channels, is incompatible with popular government.' The scheme, the letter added, was like getting government clerks to run things. 'I am not in favour of handing over the almost entire control of our educational system to merely one of the bodies interested in its application. I am not in favour of making a close corporation in the interests of teachers of the most important branch of the public service.'[112]

Were, then, teachers professional men or paid public servants, rather like 'government clerks'? That question was not new in the last quarter of the nineteenth century and it would never be entirely closed. But by the early 1880s, caught between the Education Department and the school trustees who hired and fired them, teachers found themselves in a limbo that no amount of learning, training, or professional aspirations could resolve.

The feminization of the occupation threw up a second source of ambiguity. As Alison Prentice demonstrated some years ago, the number of women teachers had grown steadily since mid-century, and by the early 1880s women constituted something like half of the teachers in Ontario, and were to be found at nearly every level of the occupation.[113] Young women taught, on temporary third-class certificates, as their male peers did, throughout the rural countryside; but they were also well represented among the highly educated and well-trained cadre of teachers who were carving out careers in the urban school systems of the province. Toronto, where by 1881 women constituted 84 per cent of public-school teachers, would appoint its first woman principal in 1882, and women had been active members of the Toronto Teachers' Association from at least the late 1870s.[114] Their long-standing presence in the school system, in other words, was a brute, observable fact.

To the creators of the school system, however, a woman teacher was not part of the natural order of things, or at least, as things should be. Their reaction to the steady march of feminization was sometimes hostile, sometimes begrudging, but mostly a determined reluctance even to acknowledge it was happening. And that stance persisted into the last quarter of the century as well. Consider some typical examples of the rhetoric of the time. Should women be required to contribute to the teachers' superannuation plan? No, said the minister of education in 1881: the idea had been discussed in cabinet and had been rejected 'as their circumstances are so different from those of male teachers. Female teachers must, at best, be regarded as a transitory class, since in the large majority of cases ... teaching was to them but a step towards ... the responsibilities of marriage.'[115] Why did teachers need more professional training? the senior high-school inspector, James McLellan, asked in 1878. 'Scholarship alone is not sufficient to make a true teacher. A man may know much of mathematics, science, literature ... but to be a successful teacher, he must [also] know how to organize, how to govern a school.'[116] Why were better salaries needed? Because, said the author of a paper given at the Toronto Teachers' Association in 1877, 'the position of a teacher demands that he and his family shall appear respectable always.'[117]

We do not believe, we may say, that such language was merely a matter of conventional usage, incorporating women within the generic term 'teacher.' The phraseology is too often explicitly exclusive to allow so convenient an explanation. When male teachers spoke of the nature of their profession, women were either dismissed as transitory or were invisible. The reason for this lies in the meaning of 'profession' itself. Could an occupation be called a profession if it was filled with women? The answer is no – or, at least, that professional men could not reconcile their notion of a learned profession with work that might be done by either men or women. Towards the end of the nineteenth century, it remained, as at the beginning, a fundamentally gendered concept, and one in which the idea of a 'professional woman' was a contradiction in terms. But that, in turn, had its own consequences for the aspirations of male career teachers themselves, and it was an American woman who best put her finger on it. Listening to a group of male teachers debating why they lacked the kind of respect accorded to other professional men, Susan B. Anthony offered them her own answer: 'None of you quite comprehend the cause of which you complain. Do you not see that so long as society says a woman is incompetent to be a lawyer, a minister or doctor, but has ample ability to be a teacher, that every man of you who chooses that profession tacitly acknowledges that he has no more brains than a woman ... Would you exalt your profession, exalt those who labor with you.'[118] The exhortation may have fallen on deaf ears; but her analysis of the plight of male teachers is devastating in its logic. Their social ambitions could not help but be diminished and their claims to be professional men rendered ambiguous when they had to participate in an occupation filled with women, and women as well qualified, and as competent, as themselves. Only by changing the meaning of 'profession' itself could that ambiguity be resolved.

Yet there was another and even more fundamental impediment confronting those who sought to make teaching a profession, and that was the role teaching played in the larger market for educated labour during the last quarter of the nineteenth century. As many historians have remarked, the movement from rural to urban work, and from the traditional artisan crafts into new forms of white-collar work, was one of the most fundamental demographic characteristics of the second half of the nineteenth century. Ontario's education system was a major conduit for that shift. The very existence of public education, and above all the multiplication of the high schools, ensured that large numbers of young people, boys and girls alike, would be able to obtain the credentials required for all manner of white-collar jobs.

The impact this had on white-collar work of many different kinds was enormous; its effect on teaching was devastating. If students could survive the rigorous examination system of the high schools, and if they had the financial resources, parental or otherwise, to afford the opportunity costs of staying in school a few years longer than the vast majority of their peers, then access to the requisites of a third- or even second-class certificate was relatively easy. The two most critical requirements were cheapness and accessibility. The high school was local, and either it imposed modest tuition fees or it was free. The same was true of the county model schools. A permanent certificate required a period of residence at one of the two normal schools, but even that might be financed after three years of income-producing work. Beyond that, there were no apprenticeship fees, which one might encounter in other professions, and no expensive outlay for tuition at university or a medical school. Best of all, it left other options open. To qualify for a second- or first-class non-professional certificate also qualified a student for all, or nearly all, the matriculation requirements imposed by medicine, law, or divinity. The salary of a third-class teacher might have had no promise in career terms, moreover, but it might be as much as a doctor or lawyer could make in the first years of his career. For young women, with few other options, teaching was an attractive way of earning money and gaining a few years of independence before marriage. A teaching certificate was also a tempting security blanket for both sexes. It was a hedge against the possibility of spinsterhood or widowhood. Or, as Robert Barr noted in reflecting on his own experience in the 1870s, the value of obtaining a second-class certificate was that it 'would get one into something better than a backwoods school and as first and second class certificates were tenable for life, I had always a bread-winning occupation to fall back upon, if I failed in everything else.'[119]

The result was a flood of entrants into teaching throughout the last three decades of the nineteenth century. At the OTA meetings there were near-annual complaints about 'the appalling number of applicants for any situations of low grade that are offered.'[120] Reviewing the statistics for 1871 to 1883, one prominent member of the association estimated that the number of certificates issued annually was something in excess of one-third the total number of jobs available.[121] The majority of these new teachers, however, never conceived of teaching as a career; rather, they used it as a stepping-stone to something else. In his own analysis of the students enrolled at three of the county model schools between 1870 and 1890, Stewart Hardy found that only 190 of

711 individuals ever went on to achieve second-class, or permanent, teaching certificates.[122] The rest taught for a few years, or months, or never taught at all. 'While the Model schools were seen by educators as the gateway to the teaching profession and a lifelong career,' he concludes, 'many of those who trained in the schools saw them as an opportunity for temporary employment until enough capital was accumulated for them to pursue other career goals.'[123]

In discussing the transient nature of school teaching in the last quarter of the century, most of the historical literature has focused on the third-class teacher. Contemporaries, however, were far more exercised about a parallel phenomenon: the level of transience among males who held second- and first-class certificates.[124] The effects of overcrowding, competition for jobs, and the willingness of school boards to hire equally qualified women at half the price made it an occupation in which relatively few males remained for long, regardless of their qualifications. The *Canada Educational Monthly*, in what most resembles in tone an obituary column, regularly took note of the number of experienced inspectors, principals, and teachers resigning their posts to enter other occupations.[125] 'Young men of ability and ambition,' as one experienced inspector wrote in 1885, 'are not satisfied to spend their lives in the public schools, where the emoluments are small and the prizes few. They aspire to something higher – to be high school masters, lawyers, doctors, divines, and so drift into the universities and thence into the wider fields of intellectual activity where they hope to reap a richer harvest.'[126] And the head of the dental school could remark in 1889 that 'the great bulk of our students are teachers; some of them come from the colleges, but most of them have been teachers.'[127] The flight of male teachers out of the profession can also be tracked through the census returns. Between 1861 and 1891 not only did their numbers shrink as a percentage of the entire workforce in teaching, but as well they declined in comparison with the number of clergymen, doctors, and lawyers. In 1861 male elementary-school teachers vastly outnumbered any of these other three occupational groups. By 1891 Ontario had nearly as many doctors, and more clergymen; even lawyers were outnumbered by fewer than a thousand.[128]

The people who paid the price of these developments were those men and women who, for whatever reason, looked to teaching as a lifelong career. As J.G. Althouse has demonstrated, the years between 1880 and 1900 'witnessed the worst decline in rural salaries the Ontario system has ever suffered.'[129] Though substantially better in urban communities, even there salaries were apparently not attractive enough to prevent large-scale transiency. 'It is impossible,' wrote the editor of the *Globe* in 1882, 'that the profession of teaching can ever rise to its true dignity so long as a large majority of those engaged in it are obliged or content to accept a pittance of $300 or $400 a year as remuneration.'[130]

IN THE MID-1880s, all of these accumulating grievances boiled over and found expression in two attempts to establish organizations to give teachers more control over their lives and work. One proposal was explicitly modelled on the Medical Council and Law Society. It would have created a 'College of Preceptors' (or Teachers) to assume control of the examination and licensing of all teachers in the province, and to have all the powers of professional self-discipline then possessed by the Law Society. Penal laws would prevent unlicensed practice, and a code of conduct would establish norms for professional behaviour. The college would be self-governing, and, in its relationship to the state, it would be 'analogous to that of the Law Society of Upper Canada. The state demands,' the chief proponent of the college explained,

and pays for the administration of justice as a matter of the public weal; it also demands, and for the same reason, that only those who are properly qualified ... shall be entrusted with this work; but the duty of deciding who are qualified to act as judges is left to the Law Society composed of legal practitioners ... Similarly the state demands and pays for public education as a contribution to the public well-being ... [thus] the duty of deciding who are qualified *should* be entrusted to a Society composed of teachers ... The right of teachers to control the admission of members to the teaching profession rests on the same grounds as that of the Law Society to the control of its membership.[131]

A second initiative, originating among a group of Perth County teachers in late 1885, also attracted some wider interest, and a major organizational meeting was called for the summer of 1886. In this case the proposal was to create an association, to be known as the Educational Union and later renamed the Ontario Educational Society.[132] There was talk by some teachers about the association acting rather like a trade union, and at least one or two expressed the opinion that strikes would not be out of the question.[133] In the main, however, most of the Society's advocates saw it more in terms of the conventional associative activity of the period: to provide mutual support and diffuse information, to lobby the politicians for improvements in the school law, and to establish a code of conduct that would encourage teachers to abide by common rules in their dealings with trustees. Whatever the original character of the local leadership of the movement, moreover, by the summer of 1886 the chief participants consisted of well-known schoolmen: principals of urban public schools, high-school headmasters, inspectors; men in most cases who had been long-standing supporters of the OTA but now believed something more was necessary.[134]

The brief rise and fall of both initiatives has recently been charted by Harry Smaller, and we do not intend to reiterate that history here.[135] Both sparked a flurry of interest in the educational and lay press, along with discussion within the OTA and local teachers' associations. Nor were the two proposals mutually exclusive: parallel organizations to serve each purpose – professional regulation, and mutual intercourse and support – were already emerging in some professions, notably medicine, where by the 1880s there was both the Medical Council and the fledgling Ontario Medical Association.[136] Yet both movements foundered almost as soon as they had begun. Leading members of the OTA were divided about supporting one or the other, or opposed both. County teachers' associations were similarly either divided or indifferent. And there were more powerful sources of opposition as well.[137]

But beyond all that, there was the irretrievable impact of transiency itself. Looking back on the OTA's first decade from the vantage point of 1871, one of its leading members admitted that though its success had been hobbled by a number of problems, 'the most formidable difficulty in the way of securing combined action among us was, and still is, the want of permanence in the profession. Teaching has long been used as a means of reaching other professions' and thus too many teachers spent all their spare time 'pursuing a special course of study entirely unconnected with teaching. Having put in his time and drawn his salary, he troubles himself no further about either teaching or teachers, and, of course, gives himself no concern whatever about Teachers' Associations.'[138] That same problem afflicted the county teachers' associations as well: there was, as one teacher noted, very little interest 'among the young teachers.'[139] And it also bedevilled, we suggest, the attempts to organize either the Educational Union or the College of Preceptors. Whatever the attitude of the government might have been to each initiative, in the final analysis the prime requisites for success did not exist. David Boyle, a perennial OTA activist and a man himself involved in the attempt to form the Educational Union, put his finger on the problem as early as 1882:

From the nature of the circumstances that affect teachers and their calling, more especially with regard to the means and source of supply, it is absolutely impossible for them to unite for purely business purposes, as doctors and lawyers do, or even after the manner of mechanics and tradesmen ... No attempt has ever been made by teachers in this country to form 'a ring' for self-protection; and few things are more probable than that such an attempt would fail, not because the necessity for organization is not apparent, but for the reason already assigned – the peculiarity of circumstances. Not only are there scores of ... county model-school teachers looking for situations at all times, but a host of itinerant incompetents, nomads of the profession, who seldom remain in a position more than a year.[140]

From the 1860s to the mid-1880s, in sum, prominent career teachers had attempted to rally the troops in a number of ways, from the founding of the OTA through to the abortive initiatives of 1885–7. The problem was that there were no troops to rally. Or more accurately put, they numbered not in the thousands but the hundreds. Associative activities took time and effort. Successful organizations demanded fees, collective discipline, and long-term commitments. Young men with ambition, young women on their way to marriage had little stake in any of these. And that left only a minority who saw teaching as a lifelong occupation. With so few alternatives before them, it is perhaps not surprising that some of the most vociferous voices to be heard in the *Globe* during the 1880s were those of experienced women teachers demanding better salaries, equal pay and promotional opportunities, and public recognition of their professional status.[141] The men were heard from too; but it does appear that in the main they voted with their feet so far as teaching as a career was concerned.

Even the internal development of the school system conspired to undermine the standing of male public-school teachers. Ryerson's common-school master was to be the head of an 'English College of the People,' a school teaching not only the rudiments but also an advanced English and scientific education. We have chronicled elsewhere the dissolution of this vision and labelled it 'the degradation of the public school.'[142] Forces beyond Ryerson's control, above all the growth of the high school as a multipurpose institution, providing girls and boys with all of the elements of an advanced education, classical and English alike, gradually led to the reduction of the common or public school to an elementary school, teaching younger children exclusively and tutoring them in the elements of education alone, work that had already been conceded in any case as particularly suitable to women. With the school, so went the teacher. Professions (or professions on the make), remarks Andrew Abbott, can be undermined as much by a change in the status of their clientele as by anything else.[143]

The degradation of the public school, moreover, reinforced the gap between high-school and public-school teachers. The former had their own problems to contend with, and some of them were not much different from those of their public-school colleagues. But the headmasters and many of their assistants possessed arts degrees, they were substantially better paid, and they were the gatekeepers to the learned professions and every other white-collar job that required credentials or academic skills. Even in the statistical columns of the Department of Education *Annual Reports*, high-school teachers were labelled 'Ladies' and 'Gentlemen'; public-school teachers drew the epithets 'Male' and 'Female.' One of the chief incentives to obtain a first-class public-school teacher's certificate was that teachers, male and female alike, were then eligible for jobs as assistant high-school teachers.[144] Within the education system itself, in other words, success meant moving out of the public-school classroom.

IN TOO MANY RECENT accounts of the development of teaching as an occupation, there is a tone which treats the rhetoric of professionalism as either mystification or naïve delusion. As we have tried to make clear, we are not content with either interpretation. Casting the occupational ambitions of public-school teachers in terms of a learned profession was natural, given the occupational affinities of teaching in the early or mid-nineteenth century, especially its traditional links to the churches. At a time, moreover, when the lineaments of the modern occupational order were only beginning to develop, there was no preordained place in the occupational hierarchy where teaching, or many other crafts, could 'naturally' be placed. Indeed, it was the very fact of change, of the fluidity of the social order, that created opportunities which could make occupational silk purses out of sows' ears, or, more ominously, vice versa. The question was, could teachers, or any other aspiring occupation, exploit the opportunities, or transcend those forces which might burke their aspirations?

Here, teachers were confronting overwhelming odds. First, they faced the sheer weight of numbers, including the singular fact that the pool of potential entrants was effectively doubled by the opportunities available to women. Teaching was also a profoundly segmented occupation, fragmented by the status differences between high- and public-school teachers, by the different commitments and interests of the transient majority and that minority who saw it as a lifelong career, and by the presence of large numbers of women, who, whatever else, were patently not professional men. That the rhetoric of professionalism remained so irredeemably gender-bound was, of course, not simply blindness or obstinacy on the part of male teachers; rather, it was due, as Susan B. Anthony so incisively noted, to the presumptions embedded in the cultural order itself. But so long as it remained that way, it could not help but divide an occupation which was, every year, increasingly feminized.

Finally, there was the fact that elementary- and high-school teachers were *employees*. In this respect they were the first large occupational group with professional aspirations to face the hard edge of the future. For reasons internal to the occupation itself, achieving those aspirations was an improbability from the beginning. But even had they succeeded in the organizational efforts of 1885 or 1886, they still faced a conundrum. The clergyman of the early nineteenth century also held a public office, but, in principle at least, he was not paid by the state but beneficed; his independence as well as his economic security was grounded in his belonging to one of the twin pillars of civil society. Teachers had no such claims. Nor was their relationship to the state the same as that of doctors. Government could hand over to medical men the apparatus of self-government just because it had so little at stake: 'health policy' in mid-nineteenth-century Ontario consisted of little more than identifying the good doctor; the rest was a private bargain struck between patients and doctors themselves. In contrast public education was a major initiative and a large public investment. By long tradition the power of the purse would ultimately rest with the legislature, and with it responsibility for policy making. Under such circumstances it was unlikely that teachers could ever be given the kind of independence doctors or dentists or druggists acquired in the years immediately after 1867.

Teachers were not alone in having to come to terms with the fact that they were employees. Large numbers of surveyors and engineers were in the same position, employed by government, by local municipalities, or by business. Nor can we assume that employment *per se* was a necessary bar to professional status. It might be that not all professional occupations need be just like doctors or dentists, or alternatively that the culture would consign all of these occupations to some lesser galaxy. The unlikely case of the dentists reminds us that the certitudes taken for granted by the modern reader were once only opportunities to be grabbed, claims to be asserted, ground to be held in the occupational arena. But it did mean that teachers, and others like them, could not simply draw on an earlier model of professionalism, nor could they count on the efficacy of the model to offer them a secure future even if they had achieved its trappings.

The reason was simple, even if little understood at the time. The model itself grew out of a social world consisting mainly of gentlemen, merchants, artisans, and farmers, an economy structured around individuals and families, a nexus of political values dominated by interest and patronage, a society of traditional ranks and orders, a system of rule where even the notion of a distinctive class of public employees was cast in essentially non-modern terms. Throughout the middle decades of the century, all that was changing. But mental maps change more slowly. Even in 1861 prosperous manufacturers and their skilled workmen still identified themselves, almost exclusively, as 'artisans' and the census category 'manufacturer' had yet to be invented; nor did either foresee a fate in large corporations or the assembly line. Clinging in similar fashion to the presumptions that informed the past, teachers could not predict the consequences of the growth of government, the emergence of bureaucracy, or the alternative ways of organizing work that it would throw up. Indeed, even in the 1880s, as Gregory Kealey and Bryan Palmer remark of another problem altogether, 'the state, but recently arrived, was actually obscured ... by its essential unfamiliarity.'[145] Whether they knew it or not, teachers were part of a 'new model army' of occupations whose conditions of work were being cast in a crucible very different from that which had existed only a few decades before.

11
Professions 'Overcrowded'

Like their counterparts in other occupations, lawyers, dentists, doctors, and clergymen could not expect to escape unscathed from the multiple transformations engulfing the province throughout the latter half of the nineteenth century. Nor did they. In the 1860s and early 1870s, for example, doctors and lawyers had tried to tackle the problem of 'overcrowding' through a series of institutional innovations designed to tighten entry to their crafts. For a short period of time, it appeared to work. In the immediate aftermath the number of new recruits declined and, compared with the 1860s, the overall rate of growth slowed in both occupations. As tables 2 to 4 in the appendix demonstrate, nonetheless, absolute numbers increased even during the 1870s; in the two decades that followed, the rate of increase far exceeded either population growth or that of the Ontario workforce. Entry standards might be raised, examinations made more difficult, and the costs of professional training increased in various ways; the only consequence was that students stayed in high school a little longer to meet new matriculation requirements, or taught a few more months to earn extra money. Inexorably, year by year, the number of newly minted lawyers inched upwards, and particularly during the 1880s those entering medicine climbed precipitously. Though its effect was less devastating than in teaching, public education was a Trojan horse for all the professions, threatening by the sheer number of qualified applicants it ground out to undermine the advantages their legal monopolies over practice had been designed to confer.

Accompanying this increase in overall numbers was an equally important phenomenon which had been going on, largely unnoticed, for decades: the diaspora of professional men into the small towns, villages, and hamlets that dotted rural Ontario. Between 1857 and 1870 the number of lawyers in Ontario's county towns (excluding Toronto) almost doubled, while the number located in other, mostly smaller communities nearly tripled; between 1870 and 1900, they nearly doubled and tripled again.¹ This penetration into the countryside has also been documented by Jacob Spelt. In his classic study of urbanization in south-central Ontario, he defines the smallest urban unit, the 'rural village,' by the presence of only one of five urban services; invariably it was the physician. Lawyers rarely followed doctors into these small communities but were increasingly to be found in Spelt's next-largest unit, the 'urban village.'²

Yet another way to measure the diaspora is to link the addresses given in the law lists or medical registers to particular communities within a given county.³ Still overwhelmingly rural and only just past the first stages of settlement, Perth County had only four barristers in 1858, all residents of Stratford, where the county courts were located, and additionally, two attorneys living in the next-largest urban community. By 1870 there were fourteen lawyers in Stratford, eight in St Mary's, and two more in Listowel. By 1882 the number in Stratford had more or less stabilized at fifteen, and in St Mary's it had actually declined to five. But Listowel now had six lawyers, and three more communities had acquired them as well. Overall numbers in Perth County rose from six in 1858 to thirty-three by 1882. The first comprehensive medical register, published in 1872, tells us that Perth already had thirty-two doctors; a decade later there were forty-seven, and by 1892, fifty-eight. In the early 1870s, moreover, doctors were already scattered over thirteen communities, some of them mere hamlets. By 1892 that number had risen to nineteen urban centres, twelve of which had two or more practitioners. For dentists, the census returns are indicative of a parallel development: in 1861, in Perth County, there was only one dentist, located in Stratford; twenty years later there were ten, and by 1891, thirteen; and they were to be found in most of the towns and larger villages.

We have, then, two overlapping demographic trends: a rapid increase in the overall number of professional men in the last half of the nineteenth century, and their dispersal downwards throughout the urban hierarchy. What was the combined impact of these developments? Consider the implications in Perth County. Sometime in the 1870s the small communities of Milverton, Kirkton, and Dublin acquired their first doctor. By 1892 Milverton had three, Kirkton and Dublin two. None of these doctors could expect to live off the population of the village itself. As Spelt remarks, it was not the size of the village *per se* that drew basic services to it:

> The demand for services increased with the growth of a municipality, but services appear sooner in a centre which attracts the population of a large surrounding district. In 1881, there were a considerable number of places with

a population of 200 to 500 which had not yet reached the service status of a rural or urban village. On the other hand, many smaller hamlets which are not shown on [a conventional] map were already rural villages and appear on [Spelt's] map of the service centres.[4]

The rural village, the reader is reminded, was *defined* by the presence of the physician; the physician, in turn, was dependent not only on the population of the village but on its hinterland as well. If Kirkton or Dublin acquired a second doctor, if Milverton acquired yet one more, the consequences are obvious: the volume of practice must increase, each doctor must receive a reduced share, or one must fail and leave.

IT WAS NOT, however, easy to increase the volume of practice. In the nineteenth century, as we noted in an earlier chapter, people rarely consulted a doctor except in serious cases of illness, injury, or childbirth. In part this was so because the doctor's armament against most common illnesses was limited, and self-dosing nearly universal. But it was also attributable to the costs of medical treatment, especially in the countryside. As Paul Starr has argued, charges for visits and simple procedures were generally modest, but what drove costs up were the additional expenses of travel. Doctors charged a basic fee for a visit and so much per mile in addition; someone had to be sent to call a doctor and travel back with him. 'Dispersed in a heavily rural society,' writes Starr,

lacking modern transportation, the great majority of the population was effectively cut off from ordinary recourse to physicians because of the prohibitive opportunity cost of travel. For a farmer, a trip of ten miles into town could mean an entire day's lost work ... Even at relatively short distances, the share of the total price due to travelling and opportunity costs exceeded the physician's ordinary fee; at a distance of five or ten miles, the mileage charges typically amounted to four or five times the basic fee for a visit ... So indirect prices especially limited use of physicians' services in routine illness. In rural areas, many families would not think of calling in a doctor except under the most grave conditions.[5]

Though Starr is writing here of nineteenth-century America, the argument is equally pertinent for Ontario. Tariffs of fees routinely included mileage charges; prolonged obstetric cases might bring additional charges; night visits were more expensive than those carried out during the day. A combination of circumstances – a prolonged delivery at night in a country farmhouse, for example – might cost many times the fee for the service itself.⁶ A new practitioner arriving in Dublin or Kirkton, in other words, had to carve out a living from a relatively inelastic market which might or might not accommodate him, or alternatively might parcel out work in such a way as to leave both practitioners worse off than before.

But why not, then, settle in Stratford, or any one of the rapidly urbanizing industrial towns scattered across the Ontario landscape in the later nineteenth century? Here, presumably, there was a new market to be penetrated: expanding numbers of white-collar workers, including a prosperous middle class, and an agglomeration of skilled and unskilled labourers who, if not prosperous, would at least be spared the opportunity costs farmers encountered when calling upon a distant doctor. This was obviously a strategy that many physicians adopted.⁷ But here again one has to ask about the net effect of market constraints. A growing population will not necessarily provide work for even an equivalent growth in the number of doctors. What is critical is not population growth but effective demand – people who can actually pay for services rendered. Throughout the last two decades of the nineteenth century, it was widely taken for granted that large numbers of unskilled and even skilled workers could not afford the expense of a visit to a doctor's office, the price of the medicines he might prescribe, or the cost of having that prescription made up in a druggist's shop.⁸

The nature of medical practice imposed its own limits. Paul Starr estimates that the average American doctor saw five to seven patients a day, perhaps a handful more in urban areas, or fewer in the countryside.⁹ Though it is probably true in many cases, this situation was not simply the result of there being too few patients to go around. In the late 1860s R.M. Bucke had established a successful general practice in Sarnia but normally saw only ten patients a day. Still he complained that 'I work an average of 12 to 14 hours a day.'¹⁰ Over the course of his long practice in Richmond Hill, James Langstaff's typical patient load rose from seven a day in his fifth year to just under ten in later years; but he too ran a back-breaking schedule.¹¹ Even though established in thriving urban communities, both had to service the nearby townships as well. The habit of visiting patients in their own homes, the travel time that involved, the lengthy processes of evaluation and treatment, the serious nature of most calls upon a doctor's time – all restricted the number of consultations he could carry out and, concomitantly, the overall income he could derive from his practice. A beginner attempting to build a practice could have a much harder time of it: in his first year, Langstaff averaged only one visit a day, and in his second, hardly more than two.¹²

In the very decades that doctors spilled out into the countryside, moreover, much of the rural population was pulling up stakes and going somewhere else. Historians have generally agreed that the overall decline of the farm population was a modest one in the late nineteenth century, though its effects were uneven, and in some counties dramatic.[13] They also agree, however, that the rural non-farm population declined sharply, whole villages and small towns losing a fifth, a third, or even more of their businesses, their manufacturing capacity, or their population. Nor was it only Spelt's urban and rural villages that were hard-hit; he himself provides a remarkable list of old and hitherto thriving south-central Ontario towns which lost population in the same proportion.[14] This could not help but have a depressing effect on local markets for professional services: fewer grocers, shoemakers, clerks, dry-goods merchants, small manufacturers to sustain a medical practice or offer the newcomer a niche in the community. Again we illustrate with Perth County. Excluding Stratford, by far its largest town, Perth lost 21 per cent of its population between 1881 and 1891, and another 5 per cent to 1901. During the 1890s the only two urban communities to experience *any* population growth were Stratford and Milverton. Yet the number of doctors locating in Perth (again excluding Stratford) grew by *44 per cent* between 1882 and 1892, from 34 to 49, and only began to decline in the decade after that. In the process, a few communities lost the services of a doctor altogether, and many saw one or more of them leave for greener pastures. But there were still more doctors in rural Perth in 1903 than there had been in 1882, and the ratio of doctors to population had dropped from 1:1,375 to 1:899.

To put these developments in perspective, a modern comparison is perhaps useful. In 1892 the whole of Perth, including Stratford, had 58 doctors; in 1966 it had 54. For every 10,000 persons living in the county in 1892, there were 12.5 doctors; in 1966, that figure stood at 8.9. Despite the constraints on medical care in the later nineteenth century, in other words, and despite the growth in personal wealth and improved communications following the Second World War, Perth actually had more doctors per population in the former period than it did in the mid-twentieth century.[15]

The number of lawyers increased less rapidly than did doctors and they dispersed less widely. Yet by 1900 nearly a third of them were located outside Toronto and the county towns, dependent for a living on the routine work of conveyancing and what could be garnered from the small cases entered in the local division courts. Wherever they worked, lawyers met the universal constraint of law costs. Only a relative handful of firms or individuals could afford to turn to a lawyer without regard to the financial consequences; most people had to weigh the gains against the losses and tried to avoid it if they could. There were, of course, comfortable and even affluent livings to be made from the law. But new practitioners and country lawyers often found it difficult, and those difficulties increased during the hard times of the 1890s. In his own close study of the number of cases entered in the lower courts, Curtis Cole has identified a dramatic decline in the amount of court business available to Ontario lawyers in the 1890s, and particularly in the division courts, something which would hit hardest at the neophyte and those located outside the larger towns.[16] At the same time, rural depopulation cut into the lawyer's business just as it did the doctor's. The loss of the village or small-town merchant or manufacturer meant not only fewer suits but fewer wills, deeds, and mortgages. During the 1890s, nonetheless, the number of lawyers in Ontario increased by nearly 300, a growth rate of 18 per cent in a decade when the population increased by only 3 per cent, and when the *Canada Law Journal* repeatedly bemoaned the 'dullness of business' that had overtaken the law.[17]

Dentists faced some of the same dilemmas, and others besides. Those who had led the fight for restrictive legislation and better training had based their claim to professionalism primarily on their skills in preventive and high-quality restorative work. But that kind of dental care was expensive, and when used at all was limited to the prosperous. Even then, there were deterrents: the crudities of a dental engine driven by a foot pedal, or drilling still done with hand tools; ineffective or dangerous local anaesthetics, or no anaesthetics at all; the additional costs of chloroform, which usually required the presence of a doctor to administer it; the expense and the difficulties of working with gold (one dentist estimated that it took at least an hour to insert a gold filling properly);[18] all added up to powerful disincentives to seek dental care except *in extremis*.[19] Proper treatment, moreover, required a visit to a dentist's office and the resources of his 'laboratory.' But for country people that often involved the indirect costs not only of travel and lost labour time but even of boarding one or two days while the work was carried out. Throughout the second half of the century, dentists coped with the problem by establishing schedules of visits to other nearby communities where they would set up a temporary office in a hotel, or by maintaining a branch office in another town.[20] Still, that was of limited use to those who had to make a long trip to one or another office regardless of where it was located.

The major marketing problem for dentists, however, was of another order altogether. If one had a broken leg, a doctor was likely to be called. Fading vision or some disease of the eye might provoke a visit to an oculist. But the near-universal solution to decaying or aching teeth was, simply, to have them yanked out, a custom that would infuriate and perplex dentists for decades and which they labelled, despairingly, the 'public perversity.'[21] Had people thirty-two eyes and but two teeth, wailed one, they would probably have their eyes extracted and their teeth saved.[22] The ingrained resistance to alternative forms of dental care nevertheless made it difficult to build a practice upon preventive and restorative work alone.

There was, however, one area where the market for dental services was rapidly expanding throughout the second half of the nineteenth century. Dentists could plug cavities with cheap amalgams, or extract teeth and replace them with artificial plates. Prices for plates dropped steadily during the period, driven downwards by less costly materials and by competition among dentists themselves. Thus many dentists were able to establish a niche in this part of the craft, even if there was not enough high-quality restorative work to go around.[23]

DOCTORS, DENTISTS, and lawyers, moreover, all had to share with rivals the markets in services they considered rightfully theirs alone. The medical acts of 1869 and 1874, for example, defined what constituted illegal practice but didn't eliminate it. The latter could only be done by the resolute pursuit of policies to suppress it, and that took decades, not years. Meanwhile, except for the fact that the homeopaths and eclectics had been brought within the pale, regular doctors had to face a variety of competitors, some of them mainly nuisances and others of more menacing proportions. Among the former were traditional enemies – such as herbalists, bone-setters, and other peripatetic practitioners. Throughout the 1870s, though more rarely after that, country doctors in particular also complained about the prevalence of female midwives, regaling the *Lancet* with the horrors perpetrated by unskilled hands and the 'meddlesome interference on the part of old women' in medical matters.[24] The fundamental issue, however, was not so much obstetrical skill as economic competition. 'Where I am located,' one doctor wrote in the pages of the *Lancet*, 'I have to contend with two of these old bodies and a quack who I must say have been pretty successful in their attendance on such [obstetrics] cases. They charge $2 (while I have $5) ... and they get 60 cases a year, which would amount in my hands to a very decent living for my small family. No doubt all of this would pass into my hands were it not for them, as I am the only doctor within reasonable reach.'[25]

In rural and urban areas alike, however, doctors also faced more formidable competitors. Among them were the druggists, who routinely indulged in 'counter-prescribing' and who, because of their accessibility and their prices, were particularly successful in attracting the patronage of the urban working class. During a well-publicized prosecution of a druggist in 1882, it was universally conceded that the guilty party was only doing, as the *Globe* put it,

> what every druggist in the Dominion is in the habit of doing. The fact is that the druggist is in the case of many of the lesser ills that the flesh is heir to the poor man's physician. His knowledge of the properties of the *Materia Medica* puts him in a position to give intelligent and useful advice in a great variety of cases. His shop door stands conveniently open by day and by night ... The poor man who has need of some simple remedy of a common ailment for himself or some member of his family knows he can consult his physician only at stated hours, possibly very inconvenient for him. Consultation, moreover, means a fee which he may be unable to afford, and then the expense and trouble of getting the prescription put up at a druggist's in addition. There is no doubt that in many a case, by stating simple facts to an intelligent druggist he can obtain without delay and at trifling cost a remedy quite as effective as that got with so much expense and trouble in the regular course.[26]

And then there was the rapid expansion of the patent-medicine industry, promising cures from a bottle (or by some other means) without the need to consult a doctor.[27] In the modern world the market for patent medicines and that for medical services, while not entirely distinct, are distanced from each other, the one catering to a limited range of minor and routine ailments like the common cold, the other dealing with complaints that don't quickly respond to aspirin and nasal sprays. In the late nineteenth century, however, the two markets overlapped substantially, patent medicines often aggressively challenging the ability of the medical practitioner to cure a wide range of major as well as minor illnesses.

The industry's wares were hawked most insistently in the daily press, where their advertisements occupied an enormous amount of space, whole pages indeed, with the same advertisement running for weeks or even months at a time;[28] but the clerical journals were often full of them as well. Typical of these advertisements was one appearing in the *Presbyterian Review*, headed in extra-large type by the following: 'WAS A PATIENT IN ST. JOSEPH'S HOSPITAL, HAMILTON, ONT. THE DOCTORS SAID A SURGICAL OPERATION WAS NECESSARY TO EFFECT A CURE. THE LADY LEFT THE HOSPITAL AND DOCTORS. SHE USES PAINE'S CELERY COMPOUND *AND IS CURED.*' In smaller type below, the conventional few paragraphs described her case and ended with the punch line: 'Several doctors treated me ... [but] I obtained no relief from medical treatment. The doctors said unless I had the ovary taken away I could not be cured. Instead of submitting to the operation, I used Paine's Celery Compound, and I am thankful your valuable medicine cured me. I feel like a new woman, and I would like all sufferers to know just what this great medicine has done for me.'[29]

The reader may giggle. Nineteenth-century doctors could not afford to. The bulk of a doctor's business lay in medicine rather than in surgery or obstetrics. And it was in the field of medical advice and treatment that the patent-medicine industry offered pervasive competition. Who were the *real* doctors to the people in late nineteenth-century Ontario? Regular medicine failed, such advertisements repeated interminably; cures were effected by Paine's Celery Compound or Dr Williams' Pink Pills for Pale People.

Just as the doctors faced their own forms of competition, so dentists had to contend with the doctor, who was exempt from the penal clauses of the dental act. We have found no evidence that doctors ever set up as restorative dentists, though on more than one occasion the medical journals suggested that young physicians would do well to pay more attention to dentistry as a means of building a practice.[30] But what doctors did do, complained dentists, was pull 'thousands of good teeth' every year; pull them indeed 'by the quart.'[31] This reduced the amount of extracting to be done by the dentist; but more important, it removed teeth, that in his hands, could be *saved*. There would be no overcrowding in the profession, said one dentist plaintively, if physicians would send patients to dentists rather than just extracting teeth themselves.[32]

Like doctors, on the other hand, dentists also had to contend with the unlicensed practitioner. Some of these operated on a commercial basis, ducking the law by promising 'free extraction' (it was only illegal to do it for gain or hope of reward) and then charging for some other service such as a nostrum, or simply taking payments under the table.[33] But probably the most ubiquitous competitor was simply the neighbour who had gained some reputation as a skilled tooth-puller. Writing of his own rural childhood, Ontario's dental historian D.W. Gullett remarks that, 'as late as 1904, it was a debatable point among the populace whether it was better to have a local farmer extract an aching tooth with his turnkey or drive six miles to a dentist with his cruel forceps.'[34]

For lawyers, the equivalent of unlicensed practice in medicine and dentistry was lay conveyancing, a term applied when non-lawyers earned income from drafting wills, deeds, mortgages, and other similar documents. Though a long-established practice in Upper Canada, it probably took even firmer root as commercial life quickened in the decades around mid-century. Small transactions involving land or commerce needed documentation, lawyers only slowly moved beyond the county towns, and laymen who could do the job were not only more accessible in the countryside but in town and country alike were willing to do it at cheaper rates.[35] Lawyers themselves often referred to it as 'unlicensed practice'; but it was in fact perfectly legal for laymen to perform such tasks and charge fees for it.

So long as the number of lawyers remained small and most practised in the larger towns and cities, there was apparently enough work for both professionals and laity, and thus conflict between the two groups remained muted. Lawyers controlled the county and superior courts, carried on most of the complex or special conveyancing, and more generally could rely on the routine business of all those prosperous citizens who wanted professionals to tend to their affairs. Laymen tended to pick up any remaining business, combining conveyancing with a variety of other services such as land surveying, insurance, real estate, accounting, or similar activities. Since lawyers and laity didn't compete against each other, professional complaints about lay conveyancing, though frequent enough from the mid-1850s to the mid-1870s, tended to take the form of sporadic grumbling rather than insistent or concerted demands for protection.[36]

Any complacency that may have existed in the two decades after mid-century, however, began to disappear as the press of numbers made itself felt during the 1870s. Everywhere, more lawyers, especially the new entrants to the profession, had to find work where they could, and they depended as a first resort on the routine paperwork involved in conveyancing. It was a particularly important source of income to those who proposed to move beyond the larger urban centres and establish a practice in villages and hamlets never before graced by the presence of a lawyer's office. To their dismay, however, they quickly discovered that they were entering occupied territory. 'I have been practising law for the last nine years in a country town,' an 'Old Subscriber' to the *Law Journal* explained in 1880; 'besides myself there are two other professional men, and three (at least) so called "conveyancers".'[37] Not to be outdone, 'Scriptor Sine Scriptum' wrote in the next issue that 'Old Subscriber' had only 'practised nine years in a country town; I have practised at least eighteen. There are two other professional men in our town as in his; *he* has to contend with three conveyancers, and I alas! with thirteen.'[38]

Nor could country lawyers cling to the self-deceiving shibboleths of earlier decades which dismissed lay practitioners as broken-down tradesmen or half-literate grocers, marginal men who attracted clients only because no reputable professional man practised nearby. 'Schoolmasters, magistrates, clerks of the Division courts ... MPs, township officers and some others, have monopolized the principal part of the conveyancing business in this county,' wrote one lawyer.[39] Others added clergymen, general merchants, deputy clerks of the Crown, county registrars, postmasters, and druggists to the list.[40] In a revealing letter written in 1881, Fred Rogers, a lawyer who had settled in Wingham, described the origins of lay practice in Huron County: 'They resided in the county long before solicitors came into it – they have grown up with the country, and have the confidence of the old settlers – they in fact got the business before any lawyers came here, and they mean to hang onto it and keep it in spite of the Law Society, or as Mr. Scott (a "prominent" conveyancer here, who keeps several clerks writing for him) told me when I came here, "We have a vested interest in the conveyancing!"'[41]

Lay practice was all the more threatening because it extended far beyond conveyancing narrowly defined. Laymen offered legal advice on a wide variety of matters, called themselves lawyers and were taken as such by local people, and routinely acted as advocates in the division courts. True, lay agents could not sue for costs or be awarded payment if a tariff of fees applied, but they did have the right to represent themselves or act for others in those courts.[42] Some even took surrogate court work, an area unequivocally restricted to either lawyers or those acting on their own behalf. 'At least one attends every funeral within twenty miles,' an irate lawyer informed the *Law Journal*, '[and] is said to hunt in couples with the tombstone man ... "You will have some surrogate work to do," he suggests to the survivor ... "No use going to lawyers; they are great rogues. I am an honest man and will put *thy* business through for one-half of what it will cost thee, if thou employest a lawyer."'[43]

Unlike the situation in the cities, or even in the smaller county towns, lay practitioners posed a serious economic threat to country lawyers because both groups competed for the same scarce dollars. 'A country solicitor's practice is to a great extent built up by conveyancing: but the fact is, nearly all the conveyancing outside the cities is done by non-professional men,' said one; 'take away from a country solicitor his conveyancing, his surrogate practice, his collecting, and a great deal of his Division Court work, and often his advising, and what, I say, have you left him?'[44] By the early 1880s, indeed, the editor of the *Canada Law Journal* could declare that lay conveyancing, or 'Professional Invaders' as he called them, was the 'burning question amongst country practitioners.'[45]

AND WHAT OF THE CLERGY? Did they experience the same patterns of dispersal and growing competition? Though there were complaints from Anglicans and Presbyterians during the middle decades of the nineteenth century about a shortage of ministers, their numbers rose steadily throughout the second half of the century,[46] and, as we have already seen, the Methodists had more than enough from at least the 1860s onwards. According to the census, moreover, between the 1850s and the 1870s the number of ministers of all denominations grew more rapidly than the general population, and at roughly the same rate during the 1880s. By 1891 Ontario had some 3,200 ministers and priests, exceeding the total of male elementary-school teachers, *or* of doctors, *or* lawyers.[47] To turn once again to Perth County, by 1871 it already had fifty-four ministers, compared with thirty-three doctors and twenty-four lawyers. In the towns and villages, ministers were thick on the ground: in 1881 Stratford, with a population of 8,239, had 25 clergymen compared with 12 doctors and 15 lawyers. But the ministry was also very widely dispersed throughout the countryside. Even doctors were to be found in only thirteen communities; ministers were located in every township and in nearly every hamlet in the county.[48]

How are we to account for this plethora of preachers? The pressure of denominational competition was an obvious cause: if each church didn't field a local candidate it risked losing potential adherents to others. But there is also a more fundamental explanation, and one that renders all conventional formulas governing the relationship between supply and demand largely irrelevant in the case of the clergy. The ministry did not live by the precept that directed other professional men to 'go ye forth' and find communities which not only needed their services but could also provide them with respectable livings. The biblical injunction was to 'preach the gospel to every living creature.'

Were there enough ministers, for example, to serve all the needs of the Free Church's London presbytery? By one means or another, its committee on Home Missions reported in 1865, all existing congregations were provided for; and yet 'the amount of supply given may serve the purpose of keeping together and preserving in connection with the Church those who are decidedly attached to it, but cannot possibly accomplish what is the proper mission work, the gathering in and establishing in religious habits the ignorant, careless and worldly of the community.'[49] The conviction that the presbytery faced a shortage of ministers, in other words, was rooted not just in the recognition that there were a specified number of vacant parishes, or congregations yet to be organized; more fundamentally, it arose from the divine injunction laid upon the Christian Church to carry its message to all of humankind. In this sense, there could never be an excess of men entering the ministry.

But that injunction was not devoid of economic implications. Reporting on his mission trip to Grey County a decade earlier, one minister wrote that in Owen Sound, with its population of 1,300 souls, 'there are places of worship belonging to the Church of England, the Disciples, the Wesleyans, the Free Church, the United Presbyterians, the Congregationalists and the Baptists'; he was there to scout the prospects for the Kirk.[50] Did Owen Sound, then, have too many or too few? And did it need one more? Perhaps it did, to minister to a small band of the faithful who wanted a minister of their own kind. Yet the financial consequences were plain. Only the largest communities could sustain such fractured allegiances and still reward their ministers generously. The churches continued to press into communities large and small, nonetheless. As the editor of Victoria College's student journal remarked in 1887, 'Many circuits have been so divided up as to make it impossible for them to support their ministers. Men must be furnished with appointments, and consequently circuits which were only able to support a married man and a single man have been cut in two, and two married men sent to labor on them. In towns and cities also, some churches are kept open for which the only apparent need is to supply a minister with a place.'[51] And all that during decades when the population of rural hamlets and villages was shrinking everywhere, a development that hit at clergymen even harder than at doctors or lawyers just because there were so many more of them.

The result, in economic terms at least, was a surplus of ministers, which drove salaries down in much the same way as it had for public-school teachers. Large numbers of ministers lived at or below the figures their denominations established as the *minimum* acceptable stipend; large numbers of others, barely above it. By the last two decades of the century, moreover, it brought clerical underemployment and even outright unemployment in its train. Wrote the editor of the *Presbyterian Review* in 1886, 'comparatively very few even of our ministers are aware of the large number of probationers who, like horses in a treadmill, go the ceaseless round of preaching in vacancies but are never called by any congregation.'[52] More than a decade later the editor of the *Globe* drew attention to the same phenomenon. In the Presbytery of

Professions 'Overcrowded' 261

Toronto alone there were thirty-seven ministers who had no charge. Many were retired but of these only a few were 'wholly incapable of preaching ... Of those who are waiting for something to turn up,' he continued,

one man, a master of arts, said pathetically the other day that he loved the ministry, but as he could not get a charge would have to enter some other employment. Another man, still in the prime of life, said that when he graduated he had the choice of three calls, but now cannot even get a chance to preach ... One of the number gave up the ministry and entered medicine.

Not only are these men without calls, but they do not even get chances to fill 'supplies.' It is not infrequent for some of them to offer their services gratuitously rather than get entirely out of touch with the pulpit.[53]

The most difficult problem confronting the stationing committees, as one leading Methodist said in 1898, was 'the crowded conditions of the Conferences; ... [they] cannot put eleven men into ten men's places.'[54]

The schools and colleges, then, threw up their graduates, and the churches tried to find places for them. But the laity had to pay the bills, and their allegiance was divided, not just among three denominations but among others besides. The churches were not unaware of that reality; indeed they acknowledged the economic impact of pluralism often enough.[55] In this respect there were, as one editorial put it, 'TOO MANY MINISTERS.'[56] Yet it remained hard to square that with the gospel call. 'There is not the slightest danger of overcrowding the sacred calling,' the editor of the *Presbyterian Record* could write in 1886: 'The field is everwidening; indeed, it is practically unlimited, for it is co-extensive with the human race.'[57]

HOW DID INDIVIDUALS COPE with the growing number of competitors they faced within and without their occupations? Not surprisingly, they adopted a wide variety of survival strategies, attempting to locate new markets for themselves or corner old ones by innovative approaches. Of the various ways to find new markets, the most notable was emigration. Like many of their fellow Ontarians in the last quarter of the nineteenth century, professional men left for the United States and the Canadian west to seek out opportunities where their education and skills would bring them better, or quicker, returns, and a more secure future. And they left in staggering numbers.

In the case of medicine, for example, the published medical registers tell us that, in 1892, 25 per cent of all Ontario registrants either practised outside Ontario or were listed as 'residence unknown.' By the end of the century, these two categories totalled 30 per cent. Dentists' skills were as portable as doctors', and there is no reason to think they didn't follow suit, especially when one considers the pattern in a similar occupation, that of pharmacy. In 1889 the editor of the *Canadian Pharmaceutical Journal* estimated that something like 75 *per cent* of all druggists who had graduated since 1868 had gone to the United States or the Canadian west.[58] Ontario's lawyers tended not to go to the United States, where their training was less relevant, but they constituted a large portion of the early bar in the western provinces, and at the end of the century one commentator could speak of 'the departure of scores of young barristers for other places, chiefly for Western Canada, where they will grow up with the new towns and cities and doubtless do better than they would have here.'[59] That indeed was exactly the sentiment expressed by one young Ontario lawyer in a letter to his future wife in 1882: 'I am going to Manitoba the reasons for this change are many chiefly the opportunities of advancement twofold more than here where everything is settled and it takes a long time to make that progress which ... young men are ambitious for.'[60]

Clergymen also emigrated in large numbers. Like those in law or medicine, young (and not so young) men trekked west to staff the urban churches and the rural missions being established in Manitoba and beyond. Others joined the ranks of missionaries flocking to Africa and India, China and Japan, and the myriad islands of the great South Seas. Indeed, without casting doubt upon the intensity of the evangelical fervour which motivated them, one can at least speculate that the flowering of the missionary movement at home and abroad, and the surplus of pious and educated young men, was no coincidence. Technically, of course, they were not emigrants but members of denominations increasingly pan-Canadian in scope and committed to an international mission besides. But they were lost to Ontario nonetheless. There was, moreover, a steady stream of clerics going to the United States, especially in the 1890s. Some of these were experienced men with high reputations, leaving pulpits in Ontario's most prominent churches.[61] Others were young men attracted by better starting salaries than they could hope to earn at home.[62] In 1895 the *Canadian Churchman* would refer to it as this 'distressing exodus' and the *Presbyterian Review* would ask, 'Are our Colleges to become largely sources of supply for American pulpits?'[63]

A 'distressing exodus' indeed. A recent study of those who graduated from Queen's College between 1895 and 1900 reported that something like 56 per cent of health professionals (including both males and females) left Ontario, 21 per cent for the west and 35 per cent for the United States; 54 per cent of the graduates who became lawyers went to the Canadian west (though none to the United States); of those who entered the ministry, 30 per cent left the province; for those who entered teaching, the figure was 40 per cent.[64] Some of these graduates undoubtedly went because they chose to, responding as the young perennially do to the beckoning call of faraway places and strange-sounding names. And yet the history of other mass emigrations tells us that the majority left because of dimmed expectations and blighted hopes at home. Not for the first time, in any case, Ontario's schools, colleges, and professional schools were producing huge numbers of graduates who, finding no easy foothold in the province itself, left for greener pastures elsewhere.

Those who stayed home pursued other strategies to expand or secure a clientele. Probably the most common were various forms of self-promotion. They circulated 'cards,' placed advertisements in the newspapers, or printed up flyers and posters drawing attention to their credentials, talents, and, often enough, fees lower than their rivals charged. Doctors saw to it that their successful operations or cures were reported in the newspapers, and lawyers were occasionally accused of doing the same with their court cases.[65] Lawyers seem to have been the most circumspect in these matters, and dentists the most flamboyant, the latter using everything from large posters installed on the main roads leading into the cities and towns, to woodcuts of full sets of plates with prices attached, promises of 'painless extraction,' and showcases of their work located at the gateposts to their offices and even at local fairs. If the clerical press is to be believed, the ministry was not far behind them. 'A pulpit that can draw is the cry,' one Toronto Methodist minister declared in 1891.

Claptrap titles to sermons, claptrap illustrations, and claptrap methods of delivery spiced with a Gospel solo, often only a jingle of claptrap words, with a request that the congregation unite in the still more claptrap chorus ... Brevity is in such demand that in one church the minister advertises that his sermons will take only twenty minutes in delivery ... The treatise has given place to the sermon, the sermon to the sermonette and one alternative only remains, either the sermonium or obliteration.[66]

Variations on that theme were heard from Anglicans, Presbyterians, and Methodists alike.[67] 'A fairly accurate idea of this catch penny pulpit style,' wrote the editor of the *Evangelical Churchman* on one occasion, 'may be gleaned by a walk up Yonge Street, in Toronto. At every street corner huge placards, badly conceived and executed, advertise to the passersby that the Rev. Mr. So and So and his choir will make a show of themselves so as to *draw* a crowd on Sunday next.'[68]

Both dentists and doctors experimented with new organizational forms. In the larger towns and cities, the former established 'dental factories' where cheap plates were manufactured on a high-volume, low-cost basis.[69] Alternatively they created 'dental parlors' with several chairs staffed by students or other employees.[70] In the 1890s some found work in department stores or as part of other commercial ventures owned by non-dentists.[71] Doctors created 'medical syndicates' which offered initial 'free consultations' and ready access to specialists in a wide variety of diseases.[72]

Physicians more commonly adopted two other strategies, however: establishing themselves as specialists, or entering into contract practice. Specialization came slowly to Ontario in large part because small urban populations simply could not sustain it. First in Toronto, nonetheless, and then in the larger county towns, a few doctors could begin to limit their work to one or another specialty. Noting a recent decline in surgical operations at the Toronto General Hospital, the editor of the *Canadian Practitioner* explained in 1886 that 'a great number of the medical practitioners throughout the province are now skilful surgeons, and many patients who formerly came to Toronto are now operated on at home. There is a surgeon in every district of the Province who can perform even the most severe operation, with skill and success.'[73] Beyond surgery there was gynaecology and obstetrics,[74] those who specialized exclusively in eyes (the oculists), or more commonly in ear, eye, nose, and throat, and by the 1890s a variety of other organs and diseases.[75]

Some doctors may have learned their specialist skills in Ontario through extra hospital attendance or simply have been able to establish a reputation because of their 'knack' in a certain area. But what has impressed us in the medical record, and it is something unique among our professional men, is the large number of doctors, already licensed in Ontario, who went off to study in one of the specialist hospitals in London or elsewhere in Britain.[76] There is no reason to think their motives were narrowly economic. Idealistic young men committed to the cause of medical science undoubtedly went abroad because they were eager to master the techniques and the knowledge that would put them at the forefront of their field. But, at the same time, they could not help but be aware of the social and economic advantages that might be thus obtained – the chance to secure a special niche in the medical market, to distinguish themselves beyond their peers, or to obtain appointments as specialists at the small but growing number of general hospitals scattered about the province. It was also one of the surest routes to an appointment as a professor at one of the medical schools: by 1890 most of the medical instructors at Trinity and many at the University of Toronto and Queen's had British qualifications, and while some of these men were born and educated in Britain, there were also a number of young Canadians who had finished their education in one of the British hospital schools.[77]

The second strategy was contract practice. In some cases this involved working for municipal councils, railway companies and other large industries, or commercial enterprises like department stores where owners would arrange cheap medical services for their male employees or their 'shop-girls.'[78] But the main market for contract practice was with the fraternal lodges, benefit societies, and workingmen's clubs. Our labour historians in particular have described the importance of these institutions in Ontario's industrializing towns and cities during the second half of the nineteenth century; one of their drawing cards, though not the only one, was their ability to make available to those who could not otherwise afford it such services as cheap life insurance, sickness benefits, and medical care. 'We have in Ontario a very large number of labourers, skilled mechanics, and even employers of labour, who belong to these various organizations,' wrote the editor of the *Canadian Practitioner* in 1885.

When a new lodge is opened, or a vacancy occurs in one already in existence, the names of a number of physicians are proposed by members, an election takes place, and the medical man who obtains the largest number of votes becomes the lodge physician. He holds office for one year only, and may be superseded at the end of that time. As a general rule, however, the lodge retains the same physician for a number of years.

The fees paid are usually one dollar a year from each member, and when medicines are provided the amount is a dollar and a quarter. In many instances, however, very much smaller fees have been accepted.[79]

By the 1890s even its opponents had to concede that lodge practice was deeply embedded throughout the province, and for good reason.[80] It offered the neophyte the promise of a ready-made male clientele; it offered a supplement to a struggling practice; but, above all, it provided a base for gathering in a family practice through the contacts made with the lodge members themselves.[81]

RISING NUMBERS, market constraints, a variety of lay competitors, the internal struggle within each occupation to find a niche which would provide a respectable income – all of it together found expression in the cry of 'professions overcrowded.' The timing of such complaints differed by occupation and in volume. Among doctors it was recurrent from mid-century onwards and grew increasingly shrill throughout the last two decades of the century. Clergymen only gradually reconciled themselves to the idea that such a phenomenon could exist at all. Having survived the crush of the 1860s, lawyers rarely raised the issue of numbers until the 1890s, but the vociferous attack on lay conveyancing is a kind of surrogate for it: work sequestered by the laity meant that there were too many lawyers for the amount left over for them. And if the professional journals themselves sometimes played down the issue, it was, not surprisingly, a recurring source of worry in the student press, the young editor of *Acta Victoriana* commenting in 1879 that

Canada is flooded with briefless barristers and doctors looking in vain for patients. The teaching profession is so full that the most ordinary position in a high school is sought for by thirty or more applicants. The ministry of the Methodist Church at least is already overcrowded ... There is, of course, always plenty of 'room in the upper stories' in all of the so-called learned professions; yet before entering on what may be a life-long struggle, a man should consider well what the odds will be against him, and not attempt what he is unequal to.[82]

Yet the notion of 'overcrowding' begs for interpretation. Writing about 'the problem of an excess of educated men' in Western Europe during the first half of the nineteenth century, Lenore O'Boyle remarks that 'it is meaningless to say that there were too many trained men for the needs of society; the mass of the population, for example, could have used far more doctors or teachers than were provided.' O'Boyle goes on to suggest that what it seems to have meant in Britain and Europe was that there were too many men entering a handful of relatively prestigious occupations to maintain all of them according to their expectations; the disparity between expectations and reality was then interpreted as 'overcrowding.'[83] This we find a plausible interpretation for nineteenth-century Ontario as well. The issue is not so much supply as effective demand – the ability of individuals, or the society as a whole, to pay for such services at a price at which professional men are willing to provide them.

Nor is 'overcrowding' a synonym for a contracting, or even stable, market in professional services. While we have no systematic evidence on this point, it appears from the surviving medical tariffs that fees remained remarkably stable across the entire second half of the nineteenth century, and may have actually fallen off somewhat, despite a general rise in the price of most commodities, wages, and salaries. Medical services also became steadily more accessible geographically. Though the evidence is thinner, dental fees appear to have followed the same course, and while, for most people, high-quality dental care may have been out of reach, many more people could afford cheap fillings or artificial plates at the end of the century than fifty years earlier. Despite complaints about inadequate salaries or unfair competition, more clergymen and more lawyers found work in Ontario than ever before. There is good reason to think, in other words, that the market for professional services grew substantially over the last half of the nineteenth century.

But not fast enough. Too many people too poor to avail themselves of such services; the grip of traditional customs like self-dosing and extraction; the limits of effective therapeutic or surgical skills; the opportunity costs involved in providing care in country areas – given such constraints, rising numbers meant more competition within each occupation for the limited clientele that did exist. In the search for expanded markets, moreover, professional men increasingly found themselves on overlapping turf, doctors and dentists competing with each other over extractions, for example, or doctors attempting to capture a clientele that had been traditionally left to the druggist. Then there were lay competitors, some merely a local nuisance and some representing powerful interest groups. For clergymen, the situation was only somewhat different. Their clientele was precommitted; but it might be too small to sustain them according to their expectations and it was always subject to the depredations of predators representing some other denomination, or a new vision of the true faith.

12
Clergymen and the Ascendancy of the Laity

The Christian Church, it goes without saying, has purposes other than providing its ministers with decent salaries and working conditions. But its governing bodies also have, as one of their first responsibilities, the recruitment and placement of an efficient workforce, securing for it some degree of financial security and regulating the relations between the shepherd and his flock. Certainly the churches were not oblivious to the implications of denominational competition, the multiplication of numbers within their own ranks, or the dangers that low stipends posed to both doctrines and assumptions about the relationship of the clergyman to his society. Indeed, great efforts were made to mitigate their worst effects. Yet it proved remarkably difficult to contain the forces unleashed by pluralism and voluntarism, and increasingly in the later nineteenth century, the consequences seemed to be eroding the very foundations of the clerical order itself.

One obvious challenge was the existence of too many small congregations, straining lay finances, draining resources from the larger work of the church, and depleting ministerial pocketbooks. A problem even in the middle decades of the century, it progressively worsened with the depopulation of the countryside. Equally, urbanization forced the churches to multiply buildings and find ministers for the burgeoning towns and cities. The impetus to church union constituted one response to these pressures. Between the 1860s and the 1880s, a series of mergers between various Presbyterian and Methodist groups gradually created united, and much larger, denominations. The union movement made many clergymen uneasy, and with good reason: when two or three congregations in a small community were reduced to one, they worried, naturally enough, about their jobs. But carefully drawn agreements, the promise of better stipends through consolidation, along with the opportunities available in the cities and the west, all helped reduce anxieties and smooth the transition.[1]

While these intradenominational unions limited some of the worst excesses of competition, the pressures remained, especially in northern Ontario and the rural countryside, and in some places at least Methodists and Presbyterians began to divide up the territory between them to ensure the survival of one viable congregation, and one decent stipend for its minister.[2] More important, there was increasing talk throughout the last two decades of the century of yet larger unions combining the resources of two or more denominations, or even the whole of Protestant Christianity – talk that would begin to result in concrete action at century's close.[3] High-toned it usually was, but one correspondent to the *Globe* put the issue in plain language, and in keeping with the spirit of the age. The amalgamation of the churches was 'in line with the present trend of business. The small tannery, the small manufactory, the small store are gone or going. Everything must be on a big scale.' But when it came to religion

> we do not proceed on the same plan. Here are two churches, the Presbyterian and the Methodist, ... preaching the same plan of salvation, following the same methods of work ... Why, then, in the name of common sense, if for no higher reason, should we in small villages go to the expense of having two churches heated and lighted, two ministers poorly supported, two organs, and two little knots of worshippers, when one of each would be far cheaper and have greater drawing power?[4]

Church unions, nonetheless, were an organizational innovation designed to rationalize resources, not create them. Money still had to be found to pay salaries and provide for all the other projects the churches were committed to. Many Anglican ministers, of course, could count on the commutation fund for the largest portions of their stipends, and so indeed could those who had belonged to the pre-union Kirk. In both cases, moreover, some new ministers would benefit from the surpluses the commutation funds generated from the early 1860s onwards. But that was never enough to meet the whole cost of supporting additional recruits, and in 1867, in any case, the Kirk had been dealt a devastating blow when much of its commutation (as well as its university endowment) fund was wiped out by the failure of the Commercial Bank of Kingston.[5] Thus the forced march towards voluntarism continued throughout the second half of the nineteenth century. The churches could not do much about the general run of ministerial stipends, which were largely determined by what each local congregation was able or willing to pay. But they did try to establish minimum figures below which no stipend was supposed to fall, and, no less important, they established a variety of special funds, raised from the laity but controlled by the governing bodies themselves, to provide additional degrees of security – to underwrite the salaries of those who received less than the stipulated minimums, especially on the home mission field; to create pension funds; to provide subsidies for the education of clergymen's children; or to rescue their widows and orphans from destitution.[6]

Financial innovations designed to help buffer the clergy from the effects of voluntarism were paralleled by attempts to ensure the orderly placement of recruits and the preservation of career paths. Whether it was done by the Anglican bishop or the stationing committee of the Methodist Conference, jobs were assigned, in principle at least, by some clerical authority, and allocated in ways appropriate to the life-cycle: a mission or rural circuit for the young ordinand, a village pastorate that would support a growing family, or a post that was not too taxing for the elderly. Merit, as judged by one's peers, would lead to promotion for some; but, by one means or another, all would be provided for. Presbyterian ministers were initially 'called' by a congregation, but the presbytery had to approve (or moderate) the call. The doctrine that underpinned these notions in all three denominations, in any case, was that a minister was sent by God and his church to labour among the laity, not 'hired' as one might hire a mechanic or labourer.[7]

The clergy, moreover, made prodigious efforts to maintain these principles. Despite enormous pressure from the laity, as we have already seen, Anglican clergymen in the Diocese of Toronto were able to secure a canon which put 'patronage' in the hands of the bishop, though he was also supposed to consult with representatives of the congregation as well. During negotiations over union in the 1870s among Methodists, the Wesleyans had to agree to give laymen a voice in the new General Conference, which was the highest policy-making body of the church – something they had traditionally been loath to concede.[8] But the clergy successfully fought off the admission of the laity to those committees of the regional 'annual conferences' which dealt with the crucial areas of internal discipline and the stationing of the ministry. Presbyterians had less leverage because of the central role of the congregational call, but by the 1870s the General Assembly created its own committee to supervise the orderly placement of probationers who were without churches or those who had been 'loosed from their charges,' individuals who were supposed to get first crack at each vacancy as it became available. In effect the committee's responsibility was to put a safety net under the calls system to ensure that all its ministers had jobs.[9]

'THE MINUTE A MAN begins to put his hand in his pocket,' one clerical correspondent remarked in the pages of the *Evangelical Churchman* in

1888, 'he consciously or unconsciously claims the right of a voice in the disposal of his money.'[10] And he was right. Regardless of the best-laid plans of the clergy who dominated the governing councils of the churches, voluntarism made the laity, as one fearful Anglican had once said, both 'patrons and paymasters.' Among Presbyterians, congregations simply bypassed the committee on placement, calling new graduates or those who were already settled, without even informing the committee, and these calls were simply rubber-stamped by the local presbyteries; those left on the committee's list descended into a pool of underemployed clerical labour, eking out a living by supplying congregations between calls, or giving up and leaving the ministry entirely.[11] Among Methodists, the 'invitation system' spread steadily, congregations picking and choosing potential candidates and then exerting pressure on the various stationing committees to accede to their request.[12] In the mid-1870s, Benjamin Cronyn, Bishop of Huron, could concede that 'the canon on Patronage is practically of little or no value, owing to the unfortunate state of feeling that prevails in most localities, that each congregation should have the choice of their clergyman.'[13]

The laity acquired their clout in these matters quite simply. An unpopular minister would be rewarded with a declining stipend and a dwindling congregation. Even when the assignment might be a relatively brief one, as was the case with Methodism, a congregation could be 'ruined' in short order by an unwanted appointment.[14] Anglican and Presbyterian congregations had no power to remove an incumbent. Indeed, the notion of a 'settled ministry,' where a clergyman held a position for life, was regarded by Anglicans especially as one of the central principles of church polity, and a critical prop for the independence a clergyman must have in order to exercise his office properly. But voluntarism put even that security at risk: without resources independent of the congregation, an unwelcome appointee could be 'starved out,' the laity simply refusing to contribute to his support, or melting away to other churches.[15] It was, in other words, not in the interest of the minister, congregation, or denomination itself to impose the one without the consent of the other, and thus all three denominations descended, to one degree or another, into a kind of *de facto* congregationalism.

Though not without a fight, predictably enough, in the Anglican Diocese of Toronto. Bitter divisions between high and low church over many issues, including the patronage question, had blighted synod meetings throughout the 1870s, but matters came to a head in 1878 when the Rev. C.C. Johnson, a senior high church minister, was appointed to St George's, Oshawa, without any consultation with the local congregation, against their clearly expressed preference for another candidate, and despite the canon of 1871 on patronage, which seemed to require consultation. When the new appointee 'appeared at the church to take services,' writes Alan Hayes, 'the wardens barred his entrance. The diocese smelled a heaven-sent opportunity "to fight the battle of the Church," and Johnson sued the wardens.'[16] Much to the consternation of the high church party, he lost his case on the grounds that the spirit of the canon clearly directed the bishop to make no appointment until '"after the bishop has consulted with the representatives of the congregation" for guidance in the appointment.'[17] The reaction was no less predictable. To the *Evangelical Churchman* it was a decisive defeat for clerical despotism, and a victory for the voice of the laity in the councils of the church.[18] The decision, moaned the *Dominion Churchman*, virtually placed 'the inspiration of the multitude above the inspiration of Scripture, and substituted the conscience of an individual congregation for the conscience of the whole church of the past ... *"Divine right pales before ... the cogent argument of the purse!"*'[19]

Be that as it may, the Oshawa court case didn't resolve all of the conflicts between bishops and their people. The Anglican journals are littered with accounts of warfare over appointments throughout the last two decades of the century. In one spectacular case, a congregation confronting an unpopular appointment voted to reduce the stipend to one dollar a year; in another they tried to defeat a new incumbent's ritualistic innovations by drowning out the choir with evangelical hymns.[20] But, in the main, these were disputes tinctured with the sectarianism of warring theologies. Whatever the high churchman might think of it, even among Anglicans, clergymen were increasingly both 'sent' and 'called'; and when they were not 'called,' mostly they weren't 'sent.'

GENEROUS IN THE ASSERTION of their own influence, the laity was a good deal less so when it came to the financial support of their ministers. In many cases, of course, small congregations had to struggle to raise even the minimum amounts. The laity, moreover, was besieged by causes: aside from their own minister's stipend, they were asked to contribute to everything from the construction of grand new city churches to innumerable missions to Christianize the heathen or rescue Quebec from Catholicism. The sheer amount the churches raised through voluntary donations in the last quarter of the nineteenth century is itself testimony to lay devotion, but it is also telling of lay priorities and tastes. Foreign missions proved a huge success; much less was forthcoming, however, for the various funds which mattered most to their clergyman's material well-being and peace of mind: salary supplements for home missionaries and others who fell below the stipulated minimums, retirement funds, or support for their widows and orphans.²¹ Though cajoled from the pulpit and in the pages of the clerical press, year in, year out, the laity responded with faint enthusiasm, and these funds were perennially undersubscribed. The 1897 report of the Presbyterian Committee on the Aged and Infirm Ministers' Fund is typical:

> It is to be feared that the claims of this most important fund are largely left out of sight when moneys collected for the Schemes of the Church are being distributed, and in probably too many instances it only gets what happens to be left over after all the other Schemes have been considered ... The Committee earnestly press ... upon congregations the claims of those ministers on the fund who, after rendering faithful service to the Church, have been compelled on account of age or infirmity to retire from active work with, in most cases, but small incomes outside of what this fund gives them to procure the necessaries, we dare scarcely say the comforts, of life.²²

THE ASCENDANCY OF THE LAITY, moreover, struck at both the clergyman's self-image and the structure of the clerical career. There was, for example, the conviction that the 'invitation system,' in all its forms, invited grandstanding and the lesser arts of the rhetorician, put a premium on glitter rather than substance, and discounted the standards that peers might have applied in evaluating merit. 'The system of "popular election",' wrote one Presbyterian minister in 1868, was one which 'tends to degrade the ministerial office' by requiring them to appear before vacant congregations 'to show their "points," much after the manner in which a horse, when offered for sale, is inspected. Not only is the sermon ... subjected to the criticism of the vulgar, but likewise the age, the voice, the action, the colour of his hair, and the general appearance ... closely canvassed. The wonder is that any Christian minister should submit to such a strange, humiliating test.'²³

Still, submit they did. As one Presbyterian described it in 1888, 'If the "vacancy" is at all a good one there is generally quite a competition among those who are eligible for a call, and who are therefore anxious for "a hearing." The whole thing is too frequently turned into an eager and a not very seemly "preaching match" ... Wire-pulling and other worldly ways are often not wanting, and even bare-faced canvassing has not in some cases been altogether unknown.'²⁴ One Presbyterian correspondent to the *Mail* said she'd heard seventy-five trial sermons in a row. Citing this, a correspondent to the *Evangelical Churchman* added that he'd witnessed another case where a Presbyterian congregation had heard twenty-five candidates before 'the choice fell upon the 26th with great applause and self-congratulation.'²⁵ Though the most frequent complaints on this score came from Presbyterians, it was, apparently, no less a problem for Anglicans and Methodists. The practice of 'candidating,' as it was called, of giving 'trial sermons,' of going on ministerial 'fishing expeditions,' was routinely condemned as degrading and unprofessional by editors and correspondents in all the clerical journals.[26] Yet it was an inevitable by-product of a situation where many ministers were looking for better jobs not merely to advance their own reputations but to find the means of adequately supporting their families.

But it also contributed to the fear that the minister was being reduced to a 'hired hand.' As the editor of *The Presbyterian* put it on one occasion, the people

have come to talk of 'hiring' a minister, as if he were a ploughman, and offer him 'wages' ... sadly inadequate for the support of a thoroughly trained minister, who ought to be a gentleman, in the true sense of that term. The general standard of income being lowered, ministers have been compelled to resort to expedients to keep the wolf from the door, which still further help to deprive them of the respect of the people, and so the work goes on till those who would be an ornament to any Christian Church are afraid to enter on the work.[27]

To make the laity both patrons and paymasters, in sum, seemed to 'commercialize' the ministry and to undermine both the dignity and the independence of the office itself. 'A people-elected minister,' said one pithy Anglican, 'is literally "on trial" every day of his life; the sheep stand round him not for food but to see him perform tricks with his pastoral crook.'[28]

Clergymen found it difficult to come to terms with the 'shock of the new' not simply because it undermined conventional assumptions but because it directly challenged doctrine, or, at least, introduced contradictions between doctrine and practice. In the last quarter of the nineteenth century, Methodist ministers stood firm against repeated lay attempts to gain access to a variety of conference committees, above all, the stationing committees, and concomitant pressures to extend the term or even abolish the itinerancy system altogether.[29] Still the 'invitation system' took powerful hold, while some ministers managed to extend their stay on congenial circuits beyond the three-year term, and 'rings' of city ministers were accused of manipulating the stationing committees so that they simply exchanged pulpits among themselves, thus retaining the choice pulpits and salaries.[30] For high church Anglicans the whole trend of the times seemed to pull down the spiritual pillars of the Church itself, and they, above all others, fell into a profound pessimism, reflected in page after page of the *Dominion Churchman*.³¹ Indeed, the principle of a 'settled ministry' itself began to evaporate as those who were already incumbents deserted one congregation after another in search of greener pastures. In the early 1860s Bishop Lewis of the Anglican Diocese of Ontario had warned that any system of clerical appointments by the laity would reduce 'a clergyman to a mere marketable commodity, here today and gone tomorrow.'³² It was a prescient remark: by the last two decades of the century, Presbyterian and Anglican spokesmen alike noted that their clergy changed pulpits, on average, nearly as often as Methodists did.³³

The existence of a market for clerical services chipped away at yet another traditional assumption. Rather as lawyers had, both Anglican and Presbyterian clergymen conceived of themselves as constituting something like a gentlemen's club – a fraternity of equals, each of whom participated in forms of collegial self-government. And that sense of fraternity had at one time been rooted in a degree of economic equality, and in the independence conferred by a fixed stipend. Voluntarism, however, struck at the heart of this convention. A country clergyman was no longer simply one who happened to serve a country parish; he was also a *poor* clergyman, unable to sustain the lifestyle his city brethren assumed to be appropriate or, indeed, consonant with his own presuppositions. Protesting against the growth of such disparities within the Kirk, one clergyman wrote that he hoped 'no one will attempt to defend this condition of affairs as healthy and legitimate. It is a practical violation of the first principles of Presbyterianism; and no one at all acquainted with Church history needs be told that it was by beginnings like this that the first encroachments were made upon the purity and simplicity that belonged to the clergy of the primitive church. *Prelacy* is not so bad a thing *as Presbyterianism with ranks and gradations.*'³⁴ In the London Conference, an 'Old Methodist' noted in the pages of the *Christian Guardian* in 1887, salaries ran from $313 to $2,040. 'Why should there be such a difference ...? Is this the connexional brotherhood of Methodism? or is it not Congregationalism, pure and simple? It is not to be expected that salaries in large cities and country circuits should be the same. Ministers in cities have many calls on them, and many expenses, which those in the country are free from. Still, making due allowance for these, the discrepancy seems to be too great.'³⁵

Notions about the 'brotherhood of Methodism' or the ideal of a settled ministry were not only casualties of economics, however, but were undermined as well by the meritocratic ideology of the age. A country clergyman was not just a poor clergyman, he was a *failed* one. Wrote the editor of the *Globe* in 1877, there was nothing surprising or untoward about the number of pastoral changes that took place year in, year out, in all parts of the province.

> A young man displays in his first rural charge marked ability as a pulpit orator. His fame soon spreads, and he is invited to preach trial sermons elsewhere ... By a process of selection, easily understood and capable of being readily traced, the best minds in the pulpit of each church find themselves gravitating towards the wealthiest or most liberal localities ... Nor from a layman's point of view is there much to regret or find fault with in all this. There is no good reason why a clergyman should not have the same privilege as the poorest of his parishioners – that of substituting a more for a less congenial field of labour whenever he can do so without interfering with the rights of others or acting contrary to the dictates of his own conscience.[36]

Synods, assemblies, and conferences, then, had limited powers to preserve either traditional roles or tacit assumptions in the face of the corrosive effects of voluntarism. All of the assertions of clerical authority in the world could not constrain the power of the purse, reduce the competitive pressures at work, maintain orderly career paths, or prevent the reduction of the clergyman to 'a mere commodity.' Voluntarism, indeed, was a Pandora's box of spiritual, social, and economic implications which, once loosed, preyed upon the whole body of beliefs and convictions the clergy had inherited from the eighteenth century, and wrought manifold changes, some dramatic, some more subtle, throughout the century that followed. And no mere convocation of clerical gentlemen, lacking even the legal sanctions possessed by dentists or doctors, could contain them.

THE CUMULATIVE EFFECTS were to provoke a crisis of confidence about the clergyman's place in his society that, in its intensity at least, has no parallel among our other occupations. It began with the impact of material conditions on individual clergymen and their families. In 1867 one Methodist minister set out what he considered to be a reasonable yearly budget for 'a minister with a wife and four children on a country circuit, and residing in a village,' with 'a total of allowances amounting to $700.'

> Let us look at his yearly expenditure; as a first payment ... there will be one-tenth to the Lord, $68. It is generally admitted that every minister should have

his life insured and which will cost say $40. That a wife may occasionally accompany her husband in visiting the people, and for other reasons a servant is necessary, her board and wages will be $100. Horse keep $70, wear and tear of buggy, harness, etc., $25, wood and cutting $70, books and periodicals for a minister to preach, must read and study, at a moderate computation, $25, stationery and postage $20, clothing for self, wife and children, in the exercise of greatest prudence and economy, $150 ... will leave $137 to provide food for six persons in one year ... a shade more than 2 cents a meal for each person ... But $3 per week, or 14 cents per meal [is the minimum necessary] ... it will be observed that no estimate is made for contingencies, such as accidents, sickness, etc., and none for the education of a minister's family.[37]

Given the effects of pluralism and the growing number of men entering the ministry, such an estimate may have been wholly unrealistic, an aspiration for a lifestyle beyond his means. But put in juxtaposition with what we already know about the general run of clergymen's salaries, two potent messages ring through that passage, as they do in others of the same kind.[38] One is that clergymen expected an income that would allow for expenditures on education, books, life insurance, servants, savings for old age and sickness – provide them, in short, with the wherewithal to maintain their proper station in life. The second is that large numbers of them lacked the resources to achieve these goals, or lived close enough to the edge that they could be met only by penny-pinching and scraping by.

The gap between the two, in turn, is the measure of diminished expectations expressed by so many clergymen throughout the second half of the nineteenth century. There were probably always clergymen who were objectively 'poor,' especially the young and those serving on mission fields. But were most clergymen poorer than mechanics, grocers, or labouring men? In the case of our Brantford clergymen at least, they can hardly be described as 'poor' by the general standards of the community, nor were the minimum stipends established by the churches set at the levels suitable to mechanics or labouring men. But those were not the pertinent standards that clergymen judged themselves against in any case. Methodist ministers compared themselves, to their own disadvantage, with public- or high-school teachers.[39] For Anglicans and Presbyterians it was more likely to be doctors or lawyers. 'Of all the learned professions,' one Presbyterian remarked in 1871, 'precedence in *status* is freely conceded to "the Church"; in the scale of emolument it ranks the lowest.'[40] Their expectations were not yet hitched to the notion of a market for their services, but to assumptions about the rewards that should accrue to the intrinsic value of their education, their services, and their social position.[41] And it was by that standard that they saw themselves losing ground.

Inevitably, diminished material expectations were translated into deep foreboding about their social standing: the humiliation of a wife and children in shabby clothes facing a well-dressed Sunday congregation, or of a minister himself in worn broadcloth making his pastoral visits, the deprivation resulting from a lack of intellectual sustenance, the loss of 'efficiency' in a minister borne down by the weight of debt or worry, the fear of a future which promised only abject penury, the conviction that the office itself was being degraded, and with it the man. The sense of dignity lost and independence compromised is palpable in passage after passage, as ministers poured out their woes in the clerical journals or the secular press.[42]

But the consequences also extended beyond the plight of individuals, seeming to challenge the social and cultural authority of the Church itself. 'My solicitude' about stipends, explained John Travers Lewis, Bishop of the Diocese of Ontario, to Synod in 1869, '... springs not only from a desire to see the temporal wants of our Missionaries supplied, but also from the conviction that if the standard of our clergy, socially and educationally is to be maintained, remuneration for their services must be improved. It was the remark of Dr. Chalmers,' he continued, 'that a scandalous maintenance makes a scandalous Ministry, and what more grievous scandal to the Church can arise than that her Ministers shall not be maintained respectably.'[43] The following year, A.N. Bethune, Bishop Strachan's successor, spoke his mind on the same subject. It was 'utterly insufficient' to ensure merely that a clergyman with a family had 'the ordinary comforts of life.' *Every* clergyman, Bethune argued,

> educated as he has been, and with so important a trust delegated to him, should be able to maintain the due respectability of his social position; and if he cannot do so, we must look too speedily for a diminution of his influence with all classes of his parishioners. The individual of humble grade and of narrow means may look with compassion, but not with confidence or respect, upon a clergyman reduced to a social equality with himself; and the compassion of those of higher standing and ample supply of the comforts of life, is, in many instances, apt to pass into contempt.[44]

A correspondent to *The Presbyterian* noted a few years earlier that a minister must 'maintain a standing in society which shall not place him in social position below any of his Flock, and this he cannot do without a stipend to meet his necessarily large expenditures.'[45] For the editor of the *Christian Guardian*, 'Ministers, as leaders and teachers in the community, whose mission is to the rich as well as to the poor, should receive a support which will place them in a condition of social respectability, not out of harmony with their office and work. They will not otherwise command the respect which is essential to make their influence potent for good in the community.'[46]

Among Anglicans and Presbyterians particularly, inadequate stipends posed yet another threat. Both churches clung tenaciously to the principle of 'a learned ministry,' a phrase that meant not just theological training but the acquisition of a liberal education as well. Yet to acquire such an education demanded a substantial investment of time and money. Thus, while it was always assumed that careers must be open to talent, and provision made to enable the poor but intelligent boy to enter the ministry, it was also taken for granted that the main pool of recruits would come from the higher classes. The educational standards of the churches, in other words, served at one and the same time as intellectual and social sieves, ensuring that the next generation of ministers would be drawn, in the main, from the same social circles as those who provided leadership in secular society generally.

But they recognized as well that respectability was grounded in a secure material base, and without that they could not hope to attract either the talented or the affluent, however pious, to a career which promised so little earthly reward. 'Unless the slender pittance of the clergy was secured in some legal way,' said one Anglican in 1868, 'it would be almost impossible to find young men well qualified who would enter the ministry, and its ranks would ultimately be filled from the riff-raff of the province.'[47] To the editor of the *Evangelical Churchman* in 1876, it was 'painful that few of our young men, especially very few among our wealthier and more cultivated classes are found offering themselves for the highest and noblest work which God permits his children on earth.'[48] The editor of the *Presbyterian Record* concurred: poor pay 'practically cuts off from the ministry young men of the higher and even the middle classes of society.'[49]

EVEN AS THEY FRETTED about the threat of social declension in its manifest varieties, the clergy were under siege in other ways as well. During the 1880s and early 1890s, a variety of new 'sects' appeared on the scene – above all the Salvation Army, but Christian Scientists, Swedenborgians, and others besides. They provoked much debate and some alarm, the Army especially because it seemed to be cutting a wide swathe among working people traditionally attached (if at all) to the mainstream churches. But their advent raised other issues besides, such as that encapsulated in a brief war of words between an Anglican minister, on the one hand, and the editor of the *Globe* and some of his readers on the other. In the summer of 1882, an Ottawa doctor had laid charges against a counter-prescribing druggist, a case widely reported in the press. In the midst of it the clergyman imprudently, and with heavy-handed irony, asked why, if regular doctors were to be protected in this manner, similar provision was not made to protect 'the regular clergy' against the horde of 'Cheap Jacks' and religious 'quacks' invading the province. Editor and correspondents had a field-day at his expense, but the essential message could not be missed either: the day of religious privilege, of established churches, was dead and gone; 'all attempts to determine matters of religious difference otherwise than by a full admission of the right of private judgement' were futile.[50] Now there is nothing surprising here, especially coming from the *Globe*. Yet it was a reminder to clergymen, and to all other readers as well, that even if some were more equal than others, all ministers were alike in one essential respect: they hawked their ideas in an intellectual marketplace where choice was exercised, without constraint, by the laity, and any new doctrine or messiah that might appear was as good as, or maybe even better than, the old ones.

Indeed, it might give the advantage to those bereft of the very values which distinguished the professional gentleman. Confronted by clerical criticism of the Salvation Army in 1887, the *Globe* replied that

> some may say that they show shockingly bad taste in many of their ways and words. That may be but good taste is not everything. Some things which pass for good taste in certain circles are very far from having anything to do with the original article ... Some of the most successful workers in the field of religion and practical benevolence have not been gifted with much 'good taste,' but they have had something better and greatly to be preferred. They have had consuming earnestness, dauntless energy and a facility for persuasion which many of their more cultivated brethren might well have envied ... if souls are saved among the wicked and the sinner, it matters very little, if vowels be sadly misused, and the grammar is such as would have made Lindley Murray go into fits.[51]

But did it matter very little? Perhaps in the eyes of the *Globe*; yet to those who believed their cultural authority rested not simply on 'accomplishing practical salvation' but on their education and sense of decorum, such assessments could not help but demean them.

Nor were the clergy insulated from the politics of the age. The struggle over Sunday streetcars in Toronto, as Christopher Armstrong and

H.V. Nelles have demonstrated, ended in a defeat for the Protestant ministers who had led the opposition.[52] Less familiar is the attack on clerical tax exemptions.[53] By long tradition, ministers had enjoyed an exemption from full municipal taxation of their real and personal property (which included their salaries). They defended this situation by arguing that they did not minister merely to individuals but to society as a whole; that, like public education or government itself, the Church deserved exemption because it was a guardian of the public good.[54] Their critics replied that exemptions were just one of the last vestiges of special privilege, and that the minister had no more right than any other citizen to escape the burdens entailed in the administration of local government. Swelling in volume during the 1880s, the attack on clerical exemptions culminated in their abolition in 1890. And it could hardly be read otherwise than as one more symbol of a loss of place.[55]

DIMINISHED MATERIAL expectations, the loss of cultural authority, and the ominous spectre of social declension; to readers familiar with recent accounts of Protestantism triumphant in the three or four decades after mid-century, the preceding pages must seem bizarre. How are we to square our tale of woe compounded with the burgeoning number of the faithful, the fine new buildings, the outpouring of missionary work at home and abroad, the pervasive influence of the churches in Ontario life, presented to us by historians such as William Westfall and John Webster Grant? How, in other words, to interpret the meaning of the clergy's own conviction that the sky was falling in?

The sheer success of the churches, the fruit of both their laity and their ministers, is not to be gainsaid. But what seems to have been more halting, more difficult, was the reformulation of what it meant to be a clergyman in a changed society. The complex of inherited assumptions remained remarkably resilient among Anglican clergymen even in the last decade of the nineteenth century, could still evoke strong loyalties among an older generation of Presbyterians, and had their influence among Methodists as well. The servant of God was 'sent,' not 'called.' Because of the nature and demands of his office, he must maintain his spiritual independence from the laity and could not be reduced to a hireling who worked for wages. He had a right to a respectable maintenance which would underwrite that independence and sustain a lifestyle appropriate to its dignity.

During the course of the nineteenth century, however, all of these assumptions had been cut loose from their economic underpinnings. There was no parish in the establishmentarian sense to provide for a clergyman through tithes, taxes, or endowments. There were no large pools of wealth at the command of the churches which could be used to underwrite a respectable maintenance for each of their clergymen. If the Clergy Reserves had not been lost, such aspirations might have been realizable. Even voluntarism might have sustained them had Ontario had but one or two 'national' churches. The fragmentation of resources which accompanied religious pluralism, however, put paid to all such notions. From at least mid-century onwards, the clergy of the Anglican and Presbyterian churches competed in an open market against all comers, and so indeed did Methodists as well. They had little to sustain them beyond the price the laity was prepared to pay for their services. Coming to terms with that reality was hard. How, in these circumstances, was the social standing of the clergy to be maintained? How could the churches continue to attract enough recruits of the right sort? How could they maintain the social and cultural authority necessary to their sacred calling? It was, in other words, the severance of the linkage between economic base and social expectations that haunted so many clergymen of the time. And so long as they continued to see the present through the prism of the past, their sense of disorientation would persist. The ideal of the professional gentleman, in sum, seemed to be receding beyond their grasp. And less so because of internal forces than because of the inexorable logic imposed from outside by the pressures of pluralism and voluntarism. Alone in the quiet of their studies on more than one dark night, our clergymen must have echoed the sentiments of Emerson's bleak aphorism: 'Things are in the saddle, and ride mankind.'

13
Professional Organizations at Bay

Did lawyers, doctors, or dentists experience the same kind of disquiet that seems to have been so pervasive among the clergy? The answer, we think, is yes, though it found expression in a different way. And it also had different consequences. Confronted with the dilemmas of pluralism and voluntarism, clergymen rarely blamed their synods or conferences for failing to rescue them; the pressures, they recognized, came from the larger forces at work in society, not just from within their own ranks. Other professional men reacted differently, turning upon their professional organizations when the latter failed to protect them from the depredations of rising numbers and external competitors.

If clergymen translated diminished material expectations into forebodings about their social standing, lawyers, doctors, and dentists read the effects of excessive competition in terms of the spread of 'unprofessional conduct.' For doctors the debate over the purported decline of medical ethics focused primarily on two sorts of behaviour. There were, in the first place, those practices which violated the rules of 'professional etiquette': such things as 'patient stealing,' underbidding, challenging the reputation or skills of another doctor in public, or instigating malpractice suits against colleagues.[1] By far the greatest bulk of complaints, however, arose from the 'commercialization' of medicine that seemed to be taking place in the last quarter of the nineteenth century: advertising or various other forms of self-promotion and, by the 1890s especially, contract practice.

In a competitive medical marketplace, operating within a social context where entrepreneurial values were increasingly prized, why was such behaviour condemned at all? Why shouldn't doctors advertise like other businessmen, compete with each other as grocers did, take paid employment with the lodges, or invent new forms of corporate organization, as others were doing at the same time? To put the question another way, what motivated the attacks on unprofessional conduct which crowded the columns of the medical press, and found expression year after year at the meetings of the Medical Council, or in other forums where medical men debated the state of their craft?

One common response in the historiography of the professions has been to view the concern about professional ethics as part of a larger project designed to promote group upward mobility. Our own view is that it has much more to do with the past than the future, with an attempt to restore or maintain traditional values in the face of unsettling changes. What needs to be done, we suggest, is to listen carefully to the tenor of the language used by doctors themselves and thus to hear the way they interpreted their own experience.

As their numbers multiplied and competition got tougher, as new men unlearned in the traditional codes of respectable behaviour entered practice, as doctors established themselves in the countryside and were isolated from the benefits of association with their brethren, the codes appropriate to a learned profession, and taken for granted within a small, closely knit social world, were perceived to be breaking down. Reflecting on 'Our Medical Ethics,' John Fulton, the editor of the *Lancet*, described the problem in the following terms in 1870. 'In Great Britain there is no written code of ethics, but there is, what is far more effective, a public opinion, both in the profession and out of it, which keeps everyone, except the very lowest, from any flagrant breach of courtesy.' But in Ontario the situation was different.

In the cities, as a rule, people have some notion of professional etiquette, and flagrant breaches of it are comparatively rare. But then we have in every large town a class of people, well-to-do mechanics and small tradesmen, who have worked themselves up from nothing to their present positions. These men cannot understand that a professional visit, occupying perhaps a quarter of an hour, can possibly be worth a dollar ... On the other hand there are a large number of medical men, trying to struggle against enormous competition, into a practice sufficient to keep themselves and their families in comfort ... In country practice we see the evil cropping up in even a worse form. The utter ignorance in a large proportion of the people, of the difference between a profession and a trade prevents their understanding the necessity, in the former, for a high and honourable course of action.[2]

The inevitable result of such circumstances was the proliferation of unprofessional conduct in all its forms. 'A degrading competition takes place,' wrote Fulton a few years later, 'instead of that professional self-respect which exacts a proper honorarium for the services of science and skill; and we find conduct only to be expected of hucksters and pedlars, taking the place of that gentlemanly deportment, which the members of a liberal profession owe to one another ... Overcrowded as the profession may be ... there is no reason why the lower arts of competing tradesmen should be adopted by professional men.'[3]

To parade before the public blatant accounts of this or that wonderful success in surgery was no more than '*ad captandum*' self-advertising, Fulton argued, and 'degrading to its author. The man who follows such a course follows a mistaken path to eminence.'[4] Not surprisingly, then, all other forms of advertising came under attack as well. It was one thing to make a tasteful public announcement, said Fulton of one doctor's notice that he was relocating his office, but these posters 'seem as if intended to be nailed up on gate posts, telegraph poles, or in barrooms, etc.'[5] As for contract practice, it was merely a scheme 'for securing the services of medical men at labourers' wages,' another doctor contended in the pages of the *Lancet*. Beyond that it reduced the professional man to an employee, robbing him of his independence and making him the servant of the laity and of every 'noisy demagogue' belonging to the 'society.' It would inevitably lead to the 'rapid decay of medical science, and the lowering of the social status of the profession.' Indeed, it would reduce the medical man to 'very much the status of the Russian clergy, who are more the slaves than the religious instructors of the gentry, and even of the middle classes.'[6] Again, there was the issue of what it meant to receive a professional fee. Doctors had a right to an 'honorarium,' but they could not be *paid* for their services because no price could be fixed upon the value of their knowledge and skills. The distinction was virtually explicit in a comment made in passing by Fulton, in an editorial of 1886 about a case of unprofessional advertising which involved price-cutting: 'The term professional charge is hardly the proper one to use – price would be a better word to apply to the money for such jobs.'[7]

Doctors, then, were not tradesmen or entrepreneurs. They did not advertise their wares or compete against one another in the marketplace like grocers or butchers. They did not charge a 'price' for a 'job' but were entitled to a professional fee as a recognition of a priceless service rendered. Nor, as gentlemen, could they be the hired servants of others. The traditional values of the Georgian gentleman, in other words, continued to inform the rhetoric of the medical élite, and probably many others as well, as they struggled to come to grips with new social forces and changing economic circumstances.

THOUGH ADVERTISING was a recurrent source of complaint among lawyers, it does not seem to have assumed the proportions it did in medicine, and lawyers seem to have been less prone than doctors to other varieties of 'unethical behaviour.' There were probably several reasons for this. One was that accepting a salary in lieu of fees was not simply unprofessional but of doubtful legality, so that the most 'degrading' features of contract practice were less likely to occur.[8] There were, moreover, built-in constraints through the forms of discipline exercised by the courts. Business conducted there was subject to tariffs of fees set by either the legislature or the judges, so price competition was less likely to occur. Conduct could be scrutinized by the judges, who had power to discipline those who offended the dignity of the courts. And beyond that there was the effect of the constant round of social *cum* business activity that centred on the courts themselves. Though it is hardly more than a speculation, it seems reasonable to think that such activities not only socialized the young to appropriate standards of behaviour but allowed informal peer pressure against those who violated the norms.

There are, nonetheless, telling parallels in the tone, if not the volume, of the rhetoric, and it focused especially on practices common in conveyancing, which lay outside the purview of the courts. 'A legal firm not 200 miles from Toronto,' the editor of the *Canada Law Journal* lamented in 1872, 'has propounded and distributed a printed circular which is more in the green grocer line of advertising, than anything we have seen for some time.'[9] He described another lawyer as 'one, who puts half the alphabet after his name, issues a circular, reminding us of the effusion of a travelling dentist ... The amount of colour displayed suggests the thought of a Barrister appearing in court in a velveteen coat, a red flannel shirt and a white tie.'[10] Price competition, one correspondent had warned a few years earlier, was the road to ruin. 'If each professional man is to charge whatever he pleases – is to *beat down* the price of his fellow practitioners – and in other words (to use a vulgar phrase), act upon the "dog eat dog" system, conveyancing, which ought to be an honourable and remunerative part of a lawyer's business, will be degraded.'[11] Thus, once again, we have the standards of the professional man pitted against those of trade. If lawyers were to act like greengrocers or travelling dentists, they would degrade themselves and the profession they represented. After advertising, what next? A 'red flannel shirt and a white tie' in court.

LAWYERS, AND EVEN MORE SO, doctors, fretted about the dangers of degradation. To leading dentists it was an impending reality. They had set out with high hopes in the late 1860s and early 1870s to turn a craft into a profession and a group of artisans into gentlemen; a daunting task to be sure, but the tone of their first journal, the *Canada Journal of Dental*

Science, was optimistic: it could be achieved by raising educational standards, creating a training school, building a body of scientific knowledge, focusing the work of the dentist on preventive and restorative work, and explaining to dentists how they must now behave. The dental journal collapsed in 1872 and, except for a few issues in the late 1870s, was not resuscitated until 1889. But when the record does resume, it is marked by a mood of near-unrelieved pessimism. The reason was, quite simply, the nature of the market in dental services and the competitive pressures at work. The demand for high-quality preventive and restorative work was limited, and to make a living the growing number of dentists had to turn to the one market that did exist – the manufacture of cheap plates, or, for restorative work, the use of cheap amalgams.

For the editor of the newly established *Dominion Dental Journal*, however, and indeed for most of his correspondents, who liked to identify themselves as 'ethical' dentists, this situation posed two related threats. First, a practice based on the sale of plates invited an excrescence of outrageous advertising and price competition.[12] The differences in tone adopted by the editors of the various professional journals are instructive here. Confronted by advertising lawyers, the editor of the *Canada Law Journal* expressed his dismay in language redolent with world-weary condescension; John Fulton of the *Lancet* fulminated; the editor of the *Dominion Dental Journal* and like-minded correspondents foamed at the mouth. Routinely they used such phrases as 'the advertising liar and fraud,' 'professional tramp,' 'Cheap John,' 'gutter dentists,' or 'barber dentists' (for those who set up shop with several chairs).[13] Second, there was the nature of the dental business itself. The manufacture and sale of plates meant that dentists were primarily engaged in producing and selling a commodity rather than offering a service. It put the emphasis, moreover, on the 'mechanical' rather than the 'professional' side of the occupation. 'The surgeon does not make wooden legs or trusses,' said one dentist plaintively; 'why not separate the "work" of making artificial sets of teeth from the science and skill required to save them?'[14] As another wrote, in a vein typical of dozens of others, those who advertised 'painless extraction and extremely low-priced plates, are practically placing a premium upon the sacrifice of the natural teeth ... It needs no argument to convince us that this line of action, while it may temporarily enrich the individual who carries it on, must necessarily have a weakening and disastrous effect upon the profession as a whole, dragging it down to a mere trading institution.'[15]

In the last quarter of the nineteenth century, then, numbers multiplied and competition increased everywhere. As it became more difficult to make a living, the search for economic security threw up behaviour that challenged traditional notions of what it meant to be a professional man. The sense of things going awry, though it existed there too, was least palpable among lawyers. To the guardians of the professional ideal in medicine, however, and more especially in dentistry, there was the pervasive, brooding fear that competition was undermining the fundamental codes of behaviour that were supposed to define them as professional gentlemen in Victorian society.

AND, NOT SURPRISINGLY, they expected their professional organizations to 'do something' about it. But what could the Medical Council, the Royal College of Dental Surgeons, or the Law Society actually do to control competition and mitigate its degrading impact on values and morale? Our own answer to that question is precious little.

Consider first the issue of 'unprofessional conduct' itself. The dental act had given the Royal College of Dental Surgeons the right to make regulations for the 'better guidance, government, and regulation of [the] ... profession of dentistry.' Sweeping powers on the face of it, but all regulations were subject to approval by the lieutenant-governor-in-council, and the act included no penal clause by which such regulations could be enforced.[16] The Medical Council had no general disciplinary powers until 1887, when legislative amendments allowed it to erase a licentiate's name from the medical register for 'any infamous or disgraceful conduct in a professional respect,' a clause which, though hedged about by the right of an accused to appeal to the courts, did give the College of Physicians and Surgeons some influence over the behaviour of its membership.[17] The Law Society was in the strongest position in this respect. Long responsible for the internal discipline of the bar, in 1876 it had also acquired equivalent control over attorneys and could 'disbar' lawyers, the equivalent of striking a doctor from the medical register, for unprofessional conduct.[18]

But under what circumstances would such powers be exercised? As Curtis Cole's analysis of the activities of Convocation and its disciplinary committee suggests, apparently neither body considered advertising worthy of notice.[19] If complaints about it were registered, and not even that is clear, no formal steps were taken to curb it. What did provoke action were much more serious offences ranging from fraud and breach of trust to failing (we cannot resist noting) to pay Law Society fees. Given its weak mandate, it is perhaps not surprising that the Dental College apparently never attempted to introduce any sort of disciplinary regulations. After the enabling legislation of 1887, the Medical Council set up a disciplinary committee, and, in the years that followed, it did indeed issue reprimands and in a few cases strike names from the register. But the kind of cases it dealt with were those which might best be described as ones of gross abuse: Ontario doctors fronting for peripatetic medical syndicates which could not legally operate in the province on their own, for example; guaranteeing cures and taking money for it when no cure existed; being convicted of an illegal abortion; or advertising access to a team of specialists when no one was found on the premises but the doctor himself.[20] Indeed, as late as the second decade of the twentieth century, the CPSO's legal counsel could declare that no one had ever been struck off its rolls for advertising, except in cases of patently *false* advertising.[21]

In both law and medicine, we suggest, the reason is fairly straightforward. Advertising one's credentials or fees, even in broadsheet, might be repugnant, but it was hardly the sort of offence which merited erasure or disbarment.[22] Rather, it fell within another category: it was an affront to 'professional dignity.' As the editor of the *Canada Law Journal* remarked of one advertisement that came to his attention, 'it is difficult to say, and especially so in a new country, where bad taste in matters professional ends, and where unprofessional conduct begins; we are concerned to discountenance both; the former, if unchecked, soon takes the more aggravated form of the latter.'[23] 'We know of no written law defining the nature of an appropriate professional sign,' said the editor of the *Canadian Journal of Medical Science* in 1882; rather 'it is generally considered simply a matter of taste.'[24]

That being the case, no one expected the Medical Council or the Law Society to use their legal authority to regulate normal forms of advertising; indeed, they had no powers to do so. During the 1890s contract practice was a far more fruitful source of complaint than advertising and it led to demands that the Medical Council declare it 'disgraceful conduct.' The council was entirely in accord with such sentiments, but, probably on advice of its counsel, it had to concede that contract practice, however 'unprofessional,' did not fall within the purview of the disciplinary clause.[25] Thus, even less could be done about vulgar fanlights or corner posters graced with a large finger pointing the way to a doctor's office, however much the editors of the medical press might rant about such practices.[26]

There were, indeed, those prepared to actively defend them. Though he himself had never advertised, one medical man wrote in the *Lancet* in 1881,

I hold that the physician or surgeon has a perfect right to advertise and use every legitimate means at his command to bring himself before the public as such. He spends some of the best years of his life, and considerable money in acquiring his profession, and to ask him after having done so, to rent an office at a good figure, to provide himself with the necessary instruments, etc., for practicing his profession, to clothe himself in decent apparel, and to sit in his office until his latent ability, like the attraction of gravitation shall draw him practice, is, to use an Americanism, 'too thin.'[27]

Two decades later, a dentist who signed his letter 'Sensational Advertiser' told the editor of the *Dominion Dental Journal* that 'I think you would find it would make you more friends if you would drop your constant attacks on dentists who do not see if respectable merchants use sensational ways of attracting attention in the papers, why dentists may not do it too.'[28] Similar arguments were heard from medical men about contract practice. It was, said one,

the right of every citizen – physician included, to arrange his business engagements, to make and fulfil contracts, whether profitable or otherwise, without the necessity of consulting his business opponents, or of explaining his motives ... That lodge practice is antagonistic to the general profession is indisputable on the same grounds that every physician is a business antagonist to his neighbouring physician, but no amount of business antagonism justifies one in abusing the other, or ascribing to him unworthy motives.[29]

There was, then, no easy solution to the problem of 'unprofessional conduct' during the last quarter of the nineteenth century. Gross abuses could easily be dealt with, in law and medicine at least. But the most common cases had more to do with what might best be described as conduct unbecoming of a gentleman. Here the professional organizations had limited legal sanctions they could bring to bear, or none at all; nor was there enough unanimity to maintain solidarity in the face of centripetal individualism.

ONE MIGHT EXPECT the case to be different when it came to other matters like external competition or the number of new entrants to the professions. On the face of it at least, the jurisdiction of the Law Society, the Medical Council, or the Royal College of Dental Surgeons over such matters was more secure. Each had unqualified formal control over entry requirements, the right to issue a licence to practise, and penal laws, or their equivalent, to protect practitioners against unlicensed invaders. Yet here again, a variety of constraints crippled the capacity of all three governing bodies to deal with such issues.

One of these lay in the inability of professional organizations to exercise effective control over an area of work that lawyers, doctors, or dentists claimed was rightfully theirs. The extreme case is the legal profession. Lawyers had exclusive jurisdiction over work in the county and superior courts, and they confronted no serious rivals in those arenas. As well, they probably had effective control over conveyancing for large firms, governments, and wealthy individuals. Yet they had no monopoly over conveyancing as such, the very issue which, by the late 1870s, was of urgent concern to country practitioners in particular. Possessing no legal prerogatives in this area, however, the Law Society could not come to their rescue. If lay conveyancing were to be suppressed, professional power had to be extended. But that could only be done by the legislature and not by any act of the Society itself.

Formally at least, doctors and dentists seemed to be in a more favourable position. The medical and dental acts had defined what constituted professional work in these fields, in a fairly broad fashion, and then gave powers to the Medical Council and the College of Dental Surgeons to police it. On the face of it, then, all they had to do was to bring the law to bear against unlicensed practitioners. But that was not as easy as it sounds. Violators had to be identified. Flagrant cases were easy, but what about female midwifery in the countryside, where a doctor was never called in? Charges had to be laid in the courts, and someone had to pay for the costs of a prosecution. What if the midwife or counter-prescribing druggist asserted, with witnesses, that money had not changed hands – that practice was not being carried out 'for hire, gain, or hope of reward'? What indeed constituted illegal practice in the eyes of the courts? In one case it might be defined as prescribing drugs; in another a defendant might be found not guilty 'since he prescribed no drugs on his visits but claimed he could cure merely by looking at the patient.'[30]

We pose these questions for good reason: they point to the real dilemmas in enforcing the penal laws in both medicine and dentistry. First, prosecutions cost money. But during the 1870s and early 1880s especially, neither the Medical Council nor the Dental College had the financial means to pursue quackery vigorously or consistently. From 1874 doctors (though not dentists) were required to pay an annual fee to their professional organization, but large numbers never bothered, and the Medical Council had no way of enforcing payment except to sue a doctor in the local courts, which, aside from the expense involved, provoked a good deal of disapprobation among doctors themselves.[31] Thus the Medical Council (and even more so the Dental College) drew most of its revenues from student examination and registration fees, and so long as student numbers remained modest its resources were generally constrained. Without aggressive action by the council itself, complaints had to be initiated by local practitioners, who were often loath to do so. Why, one correspondent to the *Lancet* asked rhetorically, did he himself not lay charges against a local quack?

If I should do so, I might as well remove to some other quarter at once, for he has an extensive family connection which would rise *en masse* against me if I were to prosecute, and through their influence I would lose my business, which is a good and paying one, and no man is so foolish to destroy his practice in this way. This man is a quack in the widest sense of the term and should be prosecuted, but the various physicians residing nearest to him will not prosecute.[32]

Even when prosecutions were successful, unlicensed practitioners would sometimes treat the fine as the price of doing business and be back at it the next day.[33] Judges and JPs in the division courts, moreover, frequently interpreted the meaning of illegal practice in ways which allowed quacks to escape punishment; witnesses lost their nerve; or the case was dropped for some technical or other reason.[34] In tackling medical or dental 'quackery,' then, the Medical Council or the College of Dental Surgeons had advantages that lawyers did not. Unlike lay conveyancing, much of it was subject to the penalties of the law. But that did not mean that control over an area of work could be easily or quickly established. For both professional organizations, policing their legal jurisdictions proved a difficult, frustrating, and sometimes fruitless task.

THE GOVERNING COUNCILS of law, medicine, and dentistry also failed to take aggressive action because, in many respects, they were remote from the immediate concerns of their members. This was in part a legacy of the presuppositions implicit in their origins. Some modern views to the contrary notwithstanding, professional organizations were *not* created as close corporations merely to secure the economic or social interests of a handful of privileged occupations. Rather, they were conceived to be a part of public policy, intended to protect the citizen against the untrained, the incompetent, the dangerous. The power of regulation was conferred upon them to promote the public good and not private advantage. It is easy to be cynical about such notions, but had it been otherwise, politicians and other influential figures in the middle decades of the nineteenth century would have proved far more resistant to such legislation than they were. Indeed, this was the very ground upon which the laity rested its case for medical regulation in 1859, 1861, or 1869: the preservation of therapeutic diversity was one thing; 'unqualified quackery' was quite another. And the same principle was also deeply ingrained among the professional élite. The Law Society's duty, said Edward Blake in 1889, was to ensure 'guarantees for skill, for learning, for integrity,' not to guard the profession's own privileges but to protect the rights of the public.[35] In the early 1890s, when much of the medical profession was in a near-panic over the flood of new entrants, one schoolman from Queen's rebuked the profession in the following manner for its attacks on the Medical Council:

The complaints about it frequently take the form of asserting that the profession is not sufficiently protected ... and that it is the duty of the Medical Council ... to protect those who form its constituency from undue competition. This view ... is, I think, erroneous ... The object of the Medical Council is the protection of the public, by ensuring to the people that those having its imprimatur are competent to perform the duties they undertake; any advantage in the way of protection that the members of the profession receive, is incidental. If we adopt any other view, and by changes and regulations, seek to provide for our own interests, we shall lay ourselves open to the charge of being a close corporation and to the risk of having the whole thing done away with, and free trade established. This would probably not be an advantage to the country, and would certainly be disadvantageous to ourselves.[36]

Now there was nothing glib or shallow in that message; indeed, such sentiments remain the fundamental justification for professional self-governance in modern Ontario.[37] But 'the burning questions' of the last quarter of the nineteenth century were bread-and-butter protectionist issues: external competition and internal numbers. Here, on the other hand, were influential spokesmen denying that the job of the professional organization was primarily to protect its own. With friends like that, some hard-pressed practitioner in Thamesville or Vankleek Hill probably reflected, who needs enemies?

But there were also more mundane reasons why the professional organizations were distanced from their membership. The Law Society, the Medical Council, or the Dental College touched students' lives at every point. They made the regulations which governed education, conducted examinations, and licensed new practitioners. But, after that, any relationship with the pertinent governing bodies was very limited. A doctor might cast a vote during Council elections every five years. A lawyer would certainly pay his annual fees of $15 to $18, though doctors were less likely to remit their one-dollar assessment. Beyond that, contact between individual practitioners and Convocation or the Medical Council was rare. For dentists the link was virtually non-existent:

for most of the 1870s and 1880s, there was no dental journal, no annual assessment, and only the most modest changes in policy to keep informed about in any case. These were not organizations, we reiterate, designed to mobilize an occupation; their functions lay elsewhere. But that very fact made them remote from the ordinary practitioner.

THE DIASPORA of professional men throughout the province bred its own problems. However much common ground they might continue to share, inevitably the perspective of those located in Brockville or Ottawa, let alone Wingham or L'Orignal, would be different, on some issues at least, from that of Toronto practitioners. Inevitably as well, similar differences would arise between the young and the established, the country doctor or lawyer and those in the cities. Divisions of this sort would have a profound impact on all three occupations in the later nineteenth century; but because the law was already organized, they emerged earliest among lawyers.

The first major conflicts occurred over legal education.[38] An apprenticeship in the law was not only an educational but an economic relationship. Before the days of specialized office labour, the legal apprentice was secretary, office manager, errand boy, and general amanuensis to his principal. As a consequence, lawyers did not take kindly to policies which dragged their clerks off to Toronto even for judicial terms, let alone for more extended courses. Nor did they appreciate innovations which provided incentives for students to serve all or part of their terms of service in Toronto. Indeed, it was precisely these kinds of arguments that had led to the abolition, in 1868, of the rule that required students to attend the judicial terms in Toronto,[39] and also help explain the succession of *voluntary* law schools between the 1860s and 1880s. Reflecting on the history of formal instruction over the previous twenty years, one senior Bencher, Aemilius Irving, remarked in 1881 that

> we would have had a law school long ago had it not been for the opposition of the country members of the profession. They contend that by the establishment of such an institution in Toronto they are robbed of their students. The latter do not care to work in a village or country office when they can get the advantage of a law school here ... the difficulties in the way of a Law School are many and hard to surmount. The greatest opposition comes from the country members of the profession.[40]

Though we have argued in an earlier chapter that a full explanation is somewhat more complicated than this, there is no lack of evidence that Irving's assessment was an accurate one. It was over educational policy, in any case, that the extent of sectional factionalism within the Law Society first began to display itself.

Nor did the introduction of elected Benchers in 1871 provide the mechanisms for reducing such conflicts. The first version of the bill presented to the legislature had included representation by region: Ontario (outside Toronto) would be divided into five districts, and the lawyers in each would elect five Benchers.[41] But during passage, the bill emerged from a select committee, composed mostly of lawyers, with a critical amendment. The clause calling for territorial representation had been struck out and replaced by one providing for the province-wide election of all thirty Benchers.[42] The original clause, possibly modelled on the medical acts of 1865 and 1869, would have guaranteed that those elected would represent particular constituencies, and that in turn would have given the opinions of ordinary lawyers much greater weight in the Society's affairs. The final version of the clause, however, conferred the advantage on those lawyers with well-established reputations who could draw votes from across the entire province. It could not help, moreover, but favour candidates from Toronto, where a disproportionate number of lawyers resided. And the first election reflected these realities. Twelve out of thirty of the newly elected Benchers were from Toronto, nineteen had been Benchers under the old regime, and the entire winners' list read like a 'who's who' of the contemporary bar.[43]

Yet men such as these were the least likely to share the concerns and anxieties of the rank and file. In late 1878, for example, when a group of country lawyers announced their intention to hold an organizational meeting in Toronto, one of them explained their purpose in the following way: 'At present, while almost every other profession or business has annual meetings of its representatives to consider matters of common interest, the legal profession has no such meeting.'[44] The Benchers, in other words, were simply not seen to represent those interests. Indeed, that was the opinion of the editor of the *Law Journal* as well. 'The difficulty,' he wrote in 1880,

> is that the Benchers are not in truth a *representative* body, although elected by the very men who now, with great reason, complain of the evil ... They are composed mainly of eminent counsel or practitioners with large business in the principal cities, who do not feel, and seem unable to comprehend, or are too busy to think about the difficulties of their brethren who are struggling for existence against overwhelming odds in the numerous small towns and villages in the Province.[45]

THOUGH THE PARALLELS are not exact, similar circumstances existed in dentistry and medicine. Like Convocation, the Board of Directors of the Royal College of Dental Surgeons was elected on a non-territorial basis by all registered dental licentiates. But, in the case of law, that election was at least carried out by a mail ballot. The dental board was nominated and elected directly by those licentiates actually present at the biennial election meeting, always held in Toronto, and, except for Toronto dentists, few licentiates bothered or could afford to attend. In the mid-1870s, for example, only twenty to twenty-five dentists attended;[46] even as late as 1889, when college affairs were of much greater interest, the number stood at only sixty, and, the editor of the *Dominion Dental Journal* noted, most of them were from the city.[47] Indeed, the reaction to proposals by the college in 1886 for some new initiatives to enlarge its role was potent testimony to the extent it had lost touch with a large portion of its membership over the intervening fifteen years.[48]

The constitution of the Medical Council had been determined initially by a set of compromises between leading practitioners and schoolmen, and then by the insistence of the legislature that the eclectics and homeopaths be included as well. The result was a body composed of twelve practitioners elected by mail ballot on a territorial basis, of representatives appointed by the medical schools and universities, and others elected by the old 'irregulars.' During the late 1860s and early 1870s, the practitioners held a majority on Council, but that edge gradually disappeared as additional colleges acquired the right to grant medical degrees and thus obtained seats as well. By the 1880s the council consisted of the twelve territorials, five homeopaths, and ten schoolmen, leaving the territorial representatives in a clear minority on a number of issues they considered of critical importance.[49] As the number of new entrants began to rise rapidly from the late 1870s, for example, there were recurring fulminations about burgeoning medical-school enrolments, and demands that educational standards be raised as a means of limiting excessive numbers.[50] The schoolmen on the Medical Council nonetheless were able to thwart these initiatives, arguing that such standards were either unrealistic or unnecessarily high. Until 1887, indeed, entry standards remained set at the equivalent of a third-class teacher's certificate, which required only two years of high school.[51]

The schoolmen had their own good reasons for pursuing such a policy. Though frequently accused of mere pecuniary self-interest, they were, as we have already suggested, deeply committed to improving the quality of medical education throughout the 1870s and 1880s. Financed entirely by student fees, however, the medical schools they represented had to be self-sustaining, and thus their success rested on the number of students they enrolled. To the schoolmen, then, a ruthless winnowing of the number of students represented a direct threat to standards of excellence in medical education.[52] That, however, hardly placated practitioners, nor did the schoolmen endear themselves when they responded to complaints about overcrowding with reassurances which must have seemed outrageously complacent. In a survey of opinion about changes in medical education published in the spring of 1887, several prominent doctors pointed to the excessive number of new graduates the schools were grinding out, to the detriment of the profession generally.[53] Replied one leading schoolman (in a manner reminiscent of the Gospel injunction itself),

People say we are turning out doctors too fast and that Ontario is oversupplied with them, but they must take a broader view of education. We are educating the young men to go to all parts of the world. We are sending them to Australia, New Zealand, British Columbia, Jamaica and the West Indies. Then there is our own great North West and the Western States of America. The surplus of medical graduates go abroad, and carry with them the imprimatur of the Canadian Colleges and Universities. We are proud to be in a position to supply these outlying districts.[54]

The council had an equally mixed record when it came to the pursuit of 'quackery.' From the early 1870s onwards, the pressure to do something to protect registered practitioners had been swelling.[55] Short of funds, the council decided to retain a prosecutor but, in lieu of a stipend, allow him to keep all the fines he was able to collect from successful prosecutions. 'Detective Smith' was duly appointed in the summer of 1876 and within six months had become 'a terror to all quacks and unregistered practitioners.'[56] For the next few years, he criss-crossed the country, making his impact felt in town and country alike.[57] His success, however, brought a diminishing income from fees, and in 1882 he demanded a salary for his services. The council decided they could not afford it, Smith resigned, and he was not replaced.[58] The work of suppressing quackery was once again left to the efforts of individual doctors or to the divisional associations. And despite a renewed flurry of complaints in the mid-1880s – despite, indeed, Council's own admission that there were still 'a large number of quacks who infested the province' – a majority of its members voted against a motion to appoint a new prosecutor on the grounds that Council was 'not a detective bureau.'[59] Certainly, neither the editors of the medical journals nor the members of Council condoned illegal practice; but they didn't consider it a priority either. Rather like their *confrères* in law when it came to conveyancing, the leading lights of the medical profession were not especially attuned to the concerns of ordinary physicians.

For a whole variety of internal reasons, then, the governing bodies of the Law Society, the College of Physicians and Surgeons, or the College of Dental Surgeons proved ineffective in coming to terms with some of the most serious issues confronting many ordinary practitioners during the 1870s and 1880s. We are not arguing here, we want to emphasize, that they were irresponsible oligarchies or that they left a record of 'do-nothingism.' Neither is in fact the case. But, because of the nature of their mandates, the formal and informal limits of their jurisdictions, the biases and priorities of the leadership, and for other reasons besides, the institutions established to ensure professional self-government were unable to address those problems which constituted the 'burning questions' among so many of their members.

INEVITABLY THAT inability bred dissent, division, and internal conflict in law, medicine, and dentistry alike. Among lawyers the flash-point was Oliver Mowat's Division Courts Act of 1880, which decentralized civil law by transferring a large category of cases from the county to the local division courts. The act posed a threat to young and struggling practitioners everywhere, but especially so for country lawyers, because it actually increased the range of cases laymen could conduct in the division courts.[60] Though complaints about the impact of lay conveyancing had been growing since the mid-1870s, the act crystallized all the accumulating grievances and provoked a torrent of protest in both the daily press and the *Law Journal*.[61] The Benchers were not entirely unsympathetic, establishing committees to consider the matter in 1881, 1882–3, and again in the early 1890s; but, in each case, the conclusion was that nothing could be done except by the provincial Parliament.[62]

The result was simmering discontent directed, not only at the lawyer-politicians who seemed reluctant to move against the conveyancers, but at the Law Society itself. At each of the quinquennial elections of Benchers between 1881 and 1896, organized attempts were made to elect a more responsive group of Benchers, but with only modest success.[63] Country lawyers by the dozen asked, what use to them was a great library at Osgoode Hall? What use the ethical imperatives of complacent and comfortable city practitioners? What use, indeed, the Law Society if it failed to protect their interests? In a fiery condemnation of the Benchers published in the *Globe* in 1886, one country practitioner summed up the multitude of grievances that his colleagues were expressing throughout the era. He had spent three years at a county grammar school and another three at Upper Canada College, then five years in a law office, and had paid in all something like $150 worth of fees to become a barrister and attorney.

Upon commencing business I found myself in the matter of drawing deeds, mortgages, contracts, etc. and in protesting notes and bills no better off with my certificates as a barrister and solicitor than if I had stayed at home, gone into some local conveyancer's office at the age of eighteen, and taken a six-months' course in copying deeds. All the main business of a solicitor I found myself deprived of by outside competition.

As to suits, all I can do, if the case is an important one, is to take a few preliminary steps of small importance, after which the matter goes to the Toronto agents, who take all the best of the fees, and virtually become the principal conductors of the case.

It was, he continued, fundamentally wrong that lawyers paid large annual fees and yet received no benefit. 'Let the Law Society be entirely abolished, or the solicitor protected like other callings.'[64] Another lawyer put the argument more pithily in 1891. If conveyancers weren't to be restricted, then lift all restrictions on lawyers, including the commandment, thou shalt not advertise. 'I object to pay a tax to maintain a library for Toronto lawyers, pay for lunches for benchers and dancing parties for Toronto swells, and get nothing for it.'[65]

Lay conveyancing was not the only issue which created conflict. Over the years there had been sporadic demands by lawyers in cities other than Toronto for the decentralization of the superior courts, or for an increase in the jurisdiction of the county courts – measures that would increase the amount of work for those outside Toronto. And in the mid-1890s both these issues produced bitter conflict between Toronto-based lawyers and those located elsewhere.[66] But it was, above all, the impact of lay conveyancing and the Division Courts Act that created fissures within the occupation where other grievances could lodge and fester.

During the 1890s, in both dentistry and medicine, disaffection culminated in outright revolt. In dentistry the immediate cause was a proposal by the Board of Directors of the RCDSO to impose an annual levy on all its licentiates to pay for improved educational facilities in Toronto. Practitioners, in other words, were being asked to pay a fee intended for the production of more competitors, as one angry dentist was quick to point out.[67] But beyond that, there was the sense, widely shared among dentists outside Toronto, that the board was an unrepresentative body, too much under the thumb of the schoolmen. Led by an eastern Ontario group, a majority of dentists across the province demanded an entire overhaul of the RCDSO, and in 1892 they succeeded in convincing the legislature that they were right.[68] A new dental act was passed which partitioned the province into seven divisions, a representative from each to be elected to the board by resident dentists through a mail ballot. The result was a far more representative board of directors and one where the schoolmen had but a single representative.

Compared to what happened in medicine, however, the 'revolt' in dentistry was a tepid affair. Militancy, fed by a host of grievances over quackery, excessive numbers, and the dominance of the schoolmen in professional affairs, had been increasing in the late 1880s and early 1890s, forcing Council once more to hire a prosecutor in 1887 and raise entry standards in the same year, and again in 1891.[69] Early in the following year, however, opposition coalesced around a group known as the Medical Defence Association (MDA), founded by Dr J.H. Sangster, a Port Perry practitioner.[70] Its central aim was to obtain 'representation by population' – a reorganized council that would exclude the schoolmen and ensure that the voice of the practitioner would be dominant. The MDA, in other words, sank its teeth into a long-standing grievance among a large number of doctors, including a long line of territorial representatives on Council.

The MDA did not get everything its leaders wanted, but it was powerful enough to extract substantial concessions from the council, convincing the legislature to agree to a reorganized constitution for the College of Physicians and Surgeons which increased the territorial delegates from twelve to seventeen, giving them a clear majority on the Medical Council. The sheer level of unrest among the profession was confirmed by the results of the council elections of 1895. As Dan McCaughey remarks, 'Of the 17 Territorial Divisions, 10 were contested, a remarkable change from the 2 in 1890. Just as striking, 13 of the 17 ultimately elected were newcomers to the Council ... Six declared members of the Medical Defence Association were elected,' including Sangster himself.[71]

In medicine and dentistry at least, militancy brought in its train not simply a more representative governing council but substantive gains as well. A vigorous prosecution policy by the Medical Council began to eliminate some traditional forms of unlicensed practice, and in both occupations matriculation standards were raised substantially. Yet, as in the past, only so much could be done. The limited scope of the meaning of 'disgraceful conduct' prevented any broad assault on normal forms of advertising or contract practice. Blatant cases of counter-prescribing by druggists could also be dealt with, but the practice continued because of the ambiguities of the law. During the 1890s, moreover, 'doctors of refraction,' jewellers turned opticians, began to prescribe corrective lenses, bypassing both the general practitioner and the licensed oculist.[72] 'Drugless practitioners' like osteopaths and chiropractors appeared on the scene as well, and attempts to suppress them failed when the courts declared, early in the new century, that to diagnose and then manipulate did not amount to the practice of medicine.[73] Nor was there any simple remedy to 'overcrowding.' The Medical Council or the Dental College might well raise new barriers to entry, but candidates responded, as they had in the past, by remaining in school that much longer. It was a puzzling and frustrating chain reaction. Said the editor of the *Lancet* early in 1893, the Medical Council 'have been continually at work for the past ten years at the Matriculation Examination, and although it is higher today than the Matriculation Examination required by any licensing body in Europe the influx still continues. The Matriculation Examination and the subsequent portion of the curriculum is today nearly three times as difficult as it was ten years ago, and yet the number of students entering the profession is thrice as great.'[74] Determined to deal with the numbers problem nonetheless, the newly elected Medical Council of 1895 pushed up matriculation standards yet again, and, just to be sure the gates were shut fast, tied entry to the current high-school leaving certificate, excluding all equivalencies.[75] Thus those who held a matriculation certificate conferred by some university rather than the Department of Education itself, or those who had left high school a year or two earlier with a different certificate, could not meet the new letter of the law.

It proved a stupid blunder. Petitions pleading for exemption inundated the council and, more important, the legislature. To students and the public alike, it simply appeared a ruthless and patently unjust means of closure, and George Ross, the minister of education, immediately stepped in, introducing in the spring of 1896 his own bill prescribing a lower standard and a much more open one.[76] In effect he was proposing to strip the Medical Council of one of its most fundamental powers – control over matriculation. Faced with that threat Council representatives met with Ross in an attempt to protect their interests, and he agreed to withdraw the bill on condition that the council pass by-laws conforming exactly to its every clause. Said the editor of the *Lancet*, 'The Council had the choice offered of committing suicide, so far as the control of matriculation was concerned, or of submitting graciously to the gentle hand of Parliament controlling the guillotine.'[77]

THE REORGANIZATION of the governing councils in medicine and dentistry, then, offered no easy solutions to the challenges professional men faced in the late nineteenth century. And even had the attempts to elect more representative Benchers been successful, the outcome would probably have been the same. The fact of the matter was that, in all three cases, the professional organizations had bumped up against the formal and informal limits of their legal jurisdictions. Lay conveyancing, quackery, unprofessional conduct, and other things besides lay beyond that jurisdiction: in the hands of the courts and, above all, the legislature. And now, in medicine, even control of entry standards had been compromised. Creatures of the state in the first place, professional monopolies rested, as they always had, in the hands of the politicians, and, more generally, within the domain of a political culture that conferred legitimacy upon them. Yet that conclusion simply begs another question. In the 1860s and early 1870s, professional men had been notably successful in extending their legal jurisdictions; why not, then, simply return to the legislature and ask for additional powers to deal with the 'burning questions' they faced?

14
The Impact of a Changing Political Culture

In the spring of 1891, a group of prominent undertakers appeared before the provincial legislature with a bill to establish 'the Ontario College of Embalming and Organic Chemistry.' As one of its sponsors explained to the House, the bill 'did not in any way refer to the business of the undertaker but to the science of embalming.' Thus the purpose of the college was to provide instruction in that science, along with 'the nature of post-mortem appearances and the disinfectant treatment of diseases,' as well as 'to collect data on cremation and other methods for the disposition of the deceased.' A representative council would be appointed to superintend the work of the school, to organize examinations, and to grant diplomas twice a year. New graduates, and those already in practice who met the requisite educational standards, would have the exclusive right to identify themselves by the title 'Registered Undertaker and Embalmer.'

A school, offering a course of training grounded in the relevant sciences; a governing council to set educational standards and certify that they had been met; a restricted title to guarantee that the public could tell the difference between the competent and the quack; emphasis on public service rather than commerce: the undertakers had tried to strike all the right chords. The bill met concerted opposition nonetheless. Referred to a select committee, it was attacked by a group of dissident embalmers who feared it would exclude them from their craft. Representatives of the Toronto Trades and Labor Council, including Alfred Jury, a leading member of the Knights of Labor, also spoke against the bill. Jury, the *Globe* reported, 'gave a particularly able and interesting speech,' handling the question 'without gloves.' It was, he said, supposed 'to be an age of competition and individualism,' yet

trade after trade came and asked that so far as it was concerned the rule of competition should be done away with. While the workingmen were warned against Socialism they found that Socialism was in force in favor of certain parties while they were excluded from such benefits as it conferred. He asked why certain trades should be given the benefits of a close corporation while others were excluded ... 'Why,' he went on, 'I would undertake to get up a better case for the men who put down the sewers in this city than can be made out for the undertakers. We all know how necessary it is for the public health that we should have the sewers well made. Why not have every man who assists in making them pass an examination and receive a license?'

Despite Jury's attempts to bury the bill outright, compromises were struck between the contending factions of undertakers and a much modified version was sent back to the House. There, however, it met a barrage of criticism from the politicians, one declaring that 'it was nothing but a combine.' Bowing to the prevailing mood, its sponsor agreed to withdraw the bill, though not without promising that he and the undertakers would be back with a revised version next session.[1]

DURING THE SAME SESSION the House also had before it an incorporation bill submitted by the Association of Stenographic Reporters, a group comprised of those who provided verbatim reports of court proceedings, or of any other meeting where such a record might be required. Explicitly and carefully modelled on an act passed in 1883 incorporating the Institute of Chartered Accountants, the bill endowed the association with powers to establish educational standards and examinations for those who chose to take them, and created the restricted title of 'Chartered Stenographic Reporter.' Unlike the undertakers' bill, this one became law without any apparent dissent or debate.[2]

The year before, in 1890, the legislature had approved a similar act for the architects. Sponsored by the recently established Ontario Association of Architects (OAA), the original version of the bill sought powers similar to those possessed by the legal and medical professions. It provided for occupational self-government through an elected council, control over entry standards and professional training, and a restricted title: no one, under threat of a fine, could designate himself an 'architect' unless he was a member in good standing of the OAA. The bill was gutted by the politicians, however, and even the restricted title was changed from 'architect' to 'registered architect.' To the leadership of the OAA that modification in particular was a disaster. The latter term meant nothing to those outside the association, while the traditional identification for the craft, the simple word 'architect,' could continue to be used by anyone who wished to designate himself as such. Bitterly disappointed, the association would return to the legislature seeking amendments five times between 1892 and 1897. In each case their efforts met with a firm rebuff. The legislature was willing to give those who asked for it a singular title if they wished; but it was resolutely opposed to bestowing a monopoly on any group by excluding others from calling themselves, or practising as, architects.[3]

The architects were not the only occupation which had to face that reality. Between 1880 and 1900 no fewer than eleven bills were introduced to impose some form of control over the qualifications of 'stationary engineers' – those who tended and repaired steam engines. Initially these bills were promoted by individuals or *ad hoc* groups. In 1891, however, the same year in which the undertakers and stenographers were importuning the House, an act was passed incorporating the Ontario Association of Stationary Engineers. But the experience of the architects was recapitulated. During passage the original draft was much modified and all forms of compulsion or monopoly removed. The association was to be purely voluntary, and membership conferred no statutory advantage. Indeed, while the association could establish educational standards and set examinations, there was not even provision in the act for a designated qualification, let alone a restricted title, recognizing the acquisition of the association's credentials. Once established, the association itself assumed the initiative in seeking legislation which would lead to the inspection of steam engines and the licensing of their operators. Almost annually through the 1890s, the executive reported that the political winds were changing and such a measure would now be welcomed in the legislature. Just as regularly the most recent bill would be rejected, or withdrawn upon advice from some senior politician that the House was not even prepared to contemplate that kind of regulatory interference.[4]

There are other examples of similar initiatives as well. In 1892 not only the surveyors' bill came before the House but one to establish examinations and qualifications for railway engineers, conductors, and brakemen.[5] During the second half of the 1890s, as we have already seen, the Canadian Society of Civil Engineers was engaged in promoting its own incorporation bill. When the third OAA bill failed in 1893, the executive laid the blame on the hostility to all such measures aroused by another bill from the undertakers and one asking that only qualified milkmen be allowed to sell milk.[6] There were, in other words, a remarkable number of these legislative initiatives by a variety of occupations during the last two decades of the nineteenth century, and especially in the 1890s.

ARCHITECTS, ENGINEERS, and surveyors perhaps; but undertakers in a volume on the learned professions? Boiler-tenders, stenographic reporters, and milkmen besides? What occupations, then, are to be excluded?

Where does one draw the line? That indeed was the question which confronted those who tried to make sense of the place of the professions in the emerging occupational order of the late nineteenth century. Once there had been a cluster of characteristics which distinguished, more or less, the three learned professions from other occupations. These distinctions had already been compromised as law and medicine became more inclusive, as the term 'clergyman' tended towards the generic, as parvenus like dentists and druggists laid hands on the institutional structures of professionalism. Later developments supplemented and amplified these trends. The variety of occupations continued to multiply, and some, both old and new, became more closely linked to sophisticated technologies, more dependent upon advanced levels of technical training, more closely tied to the credentials proffered by the high schools, more critical to the well-being of individuals or the progress and prosperity of an urbanizing society, or, simply, more able to carve out, from the rising prosperity of others, a niche for themselves in the retail or service trades. Though such occupations did not belong to the traditional professions, the lines of convergence were sometimes striking and substantial.

If a prolonged preliminary education was a hallmark of a profession, for example, then what of the claims of public- and high-school teachers? A few decades earlier it would have been rare to find a teacher in possession of an advanced education unless he was a professional man himself, most likely an Anglican or Presbyterian clergyman. By the 1870s or 1880s, the elementary-school teacher was as likely to have as good a preliminary education as most professional men, and the high-school teacher a better one. Perhaps teaching was not yet an established profession; but teachers had obtained what had long been one of the signal attributes of a profession. Nor were they alone in this: accountants, stenographic reporters, and others besides, had acquired a level of education far in advance of the vast majority of their peers. If the distinction between a classical and an ordinary English education was breaking down, if an acquaintance with the classics was no longer the singular mark of the professional gentleman or the educated man, then why couldn't those trained in English or mathematics demand the same respect, and the same privileges, as doctors or lawyers? If the quality of technical training was a criterion, surely the architect, the engineer, the accountant, was at least the equivalent of the dentist and the druggist? If the druggists, still immersed in the world of retail trade, could lay claim to a science and a self-governing college, why couldn't the undertakers? Indeed, if monopolies were justified primarily in terms of the public interest, then why exclude the stationary engineers, whose entire case was built upon the mayhem caused by boiler explosions, the cost of which, in terms of lives and property, was documented in the newspapers with depressing regularity. Surely their claim was more plausible in this respect than that of the dentists? But then could not the same be said, as Alfred Jury maintained, for the sewermen?

We are not arguing that differences in status, in levels of education, in public esteem and the like were being systematically washed out. That would be silly. But by the late nineteenth century, not only had the spectrum of occupations expanded but many of them could legitimately claim characteristics similar to those of the established professions. The consequence was to blunt distinctions and dilute differences between categories of work, and to construct new conceptual categories which transcended them, above all the comprehensive one we now identify as 'white-collar work.' Internally stratified that emergent designation might well be; yet to the extent that 'the professions' became a subcategory within 'white-collar work,' the singularity of 'the learned professions' was diminished and the term 'professional gentleman' became more open to expropriation through the mechanism of social proximity.

We want to avoid a simple functionalist explanation here, however, for there was also a *politics* of change, as occupations actively tried to shape or reshape their place in the world. A growing number of individuals engaging in the same occupation, the steady urbanization of the workforce, and the increasing ease of transportation and communication bred a sense of common identity and shared interests. The result was the ubiquitous craft and trade associations of the later nineteenth century, the leaders of which could articulate rationales justifying special privilege before the legislature or in the press, and appear before cabinet or at select committees claiming to represent the collective voice of hundreds of like-minded colleagues. They could afford to hire lawyers to draft incorporation legislation or otherwise advise them on the best means of procuring their political goals. And they could mobilize a province-wide constituency to lobby individual politicians at the local level. Increasingly, then, a growing number of *organized* occupations possessed the collective resources to make their influence felt in the public arena. Each had its own agenda, but all, in the broad sense, were trying to manage change. Sometimes this took the form of a bold attempt to exploit an opportunity, an aggressive foray into new terrain; more often it can be read as the kind of 'flight from competition' so vividly described by Alfred Jury and identified by Michael Bliss as 'the protective impulse.'[7]

To aspire to professional status, indeed, incorporated both sorts of objectives. As the case of the undertakers demonstrates, to be identified as a businessman or a retailer was no match for the prestige to be won from an alliance with 'science,' formal professional training, and the other trappings of professional status.[8] But there was a more mundane motive for a legislative initiative as well: the close corporation was a particularly attractive mechanism for institutionalizing the protective impulse. Combines and unions could be powerful instruments, but because they depended on voluntarism they could also be evanescent or, alternatively, long-enduring but impotent. Statutory measures which sequestered an occupational title, or better still the work itself, were not foolproof devices, but they offered an obvious advantage. Thus it is not surprising that we find undertakers and architects, stationary and civil engineers, surveyors and stenographers, all looking to the legislature to lend sanction to their economic goals or their quest for enhanced social status. Before the last quarter of the nineteenth century, only a handful of occupations had sought such privileges; by the 1890s a horde was clamouring at the door.

THE EXPANDING NUMBER of occupations which shared some similar characteristics; the fact that large numbers of occupations, professional or not, had their 'associations'; the sheer number of them that turned up as supplicants before the legislature – all tended to blur distinctions further, in the public mind at least. Sometimes politicians and editors could be genuinely confused about the differences, muddling up those which had legal privileges and those which did not, as well as the extent of the privilege obtained.[9] But, equally, it encouraged people to collapse categories for the sake of convenience or because they had come to view a large grouping of occupations in roughly the same light. 'There was much to be said,' one MPP contended in 1891, 'in favour of an association to examine and give certificates to [stationary] engineers on the same basis as was now done in the case of architects.'[10] Said another during the debate on the surveyors' act, he 'saw no reason why the surveyors should not be incorporated as well as the medical men.'[11] Those who were bitter opponents of occupational privilege did the same sort of thing. Consider this diatribe from William Balfour, a prominent Liberal who was eventually to serve as Speaker and then Provincial Secretary in 1895–6. Confronted by the second attempt by the undertakers to get themselves an incorporation act, Balfour cast his own net widely indeed.

They heard a good deal about the salt combine, the binder twine combine and other combines ... There was a growing feeling ... that law was being made so expensive that men would rather submit to impositions than take the chances of a law suit ... the people felt that they had been oppressed by the manner in which the legal machinery of the country was being worked, and they felt that the Law society was one of the greatest of combines. Privileges had not only been given to the Law society but to the medical men of the country. They had not been satisfied with what they had got, but had come back and asked for more concessions, that the law might act more stringently against everybody who did not belong to their organizations. The people of the country were rebelling. This was one of the reasons that the Patrons of Industry excluded professional men from membership in their organization. The architects had come to the house and asked permission to call themselves 'registered architects.' Now they had a bill before the house to enact that nobody who did not belong to their association should call himself an architect even. The undertakers asked to be allowed to call themselves 'registered embalmers,' but next session they would come to the house and ask that nobody be allowed to call himself an embalmer who did not belong to their combine. As an instance of the way in which special concessions are got he cited the pharmacy bill, which when introduced was said to be unobjectionable and which after passing through the hands of a committee of the house would practically prohibit a large number of people throughout the country from selling patent medicines. This was the way it was worked. Special privilege after special privilege was obtained, but the people of the country would rise in their might and say that they would have no more of it. If it was right to extend privileges to any class why not to all classes and to every trade?[12]

Balfour, the reader will notice, does not single out undertakers alone; rather, they are treated simply as one of a larger class of occupations which included not only pharmacists and architects but doctors and lawyers as well. They are not all unequivocally identified as professional men, for residual distinctions survive, marking off doctors and lawyers from the rest. But we are no longer dealing with assumptions about a society of ranks and stations where professional gentlemen possess prerogatives that rightfully belong to them, and where the distinctions between the learned professions and all other occupations are taken for granted. What Balfour describes is an unseemly scramble for power and place by contestants who all deserve to be treated in much the same way.

Equally here, the meaning of profession is reduced to a single dimension, the possession of legal privileges not shared by the occupational order at large. It was not simply laymen who engaged in such reductionism, moreover. Alan Macdougall, the leader of the Ontario wing of the Canadian Society of Civil Engineers, could use the following phraseology in a preface to his own argument for an incorporated profession: 'The Province of Ontario has passed several acts in late years regulating the practice of a number of businesses, thereby forming them into professions, and granting them close corporations.'[13] In the light of what had happened since mid-century, this was a perfectly reasonable way of seeing things. But it is the distilled essence of the changes overtaking the meaning of profession by the mid-1890s. A century earlier or less, a profession was an occupation fit for gentlemen, who held that rank not by virtue of their occupation but through their prior membership within the gentry class. Self-government was not a hallmark but the concomitant to a larger sense of 'ruling-class egalitarianism,' and it was manners and a liberal education which made the professional gentleman. Now politicians, by a wave of their legislative wand, could transform any 'business' into a 'profession.' Macdougall was hardly alone in expressing such views; indeed, they would become the conventional wisdom of the twentieth century. Robert Baldwin or John Strachan, John Rolph or John Beverley Robinson, or perhaps even the Methodistical Egerton Ryerson, would have turned over in his grave.

'THE PEOPLE of the country were rebelling,' William Balfour had warned in 1893, and a few months later the Patrons rode out of the west, captured seventeen legislative seats in the general election of 1894, and showed surprisingly high levels of electoral support in many constituencies they lost.[14] They had bigger fish to fry than the organized professions, but the latter were not exempt from their list of monopolies that fattened off the fruit of the land. And Balfour was right about something else as well: those banned from membership included 'all persons of immoral character ... lawyers, doctors ... Liquor Dealers' and others 'whose interests conflict with those of Farmers and labourers.'[15] In their first session in the legislature the Patrons ripped into the doctors, proposing a bill that would have effectively destroyed the Medical Council, taking out of its hands control over matriculation, leaving its representatives in a minority on the licensing board, and opening registration to anyone who held a Canadian or British medical degree. Adding insult to injury, they even proposed to license female midwives.[16] Not surprisingly, the Patrons were condemned emphatically in the medical press and by the Medical Council. The bill would create 'free trade in medicine' and would bring a retrogression to the state of things in 1850, said one leading Toronto doctor.[17] And when J.H. Sangster called for a general rebellion against the medical establishment, he certainly didn't mean one of this sort, dismissing the Patrons' leader in the House as a 'political charlatan' and the medical bill as an 'absurd fiasco.'[18]

The bill was defeated handily, Liberals and Conservatives voting against it almost to a man. The big guns on both sides of the House uniformly condemned it, Oliver Mowat characterizing it as 'revolutionary,' 'not in the public interest,' and an unwarranted attack on a 'learned' and 'honourable' profession.[19] The doctors did not get off scot-free however. In what was clearly a concession to the Patrons, who had hold of a popular issue, the government supported a private member's bill which repealed the section in the Medical Act giving the divisional associations powers to establish a uniform tariff of fees. In place since 1874, the tariff was not compulsory, but it established a benchmark of prices to be used by judges when disputes over fees arose between doctors and patients. Though hardly of the proportions the Patrons' bill represented, the repeal of the clause was, itself, seen by doctors as a major blow.[20]

To professional men generally, the Patrons were a scary bunch. As a run up to the coming election of Benchers, members of the junior bar in Toronto met in early 1896 to call for changes in the constitution of the Law Society that would make it more responsive; but as the *Globe* report noted, 'Many present believed lawyers should not go to the legislature for fear the Society's powers would be curtailed.'[21] Why had it taken so long for dentists to adopt more aggressive policies against the rising number of new entrants? The only reason, said the editor of the *Dominion Dental Journal* in the same year, was 'the fear that the Patrons in Parliament would succeed in an agitation to open the practice of dentistry to all comers if there was any movement on the part of the profession to restrict the production.'[22] The Patrons, in other words, encouraged professional men to keep their guard up and their heads down. The effect on leaders of aspiring occupations was much the same. In some cases, groups like the architects, stationary engineers, or the representatives of the Canadian Society of Civil Engineers saw their bills unceremoniously thrown out. In others they were told in no uncertain terms by some senior politician that, given the mood of the House, there was no point in attempting to introduce them. Alternatively those promoting such bills decided it would be the better part of valour to put off their initiatives to a brighter day.[23]

A SCARY BUNCH the Patrons might be. But they hadn't appeared on the scene until 1893, and by 1896 or 1897 their political clout was already waning. Even at the height of their influence, they were a relatively small third party, easily beaten back when the Liberals or Conservatives put their minds to it, as the resounding defeat of the medical bill demonstrates. Yet during the Patrons' glory days, architects despaired of ever seeing their registration act given teeth, the Medical Council heaved a collective shudder, and even the august editor of the *Canada Law Journal* waxed hysterical: 'We may consider ourselves lucky if we can keep Osgoode Hall over our heads, and be allowed to conserve for a little longer the limited privileges we enjoy.'[24]

Now what, one must ask, could provoke such lamentations, which seem, in hindsight at least, all out of proportion to the actual threat the Patrons posed? It was not the Patrons *per se* that spooked professional men, we want to suggest, but the deeper currents of public opinion they tapped into. During the last quarter of the nineteenth century, there had been growing opposition not only to the kind of close corporations possessed by lawyers and doctors, dentists and druggists, but to the entire body of assumptions which had thrown up those institutions in the first place. The Patrons, indeed, had no monopoly on anti-professional rhetoric. It was not a Patron but William Balfour who, even when he was Speaker of the House, attacked virtually every proposal to extend privileges for any occupational group, from doctors and lawyers, to architects, surveyors, and undertakers.[25] It was not a Patron but a Conservative politician who, in one legislative debate, described doctors as a 'parasitic fungus.'[26] The Patrons might oppose any prohibitions on contract practice, but before they came along, one doctor had already warned against any attack on the companies and lodges themselves: 'If we try to relieve ourselves from this injustice on that line, we will find ourselves fighting the most powerful and wealthy societies and companies in the land.'[27] Even before the elections of 1894, the editor of the *Canada Law Journal* was bemoaning the fact that 'we are compelled, unhappily, to pay some attention to the lay element in the House, as they are the exponents of the levelling spirit of the age, and they have votes, and party politicians exist on those votes.'[28] The Patrons, in other words, were simply the 'rough edge' of a political culture which had become sceptical and suspicious of, and in some cases profoundly hostile to, what professional men saw as their traditional prerogatives and their preordained place in Ontario's social structure.

This shift in the political culture originated in part from the cumulative impact of generational turnover, as men who had grown up in the decades around mid-century began to take over the reins of power, and not just in politics but in all those institutions which shaped and expressed influential opinion. Concomitantly, what had once been an insurgent ideology directed against the 'abuses' of the *ancien régime* became the dominant strain of social thought for a succeeding era. The Liberal election victory of 1871 or the coming to power of Oliver Mowat are probably appropriate symbolic turning-points, but it should not be tied too closely to the ideology of a particular political party in any case. Increasingly through the last quarter of the century the rhetoric of 'every tub on its own bottom,' of 'productive versus unproductive labour,' of anti-monopoly, of opposition to 'class legislation' ran deep, cut across party lines, and could be heard in a wide variety of political and social movements from the Grange, and later the Patrons, in the countryside, to labour in the towns. It fed off the dislocating effects of agricultural change, urbanization, and industrialization, and off the widespread hostility to industrial combines and public-utility monopolies. It found voice in the rising influence of a populist penny press and in such high-toned exponents of liberalism as the *Globe* and *The Week*. It even cropped up in the complaints of businessmen dismayed by the lack of respect they encountered compared with the prestige which seemed to accrue to the 'unproductive' professional man.[29] During the last two decades of the nineteenth century, in sum, professional men faced more articulate and sustained opposition than they had had since the years immediately around mid-century.

CONSIDER ONCE MORE the issue of lay conveyancing. It may be true that, during the late 1870s and early 1880s, the Benchers were less concerned about the problems of country practitioners than they might have been, had the internal organization of the profession been different. But supposing the Benchers had launched a vigorous campaign against lay conveyancing, would it have made any difference? Within the profession it might have had some symbolic importance, muting internal criticism, containing disaffection, or deflecting charges by country practitioners that the Law Society was merely 'inert.'[30] But the fact of the matter was that Convocation itself had no power whatever to outlaw lay competitors. That rested with the legislature alone, and it was in the political arena where the real resistance lay. Lawyers might be well represented in the House and even more so in the cabinet. But lawyers who were also politicians had responsibilities to wider constituencies. And the debate over the Division Courts bill first introduced in 1878 revealed a reservoir of anti-lawyer sentiment, in both the legislature and the press, which not even lawyers could ignore.[31] Letters poured in to the papers defending the competence of lay practitioners, and the rights of poor men everywhere to pursue cheap justice unencumbered by fee-hungry lawyers. Said one conveyancer from Paisley, in a tone that eerily evokes the ghost of William Lyon Mackenzie, 'We are the law Grangers who rescue the poor man from the fangs of the lawyer ... If we can stop the work of country lawyers, they and their dependants, the noble 260 who thrive in Toronto, will be simultaneously starved out ... We cover the land in every quarter. Go where one will, he will find a conveyancer every five miles in the country engaged in the noble work of peace-making by repressing all litigation, and by advising settlement of all disputes by arbitration.'[32] Solidly behind the Mowat government on this issue, as indeed on most others, and reading the popular mind reflected in his own correspondence columns, the editor of the *Globe* had great fun at the lawyers' expense. At a meeting of 'the junior bar' of Toronto, the press reported, one young turk had suggested that should a lay advocate propose to participate in a case, the barristers present should 'throw off their robes and mingle with the Crowd.' The *Globe* was convulsed: 'Terrible, terrible prospect! An organized strike of lawyers against the humane practice of taking fees would perhaps bring the public to their senses, and convince the legislature that young men who long for conveyancing and practice in the division courts should be allowed to make all the laws. The fearsome spectacle of even one Barrister throwing off his robes and mingling with the common herd might produce incalculable results.'[33]

Opposition to lawyers' ambitions, in any case, extended far beyond the pages of the *Globe*. The committee appointed by the Benchers to examine the question of lay conveyancing reported in 1883 that they had consulted with leading lawyer-politicians on both sides of the House, and the consensus was that there was no chance of getting a restrictive measure through the legislature.[34] Nearly a decade later, when the Law Society appointed yet another committee to review the question, things seemed worse, not better. As its chairman put it in a confidential letter sent out early in 1892 to the presidents of the county law associations, 'several of the Benchers who are members of the Legislature, stated that there was not the slightest prospect of obtaining legislation which would have for its plain object the protection of the profession against outside conveyancers; and if anything of that kind were attempted, it would probably make an opening for legislation of quite an opposite character and to the decided and permanent injury of the profession.'[35]

In the case of law the weight of public opinion made itself known when lawyers proposed to extend their jurisdiction to new areas of work. In medicine it was felt when doctors tried to enforce the penal laws by laying charges against midwives or counter-prescribing druggists. In any particular instance they might or might not get a conviction, but either way they brought down upon themselves a storm of condemnation.[36] When, for example, in 1882 an Ottawa doctor prosecuted a local druggist, not only the *Globe* but even editors who were normally favourable to the Medical Council expressed their unease. He wanted no quacks practising medicine, wrote the editor of the *Toronto Daily*

News, but 'the difficulty is in drawing the line. Many druggists are as well able to prescribe for some of the ills that flesh is heir to as some doctors are. Simple derangement of the stomach, many infantile complaints, yield to the skill of the druggist as surely as to the skill of the physician, and it is hard that the poor cannot avail themselves of the cheaper means of cure.'[37]

Thus whatever the pressures exerted by their own constituency, and at times it was intense, the Medical Council always had to tread cautiously, and occasionally retreat. In the late 1870s, for example, it had been forced to order its 'detective' to abandon his prosecutions of female midwives because of the political risks entailed,[38] and in the mid-1880s, when renewed demands for vigorous action against quacks were being heard, the editor of the *Lancet* warned that the force of public opinion could be ignored only at the profession's peril: 'The people were not always able to see why all the pretenders should be exterminated. A policy of tolerance was also stoutly maintained by influential organs of public opinion. Under such circumstances a relentless prosecution of the quacks might have resulted in tumbling the whole fabric over our heads.'[39]

WHILE THE POPULISM of the Patrons captured anti-professional sentiment *in extremis*, then, it was not an isolated or merely short-lived phenomenon. Beginning in the 1870s and culminating in the 1890s, such views had sunk deep roots in Ontario, deep enough at least that when lawyers or doctors, dentists or druggists did approach the legislature in the last two decades of the century, they were greeted with suspicion and hostility. True, they did not always walk away empty-handed. The legislature was prepared to consider and pass amendments which dealt with the internal affairs of the various professional organizations, to intervene, for example, in what one politician termed 'domestic brawls' over the composition of a governing council, or the method by which it was selected.[40] Even here the House was chary and would proceed only when satisfied that a majority of the rank and file supported the measure.[41] In a handful of instances, it was prepared to go farther, allowing the doctors an amendment in 1887 which gave the Medical Council the right to erase from its register the names of those found guilty of 'disgraceful conduct,' giving druggists in the mid-1890s a little more control over the sale of poisons,[42] or offering a group like the architects a registration act. But, in the main, the legislature was not prepared to entertain a substantial extension of existing monopolies or to create new ones.

Opposition came from three sources. The first manifested itself through vigorous lobbying by those who believed they had something to lose if such bills became law. If pharmacists sought to extend their control over the sale of poisons (often basic ingredients in patent medicines, fungicides, or pesticides), a wail arose across the land from the grocers who also sold these products; farmers joined in, warning of the dire consequences in terms of cost and inconvenience if they had to ride all the way to town to purchase 'Rough on Rats' from a druggist rather than from their friendly neighbourhood grocer.[43] Builders persistently opposed the attempts of the OAA to amend their act, fearing that it would force them to hire qualified architects to design their buildings and housing developments; the architects were equally opposed by the Toronto Trades and Labor Council, who wanted to protect master carpenters and other tradesmen from exclusions of a similar kind.[44] The stationary engineers ran smack into the lumbermen, the oil producers, and other manufacturing interests who wanted no truck with qualifications which would prevent them from hiring whomever they liked to run their steam engines.[45]

Second, there was a barrage of criticism based on liberal anti-monopoly political thought. A composite version of the kind of arguments heard in the House or in the correspondence and editorial columns of the *Globe* or *The Week* went something like this.[46] The proposed (or existing) close corporation was to be compared to other discredited institutions of the past, to the oppression and spiritual lassitude which invariably accompanied an established church, or to the unnatural restraint of trade imposed by the medieval guilds, of which the close corporations of professional men were simply an anomalous surviving vestige. Progress in all of the arts and crafts, including those like medicine and engineering, was made through the free flow of ideas and the challenge of competition which allowed merit, creativity, and innovation to find their own reward. There was also the right to sell one's labour on an open market and, concomitantly, the right of individuals to choose freely within that market. Beyond all that there were the arguments already quoted earlier in this chapter: give special privilege to one group, Alfred Jury had remarked, and how can you legitimately deny it to others? Or as William Balfour maintained, give any of them an inch and they will be back next year wanting a mile.

Finally, though not easily distinguished from the precepts of late nineteenth-century liberalism, there was the existence of what we will call an 'uninstructed' public. In an attempt to explain the growing authority of expertise in the United States during the latter half of the nineteenth century, Thomas Haskell has coined the phrase 'the recession of causation' to encapsulate a cumulative sequence of developments, such as the growing complexity of new technologies, organizations, and scientific breakthroughs, which undermined people's sense of mastery over their own destiny and made them increasingly dependent on the expertise of others.[47] It is in some respects a powerful explanatory tool and has been used since by many scholars, including some Canadian historians. We do not dismiss it lightly. But, in our own review of the public mood in the last two decades of the nineteenth century, what has impressed us most is the lack of acquiescence to the authority of experts, and the resistance to being instructed by them alone. As the editor of the Clinton *New Era* had put it in 1875, 'We are not a pack of children or imbeciles that we cannot exercise our judgement in discerning who is or is not capable of attending to our wants in the case of sickness or accident.'[48] And it is that kind of rhetoric that flows through the period, in the bills proffered by the Patrons, in the *Globe*, *The Week*, and the populist press, in speeches of Liberals and Conservatives in the legislature. It was not just the technicalities of the law which allowed 'quackery' to flourish in medicine, in other words, but also scepticism among large portions of the public about the superior therapeutic efficacy of licensed practitioners – or as one doctor put it, 'the caprices and credulity of people who seem bound to exercise their own judgement by resorting to quackery and patent medicines.'[49]

This argument needs nuance, of course. We are not dealing with some massive rejection of the expertise professional men might have to offer, but simply with the laity's right to judge and choose, much as it did among denominations. When it came to health care, most people probably exercised that right prudently. We, at least, have not located a single complaint about 'quack' surgery. An exclusive jurisdiction here arose not because a law existed but because people looked to the qualified for all but their most minor concerns. There were other areas of medicine and dentistry, however, where it was not clear that the professional man had an edge in anything except his legal prerogative. The simple extraction of teeth is one example. Childbirth without complications, an area where the experienced midwife might be routinely successful, is another. So was the diagnosis and cure of illness and disease in an era when medical therapeutics remained an uncertain art, and competitors could make plausible claims for efficacious remedies of their own. In such cases as these, individuals might still prefer to see a doctor, but they kept their options open, insisting on the right to consult the chiropractor, the Christian Scientist, the druggist, if they chose to do so, or to resort to the cures promised by patent medicines. Much the same was true in the case of lay conveyancing. Only a relative handful of critics was prepared to advocate the wholesale repeal of existing monopolies; but large numbers of more moderate people balked at the extension of monopoly, or the rigorous enforcement of existing penal laws.

That sort of tempered liberalism was common among key politicians as well. Whatever his commitment to liberal principles, 'the people's premier' was also one of the most distinguished Chancery lawyers of his generation, a leading Bencher, and a child of the pre-Victorian era. He was not about to raze Osgoode Hall or join the Patrons' assault on the Medical Council. Nor indeed was the *Globe* itself. 'The Ontario legislature has awakened to the evil of conferring exclusive privileges on certain occupations and creating close corporations for the benefit of private citizens,' its editor wrote of the plethora of such bills that had come before the House in 1892 and 1893; 'the professions which have already secured such advantages are fortunate, as all future legislation tending in that direction will be closely scrutinized.'[50] To the editor of *The Week* this was a classic case of weak-kneed liberalism. 'The Province is to be congratulated,' he replied,

on this indication that the Legislature, which means, we suppose, the government, ... has seen the error of its course in regard to a species of class legislation against which we have repeatedly protested ... But when the *Globe* says that the professions which have already secured such advantages are fortunate, does it mean to intimate that these have acquired vested rights in special privileges which are admitted to be unfair and indefensible, and that the members of these professions are henceforth to enjoy in perpetuity such special privileges while members of all other professions are to be denied them?[51]

The answer to that rhetorical question was yes. The established institutions and vested interests obtained by earlier generations remained intact and, as a consequence, remained touchstones of what full professional status meant far into the twentieth century. Had the more radical liberalism of the editor of *The Week*, the Patrons, or some of Mowat's own colleagues prevailed, the history of the professions in twentieth-century Ontario might have been different.

AND YET, the reader may say, even after all our qualifications have been made, there are still discrepancies in our account. Flawed though it might be, the architects did in fact get a registration act, and so did others as well. The surveyors, indeed, achieved the full panoply of a close corporation between 1887 and 1892, the very years when anti-professional sentiment was nearing its peak. Given the tenor of our argument in this chapter, how can we account for that accomplishment?

We would be less than forthright if we claimed to have a solid explanation; there is simply no documentation to explain it, and all we can do is suggest some plausible hypotheses. Surveying had been a regulated occupation from the beginning of settlement, and had had its own examining board, a restricted title, and an exclusive legal jurisdiction since at least mid-century. The act of 1887 *restored* a penalty clause to give that jurisdiction teeth; the act of 1892 transferred control over the examining board and professional affairs generally to surveyors themselves, reducing the government to a minority voice. The surveyors' act, in other words, made relatively modest changes to what were long-established practices, so that it may not have been seen, by those politicians who supported the bill, as a new departure.

A corollary argument has to do with the perception of surveying as a distinctive sort of occupation, one holding a special relationship to the state and thus exempt from the principle applied to most other occupations. An 1895 resolution of the CSCE, attempting to distinguish between engineers' work and that of surveyors, reads as follows: 'Land Surveyors are specially licensed for the practice of their calling because in every civilized country the guardianship of its landmarks is properly a function of the Government and Law Courts of the country and to that end, in all questions of boundaries the Licenced Surveyor is *de facto* the sworn servant of the Crown or State.'[52] A more mundane reason may be that many influential people had a large stake in ensuring that the surveyor got things right, including the prosperous farmers who became MPPs; the politician-lawyers, well aware of the mischief caused, and the legal and other expenses entailed, in boundary foul-ups or 'arbitrations' under the various drainage and municipal improvement acts; and those men of commerce involved in land speculation and real estate development. Competence among surveyors, in other words, may have been seen as essential to private interests as well as to the public interest in a way that most other occupational regulation was not.

Finally, it is possible that the politicians were unusually responsive to the claims of the surveyors because the latter were also engineers, one of the chief occupational beneficiaries of the 'theatre of science' in the nineteenth century, and men who played a key role in carrying out some of the great projects of rural and urban development that marked the era. The surveyor-engineers were not the only sort of engineers whose prestige was on the rise during the last quarter of the nineteenth century, but because they were engaged in the task *and* got there first, they had the good fortune to have a close corporation bestowed upon them. Exceptional they were, in any case, for that was something many others coveted in the late nineteenth century but could not achieve.

The consolation prize was the restricted title awarded by a qualifying association like the OAA. This device was hardly a new one in the late nineteenth century. Indeed, it was the instrument of choice in mid-Victorian Britain. Unwilling, almost without exception, to restrict the practice of a trade to an exclusive group, successive British governments had reconciled the demand for occupational protection and the public interest through legislation permitting an exclusive title alone. Medicine is a good example. Britain's major nineteenth-century medical act, passed in 1858, restricted the use of titles like 'doctor' to those practitioners licensed by the General Medical Council. It also reserved for those who were licensed a variety of other advantages such as certain government appointments as medical officers. But it did not exclude others from practising medicine. The principle at issue here was intimately linked to the larger liberalism of the age.[53] The public interest might demand that people be able to distinguish between the qualified and the unqualified, to make decisions on the grounds of informed choice. But it was to be their *choice*. Anyone was free to hawk a claim to cures in the marketplace, and the consumers were to be free to purchase that service if they wished.

In Ontario there had been early experiments with this form of occupational regulation. The medical legislation of 1865, for example, had introduced reserved titles, but the penal clauses applied only to the use of those titles and not to the practice of medicine itself. The same arrangement held for the 'veterinary surgeons,' who had obtained a restricted title between 1868 and 1871.[54] But the medical act of 1869, as well as the dental and pharmaceutical acts, reverted to the close corporation as the model upon which professional status was to be built. To see the two forms of regulation in historical juxtaposition is to illuminate the significance of the change from one to the other in the late nineteenth century. Among its other purposes the close corporation was intended to provide a maintenance for the regularly bred. Just as law and medicine were self-governing (or should be so) *because* they were modelled upon the more general practice of ruling-class egalitarianism, so they were close corporations to ensure livings for professional gentlemen. To move to the restricted title and the qualifying association is to shift from the Georgian to the Victorian, from ascription to merit, from the ascendancy of the gentry to the values of the middle class. So far as the professions were concerned at least, this transition came late to Ontario, but it came nonetheless. And once in place, it persisted. During the first quarter of the twentieth century, aspiring occupations like the nurses or the engineers, to take but two examples, might be rewarded with their own registration acts, but it would be the middle decades of that century before any group would sequester a new legal monopoly over work in Ontario.

15
'Who Was Then a Gentleman?'

In the spring of 1891, Clara Brett Martin presented her application for admission as a student of law. It would, the editor of the *Canada Law Journal* predicted, provoke 'a battle royal,' and he was right.[1] The Law Society denied her application, and as a result a bill, introduced by none other than William Balfour, was pushed through the legislature, effectively overriding the Society's decision and forcing it to admit her, though only as an articling clerk. When, a few years later, she applied to be received as a barrister, the same legislative pressures had again to be brought to bear. It was almost certainly against the better judgment of the majority of Benchers and probably of a large proportion of the rank and file;[2] but by 1897 Ontario had its first woman barrister.

Martin's achievement was singular in that she was the first woman to breach one of the more impregnable bastions of male prerogative in late nineteenth-century Ontario. She was followed almost immediately, nonetheless, and with much less fanfare, by a Port Arthur woman, Eva Maude Powley, who was admitted to the bar in 1902.[3] They, in turn, were simply part of a larger movement, gaining impetus since at least mid-century, in which a growing number of women sought paid employment in a variety of traditional and non-traditional jobs.[4] Those who had the advantage of more education than most of their peers had also a wider range of opportunities. Many of them found work in the expanding elementary-school system, a smaller number in the high schools, and a few began to enter such fields as pharmacy, medicine, and dentistry. The first register of licensed pharmacists, issued in 1871, included the names of five women, and more would be added to the list in the decades that followed.[5] Dr Jennie Trout was admitted to membership in the College of Physicians and Surgeons in 1875, and in succeeding years others would join her as licensed physicians.[6] Ontario's first female dentist, Josephine Wells, was admitted as a licentiate of the

Royal College of Dental Surgeons in 1893.⁷ Women also began to enter full-time work in the churches as foreign and home missionaries, and as deaconesses or other kinds of church workers.⁸

The entry of women into these sorts of jobs was due, in part at least, to causes we have canvassed in earlier chapters. Though the evidence is scanty or flawed, it is remarkable how often the same pattern emerges in the work of authors writing about different occupations: young women who entered medicine or the service of the church, for example, tended to come from farm backgrounds or from families who belonged to Ontario's small-town middle class, especially from those of its professional men.⁹ Economic change, above all the combined effects of urbanization and rural depopulation, pushed girls as well as boys off the farm and out of the villages and small towns, and at the same time provided a growing volume of work for them to do. The accessibility of the high schools also offered opportunities which had not been available earlier in the century. From the late 1860s onwards, a growing number of girls could, without undue sacrifice, achieve the same kind of qualifications as boys for all kinds of white-collar work, including the matriculation certificates required by the universities and the professions.¹⁰

They entered the workforce for the most conventional of reasons: they had to find the means to support themselves for a period before marriage or through a lifetime as a single woman. But some also picked a career for the sheer adventure of it, the physical or intellectual challenges promised by the study of medicine, the law, or the call to service in a foreign land.¹¹ As Veronica Strong-Boag writes, moreover, 'The development of the Canadian women's movement ... gave cause for good cheer. The emergence [in the 1870s] of the first branches of the YWCA, the WCTU, and various foreign missionary societies, together with a host of more local associations, raised up new sympathizers for female initiatives. Medical education was a particular beneficiary of this more receptive environment ... Support was all the more likely when medical pioneers like Emily Howard Stowe and Jennie Kidd Trout became leaders of groups such as the Toronto Women's Literary Society, later the Women's Suffrage Club.'¹² That was true not only for medicine, however: the feminist impulse, whatever the particular form it took, played a role in the development of nurse training, and in women's work in the churches.¹³ Constance Backhouse has demonstrated, moreover, that the organized voice of women in the political arena was critical to Clara Brett Martin's victory over the Law Society.¹⁴ There was more involved to women's entry into these areas of work, in sum, than just the push and pull of a changing economy.

The preceding paragraphs are, we must say, nothing more than the briefest gloss on a well-established literature that stretches back some twenty-five years and now consists of a considerable volume of dissertations, essays, and monographs. It is not our intention, then, to reiterate this literature in any greater detail. But we do want to draw on it in order to illuminate two questions pertinent to the larger themes of this book. First, how were these careers for women integrated into the occupational order that was emerging during the latter half of the century? And second, what consequences did their entry portend for the ideal of the professional gentleman?

WHEN WOMEN ATTEMPTED to enter occupations traditionally closed to them, the level of opposition they encountered was highly variable. It was, apparently, never a serious issue in pharmacy, and despite all the gnashing of teeth about other matters in the 1890s, the *Dominion Dental Journal* took no notice of it at all. When Emily Stowe applied for a licence to practise medicine in 1870, she was rejected on the same grounds as those males who had also been trained in the United States: the Medical Council required at least one term in an Ontario medical school (or the equivalent). But, at the same time, the council agreed almost unanimously to admit women on the same terms as men,[15] and, beginning in 1877–8, a footnote was added to its annual announcement, specifying that 'the masculine pronoun is used here and throughout the Regulations with reference to "students" and "Candidates," nevertheless these terms are to be construed as applicable to either Sex.'[16] Though the experiment didn't last long, women *were* admitted to the existing medical schools; indeed, it was by that means that both Emily Stowe and Jennie Trout qualified for registration as licensed practitioners.[17] Only the Law Society attempted to exclude women entirely, basing its initial rejection of Clara Brett Martin on the grounds that, according to the original intent of the Law Society Act, women were not to be understood as 'persons.'[18]

Even the conflicts which took place in 1882–4 over medical education for women at the Royal College in Kingston need to be interpreted with some care. A coterie of male students, abetted by one professor, certainly heaped punishment upon Elizabeth Smith and the handful of other women in the class, just because they dared to be there.[19] But the miscreants were thoroughly savaged by the local press, by newspapers across the province, and by leading lay and medical opinion as well.[20] The result was not the denial of access to medical education but the establishment of separate medical colleges for women in both Kingston and Toronto.[21] Moreover, if the initial impetus for access to professional training came from women themselves, it must also be said that they had powerful support from some influential males, ranging from the editor of the *Globe* through to Principal Grant of Queen's, and, in the case of Clara Brett Martin, Oliver Mowat himself.[22] Ambitious and able young women, in other words, did not face an implacable male 'establishment' opposed, under any circumstances, to women doctors or lawyers. Rather, opinion on the matter was divided, and if there was both overt and covert opposition, there were also those prepared to promote the right of access to higher education, including professional training.

Access, nonetheless, was almost universally mediated through the rhetoric of the separate spheres, a set of 'ideological constructions about propriety'[23] which offered, at one and the same time, both opportunities and constraints. Opportunities because it could be used to pry open areas of work traditionally closed to women – the licence to practise medicine, for example. As Strong-Boag remarks, entry to medicine 'could be justified as a "natural" outlet for women's nurturing instincts.'[24] Given the innate modesty of women, moreover, there would necessarily be a need for female physicians, since many women would be unwilling, even to the point of death, to consult a male physician about their most intimate bodily ailments.[25] It probably mattered too that doctors performed most of their work in the home and had no 'public' forum like the courtroom or the pulpit. The tone of the rhetoric makes the constraints obvious as well. Women might enter medicine, but they were especially suited to the tasks of caring for women and children, or to those involved in foreign missions where women doctors alone had access to those of their own sex.[26] In law the struggle was of a different order since not only the worksites but the entire culture of work left few niches where women's claims could be lodged except for the blunt and radical one of equal rights, something that directly challenged the doctrine of separate spheres itself.[27]

A doctor was a doctor nonetheless, and women were licensed to practise the same skills as men; in this respect a level of formal equality existed in medicine, and, by 1897, in law as well. In the realm of religion, it was rather a different matter. Throughout the last quarter of the nineteenth century, leading clergymen of the Anglican, Presbyterian, and Methodist churches were eager to mobilize the agency of women for a wide variety of activities ranging from home and foreign missions to deaconess orders. But here the rhetoric of women as 'helpmeets to men' was virtually unqualified.[28] As they entered full-time church work, women might find themselves performing much of the work ministers did, such as pastoral visits and even the conduct of Sunday services when no males were available to do it.[29] On the mission fields particularly, they might find opportunities to carve out a substantial degree of autonomy 'within the patriarchal religious institution from which they operated.'[30] Organizations of lay women, like the Methodist Woman's Missionary Society, might also win a virtually independent role within that larger framework.[31] But in the various church courts, women remained outsiders, influential voices perhaps, but never direct participants in policy making.[32] Equally, there was virtually no talk of the ordination of women in any of the three denominations. In this respect, the clerical order remained even more of a closed shop than the Law Society itself.

Whatever their level of ambivalence might be about women physicians, male doctors were in the vanguard of the movement to promote nurse training.[33] In the nineteenth century, the reader is reminded, nurses (like doctors) rarely worked in hospitals, but rather in other people's homes. Once a medical crisis had been met by the doctor, it was often the nurse who took over, tending to the more routine but essential tasks of patient care. Thus doctors (and patients) had a sizeable stake in competent nurses, which meant those who could not only cook or keep house but could monitor the patient's condition, recognize symptomatic change, and administer medication in a knowledgeable way. The chief virtue of a nurse, however, lay in her ability to understand and follow the directions of the physician and to know the limits of independent judgment. Promulgated in the first instance by Florence Nightingale herself, nurse training, which began in the province in St Catharines in 1874, was rigorously demarcated as a calling peculiarly suited to the natural abilities of women but also as one in which the nurse was the helpmeet of the physician. Prominent nurse superintendents might share that viewpoint, or have other notions about the means of turning nursing into a respectable profession. But 'the fact that modern nursing made its entry into Canada at the invitation of a physician,' writes Lauretta Hazzard, 'is, in itself, significant. Nursing education ... was, from the moment of its inception, incorporated into the domain of physicians and the hospital.'[34]

Beginning around mid-century, then, women, for a whole variety of reasons, sought entry to old and new occupations alike, and obtained a portion of success. The price was, in the main, demarcation or subordination,[35] in an occupational order structured around the ideology of separate spheres. But as Linda Kerber remarks, that ideology itself must be understood 'as a metaphor for complex power relations in social and economic contexts.'[36] The nature of those power relations is not at issue here. It was males – and, it should be added, males of a certain class – who controlled all the entry points and had the wherewithal to shape social institutions as they saw fit. Women had to accommodate themselves to that bedrock of social fact, and to work, and organize, within and around it. What we want to explore further, however, is how women's entry into professional work might threaten to undercut the nexus of material circumstances and the gendered assumptions on which those power relations rested.

GIVEN THE LARGE VOLUME of complaints about 'professions overcrowded' in the last quarter of the nineteenth century, it is remarkably uncommon to find explicit reference to professional women as potential economic competitors. We want to suggest, nonetheless, that there was far more unease on this score than the public record admits, and it is most apparent in the mediative language of separate spheres itself. In passages primarily designed to justify the place of women within an occupation, commentators would remark, for example, and almost in passing, that women would pose no threat because they would not become permanent members of it in any case. 'We do not think that lady pharmacists will ever be a numerous class,' the editor of the *Canadian Pharmaceutical Journal* wrote in 1872; 'Our churlish bachelors may rest perfectly easy on that score. No department of labor, or sphere of life, seems so adapted to females as the domestic, and generally speaking, ladies themselves are not slow in finding this out. It has almost invariably been found ... that however proficient a female may become in any avocation, she seldom becomes attached to it to such a degree that she will not desert it for the charms of the domestic hearth.'[37]

Even if women did opt for a career, the natural demarcation of their work would have its own effects. Reviewing the most recent calendar for the Kingston Women's Medical College, the editor of the *Queen's College Journal* took note in 1885 of its assurance that 'the sphere in the medical world intended for the ladies is to be exclusively confined to their own sex.'[38] Similarly 'a gentleman who has taken some interest in' the women's medical school in Toronto was reported in the *Globe* as saying that 'it isn't proposed that these Ladies shall enter the field as competitors for the ordinary practice now in the hands of men. But there is work to do attending the sick among their own sex and among children.'[39] Those women who chose to enter the professions would, in any case, represent only a 'few choice spirits';[40] as Oliver Mowat would put it in the legislature in 1895, 'Very few women ... would be likely to avail themselves of the privilege, and the men would not likely to be embarrassed by an overflow of women into the profession.'[41] Rare the explicit references might be, in other words, but the very way in which the language of separate spheres was used reveals the unease shared by many professional men about the economic threat that professional women might pose.

One didn't have to be explicit about it in any case: doctors or lawyers could listen and read, like others in their society, and draw appropriate conclusions. By the 1870s and 1880s, as we have suggested in an earlier chapter, the consequences of doubling the pool of candidates for teaching jobs was well understood. Or, to take another example, in 1893 J.L. Payne contributed a piece to the *Canadian Magazine* entitled 'The Displacement of Young Men.'[42] Women, he argued, were flooding into jobs in offices and shops, taking on work traditionally done by males, and forcing young men to compete ever more fiercely for those jobs in commerce which remained male preserves, thus driving salaries even in those jobs inexorably downwards. Payne said absolutely nothing about the professions, but the lesson could hardly be missed.[43] It was not just that women themselves might enter the professions, but that, crowded out from avenues of work traditionally their own, young men would set their sights on medicine or law and further exacerbate the effects of internal competition. In two respects, then, women might create an enlarged pool of potential competitors and thus raise fears on that score alone.

Yet we think the story is more complex than this, in large part because of the visceral male reaction in classrooms or worksites to the mere presence of women, a reaction that seems all out of proportion to their modest numbers. If the conflicts over coeducational medical education at Kingston in the early 1880s had constituted a singular incident, one might be able to discount their significance. But, as Constance Backhouse points out, they did not. Having broken through what Clara Brett Martin thought was her most impenetrable barrier, admission to the Law Society itself, she became an articled clerk in one of Toronto's élite law firms. 'When I put in my appearance,' she later wrote, 'I was looked upon as an interloper, if not a curiosity. The clerks avoided me and made it as unpleasant for me as they possibly could (I dislike to make such a charge against the young gentlemen of Canada) and for a time it looked as if I were doomed to failure through a source with which I had not reckoned.'[44] Nor was her experience at the law school any better. Martin described her classes 'as having been deliberately structured to place "unnecessary emphasis upon certain lecture points in the thousand ways that men can make a woman suffer who stands alone among them." Her alienation was compounded by mean-spirited male students, who were in the habit of hissing loudly when she entered the classroom.'[45]

What was it that provoked this behaviour? No matter what assurances might be offered by their seniors or betters, these young men could hardly help but see such women as their competitors in an era when their own economic expectations seemed at risk. But it also mattered that these particular competitors were *women*. Writing about the dangers inherent in the displacement of young men, J.L. Payne had remarked that it was 'one of the inexorable laws of creation that man alone shall be the breadwinner in the economy of domestic affairs, and the violation of this mandate can only bring retribution and sorrow.'[46] Professional men added their own gloss: when a woman 'entered the learned professions,' said one, 'she not only stepped outside her natural sphere, but also unduly interfered with man's power to support his natural dependents.'[47] Their male counterparts, both Elizabeth Smith and Clara Martin declared bitterly, had failed to act like 'gentlemen.' Understandably so. 'When young men cannot find work,' write Michael Roper and John Tosh of a somewhat different historical problem, 'not only their income but their masculinity is threatened.'[48] In an era when many professional men were confronted with the spectre of diminished expectations, they were also confronted by the violation of 'the inexorable laws of creation.' The intrusion of women into the medical school or the law office posed a threat to masculine identities simply because it challenged the power relations, economic and otherwise, embedded in the ideology of the separate spheres.

ECONOMIC *and* otherwise. The notion of the professional gentleman, we suggested in our opening chapter, was a profoundly gendered concept. Among other things, that means it was a '*relational* construct'[49] which defined the attributes of men of a certain class as against those of women (in this case mostly of the same class), and those attributes reached far beyond the economic. Consider the content of some typical male commentary on the entry of women into the professions or the universities. In a leader of 1877 on the place of women in the church, the editor of the *Christian Guardian* cautiously welcomed their increasing role but warned that 'those who maintain that women are just as fit to be ministers, legislators, engineers and judges as men, must deliberately shut out from sight constitutional and mental differences which the Creator has stamped upon each sex.' The editorial concluded, moreover, with the following remark:

It is difficult fully to express in words the instinctive repugnance which most men of refinement feel to women coming to the front in the professions, and mingling in the rough conflict, such as takes place between man and man. As the whitest linen is the most easily soiled, the very delicacy and attractive grace of womanhood render any work, not entirely in harmony with that retiring modesty which is the great charm of the gentler sex, inconsistent with delicate womanliness.[50]

It was inappropriate to award university degrees to women, the editor of the *Queen's College Journal* had argued a year earlier, because such degrees 'have reference solely to public life. Their conferment implies that the objects of it are to go forth and push their way in the outside world, and there acquire *ipso facto* a certain acknowledged position.' Women, however, 'because of the delicate grace and beauty' of their character, did not belong in that world, and thus their education should be of a different kind. Though their minds should be cultivated, that culture 'should not be what is regarded as distinctively intellectual. It should be governed with reference to elegance as well as strength, to the development of the tastes and affections as well as the mere reasoning faculties. Let a woman rather acquire the modern languages than the ancient, and let her study music, poetry and painting than the problems of mathematics and metaphysics.'[51]

Reflecting some years later on Clara Martin's success in mathematics at Trinity College, a Toronto newspaper would note that she had 'a real masculine penchant for mathematics ... It was with great supercilious regret that the male mathematicians of those days admitted that a woman could master the binomial theorem or the integral calculus.'[52] According to a columnist in the *Globe* in 1886, a recently interviewed 'lady doctor' had shown no 'evidence of that loss of womanly attribute which is so necessarily a result of a medical course ... She didn't stride, she wasn't a guy, she didn't use slang, her manners weren't aggressive.'[53] One could not expect too much, on the other hand. 'It should be borne in mind that medicine requires peculiar natural as well as acquired qualifications,' wrote the editor of the *Christian Guardian* in 1883. 'We have no idea that female doctors will ever, to any large extent, compete with their brethren of the noble art in surgery, or the severe toils of the profession.'[54] Nor would they find their *métier* in generating new knowledge: 'Intellectual initiative seems exclusively the province of the male mind,' wrote a *Globe* columnist, and

we need look for little advancement along the lines of scientific investigation from women for some time to come. Here, as elsewhere, however, we may expect careful and conscientious study of research, insofar as it has been carried, and unerring application of truth so apprehended. Of course, the young woman who would be an MD must feel special fitness for the calling to offset the special difficulties which will beset her in following it. Closely akin to it, and gained without expense, is the profession of nurse, well paid and honorable.[55]

Though sentiments like these were not universal in the period, they were pervasive enough; and they have been used by a generation of feminist historians as so many exemplars of the attempt to keep women in their proper sphere. They are indeed that. But they also offer an *entrée* to the language and behavioural codes by which professional men construed their own masculinity. From childhood they received an education unlike that of women. Above all, they were initiated into the mysteries of the classical languages and higher mathematics – the liberal education suited to the learned professions. Through that education they acquired not only esoteric knowledge but that quality of mind which provided them with 'intellectual initiative' and disciplined rationality. Some went on to learn the secrets of their craft, along with its manners and mores, in offices or other worksites which were the exclusive preserve of males. Others attended the equally closed world of the university, with its learning and degrees which 'have reference solely to public life' and which thus enabled them to 'push their way in the outside world, and there acquire *ipso facto* a certain acknowledged position.' Beyond the classroom there were the clubs, the student newspapers, and the rest of the non-formal curriculum which constituted the student subculture of the age. Though it was not confined to them, medical students seem to have been a particularly gregarious and rowdy lot, indulging in everything from the disruption of their classrooms or university convocations, to 'harmonic street parades' and stringing up corpses in front of shop windows.[56] But genteel or not, it was all part of learning to be 'guys.' They also learned, among other things, self-control and physical stamina in order to move, for example, from the dissecting room to the surgeon's table, from the classroom to the 'severe toils of the profession.' Their public arenas, whether the legislature or the courts, necessarily involved them in the 'rough conflicts between man and man.' Even vestry or synod meetings constituted a 'battlefield of discussion and contention.'[57]

In the last three decades of the nineteenth century, however, women were invading this turf, intruding into the physical and psychic spaces that men claimed as their own. Like the men, they now learned Latin in order to pass their matriculation examinations before the university or the Medical Council. Clara Martin graduated with high honours in mathematics, the special province of the male mind. Students at the Toronto Woman's Medical College were told that they too must learn to control their emotions, to be physically strong and mentally capable.[58] Challenged to make their own contribution to a vivisection lesson, and taunted 'by a delicate allusion to old maidism,' Elizabeth Smith's female compatriots 'resurrected' four cats and dumped them at their instructor's door, proving that they could assimilate themselves within the medical student's subculture.[59] At least two women ran (though without success) for seats in pharmacy's governing council.[60] An 'interloper' or not, Clara Martin was learning her craft in a law office and the courts, alongside other law clerks. Their numbers may have been token and their entry largely symbolic, but women like Martin and Smith were demanding, and gaining, access to the variety of specialized knowledge and craft skills men had claimed as their own. 'Knowledge is power,' declared one of the most pervasive clichés of the nineteenth century, and that power was now to be shared, not only among men, but with women as well.

Why should 'men of refinement' feel such 'repugnance' to women entering law, medicine, or any like occupation? What drove medical students or law clerks to conduct unbecoming of a gentleman? It was not simply the threat of economic competition, though that is not to be discounted. The ideal of the professional gentleman incorporated, among its other elements, images about a particular form of masculine identity, about the gendered distribution of knowledge and authority in both the 'public' and the 'domestic' sphere, which the entry of women on equal terms necessarily challenged. And the consequences of that challenge could not be foreseen. It might be that professional men, by one means or another, could maintain that private preserve they dubbed the public sphere. More ominously, the entry of young women might change the nature of an occupation fundamentally and forever. As George Wrong would remark, in oracular tone, in 1907, 'Experience has made quite indisputable the general law that in occupations where women predominate the men tend to disappear, and where men predominate the women tend to disappear. Neither sex likes the predominance of the other in its chosen sphere of labour.'[61] By the late nineteenth century, the ideal of the professional gentleman was being attenuated by a variety of forces at work within the social order; when women too became 'professional gentlemen,' that ideal could not help but become more attenuated and ambiguous still. Nor could it help but raise anxiety among professional men themselves about their own future and their place in the social order.

FOR THE CLERGY, gender was also an issue of some importance but for a rather different reason. Here the problem was less the present women than the 'missing men.' From the early 1880s onwards, there had been growing unease over the apparent failure to attract or hold large numbers of male adherents.[62] The bulk of the rhetoric focused on young men, who seemed to lose interest in the message of the gospel (or, more likely, in attending Friday prayer meetings or Sunday school) when they reached adolescence. But by the 1890s there was also concern about the apparent indifference of mature males as well. As one Anglican clergyman commented in 1892, 'Whatever be the reason, the impression one receives from talking with the average professing Christian man of today is that religion is a good thing – for clergymen and women; that they like to see them interested and active in good works, and that they think it right to see the ordinances of religion supported in a becoming manner, but that they have no time or talent for personal religion or religious work.'[63]

We are concerned here, however, not with the case of the 'missing men' *per se*, but rather with the way the issue redounded upon self-images and lay perceptions of the clergy. In the main, not surprisingly, ministers tended to blame the problem on lay worldliness or the distractions of secular pursuits. But for some influential laymen, the culprit lay elsewhere. 'Business and professional men of today, both young and old, are of necessity practical and proportionately keen and critical,' one Anglican layman wrote in the pages of the *Canadian Churchman* in 1894. 'The six day struggle for life so sharpens their wits that when they go to church on Sunday they naturally look for a service and sermon that ... are abreast of the times in the same way their businesses have to be kept abreast of the times.' Instead, they were fed a diet of 'platitudes and high-sounding phrases,' and 'exhortations to lead a life of impossible simplicity without the faintest attempt to explain how the actual hourly trials met with in these days of complexity, hardship, vice, trickery and so forth are to be faced.'[64]

Strong enough language, one might think, but even stronger was to come in the following year by way of an influential article written by the American journalist Edward Bok, published in the pages of *Cosmopolitan* and reprinted in the *Evangelical Churchman*. To Bok, 'the average minister' was 'wholly out of touch with the times in which he lives ... The pulsations of the great business world, in which men of his congregation move every day, and where they have the greatest need of the ministrations of his office, are unknown to him. He never goes into it; he never speaks of it. He lives with his books, rather than men.' Bok went on to lambaste the clergy for their patronizing, vapid, irrelevant sermons, and their sheltered upbringing. 'We educate the goody-goody boys of our families to be ministers. Let a boy give indication that he is apart from the great world, is studious when others are at play, has inclinations for ethereal rather than material things, and that boy is at once destined for the ministry.'[65] Not everyone agreed with Bok, but his thesis sparked a vigorous correspondence in Ontario's clerical journals, he found his share of support, and his attack on the clergy resonated through other critical commentary.[66] In 1898, for example, a leading Methodist layman piled into his own ministers in similar terms. 'Sunday after Sunday, the veriest theological twaddle is poured forth from a multitude of our pulpits,' he wrote in the pages of the *Christian Guardian*. 'The average preacher apparently knows nothing of the battle within and without which every man must encounter in these days of stress and storm. We are fed from the pulpit with husks, if not with sawdust, by men who are too indolent, or too stupid, to appreciate the needs of the day. What wonder, then, that congregations dwindle away until few but women, with their religious instincts, are found in attendance?'[67]

Left with 'few but women.' There was an 'urgent necessity' for keeping young men in the church for 'none but they can do certain kinds of difficult work which is all important to have done.'[68] It was no less essential to hold the loyalties of the intellectual, social, and financial leaders of their communities. Yet the clergy were said to be 'out of touch' with the world these men, both young and old, inhabited. By the end of the nineteenth century, there were a wide variety of reasons why clergymen might shrink before the spectre of intellectual and cultural marginalization. But the furore over the 'missing men' must have made them especially anxious. Not only did it subject them to sharp criticism from prominent members of their own flock, but it raised the fear that they might be reduced, from being leaders within the community of men, to the status of domestic chaplain of its wives and daughters.

16
Portents Bleak, and Promising

For professional men, the nineteenth century ended with neither a bang nor a whimper but a wail. Confronted by external enemies, internal discord, and socio-economic changes they could only half-understand, they poured out their troubles in the pages of their professional journals, editors and correspondents alike bemoaning a precarious present and an uncertain future. 'In former days,' the editor of the *Lancet* wrote in 1895, 'the doctor had a very much higher standing in the community than at the present time when education is so cheap and common that the professional ranks are filled with men who have no real qualifications for the calling other than the parchment containing their easily won degrees.' Only a few doctors now made large incomes, he added, 'the great majority barely paying their running expenses and many not even that.'[1] In the same year the editor of the *Canada Law Journal* could speak of 'half starving solicitors throughout the cities and country.'[2] Two years earlier he had complained that 'candidates for judicial honours' continued to press into the occupation, 'including Indians, Italians and tramps ... And we must remember how largely the business which should be done by the profession is cut into by a vast army of irresponsible agents, camp followers, and pirates of every description; eating up, like locusts, every green thing.'[3]

Who was to blame? Everything and everybody. Within each occupation there were those who failed to act as gentlemen should. There was the levelling spirit of democracy abroad in the land. There were the élites who dominated the professional organizations and seemed indifferent to the plight of country practitioners or the struggling young. There were powerful industries or lodges whose malign influence made itself felt in the legislature or the press. In the 1890s professional men turned on the education system itself. 'The public school system of the province is one of our proudest boasts,' said one doctor, himself an ex–

high school-teacher, 'but the high schools are doing a work which has both a good and an evil side. An experience of seven years in the work of the high school system satisfies me that these schools are responsible for turning into physicians a great many who would have been excellent farmers and workingmen and businessmen.'[4] The editor of the *Lancet* concurred, blaming declining incomes and falling prestige on the influx of 'school teachers and farmers' sons.'[5] And so, indeed, did the editor of the *Canada Law Journal*: 'High class education for the masses is a fine thing in theory, but it has manifest disadvantages, if (as it does) it takes young men unduly from tilling the ground from whence they came, or from the ranks of mechanical labor (avocations both honorable and independent) to a profession overcrowded to excess, and in which few of them can expect to make more than a bare and uncertain subsistence, and which many will have to abandon, to obtain elsewhere a means of existence.'[6]

While there was discontent and dissension among lawyers, it was in medicine and dentistry where the most pessimistic assessments prevailed. Despite some successes by the Medical Council's prosecutor, druggists continued to find ways to counter-prescribe and engaged in other activities which brought them into competition with doctors. The patent-medicine industry continued to hawk its cures, and to trumpet claims in the pages of the daily press of superior therapeutic efficacy. No sooner did some traditional forms of quackery begin to disappear than new ones popped up. Contract practice continued to flourish as well, threatening to reduce the status of the doctor to that of a hired hand. 'Today, mechanics, artisans, and men of almost every calling are organizing for self-protection, that they may obtain a recompense for their services,' one correspondent wrote to the *Ontario Medical Journal*, and yet medical men could not even unite against 'taking patients for a dollar a year.'[7] The growth of specialties was challenging the ideal of the general practitioner itself. 'Where is the family physician of the past?' asked one prominent doctor in 1897:

A quarter of a century ago he was as much a social as a professional factor in family life. To-day, except in the country, he exists more as a 'holy memory' than as an active and trusted quantity. He may still be retained as an occasional family adviser, in a sort of an abstract way, but his laurels are already on the brow of his juvenile coadjutor – the hustling specialist. This may be for the public weal, or the public woe, but the fact remains that the old and trusted family physician is passing into oblivion.[8]

In the fading years of the century, yet other menaces loomed up. Doctors suddenly found themselves confronted with a proposal, emanating from the wife of the governor general no less, to found the Victorian Order of Nurses, which general practitioners feared would raise up a whole new species of 'half-trained' women to invade their obstetrical turf.⁹ Even the rise of the general hospital seemed ominous. It was one thing for free dispensaries, clinics, and hospitals to provide services to the poor, as they had long done. But there was a growing tendency, or so at least doctors believed, for hospitals to admit to the public (or charity) wards, patients who could well afford to pay. The result was 'to pauperize a large portion of the community, who have no desire to become objects of charity as far as their food, clothing etc. are concerned, but are quite willing or anxious to get medical attendance without paying for it.'¹⁰ This, said the editor of the *Canadian Practitioner*, was 'an outrage.'

> It was never intended that a patient in good circumstances could make use of these wards and claim free attendance because he did so. This is a clear perversion of the spirit in which public wards were founded. Charity is for the pauper – not for the pauper in spirit, the imposter, who desires to receive what he does not pay for.¹¹

Concluded the Ontario Medical Association in 1899, 'successive changes in the law [relating to hospitals] tend toward the socializing of the profession and the curtailing of the domain of the private practitioner,' and it set up a committee to review 'the operation of "The Charities and Public Health Acts" and their effects upon the status and emoluments of the profession.'¹² Altogether, then, doctors saw themselves as a profession under siege. As the editor of the *Canadian Practitioner* put it in 1898, 'Most physicians will agree with Drs. Sangster and Spence that, between the practice of druggists, the sales of patent medicines, free treatment in hospitals, and lodge practice, the medical profession is being encroached upon on every side.'¹³

Dentists debated whether they were in fact a profession at all. Some claimed dentists had achieved that status in the eyes of 'the intelligent public' at least.¹⁴ Others thought differently: 'The mischief of it is, there are so many in the community who look upon dentistry as a sort of bastard profession, little better than a trade, and there are many dentists who, by their conduct and advertisements, justify this criticism.'¹⁵ The founding fathers had set out not simply to establish a formal organization or a school but to re-educate dentists to their new role as professional gentlemen, to change even the language they used to delineate the nature of their work. But as the new century dawned it was still not clear whether dentists had patients or customers, charged fees or prices, sold goods or professional services, had laboratories or workshops. The larger forces at work in the last quarter of the nineteenth century had left them in limbo.

Nor did the turn-of-the-century political arena offer any more promise than it had a few years earlier. With the demise of the Patrons, doctors, lawyers, and dentists went back to the legislature hoping that they would get a hearing from a less antagonistic House. It didn't work out that way, however. In 1896 the Medical Council passed resolutions and initiated a petition calling for the restoration of the medical tariff and the introduction of the rescinded matriculation standards of the previous year. Over the next few months, some 2,000 doctors signed the petition, and George Ross was conciliatory, making no objection to a new matriculation by-law.[16] Because it was an election year, however, he urged that the matter of the tariff be left until 'the objectionable element [in the House] will be wiped out or at least minimized.'[17] With that reassurance the council drafted its amendment, expecting an easy passage after the election.[18] But the new Ross government showed no enthusiasm for it. The matter was not raised again until 1903, no bill was submitted to the government until 1906, and at that point the Medical Council had to concede that no measure to establish a tariff was likely to pass the House.[19] The ambitions of other occupations met much the same fate. Dentists attempted in 1900 to add a discipline clause to their act, and this too was rejected.[20] During the second half of the 1890s, there had been no cessation of complaints about lay conveyancing and in the early years of the twentieth century, Convocation made repeated efforts to find some way of controlling it. As had been the case for twenty years, nonetheless, the legislature simply rejected all attempts to extend the Law Society's powers in this area.[21] The professions had survived the Patrons relatively unscathed. But Ontario was a different place at the turn of the century than it had been in the 1860s and early 1870s, and this time there was to be no easy acquiescence in the extension of professional prerogatives. Politically, it was simply not on the cards.

THE BROODING PESSIMISM that infected so many clergymen had deeper roots than the politics of the 1890s, but the last decade of the century made its own contribution as well. The impact of economic depression could only fuel gnawing insecurities about material circumstances, as lay contributions to all of the churches' programs declined or levelled off. Anglicans fretted about the unwillingness of young men to take ill-paid country pastorates, while Methodists worried about never escaping from them: 'There is no security,' said one, 'that you will not be sent to "Hill Top Circuit," or to "Hardscrabble Ridge," or to "Splendid Isolation on Peninsula Point.'"[22] There was also the fear that low stipends were attracting only 'third-rate' men into the ministry,[23] an inevitable outcome, some ministers thought, when the laity failed to provide for their most basic material expectations. 'Men who deliberately enter a profession which pays them merely *not starvation* rates during their lifetime,' the editor of the *Evangelical Churchman* remarked in 1899, 'have at least the right to expect that their orphan children shall receive some protection ... The protection which the Church of England in Canada ... gives to the widows and orphans of deceased clergy is a crying scandal.'[24]

Anglican morale was particularly hard hit by the results of the census of 1891, which revealed a relative decline in their numbers throughout the province.[25] They were, it appeared, losing the countryside to other denominations and barely holding their own in the cities, and that provoked years of anxious soul-searching about the future of the Church, culminating in the late 1890s in a vigorous debate over the causes and consequences of what was described as a 'Church in Crisis.'[26] Anglicanism was, as one clergyman put it, 'confronted with a state of things pregnant with disaster'; nominally episcopal, 'we are in reality the weakest of weak congregationalists and the Bishop has about as much control over the life of the Church as he has over the Gulf Stream.'[27] It hardly helped that Anglicans remained as deeply divided as ever between high church and evangelicals, each side blaming the other for the difficulties the Church was facing.

Presbyterians and Methodists, generally speaking, were less hard hit by the depression of the mid-1890s, and less pessimistic about the future. But they were not immune. In 1898 a provocative piece by W.J. Robertson, a prominent Methodist layman, on the 'Decline of Methodism,' identified the causes as the growth of doubt in the wake of Darwinianism, materialism, the dilution of Methodist doctrine by the Church's theologians, and the lack of educated, cultivated clergy who could cope with the demands of increasingly well-educated congregations.[28] Much of the blame for the decline in membership, in other words, was laid at the feet of the clergy. In succeeding issues of the *Christian Guardian*, his argument was dismissed by some and supported by others, but what the subsequent flood of correspondence reveals is a good deal of unease about the quality of the clergy, their training, and their ability to lead their flock.[29]

That unease, of course, was also rooted in developments which lay beyond the doors of the church itself. The lost struggle over Sunday streetcars in Toronto stood as one symbol of the creeping secularization of the age, but there was also the flood of cheap literature, the attractions of popular entertainments, the growing preoccupation of the daily press with things secular and the conviction that its influence was far outdistancing that of the pulpit.[30] Perhaps better preoccupied with other things, indeed, than in running a 'Popular Preachers Contest' as the *Mail* did in 1891, scandalizing many clergymen who saw it as but one more proof of the 'commercialization' of their role.[31] Even if they rejected its premises, moreover, the debate over the 'missing men' could hardly be read otherwise than as an indicator that the cultural authority of the ministry within the larger community of men was at risk. More fundamentally, perhaps, there were the inroads of doubt and scepticism, the challenges to traditional theology mounted by the exponents of evolutionary theory and the higher criticism, the alternative explanations for human history and behaviour beginning to emerge from one or another of the social sciences, and equally from natural science itself.[32] To cite but one minor but characteristic example, by reiterating a passage from an earlier chapter: doctors' skills were to be valued, the *Christian Guardian* had argued in the mid-1830s, but it was above all the Divine Agency which had to be taken into account in any understanding of illness and disease; by the 1890s that explanation was increasingly being challenged by the mysterious agency of invisible 'bugs.'

Nor was it easy to know how to confront such issues. Some ministers, the editor of the *Presbyterian Review* wrote in 1896, simply turned their backs on controversial subjects out of a mistaken sense of piety or a fear of controversy. But

> our people are receiving the new theories of modern thought and research from sources that are not friendly to Christ and in forms exaggerated and distorted. Would it not be better if they heard them stated by ourselves in truer form and with sufficient explanations? The people ... naturally look to us for clear and honest statements concerning these things. And if these are properly given they will in the end confirm the faith of the people and secure for the preacher the confidence and respect of the pew.[33]

Yet the attempt to be pertinent to the age could draw criticism as well. Said the editor of the *Evangelical Churchman* on one occasion, the problem with the modern pulpit was that too many ministers 'preach on anything and everything but the Gospel; they lecture on the late war, on the future of Islam, of Judaism, of Anglo-Saxonism, Shakespearianism, Browningism, Buddhism, and all the other isms; on the telephone as a factor in civilization, on steam and electricity, on evident destiny and destiny not evident – on everything but the one thing which Jesus

Christ told his Apostles and their successors to preach to all nations.'[34]

At the end of the century, then, the rhetoric of professional men ranged from pessimism to hysterical jeremiad, and the mood darkens as one observes the various occupations in sequence – the unease among lawyers, the more urgent sense of menace besetting doctors and clergymen, the uncertainty among dentists that they had even begun to enter the promised land. Nor were they alone in this. It infected others as well, architects, for example, especially hard-hit by the effects of depression in the construction industry and, at the same time, burked of their aspirations to obtain a closed shop and the other accoutrements of professional status.[35] Caught up like so many others in a changing society, they all confronted what they saw as perplexing and sometimes ominous dilemmas, and there seemed to be no straightforward way of stemming or channelling the currents that pressed around them.

THE PORTRAIT we have painted in the preceding pages is, almost without qualification, a bleak one. Accurate in its own way perhaps, it now needs tempering. Whatever their difficulties or dilemmas, our professional men, with all their ambitions and aspirations, had never been inclined to lapse into inert melancholy. Besides, the challenges of the age offered not just the prospects of marginalization or defeat, but opportunities as well.

If for lawyers, doctors, or dentists the political arena held no promise, there were other strategies that might be pursued with more hope of success. One of these, for doctors and dentists at least, was 'Dominion Registration.' Like Ontario, most other provinces had established their own licensing authorities, and the restrictions all of them put in place made interprovincial mobility difficult. Dominion registration would remove that barrier by creating licensing reciprocity across the country. One of the 'hot topics' in the medical journals throughout the 1890s, it was attractive for a variety of reasons. For some the chief motive was patriotic. A national standard of medical education not only would foster a united Canadian profession but was a prerequisite for imperial registration. But, in Ontario, it was also seen as an important means of relieving overcrowding by providing automatic access to practice in other parts of Canada. The drawback was that it would also open the way for doctors from other provinces to practise in Ontario. Thus, within the province, opinion on the merits of Dominion registration was divided. And so indeed it was elsewhere, doctors in other provinces fearing that Ontario was about to solve its own overcrowding problem at their expense. The issue was fought out on the ground of educational standards, Ontario doctors insisting that everybody else meet their high qualifications for entry, and others proposing that existing standards in each province become the measure of the rule. In 1902 the Canadian Medical Association was able to broker an agreement for all the provinces, but reservations held up its implementation in Ontario until 1912.[36] It was much easier in dentistry. Something like half of all Canadian dentists were resident in Ontario, large parts of the country had few of them, and thus there was less fear of a flood from Ontario. A plan for a Dominion dental council was in place by 1903, and in 1905 the Royal College of Dental Surgeons approved reciprocal licensing for Ontario.[37] Though the impact of Dominion registration in both cases would not be felt in the short term, it would establish a national market for practitioners, increasing their choices about location and ensuring that Ontario professional schools could claim to be national in their function and purposes.

Another option for doctors lay in the public-health movement and the various purity campaigns of the period. Heather MacDougall and other historians have described these developments, and we will not reiterate the details here.[38] But their significance should not be overlooked. They provided new jobs for a few medical men throughout the province, but, more important, they offered a public platform upon which doctors could display their expertise and lay claim to a leadership role in a crusade which gave them a degree of visibility they had rarely had before.

Beginning in the second half of the 1890s, dentists began to debate the possibility of tackling their central marketing constraint – the 'perversity of the public' in preferring extraction to preventive and restorative work – through a campaign of public education. Since the inception of the *Dominion Dental Journal* in 1889, its purist editor and some of his like-minded correspondents had warned against using the daily press to diffuse knowledge about dentistry because they classed such activities as but one more example of advertising and self-promotion. In their view the only legitimate form of public education was to be carried out, on a one-to-one basis, between a dentist and his patient.[39] Cautiously, however, some dentists began to suggest that this was misguided. As one put it in 1898, 'The masses read the newspaper when they read anything; therefore to ignore this channel for circulating information is to shut out the dawning hope of popular dental education. The newspapers are our best friends and would, I am sure, be glad to insert well-written articles.'[40] A second line of attack was to educate the medical man. 'The influence of the physician in the family can scarcely be overestimated,' argued another dentist in 1897; at present doctors were all too often indifferent to the importance of the conservation of the teeth; change their minds and they would be more willing to advise families to attend a dentist rather than settling for wholesale extraction.[41] And finally, following a tactic pursued for years by doctors and others involved in the public-hygiene movement, dentists also began to talk about preaching the gospel through the school system by the introduction of regular dental inspection, the publication of pamphlets to be distributed to pupils and thence to their families, and the dental education of teachers themselves through hygiene textbooks with chapters 'on the teeth and their proper care.'[42]

At the end of the century, such initiatives as these still commended themselves to only a minority. But they had one great virtue. Throughout the 1890s the most creative response the *Dominion Dental Journal* could offer to the disarray among dentists was that they should voluntarily abjure advertising and price competition by acting like gentlemen regardless of the realities of the marketplace. A campaign of public education, on the other hand, offered the hope of an expanded market, and that in turn would allow dentists to slough off the 'merely mechanical work' of plate making, along with its attendant competitive excesses, and turn them, more definitively, into 'dental surgeons.' Here among the platitudinous hand-wringing of the *Dominion Dental Journal* was an idea that would eventually prove a fruitful strategy for securing the place in society that dentists craved.

FOR DECADES, prominent doctors had tirelessly advocated the virtues of associationalism as a prime means of overcoming the problems confronting professional men. Local medical societies, as John Fulton put it on one occasion, were essential 'in promoting harmony and good feeling amongst various members of the profession; in determining the rules of etiquette; in regulating to a certain extent the tariff of charges; and in driving from the ranks men who are unworthy of their calling.'[43] The origins of this impulse, we want to suggest once again, lay not so much in a new departure but in traditional notions: as practitioners came to know each other and re-established the bonds of community in new terrain, the values appropriate to the professional gentleman would naturally prevail without the need for legal sanction. The Canadian Medical Association had been founded in the 1860s to pursue such goals at the national level, and one of its first initiatives was to adopt, holus-bolus, the Code of Ethics formulated two decades earlier by its American counterpart.[44] The same sort of arguments underpinned the creation of the Ontario Medical Association (OMA) in 1880 and the refounding of the provincial dental association in 1889.[45] 'Besides the advancement in professional knowledge,' the president of the OMA declared in 1886, 'we have great social benefit in meeting and knowing each other. We get out of a narrow selfish channel, which rural practice at least is apt to engender, and have broader and higher sympathies for each other, and establish in our hearts that principle of respect for each other which is the foundation of medical ethics.'[46] The Ontario Dental Society, said one leading dentist, was the chief 'bulwark' in maintaining ethics; it was the 'isolated' dentist who resorted to unethical work.[47]

Even among the medical élite, however, a national organization like the Canadian Medical Association had little influence in Ontario until well into the twentieth century. When it met within the bounds of the province, as it did in 1883, only eighty doctors attended from the entire Dominion.[48] Three years before, Fulton had remarked of the CMA Code that, 'although nominally in force for a number of years, no effort has hitherto been made to bring it under notice of the profession generally, and we venture to say that the majority of medical practitioners in the country have never read it.'[49] Founded in 1880, the Ontario Medical Association had far greater influence. Within fifteen years of its creation, it had 700 members, something like a third of all doctors practising in Ontario.[50] Still, that meant that two-thirds of Ontario doctors didn't belong, and only a minority of those who did, roughly 150–200, attended its annual meetings.[51] And what was the effect of its Code of Ethics, adopted in 1887?[52] In 1892 the president of the OMA declared that 130 of its own members were in violation of the clauses respecting advertising.[53] We have no knowledge whatever of the number of dentists who belonged to the Ontario Dental Society, only a litany of complaints throughout the 1890s that most of them didn't. Of the small group that were present at its first meeting, in any case, three were hauled up two years later for violating its code.[54] The problem with associationalism, then, was voluntarism. Nobody had to join; most did not; even those who did could not be counted on to abide by its rules; and the gravest punishment that could be mustered was to expel a violator from an organization to which most professional men didn't belong in the first place.

The politics of the 1890s nonetheless gave associationalism an impetus it had lacked before. The medical militants, and especially the leaders of the Medical Defence Association, were probably the last group to pin their hopes for aggressive protectionism on the College of Physicians and Surgeons. As we have suggested in a previous chapter, the college could not bear that burden. The logical alternative was the Ontario Medical Association. Already by the late 1880s it was beginning to adopt a more aggressive protectionist approach, pressing the Medical Council to take action on a wide variety of issues, and by the late 1890s adopting its own lobbying strategies with the legislature.[55] While it still represented a minority of doctors, its rapid growth during that decade suggests that practitioners were beginning to see the association rather than the college as the voice of organized medicine in Ontario, and that tendency would gain impetus in the decades that followed.

Tardily, the lawyers followed suit. Though much of the grumbling in the 1890s continued to focus on the expectation that Convocation could do something about lay conveyancing if only it would act with assertion, or if some reform took place in its composition, in 1896 one young Belleville lawyer suggested another course of action. In an open letter to all lawyers published in the pages of the *Canada Law Journal*, W.C. Mikel proposed the establishment of a provincial law association. 'It has seemed difficult in the past,' he wrote,

to procure regulation or legislation beneficial to the profession, particularly outside of Toronto, because the profession has been unable to emphasize their desire in concerted united effort ... A great many of the profession have felt that they have suffered an injustice by reason of every Tom, Dick and Harry being allowed to do conveyancing and other similar work that should properly be done by the profession ... These, and other grievances arising from time to time, might be dealt with by the Association as above suggested, and the influence resulting from the united effort throughout the Province would certainly be more efficacious in accomplishing the desired result, whether asked for from the Judges, Benchers or Legislature, than at present.[56]

The editor's response was to suggest that lawyers lacked the cohesion to sustain such an organization, and initially he appeared to be right. Nothing much happened for the rest of the decade; but, early in the new century, the idea was resurrected, and in 1907 the first meeting of the Ontario Bar Association convened at Osgoode Hall.[57] It took time to build effective voluntary associations among professional men, but over the long haul collective solidarity would provide a platform for the expression of shared occupational interests and for promoting those interests in the wider public arena.[58]

SOME OF THE MOST THOUGHTFUL and thorough analyses of the response to social and intellectual change in the late nineteenth century have come from Canadian historians of religion and have focused on the clergy; for that reason, we will not treat the subject in any extended way here. There was steady progress towards church union, which, among other things, was intended to consolidate revenues and deploy manpower more efficiently, something that also held the promise of improved material circumstances for clergymen and their families. Given our own account of the plight of the clergy, it should not come as any surprise that among Presbyterians, for example, the greatest enthusiasm for union was to be found in the country districts, where resources were scarcest and where rural depopulation exacerbated the damaging effects of interdenominational competition.[59] In the cities the clergy were promoting church extension, settlement houses, and missions to the poor, and a few were beginning to formulate the embryonic doctrines that would become the social gospel. And in the colleges their theologians were assimilating the new knowledge and attempting to shape it to overarching Christian purposes.[60] Moreover, in all three of our denominations, efforts were being made to acquaint the working clergy with developments in the social sciences and changes in theology through regular clerical retreats and week-long seminars, usually organized by the theological colleges themselves.[61]

THE 'STRATEGIES' we have been discussing in these past few pages, like the political initiatives that dominate some earlier chapters of this book, were the self-conscious inventions of men pursuing their aspirations and interests. Over time, some of them turned out to be powerful tools, while others fell by the wayside. But they offered little relief in the short term, and hardly addressed, in any case, the brute reality of a political environment which ranged from the unsympathetic to the overtly hostile. At the end of the century, indeed, they seemed to lead nowhere but up a blind alley.

What was it, then, that might dissipate the angst that beset professional men? In their recent study of Canadian public utilities, Christopher Armstrong and H.V. Nelles remark that these monopolies 'were made, not born ... At critical junctures monopoly was the product of purpose, choice, policy, influence, tactic, and human effort.'[62] But that was not in itself enough to secure success; 'the economic pressures to produce and sell are readily understood. But markets must also be made in minds. What made people want to buy?'[63] Whether one is writing about gas, water, and electricity, or about medical, legal, or dental services, the problem remains somewhat the same: markets cannot be constituted merely from legal entitlements or the other products of active effort; they must also be 'made in minds.' Were there, then, circumstances which might persuade people that they should buy more (or fewer) professional services in late nineteenth- or early twentieth-century Ontario?

For doctors, paradoxically enough, one stimulus lay in the overcrowding phenomenon itself. Before mid-century large parts of the countryside were entirely undoctored, and people took it for granted that they would either look after themselves or seek out alternative forms of medical care. By 1900 licensed practitioners were common nearly everywhere in the countryside, while, in the cities and towns, contract practice had broadened the clientele by making doctors' services available at prices more people could afford. Consider obstetrics, for example. Wendy Mitchinson has argued that the male doctor replaced the female midwife because he was able to offer women 'an alternative portrayed as safe and scientific.'[64] We find her elucidation of this argument persuasive; but it is not enough in itself, for the transition was dependent upon the sheer availability of doctors as well. In her own work on female midwifery, Lesley Biggs provides indicative evidence of this. At the end of the century, upwards of 50 per cent of women living in new or developing counties, where doctors were few and far between, still gave birth unattended by a physician, and it strikes us as plausible to suggest, as Biggs does, that far more of these were attended by midwives than the extant statistics suggest. In old established counties like York, on the other hand, something like 96 per cent of all births were recorded as being attended by a physician.[65] Regardless of the rhetoric of scientific childbirth, had the number of doctors not increased so rapidly in the later nineteenth century, they might not have captured the market for obstetrical services as easily or as quickly as they did. Indeed, their absence might have provided the economic base for the growth of an alternative profession of licensed midwifery. As doctors multiplied, however, they were used by an ever-increasing portion of the population. Access bred familiarity and confidence, and the licensed doctor gradually became conventionally identified as the person one turned to for medical services. In this respect, the twentieth-century 'golden age' of the family doctor was rooted in the crisis of overcrowding a generation or two earlier.

The zenith of discontent among professional men coincided with the hard times of the 1890s. Whatever other market constraints might exist, falling personal incomes, unemployment, business failures, recession, and depression invariably mean that the demand for professional services will decline, whether we are talking about the 1890s, the 1930s, or other periods.[66] As prosperity returned towards the end of the 1890s and built towards the economic boom of the decade before the First World War, the market for services rebounded, providing professional men with better incomes and the prospect of a more secure future. Not surprisingly, the internal discord, the disaffection, and the pessimistic rhetoric that had marked the 1890s declined concomitantly. But it was not simply economic growth that mattered; so too did the reorganization of the economy, under way since at least the 1880s. The expansion of industry and the transition from the family firm to limited-liability companies, corporate mergers and concentration, the growth of government regulation – municipal as well as provincial and federal – and the proliferation of new forms of financial services generated more work for lawyers and made them indispensable in ways they had not been before.⁶⁷ Large organizations like the lodges, railways, streetcar companies, department stores, and industrial establishments created work for doctors at a time when overcrowding was hurting most. However much the professional élite might rail against it, contract practice was clearly big business and a hedge for many doctors against the pressures of competition until that time when they could support themselves by private practice alone.

The problems that beset professional men had also arisen because of the demographic imbalance in rural Ontario: just as professional men began to spread out into the countryside, large numbers of people were leaving for the cities and towns. This too began to right itself in the early decades of the twentieth century. In the case of lawyers, for example, Elizabeth Bloomfield has traced the shift out of small communities between 1900 and 1920, along with the growing number of lawyers concentrated in a few large cities, above all Toronto. But this was more than a simple realignment of the balance between the location of lawyers and that of the population; lawyers congregated where there were rapidly growing opportunities for work. 'How can we explain the parallel trends of contraction and concentration of legal services between 1900 and 1920?' asks Bloomfield.

While the administration of justice and the system of local government remained decentralized, much as they had been established in the early to mid-nineteenth century, processes of business activity changed substantially between the 1890s and 1920 and had significant implications for legal practices ... Land subdivision and agriculture, which provided small-town lawyers with their bread-and-butter probate and conveyancing work, contracted in relation to other sectors of the economy, and rural and village populations actually declined in this period. New forces of industrialization concentrated business growth and provided opportunities for specialized corporate legal practices in the larger cities, especially those with head offices.⁶⁸

Urbanization also had its effects upon the indirect costs of delivering professional services. In towns and cities more doctors could attend more patients with less investment of time; equally, the indirect price of calling a doctor fell: one no longer had to ride miles to the nearest village in order to obtain his services. A range of disparate innovations helped mitigate nineteenth-century market constraints as well. In the countryside, better roads meant quicker round trips. In the United States at least, and probably in Ontario too, the coming of the automobile not only speeded up this process but actually cut direct costs: automobiles, doctors found, were cheaper, mile for mile, than horses.[69] The telephone allowed people to ascertain whether or not a doctor was at home, or to arrange a visit, saving the opportunity costs of a trip to find him. Doctors could maximize the effective use of their time by calling up their offices or the local drugstore – an early communications centre for this purpose – to pick up messages rather than returning to home base after each individual visit. Specialists, who may have been the first group to adopt the appointment system, meeting their patients at prearranged times of the day, were assumed to have phones in the late 1890s, and dentists probably adopted the system about the same time as well.[70] Thus it's not surprising to find, in a recent study on the social diffusion of the telephone in Kingston between 1876 and 1914, that professional men had very high usage rates virtually from the time the system was established.[71]

Professional *men* could also take heart from portents which failed to materialize. Between 1883 and 1906 Ontario's two medical schools for women trained more than a hundred doctors, but by the latter date both had closed their doors, leaving women who wanted to study medicine, in Ontario at least, with access only to the faculty of medicine at the University of Toronto.[72] And instead of their numbers increasing in the early decades of the twentieth century, they appear to have declined. Those who followed in the footsteps of Clara Brett Martin and Eva Maude Powley would constitute 'more of a trickle than a flood,' Constance Backhouse remarks, 'and years often passed with no addition to the slim stream of female barristers and solicitors.'[73] Between 1900 and 1914 twenty-three women enrolled in the Ontario College of Pharmacy, a significant increase over earlier decades but still hardly more than a handful.[74] And until 1920 only eight additional women followed Josephine Wells into dentistry.[75] Why this was the case is not at all clear, and the issue now deserves the kind of intensive research work devoted over the last two decades to that generation of women who broke the initial barriers in medicine, law, and other occupations.[76] But its significance for men is not to be gainsaid. It effectively eliminated the threat of a 'double pool' of candidates for entry to these occupations, ensuring that one critical variable in the production of 'excessive competition' would not be a factor in the continuing search for economic security.

For doctors another development taking shape in the last quarter of the century would be of long-term importance as well. Beginning in the 1870s general hospitals began to be established in a growing number of communities, and they would multiply decade by decade far into the twentieth century. Initially doctors – or at least those editing and writing to the medical journals – paid little attention to this development, probably because it was viewed in a traditional way – local communities simply providing for their own poor as places like Toronto and Kingston had done for decades. But three circumstances changed that indifference. One was the slow but steady growth of medical technology, including laboratories and machinery too expensive for the private practitioner to acquire on his own.[77] Second, the recognition of the critical importance of antisepsis and asepsis along with the growing range of major surgery made the hospital a more attractive theatre for operations than the home, let alone the farm field or the workshop floor. But third, and perhaps most important, there was the fact that paying patients were increasingly using the hospital; doctors could either follow them there or allow an alternative source of medical care to grow up in their midst. It was this fear, indeed, which had provoked the brief panic about 'the abuse of charity' in the closing years of the century. Though we are not concerned with the details of the story here, what doctors did was to make sure that they would have access to their patients in the hospital itself so that the general practitioner would not lose out to a closed circle of specialists and resident medical and nursing staff.[78] That having been accomplished, Ontario doctors could now anchor themselves in a public institution which was of growing importance to all members of the community. Though at first the hospital was primarily a place where surgery was carried out, rather than a locale for obstetrics or medical therapeutics, doctors had finally gained, in effect, a theatre for their craft, analogous to the courtroom or the pulpit, where expertise, esoteric knowledge, and the authority of the profession could be put on public display.

FINALLY, both doctors and dentists would benefit from a series of technical and scientific advances which would improve the efficacy, and enhance the value, of their services. In medicine there was, above all, the 'germ theory' of disease. As S.E.D. Shortt writes,

It was the gradual acceptance of the microbial origin of infectious diseases that led to a revolution in abdominal and gynecological surgical techniques and to the discovery, by the early 1880s, of the etiological agents for gonorrhea, cholera, typhoid, tuberculosis, and diphtheria. If treatment for most of these diseases remained supportive, diphtheria anti-toxin introduced in 1894 and the anti-syphilitic, salvarsan, available by 1910, were both powerful therapies and apparent harbingers of other curative discoveries ... And to these treatments for common life-threatening disorders were added more esoteric and startlingly effective endocrine therapies, beginning with the use of thyroid extract in 1891.[79]

In the 1890s there was as well the invention of the X-ray machine, which almost immediately promised large gains in both surgery and medicine.[80] Beyond that there was the routinization of all kinds of procedures, great and small, which had been added to the medical arsenal throughout the nineteenth century. When one examines the medical tariffs of the middle decades of the century, one finds a short list of activities doctors might carry out. Surgery, for example, was simply divided into 'major' or 'minor' operations, and the number of either was limited. Tests were rarely listed and few references made to instrumentation. However, a surviving medical tariff of 1888 from the city of Ottawa tells a very different story. Here we find some 303 items listed, consuming some 25 pages and including everything from plastic surgery to 'microscopical examination of the urine,' 'analysis of urine for albumen or sugar,' 'vaginal speculum examination,' 'examination of the throat with the laryngoscope.' None of this was new in the late 1880s, but it suggests that such tests and procedures were now routine enough to be specified in a tariff of fees.[81]

The medical journals took virtually no notice of the impact of electricity on doctors' work, though it must have been considerable; in dentistry it excited great interest. One newly graduated DDS waxed almost lyrical in the pages of the *Dominion Dental Journal* in 1890. The electric dental drill, invented in the early 1880s, was 'the best of its kind since it gives great speed, variety of position and complete control.' But the uses of electricity extended far beyond this.

Another appliance that has been but infrequently used by us is a ventilating fan, which is suspended near the chair, and which is a positive luxury in hot, sultry weather. The fan not only keeps the patient and operator cool, but prevents the ever-troublesome fly from making a temporary resting-place of their features. To run the polishing lathe by electricity is a luxury that all could appreciate but few attain ... The mouth lamp is another and, perhaps, the most useful appliance given us by electricity; for the others, we had progenitors and have substitutes, but this stands alone as one of chained lightning's exclusive boons. It facilitates examinations and renders us independent of dark days, when delicate operations are most difficult, while for extracting at night it cannot be equalled.[82]

Of perhaps more critical importance, there was the work of the American dentist G.V. Black, who contributed major breakthroughs in cavity preparation and in an improved amalgam which would neither expand nor contract, nor would it break down as easily as had older alloys.[83] 'The beginnings of the use of baked porcelain for tooth restoration also occurred during this epoch,' writes Ontario's historian of dentistry, 'and the cast gold filling was in the experimental stage ... Many refinements have occurred since, but most of the technical adjuncts used in the modern dental office either came into use or were in the experimental stage by the end of the nineteenth century.'[84]

For doctors, the advances in science, as well as the associated technical breakthroughs, were important not just because of the specific contributions they made to surgery or medical therapeutics. More critically, they were part of a reorientation of professional identity that had been under way since the 1860s. Loyalties once rooted in abstract doctrine, or self-images resting upon long years of clinical experience and the deductions that arose from it, were giving way to experimental science and the methods of the laboratory. Writing for a popular audience in the *Canadian Magazine* in 1893, a bacteriologist employed by the Ontario Board of Health pointed to the potential dynamism of the link between science and medicine: 'Even if our study of microbes had only given us the facts which we have outlined, we might consider much had been done, but these are only a fraction of the results. Perhaps the most fascinating part of the whole field is that which bears upon the relationship of these minute creations to man and animals. Here it is that we must look for progress in the future which may, possibly, in a few years, revolutionize the medical treatment of infectious diseases.'[85] Even if therapeutic applications were yet beyond them, medical men could stake their claim to the mantle of science, the potent implications to be drawn from the laboratory, and the new role of the doctor as mediator between the disparate worlds of basic science and the bedside.[86] Others would follow suit. Though the implications of the 'biological revolution' came much more slowly in dentistry, when they finally struck they would begin to give some substance to the claim that dentists were truly 'dental surgeons' and not just manufacturers of teeth or vendors of plates.

If some occupations gained from the prestige being accorded to science and the laboratory method, nonetheless it would prove more inimical to others. The 'epistemological redefinition of science to mean critical research based on empirical verification'[87] could not help but undermine older conceptions of 'scientia' and raise doubts about the meaning of 'the *science* of theology' or 'the *science* of the law.' That might not affect the outlook of lawyers, who had reservations about the usefulness of the science of the law in any case; but together with all the other forces at work, it would inevitably devalue the cultural authority of the clergy.

HOWEVER BLEAK the closing years of the nineteenth century might appear, then, there were portents of promise for some professional men at least. And in the main, they were not to be found in the self-conscious strategies which professional men actively pursued. They resided rather in a series of disparate developments, hardly noticed or only half-understood, but which were beginning to construct effective and long-enduring markets in the minds of Ontario's citizens.

17
The Universities and Professional Education

Of all our portents, bleak or promising, perhaps the most significant lay in the relationship gradually being forged between the university and those occupations which held, or aspired to, professional status. Not every occupation needed that institutional base, and not all could secure it even if they wanted to. But to the extent that the relationship between a university and a professional education could be established, a handful of occupations were able to harness their fortunes to one of the powerhouses of the future. Though not the exclusive focus of this second chapter on the education of professional men, it is that story which will dominate it.

For Anglican and Presbyterian ministers that relationship had always been integral. Theologues were routinely expected not only to acquire an advanced secondary education but to complete a program of undergraduate studies before they entered theology, and when the churches could not provide that within the framework of their own universities, they created alternative means of achieving that end.[1] Entry standards for other occupations were uniformly lower and more variable. As grammar (and then high) schools multiplied, however, these standards rose steadily, and as they did so they became linked ever more securely to the curriculum required for university entrance. By the early 1870s the Law Society had already set its entry standard at the equivalent of junior matriculation at the University of Toronto, which meant at least three or four years of high-school study. Even in the mid-1880s the Ontario Medical Council still required only two years of high school before a student could begin medical studies, but it raised its standard to junior matriculation in 1891, and to something approaching senior matriculation after 1895 – a level approximating entry to second-year undergraduate studies. Dentists had begun from an even lower base, a 'good common school education' in the 1870s, and then two years of high school in the mid-1880s; but by the late 1890s they too required matriculation in arts.[2]

Matriculation standards rose, we have repeatedly pointed out, because of the perception of 'overcrowding.' That much is written all over the record of law, medicine, and dentistry alike. Yet it is important not to be reductionist on this point. To contemporaries, the university matriculation standard, which required Latin and maintained Greek as an option, was not simply a means of closing off entry but an opportunity to assimilate their requirements to the expectations embedded in the ideal of the professional gentleman. Throughout the nineteenth century a liberal education, which included classics and mathematics, remained the touchstone of an educated man: it constituted a training in character and culture, the necessary prerequisite to framing technical expertise within 'scientia,' and the means by which the status of an occupation could be raised through social proximity. As the rhetoric of the dentists demonstrates, such notions were persuasive not only in the middle decades of the nineteenth century but also at its end.[3]

To the modern reader, even three or four years of high-school education may not sound impressive. But at a time when the only two occupations which *required* undergraduate studies in arts were the Anglican or Presbyterian ministries, and high-school teaching itself; at a time when only 10 or 20 per cent of the entire elementary-school population ever wrote the high-school *entrance* examination, let alone passed it; at a time when the vast majority of their peers had only five or six years of elementary school and when even most high-school students left school after only one or two years of study: those students preparing to enter one of the professions constituted a small, highly educated academic élite.[4] A significant number of doctors and lawyers, moreover, had almost certainly taken at least some arts courses before, or concurrent with, their professional studies.[5] Already by the late 1870s, indeed, something like a quarter of all new lawyers held a BA, a telling comment not only on the level of academic achievement which characterized the nineteenth-century bar, but also on the social origins of young men who could afford the cash outlay and opportunity costs of an education far beyond the minimal requirements of the Law Society.[6] Throughout the second half of the nineteenth century, only a handful of doctors held arts degrees,[7] but even that was beginning to change; by 1899 the *Queen's University Journal* could report that 'more than 25% of all who have entered Queen's Medical College during the past two years have either been graduates or undergraduates completing their course. This percent is largely in excess of that of earlier years.'[8] We have, then, a growing number of individuals in law and medicine touched by an undergraduate education in one of Ontario's colleges, but we also have the *minimum* entry standards in such occupations as law, medicine, dentistry, or the Methodist ministry increasingly assimilated to those of the university. In this respect alone the links between the university and the education of practitioners in a variety of crafts had tightened during the second half of the nineteenth century.

From mid-century onwards the pre-eminent role of the classical languages in a general education began to be challenged. New subjects gradually found their way into the curriculum of the high schools and universities and onto the matriculation lists of the professions. English, science, and modern languages made especially important gains; concomitantly, fewer and fewer students took Greek rather than science or modern languages. As these changes occurred, there was a subtle shift in the relative standing of the various subjects, which, over the long term, would lead to a rough parity of esteem. Yet the key words here are 'subtle' and 'long term,' for it must be said that the idea of a liberal education rooted in the classics had enormous resilience. When the University of Toronto substantially reordered and raised its pass matriculation into medicine in the late 1870s, it required the study of Latin and two additional languages chosen from Greek, French, or German. English, history, and geography were compulsory too, as were arithmetic, algebra, and geometry. Not a single science was required or even allowed as an option. Even more revealing is the allotment of marks to the various subjects. The three branches of mathematics were worth a total of 400 marks, as was the grouping of English, history, and geography. Latin alone was worth 200 marks, the only subject to receive that accolade, and the other two compulsory languages, 100 each. If candidates opted for honours matriculation, they were required to write a paper in chemistry; it was worth 100 marks.[9] This, the reader is reminded, was for matriculation not in arts but in medicine. A decade later, in 1885–6, the same matriculation requirements were still in place. In the medical curriculum itself, the basic sciences were making rapid progress; at the level of matriculation, however, they remained of marginal importance, peripheral to the University of Toronto's vision of what constituted a sound preliminary education for medical students.

The Medical Council viewed the matter no differently. Though natural philosophy was a required matriculation subject from the late 1870s, the council at one point in the early 1880s was prepared to sacrifice it in favour of Latin if both could not be obtained because of the exigencies of high-school timetables.[10] And while the amount of required high-school science increased in the 1890s, three or four years of Latin remained necessary as well. As with divinity, law, and medicine, so with dentistry, which added Latin to its matriculation requirements in 1889. The standards of general education required of professional men even in late nineteenth-century Ontario cannot be judged simply in terms of the number of years they had spent in school. They were among the few who bore the stamp of a liberal education; they had studied the classical languages and higher mathematics at a time when these subjects were still a pre-eminent hallmark of culture.

FOR MUCH OF THE CENTURY, indeed, technical training divorced from a liberal education was routinely disparaged as narrow and unworthy of the high ideal of a learned profession, and so was the value of professional degrees.[11] By the 1870s most medical men had them, and yet consider this lament from the editor of the *Canadian Journal of Medical Science*, provoked by an approaching convocation at the University of Toronto:

We were grieved to observe, as we have likewise been on former occasions, that amongst many graduates in Arts, and members of the legal fraternity especially, the medical graduates are not generally received with that cordiality and favour which the bonds of fellowship ought to enclose ... If the members of the lower faculty be inflated with a sense of self-superiority, we can only point out that many of the medical graduates are also graduates in arts ... and others, although devoid of the literary hallmark of any university, are men whose general culture is not inferior to that of others so distinguished.[12]

The prestige of the arts degree among lawyers is apparent in many of the preceding pages. Though the LLB was to be had from one or another university through most of the latter half of the century, on the other hand, they put little store in obtaining a professional degree. Neither, for that matter, did Presbyterian ministers. While Queen's had always had the power to confer theological degrees, few students ever actually 'graduated' in theology. Until 1877 the BD was an honours award bestowed only upon those who achieved high marks in theology.[13] When the BD regulations were overhauled in that year, it was opened to any theological student of any church, not just Presbyterians, and few of the latter appear to have applied for it, even very late in the century.[14] Indeed, the idea of seeking a degree in divinity seems to have carried a certain whiff of puffery about it.[15]

Strictly speaking, a university degree in medicine, as in the case of law or theology, mattered not a whit; what mattered was the licence to practise conferred by the CPSO. Throughout the second half of the century, one could take the required courses at one of the medical schools, meet the other prerequisites of the CPSO, and then write its examinations for a licence without ever bothering with the additional examinations required for a university degree. In Britain this was a conventional route to practice throughout the nineteenth century and beyond, many practitioners qualifying themselves through the General Medical Council's examinations alone.[16] From the 1860s onwards, however, most of Ontario's medical students took medical degrees, probably because the universities generally geared their degree requirements to match the licensing regulations of the CPSO and thus ensured that there were no extra opportunity costs to obtaining a degree as against a licence. But again, one asks, why bother? We suspect the answer is that, for doctors, bereft of the prize of an arts degree, the professional degree helped shore up tł practitioner's social status, which was far more equivocal even in the later nineteenth century than that of the lawyer and the Anglican or Presbyterian minister.

Three consequences followed from this, however. As the honorific 'Dr' replaced the more plebian 'Mr,' the possession of a medical degree became an integral part of the general practitioner's professional identity, stamping him more indelibly as a member of one of the 'learned' professions, in the eyes of the laity at least, who didn't make fine distinctions about the relative value of an arts as opposed to a professional degree. As it became more common for practitioners to take degrees, medical education, in turn, became more and more associated with a university setting. At mid-century there had been options: the hospital school, the independent medical school, the university medical faculty, registration without a degree, registration by means of a degree. In the late nineteenth century, the options had narrowed down. No one was yet *required* to obtain a degree to practise medicine, but custom increasingly assumed it. Long before 'the rise of scientific medicine,' then, medical education in Ontario had become clearly identified with an education that was closely linked to the university.

But a third, and critical, consequence followed as well. If the university could confer increased status on medicine through the award of a professional degree alone, then others with less claim to recognition as a learned profession could pursue the same course. Had the Ontario universities been animated by the anti-professional spirit that pervaded Oxford and Cambridge in the middle decades of the nineteenth century, a spirit widely shared among the English upper-middle class, the history of the professions here might have more closely resembled that of England, where the professional organizations and the university went their separate ways.[17] In Ontario, however, a more utilitarian approach prevailed, and the universities proved willing to throw open their doors to almost anyone who came along and knocked. The full impact of this frame of mind, on both the university and the professions, would not be felt until much later. But medicine was the first occupation to link its fortunes to the professional degree, and as its star began to rise in the late nineteenth century, so too did the legitimacy of the professional degree divorced from an undergraduate education in arts. At the same time, specialized technical knowledge, divorced from a broader grounding in the liberal sciences, began to acquire a degree of reputability it had never had before.

THE LEADERS of other occupations, not surprisingly, were well aware of the significance of these developments and eager to emulate them. In 1888 the University of Toronto, at the behest of the College of Dental Surgeons, established a 'Department of Dentistry' and instituted the degree of 'Doctor of Dental Science.' The school, run for two decades by the RCDSO, in turn became affiliated with the university.[18] What major breakthroughs in dental 'scientia' provoked this accommodation between the university and the dentists? the reader may well ask. The answer, so far as we can see, is none. Encouraged by George Ross, who was pressing the architects to ally themselves with the university at exactly the same moment,[19] the University of Toronto was prepared to make the gesture in return for an additional complement of students for a few of its science courses. It did not even demand a distinct program of studies. Indeed, the requirements were identical to those prescribed by the RCDSO for all its licentiates, and the college remained responsible for staffing and financing the dental school itself.

To the dentists, on the other hand, a university school represented a major step forward. When the first class sat its DDS examinations in late 1889, one prominent member of the RCDSO crowed that it was 'the first examination ever held by a British University for a Doctor's Degree in Dental Surgery.'[20] The two signal achievements of the late 1880s, the editor of the *Dominion Dental Journal* proclaimed, were the introduction of a new matriculation standard which included Latin, and university affiliation. Together they meant that dentistry 'now occupies a recognized position among the learned professions.'[21] Whistling in the dark he may have been, but what matters here is the import ascribed to such symbols. A link to the university, however, did not suddenly turn dentistry into a 'science' or the dental school into a centre for the research ideal. Even the implications of the biological revolution in medicine remained *terra incognita* for the dental surgeon until the end of the first decade of the twentieth century.[22] And while there was much talk of the 'scientific spirit' in the pages of the *Dominion Dental Jour-*

nal throughout the 1890s, it was a vaguely formulated notion used almost entirely in opposition to 'the practical dentist,' as it had been thirty years before. 'Science' and the attachment to the university was, in other words, put to use as simply one more weapon against the 'unethical' advertiser, the mere 'tooth-carpenter,' or dental mechanic.[23] Dentistry nonetheless had obtained a foothold within the university, and over the long haul, if not immediately, that would matter a great deal to the status and prestige of the occupation itself.

That foothold, it must be said, was not universally welcomed. Indeed, the reaction of some medical doctors is testimony to the continuing insecurities attached to professional degrees themselves. 'The best evidence of our "Americanism",' complained one,

is well illustrated by the adoption by dentists and veterinary surgeons of the title of doctor. I do not believe that the veterinarians or dentists by any right whatever should be styled Doctor, and are no more entitled to the doctorate than barbers or chiropodists. We are, as Canadians, having too many 'Captains', 'Colonels' and 'Doctors'. The tendency of such careless designations to unworthy persons, is to break down the dignity attached to members of the respective professions.[24]

Not surprisingly, young men in possession of the degree of Doctor of Dental Surgery, awarded by the University of Toronto since 1889, took exception:

There are now Doctors of Law, of Divinity, of Philosophy, of Medicine, of Music and of Dentistry. One profession has as much right to the title as has another. The real cause of complaint has arisen from the fact that the common people with their usual ignorance have continually called physicians doctors, until even the physicians themselves have been led to believe the title is their own ... The title 'doctor' signifies the attainment of a certain knowledge in some direction. Surely the dentist is as fully entitled to it as are the theologian, the philosopher, the physician, and the musician.[25]

The universities had always had symbolic links with the three learned professions, however attentuated in reality, and that is what our medical doctor meant when he referred to a proliferation of degrees breaking down 'the dignity attached' to the 'respective professions.' By the latter phrase, he, at least, didn't mean veterinarians and dentists. Here, nonetheless, is yet one more intimation of the broadening meaning of the term. Just as governments could, by legislative fiat, turn a 'business' into a 'profession,' so indeed could occupations lay claim to that status through the acquisition of knowledge 'in some direction' certified by the university. And the utilitarian impulse left it open-ended. Philosophers, physicians, musicians, and dentists today; accountants, businessmen, and journalists tomorrow. What a profession was, in this respect, was what the university said it was, though now there were not just three but some indefinite multiple thereof.

IF DENTISTRY had limited claims to a link to the university by virtue of its 'scientia,' the case was different for engineers or architects. Engineers had no professional organization prescribing a course of study for them, and neither the Association of Ontario Land Surveyors nor the Ontario Association of Architects required that candidates for admission to their ranks prepare themselves for the examinations in any particular way. In all three occupations, moreover, an apprenticeship remained the conventional means of professional training. Despite all that, a cadre of leading engineers and scientists had been engaged since the 1870s in turfing the artisans out of the School of Practical Science and turning it into an academy for the applied sciences connected to the University of Toronto.[26] In small but growing numbers during the 1880s, students of engineering or architecture began to enrol,[27] not because they were required to, but because innovations in construction materials and related developments provided incentives to obtain the pertinent theoretical knowledge that the sciences had to offer. In the last decade of the century, the needs of the mining and electrical industries quickened the pace of enrolments as well, while John Galbraith, the hard-pressed principal of the SPS, worked tirelessly to strengthen its ties to the university. In 1889 the school was affiliated to the University of Toronto, and some fifteen years later became the Faculty of Applied Science and Engineering. Similar developments were under way at Queen's.[28] By the first decade of the twentieth century, enrolments in the applied sciences, including engineering, were spiralling upwards. Encouraged but not required to do so, young men were entering the university to master rapidly expanding bodies of theoretical and systematized practical knowledge before completing their education in the office or field.[29] Gradually differentiated from the artisan and the builder, engineering and architecture were consolidating their links with the university and, as the university itself changed, were able to slough off the invidious distinctions made in the middle decades of the century between the education suitable to the learned professions and that which might be offered to those whose future lay in the making of 'things.' Benefiting as few others had in the latter half of the nineteenth century from the 'theatre of science,' benefiting as well from the increasing ambiguities in the meaning of profession itself, engineers and others like them could increasingly look to the university as a sheet anchor for their claims to be as much professional men as anyone else.

IN MEDICINE THERE WAS yet another change which secured the link between the profession and the academy. For nearly half a century, since the University Act of 1853, the University of Toronto had offered no instruction in medicine but had simply examined, and awarded degrees to, students who had completed their education at institutions like the Toronto School of Medicine (TSM) or Trinity Medical College. In 1887, however, the TSM surrendered its independent status and entered into the union that created the University of Toronto Faculty of Medicine. The professors of the TSM became salaried employees of the university, offering instruction in all of the clinical subjects of the medical curriculum. But the basic sciences, which traditionally they had taught as well, were handed over to the existing staff of the university. A few years later Queen's and the 'Royal College' of medicine, Kingston's quasi-autonomous medical school, merged in a similar fashion,[30] and in 1904, Trinity Medical College dissolved itself and amalgamated with the University of Toronto.[31] Within a relatively short period of time, in other words, the 'proprietary' schools, which had dominated medical education throughout the middle decades of the nineteenth century, had surrendered their autonomy and become organic parts of the larger university.

This change in the institutional locus of medical education occurred for a complex of reasons, including the politics of the university question in the province, the ambitions of university administrators to secure access to greater government funding, and for a variety of other parochial reasons besides. We have reviewed the causes at some length elsewhere and will not attempt to reiterate the story here.[32] But the transition was also accompanied by a significant shift in the content and pedagogy of medical education, a theme which is important to our larger argument about the nature of nineteenth-century professional education generally. And we will attempt to illuminate its significance by zeroing in on the debate which erupted when, in the winter and spring of 1886–7, the University of Toronto first announced its plan to establish its own teaching faculty.

A great many historians have recounted the progress of the research ideal within the late nineteenth-century university – the shift from the centrality of teaching and undergraduate education to research and the dissemination of knowledge. Its first impulses were already beginning to be felt at the University of Toronto by the 1880s, and it had no less impact on medicine than it did on other fields.[33] Though the basic, or what we might now call the pre-clinical, sciences had always received attention in medical education, the particular influence and success of German research during the second half of the nineteenth century lay not just in its substantive successes but in its reorientation of the methodology of medical research – with its emphasis on the laboratory and the controlled experiment, rather than the older French tradition of close clinical observation and deductions based on patients' symptoms.[34]

In Toronto its chief proponent was R. Ramsay Wright, professor of biology at University College. An Englishman by birth, Wright came to the university in the early 1880s, and as Sandra McRae has recently demonstrated, his influence on a future generation of medical researchers would be felt throughout North America.[35] In the mid-1880s he was still one of the pioneers in the reorientation of the university towards the research ideal; but that role itself put him at the centre of the initiative to create the new medical faculty and to articulate its mission. 'The University has a higher function than the education of its own undergraduates,' he argued, 'namely the advancement as well as the diffusion of learning. While it may properly be contended that the mere preparation of a lad to enter a profession ought to cost the country nothing, it is quite otherwise in regard to this higher function of the University.' He then pointed to the German model, and not just to the doctoral studies pursued by students; of far more importance was the organization of instruction, where 'the body of teachers ... is kept so large as to subdivide the drudgery of teaching, while in the scientific branches of medicine, like human anatomy, pathology, therapeutics and hygiene, the chairs are so generally endowed as to enable the professors to dispense with practice, and thus devote themselves to research.'[36] The research ideal, moreover, meant more than research laboratories and endowed chairs. It also implied a reorientation of pedagogical practice. First, the basic sciences had to be given a far greater emphasis in medical education than ever before. 'The abnormal can only be understood in terms of the normal [and thus] it is obvious that the medical sciences fall within the domain of biology and the best introduction to the study of the former is a clear grasp of the elementary principles of the latter.'[37] But the basic sciences also had to be taught in a different way – through laboratory work itself. Forced to follow 'the same road' as the researcher, the student learned how truth was to be known and was pushed from fact to generalization.[38]

Now altogether, these were revolutionary, not to say imperialistic, claims, especially to the more conservative of the schoolmen. Research as a 'higher function' than the teaching of undergraduates; professors who dispensed with medical practice and devoted themselves to research; the basic sciences, not as handmaidens to clinical instruction, but as essential prerequisites; hands-on experience for students not just in the hospital but in the laboratory; the very notion, indeed, that biology, physics, or chemistry constituted the 'science' of medicine while clinical skills formed, implicitly at least, 'merely' its art – all of this challenged not only what they had been doing, but what they thought they *should* be doing. It was not that they were strangers to the laboratory, but it was more a place to carry out clinical tests relating to diagnosis and treatment, and to train their students to do so, than a tool to push back the frontiers of knowledge.[39] The schoolmen, in other words, were clinicians and not 'researchers' *à la mode*. And even if they wished to be the latter, they lacked the necessary resources. Good clinical teaching they might achieve, and lectures and demonstrations in the 'pre-clinical' sciences might be required of all students, but they were not equipped to pursue research, nor could they afford the facilities to train all their students through laboratory work in the basic sciences.

These competing views dominated the debate over the founding of the faculty of medicine in 1887. On the one side, there was Wright, university leaders like William Mulock and Daniel Wilson, a bevy of prominent Toronto practitioners, and the leadership of the Toronto School of Medicine and their organ, the *Canadian Practitioner*. On the other, there were also a number of voices, but the most persistent was that of Walter Geikie, the dean of Trinity Medical College, ably seconded by the editor of the *Canada Lancet*. The issues that divided them were several, but for our purposes it is the argument over the nature of medical education that counts. In his inaugural address at the opening of the new faculty in October 1887, Ramsay Wright had remarked that

facts are easily lost if not bound together by principles, and consequently it will be our aim to send out our students not only well equipped for practice but with a clear conception of the main principles of the medical sciences. These have made such progress in recent years, *especially in directions which prove the close bond of union between them and other branches of biological inquiry* as well as physics and chemistry, that it has become all the more necessary for the student to lay a broad foundation of the physical sciences and general biology before he begins to devote himself to his special work.[40]

We have put the critical phrase in italics because it focuses attention, implicitly, upon the Achilles' heel of Wright's argument. To Wright, as to many others, medical education for too long had been concentrated upon 'Madame How' rather than 'Lady Why.'[41] The biological sciences would form the new scaffolding upon which practice would be built, not only in terms of substance but in training the mind of the student so that the methods of the laboratory would inform the way he did his professional work throughout his lifetime. To modern ears it has a powerful and persuasive ring. The trouble was that, in the 1880s and for many years thereafter, physicians had more knowledge than therapeutic power.[42] The medical scientists could increasingly offer explanations of disease but comparatively little by way of cure. Wright may have been hurt by 'playful and contemptuous' references to the irrelevance of his 'frogology,'[43] but to many practitioners at least, and that included both Geikie and the editor of the *Lancet*, trained in an earlier style of medical science, biology and its progeny were not the foundations of practice but its helpmates. No one of the generation, it must be emphasized, was against 'science,' but there were different views of its uses, its place in the medical curriculum, its role as an aid to clinical training.

The sceptics, moreover, must have taken badly the phraseology used by Wright and others when they spoke of the 'mere preparation of a lad' for the profession as against 'the higher function of the University.' If the biological sciences had had more payoff before 1890, in therapeutic terms, it might have been different, but even as late as April 1887 Wright still felt it necessary to rise to the defence of biology in the pages of the *Canadian Practitioner* 'because the opinion has been freely expressed by at least one gentleman engaged in Medical Education that the knowledge required to pass the University examination in Biology is entirely useless to the medical student.'[44] The next month, nonetheless, the *Lancet* issued a direct reply to Wright's arguments (including a swipe at Wright himself, who was a biologist, not a medical doctor). Why had so few students written the University of Toronto medical examinations? 'It is easy for those who have not gone through the work required of a medical student, to philosophize [about] the beauties of science, etc.,' but those who understood the requisites of medical practice also knew that 'the time now required to be spent on biology' at Toronto 'might be better spent in, say, human anatomy, as indeed it is so spent by all other students than those whose love for Toronto University impels them to accept this additional work, for the sake of possessing her degree, a number, which we are sorry to say, is very small.'[45]

In the years that followed, the issue implicit in these two passages widened out into a clamorous debate between the University of Toronto men and those at Trinity. Occasionally it descended to the preposterous: in the *Lancet*, more derision of 'frogology' and the uselessness of studying 'salamanders' tails'; in the *Canadian Practitioner*, cheap shots about 'the positive charm of lecturing to large classes and raking in proportionate heaps of shekels.'[46] But the issue at stake was a substantive one: the place of the basic sciences in the curriculum of the medical school. In 1890, and in typical fashion, J.E. Graham voiced the case for the defence. Compare the advances made at the University of Toronto with the calendar of its medical school only six years ago:

Whereas, students were then able to graduate with a very superficial knowledge of the microscope, now they commence to learn the use of that instrument during the first month of their course. Then the instruction given in the primary branches, such as physiology and chemistry, was largely of a theoretical character; now these branches are taught in the laboratory, and the student is required to make experiments for himself.

... Many of the most important processes of life cannot be understood without practical study of similar processes, as they are found in the lower animals. It is as if a student in mechanical engineering were placed before a most complicated piece of machinery and requested to study and describe its various parts, with their movements, before he had even seen the working of more simple pieces of mechanism.[47]

In a typical riposte the *Lancet* argued that

the demands of science have in many instances thrust from the field those of practice ... The student's anatomy is to be more comparative and less of human, his physiology is to be biology, and the more it is surrounded by machinery the better: it must be scientific, to follow his course of to-day; he must be a thorough and practical electrician; his knowledge of physics be of the most perfect kind; he must be a practical photographer, a chemist and a glass-blower, a naturalist and a zoologist, a good general mechanic, understand thoroughly the construction and repairing of clocks, and a thorough optician.

No one, the *Lancet* continued, was sneering at the importance of basic science. But the key question was, did every new discovery and every new piece of apparatus need to be 'thrust into the medical course? Is there a danger of ... [converting] the medical course into a science course? In this age of clamouring for "practical courses," may not the medical students of the present become rather practical scientists than practical physicians?'[48]

HISTORY AS OFT REMARKED, has little sympathy for those who find themselves on the losing side. Over the long term, the sheer success of experimental science applied to medicine appeared to vindicate Wright or Graham and not Geikie, would undoubtedly vindicate the university medical school as a critical research centre, and, more tendentiously, would be used as a vindication for teaching the related 'unapplied' sciences to generations of medical students. But what may seem obvious to the modern reader was less so to contemporaries; those who expressed dissent, moreover, were neither reactionaries nor fools. It was, for practitioner and educator alike, a period of transition, when, as John Harley Warner has suggested, knowledge and scientific expertise were replacing experience and practice as the basis for professional identity and cultural authority.[49] But it was *par excellence* a period of transition. By the mid-1880s the proprietary schools had made remarkable progress in improving the quality and quantity of their clinical instruction. But additional 'hands-on' work in well-equipped laboratories was beyond their resources. Did it matter that medical students studied salamanders' tails? Some said not; and yet to the extent that people came to accept the proposition that the knowledge produced in the laboratory 'could direct therapeutic behaviour, not just explain it,' the idea that medical education began in the laboratory became well-nigh irresistible.[50] No one, above all Ramsay Wright, denigrated the importance of clinical training. And yet a subtle shift was taking place in the location of the theatre of medical education. In the 1850s and 1860s, it had been identified with the hospital, and above all with clinical demonstrations carried out in the hospital lecture theatres. By the early 1890s it was more closely identified with the laboratory.

A related shift was the reorientation of medicine's claim to cultural authority. For much of the nineteenth century that had rested on the ideal of 'the professional gentleman,' a man marked by a liberal education, a continuing standing in society, and, in his professional capacity, a man of probity and experience. As older notions of what constituted a liberal education began to disintegrate, and science in particular could claim that status as much as any other study, a scientific education gained in respectability and put its possessor on a par with those who knew the ancient tongues. At the same time the explanatory (and more rarely the curative) power of the biological sciences heightened the prestige of technical knowledge *per se*. Frogology won its place in the medical curriculum not least because it conferred a new degree of cultural authority, not merely upon the researcher but on the medical profession as a whole. Was there not too great a danger, Geikie had asked, of medical students 'becoming practical scientists rather than practical physicians'? To the growing band of enthusiasts of the 'preclinical' sciences, Geikie and the editor of the *Lancet* had asked the wrong question. The right one was, how could the practical physician be made into a 'scientific' practitioner, and how could the art of medicine be transformed into (a reworked version of) the science of medicine?[51]

The reorientation of medical education was not completed in 1887; rather, it had just begun, and it would take decades for all of the implications to work themselves out.[52] But the creation of the faculty of medicine at the University of Toronto and the concomitant changes at Queen's in 1892 signalled some major shifts in the nature of professional education which would begin to mark off the future from the past: the intrusion into medical education of those who were not practitioners; the new emphasis on the pre-clinical sciences as the essential foundations for the art of practice; the transition to a salaried professoriate; the idea that a medical school was not simply a teaching but a research institution; the notion that medical education was best served when lodged within the walls of a university.

Accompanying these developments was yet another: the first signal of a long recessional for the role of the professional organization in its educational affairs. Since its formation in 1866, the Medical Council had been the main forum of debate over standards of medical education, and had occupied the critical role in the implementation of change. So much was this the case, indeed, that when, in the late 1870s, the University of Toronto had attempted to move to the cutting edge of international standards by raising its degree requirements far above those demanded by the council, it found itself with a diminishing number of students and was forced to beat a substantial retreat.[53] By the late 1890s, however, the new medical faculties, backed by their university senates, were beginning to exercise a growing degree of influence. It was the universities, for example, that launched the initiative to move from a six-month to an eight-month term for classes, and, in the next decade, convinced the CPSO to begin to withdraw from the examining process as well, leaving more and more of its powers of certification to the universities themselves.[54]

IN LATE NINETEENTH-CENTURY Ontario, nevertheless, the university did not sweep all before it. The law constitutes a notable exception to most of the developments we have discussed thus far. And yet even here there are parallels worth pursuing, above all the abrupt transition from an education rooted primarily in the worksite to one that incorporated formal classroom instruction as well.[55]

In 1887, only a few months after the decision to establish a teaching faculty in medicine, the University of Toronto also launched an initiative to found a faculty of law and invited the Law Society to participate in the venture.[56] A committee representing both the Senate and the Law

Society was established to draw up an outline for a revised LLB degree, and it recommended the establishment of a teaching faculty to be managed jointly by the university and the Society. There was to be a four-year program of studies, with the university taking responsibility for the first half and the Law Society for the second. Students who completed the program would receive their LLB and would then be called to the bar without further impediment. Office practice was to be limited to the last two years of the program. The proposal was not intended to replace the existing educational requirements of the Law Society but to offer an additional route to the bar which would integrate the efforts of the university and the Law Society and bring them into closer harmony. The results of the joint committee's work were put before Convocation in February 1888, with recommendations that the county law associations and the other Ontario universities be consulted.[57]

The proposal was probably doomed from the beginning. Aside from anything else, the fires of the old University Question had flared up over university federation, and the scheme to introduce a teaching faculty in law fanned them anew. Though negotiations between the Law Society and other universities were not excluded by the terms of the proposal, there were fears that the University of Toronto would obtain special privileges through the arrangement, and the other universities made their opposition known quickly and forcefully.[58] What the Toronto initiative did, nonetheless, was to give new impetus to the wider debate over the future of legal education, which had been mired for decades in the politics of regionalism and in the still-unresolved tensions between learning, in more formal settings, the science of the law, and on-the-job training. By the late 1880s, it must be said, none of the participants was opposed to more classroom instruction, legal or otherwise. There was, indeed, a general sense that legal education in Ontario was falling behind the progress made elsewhere, especially in the United States, where reformers like T.W. Dwight at Columbia and C.C. Langdell at Harvard had wrought a revolution in legal education, summoning up their own versions of 'science' to undermine the credibility of the proprietorial law school and office training alike.[59] There was, as well, the conviction that the law was falling behind the other professions in Ontario. 'Has the time not come,' one lawyer asked in the pages of the *Globe*,

when the Law Society should insist upon as thorough course in the pedagogics of law as is now required in arts, in medicine or in pharmacy? ... What is the rule in theology? Is it not years of study under the most profound Doctor of Divinity to be found in the land? In medicine is not the rule a similar one? and so with other professions. In law what is the rule? Cram your text-books. That is all. There is neither exposition, nor discussion, nor investigation ... nothing but a dry, weary, monotonous cram of case law.'[60]

But what kind of innovations would meet the needs of the profession? At one extreme were those, including the editor of the *Canada Law Journal*, who favoured some variation of the Toronto LLB proposal with its joint Law Society–University format. The advantage of the plan, he wrote, was that by 'placing the purely theoretical, historical and scientific knowledge of law and cognate subjects before practical training in law as it is and in the details of its administration by the courts, it seeks to unite the functions of the university and the Law Society, and to make each of them auxiliary to the other in rearing a race of jurists whose knowledge of law, scientific and practical ... will reflect credit on themselves, their profession and their country.'[61]

At the other extreme were those who opposed any proposal to make lectures compulsory at the expense of office practice. Compulsory lectures given in Toronto would only drive students to seek apprenticeships there, 'Lex' argued in a fiery letter to the *Globe*. 'The Toronto offices will be filled to overflowing with superfluous students, while outside of Toronto the law offices will be depleted of those students whose time should be the most valuable to their principals. Is this a device of the enemy?' On the other hand, 'Lex' was not opposed to improved educational provision *per se*. Let the Law Society unite with the university and create an effective law department, he added, and then leave the graduate three years 'for honest work' in a law office. 'We believe that a good law school is desirable, but it is most valuable for the laying of a broad foundation on which to build, and this could be best done while the student was at college.'[62] With respect to reducing the terms of service, Lex had on his side the majority of those who expressed an opinion. As one prominent lawyer put it, the LLB proposal made the time spent under articles 'ridiculously short' and, by collapsing the science and practice of the law into a four-year program, reduced legal education to 'a 4 year cram.'[63] Lawyers also questioned the need for any arrangement with the universities at all. The Law Society, said one, 'is old enough to stand alone, and rich enough to pay all professors and teachers it may need; ... we deprecate the idea of its forming an alliance with any teaching body.'[64]

There was, then, general opposition to the LLB proposal, and especially to any shortening of the terms of service, but there was also the conviction that it was time 'to do something' about the state of legal education. In April 1888, Convocation referred the LLB proposal to a special committee with instructions to report on the whole question of legal education: whether any arrangement was desirable with *any* university; whether terms should be shortened; whether to establish branch law schools; and finally, whether to make lectures compulsory or not.[65] The resulting report recommended that the Law Society go it alone, revivifying its own school and making attendance compulsory upon all students. The committee also recommended that there be no shortening of the terms of service but, in what was a remarkable sleight of hand, added that the law-school courses should be counted as part of the five (or three) years of service under articles. These recommendations, adopted by Convocation in February 1889, underpinned the establishment of the new Osgoode Hall Law School later that year.[66]

Why, one might ask, did the Law Society opt for an independent initiative? There were, after all, alternatives. The LLB proposal might have been redesigned and extended even-handedly to include the other universities. Cooperation with the universities would have reduced the costs of legal education to the Law Society, and clearly offered a means of decentralizing all or part of the program of studies. The decision, we suggest, was in part due to the reaction of the universities themselves. Trinity responded with a notable lack of enthusiasm, fearing that the scheme would drain students out of its arts program and gut its own recently established faculty of law.[67] The reaction at Queen's was somewhat the same.[68] Perhaps in an attempt to force the Law Society's hand, the University of Toronto simply went ahead and created its own Faculty of Law in the autumn of 1888 without even waiting for the Law Society to reach a decision.[69] Thus it can hardly be said that the Law Society spurned the universities; rather, it looks as though it were the other way around.

At the same time, the Law Society had its own traditions as an added incentive to go it alone. It had been engaged in the formal instruction of lawyers since 1854, and had had a law school operating more or less continuously since 1861; admittedly only voluntary and not very successful, the school had nonetheless been a part of the Society's aspirations for decades. It mattered too that the distinction between 'academic law' and practical training in the office and courts remained sharp. As one leading lawyer argued early in 1888,

Improvement I freely admit, is desirable in the course both of the Society and the Universities, but have they not each a distinct field of work which cannot profitably be amalgamated? To the Law Society is committed the charge of supplying such instruction as will fit a man for the practical work of the lawyer ... while to the University it would appear fitting to encourage the scientific study of the principles of the law. Let each equip itself for its own work ... and we shall then have skilled practitioners emanating from the one and learned authors from the other; but let us not, by making a jumble of the work of both, produce men of whom ... it may be said that they are 'Jacks of all trades and masters of none.'[70]

Finally, one must ask, what need did the profession have of the academy? Despite the fact that lawyers often enough looked over their shoulders at the progress other professions were making, they remained the most prestigious of the 'learned professions' in the late nineteenth century, with the possible exception of the clergy. Even though lawyers sometimes disparaged their own entry standards, those standards were higher than nearly all the rest. Their professional education was more prolonged, their 'stars' dominated politics and were prominent in many other public roles, and many of the leading lights among the younger generation had BA degrees besides. Medical men, with their professional degrees and professional schools, could claim nothing like that and envied them for it. The university could do even more for such parvenus as dentists and pharmacists. In social terms lawyers had the least to gain from a university professional school and would be the least tainted by establishing one of their own, independent of the universities.

The establishment of the Osgoode Hall Law School was in many respects a radical departure from the past and yet at the same time a departure consonant with the British-Canadian traditions that had developed over the course of the nineteenth century. It was radical in that it shifted the traditional balance between learning on the job and learning about the job in school. If one sets aside the two or three months of lectures during the judicial terms which all students were required to undergo between 1854 and 1868, law students had never before been *required* to attend school; from 1889 their first responsibility, for at least sixteen months of their articles (and for Toronto students, twenty-four months), was schooling. By the end of the century it was twenty-four months for all.[71] One had to pass each course of lectures before proceeding to the next, and success in the program was a prerequisite for admission to the bar. Before 1889 the vast majority of students learned their law exclusively in the office, in the courts, and by directed study for the Law Society's various examinations. Now, they prepared for the examinations in class. The Law Society, in sum, had decisively committed itself to formal instruction and the legitimacy of the classroom as one central forum for legal education.

Classes, however, were to be held either early or late in the day in order to allow students to carry on work in the Toronto law offices they were attached to. And for matriculants at least there still remained two full years of office training before their classes began. The principle of an apprenticeship in the law, in other words, was not abandoned. The politics of the profession undoubtedly played a role in that outcome. Regionalism and the interests of country practitioners were important considerations for the Benchers, and made it all the more certain that the views of those who favoured the status quo were taken into consideration. But it wasn't the status quo which carried the day, and the outcome wasn't the result of politics alone. The new program of legal education, taken as a whole, was a moderate blending of tradition and innovation, a judicious mix of apprenticeship with formal schooling in the principles and the practice of the law. Even the editor of the *Canada Law Journal*, a warm advocate of schooling throughout the debate, worried, in its aftermath, about getting the balance right. He was disappointed there wasn't more in the curriculum on 'the science of jurisprudence' but at the same time uneasy about the extent to which classes would disrupt the acquisition of the necessary experience of the office and the courts. Care about such matters was essential, he warned. 'We point out the danger, not because we are sure that it is inevitable, but because, ardently desiring the success of the school, we wish the evil to be guarded against. The enthusiasm, judgement and skill of the Principal and Lecturers will, we doubt not, be exercised to avert it.'[72]

STILL, ONE HAS TO POSE one other question here: if learning by apprenticeship was such a rooted tradition, if it was also grounded in the economics of the law office itself, why then did the shift to schooling take place at all? We have already suggested some of the answers in the preceding narrative. Yet there are three other explanations which need to be canvassed as well. First, there was the impact of the new examination requirements introduced in the early 1870s. To that point it had been rare (though not entirely unknown) for students to complain about their educational arrangements; after that, however, objections multiplied in the pages of both the lay and the professional press.[73] The reason, we suspect, is that higher examination standards, more reading to be done, and an increase in the number of examinations during their term of articles all made it more difficult for students to master the material and pass the examinations through self-preparation. It also tended to vitiate the informal instruction traditionally offered by their principals. To meet the new demands, some leading lawyers at least recognized that more formal methods of instruction were not only necessary, but long overdue.[74] A second answer may lie in the sheer growth in the number of lawyers and in the diaspora into the countryside. Because of the more restricted nature of their business, their students would not be exposed to the wide range of activities available to earlier generations or to the round of court appearances and other formal duties routinely experienced by the young Henry O'Brien or our other mid-century diarists. Numbers and dispersal, in other words, made such gradual socialization into the law less efficacious.

That, we must say, is pure speculation, for we have no evidence to sustain it at all. And so, indeed, for the most part, is a third possibility, though here there is some shred of support to be found in the sources. In the 1860s and 1870s, large numbers of practitioners, and especially country lawyers, had vociferously opposed a compulsory law school, and especially compulsory lectures centralized in Toronto. By the end of the 1880s, however, there were few voices opposed to compulsion *per se*. While undoubtedly attributable to a number of things, that shift may also have occurred because of changes within the law office itself. One of these was the application of new technologies to the work traditionally done by law students. 'Lex,' one of those who opposed compulsion, had remarked in passing, 'the pressure to get into leading [Toronto] offices is so great that in some offices the students have desks, but have nothing to do. The use of shorthand and typewriters has taken from the students much work, by some called drudgery, but withal, work which was rich in instruction.'[75] It is possible, in other words, that these sorts of innovations made the presence of students less useful to principals, who now needed, or could make more use of, specialist skills that students lacked. Similarly, the editor of the *Canada Law Journal* noted in passing that the impact of the school would 'detract materially' from the value of the student 'as an office assistant,' adding that 'young lawyers and paid clerks will probably find themselves in greater demand.'[76] That trend may well have been already under way, even in smaller law offices. As the amount of business expanded, one can at least speculate that lawyers might have come to prefer the experience of a newly qualified lawyer and a paid clerk to the help of an inexperienced student. A reasonable level of profitability, moreover, might have allowed that preference to compensate for the relatively cheap labour of the articled clerk. Even if such changes had been confined to offices in the county towns and in Toronto, where most lawyers were located, they might still have reduced the volume of opposition to a compulsory law school.

Our own analysis of Brantford hints at the same development. In 1861 the census for the town listed twelve lawyers and fourteen law students; twenty years later, there were twenty lawyers but still only fourteen law students. The changing ratio of lawyers to students might be due to many things, but it is suggestive nonetheless. At the end of the century, in any case, the evidence is more conclusive. At a meeting of the Osgoode Legal and Literary Society, one speaker remarked that articled clerks had, for all practical purposes, ceased to be useful, and he threw the blame on the Law School, which tied up so much of their time. Replied another, 'practitioners were apt to look back to some 15 years ago, when the student was part of the office machine, and did a great deal of routine work, copying etc. Now the student was of little use in the office. This change would have taken place even if there had been no school, owing to the adoption of the principle of large firms with junior partners to do the specialized work of modern practice and to the introduction of the shorthand writer and typewriting machine.'[77] In the larger world beyond the confines of the professions, technology and the reorganization of the workplace were reducing the efficacy of apprenticeship and promoting the transfer of skill-training to schools of various kinds. Less could be learned in the shop; the production process undercut the role of the apprentice, and learning a craft became something that was more likely to happen in school. And so, perhaps, in the case of law. Though apprenticeship was not abandoned, its declining economic value encouraged those who had formerly opposed classroom learning to acquiesce in the new departure at Osgoode Hall.

The reorientation of legal education in the late nineteenth century, in any case, established a pattern that would persist for decades in Ontario, persist indeed until well after the Second World War.[78] With little need for the prestige the university could confer, and with its own potent traditions of legal education to guide it, the Law Society went its own way, turning its back on the model that proved a siren song to others, the university professional school and the professional degree that accompanied it.

DID OTHERS DO the same? Yes, but with far more consequence for the future of their occupation. During the 1880s and early 1890s, there had been much talk of professional training for secondary-school teachers, and here again the universities proved amenable, establishing a Bachelor of Paedagogy degree and faculties of education for that purpose.[79] Already required to have an arts degree, or some approximation to it, high-school teachers could now, like doctors or dentists, claim a professional training carried on within the walls of the academy. For elementary-school teachers it was a different story. By the early twentieth century, the massive oversupply of teachers encouraged the ministry to abolish the county model schools, create a system of normal schools across the province, and require all candidates to complete a full year's training in them. It was, no doubt, an improvement. Yet it also put paid to any lingering notion that elementary-school teaching was, or could be, a profession 'like the others.' At the very moment when the training of professionals was being gathered in by the university, elementary-school teachers were left outside that charmed circle, consigned to what would come to be seen as an inferior, 'second-rate' form of professional education. Lawyers could afford to spurn the academy in the late nineteenth or early twentieth century; others could not.

Even the massive rise in matriculation standards in such occupations as medicine or dentistry conspired against the public-school teacher. In the 1870s or 1880s, large numbers of them held academic qualifications as good, or better, than most matriculants in medicine, dentistry, or pharmacy, and many of those in law. But as entry standards were driven up in the 1890s by the pressures of overcrowding, a gap began to open up, one that would widen steadily in the decades to come. Doctors, lawyers, or dentists would complete high school and graduate from the university preparatory stream with its emphasis on advanced mathematics or science and its dollop of Latin and modern languages. They would then go on to ever-lengthening programs of professional training and even pre-professional training in the universities as well. The education of elementary-school teachers would remain frozen at senior high school; they would matriculate with different qualifications, and then go on to a nearby normal school for a short session of preparation for their craft.

By their ties to an academic discipline, by their possession of undergraduate degrees in arts or science, by their professional education conducted under the aegis of a university, by the very fact that they were the gatekeepers to the university itself, secondary-school teachers would remain 'ladies' and 'gentlemen,' linked to the fortunes of Ontario's burgeoning class of professional workers. Elementary-school teachers would remain 'males' and 'females,' taking their place among others consigned to a less prestigious stratum in the emerging world of white-collar work. They would, of course, not be alone in that fate. Nurses, trained in the expanding number of local hospital schools, would soon join them, along with many others as well. The increasing social stratification of white-collar work was not simply the result of where one's professional training came to be located. But in the late nineteenth and early twentieth centuries, the university was becoming ever more deeply implicated in that process.

18
Retrospect

Just before the close of the nineteenth century, the Rev. Featherstone Osler died at the ripe old age of eighty-nine. Born in 1805 into an English shipowning family, he had served in the Royal Navy and then, without 'friends' to further his naval career, had entered Cambridge to study for Holy Orders. 'His first thought,' according to one of his biographers, 'had been of a comfortable living in England,' but 'with some reluctance' he accepted, in 1834, an appointment to Tecumseth and West Gwillimbury townships in Upper Canada, where for twenty-odd years he ministered as Anglican missionary to a widely scattered population only just emerging from the first stages of settlement.[1] Above all else, Osler was a clergyman of the Church of England; but he was also a jack-of-all-professional-trades, pulling teeth, bleeding the sick, drafting wills and deeds. He engaged in these activities, to some extent at least, because there was no one else available to do them. But they were also part and parcel of the duties of a parish priest in the Georgian era, and of the gentleman's conception of *noblesse oblige*.

Featherstone and his wife, Ellen, raised a family of six sons and three daughters. Among the former were William, who became one of the most distinguished physicians of his generation, finishing his career as Regius Professor of medicine at Oxford; Britton Bath, one of Canada's most prominent criminal lawyers; Featherston, another lawyer and later a judge in Ontario's highest court; and Edmund, an eminently successful banker and federal politician.[2] There is no indication, however, that William ever drafted wills, that B.B. pulled teeth, or that Edmund provided medical care for his neighbours or clients. That was not because they failed to inherit their parents' sense of service and vocation;[3] rather, these values found expression in careers where the range of tasks was more narrowly focused. As others in the society began to offer services in these areas, there was little need for them to do so. And it is doubtful that they would have felt competent to perform them in any case.

In that, at least, the younger Oslers were typical of their generation, as Featherstone and Ellen were of theirs. For one of the hallmarks of the latter half of the nineteenth century was the growth of occupational diversity and specialization. To take but a handful of other examples. The overlapping tasks of the architect, engineer, surveyor, and builder, so often carried out by a single individual during earlier decades, were becoming increasingly distinct, and by the late nineteenth century, in large urban areas at least, architects could begin to identify themselves as specialists in aspects of design and construction. The steam engine grew more sophisticated, was put to more diverse uses, and produced, in the process, an occupational subgroup responsible for supervising its operation. A new technology suddenly burst upon the scene and created the electrical engineer. Esoteric new building materials like iron and steel demanded specialist knowledge beyond that required for construction with wood or stone, and that had been accessible indiscriminately to the trained architect, the 'C.E.,' or the builder who had learned his craft as a carpenter or stone-cutter. The administrative revolution produced a demand for an undifferentiated mass of clerks, but also created specialists like the accountant or the stenographic reporter. Greater prosperity, though no doubt changing cultural attitudes as well, made room for the embalmer. Urbanization, scientific theory, and new technology combined to create work for public-health officers, sanitary engineers, and master plumbers, three occupations virtually unknown before 1875. After reviewing the expansion of non-farm, non-labouring work over the century following 1850, Ian Drummond remarks that, 'viewed in the light of these statistics, Ontario's Industrial Revolution looks remarkably like a white-collar revolution.'[4] It consisted of more than sheer numerical growth, however; it also included greater occupational diversity, more specialization, and an increasing level of technical knowledge embedded in some forms of work at least. If 'deskilling' was one side of the occupational coin in the latter half of the nineteenth century, the other was the 'skilling' and 'reskilling' of other portions of the workforce.

As individuals or whole occupations experienced that revolution, they found themselves entering a no man's land where the occupational order had yet to be fully charted in terms of hierarchies of prestige or cultural meaning. Not only did the upper and lower boundaries remain nebulous, but the vertical and horizontal strata had yet to congeal, and the positioning of occupations within the grid of 'white-collar work' was still uncertain. Even at the end of the nineteenth century, for example, prominent elementary- and secondary-school teachers still conceived of themselves as legitimate claimants to professional status; yet as lines of internal stratification began to harden, secondary-school teachers would remain on one side of an invisible divide, while public-school teachers, for a whole variety of reasons which had little to do with their own aspirations, found themselves consigned to the other. They were hardly alone in this. Dentists remained uncertain about their own place in society, while pharmacists, with their storefront windows stuffed with paints and perfumes, and their counters stacked with everything from dog soap and photographic chemicals to patent medicines, remained as puzzled as they had been in 1871 about whether they were 'professors of pharmacy' or 'vendors of drugs.'[5] Indeed, it was not clear that they would be able to retain control over even these areas of work: large department stores were attempting to hire them as employees, or offering to fill and mail prescriptions at cut-rate prices to anywhere in the province.[6] General practitioners felt themselves 'encroached upon on every side,' threatened by everything from the patent-medicine industry or the 'hustling specialist' to the 'abuse of charity' perpetrated by the hospitals. If in the end some of these fears proved groundless, they are nevertheless important in illuminating the uncertainties about the nature of that new terrain and the dangers it posed for those who had to make a place in it.

IF THE PRESENT was troubling and the future uncertain, it was not only because the lineaments of the occupational and social order were changing but because the mental maps which were supposed to order that landscape no longer provided a sure guide. Even in the 1890s the ideal of the professional gentleman remained a potent image that could encapsulate the aspirations of occupational leaders, and probably of large numbers of the rank and file. It rings interminably, for example, through the pages of the *Dominion Dental Journal* or the proceedings of the Ontario Association of Architects. The yearning for legal privilege of engineers like Alan Macdougall was phrased in terms of the ideal, while clergymen and doctors formulated their fears of social declension as a departure from its norms. Yet the inherent ambiguities of the ideal had always left it open to expropriation and dilution. Though druggists or dentists might obtain a legal monopoly, they were hardly 'gentlemen' in the old-fashioned sense, nor, it might be added, were large numbers of doctors or the attorneys absorbed into the Law Society during the 1860s and 1870s; but stripped of its connotations relating to governance, and reduced to an amorphous mix of education and good manners, the meaning of 'gentleman' in the old-fashioned sense had ceased to exist in any case. The relationship between a liberal education and the learned professions had also been modified. On the one hand, the former had ceased to refer reflexively to a primarily classical education; on the other, a much larger proportion of people could claim the kind of education once the exclusive preserve of the gentry and the learned professions alone. Some of them were even women. There were far more occupations whose leaders could argue, with a degree of plausibility, that some form of legal privilege was in the public interest. Yet there were also grave doubts that the public interest could be served by giving such privileges to *any* occupation. The presuppositions of Georgian professionalism, in other words, were increasingly being attenuated, or rendered irrelevant by changed circumstances.

There were also subtle shifts in meaning which began to give greater weight to technical expertise itself. Professional men had always possessed expert knowledge, but it had been embedded in a larger matrix of values and assumptions which gave authority to expertise. The sheer success of scientific and technical achievement over the course of the nineteenth century underpinned the rising prestige of medicine and engineering alike. Indeed, long before they achieved anything remotely resembling a legal monopoly over their work, engineers conventionally came to be referred to as professional men, much like the others – and that despite a good deal of nonchalance about the requisite norms. Many engineers, for example, remained outside the orbit of professionalism, indifferent to preliminary education, priding themselves on being practical men, uninterested in or even antagonistic to the ambitions of those like Alan Macdougall who wanted their crafts to resemble a traditional 'learned profession.' Yet they garnered impressive gains in prestige from their contributions to economic development, to building the infrastructure of the nation, and, especially in the case of electrical engineers, from their starring role in the spectacle staged by the late nineteenth-century 'theatre of science.'[7] The gospel of progress itself could now begin to bestow cultural legitimacy upon expertise without the other requisites that had marked the professional gentleman of an earlier era. It also mattered, however, that they were in demand and made good money: professional status had always rested on a firm material base.

STILL, WE ARE TALKING here about shifts in emphasis rather than any wholesale departure from an ideal. In the first place, the prestige of the three traditional learned professions remained unchallenged. What made young men unwilling to enter the trades? the editor of the *Globe* asked rhetorically in 1890. 'Educated boys prefer professions to trades because the pay is better and because the world holds a doctor, a lawyer, or a divine in greater estimation than it does a bricklayer or a carpenter.'⁸ A few years later the same editor would cast his eye over the examination lists and remark that Osgoode Hall had just produced eighty-four new barristers, and the University of Toronto, fifty-one medical graduates. 'Yet while young men in hundreds are entering overcrowded professions the examination lists [also] show that only seven students at Toronto University graduated as bachelors of applied science and only three as civil engineers.'⁹ It would be decades, not years, before other occupations could even pretend to parity of esteem.

In many respects, moreover, traditional habits of thought were simply poured into new organizational or intellectual vessels. Customary rules of gentlemanly behaviour, for example, were translated into occupational codes of ethics which preserved values antipathetic to those of the marketplace. The notion of 'vocation' survived as well: even the new applied sciences were to be put to work not just for the private benefit of individuals but in the service of humanity at large. The claim to an independent maintenance was now rarely made, but the associated principle, that professional men must be free to render an independent judgment, remained a potent force, allowing them to see themselves as something of an independent estate, not the servants of commerce or industry, labour or capital, but the critics and reformers of their society.¹⁰

The decline of the notion of the 'gentleman' as an ascribed status, moreover, was accompanied by the rise of a variant, the idea of 'nature's gentleman.' Entrée to an occupation now had to be 'earned' by dint of ability and hard work, and the tests were meritocratic ones. Those who could pass the tests nonetheless were still to be protected by restricted titles or outright monopolies, and they were even deserving of extended subsidies for their education. Why should the universities be subsidized from the public purse? the editor of the *Christian Guardian* asked in 1887. There was a difference between the professions and other occupations, he argued, which rested in the culture needed by the former and which only the university could provide.

In the interests of all the people, that the people may be served by the men to whom Providence has given the gifts for the highest service, their doors must be kept open to rich and poor alike. The free university is now and ever has been pre-eminently the friend of the poor man's boy, and through his often superior gifts and abilities the friend of the whole nation. But in the same way the free university is the only effective bulwark of democratic institutions and the democratic spirit. Men easily learn to be aristocrats ... The only safeguard against this tendency is that the whole people should join to keep open the great university highway, by which the lowliest, who are of the people, and to whom God has given the great heart, and moral strength, and thought, which sums up in their own genius the spirit and power of the age, can ever climb to the top, and by right of being truly the best, fill the best seats in all the land. The relation of the university to the general civilization of a country is neither small nor insignificant.[11]

This line of argument did not go uncontested in the last two decades of the nineteenth century. The editorial was itself a response to the growth of a body of opinion vociferously opposed to any further subsidies from the public purse to either secondary or university education.[12] But what is of interest here is the argument itself. The production of nature's gentlemen was expensive to be sure; but the good of the commonwealth and the survival of democratic institutions depended on it. The language of the Georgian professional gentleman, which is where this book began, has been transmuted but not abandoned, and in these new forms would survive far into the twentieth century. Indeed, rather than being eclipsed by the forces of 'a materialist society based on capitalist production,' the political language and social assumptions of the Upper Canadian gentry tradition would be preserved, albeit in much modified form, within the ideology of modern professionalism.[13]

There were other sorts of continuities as well. We have already had something to say about the social origins of professional men and the social complexion of the three traditional learned professions, if not some of the other occupations we have been dealing with. It may be that towards the end of the century there was some broadening out of the backgrounds of those entering the professions, and certainly the attacks on the school system in the 1890s suggest that contemporaries sensed an influx of candidates whose social standing was lower than had been the case in earlier decades. But was even the Law Society, in the graceless language of the editor of the *Canada Law Journal*, being infiltrated by 'Indians, Italians and tramps'? If surnames are any indicator, the Law Lists don't reveal it to be so. True, by 1900 there had been at least three black barristers practising in Ontario, but one of them, Delos Rogest Davis, had had to be admitted by a special act of the legislature because he had been unable to find anyone willing to take him on as an articled clerk.[14] Medicine also had at least one black, A.R. Abbott,[15] and one Native Canadian, Dr Oronhyatekha, born on the Six Nations reserve near Brantford. By the 1890s the latter was a prominent individual, holding the position of Supreme Chief Ranger of the International Order of Foresters (from which office he was able to slam into those doctors who condemned contract practice for wishing to deny medical services to those who otherwise could not afford them).[16] Both law and medicine had also been forced to admit women; but two women barristers and a handful of women doctors can hardly be translated, except perhaps as an apparition, into an encircling horde. In fact the professions remained at the close of the century much as they had been at the beginning: resolutely white; resolutely of British stock; resolutely male; and largely from comfortable, if not privileged, backgrounds.

During the 1890s, indeed, the professions may well have become less accessible than they had been before. Rapidly rising matriculation standards and longer courses of professional education in both medicine and dentistry necessitated more years of schooling. The shift in medicine, from a six- to an eight-month term, meant less opportunity for summer employment. And the requirement that all students attend law school in Toronto for a goodly portion of their term of apprenticeship may also have made that occupation more expensive to enter. The research required to answer these questions lies beyond the scope of this book. But it is plausible to suggest that there was greater social closure, in medicine and law at least, than there had been since the 1850s.

THE RECONSTRUCTION of the professions, and of the meaning of 'profession,' was nothing like complete at the end of the century; indeed, in many respects it had only just begun. But the process itself encapsulated elements of both consolidation and, paradoxically, dissolution. Except in the case of the clergy, traditional 'professional establishments' survived and even multiplied: a handful of occupations retained a monopoly over an area of work, and a few more achieved a restricted title. Nineteenth-century radicalism, in its manifest varieties, had failed to dislodge special privilege in this respect, and thus it would stand as a beacon for other aspiring occupations throughout the twentieth century, with its promise, as Alfred Jury had intimated, of a form of socialism for the middle class. Consolidation also incorporates another theme that runs throughout this text: the wedge between the professional man and the laity was being driven ever deeper. This was, of course, the intent of occupational legislation, but it didn't occur simply because of that. The Methodist lay preacher was marginalized for other reasons entirely; the sheer spread of specialization in so many crafts and occupations had its own momentum; technical innovation gave a credence to the authority of some experts that had not existed before.

The notion of profession, on the other hand, had lost the kind of conceptual coherence it had had in the early nineteenth century. Many more people were now 'learned' but lacked the legal prerogatives of medicine or law. The differences between dentists or druggists and other occupations made its meaning harder to discern. The legal entitlements that gave some a monopoly over an area of work and others only a restricted title blurred distinctions further. Engineers and high-school teachers, and many others besides, were 'employees' in large organizations. Doctors and lawyers might both operate on a fee-for-service basis, but a growing number of the latter worked in firms. The reshaping of the universities included professional schools not just for theology or medicine but for dentists and engineers, and, just over the horizon, for would-be businessmen, social workers, and librarians. At mid-century contemporaries could speak confidently of the distinctive character of the three learned professions. They could describe them as 'the tripod of a country's erudition' or write that 'the learned professions in this colony represent the aristocracy of intellect.'[17] By century's close the 'tripod' was already fractured, and a variety of new aristocrats of intellect were making their voices heard, often enough laying claim to areas of erudition hitherto the exclusive preserve of medicine, law, or divinity. And that included, above all, one late nineteenth-century occupation on-the-make which we have had altogether nothing to say about: the academic profession.[18] Both the conceptual clarity and the social coherence of the notion of 'profession' were fragmenting, and that process would continue far into the twentieth century. And not even the King's men, let alone the sociologists, would put Humpty-Dumpty back together again.

THE EMPHASIS THAT HAS fallen, in so many of the preceding chapters, on the establishment of occupational monopolies enshrined in law should serve as a forceful reminder of the linkage between the growth of the professions and the growth of the modern state. It was the latter that chartered the various colleges, delineated their powers, made unlicensed practice an offence against the law, and defined who was a legitimate practitioner and who was not. Despite the emphasis in much of the existing literature on the parallel but distinct and often antagonistic growth of autonomous professions and bureaucratic state, it should be clear from our argument that the histories of the professions and of the state are integrally linked, and are part of the same process of state formation. The public good having been defined, the police power was to be exercised sometimes by the direct arm of government and sometimes by 'private' agencies chartered by it. In effect these agencies administered a portion of the public domain, even to the point of sending their 'detectives' to ferret out illegal practice, a role not entirely unlike that of the school inspectorate. As Bruce Curtis has persuasively argued in the case of the school system, moreover, such agencies were also engaged in establishing norms which to future generations would become part of the natural order of things.[19] Between 1865 and 1874 legislation defined the good doctor, dentist, or dispenser of drugs. It also institutionalized the means of identifying the good practitioner in terms of both competence and professional probity, and put the administrative apparatus of professional life into 'safe' hands. In principle at least, the public was to be deprived of its quacks and its charlatans in medicine and dentistry, in much the same way as it had long been deprived of its right to employ whomever it pleased to plead legal cases in all but the lower courts. The new professional organizations, as much as the school system itself, were part of the impulse to enlarge, systematize, and consolidate a new conception of the social order, one in harmony with the moderate liberalism and the religious moralism of the respectable men who had governed Upper Canada and then guided the destinies of the new province. Whether one describes this as 'state formation' or as the construction of a new kind of social infrastructure parallel to the opening of the north or the building of the railways, the history of the professions in nineteenth-century Ontario (and the fate of aspiring occupations as well) needs to be seen as part of that process and not as something independent of it.

One can, indeed, even extend this line of analysis to the clergy themselves. As we have already remarked, the process of disestablishment eliminated one of the central lineaments of traditional society – the role of the church as an integral part of the constitution of civil society. New norms took its place – that church and state were independent entities, that all religions were (more or less) equal, that religion was a private matter, that the realm of the sacred and that of the secular were separate compartments of public life, that clergymen must be dependent on the faithful rather than independent of them. So rooted now are these once-contested social norms that, as John Webster Grant remarks, it takes a leap of historical imagination to realize that the role of an established church in Upper Canada was once a 'logically compelling' vision.[20]

There is also a related point worth noting here: the growth of centralization and bureaucracy within professional organizations themselves. It is not just in public education where we see these developments. All three of our denominations became more bureaucratized in the period: the growth of central offices and standing committees to supervise mission activities, sustentation funds, other sorts of administrative responsibilities, along with the establishment of central boards to examine students – all meant greater centralization of power. With the creation of the CPSO or the RCDSO, rules governing the preliminary education, training, and conduct of professional men proliferated. Policy, moreover, was made in Toronto; their buildings, administrators, and most of their schools were located there; and Toronto interests often held the upper hand in their governing councils. It was not only patterns of trade and the railways that secured the predominance of the city over its hinterland; it was also policy making and administration in government and the professions alike. This, of course, would create its own tensions. The interests of Toronto lawyers and doctors increasingly diverged from those in Wingham or Vankleek Hill, nor did the interests of the professional élite in the various occupations always coincide with those of the rank and file. From the beginning, nevertheless, the very act of organizing an association or seeking legislative privilege promoted both centralization and bureaucratization within the occupation, and thus within the larger society as well.

WHILE THE ROLE of the state is important in constructing professions, that role cannot be torn out of its historical context, or abstracted from the contingent nature of history itself. It should be clear from our account, for example, that the legislature was much more responsive at some moments than others, above all during the years between 1867 and 1872 – the inaugural era for the new province of Ontario and, until 1871, the years of the Sandfield Macdonald government. By legislation passed between 1868 and 1872, lawyers finally established full control over entry and examination standards for both intending barristers and attorneys, and introduced the elective principle for Benchers. The critical medical act was passed in 1869. Dentists and druggists achieved their charters in 1868 and 1871 respectively. The professionalization of educational administration was carried out in 1871. Viewed piece by piece, there were as many important statutes passed outside this period as within it, but what is impressive is the sheer volume of legislation concentrated in the first few years of the new province's history. Among the many other social and economic initiatives taken up during Sandfield Macdonald's years as premier, the extension of the privileges held by a small number of occupational groups is a notable one.

How is this conjuncture of events to be explained? First, we want to draw attention to the cultural milieu which gave much of the nineteenth century its particular ambience. It would hardly be sensible to discount the potent forces of modernity being unleashed in the middle decades of the nineteenth century, including the corroding influence of mid-Victorian liberalism on old institutions and assumptions; we ourselves have already stressed its impact on professional institutions in the years around mid-century, and again in the last two decades of the century. At the same time we continue to be impressed by the resilience of the Georgian frame of mind far into the nineteenth century. Perhaps that is not very surprising. Sandfield Macdonald, to take but one example, was already a young law clerk the year that Victoria came to the throne. His formative experiences at home, church, and school were Georgian in form and content, were *experienced* in an Upper Canada that was, to use William Westfall's phrase once again, 'a curiously eighteenth-century world.' That was also the case with many other influential men of his generation. An analysis of all the professional entries included in the *Dictionary of Canadian Biography* for the entire nineteenth century is, indeed, a sharp reminder of the Georgian roots of nineteenth-century Ontario's cultural and social order. A full 68 per cent of these professional men were born between 1770 and 1819, and thus would have reached adulthood by 1840 at the latest.[21] A substantial majority, in other words, of the most prominent and influential men *throughout the nineteenth century* were born and raised, read their texts and learned their manners, before Queen Victoria's accession. It is never easy to sort out the intellectual and social origins of the ideas and assumptions which guide human behaviour; but however important it is to take account of the new ideas that were indubitably making their influence felt by the middle decades of the nineteenth century, it is no less so to acknowledge the bedrock of intellectual and social assumptions which contemporaries used to construct and interpret their world. Traditional assumptions about the place of the professional gentleman in society, his role and prerogatives, could still claim allegiance in the 1860s and 1870s, and even beyond, from those to whom it was 'bred in the bone.'

Invoking the potent influence of the Georgian frame of mind, nonetheless, does not by itself explain the precise timing of the legislation we are concerned with here. Or to put it another way, why is the legislation bunched, as it is, between 1868 and 1872? We have little to offer by way of explanation except speculation. We are not alone in this; other historians have described the remarkable record of institution building during the J.S. Macdonald years but have also failed to explain why it occurred at that particular juncture in our history. One plausible interpretation is that issues long deferred by the political stalemates of the pre-Confederation period, and the focus on nation building which preoccupied the politicians in the mid-1860s, finally found their way onto the political agenda after 1867. Certainly this matches the record in education, where Ryerson's general attempts to reorganize the school system between 1860 and 1866 were repeatedly derailed by the exigencies of politics. Equally, occupational ambitions may have been put on hold pending critical decisions about the locus of power. At least some leading doctors and druggists, for example, initially saw their future in pan-Canadian organizations legitimized by the Dominion government, and only in the years immediately following Confederation did it become clear that the provinces had unqualified jurisdiction in the areas that affected them. Yet another plausible explanation is that Confederation itself – and the creation of the new province of Ontario with it – unleashed a burst of energy directed at completing the social and economic infrastructure which had gradually been taking shape in Upper Canada. The Macdonald years, as Bruce Hodgins and J.M.S. Careless have both suggested, were not so much the beginning of Ontario's history as the culmination of Upper Canada's.[22] Obviously these three hypotheses overlap, but together they may help to explain why so much new legislation affecting the professions was put in place between 1868 and 1872.

Whatever the exact explanation, dentists and druggists, and one might even add doctors, had the great good fortune to organize themselves and press for protective legislation at the very moment in the second half of the nineteenth century when politicians and the press were most receptive to it. To use some modern jargon, a 'window of opportunity' opened during the late 1860s and early 1870s which allowed doctors and lawyers to consolidate their position, and dentists and druggists to acquire the social structure commonly associated with professional status – self-governing colleges and control over the licence to practise. Others followed them, seeking the same privileges; but as the political culture of Ontario began to change in the last quarter of the century, most would not be so fortunate.

MUCH OF THE HISTORIOGRAPHY of the professions in Canada, as elsewhere, has been driven by models of 'professionalization' which posit schematic 'stages' of progress, and measure the latter on a scale graduated by a set of predetermined traits. Other accounts construct explict or implicit conspiracies against the public interest: restrictive legislation is wrested from the public terrain, codes of ethics are promulgated, professionals close ranks and, largely through internal momentum, go from strength to strength.[23] Both versions of the story have, at best, all the faults of Whiggism, and at worst, amount to little more than scorecard history. Having established the rules of the game beforehand, one totes up fifty or a hundred years of legislation, and declares a winner: doctors (or lawyers or dentists) 10, laity or competitors, 0. Alternatively, one arrives at a scorecard for occupations themselves: some develop into 'real' professions; others wind up lower down the scale as 'semi-professional' pretenders, or outright rejects.

Such approaches simply overlook the nature of a particular historical milieu or the contingencies of social change. They conflate sources of strength (or weakness) over time, conveniently ignoring the fact that resources at the command of one generation may not be available to another. They take no account of the fragility of new organizations, the potential for internal fissures which turn into irreparable ruptures, the competing interests thrown up within an occupation by new forms of work or ways of doing it, the sheer strength of potential predators intent on capturing a hitherto secure area of work. Professions are not Platonic archetypes. Dentists and druggists had no more natural right to the title 'learned profession' than a dozen or more other skilled trades animated by the protective impulse during the second half of the nineteenth century. Historical contingencies, nevertheless, pushed them in that direction and provided an opportunity which, under the right circumstances, might be exploited still further. A legal monopoly alone, on the other hand, could not by itself guarantee the future of an occupation. The surveyor-engineers were the only group among many late nineteenth-century supplicants to gain a monopoly over practice. Yet, in the end, the members of the Association of Ontario Land Surveyors did not become 'the Civil Engineers of Ontario.' It remained to others to create the modern profession of engineering in the province, and along different lines than those envisaged by either Alan Macdougall or the promoters of the surveyors act of 1892.[24]

In one of the best recent books on the modern professions, the American sociologist Andrew Abbott has argued persuasively that control over an area of work is neither inevitable nor immutable.[25] It is won or lost in recurring jurisdictional battles waged in the workplace and the political arena, and in neither do the professions have unassailable strategic advantages. The outcome can also be determined by contingencies wholly outside their control, by the sudden appearance of a new technology, the reorganization of economic life, or a major shift in cultural values. In the last quarter of the nineteenth century, doctors, for example, didn't know they were on the road to becoming what some modern scholars define as a 'sovereign profession.' Indeed, what strikes us most about the period is the level of insecurity about that future in the face of forces they seemed unable to control or even to contain. Nor could those theologians busy reconciling their evangelical faith with the new higher criticism or evolutionary theory anticipate the consequences of their endeavours, or foresee the larger forces that would, over the long term at least, begin to marginalize them. And who, it might be added, last heard of the Chartered Stenographic Reporters?

WITH ALL THAT SAID, we take leave of our professional men, still at the edge of a new century, clinging to their aspirations and fretting over their anxieties. They had none of the hindsight available to the historian a century later and no more ability than we to predict the future. If there were clergymen whose faith had been shaken by the higher criticism or the implications of the new sciences, there were others who could reassure ministry and laity alike that the gospel was not in conflict with modernity. If there were pockets of agnosticism or atheism here and there among disaffected intellectuals, the churches could still attract large numbers of the faithful. Torontonians in the 1890s could sustain (admittedly with varying degrees of success) 102 churches,[26] and the debate about the 'decline' of Methodism was not so much about a loss of adherents as about its failure to grow at the substantial rate of previous decades. Some ministers may have taken umbrage at the tone of the *Mail*'s 'popular preacher contest,' but the mere fact that it could occupy the pages of a major daily newspaper is telling in itself. And so is the fact that in 1895 a high-toned journal like *The Week* could run a less sensational series of in-depth portraits of Toronto's prominent ministers.[27] Even if some battles had been lost, and some ground given up to others, clergymen remained among the best-educated of professional men, and exercised a degree of influence in their communities that few others could command.

The laity, it is true, had asserted their own authority in church affairs, and could occasionally be vociferous critics of clerical pretensions. But that was true in the case of other professional men as well. Though lawyers might occupy the high ground of the courts, many of them faced not only the 'law grangers' but those perfectly willing to hire the latter to transact their legal business. Dentists could make a living by manufacturing and selling plates but could not convince people to invest in restorative work. Doctors had already succeeded in constructing a substantial market in the minds of many Ontarians. Midwifery largely belonged to them, and surgery exclusively so. In medical therapeutics, however, the battle had hardly begun. And in the 1890s at least, its outcome remained uncertain. Historians justly celebrate the great achievements of late nineteenth-century medical science, but they are inclined to overlook the equally spectacular failures or miscues of the era, which drew as much contemporary attention and fed the extant reservoirs of scepticism.[28] Already, there were forces at work which would, over the long haul, begin to sustain the aspirations of some groups of professional men at least, and lend increasing legitimacy to their claims to both expertise and greater cultural authority. But at century's close the laity itself reserved its right to choose alternatives and to judge the efficacy of the advice of experts. An 'uninstructed' public remained the most formidable challenge that confronted professional men as they sought to extend, or even consolidate, their place in Ontario society.

But that was not the only impediment. In the countryside, good roads and easy access to medical care would not be achieved until the prosperity and the great road-paving programs of the 1950s and 1960s. Neither doctors nor dentists would become rich from their work until the era of prepaid insurance and medicare. Though the revolution in bacteriology and virology had begun in the late nineteenth century, it would not add much to the therapeutic arsenal before the 1930s and 1940s. Oral sepsis was hardly an issue among dentists until after 1910, and those prescient dentists who advocated a campaign of public education about preventive and restorative work would not see much success in their own lifetimes: as late as the early 1950s, it was estimated that the number of people who sought annual dental care in Ontario ranged from a high of 40 per cent to a low of 20 per cent.[29] Nor did any of the professions make great breakthroughs in the political arena during the decades immediately following the turn of the century. Nothing followed from the campaign to do something about lay conveyancing; and though the Royal College of Dental Surgeons finally gained powers over internal discipline in 1912, advertising was still a source of embarrassment far into the 1920s.[30]

Some years ago, G.P. de T. Glazebrook remarked that, in many respects, the twentieth century did not begin in Ontario until 1945. A perceptive insight, we think, but one that can also be stood on its head: in some respects, it began in the 1870s and 1880s. There were, for example, significant continuities (there were, of course, discontinuities as well) between the medical practice of James Langstaff and that of the general practitioner in the first four decades of the twentieth century described by S.E.D. Shortt. The changes that had taken place in dentistry during the century after 1850 were substantial but equally startling to those who viewed them from either 1885 or 1950.[31] If in the 1890s things looked bleak for medical men, so indeed they had in the 1850s and would again in the 1930s. During the 1860s and 1870s especially, modern Ontario's professionals had begun to consolidate their place in society, and forces had been set in motion which would sustain as well as contain their aspirations far into the twentieth century. A profound change in their circumstances would have to await the explosion of economic change, personal wealth, scientific innovation, and government intervention that would follow the Second World War.

Appendix: Procedures and Sources for Quantitative Analysis

A. The Dictionary of Canadian Biography

While we have used the *Dictionary of Canadian Biography* (*DCB*) extensively in consulting individual biographies, we have also used it in two other ways, both of which involved 'collective biography.' The *DCB* is less than a perfect source for such a project. The criteria for selection are variable and not designed to produce a 'representative' group, if that were possible, even of 'notables.' Among professionals, for example, lawyers are substantially overrepresented and doctors the reverse – presumably because so many lawyers played some role in the province's or nation's political history, however small.

In mining the *DCB* for an exercise in collective biography, in any case, we first created a file from the entries in volumes 5 to 12 (1801 to 1900 by date of death) on all professionals who lived in Ontario. (Volume 13, 1901–1910, was not yet available when this book was completed.) The file consists almost entirely of the names of lawyers, doctors, clergymen, engineers, architects, and surveyors. It does *not* include the names of educators or of journalists. One purpose of the exercise was to ascertain the age cohorts of influential professionals throughout the nineteenth century. The 'Georgian' roots of the culture of nineteenth-century Ontario can be assessed in an examination of table 1.

Another way in which we have used the *DCB* for collective biography, primarily in chapter 9, is to examine birthplace and father's occupation for lawyers, doctors, and clergymen. Birthplace is very well documented, with nearly all entries providing this information, and thus presents no serious difficulties. There are, however, several problems with establishing the occupations of fathers. First, the percentage of

TABLE 1
Birth Dates of Ontario Professionals in the *DCB*

	Number					
	Clergy					Engineers, architects,
Date of Birth	CE	Presb	WM	Lawyers	Doctors	surveyors
Before 1770	2	5	1	7	4	8
1770–1819	36	28	36	67	35	46
1820–9	2	3	—	15	7	12
Others	4	2	2	28	7	13
Subtotal	44	38	42	—	—	—
Total		148		117	53	79
	Percentage of occupation					
Percentage born 1770–1819	82	74	86	57	66	58
Percentage born 1770–1829	86	82	93	70	79	73

NOTE: CE=Church of England/Anglican; Presb=Presbyterian/Church of Scotland/Free Church; WM=Wesleyan Methodist.
SOURCE: *DCB*, vols. 5–12

unknown cases corresponds exactly to how 'Canadianized' each of the three professions was. For example, lawyers' fathers are the best known (with only 30 per cent of cases missing information on their occupations), while occupational information is omitted most often for the fathers of clergymen (56 per cent of cases). We know most about lawyers' parents precisely because they were much more often born or at least settled in Upper Canada or some other part of North America themselves, whereas clergymen's fathers were more often likely to be residents in the old world and their records were therefore less accessible to the biographers of the sons. In using the occupation of a father as a surrogate for social standing, therefore, we are most limited in what we know about the clergy, and least limited for lawyers.

Second, even when a biography gives the father's occupation, there are problems with classification. Should, for example, army surgeons be classed as military officers or as doctors? We have generally classified them as the former but in one or two cases have included them in the category of doctors. Moreover, though some occupational designations indicate social standing and/or prosperity as well – for example, 'judge' or 'carriage manufacturer' – others, like 'farmer' or 'merchant,' tell us nothing about the prosperity of the father. Many biographers provide clues by the use of such phrases as 'prosperous' and 'well off.' But generally in attempting to attribute status to the occupation, we have simply followed Michael Katz's socio-economic scheme whereby occupational designations are ranked in social categories.[1]

Still, there are a large number of unknowns because often a father's occupation is either missing or too vague to classify. A significant minority of fathers were British residents whose sons emigrated as young adults, though even here the nature of the son's educational qualifications obtained in Britain indicates that their fathers were men of means. We have nonetheless left such cases among the unknowns.

B. Lawyers, Doctors, and Dentists: Numbers and Dispersal

1. Numbers

One source for our analysis of the number of lawyers, doctors, and dentists in Ontario between 1851 and 1921, and for other occupational groups as well as for the total population and workforce of the province, is the printed *Census of Canada*, 1851/2–1921. The census data allow us to compare the rate of increase between different occupations and with the growth of the population generally. The figures, however, need to be treated as approximate only. For example, the 1861 census does not include the number of doctors in some cities, so the exact rate of increase must be estimated. On the manuscript census some people used the title (or were called by the enumerator) 'conveyancer,' which was almost always the designation for a non-lawyer; but the same persons were given the designation 'lawyer' on the assessment rolls of the municipality, and we suspect that they may have been included in the category 'lawyer' by the compilers of the printed census. Certainly the printed census totals for lawyers are invariably larger than the corresponding Law Lists, which suggests that conveyancers are included in the census figures. The same problem arises with other occupations: a 'medical electrician' on the census, for example, might or might not be a registered physician. The percentages represented by the rates of growth, then, and not the numbers themselves, are the main point of table 2, and this table, using census data, should be read in conjunction with table 3, using data from the professional registers.

TABLE 2
Selected Occupations, Ontario, 1851–1911: Numbers and Rate of Increase by Decade

	1851	1861		1871		1881		1891		1901[a]		1911[b]	
	No.	No.	% incr.[c]	No.	% incr.	No.	% incr.	No.	% incr.	No.	% incr.	No.	% incr.
Doctors	382	886	132	1,565	77	1,778	14	2,266	27		—	3,053	—
Lawyers	302	632	109	1,152[d]	82	1,394[e]	21	1,886	35		—	1,678	—
Dentists	36	114	217	230	102	365	57	465	27		—	1,127	—
Clergy	963	1,716	83	2,211	29	2,876	30	3,283	14		—	3,975[f]	—
Common-school teachers[g]													
Male	2,541	3,031	19	2,641	13	3,362	27	2,621	22	2,375	-9	1,409	41
Female	847	1,305	54	2,665	104	3,660	37	5,076	39	6,301	24	7,940	26
Total	3,388	4,336	28	5,306	22	6,548	23	7,697	18	8,676	13	9,349	8
Grammar-/high-school teachers	—[h]			123		174	42	333	91	484	45	579	20	898	55
Druggists/chemists/pharmacists	108	355	228	811	128	1,275	57	1,276[j]	0	—	—	218[i] 1,035[k]	—
Ontario population	952,004	1,396,091	46	1,620,851	16	1,926,922	19	2,114,321	10	2,182,947	3	2,527,292	16
Ontario workforce	245,120	339,432	38	463,424	37	630,762	36	750,484	19	779,316	4	991,013	27

a No totals available for occupations marked with a dash. Rates of increase from 1891 to 1901 cannot be calculated for them.
b For occupations missing 1901 figures, rates of increase for 1901–11 cannot be calculated.
c Rate of increase
d 'advocates and judges'
e 'lawyers and judges'
f Including Salvation Army
g Figures are drawn from Ontario Department of Education *Annual Reports* for all teachers.
h The first grammar-school returns in the *Annual Reports* date from 1855.
i Continuation school
j 'apothecaries, pharmacists and dealers in drugs and chemicals'
k 'merchant and dealers, drugs and perfumes'

SOURCES: *Census of Canada*, 1851–1911, for all figures except teachers; the numbers of teachers are taken from the *Annual Reports*, Ontario Department of Education. No figures for specific occupational categories are recorded in the printed 1901 census.

TABLE 3
Ontario Doctors and Lawyers, 1870–1903: Numbers and Rates of Increase, from Professional Registers

	1872[a]		1882[b]		1892[b]		1903[b]	
	No.		No.	% incr.[c]	No.	% incr.	No.	% incr.
Doctors	1,271		1,658	30	2,330	41	2,452	5
	1870		1881		1891		1901	
	No.[d]	% incr.	No.[e]	% incr.	No.[e]	% incr.	No.[e]	% incr.
Lawyers	875	–	1,201	37	1,497	25	1,770	18

a Ontario residents
b Ontario residents (excluding 'unknown' and those with non-Ontario residences)
c Rate of increase
d Number cited in Elizabeth Bloomfield, 'Lawyers as Members of Urban Business Elites in Southern Ontario, 1860 to 1920,' in *Beyond the Law: Lawyers and Business in Canada, 1830 to 1930*, ed. Carol Wilton (Toronto: The Osgoode Society 1990), 116. Our own count from the 1870 Law List results in a figure of 893, which gives a slightly lower rate of increase of 34 per cent over the following decade.
e Numbers cited in Curtis J. Cole, '"A Learned and Honorable Body": The Professionalization of the Ontario Bar, 1867–1929' (PhD diss., University of Western Ontario 1987), 67

SOURCES: *Ontario Medical Registers* and *(Ontario) Law Lists*

The printed census figures are defective in another respect. In 1891 occupational totals alone are given for each province, so that we can use the census only for provincial trends. And in 1901 even this provincial information is entirely missing: occupations have been collapsed into categories, like 'professional,' whose content we have no way of knowing. Thus table 2 has a gap for most entries of twenty years between 1891 and 1911; although ratios can be calculated, as in table 4, it is impossible to give comparable rates of increase for those two decades.

It therefore becomes all the more important to supplement the census information with data drawn from other sources (see table 3). The *Ontario Medical Registers* for 1872, 1882, 1892, and 1903 have yielded a rich store of data on doctors' names and places of residence. For lawyers, we have used the Law Lists, which give the designation 'barrister' or 'solicitor' in the middle decades of the nineteenth century, as well as name and residence in all of them, as follows: J. Rordans, *The Upper*

TABLE 4
Doctors, Lawyers, and Dentists: Ratios to Ontario Population, 1851 to 1911

	1851	1861	1871	1881	1891	1901	1911
Doctors	1:2,492	1:1,576	1:1,275	1:1,162	1:907	1:890	1:828
Lawyers	1:3,152	1:2,209	1:1,852	1:1,604	1:1,412	1:1,233	1:1,506
Dentists	1:26,445	1:12,246	1:7,047	1:5,279	1:4,547	–[a]	1:2,242

a No figures are available.
SOURCES: *Census of Canada*, 1851–1911, and professional registers

Canada Law Directory for 1858; J. Rordans, *The Ontario Law List and Solicitors' Agency Book*, 1870; J. Rordans, *The Ontario Law List and Solicitors' Agency Book*, 1882; E.R. Hardy, ed., *The Canadian Law List, 1891*; Hardy's *Canadian Law List 1900*. As well, we have drawn on the data recorded and analysed from the Law Lists by Elizabeth Bloomfield in 'Lawyers as Members of Urban Business Elites in Southern Ontario, 1860 to 1920,' in *Beyond the Law: Lawyers and Business in Canada, 1830 to 1930*, ed. Carol Wilton (Toronto: The Osgoode Society 1990), 114–20; and Curtis J. Cole, '"A Learned and Honorable Body": The Professionalization of the Ontario Bar, 1867–1929' (PhD diss., University of Western Ontario 1987), especially 67–73 and Appendix A. We have also reworked some of the data in the Cole thesis. The figures in each of these three analyses (Bloomfield, Cole, and our own), though taken from the same sources, are sometimes apparently inconsistent. For example, Bloomfield lists 875 lawyers in the 1870 Law List, while we arrive at a figure of 893. Cole records all lawyers in Brant County from 1881 to 1921 as living in Brantford and Paris, though we have traced them in three other places in the county in 1882. Nor do our totals and record of dispersal agree with Cole's for Perth County. However, though we may differ slightly in our numerical listings, the percentages and overall trends of increase or decrease remain much the same in all three analyses. Thus, with these discrepancies in mind, we can draw on all three where appropriate.

The professional registers have their own defects, however. For medicine they do not even begin until 1867. For the number of licensed doctors in 1851, see the *Upper Canada Journal*, Prospectus, 2 Apr. 1851, and *Christian Guardian*, 2 Jul. 1851. Our estimates of the number of doctors before the 1860s are also based on lists of licentiates published in the *British American Journal of Medical ... Science* 3 (1847), 247–50, 314; and *British American Journal* 2 (1861), 44–5. Some of the *Medical Registers* are incomplete. The 1867 and even the 1872 registers are probably too early to record the full number of doctors in the province, as it was not until perhaps the mid-1870s that an efficient and accepted system of registration was established; and the 1892 register probably reflects a high level of alienation and non-registration, as many doctors refused to pay the annual levy to the College. As well, for the purpose of getting a rough estimate of the practitioner/population ratio in table 4, we have matched the registers between 1870 and 1903 for lawyers and doctors to the nearest census year; this obviously gives an approximate figure in some cases. On both Law Lists and *Medical Registers*, there are some practitioners whose addresses were unknown; it is possible that they may have been practising in the province and thus should have been included in our count. It is more likely, however, that they had emigrated (or died) and the College or Law Society was unaware of this.

2. Dispersal of Lawyers and Doctors Throughout the Province

The professional registers have been crucial to mapping the diaspora of lawyers and doctors from the main urban centres in the mid-nineteenth century to the nooks and crannies of the countryside by late in the century. We have used Bloomfield's analysis to establish the parameters of this dispersal for lawyers. However, we have also used the Law Lists to analyse the pattern for two counties, Brant and Perth, from 1858 to 1900. For the same two counties, we used the *Medical Registers* to gauge the spread of doctors through the countryside from 1872 to 1907. For both counties, we have used standard nineteenth-century maps (for Brant County, from the *Brant County Historical Atlas*, published in 1875; for Perth County, from the *Perth County Historical Atlas*, 1879) for *every* year listed; this standardization eliminates the possibility of numbers being affected by changes in the county's boundaries. As well, these maps often identify small hamlets that have since disappeared, where in the late nineteenth century a doctor or lawyer might still make a living.

C. Assessment Data

There are chiefly three sets of assessment records which we used in establishing the wealth of professionals. First, in researching our account of secondary education in nineteenth-century Ontario, we gathered a large amount of quantitative data for five Ontario towns in 1861. This project is described in some detail, which we will not recapitulate here, in chapter 6 of our *Inventing Secondary Education: The Rise of the High School in Nineteenth-Century Ontario* (Montreal and Kingston: McGill-Queen's University Press 1990). But essentially we collected the census and assessment records for all household heads who had children aged ten to twenty in their households in the five communities, and for the entire population in Brantford, and analysed the data in a number of ways, including the distribution of occupations and wealth.

The second set of records on wealth consists of the Brantford assessment rolls for the census years 1871 to 1891. And the third consists of the lists of the personal property and income of various occupational groups in Toronto, published in the *Globe* in the summer of 1886, and taken from the assessment rolls for that city.

1. General Problems

There are several problems associated with nineteenth-century municipal assessment data which create great difficulties in interpreting them. In one way or another, the data are very incomplete. The assessment was also biased towards the reporting of real estate rather than personal income or property. We will not attempt to review all of the problems here, though the interested reader will find a perceptive and detailed analysis in the work of Gordon Darroch. As he warns, the researcher (and reader) must be aware of the limits of the data and guard against 'the tendency to interpret quantitative values ... as if they are valid and precise indicators of actual values. The wise course is to consider the distributions and the values ... as estimates of, or better still, as judgements about, the actual values. At the same time, I doubt that these data are more demanding of careful interpretation than many other historical sources: on the contrary, their biases are perhaps more systematic and readily detected.'[2]

Keeping in mind that general warning, we will only point to some of the issues particularly relevant to the study of professional wealth, among which, for professionals, exemptions and underreporting are the more important. There was a long list of exemptions from municipal taxation throughout the nineteenth century. Personal property and annual income under a minimum amount were untaxed ($100 and $200 respectively in 1861, rising to $400 from any source, or $700 earnings, by 1891). In 1871 only the amount of personal property and income over the limit was assessed; in 1881 the whole amount, if enough to go over the limit, was supposed to be liable to taxation, but many in this category were thought to continue claiming exemptions for the amount up to the minimum.[3] Clerical incomes were exempt from taxation as follows: in 1861 up to $1,200, and in 1871 and 1881 up to $1,000. The Revised Statutes of 1877 state that the exemption applied to the 'stipend or salary of any clergyman or minister while in actual connection with the church, and doing duty as such clergyman or minister,' up to $1,000, and the parsonage and land, to $2,000. The exemption was further clarified in 1885 by a judicial decision that it applied to all ministers regularly connected with churches, to professors in theological institutions, and to superannuated ministers (but not, for example, to editors of religious papers).[4] The clerical income exemption was finally removed in 1890, and the 1891 assessment reflects this by a sharp increase in clerical assessments.[5]

Given these various exemptions, some professionals were not assessed at all. Until 1891 the clergy as a group had noticeably fewer assessments than did other occupational categories. The young and the poor (frequently, but not always, the same thing) very often escaped assessment because they could shelter under the minimum level. This was also true of the entire population: for example, 944 persons in Brantford in 1861 were assessed for real and personal property (they might have had either, and the majority were in fact assessed on their real property, either as freeholders or tenants); but there were some 1,500 adult males in the city, most of whom presumably were earning wages. As well, some professional men may have been too mobile to be caught by the city assessor. This may have been true, for example, of the itinerant Methodist ministry, who conceivably might have had property in some other municipality. Or to cite another case, in 1861 and 1871 a number of young lawyers in the Brantford city census were boarders, and therefore not assessed. However, we do have assessment data for a high percentage of both doctors and lawyers in all years; simply because so many were assessed, this reinforces the point that these professional men were better off than the average wage-earner. It also means that we can feel reasonably confident that the data are representative for the occupation.

The accuracy of income and personal-property records presents another problem. First, there were loopholes in the law itself. For example, in 1861 income was reported in ranked categories: if it fell between a higher and a lower limit, it was reported as the lowest point of that category. Thus, if it fell anywhere between $100 and $200, it was set down as $100. The higher the amount, the greater the spread in the category: for example, between $1,000 and $2,000, it was reported as $1,000. Obviously this means that the true figure in many cases could have been much higher.

Second, income and personal property in all years was chronically underreported. Suspiciously round figures are commonly given: $400, $1,000, and so on. More serious is the fact that much income escaped assessment because it was simply not reported, or reported as much less than the true figure. Those who were self-employed were able to take advantage of assessors' neglect, incompetence, or simply lack of knowledge, in this respect, more easily than those receiving salaries or wages; thus, among professional men, doctors and lawyers could hide much of their wealth if they were so inclined. In Brantford lawyers always had more assessed wealth in the form of real estate than doctors, and a lower proportion of it in the form of income. Lawyers were less likely to report personal property as well (which included money, notes, goods, shares, etc.). But both groups were able to underreport income and personal property, which means that probably both had more total wealth than appeared on the assessment rolls. This contention, at least, lay at the heart of a muckraking attack by the *Globe* during the summer of 1886 on the underreporting of income and personal property, and the consequent disproportionate weight of assessment on real estate, in the Toronto rolls.[6] The newspaper's exposé provides a cautionary reminder about the limits of these data. Nevertheless, despite all the problems, we believe that the assessment figures can be used, with due regard to their built-in biases, to establish relative, if not precise, rankings within and between occupations. In Darroch's words, 'assessment evidence is best understood as a means of approximating the relative standards of accommodation and daily living of families, rather than as estimates of the amount of wealth they hold.'[7]

2. The Brantford Assessment Records

The database for Brantford includes the census records for the entire population from 1851 to 1881, and for professionals in 1891. We have also collected complete assessment records for the town's population in 1861, and for professionals only in 1871, 1881, and 1891. (The 1851 assessment data were too incomplete to use.) For 1861, then, we have been able to generate our own wealth distribution based on these assessment records, and can establish an individual's standing by percentile ranks. This in turn enabled us to divide household heads into three groups, consisting of those who were very wealthy, those who were 'middling,' and those who were poor. For 1861 the details of these distributions can be found in chapter 6 of *Inventing Secondary Education*. For 1871 to 1891, we rely on municipal returns (published in the Sessional Papers of the Ontario *Legislative Journals*) to provide figures for the average assessment of ratepayers in those years; we can then rate professionals according to whether they were above or below (or roughly equal to) this average, but cannot tell what percentile they fell into. However, comparisons of standing within an occupation are not affected by this lack of precision, so that we can get an idea of the range of assessed wealth in each professional occupation, in each of the years examined.

D. Relative Incomes: Professional Men and Others

As we suggest in chapter 12, there is some scattered evidence that the cries of anguish over inadequate incomes, voiced most loudly by the clergy but perhaps shared by other professionals as well, were based as much in a *perception* of relative decline as in its reality. The standard of living in late nineteenth-century Ontario has been examined by several authors, who agree that, while deep inequalities in the distribution of wealth remained firmly in place throughout the period, those decades also witnessed social and economic upheavals which had far-reaching effects on every level of society, and which threw up new opportunities for some, as well as the possibility of social declension for others. Most of the commentary focuses on working-class earnings and living costs. Ian Drummond suggests that, though real earnings of Ontario industrial workers rose throughout the last decades of the century, and many were 'nowhere near the poverty line,' others, especially householders, were merely 'not comfortable.'[8] In a recent article Rosemary and David Gagan suggest that, in late nineteenth-century Ontario, 'working-class families, through their members' combined diligence, appear to have been able to accumulate modest savings, to have enjoyed an increase in the purchasing power of their collective wages relative to the basic cost of living and even to have acquired tangible wealth in the form of rateable real or personal property.'[9] Compared with the incomes of our professionals, working-class incomes certainly remained much lower, but they appear to have increased somewhat through the 1880s. Moreover, prices of some basic commodities seem to have declined, so that a higher standard of living was perhaps accessible for more people.[10]

The evidence on incomes generally is very thin and unsystematic. On working-class incomes in the nineteenth century, we offer the following indicative findings which other historians have made. Around mid-century, according to Douglas McCalla, annual artisan incomes may have ranged from perhaps £40 to £60 ($160 to $240) or more.[11] Michael Piva calculates that the average salary of unskilled workers in the civil service of the Province of Canada in 1861 was $434.[12] Paul Craven and Tom Traves estimate that most railway workers on the Great Western and the Grand Trunk in the mid-1850s were paid for a day's labour something like $1.00–$2.50, and some trades received monthly wages of between $30 and $60.[13] By the 1870s, Gordon Darroch estimates, skilled labourers or artisans might have earned $700 (but probably much less) and common labourers perhaps $250 if fully employed.[14] Rosemary and David Gagan calculate the average wage to have been $450 in 1889 for Canadian workers in various trades, though they stress that real income for half the workers was higher as a result of overtime.[15] They also suggest that average annual wages generally improved or remained the same in the 1880s; if they did not improve vastly, periods of declining prices would still have enabled workers to consume, and save, more.

White-collar occupations also seem to have experienced wage increases. For example, station and freight agents on the Grand Trunk in 1856 made salaries of £25 to £350 ($100 to $1400); clerks on the Great Western, between £50 and £150 ($200 to $600).[16] The average salary of clerks in the civil service in 1861 was $966, compared with $1,613 for 'professionals' (architects, engineers, and surveyors).[17] These figures for clerks undoubtedly reflect the presence at mid-century of male, highly skilled clerks; by 1901 the average wage of male clerical workers was $496, of female clerical workers, $264.[18] Accountants in Brantford in 1891 were assessed on taxable incomes ranging from $400 to $1,500; according to the Gagans, in 1889 accountants in the industrial sector in Ontario averaged $665 a year.[19]

Or to take another occupational group, teachers. High-school teachers had always been a highly educated group compared with their peers, and socially a cut above their elementary-school colleagues; and they always reaped financial rewards commensurate with that position. The headmasters of the high schools in five southwestern Ontario towns, for example, earned in 1885 between $1,200 and $1,500 a year, and their male assistants, between $1,100 and $400. The average wage of other high-school teachers was $740. By comparison, public-school teachers earned much less and were more on a par with other white-collar workers. In 1880 male teachers in city public schools were paid an average of $743, and in towns and rural areas, much less. Women public-school teachers in the cities earned only $324 on the average, and again much less elsewhere.[20]

In 1881 the average amount of assessed income and personal property for lawyers in Brantford was $1,140, and for doctors, $1,145. In other words, their assessed incomes were not far off the averages recorded for other occupations (though caution must be exercised because of the possibility of underreporting of assessed income – see section C above). And as we have argued in the text, the incomes earned by doctors, lawyers, and clergymen during the second half of the nineteenth century spanned a wide range which included some very small amounts as well as some very high rates of remuneration. It would thus appear that those professional men at the low end of the income scale for their occupation could well have been making not much more than clerks or other white-collar workers, or even skilled artisans. Small wonder that the rank and file of professional men in these three occupations, the struggling and moderately successful, the young men starting careers or the misfits and failures eking out a living, might have been threatened by this fact.

Notes

Abbreviations

PERIODICALS

BAJ	*British American Journal*
BAJMPS	*British American Journal of Medical and Physical Science;* continued by *British American Medical and Physical Journal*
BHM	*Bulletin of the History of Medicine*
CAB	*Canadian Architect and Builder*
CBMH	*Canadian Bulletin of Medical History*
Cdn Chman	*Canadian Churchman* (successor to *Dominion Churchman*). There was also a short-lived Anglican journal in the 1860s titled *Canadian Churchman*. It is cited in full in the notes.
CEM	*Canada Educational Monthly*
CG	*Christian Guardian*
CJDS	*Canada Journal of Dental Science*
CJMS	*Canadian Journal of Medical Science* (continued as *Canadian Practitioner*)
CLJ	*Canada Law Journal*
CMJ	*Canada Medical Journal*
CMJMR	*Canada Medical Journal and Monthly Record*
CP	*Canadian Practitioner*
DC	*Dominion Churchman* (continued as *Canadian Churchman*)
DDJ	*Dominion Dental Journal*
DMJ	*Dominion Medical Journal*
DMM	*Dominion Medical Monthly*
EC	*Evangelical Churchman*
EMR	*Ecclesiastical and Missionary Record*
JCCHS	*Journal of the Canadian Church Historical Society*

JEdUC	Journal of Education for Upper Canada
JHM	Journal of the History of Medicine
Lancet	Canada Lancet
OMJ	Ontario Medical Journal
QCJ	Queen's College Journal
UCJ	Upper Canada Journal of Medical, Surgical, and Physical Science
UCLJ	Upper Canada Law Journal

OTHER

AO	Archives of Ontario
AR	Annual Report of the Normal, Model, Grammar, and Common Schools in Upper Canada (to 1875); Report of the Minister of Education (Ontario) (after 1875)
DCB	Dictionary of Canadian Biography
DHE	J.G. Hodgins, ed., Documentary History of Education in Upper Canada, 28 vols. (Toronto 1894–1910)
JLAC	Journals, Legislative Assembly of Canada
JLAO	Journals, Legislative Assembly of Ontario
JLAUC	Journals, Legislative Assembly, Upper Canada
JLCUC	Journals, Legislative Council, Upper Canada
Legislative Debates	E. Nish (Gibbs), ed., Debates of the Legislative Assembly of United Canada, 1841–1856, 13 vols. (Montreal: Les Presses de l'École des Hautes Études Commerciales 1970–88)
LSUCA	Law Society of Upper Canada Archives
MTRL	Metropolitan Toronto Reference Library
NAC	National Archives of Canada
OTA Proceedings	Proceedings of the Ontario Teachers' Association
Parliamentary Debates	[Canadian Library Association] Parliamentary Debates
PRO	Public Record Office (England)
Proceedings, AOLS	Proceedings of the Association of Public Land Surveyors of Ontario/Association of Ontario Land Surveyors
QUA	Queen's University Archives
Transactions, CSCE	Transactions of the Canadian Society of Civil Engineers
UCA	United Church Archives
UWORC	University of Western Ontario Regional Collection

Toronto Academy of Medicine Archives: After we had completed our research, the building housing the Toronto Academy of Medicine was sold and its Museum and Archive Collection was sent to the Toronto General Hospital, where it is now stored. We have documented all references to this collection as it was arranged in the Academy Archives.

PREFACE

1 *Oxford English Dictionary*, 'Profession'
2 There are a number of good introductions to this literature which include, as well, an analysis of the problems embedded in it. Among the best is Eliot Freidson, 'The Theory of the Professions: State of the Art,' in *The Sociology of the Professions: Lawyers, Doctors and Others*, ed. Robert Dingwall and Philip Lewis (London: Macmillan 1983), 19–37. See also a revised version of this paper in Freidson's *Professional Powers: A Study of the Institutionalization of Formal Knowledge* (Chicago: University of Chicago Press 1986), ch. 2. A more recent survey and critique is Andrew Abbott, *The System of Professions: An Essay on the Division of Expert Labor* (Chicago: University of Chicago Press 1988), ch. 1.
3 See Daniel Duman, 'A Social and Occupational Analysis of the English Judiciary: 1770–1790 and 1855–1875,' *American Journal of Legal History* 17 (1973), 354. The situation in the United States was similar. See E. Lee Shepard, 'Lawyers Look at Themselves: Professional Consciousness and the Virginia Bar, 1770–1850,' *American Journal of Legal History* 25 (1981), 1–23.
4 See Raymond Cocks, *Foundations of the Modern Bar* (London: Sweet and Maxwell 1983), ch. 8.
5 G.L. Geison, 'Introduction,' in *Professions and Professional Ideologies in America*, ed. G.L. Geison (Chapel Hill: University of North Carolina Press 1983), 6. For a similar argument see Wilfrid Prest, ed., *The Professions in Early Modern England* (London: Croom Helm 1987), ch. 1; and Laurence Veysey, 'The Plural Organized World of the Humanities,' in *The Organization of Knowledge in Modern America, 1860–1920*, ed. Alexander Oleson and John Voss (Baltimore, MD: Johns Hopkins University Press 1979), 58. A book that came to hand too late to exercise a direct influence on our own work but which we believe will have a major impact on the understanding of the changing meaning of 'profession' is Bruce A. Kimball, *The 'True Professional Ideal' in America: A History* (Cambridge, MA: Blackwell 1992). For his own critique of the 'presentist' bias in nearly all the extant scholarship, see his concluding chapter, 301ff.
6 See Freidson, 'The Theory of the Professions,' 31–6.

CHAPTER 1 *Images and Transcripts*

1 Kingston Gazette, 30 Oct. 1810
2 *Kingston Chronicle*, 4 Feb. 1825. Similarly, see Egerton Ryerson's definition in *CG*, 1 Oct. 1831.
3 *Legislative Debates* 12 (1854–5), Part III: 1200. For the importance of the military in early Upper Canada see J.K. Johnson, *Becoming Prominent: Regional Leadership in Upper Canada, 1791–1844* (Montreal and Kingston: McGill-Queen's University Press 1989), 68ff.

410 Notes to pages 3–6

4 See W.L. Burn, *The Age of Equipoise; A Study of the Mid-Victorian Generation* (London: Unwin University Books 1968), 263–4. Similarly, see Gwyn Harries-Jenkins, *The Army in Victorian Society* (London: Routledge and Kegan Paul 1977), 102; M. Jeanne Peterson, *The Medical Profession in Mid-Victorian England* (Berkeley: University of California Press 1978), 284; Robert Robson, *The Attorney in Eighteenth-Century England* (Cambridge: Cambridge University Press 1959), 153.

5 We explore the meaning of a liberal education in early Upper Canada at more length in R.D. Gidney and W.P.J. Millar, *Inventing Secondary Education: The Rise of the High School in Nineteenth-Century Ontario* (Montreal and Kingston: McGill-Queen's University Press 1990), ch. 2.

6 *Colonial Advocate*, 19 Aug. 1824

7 William Canniff, *The Medical Profession in Upper Canada, 1783–1850* (Toronto: William Briggs 1894), 52. For other examples see pp. 60 and 63.

8 Quoted in William R. Riddell, *The Legal Profession in Upper Canada in Its Early Periods* (Toronto: The Law Society of Upper Canada 1916), 39

9 Canniff, *The Medical Profession*, 63

10 MTRL, Baldwin Room, R.B. Baldwin Papers, A69-32, J.H. Samson to R. Baldwin, Kingston, 20 Jun. 1819. On the role of the classics in defining the gentleman, see also Victoria Glendinning, *Trollope* (London: Pimlico ed. 1993), 57–8.

11 For the meaning of a liberal education and the role of the classics in Georgian England, see Sheldon Rothblatt, *Tradition and Change in English Liberal Education: An Essay in History and Culture* (London: Faber and Faber 1976), esp. chs 3 and 5.

12 See for example William Leitch's distinction between theology as a science which all educated men would be familiar with and theology as a professional study: *The Presbyterian* 13 (Dec. 1860), 182–3; see below, chapter 8, 176–7.

13 Donald Maclean, *On the Medical Profession and Medical Education in Canada: Address delivered at his Installation as Professor of the Institutes of Medicine* (Kingston 1865), 21

14 Robert L. Fraser, 'Like Eden in Her Summer Dress: Gentry, Economy and Society in Upper Canada, 1812–1840' (PhD diss., University of Toronto 1979), 214–15, and generally, chs 5 and 6. Fraser's argument can now be read in conjunction with that of S.J.R. Noel. The latter draws on Fraser's work and broadens it in certain respects. Though he does not note it because it is not pertinent to his argument, most of his 'grand patrons' were well educated and several were 'professional gentlemen' – Buell, Sherwood, and Dunlop, for example. And when they were not – like W.H. Merritt, for example – they ensured that their boys received an appropriate education at Upper Canada College or elsewhere. See Part I of S.J.R. Noel, *Patrons, Clients, Brokers: Ontario Society and Politics, 1791–1896* (Toronto: University of Toronto Press 1990).

15 Quoted in Fraser, 'Eden,' 215
16 See for example the general discussion in G. Kitson Clark, *The Making of Victorian England* (London: Methuen University Paperbacks 1965), 251ff.; Burn, *The Age of Equipoise*, 253ff. For the ideal of gentility in particular occupations and their relative status see Brian Heeney, *A Different Kind of Gentleman: Parish Clergy as Professional Men in Early and Mid-Victorian England* (Hamden, CT: Archon Books 1976), esp. 23ff.; G.F.A. Best, *Temporal Pillars: Queen Anne's Bounty, the Ecclesiastical Commissioners, and the Church of England* (Cambridge: Cambridge University Press 1964), esp. 69ff.; Daniel Duman, 'The Creation and Diffusion of a Professional Ideology in Nineteenth-Century England,' *Sociological Review* N.S. 27 (1979), 115–16; Daniel Duman, 'The English Bar in the Georgian Era,' in *Lawyers in Early Modern Europe and America*, ed. Wilfrid Prest (London: Croom Helm 1981), 86–107; Robson, *The Attorney in Eighteenth-Century England*, 134–54; Irvine Loudon, *Medical Care and the General Practitioner, 1750–1850* (Oxford: Clarendon Press 1986), 18–21, 68, 199ff.
17 A.J. Engel, *From Clergyman to Don: The Rise of the Academic Profession in Nineteenth-Century Oxford* (Oxford: Clarendon Press 1983), 11
18 Quoted in Fraser, 'Eden,' 216
19 G. Blaine Baker, 'Legal Education in Upper Canada 1785–1889: The Law Society of Upper Canada,' in *Essays in the History of Canadian Law*, ed. David H. Flaherty (Toronto: University of Toronto Press for The Osgoode Society 1983), II: 56.
20 Peter A. Russell, *Attitudes to Social Structure and Mobility in Upper Canada, 1815–1840* (Lewiston, NY: Edwin Mellen Press 1990), 7–9. For the English background see Robson, *The Attorney in Eighteenth-Century England*, 134–54; W. Wesley Pue, 'Guild Training vs. Professional Education: The Committee on Legal Education and the Law Department of Queen's College, Birmingham in the 1850s,' *American Journal of Legal History* 33 (Jul. 1989), 243–6, 256–7; Michael Miles, '"A Haven for the Privileged": Recruitment into the Profession of Attorney in England, 1709–1792,' *Social History* 11 (May 1986), 197–210.
21 *Kingston Chronicle*, 4 Feb. 1825
22 See Loudon, *Medical Care and the General Practitioner*, 199ff.
23 *Kingston Chronicle*, 28 Dec. 1821
24 Mary S.G. O'Brien, *The Journals of Mary O'Brien, 1828–1838*, ed. A.S. Miller (Toronto: Macmillan 1968), 24
25 C.W. Robinson, *Life of Sir John Beverley Robinson* (Edinburgh: Blackwood 1904), 179
26 See Elizabeth Gillan Muir, *Petticoats in the Pulpit: The Story of Early Nineteenth-Century Methodist Women Preachers in Upper Canada* (Toronto: United Church Publishing House 1991), 34–48; John Webster Grant, *A Profusion of Spires: Religion in Nineteenth-Century Ontario* (Toronto: University of Toronto Press 1988), 111.

27 On the latter point see Anne Witz, *Professions and Patriarchy* (London: Routledge 1992), 74–9, 106–8; Leonore Davidoff and Catherine Hall, *Family Fortunes: Men and Women of the English Middle Class, 1780–1850* (London: Hutchinson 1987), 307–8; Judith Walzer Leavitt, *Brought to Bed: Child-Bearing in America, 1750–1950* (New York: Oxford University Press 1986), 39.
28 David F. Noble, *A World without Women: The Christian Clerical Culture of Western Science* (New York: Alfred A. Knopf 1992), esp. ch. 7
29 For a parallel argument see M. Jeanne Peterson, 'Gentlemen and Medical Men: The Problem of Professional Recruitment,' *BHM* 58/4 (Winter 1984), 470–1.
30 For the wider importance of this concept in Upper Canada, see Fraser, 'Eden,' 123, 228ff.; Noel, *Patrons, Clients, Brokers*, 41, 96.
31 Quoted in Mark M. Orkin, 'Professional Autonomy and the Public Interest: A Study of the Law Society of Upper Canada' (Doctor of Jurisprudence diss., York University 1971), 356
32 *BAJMPS* 1 (Mar. 1846), 335.
33 E.A. Cruikshank and A.F. Hunter, eds., *The Correspondence of the Hon. Peter Russell* (Toronto: Ontario Historical Society 1932–6), I: 1927–8. Similarly, see John Moir, *Enduring Witness: The Presbyterian Church in Canada* (n.p.: [Presbyterian Church of Canada] 1987), 74.
34 *UCLJ* 7 (Dec. 1861), 305
35 See Harold Perkin, *The Rise of Professional Society: England since 1880* (London and New York: Routledge 1989), esp. 2–9. For an extended treatment of his argument see his essay *Professionalism, Property and English Society since 1880* ([Reading]: University of Reading Press 1981).
36 *JLAUC*, 1830, Appendix: Report of the Select Committee on the Administration of Justice, 55
37 Donald M. Scott, 'The Profession that Vanished: Public Lecturing in Mid-Nineteenth Century America,' in *Professions and Professional Ideologies in America*, ed. Gerald L. Geison (Chapel Hill: University of North Carolina Press 1983), 23
38 For an introduction to these occupational guilds in England, see W.J. Reader, *Professional Men: The Rise of the Professional Classes in Nineteenth-Century England* (London: Weidenfeld and Nicolson 1966), ch. 1.
39 For the link between gentlemanly manners and occupational codes see Edmund D. Pellagrino, *Thomas Percival's Ethics: The Ethics Beneath the Etiquette* (Birmingham, AL: The Classics of Medicine Library 1985), ch. 3. Percival's code, published in 1803, would become the foundation for the medical codes of ethics formulated by a later generation throughout North America. See C.D. Naylor, 'The CMA's First Code of Ethics: Medical Morality or Borrowed Ideology?' *Journal of Canadian Studies* 17 (Winter 1982–3), 26–9.
40 Robert Gourlay, *A Statistical Account of Upper Canada* (London 1822), I: 332 (Norwich Township)

41 Thomas Radcliff, ed., *Authentic Letters from Upper Canada* (1833; Toronto: Macmillan 1952), 116
42 *Kingston Chronicle*, 11 Feb. 1825
43 AO, John Strachan Letterbook, 1844–9, Strachan to Joseph Biddle and Geo. R. Johnston, 7 Aug. 1846
44 On this point see for example Peter Earle, *The Making of the English Middle Class: Business, Society and Family Life in London, 1660–1730* (London: Methuen 1989), 60ff.
45 On the long-standing ambiguities see ibid., 5–7, and Geoffrey Holmes, *Augustan England: Professions, State and Society, 1680–1730* (London: Allen and Unwin 1982), 3–11.
46 For an example of the ambiguities see Peter Russell's discussion of the place of surveyors in *Social Structure*, 39.
47 See for example *DCB* 10, 'H.H. Killaly,' who was a university graduate and engineer; or *DCB* 11, 'Francis Shanly,' whose father was a university graduate, barrister, and estate manager.
48 William Westfall, *Two Worlds: The Protestant Culture of Nineteenth-Century Ontario* (Montreal and Kingston: McGill-Queen's University Press 1989), 196. For local government and the 'pre-industrial' traditions of local regulation see William T. Matthews, '"By and For the Large Propertied Interests": The Dynamics of Local Government in Six Upper Canadian Towns during the Era of Commercial Capitalism, 1832–1860' (PhD diss., McMaster University 1985), 133–4.
49 See *DCB* 6 (Powell, Osgoode), 5 (Elmsley). For White see Baker, 'Legal Education,' 65.
50 J.J. Talman, 'Some Notes on the Clergy of the Church of England in Upper Canada Prior to 1840,' *Transactions of the Royal Society of Canada*, series 3, XXXII, sect. 2 (May 1938), 61–3
51 *CG*, 26 Feb. 1831
52 The names and qualifications of those who received licences to practise medicine in Upper Canada were printed in the *Upper Canada Gazette* for 1831–9.
53 See *Upper Canada Gazette*, 3 Mar. 1836.
54 Over the last decade or so, the relative extent of American influence on early Upper Canada has been the subject of some important articles and monographs. For a review of this literature see Colin Read, 'Conflict to Consensus: The Political Culture of Upper Canada,' *Acadiensis* 19 (Spring 1990), 169–85.
55 For the founding and development of the Upper Canadian grammar schools see Gidney and Millar, *Inventing Secondary Education*, ch. 5. There are many good accounts of the history of King's College. Most recently, see A.B. McKillop, *Matters of Mind: The University in Ontario, 1791–1951* (Toronto: University of Toronto Press 1994), ch. 1.
56 *DHE* 1: 213
57 Ibid.

58 *CG*, 6 Jul. 1842 (italics in original). The founders of Queen's College may have originally intended to establish a university with two faculties only, but the charter included a full complement. See *British Colonist*, 15 Jan. 1840, 'Letter' by Robert McGill.

59 For details on financing the established churches in Britain see Best, *Temporal Pillars*, esp. 62ff. The economic and social status of the early nineteenth-century Scottish clergy is touched upon in Andrew L. Drummond and James Bulloch, *The Church in Victorian Scotland* (Edinburgh: The Saint Andrew Press 1975), 122–3, and in Laurence J. Saunders, *Scottish Democracy, 1815–1840* (Edinburgh: Oliver and Boyd 1950), 349.

60 For the Presbyterian position see Moir, *Enduring Witness*, 72ff. The definitive account is Alan Wilson, *The Clergy Reserves of Upper Canada: A Canadian Mortmain* (Toronto: University of Toronto Press 1968).

61 See Westfall, *Two Worlds*, 100–1; William Gregg, *Short History of the Presbyterian Church* ... (Toronto: Printed by C.B. Robinson for the author 1892), 69.

62 Quoted in J.L.H. Henderson, ed., *John Strachan: Documents and Opinions* (Toronto: McClelland and Stewart 1969), 107

63 Grant, *Profusion of Spires*, 94. For Grant's succinct statement of the case for an establishment see pp. 94–6. See also Westfall, *Two Worlds*, 86ff.

64 Cruikshank and Hunter, *Russell Correspondence*, I: 311

65 See Noel, *Patrons, Clients, Brokers*, 62.

66 For readers unfamiliar with the changing arrangements for the administration of justice in Upper Canada and the development of the Law Society, the clearest introduction is to be found in the opening chapter of Robert Fraser, ed., *Provincial Justice: Upper Canadian Legal Portraits* (Toronto: The Osgoode Society 1992). However, several important sources offer more detailed descriptions of the early period, and these, except where otherwise noted, provide the documentation for our account here. See William N.T. Wylie, 'Instruments of Commerce and Authority: The Civil Courts in Upper Canada, 1789–1812,' in *Essays in the History of Canadian Law*, ed. David H. Flaherty (Toronto: University of Toronto Press 1983), II: 3–48; and Baker, 'Legal Education,' esp. 49–67. The best single introduction to the early history of the Law Society and to its colonial and English predecessors is Orkin, 'Professional Autonomy and the Public Interest,' Part 1. See also the early chapters of Paul Romney's *Mr. Attorney: The Attorney General for Ontario in Court, Cabinet, and Legislature, 1791–1899* (Toronto: University of Toronto Press 1986). Dated but still useful is Riddell, *Legal Profession*.

67 See William R. Riddell, *The Bar and the Courts of the Province of Upper Canada or Ontario* (Toronto: Macmillan 1928), 36–8, and Baker, 'Legal Education,' 80.

68 All of the key clauses are printed in Riddell, *Legal Profession*, 9–13.

69 Blaine Baker has drawn attention to this in several articles, but see for example

'The Juvenile Advocate Society, 1821–26: Self-Proclaimed Schoolroom for Upper Canada's Governing Class,' Canadian Historical Association *Historical Papers*, 1985, 79–81.
70 See Riddell, *Legal Profession*, 15; Riddell, *The Bar and the Courts*, 64.
71 For the main clauses of the act of 1822 see William R. Riddell, 'The Law Society of Upper Canada in 1822,' *Ontario History* 23 (1926), 450–61.
72 G. Blaine Baker, '"So Elegant a Web": Providential Order and the Role of Secular Law in Early Nineteenth-Century Upper Canada,' *University of Toronto Law Journal* 38 (1988), 187
73 *Kingston Chronicle*, 14 Feb. 1823. Italics added
74 Ibid., 11 Feb. 1825
75 The number of professionals and laity can be calculated by comparing the lists of barristers and district court judges in Frederick H. Armstrong, *Handbook of Upper Canadian Chronology*, rev. ed. (Toronto: Dundurn Press 1985).
76 *JLAUC*, 1830, Appendix: Report of the Select Committee on the Administration of Justice, Testimony of R.B. Sullivan, 54
77 Ibid., Appendix: Report of the Select Committee on the Administration of Justice, 50.
78 See *UCLJ* 7 (Mar. 1861), 61.
79 Ibid.
80 See Margaret Banks, 'The Evolution of the Ontario Courts, 1788–1981,' in *Essays in the History of Canadian Law*, ed. David H. Flaherty (Toronto: The Osgoode Society 1983), II: 509.
81 *Legislative Debates* 1 (1841), 486
82 See ibid., 236, 360, 487.
83 Ibid., 4 (1845), Part I: 1303
84 Ibid., 1306
85 The standard source remains Canniff, *Medical Profession*. Canniff reports most of the legislation and the minutes of the Medical Board from 1812 but has little material beyond that for the early period. See also Elizabeth MacNab, *A Legal History of Health Professions in Ontario* (Toronto: Queen's Printer 1970), 3–7; Ronald Hamowy, *Canadian Medicine: A Study in Restricted Entry* (Vancouver: Fraser Institute 1984), 13–19. Hamowy attributes the various medical bills to continuing pressure from the medical establishment. This is plausible but is speculation nonetheless for there is no hard evidence to support it. Our own view is that initiatives may just as well have come from those laymen anxious to ensure that medicine, like law, was controlled by respectable gentlemen of assuredly loyal politics. The evidence for any interpretive stance is minimal; we simply happen to think our explanation fits the overall intent of colonial administration. Though it came to hand too late to contribute to our own account, the interested reader should also see a revisionist piece by Rainer Baehre, '*The Medical Profession in Upper Canada* Reconsidered: Professionalization, Medical

Reform and Law in a Colonial Society,' unpublished paper presented to the annual meeting of the Canadian Society for the History of Medicine, June 1993.
86 59 Geo. III, c. 13, s. 2
87 8 Geo. IV, c. 3
88 The biographies for these men can be located in vols 8, 9, and 10, *DCB*.
89 Some of the evidence for this paragraph is gathered together in the relevant chapters of Canniff, *Medical Profession*, but see also 'Christopher Widmer,' *DCB* 8, and Hamowy, *Canadian Medicine*, 35–40.
90 Colin Read, *The Rebellion in Upper Canada*, Canadian Historical Association Historical Booklet No. 46 (Ottawa 1988), 18
91 NAC, RG5, B11, Vol. 5, no. 636, R.C. Horne to J. Macaulay, 6 Apr. 1839. Similarly see *Patriot*, 5 and 12 Apr. 1839.
92 See Hamowy, *Canadian Medicine*, 38–9.
93 *JLAC*, 29 Nov. 1843
94 Ibid., 24 Nov. 1843

CHAPTER 2 *Compromises and Competitors*

1 For succinct accounts of the financial history of the Church of England see William Westfall, *Two Worlds: The Protestant Culture of Nineteenth-Century Ontario* (Montreal and Kingston: McGill-Queen's University Press 1989), 101–5; G.P. de T. Glazebrook, 'The Church of England in Upper Canada, 1785–1867' (typescript, 1982), 112ff. On the income levels for respectability see Peter A. Russell, *Attitudes to Social Structure and Mobility in Upper Canada, 1815–1840* (Lewiston, NY: Edwin Mellen Press 1990), 7.
2 See Curtis Fahey, *In His Name: The Anglican Experience in Upper Canada, 1791–1854* (Ottawa: Carleton University Press 1991), 214–15. For a contemporary and plaintive review of the situation see AO, Bethune Papers, unsigned and undated memorandum relating to SPG proposals to reduce stipends (dated by an archivist 'about 1846' and filed there).
3 Quoted in *The Church*, 11 Nov. 1837
4 See John Moir, *Enduring Witness: The Presbyterian Church in Canada* (n.p.: [Presbyterian Church of Canada] 1987), 80ff.
5 See for example Great Britain, House of Commons, *Report of the Select Committee on Civil Government in the Canadas*, 22 Jul. 1828, No. 569, Evidence of J.C. Grant, 193; Harriet Priddis, ed., 'The Proudfoot Papers,' *London and Middlesex Historical Society Papers and Records* (1915), Part I: 1832, 53; Isaac Fidler, *Observations on Professions, Literature, Manners and Emigration in the United States* ... (London 1833), 309 and 224.
6 Quoted in Peter A. Russell, 'Church of Scotland Clergy in Upper Canada: Culture Shock and Conservatism on the Frontier,' *Ontario History* 73 (Jun. 1981), 92. Similarly see AO, John Strachan Papers, Bethune to Strachan, 12 Jan. 1831.

7 UCA, Mark Y. Stark Papers, Stark to Marion, Dundas, 4 Oct. 1836
8 *The Reserve Question, or a Word for the Church* (1837), 14. Similarly see AO, John Strachan Papers, Bethune to Strachan, 12 Jan. 1831. For a more extended but parallel argument see Fahey, *In His Name*, 218ff.
9 See Glazebrook, 'Church of England in Upper Canada,' 12, 107–8. As late as 1851 congregational support for clerical stipends probably amounted to no more than a third of total salaries. See AO, John Strachan Papers, Report of the Home Rural Deanery for 1851.
10 For examples of the progressive pressures in this regard see Ernest Hawkins, *Annals of the Diocese of Toronto* (London: SPCK 1848), 122; AO, John Strachan Papers, Hawkins to Strachan, 18 May 1844, and Thos Vowler to Strachan, 3 May 1849.
11 Fahey, *In His Name*, 225
12 *Pastoral Letter to the Clergy and Laity of the Diocese of Toronto, April 2, 1851. By John Toronto*, 10–11
13 *The Church*, 27 Mar. 1851; similarly, see ibid., 8 May 1851.
14 On this paragraph see Moir, *Enduring Witness*, 91ff.
15 *The Presbyterian* 1 (Jul. 1848), 112
16 See for example the extended wail of one minister in ibid., 93–8.
17 Ibid., 3 (Jul. 1850), 102
18 Moir, *Enduring Witness*, 106ff. See also Richard W. Vaudry, 'Peter Brown, the Toronto *Banner*, and the Evangelical Mind in Victorian Canada,' *Ontario History* 77 (Mar. 1985), 6–8
19 *EMR*, Jul. 1848, 134
20 Ibid., Jul. 1851, 138–9. Compare James Croil, *A Historical and Statistical Report of the Presbyterian Church of Canada ...*, 2d ed. (Montreal: John Lovell 1868), 142.
21 See Irvine Loudon, *Medical Care and the General Practitioner, 1750–1850* (Oxford: Clarendon Press 1986), esp. 22ff.
22 William Canniff, *The Medical Profession in Upper Canada, 1783–1850* (Toronto: Wm Briggs 1894), provides some relevant information in his reproduction of the minutes of the Medical Board, but see also *JLAUC*, 1839, Appendix, Vol. II, Part 2, Correspondence between the Government and the Medical Board, 716. Of the 164 licences granted by the Medical Board between 1830 and 1837, only 5 were limited to one of the branches of medicine.
23 For an introduction see William R. Riddell, *The Legal Profession in Upper Canada in Its Early Periods* (Toronto: The Law Society of Upper Canada 1916), chs. 1–4.
24 See ibid., 14.
25 See LSUCA, Convocation Minutes, 1-1, 29 Apr. and 26 Jun. 1830, 1 Jul. 1831, 8 Feb. 1840.
26 *Colonial Advocate*, 29 Jul. 1830. For similar sentiments see William Catermole,

418   Notes to pages 32–6

Emigration; The Advantages of Emigration to Canada ... (London 1831), 20–1; Patriot, 27 May 1845; Legislative Debates 7 (1848), 168–9; 9 (1850), Part I: 351.
27 Kingston Chronicle, 14 Feb. 1823. For details of the pertinent legislation and records of the Law Society see Riddell, Legal Profession in Upper Canada, 9–20. The legal advertisements in any of the Toronto newspapers of the 1830s show the extent to which the branches were combined in the leading law firms.
28 John A. Macdonald, for example, finished his preliminary education and began articling at the age of fifteen; Donald Bethune at fourteen; Oliver Mowat at sixteen. See *DCB* 6, 'George Mackenzie'; Peter Baskerville, 'Donald Bethune's Steamboat Business,' *Ontario History* 67 (Sep. 1975), 135; C.R.W. Biggar, *Sir Oliver Mowat* (Toronto: Warwick Bros. and Rutter 1905), I: 12.
29 Though it was relatively common to attend a medical school in upper New York State or Ohio for a few months, these small schools rarely included hospital facilities. For this it was necessary to go to Boston or New York City.
30 See for example *JLAUC*, 1833–4, Appendix: Second Report of the Select Committee on Education.
31 J.R. Godley, *Letters from America* (London 1844), I: 189 and 197
32 On the links to the military see J.J. Talman, 'Some Notes on the Clergy of the Church of England in Upper Canada prior to 1840,' *Transactions of the Royal Society of Canada*, series 3, XXXII, sect. 2 (May 1938), 66.
33 See for example G.W. Spragge, ed., *The John Strachan Letter Book* (Toronto: Ontario Historical Society 1946), 72–3.
34 AO, John Strachan Papers, Report of the Theological College, Diocese of Toronto, by A.N. Bethune, 20 Nov. 1846
35 *The Presbyterian* 1 (Jul. 1848), 113
36 Quoted in Moir, *Enduring Witness*, 66
37 Quoted in Harriet Priddis, ed., 'The Proudfoot Papers,' *London and Middlesex Historical Society Papers and Records* (1915), Part I: 1832, 37. On this point see also the pungent summary comment of John Webster Grant, *A Profusion of Spires: Religion in Nineteenth-Century Ontario* (Toronto: University of Toronto Press 1988), 74.
38 See for example Walter G. Pitman, *The Baptists and Public Affairs in the Province of Canada, 1840–67* (New York: Arno Press 1980), 15; Grant, *Profusion of Spires*, 38ff.
39 NAC, SPG records, 'C' MSS, Box 4a/39, Rev. R. Rolph to Rev. A. Hamilton, 13 Jul. 1827. Similarly, see Thomas Radcliff, ed., *Authentic Letters from Upper Canada* (1833; Toronto: Macmillan 1952), 114–16.
40 See for example *JLAUC*, 1828, Appendix: Report of the Select Committee on the Petition of Bulkley Waters.
41 *CG*, 27 Feb. 1839.
42 For the figures see J.M.S. Careless, *The Union of the Canadas* (Toronto: McClelland and Stewart 1967), 31.

43 The names of all those called to the bar by the Law Society of Upper Canada between 1797 and 1841 are recorded in Frederick A. Armstrong, *Handbook of Upper Canadian Chronology*, rev. ed. (Toronto: Dundurn Press 1985), 128–32. The number of entrants annually can also be tracked in Riddell, *Legal Profession in Upper Canada*, 32.
44 For an introduction see J. Rordans, *The Canadian Conveyancer* ... (Toronto 1859).
45 See for example *Kingston Chronicle*, 14 Feb. 1823.
46 AO, Osler Family Papers, Autobiographical sketch of F.L. Osler, 1842, 23. For another example, see John Carroll, *Case and his Contemporaries* ... (Toronto, 1867), II: 46–7.
47 *Parliamentary Debates*, 29 Mar. 1860
48 *UCLJ* 4 (Oct. 1858), 221
49 See for example *CLJ* 4 (Aug. 1868), 213.
50 See *Kingston Chronicle*, 28 Dec. 1821 and 4 Jan. 1822; Canniff, *Medical Profession*, 63; *BAJMPS* 3 (Nov. 1847), 193–4; *Legislative Debates* 9 (1850), Part III: 1202.
51 For both the numbers and the tendency to settle in the larger urban areas see J.T.H. Connor, 'Minority Medicine in Ontario, 1795 to 1903: A Study of Medical Pluralism and Its Decline' (PhD diss., University of Waterloo 1989), 199 and 202; Rainer Baehre, '*The Medical Profession in Upper Canada* Reconsidered: Professionalization, Medical Reform and Law in a Colonial Society,' unpublished paper presented to the annual meeting of the Canadian Society for the History of Medicine, Jun. 1993. Even by the mid-1840s, according to Connor's analysis of *Smith's Gazetteer*, 101 of 187 listed towns and villages still had no doctor.
52 Robert Gourlay, *Statistical Account of Upper Canada* (1822; Yorkshire, England, and New York: S.R. Publishers Ltd and Johnson Reprint Corporation 1966), II: 365, 364
53 Charles G. Roland and Bohodar Rubashewsky, 'The Economic Status of the Practice of Dr. Harmaunus Smith in Wentworth County, Ontario, 1826–65,' *CBMH* 5 (1988), esp. 34–7 and n16
54 *JLAUC*, 1821, 17 Feb. 1821. Similarly see *Kingston Chronicle*, 4 Jan. 1822; *Colonial Advocate*, 9 Feb. 1826.
55 Susanna Moodie, *Roughing It in the Bush* (Toronto: McClelland and Stewart 1962), 207. For a second example not included in this edition see ibid. (Toronto: McClelland and Stewart 1923), 442–3.
56 H.H. Langton, ed., *A Gentlewoman in Upper Canada: The Journals of Anne Langton* (Toronto: Clarke Irwin 1964), 123
57 For a recent introduction to the continuum of practitioners in England before 1850 see Loudon, *Medical Care and the General Practitioner*, ch. 1. See also the essays in W.F. Bynum and Roy Porter, eds., *Medical Fringe and Medical Orthodoxy, 1750–1850* (London: Croom Helm 1987); Edward Shorter, *Bedside Manners: The Troubled History of Doctors and Patients* (New York: Simon and

Schuster 1985), 69–72. For Ontario see Connor, 'Minority Medicine.' Connor's introductory chapter includes a thorough and thoughtful review of the international literature on the subject.
58 See for example 'Peter Howard,' *DCB* 8; Charles Roland, 'Diary of a Canadian Country Practitioner ...,' *Medical History* 15 (1971), 172–3n14.
59 Toronto Academy of Medicine Archives, Aikins Papers, H. Badens to Aikins, Madoc, 6 Sep. 1853. For other examples see Ronald Hamowy, *Canadian Medicine: A Study in Restricted Entry* (Vancouver: Fraser Institute 1984), 16–17.
60 See for example the comments in *Brockville Recorder*, 12 Dec. 1844.
61 See William N.T. Wylie, 'The Blacksmith in Upper Canada, 1784–1850,' *Canadian Papers in Rural History* 7 (1990), 139, 151. Our thanks to Jennifer and J.T.H. Connor for drawing this to our attention.
62 AO, Osler Family Papers, Autobiographical Sketch of F.L. Osler, 1842, 24
63 Anne Wilkinson, *Lions in the Way* (Toronto: Macmillan 1956), 40
64 AO, Osler Family Papers, Journals, F.L. Osler, 1837, 169–70
65 See Brian Heeney, *A Different Kind of Gentleman: Parish Clergy as Professional Men in Early and Mid-Victorian England* (Hamden, CT: Archon Books 1976), 76–8. For the Kirk see Mary Jane Price, 'The Professionalization of Medicine in Ontario during the Nineteenth Century' (MA, McMaster University 1977), 15–16.
66 Edwin Seaborn, *The March of Medicine in Western Ontario* (Toronto: Ryerson Press 1944), 43–4
67 See for example the comments by W.H. Merritt in *Legislative Debates* 8 (1849), 1556, and 9 (1850), Part II: 1202. For a fine recent study of the midwife in nineteenth-century Ontario which contains far more detail than this short introduction allows, see Connor, 'Minority Medicine,' ch. 2. See also Wendy Mitchinson, *The Nature of Their Bodies: Women and Their Doctors in Victorian Canada* (Toronto: University of Toronto Press 1991), ch. 6. For an introduction and review of the historical literature on women medical practitioners see Anne Witz, *Professions and Patriarchy* (London: Routledge 1992), 74–9.
68 See for example *Colonial Advocate*, 8 May 1828 and 8 Oct. 1829; *CG*, 23 Feb. 1842.
69 *UCJ* 1 (May 1851), 63. For other examples see ibid., 3 (1853–4), 229; and *BAJMPS* 2 (Aug. 1846), 92–3.
70 AO, Osler Family Papers, Autobiographical Sketch of F.L. Osler, 1842, 24
71 Langton, *A Gentlewoman in Upper Canada*, 171–2
72 There is now a large literature on both regular practice and the doctrines and growth of the medical sects, especially in the United States. See for example William G. Rothstein, *American Physicians in the Nineteenth Century: From Sects to Science* (Baltimore, MD: Johns Hopkins University Press 1972), esp. ch. 3; Charles E. Rosenberg, 'The Therapeutic Revolution: Medicine, Meaning, and Social Change in Nineteenth-Century America,' in *The Therapeutic Revolution: Essays in the Social History of American Medicine*, ed. Morris J. Vogel and

Charles E. Rosenberg (Philadelphia: University of Pennsylvania Press 1979), 3–25; John S. Haller, Jr, *American Medicine in Transition, 1840–1910* (Urbana: University of Illinois Press 1981), chs 1–3; John Harley Warner, *The Therapeutic Perspective: Medical Practice, Knowledge, and Identity in America, 1820–1885* (Cambridge, MA: Harvard University Press 1986). For Ontario see Connor, 'Minority Medicine.' For a highly readable introduction to and evaluation of the effectiveness of all forms of therapeutics before about 1870, see Shorter, *Bedside Manners*, 38–51 and 69–72.

73 Quoted in Seaborn, *March of Medicine*, 108
74 [Catharine Parr Traill] *The Backwoods of Canada: Letters from the Wife of an Emigrant Officer* (London 1836), 43
75 AO, Jarvis-Powell Papers, Anne Powell to Eliza, 20 Jan. 1821
76 MTRL, Baldwin Room, R.B. Baldwin Papers, A81, Robert Baldwin Jr to Robert Baldwin, 8 Dec. 1848
77 *CG*, 2 Jul. 1851; *Globe*, 27 Mar. 1851
78 Connor, 'Minority Medicine,' 360–1, and generally 359ff. For a brief exposition see the same author's '"A Sort of *Felo-de-Se*": Eclecticism, Related Medical Sects, and Their Decline in Victorian Ontario,' *BHM* 65 (1991), 503–27.
79 Quoted in Connor, 'Minority Medicine,' 365
80 We return to this point in chapter 3.
81 See *CMJMR* 1 (1852), 347, 635–6; *UCJ* 3 (1853–4), 414; *Leader*, 2 May 1855; *Globe*, 3 Apr. 1857.
82 UCA, Mark Y. Stark Papers, Stark to mother, Dundas, 4 Jan. 1852
83 Compare Warner, *Therapeutic Perspective*, esp. 92–3.
84 AO, Hay Family Papers, MU766, Father Angus MacDonell to G.H. Hay, Sandwich, 7 Feb. 1837
85 *CG*, 10 Sep. 1834
86 See, for example, AO, A.N. Buell Papers, A.N. Buell to wife, 28 Jun. 1852; Telegraph, Mrs Buell to A.N., 28 Jun. 1852; Buell to Widmer, 6 Jul. 1852; Buell to Dr Jones C. Jackson, 25 May 1853.
87 For two Upper Canadian examples of the doctrines and defence of homeopathy see R.J. Smith, *Lecture on the History of Medicine and the Science of Homeopathy* (Toronto 1852); James Lillie, MD, DD, *Small and Simple Doses Contrasted with Bleeding and Confused Drugging ...* (Toronto 1855).
88 Warner, *Therapeutic Perspective*, 11–17 and 58–63.
89 *Kingston Chronicle*, 4 Jan. 1822
90 E.P. Thompson, *The Making of the English Working Class* (London: Gollancz 1965), esp. 88–101 and 746–62
91 For a catalogue of the legislature's attempts to dispose of the reserves see 'Address of the Assembly, 28 June 1850,' in *The Elgin-Grey Papers, 1846–52*, ed. Arthur G. Doughty (Ottawa: Queen's Printer 1937), IV: 1504–8.
92 See William R. Riddell, *The Bar and the Courts of the Province of Upper*

Canada or Ontario (Toronto: Macmillan 1928), 58ff. Paul Romney's work is especially suggestive on these points. See his *Mr Attorney: The Attorney General for Ontario in Court, Cabinet, and Legislature, 1791–1899* (Toronto: University of Toronto Press 1986), ch. 3, and his article 'From the Types Riot to the Rebellion: Elite Ideology, Anti-legal Sentiment, Political Violence, and the Rule of Law in Upper Canada,' *Ontario History* 79 (Jun. 1987), 113–44.
93 For some examples see *Colonial Advocate*, 13 Nov. 1828, 30 Jan. 1829, 26 Jun. 1834.
94 *Legislative Debates* 1 (1841), 485
95 Ibid., 236 and 486
96 *JLAUC*, 1839, 20 Mar. 1839, 68
97 *Colonial Advocate*, 26 Jun. 1834
98 *Kingston Chronicle*, 28 Dec. 1821. Italics in original
99 Quoted in Peter A. Russell, 'Attitudes to Social Structure and Social Mobility in Upper Canada (1815–1840)' (PhD diss., Carleton University 1981), 117. Readers should be aware that, like this quotation, much other pertinent material in the thesis is not in the book based on it.
100 Jennifer J. Connor and J.T.H. Connor, 'Thomsonian Medical Literature and Reformist Discourse in Upper Canada,' *Canadian Literature* 131 (Winter 1991), 141
101 *Brockville Recorder*, 12 Dec. 1844

CHAPTER 3 *The Moment of Mid-Century Radicalism*

1 The phrase is adapted from J.M.S. Careless, *Brown of the Globe* (Toronto: Macmillan 1959), I: 99
2 Quoted in ibid., 110
3 MTRL, Baldwin Room, Baldwin Papers, A51-25, Francis Hincks to R. Baldwin, Kingston, 15 Jun. 1843. Italics in original
4 *Legislative Debates* 11 (1852–3), Part I: 454
5 Quoted in the *St. Catharines Journal*, 19 Nov. 1846
6 *Legislative Debates* 10 (1851), Part II: 1204
7 See for example ibid., 11 (1852–3), Part I: 453.
8 *North American*, 29 Jul. 1852 (italics in original). Similarly see *CG*, 24 Jul. 1850, and *Legislative Debates* 8 (1849), Part II: 1730.
9 *Report of a Public Discussion at Simcoe on Wednesday and Thursday, July 16 and 17, 1851, on the Clergy Reserves and Rectories* (Simcoe 1851), 18
10 Ibid., 33
11 Ibid., 5–6
12 Ibid.
13 See for example *The Presbyterian* 5 (Dec. 1852), 183–4.

14 *Legislative Debates* 12 (1854–5), Part III: 1200
15 For the Kirk see for example *The Presbyterian* 4 (Aug. 1851), 127; 6 (Sep. 1853), 130; 7 (Jul. 1854), 103–4.
16 *The Church*, 9 Mar. 1854. For Strachan's reactions see for example, AO, John Strachan Letterbook 1853–4, Strachan to Carey, 4 Nov. 1853; AO, John Strachan Letterbook 1854–62, Strachan to C.C. Brough, 11 May 1854; to Rev. W. Creswell, 15 Aug. 1854; to Rev. Inglis, 4 Sep. 1854.
17 *The Presbyterian* 8 (Feb. 1855), 27
18 J.L.H. Henderson, *John Strachan* (Toronto: University of Toronto Press 1969), 84
19 See *JLAC*, 1845 and 1846, and *BAJMPS* 1 (Apr. 1845), 27–8, and 1 (Mar. 1846), 334–5.
20 See Jacques Bernier, *La Médecine au Québec; naissance et évolution d'une profession* (Quebec: Les Presses de l'Université Laval 1989), 50–7.
21 See for example *BAJMPS* 3 (Jun. 1847), 49–50.
22 See for example the Upper Canadian petition to the legislature in *BAJMPS* 1 (Mar. 1846), 335.
23 Ibid. Similarly, see ibid., 2 (May 1846), 22–3.
24 Margaret Pelling, 'Medical Practice in Early Modern England,' in *The Professions in Early Modern England*, ed. Wilfred Prest (London: Croom Helm 1987), 109–10
25 Laurel Thatcher Ulrich, *A Midwife's Tale: The Life of Martha Ballard, Based on Her Diary, 1785–1812* (New York: Vintage Books 1991); see esp. 'Introduction.'
26 J.T.H. Connor, 'Minority Medicine in Ontario, 1795 to 1903: A Study of Medical Pluralism and Its Decline' (PhD diss., University of Waterloo 1989), 202
27 Irvine Loudon, *Medical Care and the General Practitioner, 1750–1850* (Oxford: Clarendon Press 1986), esp. 208–10. See also the brief comment in Ulrich, *Midwife's Tale*, 66.
28 John Harley Warner, 'Medical Sectarianism, Therapeutic Conflict, and the Shaping of Orthodox Professional Identity in Antebellum American Medicine,' in *Medical Fringe and Medical Orthodoxy, 1750–1850*, ed. W.F. Bynum and Roy Porter (London: Croom Helm 1987), 241. Italics added
29 For a detailed account see R.D. Gidney and W.P.J. Millar, 'The Origins of Organized Medicine in Ontario, 1850–1869,' in *Health, Disease and Medicine: Essays in Canadian History*, ed. Charles G. Roland (Toronto: Hannah Institute for the History of Medicine 1984), esp. 70–5.
30 *CG*, 18 Sep. 1850 and 2 Jul. 1851
31 MTRL, Baldwin Room, R. Baldwin Papers, A47–56, Eli Gorham to R. Baldwin, 11 Apr. 1849. Similarly see ibid., A58–78, F.B. Morly to R. Baldwin, Cooksville, 14 Apr. 1849; A72–132, Robert Smith to R. Baldwin, Newmarket, 9 Jul. 1850
32 *Globe*, 18 Jul. 1850

33 *CG*, 24 Jul. 1850. Similarly, see ibid., 14 May 1851.
34 *North American*, 29 Jul. 1852; *Globe*, 8 Jul. 1852, 3 and 21 Apr. 1857; *Daily Leader*, 11 May 1854
35 See *UCJ* 3 (1853), 18; ibid., 1 (Jun. 1851), 112.
36 *Legislative Debates* 8 (1849), Part II: 1558
37 Ibid., 9 (1850), Part II: 1203
38 *BAJMPS* 8 (May 1851), 42
39 The division is printed in *Legislative Debates* 10 (1851), Part II: 939.
40 See for example *BAJMPS* 4 (Mar. 1849), 314; *UCJ* 1 (Jun. 1851), 112.
41 *UCJ* 3 (1853–4), 267
42 *BAJMPS* 6 (May 1850), 43. Similarly, see *UCJ* 2 (Jan.–Feb. 1853), 286; 3 (1853), 20, 28–9
43 See Joseph J. Kett, *The Formation of the American Medical Profession* (New Haven, CT: Yale University Press 1968), 35–64; William G. Rothstein, *American Physicians in the Nineteenth Century: From Sects to Science* (Baltimore, MD: Johns Hopkins University Press 1972), chs. 4–5, appendix II.
44 See *Brockville Recorder*, 27 Feb. 1845 and 30 Apr. 1846; *St. Catharines Journal*, 19 Nov. 1846 (quoting the *Examiner*); *British Colonist*, 6 Apr. 1849 and 22 Jul. 1851; *Globe*, 18 Jul. 1850.
45 Again, for a more detailed exposition see Gidney and Millar, 'Origins of Organized Medicine,' 75–6.
46 *Leader*, 29 Apr. 1859
47 See *JLAC*, 1859, 30 Mar. 1859 ff.; appendix 42: Report of the Select Committee on the petition of Asa Howard and others; 22 Vict. c. 47: An Act Respecting Homeopathy. For the eclectics see *JLAC*, 1861, 5 Apr. 1861 ff.; 24 Vict. c. 110: An Act Respecting the Eclectic System of Medicine.
48 See for example the editorial wail in *BAJ* 2 (1861), 179–80.
49 John D. Blackwell, 'William Hume Blake and the Judicature Acts of 1849: The Process of Legal Reform at Mid-Century in Upper Canada,' in *Essays in the History of Canadian Law*, ed. David H. Flaherty (Toronto: University of Toronto Press 1981), I: 133. For an extended history of the Court of Chancery, including its jurisdiction and problems to mid-century, see Elizabeth Brown, 'Equitable Jurisdiction and the Court of Chancery in Upper Canada,' *Osgoode Hall Law Journal* 21/1 (Mar. 1983), 275–314. Brown's article, in passing, offers a good deal of insight into the operation and jurisdiction of the common-law courts as well. Blackwell's essay is a useful supplement on the 1840s; for the 'pre-history' of the court, see John Weaver, 'While Equity Slumbered: Creditor Advantage, A Capitalist Land Market, and Upper Canada's Missing Court,' *Osgoode Hall Law Journal* 28/4 (Winter 1990), 871–914. Ontario's Court of Chancery was abolished when the courts of common law and equity were fused to create one Supreme Court of Judicature in 1881.
50 For the essence of his indictment see esp. the opening chapter of *Bleak House*, published in 1852.

Notes to pages 60–5   425

51 See for example MTRL, Baldwin Boom, R.B. Baldwin Papers, A73–9, J. Spragge to Baldwin, Kingston, 15 Sep. 1842.
52 *North American*, 15 Sep. 1853. Similarly, see *CG*, 20 Sep. 1843.
53 Quoted in Blackwell, 'William Hume Blake and the Judicature Acts of 1849 ...,' in *Essays in the History of Canadian Law*, ed. Flaherty, I: 142.
54 *Legislative Debates* 5 (1846), Part II: 1575–8
55 Ibid., 9 (1850), Part I: 120
56 See J.M.S. Careless, *The Union of the Canadas* (Toronto: McClelland and Stewart 1967), 171; Lillian F. Gates, *After the Rebellion: The Later Years of William Lyon Mackenzie* (Toronto: Dundurn Press 1988), 183.
57 For the vote and the accompanying debate see *Legislative Debates* 10 (1851), Part I: 562–70. The Upper Canadian vote was twenty-five to nine in favour of the motion but, overall, thirty-four to thirty against. Reform supporters of the ministry voted nine to four against. If one adds three Grits and two Reform independents, the result is a tie within Reform ranks of nine to nine. Of the lawyers, one Grit, two independents, and ten Tories voted in favour, and six Reformers against. The identification of political loyalties follows the tables in P.G. Cornell, *The Alignment of Political Groups in Canada, 1841–67* (Toronto: University of Toronto Press 1962), 100–3.
58 *Legislative Debates* 10 (1851), Part I: 603–7
59 See *North American*, 18 Sep. and 22 Nov. 1850. For the *Globe*'s view, see 27 Feb. 1851.
60 *North American*, 23 Oct. 1850
61 Quoted in ibid.
62 Ibid., 29 Nov. 1850. Italics in original
63 See *Legislative Debates* 9 (1850), Part I: appendix, 324; Part I: 351 and 511; 10 (1851), Part I: 363; Part II: 1203; 11 (1852–3), Part I: 339.
64 Ibid., 9 (1850), Part I: 324
65 Ibid., 10 (1851), Part I: 363
66 Ibid., Part II: 1204
67 For the debate on Notman's bill and the preceding quotations see *Legislative Debates* 9 (1850), Part I: appendix, 324–6.
68 Ibid., 368
69 Ibid., 11 (1852–3), Part I: 342
70 Ibid., 10 (1851), Part I: 373
71 Ibid., Part II: 1207
72 Each volume of the *Legislative Debates* contains a full list of the MPPs and the ridings they represented, and their names can be linked to one of two lists of barristers: that found in F.H. Armstrong, ed., *Handbook of Upper Canadian Chronology*, rev. ed. (Toronto: Dundurn Press 1985), 127ff.; and in the earliest printed Law List, J. Rordans, *The Upper Canada Law Directory for 1858* (Toronto 1858), 53ff. For the period before 1841 Armstrong's *Chronology* also contains a full list of MLAs.

73 *Legislative Debates* 10 (1851), Part I: 366
74 *UCJ* 3 (1853–4), 560
75 *The Church*, 4 Sep. 1851
76 For details see Moir, *Church and State*, 76–81.
77 AO, John Strachan Letterbook, 1854–62, Strachan to Hincks, 16 May 1855
78 *The Presbyterian* 8 (Jul. 1855), 119
79 See for example *Legislative Debates* 8 (1849), Part II: 1554–7; 1730–2; 10 (1851), Part II: 937–9.
80 See J.M.S. Careless, ed., *The Pre-Confederation Premiers: Ontario Government Leaders, 1841–67* (Toronto: University of Toronto Press 1980), 15–16. In our own analysis of five communities in southwestern Ontario in 1861, 70 per cent of the heads of families were British-born. See R.D. Gidney and W.P.J. Millar, *Inventing Secondary Education: The Rise of the High School in Nineteenth-Century Ontario* (Montreal and Kingston: McGill-Queen's University Press 1990), 130.
81 On this point see our analysis in chapter 9, below.
82 R.C.B. Risk, 'The Law and the Economy in Mid-Nineteenth-Century Ontario,' in *Essays in the History of Canadian Law*, ed. Flaherty, I: 107–8. Blaine Baker has been critical of Risk on this point, and perhaps legitimately so. But we believe with Paul Romney that Baker has pressed his argument so hard that Upper Canadian lawyers appear almost entirely indifferent to British law, legal institutions, or ideas. This we think is excessive revisionism. Baker's argument, none the less, is also enormously stimulating, and has far more pertinence for the entire nineteenth century than the title suggests; see 'The Reconstruction of Upper Canadian Legal Thought in the Late Victorian Empire,' *Law and History Review* 32 (Fall 1985), 219–92. Cf. Paul Romney, 'Very Late Loyalist Fantasies: Nostalgic Tory History and the Rule of Law in Upper Canada,' in *Canadian Perspectives on Law and Society: Issues in Legal History*, ed. W.W. Pue and Barry Wright (Ottawa: Carleton University Press 1988), esp. 136–7.
83 See J.K. Johnson, 'John A. Macdonald,' in *The Pre-Confederation Premiers*, ed. Careless, 211–13. For a full narrative account of these political developments see Careless, *Union of the Canadas*, chs. 10 and 11.
84 A.G. Doughty, ed., *The Elgin-Grey Papers 1846–52* (Ottawa: Queen's Printer 1937), III: 792

CHAPTER 4 *The Placid Progress of the Law*

1 See *JLAC*, 1856, 636–7; 1857, 144–5.
2 See for example *Globe*, 20 Feb. 1858; *Leader*, 10 Jun. 1865.
3 See for example *UCLJ* 4 (Jan. 1858), 1–2; 9 (Apr. 1863), 85–8; N.S. 1 (Apr. 1865), 110–11.
4 Ibid., 9 (Apr. 1863), 85
5 See Margaret A. Banks, 'The Evolution of the Ontario Courts, 1788–1981,' in

Essays in the History of Canadian Law, ed. David H. Flaherty (Toronto: University of Toronto Press 1983), II: 513.
6 See above, chapter 1, 20–2; *UCLJ* 2 (Aug. 1856), 154.
7 For an introduction to the origins and development of the County Attorneys Act, see Paul Romney, *Mr. Attorney: The Attorney-General for Ontario in Court, Cabinet and Legislature, 1791–1899* (Toronto: University of Toronto Press 1986), 214ff. The intent of the act was to have the county attorneys prosecute for the Crown, but, Romney remarks, the act 'in due course virtually wiped out private prosecutions' (p. 290). The clerks of the peace played a key role in organizing the business of the courts. According to the act, they were not required to be barristers, but during debate John A. Macdonald declared that it was the intention to unite the office with that of county attorney and thus to appoint only lawyers as clerks; *Globe*, 11 Mar. 1857.
8 *Globe*, 11 Mar. 1857
9 See Romney, *Mr. Attorney*.
10 See ibid., 290ff., and his 'From Constitutionalism to Legalism: Trial by Jury, Responsible Government, and the Rule of Law in the Canadian Political Culture,' *Law and History Review* 7 (1989), 121–74. For another example see Banks, 'Evolution,' 521.
11 Quoted in J.K. Johnson, ed., *The Letters of Sir John A. Macdonald, 1836–1857* (Ottawa: Public Archives of Canada 1968), I: 221. For a brief description of the activities of a notary public in the 1850s, see *UCLJ* 8 (Dec. 1862), 333–4.
12 See for example AO, RG8, I-1-D, Provincial Secretary's Correspondence, No. 1076, 9 Nov. 1871, Glass and Fitzgerald, Barristers, Solicitors, etc., London, Ontario, 8 Nov. 1871.
13 For some examples see Romney, *Mr. Attorney*, 214 and 217; R.C.B. Risk, 'The Law and the Economy in Mid-Nineteenth-Century Ontario: A Perspective,' in *Essays in the History of Canadian Law*, ed. Flaherty, I: 93ff.
14 For some typical examples see *UCLJ* 1 (Feb. 1855), 32; 5 (Aug. 1859), 177; 9 (Nov. 1863), 309–10.
15 Quoted in Paul Craven, ' Law and Ideology: The Toronto Police Court, 1850–80,' in *Essays in the History of Canadian Law*, ed. David H. Flaherty (Toronto: University of Toronto Press 1983), II: 260.
16 *Globe*, 11 Mar. 1857
17 Ibid., 20 Feb. 1858
18 Robert Baldwin also made this point in defence of the number of lawyers in the legislature in 1849. See Romney, *Mr. Attorney*, 169.
19 The following paragraph is based on the list of Benchers included in J. Rordans, *The Upper Canada Law Directory for 1858* (Toronto 1858), 36–7 and 47–8.
20 G. Blaine Baker, 'Legal Education in Upper Canada, 1785–1889: The Law Society as Educator,' in *Essays in the History of Canadian Law*, ed. Flaherty, II: 123.
21 See *Rules of the Law Society of Upper Canada* (Toronto 1859); see also *Rules of*

the Law Society of Upper Canada (York, Upper Canada, 1833). Similarly, see Baker, 'Legal Education,' 50.
22 See for example the comments of W.G. Draper quoted in *UCLJ* 7 (Apr. 1861), 88–90.
23 Most recently, see J.K. Johnson, *Becoming Prominent: Regional Leadership in Upper Canada* (Montreal and Kingston: McGill-Queen's University Press 1989), 23.
24 The 1840 figures were compiled by William R. Riddell from a Law Society report of 1840; see his *The Legal Profession in Upper Canada in Its Early Periods* (Toronto: Law Society of Upper Canada 1916), 18. Otherwise, see the appendix, section B.
25 Quoted in C.R.W. Biggar, *Sir Oliver Mowat* (Toronto: Warwick Bros. and Rutter 1905), I: 20. For similar observations see Peter Neary, ed., 'Neither Radical nor Tory nor Whig: Letters by Oliver Mowat to John Mowat, 1843–46,' *Ontario History* 71 (1979), 91, 99, 104.
26 MTRL, Baldwin Room, Henry O' Brien Diary, 10 Feb. 1859
27 See for example *Legislative Debates* 2 (1852–3), Part III: 1785 (Mr Gamble); *Parliamentary Debates*, Legislative Council, 25 Feb. 1859; *UCLJ* 1 (Sep. 1855), 162–8; 7 (Apr. 1861), 88–90; 7 (Jun. 1861), 141; N.S. 1 (Jan. 1865), 24–7.
28 See for example *Smith's Canadian Gazetteer* (Toronto 1846), 250; MTRL, Baldwin Room, MacLeod Papers, M.D. MacLeod to Hugh M. Mackenzie, 8 Mar. 1851; same to Rev. James Latouche, 4 Jul. 1856.
29 *Globe*, 19 Dec. 1863. Similarly see ibid., 25 Aug. 1863.
30 *UCLJ* N.S. 1 (Jan. 1865), 24
31 See chapter 2 above, 31–2.
32 The calculations are based on the sources listed in section B of the appendix.
33 LSUCA, Convocation Minutes, 1-1, vol. 3, 3 Aug. 1847; William R. Riddell, *The Bar and the Courts of Upper Canada or Ontario* (Toronto: Macmillan 1928), 93–4; MTRL, Baldwin Room, A55–72, Wm Lapontiere to Robert Baldwin, 15 Feb. 1848; *UCLJ* 3 (Feb. 1857), 32–5; N.S. 2 (Oct. 1866), 253. Though we know nothing of its substance, a second attempt to bring the attorneys to heel was made in the legislature in 1855, but it was equally unsuccessful. See *JLAC*, 12 Mar. and 26 May 1855.
34 *UCLJ* 1 (Sep. 1855), 162–5. Similarly, see ibid., 2 (Mar. 1856), 49–50; 3 (Feb. 1857), 37–8.
35 Ibid., 2 (Mar. 1856), 50
36 20 Vict., c. 63, An Act to Amend the Law for the Admission of Attorneys, esp. ss. 3 and 19
37 On this point see the comment in *UCLJ* 3 (Aug. 1857), 155–6.
38 See *Globe*, 20 Feb. 1858; *UCLJ* 7 (Apr. 1861), 88–90; ibid., 9 (Oct. 1863), 274–5.
39 *UCLJ* N.S. 1 (Jan. 1865), 24–5. Similarly, see ibid., 9 (May 1863), 135–6; N.S. 1 (May 1865), 138.

40 Ibid., N.S. 1 (Feb. 1865), 54
41 *UCLJ* N.S. 1 (Mar. 1865), 80–1. Similarly, see ibid., N.S. 1 (Jan. 1865), 26–7; (May 1865), 138; (Aug. 1865), 220–1.
42 *CLJ* 4 (Mar. 1868), 65; 4 (Apr. 1868), 86; LSUCA, Convocation Minutes, vol. 5, 173–5, 6 Jun. 1868. See also 31 Vict., c. 23, An Act to Amend the Act Chap. 35 of the Consolidated Statutes of Upper Canada, entitled 'An Act respecting Attorneys at Law.'
43 LSUCA, Convocation Minutes, vol. 5, 8 Dec. 1871
44 For the details of the new examination regulations of 1872 for both students-at-law and articled clerks, see *DHE* 24: 101.
45 See table 2, appendix.
46 39 Vict., c. 31, An Act to Amend the Laws respecting the Law Society. The act is also printed in *CLJ* 12 (Feb. 1876), 41–2. That the Benchers actively sought this act, see ibid., 11 (Jul. 1875), 191. In 1881 additional legislation provided disciplinary teeth. See ibid., 17 (1 Apr. 1881), 134.
47 See Curtis J. Cole, '"A Learned and Honorable Body": The Professionalization of the Ontario Bar, 1867–1929' (PhD diss., University of Western Ontario 1987), 237ff.
48 These later figures are drawn from ibid., 237.
49 Keith MacDonald and George Ritzer, 'The Sociology of the Professions: Dead or Alive?' *Work and Occupations* 15 (Aug. 1988), 257–8.
50 For those who wish to pursue comparisons, W. Wesley Pue offers both a helpful introduction to the literature and his own substantive arguments, which focus on the mid-Victorian period. See the references to his own work, and that of others, in his 'Rebels at the Bar: English Barristers and the County Courts in the 1850s,' *Anglo-American Law Review* 16 (1987), 303–52.
51 Riddell, *Legal Profession,* 4. The change was made as part of the Judicature Act of that year.
52 LSUCA, Convocation Minutes, vol. 5, 8 Sep. 1866, 88–9
53 *Globe*, 25 Feb. 1868
54 See *CLJ* 6 (Jan. 1870), 1–2; *Globe*, 2 and 17 Dec. 1869, 20 Dec. 1870; *JLAO*, 1870–1, 4 Jan.–4 Feb. 1871.
55 See chapter 1 above, 19–20.

CHAPTER 5 *Doctors and the Price of Occupational Closure*

1 Part of what follows is a much condensed and simplified version of our article 'The Origins of Organized Medicine in Ontario, 1850–1869,' in *Health, Disease and Medicine: Essays in Canadian History*, ed. Charles G. Roland (Toronto: Hannah Institute for the History of Medicine 1984), 65–95. The specialist reader who wishes more detail and documentation on the medical politics of the period 1850 to 1869 should consult that essay.
2 For our sources and calculations, see section B of the appendix.

3 As late as 1890 only 60 per cent of Ontario's municipalities had appointed medical health officers; see Richard B. Splane, *Social Welfare in Ontario, 1791–1893* (Toronto: University of Toronto Press 1965), 199.
4 See the lists of coroners in J. Rordans, *The Upper Canada Law Directory for 1858* (Toronto 1858); ibid., *The Ontario Law List*, 6th ed. (Toronto 1870); *JLAO*, 1871–2, Sessional Papers, No. 21. For a cross-check on those coroners who were doctors, we consulted the Ontario *Medical Register* for 1872.
5 The main biographical sources for this analysis are as follows: the relevant biographies in William Canniff, *The Medical Profession in Upper Canada, 1783–1850* (Toronto 1894); W. Stewart Wallace, ed., *The Macmillan Dictionary of Canadian Biography*, 3rd ed. rev. (Toronto: Macmillan 1963); *DCB*, vols 8–12; A.A. Travill, *Medicine at Queen's, 1854–1920: A Peculiarly Happy Relationship* ([Kingston] Faculty of Medicine, Queen's University, and the Hannah Institute for the History of Medicine 1988); Murray L. Barr, *A Century of Medicine at Western* (London, ON: University of Western Ontario 1977). For obituaries, we consulted the *Lancet*, various volumes, 7 (1874–5) to 39 (1905–6); *OMJ* 2 (1893–4); *CP* 2 (1877) to 19 (1894). For listings of the members of the Medical Council see the yearly record of the OMC proceedings in *DMJ* and *Lancet*. For the record of members of the Ontario legislature, see Roderick Lewis, comp., *Centennial Edition of a History of the Electoral Districts, Legislatures and Ministries of the Province of Ontario, 1867–1968* (Toronto n.d.). For educational qualifications, see *Medical Register* for 1872.
6 Statutes of Ontario, 1869, c. 45, s. 8 (2) and 25
7 See for example *Globe*, 15 Jan. 1869; *Leader*, 15 and 25 Jan. 1869. Drs Clarke and McGill, who had responsibility for the bill in the legislature, later claimed that copies of the bill had been circulated, and in any case, there had been ongoing discussion of such a measure for at least two years. Both points are true, but many doctors never saw the copies. Moreover, at the last council meeting, in 1868, members had given the legislation committee no instructions to pursue such a course. The shock and outrage in 1869 suggest that most doctors were not aware that unification was about to be thrust upon them without discussion or debate.
8 See *Globe*, 7 Dec. 1868.
9 Ibid. See also ibid., 5 Jun. 1868; *DMJ* 1 (Aug. 1869), 238.
10 *DMJ* 1 (1 Nov. 1868), 49–50. Similarly see ibid., 1 (Aug. 1869), 229–30.
11 Ibid., 1 (1869), 238
12 *Globe* and *Leader*, 15 Jan. 1869
13 *Globe*, 15 Jan. 1869; see also *DMJ* 1 (Aug. 1869), 236–7.
14 *DMJ* 1 (Aug. 1869), 236–7
15 Ibid., 238; *Globe*, 7 and 11 Dec. 1868, 15 Jan. 1869
16 *CMJ* 5 (1869), 336; *Globe*, 22 Jan. 1869. Similarly, see *CMJ* 5 (Feb. 1869), 367.

17 *DMJ* 1 (Apr. 1869), 158; H.E. MacDermot, *History of the Canadian Medical Association, 1867–1921* (Toronto: Murray Printing 1935), ch. 3
18 *CMJ* 5 (May 1869), 497
19 Ibid., 5 (Apr. 1869), 472–6
20 Ibid., 5 (May 1869), 497–502
21 The petition met a sad fate. It got lost on an Ottawa doctor's desk and sat there for a year before being forwarded for publication – a protest movement becalmed indeed. Ibid., 7 (1871), 321–3.
22 Our calculations here are based on a count of the registration qualifications in the Ontario *Medical Register*, 1872.
23 *CMJ* 5 (Apr. 1869), 472–3
24 See AO, Robert Harrison diary, 28 Dec. 1865 to Mar. 1866; AO, William Cochrane diaries, 5–10 Sep. 1870.
25 See *Mail*, 27 Feb. 1874.
26 The *Globe*'s owner, George Brown, may or may not have supported the principle of therapeutic diversity, but later in life, at least, he made use of regular doctors. When he was shot, in 1880, two regulars were called immediately, and other regulars attended him during the days he lay dying; one of them, indeed, is referred to as 'his regular medical attendant.' By the 1870s, however, his younger brother Gordon had taken over responsibility for the editorial pages, and here we have a direct link to homeopathy, for he was one of a bevy of leading citizens who organized a lay lobby in favour of the homeopathic bill of 1874. Thus our guess is that Gordon Brown's preference in medical attendants had much to do with the editorial line pursued by the *Globe*. See *Globe*, 12 May 1880; *Mail*, 27 Feb. 1874; J.M.S. Careless, *Brown of the Globe* (Toronto: Macmillan 1963), II: chs. 9 and 10, and esp. 300, 359–60; see also 399n191.
27 *CMJ* 5 (May 1869), 498
28 Quoted in *Canadian Journal of Science, Literature and History* (Jul. 1869), 211
29 See list of re-elected councillors in *CMJ* 6 (Jul. 1870), 17
30 Ibid., 17–33. The total vote was twenty to seven, but that includes the ten homeopathic and eclectic members of Council.
31 See MacDermot, *Canadian Medical Association*, ch. 3.
32 *CMJ* 6 (1870), 509–10; MacDermot, *Canadian Medical Association*, 53–7
33 *CMJ* 6 (1870), 567–8
34 *Lancet* 3 (Apr. 1871), 341–2
35 See, for example, ibid., 3 (Jul. 1871), 459; 6 (Feb. 1874), 203.
36 *DMJ* 2 (Jul. 1870), 193. In 1874 two doctors testified before a legislative committee that the numbers annually licensed in the years after 1870 remained between forty and fifty; see *Lancet* 6 (Apr. 1874), 262.
37 *DMJ* 1 (Aug. 1869), 227
38 *Lancet* 3 (May 1871), 423

39 *DMJ* 1 (Aug. 1869), 237. For similar remarks see W. Marsden in *CMJ* 6 (1870), 193ff.; similarly see ibid., 6 (Jul. 1870), 27.
40 *Lancet* 3 (May 1871), 368-9; 3 (Jun. 1871), 431-3; 4 (Sep. 1871), 29-30
41 See *CMJ* 6 (1870), 509-10; *Lancet* 3 (Jul. 1871), 458-61.
42 See *JLAO*, 13 Jan. 1874, 15. For a more extended account of these conflicts see Ronald Hamowy, *Canadian Medicine: A Study in Restricted Entry* (Vancouver: Fraser Institute 1984), 100ff.
43 That doesn't mean that peace broke out everywhere, however. In 1875, for example, a major dispute developed in London over hospital privileges, and again in 1882 when, for reasons which remain unclear, the editor of the *CJMS* reopened hostilities with a long succession of editorials condemning consultations with homeopaths. See for example *London Free Press*, 2 Sep. 1875; *London Advertiser*, 24 Aug., 7 and 21 Sep. 1875; *CJMS* 7 (Feb. 1882), 61-2; 7 (Mar. 1882), 97-8; 7 (Apr. 1882), 128-9; *Lancet* 14 (June 1882), 318.
44 See *Lancet* 5 (1872-3), 121-3.
45 See ibid., 5 (1872-3), 86-8, 121-31, and 199-201. For a more detailed account of the decline of eclecticism see J.T.H. Connor, '"A Sort of *Felo-de-Se*": Eclecticism, Related Medical Sects, and Their Decline in Victorian Ontario,' *BHM* 65 (1991), 503-27.
46 Connor, 'Eclecticism,' 37-8
47 See chapter 3 above, 55.
48 *Lancet* 14 (Sep. 1881), 389
49 Though it misses some of the more recent literature, the best single review of the issues anywhere remains S.E.D. Shortt, 'Physicians, Science and Status: Issues in the Professionalization of Anglo-American Medicine in the Nineteenth Century,' *Medical History* 27 (1983), 51-68. For a blunt application of the revisionist position see Hamowy, *Canadian Medicine*.
50 For an extended (and illuminating) review of the advances made in medicine over the entire previous century, see the *Globe*'s summary of and commentary on an article, originally published in the English *Fortnightly*, by Morell MacKenzie, 26 Jun. 1886, 8.
51 On ophthalmology see the 'state of the art' review by A.M. Rosebrugh in the *Canadian Journal of Science, Literature and History*, Jan. 1866, 1-31. For a commentary on the spread of specialisms see *Lancet* 6 (Aug. 1874), 389. On medical technology generally see S.J. Reiser, *Medicine and the Reign of Technology* (Cambridge: Cambridge University Press 1978). On anaesthetics and Listerism see two works by J.T.H. Connor: 'Joseph Lister's System of Wound Management and the Canadian Medical Practitioner, 1867-1900' (MA, University of Western Ontario 1980), and 'To Be Rendered Unconscious of Torture: Anaesthesia in Canada, 1847-1920' (MPhil, University of Waterloo 1983).
52 See Jacalyn Duffin, 'A Rural Practice in Nineteenth-Century Ontario: The

Continuing Medical Education of James Miles Langstaff,' *CBMH* 5 (1988), esp. 9–10 and 15–17.
53 Kenneth M. Ludmerer, *Learning to Heal: The Development of American Medical Education* (New York: Basic Books 1985), 78
54 See above, note 26.
55 Quoted in Shortt, 'Physicians, Science and Status,' 60
56 Christopher Armstrong and H.V. Nelles, *Monopoly's Moment: The Organization and Regulation of Canadian Utilities, 1830–1930* (1986; Toronto: University of Toronto Press 1988), 63
57 Shortt, 'Physicians, Science and Status,' 67–8
58 Wendy Mitchinson, *The Nature of Their Bodies: Women and Their Doctors in Victorian Canada* (Toronto: University of Toronto Press 1991), 163, but see more generally her discussion on pp. 162–91. See also J.T.H. Connor, 'Minority Medicine in Ontario, 1795 to 1903: A Study of Medical Pluralism and Its Decline' (PhD diss., University of Waterloo 1989), ch. 2. Though it is an American account, an indispensable and persuasive history is Judith Walzer Leavitt, *Brought to Bed: Childbearing in America, 1750 to 1950* (New York: Oxford University Press 1986). On the issues raised in this particular paragraph, see esp. 38–9.
59 William R. Brock, *Investigation and Responsibility: Public Responsibility in the United States, 1865–1900* (Cambridge: Cambridge University Press 1984), 58; on the role of religion, see ch. 2. A rewarding discussion of the relationship between religion and the marketplace is to be found in Fred Hirsch, *Social Limits to Growth* (Cambridge, MA: Harvard University Press 1976), ch. 10. Some aspects of mid-nineteenth-century Protestant social thought are treated in A.B. McKillop, *A Disciplined Intelligence: Critical Inquiry and Canadian Thought in the Victorian Era* (Montreal and Kingston: McGill-Queen's University Press 1979), ch. 2. There is a fine description of the wide variety of other sorts of licensing activity in Upper Canada in William Thomas Matthews, '"By and For the Large Propertied Interests": The Dynamics of Local Government in Six Upper Canadian Towns during the Era of Commercial Capitalism, 1832–60' (PhD diss., McMaster University 1985), esp. ch. 3.
60 Thomas L. Haskell, ed., *The Authority of Experts* (Bloomington: Indiana University Press 1984), 185
61 See Michael Bliss, 'The Protective Impulse,' in *Oliver Mowat's Ontario*, ed. Donald Swainson (Toronto: Macmillan 1972), 189–210. For the dairymen, see *Globe*, 14 Feb. 1876. See also Ben Forster, *A Conjunction of Interests: Business, Politics, and Tariffs, 1825–1879* (Toronto: University of Toronto Press 1986), 110ff., 202; Gregory Kealey, *Toronto Workers Respond to Industrial Capitalism, 1867–1892* (Toronto: University of Toronto Press 1980), esp. chs. 3–6.
62 See Harold Perkin, *The Rise of Professional Society: England since 1880*

(London and New York: Routledge 1989), esp. 6–8. For an extended treatment of his argument, see his short essay *Professionalism, Property and English Society since 1880* ([Reading]: University of Reading Press 1981). For another, not exactly parallel, argument which points in the same direction, see Paul Starr, *The Social Transformation of American Medicine* (New York: Basic Books 1982), esp. 3–29.

63 Kealey, *Toronto Workers*, 75. Similarly, see Bryan D. Palmer, *A Culture in Conflict: Skilled Workers and Industrial Capitalism in Hamilton, Ontario, 1860–1911* (Montreal and Kingston: McGill-Queen's University Press 1979), 74–5.

CHAPTER 6 *The Ministry*

1 The phrase is from William Westfall, *Two Worlds: The Protestant Culture of Nineteenth-Century Ontario* (Montreal and Kingston: McGill-Queen's University Press 1989), 119. Generally, see Westfall; Curtis Fahey, *In His Name: The Anglican Experience in Upper Canada, 1791–1854* (Ottawa: Carleton University Press 1991); C.F. Headon, 'The Influence of the Oxford Movement upon the Church of England in Eastern and Central Canada, 1840–1900' (PhD diss., McGill University 1974); Alan L. Hayes, ed., *By Grace Co-Workers: Building the Anglican Diocese of Toronto, 1780–1989* (Toronto: Anglican Book Centre 1989).

2 Fahey's *In His Name*, 197ff., is an excellent account of the road to independence. See also T.R. Millman, 'Beginnings of the Synodical Movement in Colonial Anglican Churches with Special Reference to Canada,' *JCCHS* 21 (1979), 3–19; Hayes, *By Grace Co-Workers*, 31–9; Spencer Ervin, *The Development of the Synodical System in the Anglican Church of Canada* (Amber, PA: Trinity Press 1969), 3–4; *Canons, By-Laws and Resolutions Adopted by the Synod of the Diocese of Toronto* (Toronto: Leader Office 1873), 50–1.

3 Hayes, *By Grace Co-Workers*, 45

4 Algoma, however, established a synod in the mid-1890s. For a description of its special status and unique history see Harry Huskins, 'The Anglican Church in Algoma in the Nineteenth Century' (MA, Laurentian University 1989).

5 For a summary of the various estimates of high church and tractarian loyalties among the clergy made by a number of historians see Fahey, *In His Name*, 247.

6 The best introduction to the influence of tractarianism on the Upper Canadian church is ibid., esp. 240–1. See also Headon, 'Oxford Movement,' ch. 5.

7 Westfall, *Two Worlds*, 122

8 For an introduction see Frederick V. Mills, *Bishops by Ballot: An Eighteenth-Century Ecclesiastical Revival* (New York: Oxford University Press 1978), esp. 288ff.

9 See Fahey, *In His Name*, 198–9; AO, John Strachan Papers, Rev. John Bethune to John Strachan, 25 Jan. 1836; *Canons, By-Laws and Resolutions*, 48.

10 An account of the meeting can be found in *The Church*, 8 May 1851. See also Fahey, *In His Name*, 206ff.

11 Quoted in *Echo*, 23 May 1856. Similarly, see AO, A.N. Bethune Papers, John Strachan to A.N. Bethune, 13 Dec. 1854; *The Echo and Protestant Episcopal Recorder* [*Echo*], 9 May 1856.
12 While it was probably something of an exaggeration, one observer could remark matter-of-factly in 1884 that '"Low Church" Protestantism ... includes well-nigh all the lay element of the Anglican Church in Canada': Pelham Mulvany, *Toronto Past and Present Until 1882* (Toronto 1884), 201.
13 *Echo*, 19 Oct. 1856. Similarly see *EC*, 21 Sep. 1876; 5 Mar. 1877; 5 Sep. 1878, 266. For evangelicalism generally see Fahey, *In His Name*, 254–5; D.C. Masters, 'The Anglican Evangelicals in Toronto, 1870–1900,' *JCCHS* 20 (1978), 51–66.
14 For a lengthy and illuminating contemporary commentary on these differences, argued from the evangelical perspective, see *EC*, 24 Oct. 1889, Rev. J.P. Sheraton, 'The Christian Ministry in Its Relation to the Christian People,' 291–3.
15 They were not absent, however. See, for example, Bruce S. Elliott, 'Ritualism and the Beginnings of the Reformed Episcopal Movement in Ottawa,' *JCCHS* 27 (1985), 18–47.
16 There is an excellent introduction to the list of lay demands in Hayes, *By Grace Co-Workers*, 48–51; but see also his article 'The Struggle for the Rights of the Laity in the Diocese of Toronto, 1850–79,' *JCCHS* 26 (1984), 5–17.
17 H.E. Turner, 'Protestantism and Progress: The Church Association of the Diocese of Toronto, 1873–79,' *JCCHS* 22 (1980), 9.
18 The Toronto newspapers, and especially the *Globe*, feasted on Anglican conflicts throughout the 1870s.
19 On England see Alan Haig, *The Victorian Clergy* (London: Croom Helm 1984), 248.
20 *Proceedings of Synod, Diocese of Toronto, for 1870*, 23
21 *Echo*, 1 Apr. 1858. Italics added
22 *Canadian Churchman*, 6 Aug. 1863
23 *Globe*, 25 Jun. 1875
24 A full history of the patronage question, along with the proceedings of Synod 1867–71 in the matter, can be found in *Canons, By-Laws and Resolutions*, 94–102.
25 For a full description of the pertinent canons in each diocese see *EC*, 28 May 1891, 37–42.
26 For a brief but clear introduction to the forms of Presbyterian governance see Richard W. Vaudry, *The Free Church in Victorian Canada, 1844–1861* (Waterloo, ON: Wilfrid Laurier University Press 1989), 2–4. Readers should be aware that Vaudry's book is a very much distilled version of his doctoral thesis, and on this, as on many other substantive matters, the latter contains much that the book does not. See Vaudry, 'The Free Church in Canada, 1844–61' (PhD diss., McGill University 1984), 254ff. For the role of the clergy and laity in the United Secession Churches see Stewart D. Gill, *The Reverend William Proudfoot and the United Secession Mission in Canada* (Lewiston, NY: Edwin Mellen Press 1991).
27 On this point generally see *The Presbyterian* 18 (Feb. 1865), 84.

28 The best extant account is Vaudry, *Free Church*, ch. 2. The formal titles of the two churches are both cumbrous and confusingly similar. For convenience we will consistently refer to them as the Free Church and the Kirk. For a description of the disruption in Scotland see A.L. Drummond and James Bulloch, *The Scottish Church, 1688–1843* (Edinburgh: The Saint Andrew Press 1973), 222ff.

29 For the Kirk the best introduction, though one that is also muddled and confusing in some places and dead wrong in others, is *Historical Report of the Administration of the Temporalities Fund of the Presbyterian Church of Canada ...* (Montreal 1900). Despite Presbyterian Union, the Temporalities Fund remained intact and functioned until late in the century to help those who had belonged to the old Kirk. The terms of union took no account of the existence of this fund, and it operated independently of the General Assembly or local synods after 1875; thus its existence doesn't surface in the more conventional sources for the history of the united Presbyterian Church. In the Anglican Church the commutation fund was held and administered by the diocese. Except in the case of Algoma, as each new diocese was created it received a share of the original fund. The main sources for the history of these funds are the annual proceedings of the various synods. See for example the annual reports of the 'Clergy Commutation Trust Committee' in *Journal, Church of England Synod, Diocese of Toronto*. Policy and a historical sketch can also be found in *Canons, By-Laws and Resolutions*, 1873, and in the successor volume published in 1895. See also Huskins, 'The Anglican Church in Algoma,' ch. 4.

30 A distinction which confused many contemporaries was that between the first charge on the funds, on the one hand, which was a binding legal commitment to the commuting ministers to pay their stipends, and, on the other, the commutation fund *surplus* – the amount remaining after the first charge was met – which could be disposed of as Synod saw fit.

31 See *Journal, Church of England Synod, Diocese of Toronto*, 1883, Appendix B, 82–4. We will examine salaries and incomes further in chapter 9.

32 The words of *The Church*, quoted in *CG*, 10 May 1843. For other examples see *CG*, 13 May 1833, 1 May 1839, 29 Jan. 1840. Such views were held not just by Anglicans but by Presbyterians as well; see *CG*, 30 May 1838.

33 For some parallel developments in other branches of Ontario Methodism, see Neil Semple, 'The Impact of Urbanization on the Methodist Church in Central Canada, 1854–1884' (PhD diss., University of Toronto 1979).

34 See for example the kind of lay support that Methodists could mobilize for their 'Committee for the Petition on Civil and Religious Privileges,' *Minutes*, Wesleyan Methodist Conference 1838, 195.

35 David Mills, *The Idea of Loyalty in Upper Canada, 1784–1850* (Montreal and Kingston: McGill-Queen's University Press 1988), 64.

36 *CG*, 5 Nov. 1831

37 See R.D. Gidney and W.P.J. Millar, *Inventing Secondary Education: The Rise of*

the High School in Nineteenth-Century Ontario (Montreal and Kingston: McGill-Queen's University Press 1990), 91–2.
38 See for example the editorial in *CG*, 30 Oct. 1844.
39 See *The Doctrine and Discipline*, Wesleyan Methodist Church in Canada (Toronto 1836), 130–6.
40 *Minutes of Conference*, 1855, 305–6
41 For an extended analysis of salaries and incomes, see chapter 9 below.
42 *Home and Foreign Record* 8 (Nov. 1868), 4. In fact they were probably not 'the best paid,' but what is important here is the perception and not the reality.
43 *CG*, 1 May 1867, 69.
44 For the best introduction see Semple, 'Impact of Urbanization on the Methodist Church,' ch. 3.
45 See Westfall, *Two Worlds*, ch. 3. See also Neil Semple, 'The Quest for the Kingdom: Aspects of Protestant Revivalism in Nineteenth-Century Ontario,' in *Old Ontario: Essays in Honour of J.M.S. Careless*, ed. David Keane and Colin Read (Toronto: Dundurn Press 1990), 95–117, and Semple, 'Impact of Urbanization on the Methodist Church,' 169ff.
46 See for example *CG*, 11 Feb. 1835, 28 Nov. 1838, 11 Feb. and 4 Aug. 1852.
47 The stationing of preachers became a major issue for the Wesleyans in the years after mid-century. See Semple, 'Impact of Urbanization on the Methodist Church,' 132ff.
48 Cf. ibid., 85.
49 See for example *CG*, 10 May 1837.
50 For some of the reasons see for example *CG*, 6 Apr. 1864, 58. See also *CG*, 19 Jan. 1870, 10; 2 Feb. 1870, 18; 23 Nov. 1870, 185; 6 Mar. 1872, 78; 22 Apr. 1874, 124; 5 Sept. 1877, 284. Among the Wesleyans at least, women had long since been excluded from preaching. See Elizabeth Gillan Muir, *Petticoats in the Pulpit: The Story of Early Nineteenth-Century Methodist Women Preachers in Upper Canada* (Toronto: United Church Publishing House 1991), 27, 34–6, 122, 134–5.
51 See for example *CG*, 24 Apr. 1867, 65. For the specifics in this paragraph see *CG*, 10, 24, 31 Jul. 1850 (parsonages); 8 and 29 May 1867, 2 Apr. 1873 (buggies); 29 Jul. 1858, 22 Oct. 1862 (studies and books); 9 Oct. 1878 (servants).
52 Semple, 'Impact of Urbanization on the Methodist Church,' 144
53 *Doctrines and Discipline*, 1850, 40
54 For good examples of the tensions these views imposed, see *CG*, 11 Jul. 1838, 5 Jul. 1854, 5 Sep. 1855, 16 Dec. 1863. For parallel developments in England see Dale A. Johnson, 'The Methodist Quest for an Educated Ministry,' *Church History* 51 (1982), 304–20.
55 But some of the most influential editors were also the most enthusiastic promoters of high educational standards – Egerton Ryerson and E.H. Dewart, for example.
56 See *CG*, 2 Dec. 1835; Neil Semple, 'S.S. Nelles and Victoria College, 1850–

1887,' unpublished paper, Oct. 1988. For examples of the views of E.H. Dewart, a later editor of the *CG*, see *CG*, 21 Dec. 1870, 7 Jun. 1871, 21 Feb. 1872, 9 Oct. 1872.
57 See for example *CG*, 9 Oct. 1878 and 11 Jun. 1879.
58 See Semple, 'Impact of Urbanization on the Methodist Church,' 150–1.
59 *Minutes of Conference*, 1865, 87 and 90
60 See Semple, 'Impact of Urbanization on the Methodist Church,' 152; *DHE*, 24: 43–4; 26: 145.
61 See *Journal of the Third General Conference of the Methodist Church of Canada 1882*, 198. The new standard was to come into force in 1884.
62 *CG*, 19 Sep. 1894, 594
63 See ibid., 20 Sept. 1882
64 Ibid.
65 For some examples see *Minutes of Conference*, 1861, 75; *CG*, 6 May 1863, 1 Apr. 1874, 19 Jul. 1876, 27 Jun. 1877, 19 Jun. 1878, 1 Oct. and 19 Nov. 1879, 27 Apr. and 22 Jun. 1881.
66 *CG*, 23 Nov. 1881
67 *DC*, 4 Mar. 1880, 114
68 These are our own calculations, based on a count of the qualifications of ministers in all of Ontario as listed in the various *Methodist Church Minutes of Conferences*. There is, however, some variation between conferences, the highest being Niagara, with 17 per cent holding arts degrees.
69 See for example *CG*, 26 Feb. 1873. By 1900, according to Nathanael Burwash, something like half of all active Methodist ministers had attended college for some period of time. See Michael Gauvreau, *The Evangelical Century: College and Creed in English Canada from the Great Revival to the Great Depression* (Montreal and Kingston: McGill-Queen's University Press 1991), 241 and 356n50.
70 *The Presbyterian* 18 (Jan. 1865), 9
71 To cite but a few examples, William Aikins, the head of the Toronto School of Medicine, and Michael Lavell of the Kingston Medical School; Dr Brouse, another long-standing member of the Medical Council and future senator; A.W. Lauder, a prominent Toronto lawyer and future MPP. For Aikins, see *DCB*, 12; for Brouse, see *Journal of the Third General Conference 1882*, 157; for Lauder, see *Globe*, 9 Apr. 1878.
72 *CG*, 20 Sep. 1882
73 Quoted in *The Presbyterian* 20 (Oct. 1867), 167–8

CHAPTER 7 *Professional Work*

1 Much of this is increasingly well documented, especially in the *DCB* or in full-scale biographies of individuals. For the law see also Carol Wilton, ed., *Beyond the Law: Lawyers and Business in Canada, 1830 to 1930* (Toronto: The Osgoode

Society 1990). For one doctor's business activities see Charles G. Roland and Bohodar Rubashewsky, 'The Economic Status of the Practice of Dr. Harmaunus Smith ...,' *CBMH* 5 (1988), 28–49. See also Jennifer J. Connor, 'Estate Records and the History of Medicine in Ontario,' *CBMH* 10 (1993), 3.

2 UCA, Nathanael Burwash Diaries, 1861–6. Generally, see Marguerite Van Die, *An Evangelical Mind: Nathanael Burwash and the Methodist Tradition in Canada, 1839–1918* (Montreal and Kingston: McGill-Queen's University Press 1989).

3 UCA, Henry Flesher Bland Diaries, 1870–85. There is a brief biography in the relevant finding aid, as is the case with each of the diaries referred to in the next few notes.

4 UCA, Donald McKerracher Papers, Diary 1875–81

5 AO, Rev. William Cochrane Papers, Diaries 1870–5, 1880–5, 1898–9

6 *CG*, 26 Oct. 1898, 673

7 See Sara Jeannette Duncan, *The Imperialist* (1904; Toronto: McClelland and Stewart 1990); Marian Fowler, *Redney: A Life of Sara Jeannette Duncan* (Markham, ON: Penguin Books 1985), 36–7.

8 AO, J.F. Lundy Diary, 1849–65

9 AO, Duck Family Papers, George Duck Diaries, 1854–8

10 AO, Robert Harrison Diary. There is a lengthy biography of Harrison in *DCB* 10.

11 Paul Romney, *Mr. Attorney: The Attorney General for Ontario in Court, Cabinet, and Legislature, 1791–1899* (Toronto: University of Toronto Press 1986), 37

12 See for example M.A. Garland and Orlo Miller, eds., 'The Diary of H.C.R. Becher,' *Ontario History* 33 (1939), 126. Becher noted 'some 100 ladies in court' at the assizes at Chatham in 1856. Similarly see AO, Robert Harrison Diary, 22 Mar.–3 Apr. 1858.

13 Marion MacRae and Anthony Adamson, *Cornerstones of Order: Courthouses and Town Halls of Ontario, 1784–1914* (Toronto: The Osgoode Society 1983)

14 *UCLJ* 2 (Apr. 1856), 72–3

15 See David Gagan, 'For "Patients of Moderate Means": The Transformation of Ontario's Public General Hospitals, 1880–1950,' *Canadian Historical Review* 70 (Jun. 1989), 151–79.

16 Jacalyn Duffin, 'A Rural Practice in Nineteenth-Century Ontario: The Continuing Medical Education of James Miles Langstaff,' *CBMH* 5 (1988), 6. Similarly, see Roland and Rubashewsky, 'Harmaunus Smith,' 34; UWORC, Dr James R. Anderson, Account Book, Ailsa Craig, 1874–83; AO, Dr W.R. Bowns, Ledger, 1856–72; QUA, W. Youker, Daybook, 1895–9.

17 Peter G. Goheen, *Victorian Toronto, 1850 to 1900: Pattern and Process of Growth* (Chicago: University of Chicago, Dept. of Geography, Research Paper No. 127, 1970), 132

18 Based on our own analysis of the Brantford manuscript census and assessment rolls.

19 In the case of the diarists we have already identified, throughout the rest of this

chapter we will omit precise references for many of our generalizations, for references where we are summarizing a number of diary entries, or where we give an exact or an approximate date in the text. Additional sources will be noted in the conventional way.

20 UCA, Preachers' Plans, Box 1. Our thanks to Neil Semple for drawing these to our attention. For a visual grasp of these circuits, see *Historical Atlas of Canada*, Vol. 2, plate 53.
21 McKerracher Diary, 18 and 19 Mar. 1875
22 Bland Diaries, 1 Mar. 1881
23 See for example Lundy Diary, 4 Jan. 1849.
24 Burwash Diaries, 7 Oct. 1861
25 *DC*, 1 Dec. 1887
26 Similarly see Lundy Diary, 16 Apr. 1849.
27 *Canadian Churchman*, 2 Feb. 1870, 3
28 UWORC. We have changed the names to preserve anonymity and omit any identification of the church for the same reason.
29 See for example Cochrane Diaries, 26–30 Apr. 1870.
30 Cochrane is not a singular example. Cf. UCA, Mark Y. Stark Papers, Stark to Mother, Dundas, 12 Jun. 1847.
31 *DC*, 2 Nov. 1882
32 Though to some readers this may sound implausible, one of the authors, brought up in an 'ordinarily devout' home, took it for granted that Sunday school and two Sunday services were as routine as breakfast. Attending at least one additional church meeting a week was no less so. In understanding the cultural and intellectual ambience of nineteenth-century, and much of twentieth-century, Ontario, the lasting impact on young people of listening to 1,500 hundred sermons or so over a period of fifteen years (2 x 52 x 15 would be a minimal calculation) deserves attention. It would also be a useful antidote to assessments based mainly on the secular press or other like sources.
33 For an example see *Globe*, 12 Jun. 1876.
34 *Mail*, 17 Jan. 1880; *Globe*, 6 Jan. 1875, 2
35 Harrison Diary, 4 Mar. 1860. For another example see '*A Woman with a Purpose*': *The Diaries of Elizabeth Smith, 1872–1884*, ed. Veronica Strong-Boag (Toronto: University of Toronto Press 1980), 29–30.
36 *DC*, 9 Aug. 1888, 502
37 Burwash Diaries, 14 Dec. 1861
38 Cochrane Diaries, 8 Apr. 1870
39 *CG*, 18 Jul. 1860, 114. Similarly, see *Globe*, 29 Apr. 1876, 2; 6 May 1876, 2; 10 May 1876, 2.
40 AO, J.G. Malloch Diary, 18 Feb. 1842
41 There is a nice example of this in H.H. Langton, ed., *A Gentlewoman in Upper Canada: The Journals of Anne Langton* (Toronto: Clarke Irwin 1964), 131.

42 *QCJ*, 8 May 1880, 140
43 A good example of the personal turmoil a local clerical scandal could cause was the Beattie case in Brantford. Cf. Cochrane Diaries, 15 Jan. 1883, and a number of entries following that.
44 See for example *Globe*, 28 Apr. 1880, 4; 13 Dec. 1880; 27 Jul. 1882; *Brantford Expositor*, 24 Jul. 1882. On the Beattie case as a major news story see *Globe*, 31 Jan., 2, 3, 5 Feb. 1883.
45 *CG*, 2 Mar. 1864, 38. Similarly see *CG*, 20 Apr. 1870, 63.
46 See, for example, Joseph C. McClelland, 'The Macdonnell Heresy Trial,' *Canadian Journal of Theology* 4 (Oct. 1958), 273–84.
47 *DC*, 9 Apr. 1885, 232
48 See for example Cochrane Diaries, 26–30 Apr. 1870.
49 See for example *Globe*, 12 May 1886, 4.
50 See *EMR*, May 1850.
51 Duncan, *The Imperialist*, 66
52 For a wonderful description of one Conference meeting, see *Canadian Methodist Magazine* VI (Jul. 1877), 75–9; see also ibid., XIV (Jul.–Dec. 1881), 85–6.
53 For a typical example see Bland Diaries, week of 21 May 1870.
54 See for example *Presbyterian Review*, 28 Jan. 1897, 626; *Canadian Churchman*, 16 Sep. 1863, 17 Aug. 1864, 15 Feb. and 22 Mar. 1865; *CG*, 31 Mar. 1858; 9 Apr. 1862; 12 Aug. 1868, 134; 20 Oct. 1869, 166. There is also a nice description of such a meeting in Flesher Bland Diaries, 25 Feb. 1881.
55 For an example see Lundy Diary, 18 Feb. 1849.
56 An additional indicative source here is AO, Rev. Wm. Ritchie Diaries. See the entries for 4 Mar., 9, 10, 19 Apr., 19 Aug., 3, 28, 29 Sep., 6 Oct. 1850.
57 Toronto Academy of Medicine Archives, Wm Tempest, Sr, to Mary, 16 May 1856
58 AO, Rev. John Fenwick Papers, J. Whyte to J. Fenwick, Osgoode, 17 Mar. 1860
59 When M.S. Bidwell moved from Kingston to York in 1833, for example, he offered to become agent for the Brockville partnership of Ford and Bogart in Brockville, and the ensuing correspondence leaves a nice record of the routines of agency work and the relationships it involved. See AO, Bidwell Papers, Correspondence, 1833 and 1834.
60 NAC, Hamnet K. Pinhey Papers, Records of law firm, Lewis and Pinhey/Pinhey, Christie and Hill, Series D, file 1, Correspondence, 1866–77. Much of Pinhey's business was of this sort – dealing with firms or lawyers from all over Canada with business in Ottawa.
61 AO, Benson Family Papers, T.M. Benson Journals, no. 1, 1857– . Along with the collections noted in the last few references we have also found the following useful: AO, Richard H. Holland, Solicitor, Port Hope, Docket Book 1860–72; R.J. Turner, Chancery lawyer, Toronto, Docket Book 1849–56; James Reynolds Papers; James Maclennan Papers; Thos. Radenhurst Papers; Gemmill Family

Papers; A.N. Buell Papers; Pringle Family Papers; UWORC, Partridge and Essery, Solicitors etc., Daybooks.
62 For a similar pattern of activities, see AO, J.G. Malloch Diary, 1841–2.
63 For the latter see Harrison Diary, 7 Jul. 1860. His routines can be sampled simply by reading, say, the first six months of 1860 or Aug.–Nov. 1861.
64 The circuit schedules were routinely printed in the *UCLJ*. See for example 8 (May 1862), 60; 9 (Mar. 1863), 66; N.S. 3 (Feb. 1867), 56.
65 W.H. Smith, *Canada: Past, Present and Future* (Toronto: Thos Maclean [1851–2]), I: 107–8
66 See for example *The Canadian Pocket Diary for 1875* (n.p.: n.d.)
67 AO, Pringle Papers, Series 3 (b) i, Legal documents, Printed list of cases, Cornwall Spring [Assizes], 1856
68 MTRL, Baldwin Room, Henry O'Brien Diaries, 4 Nov. 1858. Similarly see the comment in *CG*, 30 Oct. 1850.
69 MTRL, Baldwin Room, Henry O'Brien Diaries, 9 and 13 Nov. 1858
70 For a nice example see *UCLJ* 5 (Jan. 1859), 19–20.
71 AO, J.G. Malloch Diary, 2 Nov. 1842. For a comment on similar problems in the Toronto courts, see *CLJ* 5 (Oct. 1869), 253.
72 Garland and Miller, 'Diary of H.C.R. Becher,' 3 Mar. 1856
73 George W. Spragge, ed., 'A Diary of 1837 by Sandfield Macdonald,' *Ontario History* 47 (Jan. 1955), 8–11.
74 AO, Gemmill Family Papers, John A. Gemmill, Jr, to Father, 19 Jul. 1874
75 AO, J.G. Malloch Diary, 31 May 1842
76 Duck Diary, 20 Oct. 1858
77 Harrison Diary, 12 Oct. 1875 and successive entries for three weeks
78 AO, Douglas Family Papers, Wm Douglas to Jeannie, Chatham, 7 Nov. 1861
79 See for example Duck Diaries, 30–1 Oct. 1854.
80 Duffin, 'A Rural Practice'; Jacalyn Duffin, *Langstaff: A Nineteenth-Century Medical Life* (Toronto: University of Toronto Press 1993)
81 UWORC, Dr Wm. Waugh, Reminiscences of 60 Years Medical Practice in the City of London, 6 Feb. 1932 [typescript], 4–5
82 Duffin, 'A Rural Practice,' 8, 16–19
83 AO, Dr James C. Goodwin Coll., Invoices, 1823 and 1827, C. Widmer to Mr Howard
84 *Lancet* 17 (Mar. 1885), 223
85 Duffin, 'A Rural Practice,' 8–11
86 The kind of surgery done and the difference between minor and capital operations can be gauged in the many surviving 'tariffs of fees.' See for example Toronto Academy of Medicine Archives, 'Tariff of Fees ... of Medical Practitioners of Toronto, 1873'; 'Tariff of Fees of the Medical Association of the County of Simcoe' [c. 1877]; *Lancet* 7 (Mar. 1875), 220–1.
87 Toronto Academy of Medicine Archives, William Aikins Papers, Petch to Aikins, Mono Mills, 1852

Notes to pages 146–9   443

88 MTRL, Baldwin Room, 'The Memoirs of Henry Orton M.D.' [typescript], 14
89 See J.T.H. Connor, 'Minority Medicine in Ontario, 1795 to 1903: A Study of Medical Pluralism and Its Decline' (PhD diss., University of Waterloo 1989), ch. 2; Wendy Mitchinson, *The Nature of Their Bodies: Women and Their Doctors in Victorian Canada* (Toronto: University of Toronto Press 1991), 162–75.
90 Duffin, 'A Rural Practice,' 11
91 See *CP* 23 (Sep. 1898), 527.
92 MTRL, Baldwin Room, 'Memoirs of Henry Orton,' 12
93 Quoted in S.E.D. Shortt, *Victorian Lunacy: Richard M. Bucke and the Practice of Late Nineteenth-Century Psychiatry* (Cambridge: Cambridge University Press 1986), 20–1
94 Susanna Moodie, *Life in the Clearings* (Toronto: Macmillan 1959), 124
95 *UCJ* 1 (Jul. 1851), 152–3
96 *Globe*, 24 Oct. 1884, 4
97 But there were exceptions. See for example Toronto Academy of Medicine Archives, St Catharines Medical Society for Mutual Improvement, Minutes 1871–9.
98 Duffin, *Langstaff*, 31
99 William Canniff, *The Medical Profession in Upper Canada, 1783–1850* (Toronto: Wm. Briggs 1894), 658.
100 Elizabeth Bloomfield, 'Lawyers as Members of Urban Elites in Southern Ontario, 1860–1920,' in *Beyond the Law: Lawyers and Business in Canada, 1830 to 1930*, ed. Carol Wilton (Toronto: The Osgoode Society 1990), 121–2.
101 There is a particularly good surviving record of such a relationship in the Robert Baldwin Papers, where the young Adam Wilson minded the shop with the help of a bevy of law clerks and students, while Baldwin spent much of his time in government and out of it in Kingston and Montreal, offering, when he had a moment, his advice to Wilson and his counsel to clients, or occasionally appearing in the courts. See MTRL, Baldwin Room, Robert Baldwin Papers, Correspondence from Adam Wilson to Baldwin through the 1840s. For other examples see Duffin, *Langstaff*, 28–9; Toronto Academy of Medicine Archives, William Aikins Papers, Aikins to Ogden, 13 Nov. 1852; MTRL, Baldwin Room, Robert Baldwin Papers, Jas Macintosh to R. Baldwin, 26 May 1842; Baldwin Room, 'Memoir of Henry Orton,' 17–18; AO, James Maclennan Papers, 1 Feb. 1860, Articles of Partnership, Oliver Mowat and James Maclennan; AO, Blake Papers, Box 17, Misc., Env. 1, 'Memorandum of Articles of Partnership 1862–1885.'
102 AO, Benson Family Papers, T.M. Benson Letterbooks, Benson to Martin Downsford, Lindsay, 19 Jun. 1862.
103 AO, Blake Papers, Edward Blake Family Correspondence, William Hume Blake to Edward Blake, 24 Dec. 1856
104 Harrison Diary, 20–4 Feb. 1859. In the diaries there is a fairly detailed description early in 1859 of the formation of this partnership, and in 1870 of its dissolution.

105 Ibid., 17 Jan. 1860
106 Leonore Davidoff and Catherine Hall, *Family Fortunes: Men and Women of the English Middle Class, 1780–1850* (London: Hutchinson 1987).
107 See Harrison's comment on this point, 31 Dec. 1871.
108 See Canniff, *The Medical Profession*, 246. One woman who did 'manage the shop' was Mrs Rolph, while John Rolph was preoccupied with politics. William Aikins was carrying on the practice, but she is to be found advising Aikins about both the practice and the school. Cf. Toronto Academy of Medicine Archives, William Aikins Papers, Mrs Rolph to W.T. Aikins, Quebec, 1 Sep. 1852. With better sources at his command, S.E.D. Shortt suggests that, in the early twentieth century, wives frequently helped out with the husband's medical practice; see '"Before the Age of Miracles": The Rise, Fall, and Rebirth of General Practice in Canada, 1890–1940,' in *Health, Disease and Medicine: Essays in Canadian History*, ed. Charles G. Roland (Toronto: Hannah Institute for the History of Medicine 1984), 132.
109 *Canadian Churchman*, 7 Apr. 1869. For other examples see *The Presbyterian* 5 (Jan. 1852), 3; *CG*, 8 Apr. 1874, 109; 1 May 1889, 275; *DC*, 2 Dec. 1880, 585.
110 *CG*, 9 Oct. 1878, 327
111 *Cdn Chman*, 17 Jan. 1895, 41
112 *DC*, 2 Jul. 1885, 420–1
113 Lundy Diary, 9 Jan. 1859
114 Cochrane Diaries [Jennie's entries], 9 Mar., 22 Apr., 28 May 1874
115 McKerracher Diary, 17 Jan. 1875
116 Bland Diaries, 13 Jan. 1881
117 Cochrane Diaries, 6 Mar. 1874
118 Burwash Diaries, 18 Sep. 1861

CHAPTER 8 *Professional Education*

1 For a thorough review of the Scottish background see Stewart Mechie, 'Education for the Ministry in Scotland since the Reformation,' *Records of the Scottish Church History Society* XIV, Part II (1961), 115–33.
2 For a fine introduction to nineteenth-century Anglican clerical education see Brian Heeney, *A Different Kind of Gentleman: Parish Clergy as Professional Men in Early and Mid-Victorian England* (Hamden, CT: Archon Books 1976), ch. 5. A more intensive study, with a comprehensive bibliography, is Alan Haig, *The Victorian Clergy* (London: Croom Helm 1984).
3 For an introduction to the development of professional education in England generally in the nineteenth century see Arthur Engel, 'The English Universities and Professional Education,' in *The Transformation of Higher Learning, 1860–1930*, ed. Konrad H. Jarausch (Chicago: University of Chicago Press 1983), 293–305. For medical education in Britain see Charles Newman, *The Evolution of Medical Education in the Nineteenth Century* (London: Oxford University Press

1957); M. Jeanne Peterson, *The Medical Profession in Mid-Victorian London* (Berkeley: University of California Press 1978), ch. 2; Irvine Loudon, *Medical Care and the General Practitioner, 1750–1850* (Oxford: Clarendon Press 1986), ch. 2; Susan C. Lawrence, 'Entrepreneurs and Private Enterprise: The Development of Medical Lecturing in London, 1775–1820,' *BHM* 62 (1988), 171–92.

4 The history of the various universities and their theological schools is now reasonably well documented; for an introduction and guide to the literature see A.B. McKillop, *Matters of Mind: The University in Ontario, 1791–1951* (Toronto: University of Toronto Press 1994). Though outside the scope of this narrative, McGill's medical school exercised an enormous influence in Ontario by the standards it set and by the fact that a large number of its students were from the upper province and returned to practise there. See R.D. Gidney and W.P.J. Millar, 'The Origins of Organized Medicine in Ontario, 1850–1869,' in *Health, Disease and Medicine: Essays in Canadian History*, ed. Charles G. Roland (Toronto: Hannah Institute for the History of Medicine 1984), 78. For a historiographical introduction to the literature on Ontario's medical schools see Sandra F. McRae, 'The "Scientific Spirit" in Medicine at the University of Toronto' (PhD diss., University of Toronto 1987), 54ff. See also A.A. Travill, *Medicine at Queen's, 1854–1920* (Kingston, ON: Faculty of Medicine, Queen's University, 1988), a book which deserves a wider readership and better distribution than it has thus far received.

5 The sources for this and the succeeding paragraph are to be found in various published 'announcements' and calendars of the medical schools and universities.

6 Quoted in *The Church*, 14 Nov. 1850. For the development of the early hospitals see W.G. Cosbie, *The Toronto General Hospital, 1819–1965: A Chronicle* (Toronto: Macmillan 1975); Margaret Angus, *Kingston General Hospital: A Social and Institutional History* (Montreal and Kingston: McGill-Queen's University Press 1973).

7 *Medical Register for Upper Canada 1867*, 54

8 *Lancet* 3 (Sep. 1870), 32

9 The conclusions in this paragraph are based on a comparison of the annual announcements of the schools with the published *Annual Announcements* of the CPSO.

10 See *Calendar of Queen's University, 1864–5*, 66.

11 Consolidated Statutes of the Province of Canada, 1859, c. LXXVI, An Act respecting the Practice of Physic and Surgery, and the Study of Anatomy, s. 3

12 Quoted in George Spragge, 'Trinity Medical College,' *Ontario History* 58 (Jun. 1966), 72

13 Toronto Academy of Medicine Archives, William Aikins Papers, G.W. Brigham to Aikins, Tillsonburgh [sic], 8 Sep. 1856. Italics in original.

14 See *CJMS* 1 (Jan. 1876), 31–2; *Globe*, 19 Oct. 1882. For a review of the incidence of grave-robbing see Royce MacGillivray, 'Body-Snatching in Ontario,' *CBMH* 5 (Summer 1988), 51–60.

15 See *CP* 10 (Mar. 1885), 91; *Lancet* 21 (Jul. 1888), 346. We have dealt with this question in greater detail in R.D. Gidney and W.P.J. Millar, '"Beyond the Measure of the Golden Rule": The Contribution of the Poor to Medical Science in Nineteenth-Century Ontario,' *Ontario History* (Sep. 1994).
16 *CJMS* 6 (Nov. 1881), 362–3.
17 *Lancet* 8 (Nov. 1875), 85–6. Similarly see *CJMS* 2 (Dec. 1877), 418–22; 4 (Oct. 1879), 296–8; 6 (May 1881), 154–6.
18 See for example *CJMS* 4 (Oct. 1879), 296–8.
19 See for example *Report of an Investigation by the Trustees of the Toronto General Hospital ...* (Toronto 1855); *JLAO*, 1867–8, Appendix 8, Report of Select Committee ... on the Toronto General Hospital.
20 Unless otherwise noted, the information relating to the Toronto School of Medicine in the next few pages is taken from its published *Annual Announcements*.
21 *Journal of the Second General Conference of the Methodist Church of Canada, 1878*, 205
22 *Globe*, 17 Mar. 1887, 3; 9 Apr. 1887, 9
23 Ibid., 12 Mar. 1887, 8. For other evidence on this point see the opinions expressed by various Toronto doctors in *Globe*, 14 Mar. 1887, 8, and 17 Mar. 1887, 3. We have dealt in more detail with the progress of the proprietary medical schools, and their historiographical context, in R.D. Gidney and W.P.J. Millar, 'The Reorientation of Medical Education in Late Nineteenth-Century Ontario: The Proprietary Medical Schools and the Founding of the Faculty of Medicine at the University of Toronto,' *JHM* 49/1 (1994), 52–78.
24 For Queen's, see *The Presbyterian* 1 (Jun. 1848), 78; Queen's University, *Course of Study 1855–6*, 6–7; Queen's University, *Course of Study 1860*, 5–8. For Knox see *EMR*, May 1855, 106–7; Aug. 1855, 146–7; Richard W. Vaudry, *The Free Church in Victorian Canada, 1844–61* (Waterloo, ON: Wilfrid Laurier Press 1989), 81–83.
25 Edward Richard Schwarz, 'Clergy Education and the 1925 Church Union' (MA, University of Alberta 1974), 78–80.
26 George Rawlyk and Kevin Quinn, *The Redeemed of the Lord Say So: A History of Queen's Theological College 1912–1972* (Kingston, ON: Queen's Theological College 1980), 20–1
27 Quoted in Hilda Neatby, *Queen's University: Volume I, 1841–1917* (Montreal and Kingston: McGill-Queen's University Press 1978), 59.
28 See for example ibid.; *Acts and Proceedings*, General Assembly, Presbyterian Church in Canada, 1893, Appendix 8, Report of the Senate, Knox College.
29 *EMR*, May 1855, 106. For a parallel description of such activities at Queen's see *The Presbyterian* 14 (May 1861), 73.
30 *EMR*, May 1848, 107–8; compare the similar comments about the Queen's Missionary Association in *The Presbyterian* 14 (Jan. 1861), 3–4.

31 See *The Presbyterian* 4 (Aug. 1851), 114; 5 (May 1852), 66; 6 (Sep. 1853), 130.
32 UCA, Rev. Donald McKerracher Papers, Diaries, for the pertinent dates, 1873 and 1874
33 *QCJ*, 12 Feb. 1876, 2
34 We will frequently use the word 'apprenticeship' when referring to law students because of its familiarity and convenience. But it is technically incorrect, as Blaine Baker has pointed out in 'Legal Education in Upper Canada, 1785–1889: The Law Society as Educator,' in *Essays in the History of Canadian Law*, ed. David H. Flaherty (Toronto: University of Toronto Press 1983), II: 81, 132n124. To avoid undue complexity we propose to ignore entirely, throughout this chapter, the special or distinctive regulations for articled clerks (intending attorneys) who were not also students-at-law (intending barristers).
35 This, the specialist reader will be aware, is a different account from that provided by Baker in 'Legal Education.' While we admire that essay in many respects, we also have reservations about some key issues of fact and interpretation. The most significant of these is Baker's assumption that term-keeping amounted to a full year or more in Toronto. The length of term-keeping was clearly defined in the *Rules of the Law Society of Upper Canada* (Toronto 1833), 63, as a period of about a fortnight coinciding with the judicial terms. There were four of these a year, and students had to keep four terms over the course of five years. Thus we suggest two months is about right. Compare Baker, 'Legal Education,' 86–7. If we are correct on this point, and we believe the references made during the legislative debates over the abolition of term-keeping confirm it, then one important emphasis in Baker's argument that the Law Society was an 'educative' force is vitiated; see Legislative Assembly of Ontario, Newspaper Hansard, 15 Jan. 1868; *Globe*, 12 and 14 Nov. 1868.
36 LSUCA, Convocation Minutes, 1-1, Vol. 3, 13 Feb. 1855, 436–8.
37 Ibid., 7 Sep. 1854, 416–17
38 Ibid., 16 Feb. 1855, 443
39 *Globe*, 26 Feb. 1855
40 *The Upper Canada Law List* (Toronto 1862), 47
41 We explore the reasons for this action in chapter 4 above, 78–80.
42 See *DHE*, 24: 101
43 MTRL, Baldwin Room, William Elliott Papers, Diaries, 1847–9; Larratt Smith Diary (Transcripts), 1840–3; Henry O'Brien Diary, 1858–9
44 This may seem confusing since we have already said that students had to pass the Law Society's matriculation examination *before* beginning their five-year term. At this point there was no matriculation for articled clerks, so one could begin as a clerk while preparing for matriculation as a student-at-law.
45 Elliott was now a matriculated student-at-law and was not, according to Law Society regulations, supposed to be employed in any other occupation; clearly this was a rule winked at now and then, though Blake did warn him that the Law

Society was becoming stricter in this respect. See MTRL, Baldwin Room, William Elliott Papers, Diaries, 26 Jun. 1847.
46 For yet another, account of the relative roles of classroom and practice, see Terry Crowley, '"I Want to Be a Veterinarian": Student Life at the OVC 100 Years Ago,' *The Canadian Veterinary Journal* 28 (Jan.–Feb. 1987), 22–5.
47 Ruth Richardson, *Death, Dissection and the Destitute* (Harmondsworth: Penguin Books 1988); Gidney and Millar, 'Beyond the Measure of the Golden Rule.'
48 LSUCA, Convocation Minutes, 1-1, Vol. 3, Petition of the Osgoode Club, 129–33
49 See Baker, 'Legal Education,' 93–4.
50 There are three accounts of these developments and thus we have not attempted to outline them in any detail here. See Baker, 'Legal Education,' 99ff; C. Ian Kyer and Jerome E. Bickenbach, *The Fiercest Debate: Cecil A. Wright, the Benchers, and Legal Education in Ontario, 1923–1957* (Toronto: The Osgoode Society 1987), 26–9; Curtis J. Cole, '"A Learned and Honorable Body": The Professionalization of the Ontario Bar, 1867–1929' (PhD diss. University of Western Ontario 1987), 166ff.
51 LSUCA, Convocation Minutes, Vol. 5, 6 Dec. 1872, 416–18
52 Raymond Cocks, *Foundations of the Modern Bar* (London: Sweet and Maxwell 1983), passim.
53 AO, Benson Family Papers, T.M. Benson, Legal Notes, 1855 Notebook, 111–13
54 For the developments in this paragraph generally see Kyer and Bickenbach, *Fiercest Debate*, 5–11; Cocks, *Foundations of the Modern Bar*, ch. 2; W. Wesley Pue, 'Guild Training vs. Professional Education: The Committee on Legal Education and the Law Department of Queen's College, Birmingham, in the 1850s,' *American Journal of Legal History* XXXIII/3 (Jul. 1989), 241–87. See also a brief but helpful article, with a rich bibliography, by M.H. Hoeflich, 'The Americanization of British Legal Education in the Nineteenth Century,' *Journal of Legal History* 8 (Dec. 1987), 244–59.
55 Quoted in Kyer and Bickenbach, *Fiercest Debate*, 8
56 *CLJ* 24 (16 Mar. 1888), 153
57 See for example Robert Stevens, *Law School: Legal Education in America from the 1850s to the 1980s* (Chapel Hill: University of North Carolina Press 1983), 24. Even Baker, in his reassessment, gives it no close attention and concludes that it would be 'an overstatement ... to say that apprenticeship was the heart of its [the Law Society's] training operation.' Cf. 'Legal Education,' 86. It is an understatement to say that we consider this a wayward judgment. The fact is that from 1797 to 1889 all law students spent most of their time for a full five years learning in this way. See as well Kyer and Bickenbach's approach in the earlier chapters of *Fiercest Debate*, which generally denigrates learning through office practice and its advocates; for example, p. 35.

58 George W. Spragge, ed., 'A Diary of 1837 by John Sandfield Macdonald,'
   Ontario History 47 (Jan. 1955), 11
59 MTRL, Baldwin Room, Robert Baldwin Papers, Adam Wilson to Baldwin,
   31 Dec. 1842
60 *The Presbyterian* 13 (Dec. 1860), 182–3
61 *QCJ*, 15 Dec. 1877, 6
62 Ibid., 11 Apr. 1885
63 See for example ibid., 30 Jan. and 21 Mar. 1885.
64 See for example QUA, Queen's University Senate Minutes. Each April there is a list of graduands, and even in the 1890s the number listed in theology is only two or three a year.
65 For a parallel comment regarding the content of professional knowledge itself, in this case theology, see Michael Gauvreau, 'Protestantism Transformed,' in *The Canadian Protestant Experience, 1760 to 1990*, ed. G.A. Rawlyk (Burlington, ON: Welch Publishing Co. 1990), 55.

CHAPTER 9 *Making Careers, Making Money, Making a Place*

1 There is already a modest literature on the subject. For example, though he deals only with those professionals who attended university, David Keane has begun to elucidate the multiple tracks followed by students in pursuing a professional education. See 'Rediscovering Ontario University Students in the Mid-Nineteenth Century' (PhD diss., University of Toronto 1982), esp. chs. 4–6. While the difference between 'consecutive' and 'multiple' or concurrent careers remains something of a muddle, several historians have drawn attention to these phenomena. See J.K. Johnson, *Becoming Prominent: Regional Leadership in Upper Canada, 1791–1841* (Montreal and Kingston: McGill-Queen's University Press 1989), 11; Carol Wilton, 'Introduction,' in *Beyond the Law: Lawyers and Business in Canada, 1830 to 1930*, ed. Carol Wilton (Toronto: The Osgoode Society 1990), 30; Michael J. Piva, 'Getting Hired: The Civil Service Act of 1857,' *Journal of the Canadian Historical Association* N.S. 3 (1992), 106–9. The *DCB* also provides a fine resource for the study of career paths, and not only for the 'rich and famous,' since at least for professional men it includes many who were never among the most prominent of their peers.
2 UCA, Donald McKerracher Papers, Wm Anderson, Dawn Mills to McKerracher, 18 Aug. 1873; A. Campbell to same, Acton, 12 Nov. 1874; Geo. Rutherford to same, Elmira, 2 Jan. 1875. See also the comments on calls to newly graduated theologues in *Presbyterian Review* 2 (20 May 1886), 153; 5 (14 Mar. 1889), 1341; *Acts and Proceedings*, General Assembly, Presbyterian Church in Canada, 1894, Appendix 18, Report of Committee on the Distribution of Probationers.
3 See UCA, Donald McKerracher Papers.
4 Ibid., File 7, Guarantee for Minister's Stipend ... from Wallaceburg Congregation

450   Notes to pages 182-6

5 Marguerite Van Die, *An Evangelical Mind: Nathanael Burwash and the Methodist Tradition in Canada, 1839–1918* (Montreal and Kingston: McGill-Queen's University Press 1989), 66
6 See AO, Duck Family Papers, Finding Aid.
7 *CP* 19 (Sep. 1894), 640–1
8 Elizabeth Bloomfield, 'Lawyers as Members of Urban Elites in Southern Ontario, 1860–1920,' in *Beyond the Law: Lawyers and Business in Canada, 1830 to 1930*, ed. Carol Wilton (Toronto: The Osgoode Society 1990), 126ff.
9 AO, Gemmill Family Papers, John Gemmill, Jr, to Father, 2 Sep. 1870. Similarly see MTRL, Baldwin Room, MacLeod Papers, M.D. MacLeod to Archy Cameron, Toronto, 16 Jan. 1860.
10 AO, Gemmill Family Papers, John Gemmill, Jr, to Father, 6 Jun. 1871
11 AO, Benson Family Papers, T.M. Benson, Business Correspondence, W.H. Bowlby to T.M. Benson, 2 Sep. 1858
12 AO, Angus Cattanach Papers, Correspondence, A. Cattanach to Uncle, 17 Feb. 1859
13 Toronto Academy of Medicine Archives, William Aikins Papers, Aikins to Ogden, Toronto, 13 Nov. 1852
14 AO, Benson Family Papers, T.M. Benson, Business Correspondence, Adam Wilson to T.M. Benson, 19 Feb. 1859. Benson opted, however, to go it alone.
15 MTRL, Baldwin Room, Reminiscences of Dr James Richardson, 7
16 AO, Robert Harrison Diaries, 20–4 Feb. 1859. Similarly, see MTRL, Baldwin Room, Robert Baldwin Papers, John Roaf, Jr, to R. Baldwin, 25 Oct. 1849; Larratt Smith to R. Baldwin, 27 Oct. 1849.
17 AO, Gemmill Family Papers, John A. Gemmill, Jr, to Father, 23 Nov. 1869
18 On the latter point see Dr W.B. Geikie's announcement of a change of office location in the *EMR*, Dec. 1858, 32. On the value of a good marriage see Heather MacDougall's comment on William Canniff: '"Health is Wealth": The Development of Public Health Activity in Toronto, 1834–1890' (PhD diss., University of Toronto 1982), 201.
19 UWORC, [Dr] Peter Macdonald, manuscript autobiography
20 See for example MTRL, Baldwin Room, 'Memoirs of Henry Orton' [typescript].
21 See AO, Thomas Walton Papers and Finding Aid.
22 *Globe*, 16 Nov. 1896, 2 (obituary for the Rev. Dr Smellie)
23 UCA, Donald McKerracher Papers, T.S.T. Smellie to Rev. M. Hamilton, Fergus, 7 Dec. 1878; T.S.T. Smellie to McKerracher, 12 Dec. 1878; Arthur W. Wright to McKerracher, 19 Sep. 1879
24 For a good example see AO, Benson Family Papers, T.M. Benson Letterbooks 1857–63, T.M. Benson to Uncle, 1 Aug. 1857.
25 AO, Thomas Walton Papers, Thomas Walton to father, Trout Lake PO, Mar. 1870
26 AO, Gemmill Family Papers, John A. Gemmill, Jr, to Father, 14 Jul. 1870

27 MTRL, Baldwin Room, 'Memoirs of Henry Orton,' 3–4
28 UCA, Donald McKerracher Papers, T.S.T. Smellie to McKerracher, Fergus, 24 Feb. 1879. Similarly see AO, Thomas Radenhurst Papers, Wm Radenhurst, Montreal, to Thomas Radenhurst, York, 19 Jan. 1824.
29 For a good example see Toronto Academy of Medicine Archives, William Aikins Papers, W.W. Wright to Rolph, Markham, 15 Sep. 1852
30 See for example UCA, Donald McKerracher Papers, T.S.T. Smellie to Rev. M. Hamilton, Fergus, 7 Dec. 1878.
31 Michael B. Katz, *The People of Hamilton, Canada West* (Cambridge, MA: Harvard University Press 1975), 133
32 See chapter 6 above.
33 See *The Presbyterian* 7 (Jan. 1854), 10, quoting a letter published in *The Church*.
34 In 1856, for example, the average stipend for ministers of the Kirk was only £163, or about £50 above the £112 from the Temporalities Fund: *The Presbyterian* 9 (Mar. 1856), 63.
35 See for example ibid., 14 (Jul. 1861), 102.
36 Ibid., 25 (Sep. 1872), 206
37 Ibid., 26 (Jul. 1873), 173
38 See *Proceedings of Synod, Diocese of Toronto, 1872*; *DC*, 18 May 1876, 235; *EMR*, Jul. 1851, 138–41; *Home and Foreign Record*, Aug. 1867, 316–27.
39 Reported in *Cdn Chman*, 3 Jan. 1889, 4; also *EC*, 10 Jan. 1889, 430–1. Similarly see *Globe*, 4 May 1886, 6. However, it should be noted that a great many of the Anglican clergymen enjoyed additional income: for example, as the *Globe* noted, there were supplements from the commutation fund, congregational donations in addition to a stipend, the use of a parsonage, or private sources of income. The published figures, in other words, do not tell the whole story and may indeed distort the differences between the denominations as recorded in the newspapers.
40 *Acts and Proceedings*, General Assembly, Presbyterian Church in Canada, 1883, 15–21
41 See the Statistical and Financial Returns, Kingston Presbytery, in *Acts and Proceedings*, General Assembly, Presbyterian Church in Canada, 1880, 1890, 1900. Our analysis of the Presbyterian returns excludes the stipends of missionaries, who generally received very small amounts that required augmentation with church funds.
42 *Doctrines and Discipline*, 1874, 113
43 *CG*, 7 Oct. 1874, 317, and 14 Oct. 1874, 326
44 Ibid., 2 Feb. 1898, 72. See also *Canadian Methodist Magazine* XVI (Jul.–Dec. 1887), 265; *Minutes of the London Conference, 1891*, 43; *Globe*, 3 Jun. 1892, 2; *Minutes of the Niagara Conference, 1893*, 52; *CG*, 17 Jan. 1894, 35.
45 For example, among lawyers, Oliver Mowat estimated at mid-century that he received annually something 'like £3500 clear' from his Chancery practice; in the mid-1870s Robert Harrison was earning $12,000–14,000 a year; in 1888–9,

Edward Blake made close to $37,000 in fees alone. See C.R.W. Biggar, *Sir Oliver Mowat: A Biographical Sketch* (Toronto: Warwick Bros. and Rutter 1905), I: 42; AO, Robert Harrison Diary, 31 Dec. 1874, 25 Sep. 1875; AO, Edward Blake Papers, Series B, Box 17, Misc., 'Statement of Edward Blake's Account 1888–89.' Among doctors R.M. Bucke took in $3,400 in cash in 1869; James Langstaff was earning around $2,000 in 1861, and $3,000 by 1880. See UWORC, R.M. Bucke Papers, C9, R.M. Bucke to H. Forman, 29 Oct. 1869; Jacalyn Duffin, *Langstaff: A Nineteenth-Century Medical Life* (Toronto: University of Toronto Press 1993), 48.

46 For example, William Cochrane was assessed for $2,400 in 1891, and salaries at Toronto's prestigious Methodist churches were about the same. For Cochrane, see Brantford City assessment rolls, 1891; see also *Minutes of Proceedings ... Toronto Conference of the Methodist Church*, 1885, 1890.

47 Duffin, *Langstaff*, 52–7

48 See Michael B. Katz, Michael J. Doucet, and Mark J. Stern, *The Social Organization of Early Industrial Capitalism* (Cambridge, MA.: Harvard University Press 1982), esp. ch. 2.

49 David G. Burley, 'The Businessmen of Brantford, Ontario: Self-Employment in a Mid-Nineteenth-Century Town' (PhD diss., McMaster University 1983), 282–3

50 See the appendix, section C, for a more detailed discussion of these points.

51 For both doctors and lawyers, the existence of outliers, i.e., people who were *very* wealthy, can distort the analysis of the average and range of wealth. Where these outliers are extreme, we have excluded them; if they were included, the range would be even greater.

52 See the appendix, section C, for this paragraph generally. Wealth categories in 1861 are based on assessed wealth as follows: 'poor,' percentiles 1–39; 'middling,' 40–79; 'wealthy,' 80–100. See R.D. Gidney and W.P.J. Millar, *Inventing Secondary Education: The Rise of the High School in Nineteenth-Century Ontario* (Montreal and Kingston: McGill-Queen's University Press 1990), 131.

53 See for example J.R. Godley, *Letters from America* (London 1844), I: 197.

54 Jacalyn Duffin, 'A Rural Practice in Nineteenth-Century Ontario: The Continuing Medical Education of James Miles Langstaff,' *CBMH* 5 (1988), 8

55 *Lancet* 7 (Feb. 1875), 183. Similarly, see ibid., 6 (Jul. 1874), 369. Examples of surviving fee bills also indicate semi-annual billing. Cf. AO, Dr James C. Goodwin Coll., J.P. Russell, MD, with A.M. Howard, 1862; 'Thos. Galt Esq. to John Hall MD.' As late as 1886 the *CP* still took it for granted that, in cities and towns, billing would be done on a semi-annual or annual basis; *CP* 11 (Feb. 1886), 49–50.

56 For an introduction see Douglas McCalla, *Planting the Province: The Economic History of Upper Canada, 1784–1870* (Toronto: University of Toronto Press 1993), ch. 8.

57 See for example the comment in *Acts and Proceedings*, General Assembly, Presbyterian Church, 1896, Appendix No. 20, viii–ix.

58 *Acts and Proceedings*, General Assembly, Presbyterian Church in Canada, 1893, Appendix No. 19, x. Italics in original
59 See for example *CG*, 26 Apr. 1865, 66; *Canadian Churchman*, 26 Jan. 1870.
60 Duffin, *Langstaff*, 48–9; Charles G. Roland and Bohodar Rubashewsky, 'The Economic Status of the Practice of Dr. Harmaunus Smith ...,' *CBMH* 5 (1988), 38–9.
61 AO, Benson Family Papers, T.M. Benson Letterbooks, T.M. Benson to W. Bowlby, 5 Dec. 1861
62 Ibid., Account Books
63 For one example see ibid., Letterbooks, T.M. Benson to W.F. Russell, 2 May 1865. This account went back to 1857, and all Benson could do was end with the statement that he was ready 'to make a reasonable reduction from my account for cash settlement – make me an offer.'
64 See for example *UCJ* I (May 1851), 64; *Lancet* 16 (Feb. 1884), 174–5.
65 *Lancet* 13 (Sep. 1880), 23
66 MTRL, Baldwin Room, 'Memoirs of Henry Orton,' 6
67 Roland and Rubashewsky, 'Harmaunus Smith,' 41
68 William Canniff, *The Medical Profession in Upper Canada 1783–1850* (Toronto: Wm. Briggs 1894), 327
69 *EMR*, Apr. 1857, 85. In the more rural and northern parts of Ontario, clergymen were still receiving substantial parts of their income in kind into the 1890s. See for example *Cdn Chman*, 7 May 1891, 294.
70 See for example *Globe*, 9 and 30 Aug., 16 Sep. 1879.
71 *CP* 23 (Sep. 1898), 527
72 See Canniff, *Medical Profession*, 256; *Brantford Expositor*, 28 Nov. 1854.
73 See for example AO, Benson Family Papers, T.M. Benson Letterbooks, T.M. Benson to A. Davidson Parker, 24 Oct. 1862.
74 AO, J.F. Lundy Diary, 29 Jan. 1849; MTRL, Baldwin Room, MacLeod Papers, M.D. MacLeod to 'My Dear Sir,' 24 Jan. 1850
75 *The Presbyterian* 13 (Aug. 1860), 115; *Presbyterian Record* I (Mar. 1876), 62; *CG*, 29 Jan. 1873, 37; *Cdn Chman*, 2 Jan. 1890, 7; *EC*, 4 Jan. 1894, 10
76 AO, J.F. Lundy Diaries, 9 Jan. 1849
77 AO, Rev. William Cochrane Papers, Diaries, 27–30 Nov. 1871
78 For the procedures and problems here, see the appendix, section A.
79 See Burley, 'Businessmen of Brantford,' 6–8, 172.
80 See Gidney and Millar, *Inventing Secondary Education*, 126–49, 279–81; J. Anthony C. Ketchum, '"The Most Perfect System": Official Policy in the First Century of Ontario's Government Secondary Schools and Its Impact on Students between 1871 and 1910' (PhD diss., University of Toronto 1979), esp. 168–75, and appendices E1–E7.
81 See for example MTRL, Baldwin Room, Robert Baldwin Papers, Adam Wilson to Robert Baldwin, 15 Feb. and 1 Sep. 1843; see also Niagara Historical Society Museum, Letters Relating to Niagara, Misc. Vol., Robt Dickson to Mrs Campbell,

7 Feb. 1824; LSUCA, Letters of Adam Wilson, M56, Article of Agreement, 1834; MTRL, Robert Baldwin Papers, John Gwynne to Robert Baldwin, 13 May 1838; G. Blaine Baker, 'Legal Education in Upper Canada, 1785–1889: The Law Society as Educator,' in *Essays in the History of Canadian Law*, ed. David H. Flaherty (Toronto: University of Toronto Press 1983), II: 81. Dwindling references to such large fees in the second half of the century *may* indicate their gradual disappearance.

82 For the proscription on employment see Baker, 'Legal Education,' 82; 20 Vict. c. 63 (1857), An Act to amend the Law for the Admission of Attornies, s. ix; *Rules of the Law Society of Upper Canada*, 1859, 29–30. For fees see *Rules of the Law Society of Upper Canada*, 1833, 1859; *Upper Canada Law List*, 1862, 41–3.

83 See, for example, *Announcement of the College of Physicians and Surgeons of Ontario*, 1877–8, 19; 1890–1, 15; *Royal College of Physicians and Surgeons, Calendar, 1873–4;* ibid., *1888–9*; A.A. Travill, *Medicine at Queen's, 1854–1920* (Kingston, ON: Faculty of Medicine, Queen's University, 1988), 143; *Queen's University Calendar*, 1871–2, 8; *CG*, 15 Aug. 1894, 515.

84 The majority of law students listed in the manuscript census for Brantford, 1871 to 1891, were living at home.

85 See Gidney and Millar, *Inventing Secondary Education*, 25–6.

RECONSTRUCTING PROFESSION: AN INTRODUCTION

1 Michael Bliss, *Northern Enterprise: Five Centuries of Canadian Business* (Toronto: McClelland and Stewart 1987), 129–30. For a closer look at these developments in Toronto see Barry Dyster, 'Toronto 1840–60: Making It in a British Protestant Town' (PhD diss., University of Toronto 1970), 249ff. The way in which services of various sorts invaded the hinterland is best illuminated in Jacob Spelt's *Urban Development in South-Central Ontario* (1955; reprint, Toronto: McClelland and Stewart 1972).

2 As David Gagan has pointed out, this is largely, though not entirely, *terra incognita* in Canadian social history. See his 'Class and Society in Victorian English Canada: An Historical Reassessment,' *British Journal of Canadian Studies* 4 (1989), 74–87. Elsewhere in the Anglo-American world, however, the transformation is already well charted. See especially Leonore Davidoff and Catherine Hall, *Family Fortunes: Men and Women of the English Middle Class, 1780–1850* (London: Hutchinson 1987); Stuart M. Blumin, *The Emergence of the Middle Class: Social Experience in the American City, 1760–1900* (Cambridge and New York: Cambridge University Press 1989).

3 See for example Ann Wagner, 'Idleness and the Ideal of the Gentleman,' *History of Education Quarterly* 25 (Spring/Summer 1985), esp. 41–2.

4 G. Kitson Clark, *The Making of Victorian England* (London: Methuen University Paperbacks 1965), 253 and 255. Similarly, see W.G. Burn, *The Age of Equipoise*

(London: Unwin University Books 1968), 255–65; Victoria Glendinning, *Trollope* (London: Pimlico ed. 1993), 52–8.
5 See for example the comment of Robert Playfair, *Recollections of a Visit to the United States and British Provinces of North America* (Edinburgh 1856), 67.
6 Davidoff and Hall, *Family Fortunes*, 73
7 *UCLJ* 1 (Sep. 1855), 163 (italics in original). For other similar examples see ibid., 1 (Apr. 1855), 80; *JEdUC* 2 (Jun. 1849), 90.
8 *JEdUC* 14 (Nov. 1861), 175
9 For other examples see the social backgrounds of H.H. Killaly, *DCB* 10, and Francis Shanly, *DCB* 11.
10 T.C. Keefer, *Philosophy of Railroads*, ed. with an introduction by H.V. Nelles (Toronto: University of Toronto Press 1972), xiii–xv
11 See ibid., l. Not surprisingly, it was men like Keefer who played key roles in attempting to create a professional organization for engineering in the 1880s. See J. Rodney Millard, *The Master Spirit of the Age: Canadian Engineers and the Politics of Professionalism* (Toronto: University of Toronto Press 1988), 6.
12 *JEdUC* 24 (Nov. 1871), 169. For other examples of the phenomenon see ibid., 22 (Apr. 1869), 57–8, and 27 (Jul. 1874), 110; *Globe*, 10 Aug. 1875, 26 Oct. 1878.
13 Quoted in *DHE* 25: 188
14 *JEdUC* 9 (Jan. 1857), 16
15 *JLAO*, Sessional Papers, 1884, Vol. XVI, Part II, No. 5, Report Relating to the Registration of Births, Marriages and Deaths ... for 1882. This reference is courtesy of George N. Emery. Similarly see *UCLJ* 8 (May 1862), 117.
16 See for example the comments of Christopher Widmer and J.H. Cameron on this point: *JLAC*, 1852–3, Appendix GGG, 24; *Globe*, 29 Nov. 1878.
17 Quoted in Nathanael Burwash, *The History of Victoria College* (Toronto: The University College Press 1927), 275. For other examples see the editorial in *CG*, 21 Aug. 1867; William Dawson's views in *JEdUC* 8 (Nov. 1855), 166 and 170.
18 The summary arguments in this and the following paragraph are developed in some detail in R.D. Gidney and W.P.J. Millar, *Inventing Secondary Education: The Rise of the High School in Nineteenth-Century Ontario* (Montreal and Kingston: McGill-Queen's University Press 1990), 234–43.
19 For a good example of this kind of thinking, see Daniel Wilson's description of the course at the University of Toronto in 1861, quoted in ibid., 240.

CHAPTER 10 *Parvenus*

1 See D.W. Gullett, *A History of Dentistry in Canada* (Toronto: University of Toronto Press 1971), 43.
2 See Edith G. Firth, ed., *The Town of York, 1815–34* (Toronto: University of Toronto Press 1966), lxii; W.H. Smith, *Smith's Canadian Gazetteer* (Toronto 1846), 195.

456 Notes to pages 212–14

3 See table 2. The figure for 1871 roughly matches estimates made by dentists themselves in the late 1860s so it is probably fairly accurate. Compare *Leader*, 6 Nov. 1868.
4 For the role of doctors see for example Charles G. Roland and Bohodar Rubashewsky, 'The Economic Status of the Practice of Dr. Harmaunus Smith ...,' *CBMH* 5 (1988), 36; Jennifer J. Connor, 'Estate Records and the History of Medicine in Ontario,' *CBMH* 10 (1993), 14.
5 AO, Osler Family Papers, Record of the Lives of Ellen F. Pickton and Featherstone L. Osler (printed), 1838, 181
6 University of Toronto, Faculty of Dentistry Library, File Cabinet, Folder: Advertisements
7 See for example *Second Annual Announcement of the Canada College of Dentistry. Session of 1869–70* (Toronto 1869), 5–6; *CJDS* 3, 5 (Mar. 1871), 129–30.
8 Their advertisements are useful in demonstrating what dentists themselves saw as their chief business. See for example *Echo*, 17 Jun. 1858, 11 Aug. 1859; *The Church*, 2 Oct. 1850; *Brantford Expositor*, 2 Nov. 1860. For a second and much richer source see the manuscript autobiographical sketches labelled 'Early Dentistry in Ontario,' written in 1903 and held in the University of Toronto, Faculty of Dentistry Library. There are only a handful of these reminiscences, but they constitute an invaluable source for the occupation's early history. For a wonderful introduction to the eighteenth- and nineteenth-century trade in human teeth, see John R. Maestri, Jr, 'Tooth Transplantation: An Idea Whose Time Has Past,' *Bulletin of the History of Dentistry* 37 (Oct. 1989), 115–22.
9 University of Toronto, Faculty of Dentistry Library, 'Early Dentistry in Ontario,' Notes by B.W. Day
10 AO, Macaulay Papers, Ann Macaulay to John Macaulay, Kingston, 4 Oct. 1839
11 See R.D. Gidney and W.P.J. Millar, *Inventing Secondary Education: The Rise of the High School in Nineteenth-Century Ontario* (Montreal and Kingston: McGill-Queen's University Press 1990), 63.
12 AO, Dr James C. Goodwin Collection, Bill, Mr I.S. Howard from Mortimer D. French, Toronto, 18 Apr. 1860; University of Toronto, Faculty of Dentistry Library, 'Early Dentistry in Ontario,' Notes by Henry Robinson and by Chas A. Martin; File Cabinet, Folder: History – Dr J.B. Willmott, Account Book, 1861–5. According to Barnabus Day the fees in the late 1850s for a complete set of dentures built on the new and improved continuous gum process were $150 to $200. See Faculty of Dentistry Library, 'Early Dentistry in Ontario,' Notes by B.W. Day.
13 Most of the autobiographies in University of Toronto, Faculty of Dentistry Library, 'Early Dentistry in Ontario,' describe these innovations and their significance. See also the later editions of *the* basic nineteenth-century manual, Chapin A. Harris, *The Principles and Practice of Dental Surgery*, which was

already in its seventh edition by 1858. On the rubber dam see *CJDS* 3 (Mar. 1871), 132-3.
14 For an introduction see M. Samuel Cannon, Evelyn D. Kapes, and Gabriel A. Paltuki, 'Dr Black and the Amalgam Question,' *JHM* 40 (Jul. 1985), 309-13. For aspects of the debate in Ontario see *CMJ* 7 (Jan. 1870), 304-7; *CJDS* 2 (Mar. 1870), 252-3; 4 (Mar. 1878), 69-71; *Globe*, 16 Jul. 1873; *Lancet* 10 (Jul. 1878), 375-6.
15 There is a helpful introduction in *CJDS* 2 (Aug. 1870), 362-6. See also Gullett, *History of Dentistry*, 29-30. Again, the manuscript autobiographies in the University of Toronto, Faculty of Dentistry Library, are invaluable on its significance. For Goodyear himself and the history of the invention, see 'Charles Goodyear,' *Dictionary of American Biography*.
16 Barnabus Day, manuscript autobiography, which also contains a description and a sketch of the machine; see University of Toronto, Faculty of Dentistry Library, 'Early Dentistry in Ontario,' Notes by B.W. Day.
17 *DDJ* 5 (Jul. 1893), 164. Similarly see ibid., 5 (Jan. [*sic* Mar.], 1893), 93-4; 4 (May 1892), 70; *CJDS* 2 (Aug. 1870), 363.
18 See Gullett, *History of Dentistry*, 35; G.L. Elliott, *An Account of My Stewardship* (Toronto 1870), 3.
19 Though there are some minor discrepancies between the two accounts, the sequence of events is described in more detail in Gullett, *History of Dentistry*, 39-42; and James W. Shosenberg, *The Rise of the Ontario Dental Association: 125 Years of Organized Dentistry* (Toronto: ODA 1992), ch. 1.
20 University of Toronto, Faculty of Dentistry Library, 'Early Dentistry in Ontario,' Notes by B.W. Day
21 *CJDS* 1 (Jul. 1868), 38
22 See for example *CJDS* 1 (Jun. 1868), 7; 1 (Sep. 1868), 98-9.
23 Andrew Abbott, *The System of Professions: An Essay on the Division of Expert Labor* (Chicago: University of Chicago Press 1988), 224
24 The biographical sketches and related quotations in this and the next few paragraphs are all drawn from manuscript autobiographies of each individual collected in 1903 and filed in University of Toronto, Faculty of Dentistry Library, 'Early Dentistry in Ontario.' But see also 'Barnabus Day,' *DCB* 13.
25 See the passing comment in *CJDS* 1 (Aug. 1868), 84.
26 For Scott's credentials see *Second Annual Announcement of the Canada College of Dentistry. Session of 1869-70* (Toronto 1869), 2.
27 See *CJDS* 1 (Jun. 1868), 13, 20-2.
28 See *JLAO*, 1867-8, 27 and 30 Jan. and various dates in Feb. 1868. The petitions are filed in AO, RG8, I-1-D, Provincial Secretary's Correspondence, 1868, nos. 123, 163, 164, 192, 193, 224. The main petition is reproduced in *The Ontario Dental Association, A Profile: The First One Hundred Years* [1967], 12.
29 *CJDS* 1 (Jun. 1868), 14-15

30 *Globe*, 25 Feb. 1868
31 Ibid.
32 Statutes of Ontario, 1868, 31 Vict. c. 37, An Act Respecting Dentistry
33 'Historical Reminiscences by C.S. Chittenden,' *Independent Practitioner* 7 (1886), 68
34 *Globe*, 21 Oct. 1874
35 Reprinted in *DDJ* 39 (1927), 170–1. Italics added
36 *CJDS* 1 (Aug. 1868), 87. Italics added
37 Ibid., 1 (Jun. 1868), 15
38 Ibid., 2 (Nov. 1869), 124
39 Ibid., 1 (Jan. 1869), 187
40 Ibid., 3 (Aug. 1871), 297
41 By the time the dental journal started, leading dentists referred, as in their reminiscences, exclusively to 'laboratory.' But see the routine references to 'shop' in the Account Book, 1861–5, of Dr J.B. Willmott, Faculty of Dentistry Library, University of Toronto.
42 See Gullett, *History of Dentistry*, 46–50.
43 R.J. Clark, 'Professional Aspirations and the Limits of Occupational Autonomy: The Case of Pharmacy in Nineteenth-Century Ontario,' *CBMH* 8 (1991), 43–63
44 Though for our purposes it remains flawed in some respects, Ontario's land surveyors now have their own full-scale monograph, and one that is superior to many other histories of individual occupations. See John L. Ladell, *They Left Their Mark: Surveyors and Their Role in the Settlement of Ontario* (Toronto: Dundurn Press 1993). For other important introductions to surveying in Canada see Don W. Thomson, *Men and Meridians: The History of Surveying and Mapping in Canada*, 3 vols. (Ottawa: Queen's Printer 1967); C.C.J. Bond, *Surveyors of Canada, 1867–1967* (Ottawa: The Canadian Institute of Surveying 1966); Morris Zaslow, *Reading the Rocks: The Story of the Geological Survey of Canada, 1842–1972* (Toronto: Macmillan 1975). For a detailed and valuable account of the development of surveying in Great Britain see F.M.L. Thompson, *Chartered Surveyors: The Growth of a Profession* (London: Routledge and Kegan Paul 1968). The *Proceedings* of the Association of Ontario Land Surveyors (1886–) contain historical reviews as well as yearly accounts of its activities.
45 Villiers Sankey, 'The Surveyor's Act,' *Proceedings*, AOLS, 1886, 26; Ladell, *They Left Their Mark*, 75, 118
46 See Ladell, *They Left Their Mark*, 138–9, 156. In subsequent legislation two boards of examiners, one for each province, were created in 1851 (14 & 15 Vict. c. 4); the members of each continued to be appointed by the government. An act passed in 1855 (18 Vict. c. 83) required a preliminary examination for those entering surveying apprenticeships.
47 The subjects of both examinations are given in the relevant legislation of 1849

and 1855; for an assessment of the level of education necessary to pass the examinations see Gidney and Millar, *Inventing Secondary Education*, 255–6.

48 See J.K. Johnson, *Becoming Prominent: Regional Leadership In Upper Canada, 1791–1841* (Montreal and Kingston: McGill-Queen's University Press 1989), 10–11; Peter A. Russell, *Attitudes to Social Structure and Mobility in Upper Canada, 1815–1840* (Lewiston, NY: Edwin Mellen Press 1990), 39. Russell gives a useful but brief discussion of the status of surveyors in Upper Canada in this work, a point amplified in the thesis on which it is based: 'Attitudes to Social Structure and Social Mobility in Upper Canada (1815–1840)' (PhD diss., Carleton University 1981), 122–3.

49 See for example the description by W.R. Burke, PLS, in 'Hints to Surveyors about to Survey a Township for the Ontario Government,' *Proceedings*, AOLS, 1892, 80–6.

50 See for example the advertisement in Sutherland's *County of Brant Gazetteer and General Business Directory, 1865–6*, 82; Ladell, *They Left Their Mark*, 156; Thomson, *Men and Meridians*, II: 72.

51 For descriptions and examples of the overlap between all three groups, including the way in which many practitioners easily slipped from one to another related type of work, see Nancy Z. Tausky and Lynne D. DiStephano, *Victorian Architecture in London and Southwestern Ontario: Symbols of Aspiration* (Toronto: University of Toronto Press 1986), 57–66, 303; Geoffrey Simmins, *Ontario Association of Architects: A Centennial History 1889–1989* (Toronto: OAA 1989), 8–11.

52 For example, Henry MacLeod apprenticed in 1851 to a civil engineer in Kingston; after three years learning the trade, including railway surveying, he sought further training in a foundry 'to learn mechanical engineering' and wound up doing an apprenticeship with a London, Canada West surveyor. See MTRL, Baldwin Room, MacLeod Papers, 1851–5. F.F. Passmore literally walked off the boat as a new immigrant into an apprenticeship with J.G. Howard in Toronto, in architecture and surveying, and then hoped to work in 'Tully's office' [Kivas Tully, the engineer] to learn something of engineering; MTRL, Baldwin Room, F.F. Passmore letters, 1845–6.

53 In addition to the general prohibition against unauthorized surveying included in the 1849 act, the 1859 Act Respecting the Survey of Lands in Upper Canada stated that no private surveys were valid unless made by an authorized surveyor. See Ladell, *They Left Their Mark*, 171.

54 See *Proceedings*, Association of Dominion Land Surveyors, 1886, 8–9. For a description of these surveying projects see Bond, *Surveyors of Canada*, 20ff.

55 For a lucid explanation of economic change in the countryside and the reclamation of Ontario's wetlands see John C. McLaughlin, 'The Lost Lands: Land Drainage in Ontario, 1781 to 1900' (MA thesis, Queen's University 1991). See also Dennis DesRivieres, 'The Great Enniskillen Swamp: Speculation, Drainage

and Settlement,' *Western Ontario Historical Notes* 26 (1972), 25–35; Kenneth Kelly, 'The Artificial Drainage of Land in Nineteenth-Century Southern Ontario,' *Canadian Geographer* 19 (1975), 279–98.
56 Margaret Evans, *Sir Oliver Mowat* (Toronto: University of Toronto Press 1992), 84–5. For an explanation of the pertinent Ontario legislation relating to drainage see McLaughlin, 'The Lost Lands,' 34–7, 76ff.
57 For previous attempts see Ladell, *They Left Their Mark*, 182–3.
58 See for example *Proceedings*, Association of Dominion Land Surveyors, 1886, 9; Bond, *Surveyors of Canada*, 23–6; *Proceedings*, AOLS, 1886, 15.
59 See for example *Proceedings*, AOLS, 1887, 23.
60 See for example *Globe*, 1 Apr. 1875, letter from John McAree, PLS; *Proceedings*, AOLS, 1892, 40–1.
61 The 1849 act established a penalty of £10 for unlicensed practice; the 1855 act continued the authorized land surveyor's right to exclusive practice in the province but omitted the penalty.
62 Italics added. The relevant statutes are the Municipal Drainage Aid Act, 1873 (36 Vict. c. 39 s. 2), consolidated with all other municipal drainage provisions in the Municipal Institutions Act in the same year, and the Ditches and Watercourses Act, 1883 (46 Vict. c. 27 ss. 4 and 21). See also H.B. Proudfoot, 'Land Drainage,' *Proceedings*, AOLS, 1886, 30–5.
63 From 1886 to 1892 the official title was the Association of Provincial Land Surveyors of Ontario; 'Association of Ontario Land Surveyors' originates with the act of 1892.
64 For this paragraph see Ladell, *They Left Their Mark*, 192. Section 2 of the 1887 act reinstated a money penalty of $40. The act also specified 'the use and adjustment of surveying and levelling instruments, the laying out of curves ... the theory and practice of levelling' among the subjects of the licensing examination – subjects considered to be engineering knowledge necessary for railway surveying and drainage work. See the comments by the president, *Proceedings*, AOLS, 1888, 41; CSCE, *The Professional Status: An Epitome* [c. 1895], 2.
65 See Ladell, *They Left Their Mark*, 197–202; *Globe*, 24 Feb. 1892, 8, and 25 Feb. 1892, 8.
66 The key compromise lay in the composition of the Council of Management. Because the government contributed to the costs of administering the surveyors' qualifying examination (as it had since 1849), the organization had to accept continued government representation on the council and on its board of examiners. Government appointees, however, were a minority and in at least some cases were members of the association. See Ladell, *They Left Their Mark*, 202.
67 *Proceedings*, AOLS, 1895, 60
68 There is no comprehensive account of the development of the engineering profession as a whole in Canada, but for civil engineering see J. Rodney Millard, *The Master Spirit of the Age: Canadian Engineers and the Politics of Professionalism* (Toronto: University of Toronto Press 1988). For historical reviews and

yearly accounts of the activities of the Canadian Society of Civil Engineers see the *Transactions* and *Reports* of the Annual Meetings, CSCE, from 1887. For Great Britain see R. Angus Buchanan, *The Engineers: A History of the Engineering Profession in Britain, 1750–1914* (London: Jessica Kingsley Publishers 1989). There are several secondary works to draw on for American developments; see, among others, Richard M. Levy, 'The Professionalization of American Architects and Civil Engineers, 1865–1917' (PhD diss., University of California, Berkeley, 1980); David F. Noble, *America By Design: Science, Technology, and the Rise of Corporate Capitalism* (Oxford: Oxford University Press 1977), esp. Part 1; Daniel Calhoun, *The American Civil Engineer* (Cambridge, MA: MIT Press 1960); Monte Calvert, *The Mechanical Engineer in America, 1830–1910* (Baltimore, MD: Johns Hopkins University Press 1967).

69 University of Toronto Archives, James Loudon Memoirs, 'The College of Technology,' typescript, 19–20

70 Frank M. Turner, 'The Conflict Between Science and Religion: A Professional Dimension,' *Isis* LXIX (1978), 360

71 On the link between engineering and the 'theatre of science' see Christopher Armstrong and H.V. Nelles, *Monopoly's Moment: The Organization and Regulation of Canadian Utilities, 1830–1930* (1986; Toronto: University of Toronto Press 1988), ch. 3 and esp. 63–5.

72 See Gidney and Millar, *Inventing Secondary Education*, 287–92.

73 Alan Macdougall, 'A Plea for a Close Corporation,' *Transactions*, CSCE, 6, Pt. 1 (1892), 113

74 CSCE, *Annual Meeting* (Feb. 1893), 17

75 See Millard, *Master Spirit*, ch. 2. In a list of those attending the first general meeting of the CSCE, in Montreal, a majority resided in that city; *Transactions*, CSCE, 1, Pt. 1 (Mar.–Jun. 1887), v. The 1887 statute establishing the CSCE (50–1 Vict. c. 124) named 19 persons to form the corporation; 9 had Ontario addresses, including 3 at Ottawa; 7 others were listed as Montreal residents. *Charter, Bylaws and List of Members*, CSCE, 1888, lists 231 full members; of these, 92, or a third, have Ontario addresses; another 67 lived in Montreal.

76 As the specialist reader will be aware, this interpretation is very different from Millard's in *Master Spirit*. Our own views have been shaped by a comparative perspective on the different professions in Ontario and through examining the prior organization of the land surveyors in the province, a development that Millard almost entirely ignores. Millard's book, however, remains the standard reference for the CSCE itself.

77 See for example *Proceedings*, AOLS, 1886–92, for membership lists which often carry occupational designations. In 1886, 33 out of 69 members had engineering degrees or qualifications, or were listed as 'engineer' of one sort or another; in 1887 out of 99 members with Ontario addresses, 47 fell into this category; in 1892 out of 115 in Ontario, 66 were in this category or can be traced to the 1894 list of members or associate members of the CSCE (30 of them belonged to that

78 *Annual Meeting CSCE* (1896), 8
79 Ibid., 10–11 (italics added). See also ibid., 11–12; *Annual Meeting CSCE* (1894), 47; CSCE, *The Professional Status*.
80 For example, Alan Macdougall, John Galbraith, Willis Chipman, and Matthew Butler were qualified as both surveyors and engineers, and held office in both the AOLS and the CSCE. For Macdougall, see *Transactions*, CSCE, 6, Pt. 1 (1892), 115; *DCB* 12. For Chipman, see Ladell, *They Left Their Mark*, 183–4; Millard, *Master Spirit*, 141; *Canadian Engineer* 2 (Apr. 1895), 353–4. For Galbraith and Butler, see *Proceedings*, AOLS, 1886–94 (lists of members and officers of the association, including qualifications), and *Charter, Bylaws and List of Members*, CSCE, 1894. There is a brief biography of Butler in *Canadian Engineer* 3 (Mar. 1896), 302.

(Continuing note 77 from previous page:)
organization in 1894 as well as to the AOLS, according to the listings in *Charter, Bylaws, List of Members*, CSCE, 1894). See also Ladell, *They Left Their Mark*, 196; for the degree of overlap that continued into the twentieth century, see p. 230.

81 See *Annual Meeting CSCE* (1892); *CAB* 6 (Dec. 1893), 121; CSCE, *The Professional Status* [c. 1895]; *Annual Meeting CSCE* (1896), 5.
82 See *Transactions, CSCE* 2 (1888), 2; Millard, *Master Spirit*, 165n31; *Transactions CSCE* 4 (1890), 57; *Proceedings*, AOLS, 1891, 32.
83 *Annual Meeting CSCE* (1896), 8. Similarly see Chipman's initiatives: *Proceedings*, AOLS, 1896, 25.
84 *Proceedings*, AOLS, 1899, 21
85 *Report of the Proceedings*, Annual General Meeting, CSCE, Jan. 1899, 16; *Proceedings*, AOLS, 1898, 26; 1899, 12–13, 15.
86 For an account of these developments see Millard, *Master Spirit*, 72ff.
87 See ibid., 187n84: 'Both Chipman and McLeod complained of apathy among Ontario members. "The real reason why our bill [1899] did not go through the Ontario Legislature," McLeod asserted, "was that the members of the Society resident in Ontario have not taken sufficient interest in this measure."'
88 For Ryerson the comparison was explicit: a teacher was to be 'an Educational Missionary' and 'an Educational Pastor.' See *DHE*, 9: 216. For similar analogies see the address by Rev. Wm Cochrane in *Brantford Expositor*, 26 Jun. 1863, and AO, RG2, C6C, No. 5709, Geo. Elmslie to Ryerson, n.d. [received 29 Jul. 1869].
89 For the local superintendents see for example *AR* for 1862, 160; for the number of clergymen who served as grammar school trustees and thus as members of the county boards of instruction see Gidney and Millar, *Inventing Secondary Education*, 92.
90 Quoted in *DHE*, 9: 217.
91 *Globe*, 14 Sep. 1850
92 Receiving a minimum grant of £100 plus tuition fees from their students, most grammar-school masters before 1841 were as well-off as the clergy of the Church of England.

93 See Douglas Meyers, 'Scottish Schoolmasters in the Nineteenth Century: Professionalism and Politics,' in *Scottish Culture and Scottish Education 1800–1980*, ed. W.M. Humes and H.M. Paterson (Edinburgh: John Donald Publishers 1983), 76–7.

94 The mid-century vision of the teacher as a professional man is well established in the specialist literature, but the best single introduction is in an unpublished paper by Alison Prentice and Beth Light, 'From Patriarch to Public Servant? Teachers and Professionalism in Mid-Nineteenth-Century Ontario,' presented to the Workshop on Professionalization in Modern Societies, University of Western Ontario, Mar. 1981; see esp. 9–20. For a useful earlier essay see James Love, 'The Professionalization of Teachers in Mid-Nineteenth-Century Upper Canada,' in *Egerton Ryerson and His Times*, ed. Neil McDonald and Alf Chaiton (Toronto: Macmillan of Canada 1978). Compared with most occupations, teaching in Ontario has been relatively well served by historians. The classic account, first written in 1929 and still useful, is J.G. Althouse, *The Ontario Teacher, 1800–1910* (n.p.: Ontario Teachers' Federation 1967). Over the past two decades, however, the most influential body of work on the subject has been produced by Alison Prentice, along with her colleagues and students. For those unfamiliar with her contributions to the subject, an introduction can be found in Susan Houston and Alison Prentice, *Schooling and Scholars in Nineteenth-Century Ontario* (Toronto: University of Toronto Press 1988), ch. 6. See also various essays in Alison Prentice and Marjorie R. Theobald, eds., *Women Who Taught: Perspectives on the History of Women and Teaching* (Toronto: University of Toronto Press 1991); Ruby Heap and Alison Prentice, eds., *Gender and Education in Ontario* (Toronto: Canadian Scholars' Press 1991). For the nineteenth-century grammar- and high-school teacher, see Gidney and Millar, *Inventing Secondary Education*.

95 Abbott, *System of Professions*, 217

96 AO, RG2, C6C, Chairman, School Association, Eastern District, to Ryerson, 9 Jul. 1850. For similar sentiments and initiatives on the part of teachers at mid-century see *The Packet* [Ottawa], 5 and 26 Oct. 1850 (Renfrew Teachers' Institute); *Globe*, 1 Oct. 1850; *JEdUC* 4 (Mar. 1851), 36.

97 See *JEdUC* 19 (Aug. 1866), 126.

98 The following summary paragraph is based on the OTA records printed annually during the 1860s in the *JEdUC* and the *OTA Proceedings*.

99 *JEdUC* 18 (Oct. 1865), 151

100 *Ottawa Citizen*, 9 Jul. 1866

101 See for example Ryerson's proposals made at the county school conventions in 1866: *DHE*, 19: 153–4, 170–5; see also ibid., 19: 232 and 234; ibid.: 20, 250.

102 *DHE*, 23: 72

103 *JEdUC* 24 (Jun. 1871), 88

104 See Gidney and Millar, *Inventing Secondary Education*, 223–4.

105 These developments are described in detail in the early chapters of John Stewart

Hardy, 'Training Third Class Teachers: A Study of the Ontario County Model School System, 1877–1907' (PhD diss., University of Toronto 1981).
106 For one major example see Gidney and Millar, *Inventing Secondary Education*, chs. 7–9.
107 *Globe*, 14 Aug. 1877. Similarly, see ibid., 11 Aug. 1879.
108 A complete list is given in *AR* for 1890, 391–4. Note that this is a list of all those qualified and not of those actually appointed.
109 See the appendix, sections C and D.
110 *Globe*, 22 Jul. 1876, 2
111 See for example John E. Bryant, 'The Advisability of a Change in the Administration of the School Law,' *OTA Proceedings, 1883*, 33–5; *CEM* 6 (Oct. 1884), 413.
112 *Globe*, 17 Aug. 1883, 4
113 Alison Prentice, 'The Feminization of Teaching,' in *The Neglected Majority: Essays in Canadian Women's History*, ed. Susan Mann Trofimenkoff and Alison Prentice (Toronto: McClelland and Stewart 1977), 49–57; see also Marta Danylewycz, Beth Light, and Alison Prentice, 'The Evolution of the Sexual Division of Labour in Teaching: A Nineteenth-Century Ontario and Quebec Case Study,' *Histoire sociale* 16 (May 1983), 84.
114 See *Globe*, 14 Sep. 1882, 7; 15 Dec. 1877, 5.
115 *CEM* 3 (Jan. 1881), 26
116 *OTA Proceedings, 1878*, 27
117 *Globe*, 18 Dec. 1877, 3
118 Quoted in David Tyack, 'Was There Ever a Golden Age in Teaching?' *Harvard Educational Review* 57 (May 1987), 171–2
119 Robert Barr, *The Measure of the Rule*, intro. by Louis K. MacKendrick (Toronto: University of Toronto Press 1973), 70
120 *CEM* 3 (Jan. 1881), 23–4. For similar complaints see the address by John Dearness in *OTA Proceedings, 1880*, 47; *CEM* 4 (Dec. 1882), 514–15.
121 See D. Fotheringham, 'Permanency of the Teaching Profession,' *OTA Proceedings, 1885*, 71–2. Paradoxically, however, there could also be shortages in some counties. For an explanation see *Canada School Journal* 6 (Oct. 1881), 222–3.
122 Hardy, 'Training Third Class Teachers,' 251
123 Ibid., 191 and 311. Hardy's discussion includes an analysis of parents' occupations which underlines these points. The vast majority were the sons and daughters of farmers, but those in a number of artisan crafts and small businesses were also overrepresented, as were the sons and daughters of widows. See ibid., 184ff. For the high schools, see Gidney and Millar, *Inventing Secondary Education*, 279–81.
124 See for example *Globe*, 3 Nov. 1876; 25 Oct. 1877, 2; *OTA Proceedings, 1880*, 47.
125 See for example *CEM* 5 (Feb. 1883), 95–6; 6 (Feb. 1884), 95; 6 (Jul.–Aug. 1884), 313.

126 *AR* for 1885, 117. Similarly, see George Ross's analysis in *AR* for 1887, xviii.
127 *DDJ* 1 (Apr. 1889), 75
128 See table 2.
129 Althouse, *The Ontario Teacher*, 108
130 *Globe*, 20 Feb. 1882, 4
131 See George Dickson, 'The Ontario College of Preceptors,' *OTA Proceedings, 1886*, 65–73. The quotations are drawn from p. 72.
132 See *Globe*, 12 May 1886.
133 See for example ibid., 6 Apr. 1886, 4; *CEM* 8 (Apr. 1886), 126–7.
134 There is extensive reporting of the debates at the summer meetings of the Ontario Educational Society and the OTA in both the *Globe* and the *Mail* between 10 and 13 Aug. 1886. The executive of the Society was listed in *Globe*, 13 Aug. 1886, 2, but see also the names of participants in the debate.
135 See Smaller, 'Teachers' Protective Associations,' 206–30. Smaller's interpretation differs from ours, however, in that he sees the Educational Union proposal as a far more radical, militant one. Our own review of the evidence leads us to the conclusion that the sources will not support that contention.
136 On this point see *Mail*, 16 Aug. 1886, 6.
137 See *OTA Proceedings, 1887*, 43.
138 *OTA Proceedings, 1871*, 27
139 *Globe*, 13 Aug. 1884, 6
140 *CEM* 4 (Feb. 1882), 51. For Boyle's role in the Educational Union, see Smaller, 'Teachers' Protective Associations,' 207ff.
141 See for example *Globe*, 2 Feb. 1882, 9, 11; 25 Feb. 1882, 8; 1 Mar. 1882, 7; 18 Feb. 1886, 4; 20 Feb. 1886, 3. See also Harry Smaller, '"A Room of One's Own": The Early Years of the Toronto Women Teachers' Association,' in Heap and Prentice, *Gender and Education*, 103–24.
142 Gidney and Millar, *Inventing Secondary Education*, esp. ch. 10
143 Abbott, *System of Profession*, 122–4
144 See Gidney and Millar, *Inventing Secondary Education*, 302–3.
145 Gregory S. Kealey and Bryan D. Palmer, *Dreaming of What Might Be: The Knights of Labor in Ontario, 1880–1900* (Cambridge: Cambridge University Press 1982), 386

CHAPTER 11 *Professions 'Overcrowded'*

1 Elizabeth Bloomfield, 'Lawyers as Members of Urban Business Elites in Southern Ontario, 1860 to 1920,' in *Beyond the Law: Lawyers and Business in Canada, 1830 to 1930*, ed. Carol Wilton (Toronto: The Osgoode Society 1990), 113–20
2 Jacob Spelt, *Urban Development in South-Central Ontario* (1955; reprint, Toronto: McClelland and Stewart 1972), 95–6, 140, 176, and the pertinent maps of central places at the back of the volume.

3 For our procedures and sources here, see the appendix, section B.
4 Spelt, *Urban Development*, 140–1
5 Paul Starr, *The Social Transformation of American Medicine* (New York: Basic Books 1982), 66–8
6 On this point see William Canniff's comment, in *Lancet* 14 (Sep. 1881), 390.
7 Stratford experienced modest population growth in the 1880s and 1890s, and acquired a hospital in 1891. Not surprisingly the number of doctors located in the town rose in both decades.
8 See for example *CJMS* 4 (Aug. 1879), 235–6; *Globe*, 21 Jul. 1882; *Brantford Expositor*, 27 Jul. 1882; *CP* 10 (Feb. 1885), 57–8.
9 Starr, *Social Transformation*, 68
10 Quoted in S.E.D. Shortt, *Victorian Lunacy: Richard M. Bucke and the Practice of Late Nineteenth-Century Psychiatry* (Cambridge: Cambridge University Press 1986), 20
11 Jacalyn Duffin, 'A Rural Practice in Nineteenth-Century Ontario: The Continuing Medical Education of James Miles Langstaff,' *CBMH* 5 (1988), 6
12 Ibid.
13 See Ian M. Drummond, *Progress without Planning: The Economic History of Ontario from Confederation to the Second World War* (Toronto: University of Toronto Press 1987), 21, 31.
14 Spelt, *Urban Development*, 184
15 The parallel is not exact because the county's boundaries changed over the years, and no comparable figures exist for rural Perth alone. Still, it is roughly indicative of the problem. For the modern figures see R.D. Fraser, *Selected Economic Aspects of the Health Care Sector in Ontario*, A Study for the Committee on the Healing Arts (Toronto: Queen's Printer 1970), 428.
16 Curtis J. Cole, '"A Learned and Honorable Body": The Professionalization of the Ontario Bar, 1867–1929' (PhD diss., University of Western Ontario 1987), 74–83
17 See for example *CLJ* 29 (16 Jun. 1893), 386–7.
18 *DDJ* 7 (Jun. 1895), 153
19 For one painful example see ibid., 153–4. More generally here see ibid., 2 (Apr. 1890), 83–5, where the editor, writing in praise of the new material of porcelain, also gives an overview of existing methods and their problems. Novocain, the first big breakthrough in local anaesthetics, was not available in North America until 1907; see D.W. Gullett, *A History of Dentistry in Canada* (Toronto: University of Toronto Press 1971), 126–7.
20 See University of Toronto, Faculty of Dentistry Library, 'Dental Advertisements,' J.B. Willmott, Milton, 1860; ibid., 'Early Dentistry in Ontario,' Notes by Charles W. Martin, Henry Robinson, and S.M. Kennedy.
21 *DDJ* 6 (Dec. 1894), 294
22 Ibid., 8 (Mar. 1896), 90–1
23 Again, see the article on porcelain by the editor, in ibid., 2 (Apr. 1890), 83–5; see

also ibid., 10 (Aug. 1898), 283–5. Our conclusions here, however, have to be 'read' through complaints about unethical practice, rather than rational discussion about the economics of the trade: cheap platemaking was an activity of the 'unethical' and is condemned in column after column. The central role of platemaking can also be seen in advertisements in the press, where the emphasis falls on plates, not restorative work.

24 *Lancet* 6 (Jan. 1874), 150
25 Ibid.
26 *Globe*, 21 Jul. 1882
27 For a more detailed discussion see J.T.H. Connor, 'Minority Medicine in Ontario, 1795 to 1903: A Study of Medical Pluralism and Its Decline' (PhD diss., University of Waterloo 1989), 90ff.
28 See Paul Rutherford, *A Victorian Authority: The Daily Press in Late Nineteenth-Century Canada* (Toronto: University of Toronto Press 1982), 121.
29 *Presbyterian Review*, 24 Sep. 1895, 283
30 For example, see *Lancet* 7 (Mar. 1875), 216–17.
31 *DDJ* 2 (Jul. 1890), 128; 8 (Mar. 1896), 90–1
32 Ibid.
33 See for example ibid., 3 (Sep. 1891), 154–5
34 Gullett, *History of Dentistry*, 83
35 Though contemporaries often described it as a rural phenomenon, lay conveyancing had never been confined to the countryside. In our census research, described in the appendix, we have found conveyancers listed who are not on the published Law Lists. Their advertisements in the business directories for Perth County and for Stratford normally list the other services they offered as well. For typical advertisements for other urban areas see W.H. Smith, *Canada: Past, Present and Future ...* (Toronto [1851–2]), I: 53 [Toronto directory]; *Canadian Churchman*, 11 Sep. and 6 Nov. 1867 [Kingston].
36 See for example *UCLJ* 4 (Jan. 1858), 1; 4 (May 1858), 108; 5 (Apr. 1859), 74–5; 7 (Dec. 1861), 307; *CLJ* 4 (Aug. 1868), 213; 10 (Jan. 1874), 3. There were also other forms of lay practice which lawyers objected to but which caused less concern. See Cole, 'A Learned and Honorable Body,' 114–19.
37 *CLJ* 16 (Jan. 1880), 19–20. See also ibid., 15 (Jan. 1879), 4.
38 Ibid., 16 (Feb. 1880), 62–3
39 Ibid., 4 (Aug. 1868), 213
40 See for example, ibid., 13 (Mar. 1877), 94; 16 (Mar. 1880), 91–3; 16 (May 1880), 151; 17 (1 Jan. 1881), 29–30; 17 (22 Aug. 1881), 299; 20 (15 Jan. 1884), 38; *Globe*, 14 Jan. 1881.
41 *CLJ* 17 (15 Oct. 1881), 397
42 For some helpful commentary on this issue see ibid., 19 (1 Aug. 1883), 257, and 20 (16 Jun. 1884), 218–20.
43 Ibid., 16 (Feb. 1880), 63

44 Ibid., 17 (15 Jan. 1881), 50–1. Similarly see ibid., 16 (Mar. 1880), 91–2; *Globe*, 25 Feb., 9 Mar., 11 Dec. 1878; 14 Jan., 27 Dec. 1881; *Mail*, 1 Jul. 1880
45 *CLJ* 19 (15 Feb. 1883), 64
46 The figures can be traced through the minutes and proceedings of the various Anglican diocesan synods and in the *Acts and Proceedings of the ... Presbyterian Church in Canada*.
47 See table 2.
48 These comparisons, however, are rough. In the case of doctors and lawyers in Perth County, we are dealing with the medical registers and Law Lists, which we take to be fairly precise counts and which give postal addresses. We have no equivalent source for all ministers and our figures here are based on the relevant census material for 1871, 1881, and 1891, which we find generally less satisfactory.
49 *Home and Foreign Record*, Jan. 1865, 78
50 *The Presbyterian* 8 (Aug. 1855), 173
51 *Acta Victoriana* 10 (Feb. 1887), 9. Similarly see *CG*, 31 May 1882, 172; 22 Jan. 1879, 31. For the Anglicans see *EC* 11 Aug. 1892, 382; *Cdn Chman*, 1 Sep. 1898, 519; 27 Oct. 1898, 655
52 *Presbyterian Review* 2 (11 Feb. 1886), 44
53 *Globe*, 30 Apr. 1898, 10
54 *CG*, 21 Sep. 1898, 601
55 See for example *Journal, Proceedings of the Provincial Synod of the Church of England in Canada*, 1886, 113.
56 *Cdn Chman*, 16 Feb. 1893, 99. Similarly see *The Week*, 24 Feb. 1893, 301–2.
57 *Presbyterian Record* X (Jan. 1886), 1–2
58 See *Canadian Pharmaceutical Journal* 23 (Aug. 1889), 2. The journal also routinely noted the emigration of individuals: for example, see ibid., 22 (Nov. 1888), 54; 23 (Jan. 1890), 90; 24 (Dec. 1890), 66; 24 (Feb. 1891), 93. Our thanks to R.J. Clark for this material.
59 *Globe*, 9 Nov. 1899, 3. See also Richard A. Willie, '"It Is Every Man for Himself": Winnipeg Lawyers and the Law Business, 1870 to 1903,' and Jonathan S. Swainger, 'Ideology, Social Capital, and Entrepreneurship: Lawyers and Business in Red Deer, Alberta, 1900 to 1920,' in *Beyond the Law: Lawyers and Business in Canada, 1830 to 1930*, ed. Carol Wilton (Toronto: The Osgoode Society 1990), 263–7 and 377–402 respectively.
60 Quoted in Willie, 'Every Man for Himself,' 272
61 See for example *EC*, 19 Aug. 1886, 161; *Globe*, 3 Apr. 1897, 3.
62 See for example *CG*, 21 Sep. 1898, 600.
63 *Cdn Chman*, 24 Jan. 1895, 51; *Presbyterian Review*, 28 Dec. 1893, 442–3. Similarly see *EC*, 18 Aug. 1886, 161.
64 Chad Gaffield, Lynne Marks, and Susan Laskin, 'Student Populations and Graduate Careers: Queen's University, 1895–1900,' in *Youth, University, and Canadian Society: Essays in the Social History of Higher Education*, ed. Paul

Axelrod and John G. Reid (Montreal and Kingston: McGill-Queen's University Press 1989), 20.
65 The reason we know about these practices is, once again, the complaints (and apologies or defences) in the debate over medical, legal, or dental ethics. The nature of the problems is documented below in chapter 13 and there is no point in duplicating those references here. We add references only where they are not included in chapter 13.
66 *Acta Victoriana* 14 (May 1891), 8–9
67 See for example *Globe*, 26 Jan. 1892, 8; *Cdn Chman*, 16 Feb. 1893, 99; 15 Jun. 1899, 376.
68 *EC*, 18 May 1899, 313. Italics in original
69 See *DDJ* 4 (Sept. 1892), 159.
70 Ibid., 6 (Mar. 1894), 65–6
71 Ibid., 8 (Aug. 1896), 227; 9 (May 1897), 195
72 See *Lancet* 14 (Jul. 1882), 242; *Globe*, 27 Jan. 1883; *CP* 8 (Feb. 1883), 53.
73 *CP* 11 (Mar. 1886), 82
74 See Wendy Mitchinson, *The Nature of Their Bodies: Women and Their Doctors in Victorian Canada* (Toronto: University of Toronto Press 1991), ch. 8.
75 Cf. *CP* 22 (Jun. 1897), 392–3
76 One way to document this is through the 'notes' in successive issues of the medical journals. See for example *Lancet* 4 (Oct. 1871), 60; 9 (Apr. 1877), 254; *CJMS* 6 (Oct. 1881), 331. But it was also considered a common enough pattern to provoke articles and letters giving advice to those who intended to go to Britain or Europe; cf. *Lancet* 9 (Jan. 1877), 142–5, and 9 (Feb. 1877), 169–72; 13 (Dec. 1880), 97–9; 17 (Apr. 1885), 253; *QCJ*, 21 Mar. 1885, 107–8; 11 Apr. 1885, 121–3.
77 See Robert W. Powell, *The Doctor in Canada* (Montreal 1890), 209ff. (qualifications of professors at the various medical schools).
78 See for example *Lancet* 21 (Dec. 1888), 122; *CP* 18 (Dec. 1893), 949–50. Much of the attack on 'lodge practice' subsumes other forms of contract practice as well.
79 *CP* 10 (Feb. 1885), 57–8
80 See for example ibid., 18 (Dec. 1893), 946.
81 See for example ibid., 20 (Oct. 1895), 783–4.
83 *Acta Victoriana* 1 (May 1879), 7
83 Lenore O'Boyle, 'The Problem of an Excess of Educated Men in Western Europe, 1800–1850,' *Journal of Modern History* 42 (1970), 471–95

CHAPTER 12 *Clergymen and the Ascendancy of the Laity*

1 See John S. Moir, *Enduring Witness: A History of the Presbyterian Church in Canada* (n.p.: [The Presbyterian Church in Canada] 1987), ch. 7; J. Warren

Caldwell, 'The Unification of Methodism in Canada, 1865–1884,' *The Bulletin* [United Church of Canada] 19 (1967), 3–61; John Webster Grant, *A Profusion of Spires: Religion in Nineteenth-Century Ontario* (Toronto: University of Toronto Press 1988), 159, 178–9.
2 See for example *Presbyterian Record* XI (Nov. 1886), 297; XVIII (Jun. 1893), 142; *Journal*, Proceedings of the Provincial Synod of the Church of England in Canada, 1886, 113; *Acts and Proceedings*, General Assembly, Presbyterian Church in Canada, 1896, Appendix 1, Home Mission Report, xi.
3 See Webster, *Profusion of Spires*, 194–5; *Journal of Proceedings, Methodist General Conference, 1902*, Report of Committee on Church Union, 172.
4 *Globe*, 28 Jan. 1899, 10
5 See *The Presbyterian* 20 (Nov. 1867), 321; 20 (Dec. 1867), 353–4; William Gregg, *Short History of the Presbyterian Church ...* (Toronto: C.B. Robinson 1892), 115.
6 The development of these funds may be traced through the proceedings and reports of the various church governing bodies: the *Journals* of the Anglican synods, *Journals* of the Proceedings of the Methodist General Conference, and *Acts and Proceedings* of the General Assembly of the Presbyterian Church.
7 See for example *CG*, 30 Jan. 1861, 17; 8 Aug. 1888, 499; *Presbyterian Review* 2 (18 Mar. 1886), 84; *EC*, 3 Jan. 1889, 420; *Cdn Chman*, 27 Apr. 1893, 260; 24 Sep. 1896, 589.
8 Caldwell, 'Unification of Methodism,' 35–6, 46–8
9 *Acts and Proceedings*, General Assembly, Presbyterian Church in Canada, 1876, 59; 1886, 48–9
10 *EC*, 6 Dec. 1888, 366
11 See for example *Globe*, 5 Sep. 1883; 4 Feb. 1891, 8; *Presbyterian Review* 2 (11 Feb. 1886), 44; 5 (4 Apr. 1889), 1365; 10 (17 Aug. 1893), 84; *Acts and Proceedings*, General Assembly, Presbyterian Church in Canada, 1895, Appendix 20.
12 See for example *CG*, 27 Apr. 1859; 29 Apr. 1891, 259; 17 Feb. 1897, 106; *Acta Victoriana* 7 (Jan. 1884), 6–7; *Globe*, 4 Dec. 1884, 4.
13 *DC*, 6 Jul. 1876, 313. See also *EC*, 3 Jul. 1890, 98; *Cdn Chman*, 16 Jun. 1892, 372.
14 See *Globe*, 15 Jul. 1886, 4; *CG*, 11 Jul. 1888, 440; 29 Aug. 1888, 548; 24 Jun. 1891, 392.
15 See for example *EC*, 26 Apr. 1888, 606; 31 Oct. 1889, 306–7; *CG*, 28 Jul. 1898, 477.
16 Alan L. Hayes, ed., *By Grace Co-Workers: Building the Anglican Diocese of Toronto, 1780–1989* (Toronto: Anglican Book Centre 1989), 55
17 Ibid.
18 *EC*, 13 Mar. 1879
19 *DC*, 13 Mar. 1879, 125. Italics in the original

Notes to pages 272-8 471

20 *EC*, 7 Nov. 1889, 312; 21 May 1891, 30-1
21 See *Globe*, 3 Dec. 1888, 4; 24 Jun. 1893, 7; *EC*, 4 Jul. 1889, 102-3; *Journal of Proceedings*, General Conference, Methodist Church, 1890, Report no. 1, Committee on Missions; *Acts and Proceedings*, General Assembly, Presbyterian Church in Canada, 1894, Appendix I, xlix and 27-8; *CG*, 11 Aug. 1897, 498-9; *Proceedings of Synod*, Diocese of Toronto, 1898, 36.
22 *Acts and Proceedings*, General Assembly, Presbyterian Church in Canada, 1897, Report of the Committee on the Aged and Infirm Ministers' Fund (Western Section), 237. Similarly, see ibid., Report of the Finance Committee.
23 *The Presbyterian* 21 (Mar. 1868), 81-2
24 *Globe*, 4 Jun. 1888, 4
25 *EC*, 25 Jul. 1889, 139
26 For example see *Presbyterian Review* 2 (11 Mar. 1886), 77; 17 Feb. 1898, 714; *CG* 26 Mar. 1879, 102; 22 Dec. 1880, 404; 25 Apr. 1888, 260; 8 Apr. 1891, 211; 29 Apr. 1891, 259; *Acta Victoriana* 10 (Jan. 1887), 6-7; *EC*, 3 Jan. 1889, 420; 25 Jul. 1889, 139; 13 Mar. 1890, 540. See also *Globe*, 5 Sep. 1883, 4; 10 Jan. 1885, 6.
27 *The Presbyterian* 24 (Aug. 1871), 202
28 *DC*, 18 Aug. 1887, 484-5
29 These developments can be followed in the annual *Minutes*, Toronto Conference of the Methodist Church; *Journal* of the Proceedings of the Methodist General Conference. See also *CG*, various issues reporting the initiatives at these meetings, Sep. 1878, Jun. 1889, Sep. 1890, Jun. 1891, Sep. 1894, Sep. 1898.
30 See *CG*, 5 Apr. 1882, 108; *Globe*, 21 May 1887, 5; 6 Jul. 1891, 8.
31 See *DC*, 21 Jul. 1887, 456; 7 Jun. 1888, 363; *Cdn Chman*, 28 Feb. 1895, 137; 26 May 1898, 327-8; 10 Nov. 1898, 679-80, and following issues.
32 *Canadian Churchman*, 16 Jul. 1863.
33 See for example *EC*, 17 Jun. 1886, 63; 1 Jul. 1886, 90-1; *Presbyterian Review*, 16 Aug. 1894, 114; 27 Jun. 1895; *Cdn Chman*, 21 Apr. 1898, 253; 9 Jun. 1898, 364.
34 *The Presbyterian* 19 (Jan. 1866), 18-19. Italics in original
35 *CG*, 9 Aug. 1882, 254
36 *Globe*, 25 May 1877, 2
37 *CG*, 1 May 1867, 69
38 See for example ibid., 2 Oct. 1878, 319, and 9 Oct. 1878, 327; *DC*, 1 Feb. 1877, 57; *Canadian Churchman*, 5 Jan. 1870; *Presbyterian Review* 2 (8 Apr. 1886), 109.
39 See *CG*, 11 Mar. 1874, 78.
40 *The Presbyterian* 24 (Apr. 1871), 93. Italics in the original
41 For a classic exposition of this argument see *Presbyterian Review* 2 (18 Mar. 1886), 84.
42 Typically see *CG*, 25 Feb. 1874, 60; 11 Mar. 1874, 78; *Presbyterian Record* XI

(Nov. 1886), 290; *Presbyterian Review* 2 (25 Feb. 1886), 60; *Globe*, 6 Dec. 1881, 4; 26 Sep. 1887, 4; *Cdn Chman*, 13 Mar. 1890, 165.
43 *Canadian Churchman*, 16 Jun. 1869, 2
44 *Proceedings of Synod, Diocese of Toronto, 1870*, 19–20
45 *The Presbyterian* 8 (Feb. 1855), 28
46 *CG*, 12 Mar. 1879, 84. Similarly, see ibid., 12 Dec. 1883, 388.
47 *Canadian Churchman*, 24 Jun. 1868. Similarly, see the Bishop's address to Synod, Diocese of Toronto, in *Globe*, 17 Jun. 1874.
48 *EC*, 29 Jun. 1876
49 *Presbyterian Record* 5 (Jan. 1880), 2–3. For other examples see *Cdn Chman*, 30 Jan. 1890, 73; *Globe*, 26 Dec. 1873, 2; 23 Jan. 1884, 4. Methodists put less emphasis on this but were not unaware of its dangers; see *CG*, 12 Mar. 1879, 84.
50 *Globe*, 2 Aug. 1882, 14
51 Ibid., 4 Jul. 1887, 4
52 See Christopher Armstrong and H.V. Nelles, *The Revenge of the Methodist Bicycle Company: Sunday Streetcars and Municipal Reform in Toronto, 1888–1897* (Toronto: Peter Martin Associates 1977).
53 For more detail, see the appendix, section C.
54 See for example *Globe*, 11 Jul. 1890, 6; *Presbyterian Review*, 15 Mar. 1894.
55 See *EC*, 18 Dec. 1890, 385; *Globe*, 26 Nov. 1885, 5, and following issues; 18 Jul. 1892, 4; *Acta Victoriana* 17 (Mar. 1894), 178–9.

CHAPTER 13 *Professional Organizations at Bay*

1 For typical complaints about such practices see *CJMS* 2 (Mar. 1877), 104–7; *Lancet* 5 (May 1873), 476–8; 7 (Jun. 1875), 292–3; 13 (Sep. 1880), 7; 15 (Jun. 1883), 294; 18 (Jan. 1886), 153–4; 18 (Jul. 1886), 322; *CP* 9 (Nov. 1884), 350.
2 *Lancet* 3 (Nov. 1870), 83–5
3 Ibid., 7 (Nov. 1874), 87. For other examples see *CJMS* 7 (Mar. 1881), 89; ibid., 7 (Sep. 1882), 306; *Globe*, 3 Jun. 1886, 8.
4 *Lancet* 8 (Oct. 1875), 61
5 Ibid., 4 (Jun. 1872), 486–7. Similarly see *CJMS* 7 (Sep. 1882), 306.
6 *Lancet* 10 (Mar. 1878), 237–8
7 Ibid., 18 (Jan. 1886), 153–4
8 *CLJ* 15 (Nov. 1879), 276–7
9 Ibid., 8 (Oct. 1872), 239
10 Ibid., 14 (May 1878), 137–8. For other examples see ibid., 14 (Oct. 1878), 279; 17 (22 Aug. 1881), 298–9; 29 (12 Apr. 1893), 239.
11 Ibid., N.S. 4 (Aug. 1868), 214–15
12 See for example *DDJ* 10 (Aug. 1898), 283.
13 Ibid., 8 (Mar. 1896), 81; 3 (Sep. 1891), 139; 5 (Dec. 1893), 290–1; 6 (Sep. 1894): 212–15

14 Ibid., 9 (Feb. 1897), 53
15 Ibid., 7 (Nov. 1895), 288. Similarly see ibid., 8 (Mar. 1896), 81.
16 Revised Statutes of Ontario, 1877, c. 144, An Act Respecting Dentistry
17 Statutes of Ontario, 1887, 50 Vict. c. 24, An Act to Amend the Ontario Medical Act, s. 3
18 See chapter 4 above, 80–1.
19 See Curtis J. Cole, '"A Learned and Honorable Body": The Professionalization of the Ontario Bar, 1867–1929' (PhD diss., University of Western Ontario 1987), 237ff.
20 See Elizabeth MacNab, *A Legal History of Health Professions in Ontario* (Toronto: Queen's Printer 1970), 34. The actual record of cases is to be found in the annual minutes of the Ontario Medical Council. While MacNab (and others) sometimes describe charges being laid for advertising *per se*, our reading of the evidence is that they were laid for *false* advertising only.
21 Ontario Commission on Medical Education, Transcripts, Minutes of Proceedings and Submissions, 16 Oct., 1915–30 Jun. 1917, 996
22 Indeed, that was the central problem with the disciplinary clauses of the medical act: it was a case of all or nothing, and most 'offenses' were not severe enough, as the CPSO's counsel said in 1917, to justify such 'drastic punishment' as 'depriving a man of his profession.' Ibid., 955.
23 *CLJ* 10 (Jul. 1874), 185
24 *CJMS* 7 (Sep. 1882), 306
25 *OMJ* 2 (Jul. 1894), 465
26 See for example *CP* 17 (1 Mar. 1892), 110.
27 *Lancet* 13 (May 1881), 265
28 *DDJ* 10 (Jan. 1898), 29–30
29 *CP* 19 (Sep. 1894), 711–13
30 MacNab, *Health Professions*, 37–8
31 See for example *CP* 17 (16 Apr. 1892), 172; *Lancet* 25 (Nov. 1892), 94.
32 *Lancet* 7 (Apr. 1875), 230
33 See for example, ibid., 10 (Sep. 1877), 3.
34 For one spectacular case see *DDJ* 3 (Sep. 1891), 156–7.
35 *Globe*, 8 Oct. 1889, 4.
36 H.J. Saunders, 'The Medical Council and the Medical Defence Association,' *Queen's Quarterly* 1 (Jul. 1893–Apr. 1894), 61. Similarly see *CJMS* 5 (Jan. 1880), 26.
37 The arguments are thoroughly canvassed in the Ontario Royal Commission Inquiry into Civil Rights, 1968 [McRuer Report], Report No. 1, Vol. 3, 1159ff.
38 There were also earlier, minor conflicts. See for example *UCLJ* 1 (May 1855), 92–4, 98.
39 See Legislative Assembly of Ontario, Newspaper Hansard, 15 Jan. 1868; *Globe*, 12 and 14 Nov. 1868; *CLJ* N.S. 4 (Jun. 1868), 134–5.

40 *Toronto World*, 10 Apr. 1881, 1
41 *CLJ* 6 (Jan. 1870), 1–4
42 See ibid., 7 (Jan. 1871), 3–6, and 7 (Feb. 1871), 32–3.
43 Ibid., 7 (May 1871), 118–19
44 *Globe*, 23 Dec. 1878
45 *CLJ* 16 (May 1880), 150–1. Italics in original
46 See *Globe*, 21 Jul. 1875, 19 Jul. 1876.
47 *DDJ* 1 (Oct. 1889), 185
48 We will return to this later in the chapter.
49 By the mid-1880s even Regiopolis and Albert College had seats, along with other universities that had no medical schools.
50 See for example *Lancet* 12 (Feb. 1880), 156; *CJMS* 7 (Nov. 1882), 371; *CP* 10 (Nov. 1885), 343–44; 11 (Nov. 1886), 351; 12 (Sep. 1887), 293–4.
51 *Globe*, 23 Apr. 1887
52 There was another significant constraint as well, however, known as the 'British loophole,' which until 1886 allowed Canadian students to register in Ontario on the basis of their British qualifications. See R.D. Gidney and W.P.J. Millar, 'The Reorientation of Medical Education in Late Nineteenth-Century Ontario: The Proprietary Medical Schools and the Founding of the Faculty of Medicine at the University of Toronto,' *JHM* 49/1 (1994), 58.
53 *Globe*, 14 Mar. 1887, 8
54 Ibid., 17 Mar. 1887, 3
55 See for example *Lancet* 8 (May 1876), 281–2.
56 Ibid., 9 (Dec. 1876), 34
57 Ibid., 10 (Jul. 1878), 345
58 See ibid., 14 (Jul. 1882), 331–2; 15 (Jul. 1883), 347.
59 Ibid., 15 (Jul. 1883), 333–4. Similarly, see ibid., 17 (Jul. 1885), 326; *CP* 11 (Jul. 1886), 217.
60 See *CLJ* 14 (Dec. 1878), 312–17; 16 (Jul. 1880), 188; *Globe*, 12 Jan., 16 and 17 Feb. 1880; *Mail*, 14 and 16 Feb. 1880.
61 See for example *CLJ* 16 (Feb. 1880), 62; 16 (Apr. 1880), 98; 17 (15 Dec. 1881), 459; *Globe*, 14 and 19 Mar. 1881.
62 See *CLJ*, 17 (1 Mar. 1881), 101; 17 (1 Jul. 1881), 261; 17 (15 Dec. 1881), 459; 19 (1 Feb. 1883), 47; 19 (1 Apr. 1883), 127; 27 (2 Nov. 1891), 514; 28 (16 Jul. 1892): 367–8.
63 See for example *Globe*, 13 Apr. 1881; Cole, 'A Learned and Honorable Body,' 148–50.
64 *Globe*, 5 Mar. 1886, 6. For other similar examples see *CLJ* 22 (15 Mar. 1886), 93; 27 (1 Apr. 1891), 179.
65 *Globe*, 27 Mar. 1891, 4
66 See Cole, 'A Learned and Honorable Body,' 294ff.
67 See *Mail*, 21 Jul. 1886, 8.

68 See *DDJ* 1 (Jul. 1889), 118; 1 (Oct. 1889), 183–4; 2 (Jul. 1890), 118–19, 137–9; Newspaper Hansard, 21 Apr. 1891; *DDJ* 3 (Sep. 1891), 152–5; 4 (Sep. 1892), 158–9; 4 (Mar. 1892), 46–50; Newspaper Hansard, 6 Apr. 1892.

69 See *CP* 12 (Jul. 1887), 221, 336; *Globe*, 12 Jun. 1891, 8; 13 Jun. 1891, 15; *CP* 17 (16 Apr. 1892), 178.

70 For the history of the MDA see Dan McCaughey, 'Professional Militancy: The Medical Defence Association vs. the College of Physicians & Surgeons of Ontario, 1891–1902,' in *Health, Disease and Medicine: Essays in Canadian History*, ed. Charles G. Roland (Toronto: Hannah Institute for the History of Medicine 1984), 96–104; C. David Naylor, 'Rural Protest and Medical Professionalism in Turn-of-the-Century Ontario,' *Journal of Canadian Studies* 21 (Spring 1986), 5–20.

71 McCaughey, 'Professional Militancy,' 100

72 See for example *CP* 21 (Dec. 1896), 924.

73 See MacNab, *Health Professions*, 37.

74 *Lancet* 25 (Jan. 1893), 177

75 See the Ontario Medical Council proceedings in *CP* 20 (Jul. and Aug. 1895). For the implications see *Lancet* 28 (Nov. 1895), 99–100; 28 (Dec. 1895), 133–4.

76 See Newspaper Hansard, 23 and 27 Mar. 1896.

77 *Lancet* 30 (Sep. 1897), 44

CHAPTER 14 *The Impact of a Changing Political Culture*

1 Legislative Assembly of Ontario, Newspaper Hansard, 7 Mar.; 14, 15, 21 Apr.; 2 May 1891

2 Ibid., 25 Mar. and 27 Apr. 1891; Statutes of Ontario, 1891, 54 Vict. c. 30, An Act Respecting the Chartered Stenographic Reporters' Association of Ontario. Similarly, see Statutes of Ontario, 1883, 46 Vict. c. 62, An Act to Incorporate the Institute of Accountants of Ontario; see also Reginald C. Stuart, *The First Seventy-five Years: A History of the Certified General Accountants' Association of Canada* (Vancouver: CGA-Canada 1988), 14–15; Alan J. Richardson, 'Educational Policy and Professional Status: A Case History of the Ontario Accountancy Profession,' *Journal of Canadian Studies* 27 (Spring 1992), 44–57.

3 The best introduction is Kelly Crossman, *Architecture in Transition: From Art to Practice, 1885–1906* (Montreal and Kingston: McGill-Queen's University Press, 1987), chs. 1–3. The detailed record of rejected bills can be traced through the reports of the proceedings of the OAA, published annually in the *CAB* in its January or February issue.

4 In 1890 a return to the legislature recorded that some 3,300 stationary engines and 3,400 stationary boilers were in use across the province. On requests for inspection, qualifications, and related issues, see for example *Globe*, 5 Feb. 1880, 3 (legislative debates), and editorials and correspondence, 4 Feb. 1884, 5; 9 Apr.

476 Notes to pages 305-12

1887, 9; 14 Apr. 1887, 6; *Mail*, 19 Feb. 1889, 4; *CAB* 2 (Apr. 1889), 37; *Canadian Engineer* 4 (Jul. 1896), 77. For the act, see Statutes of Ontario, 1891, 54 Vict. c. 31, An Act Respecting Stationary Engineers. The subsequent history of the occupation can be followed in the pages of the *Canadian Engineer*.

5 Newspaper Hansard, 7 Apr. 1892
6 *CAB* 6 (Jun. 1893), 64; 7 (Feb. 1894), 24
7 See Michael Bliss, 'The Protective Impulse,' in *Oliver Mowat's Ontario*, ed. Donald Swainson (Toronto: Macmillan 1972), 189-210, and *A Living Profit* (Toronto: McClelland and Stewart 1974), ch. 2, 'The Flight from Competition.'
8 On the sense that the professions had a higher status than business, see Bliss, *A Living Profit*, ch. 6.
9 See for example *Mail*, 7 Apr. 1891, 2, where one politician, speaking in the House, exhibited a terminal case of muddle about who had what legal privileges.
10 Newspaper Hansard, 7 Apr. 1891
11 Ibid., 25 Feb. 1892
12 Ibid., 12 May 1893
13 CSCE, *The Professional Status: An Epitome* [c. 1895], 2
14 See Ramsay Cook, 'Tillers and Toilers: The Rise and Fall of Populism in Canada in the 1890s,' Canadian Historical Association *Historical Papers*, 1984, 1-20; Margaret A. Evans, *Sir Oliver Mowat* (Toronto: University of Toronto Press 1992), ch. 11; S.E.D. Shortt, 'Social Change and Political Crisis in Rural Ontario: The Patrons of Industry, 1889-1896,' in *Oliver Mowat's Ontario*, ed. Swainson, 211-35.
15 Quoted in Shortt, 'Social Change and Political Crisis,' 217
16 For the bill see Elizabeth MacNab, *A Legal History of Health Professions in Ontario* (Toronto: Queen's Printer 1970), 30.
17 *CP* 20 (Mar. 1895), 224
18 Quoted in C. David Naylor, 'Rural Protest and Medical Professionalism in Turn-of-the-Century Ontario,' *Journal of Canadian Studies* 21 (Spring 1986), 16
19 The debate is printed in *CP* 20 (Apr. 1895), 290-2.
20 Newspaper Hansard, 5 Apr. 1895; MacNab, *Health Professions*, 30
21 *Globe*, 25 Feb. 1896, 10
22 *DDJ* 8 (Mar. 1896), 86. For two medical examples see *Lancet* 26 (Jul. 1894), 345; *CP* 20 (Jul. 1895), 536, 614.
23 For the impact on the architects' initiative of 1895 see *CAB* 8 (Dec. 1895), 141-2; for the aspirations of CSCE promoters see *Annual Meeting CSCE* (Jan. 1894), 44-5, and CSCE, *The Professional Status*, 2.
24 *CLJ* 30 (2 Apr. 1894), 181-2
25 For some examples additional to the one quoted above, see Newspaper Hansard, 25 Feb. 1892 (against the surveyors' bill); 9 Mar. 1894 (pharmacy bill); *CAB* 9 (Apr. 1896), 49, and 10 (Jan. 1897), 9 (architects).

26 Newspaper Hansard, 29 Apr. 1891
27 *OMJ* 2 (Nov. 1893), 133
28 *CLJ* 30 (2 Apr. 1894), 181–2
29 On the latter point see Bliss, *Living Profit*, ch. 6. Aspects of these broader developments are presented in Evans, *Sir Oliver Mowat*; Christopher Armstrong and H.V. Nelles, *Monopoly's Moment: The Organization and Regulation of Canadian Utilities, 1830–1930* (Toronto: University of Toronto Press 1986), esp. chs. 1 and 2. On the link between liberalism and opposition to professional monopolies elsewhere, see David L. Cowen's pioneering essay 'Liberty, Laissez-faire and Licensure in Nineteenth-Century Britain,' *BHM* 43 (1969), 30–40. A decade and a half later, Matthew Ramsey contributed a wide-ranging essay on the same subject, comparing developments in Britain, France, Germany, the United States, and other jurisdictions: see 'The Politics of Professional Monopoly in Nineteenth-Century Medicine: The French Model and Its Rivals,' in *Professions and the French State, 1700–1900*, ed. Gerald L. Geison (Philadelphia: University of Pennsylvania Press 1984), 225–305.
30 *CLJ* 20 (15 Feb. 1884), 73.
31 See for example ibid., 18 (1 Nov. 1882), 390. For some examples in the legislature see *Mail*, 1 Mar. 1879 and 11 Feb. 1880.
32 *Mail*, 8 Apr. 1881. Similarly see ibid., 20 Jan. 1880; 11, 13 and 16 Apr. 1881; *Globe*, 9 Mar. 1880, 3 Jan. 1881.
33 *Globe*, 25 Mar. 1881. For other examples see ibid., 12 Jan.; 10, 17, 26 Feb.; 9 Mar. 1880.
34 *CLJ* 19 (1 Apr. 1883), 127
35 AO, Pringle Papers, Series 3 (a), H.H. Strathy, Chairman, Committee on Unlicensed Conveyancers, 6 Jan. 1892
36 For a good example, see the *Globe*, Aug. and Sep. 1875, when controversy over a series of prosecutions in the summer of 1875 elicited some twenty-two letters and editorials on the subject in less than a month.
37 *Toronto Daily News*, 22 Jul. 1882, 4. Similarly see Toronto *Telegram*, 24 Jul. 1882; *Brantford Expositor*, 27 Jul. 1882. For another case, see *Globe*, 9 Jun. 1887, 4.
38 *Lancet* 9 (Feb. 1877), 190; 12 (Dec. 1879), 108; 12 (Jan. 1880), 157.
39 Ibid., 18 (Oct. 1885), 55–6
40 The phrase was A.S. Hardy's. See Newspaper Hansard, 8 Apr. 1892.
41 See, for example, ibid., 8 Apr. 1892 (medicine); 6 Apr. 1892 (dentists).
42 See MacNab, *Health Professions*, 99–100.
43 See *Globe*, 25 Mar. 1893, 4 and 9; Newspaper Hansard, 9 Mar. 1894.
44 See *CAB* 9 (Apr. 1896), 49; 10 (Jan. 1897), 9; 10 (Mar. 1897), 48; 11 (Jan. 1898), 9.
45 Newspaper Hansard, 6 Apr. 1891

46 See for example *Globe*, 27 Jan. 1873 (medicine); 25 Sep. 1876 (architects); 22 Feb. 1881 (engineers); *The Week*, 4 Mar. 1892 (surveyors et al.); 8 Jul. 1892 (medicine); 30 Sep. 1892, 19 May 1893 (all occupational monopolies).
47 Thomas L. Haskell, *The Emergence of Professional Social Science: The American Social Science Association and the Nineteenth-Century Crisis of Authority* (Urbana: University of Illinois Press 1977), esp. ch 2.
48 Quoted in *Globe*, 4 Sep. 1875
49 *Lancet* 21 (Jul. 1889), 324. Similarly see *CP* 19 (Jul. 1894), 543; *Globe*, 31 Aug. 1899, 12.
50 Quoted in *The Week*, 28 Apr. 1893, 507
51 Ibid.
52 CSCE, *Professional Status*, 1
53 On this point see J.L. Berlant, *Profession and Monopoly: A Study of Medicine in the United States and Great Britain* (Berkeley: University of California Press 1975), 145ff.; Cowen, 'Liberty, Laissez-faire, and Licensure.'
54 See A. Margaret Evans and C.A.V. Barker, *Century One: A History of the Ontario Veterinary Association, 1874-1974* (Guelph, ON: The Authors 1976). The legislation is printed on p. 413.

CHAPTER 15 'Who Was Then a Gentleman?'

1 *CLJ* 27 (15 Aug. 1891), 385. For a full account see Constance Backhouse, *Petticoats and Prejudice: Women and Law in Nineteenth-Century Canada* (Toronto: The Osgoode Society 1991), 293-326.
2 See for example *Globe*, 10 Dec. 1892, 17; *CLJ* 28 (31 Dec. 1892), 609-10.
3 Backhouse, *Petticoats and Prejudice*, 337
4 Alison Prentice, Paula Bourne, Gail Cuthbert Brandt, Beth Light, Wendy Mitchinson, and Naomi Black, *Canadian Women: A History* (Toronto: Harcourt, Brace, Jovanovich 1988), ch. 5
5 Ernst W. Stieb, Gail C. Coulas, and Joyce A. Ferguson, assisted by Robert J. Clark and Roy W. Hornosty, 'Women in Ontario Pharmacy, 1867-1927,' in *Despite the Odds: Essays on Canadian Women and Science*, ed. M.G. Ainley (Montreal: Véhicule Press 1990), 121-3.
6 A.A. Travill, *Medicine at Queen's, 1854-1920* (Kingston, ON: Faculty of Medicine, Queen's University, 1988), 123. Though Emily Stowe is usually considered Ontario's first woman medical doctor, she did not actually register until 1880: ibid., 122.
7 D.W. Gullett, *A History of Dentistry in Canada* (Toronto: University of Toronto Press 1971), 87-8.
8 See Rosemary R. Gagan, *A Sensitive Independence: Canadian Methodist Women Missionaries in Canada and the Orient, 1881-1925* (Montreal and Kingston: McGill-Queen's University Press 1992); Ruth Compton Brouwer, *New Women*

for God: Canadian Presbyterian Women and India Missions, 1876–1914 (Toronto: University of Toronto Press 1990); Marilyn Fardig Whiteley, 'Modest, Unaffected and Fully Consecrated: Lady Evangelists in Canadian Methodism, 1884–1900,' *Canadian Methodist Historical Society Papers* 6 (1987), 18–31; John D. Thomas, 'Servants of the Church: Canadian Methodist Deaconess Work, 1890–1926,' *Canadian Historical Review* 65 (Sep. 1984), 371–95; Alison Kemper, 'Deaconess as Urban Missionary and Ideal Woman: Church of England Initiatives in Toronto, 1890–1895,' in *Canadian Protestant and Catholic Missions, 1820s–1960s: Historical Essays in Honour of John Webster Grant*, ed. J.S. Moir and C.T. McIntire (New York: Peter Lang 1988), 171–90; Nancy Hall, 'The Professionalisation of Women Workers in the Methodist, Presbyterian, and United Churches of Canada,' in *First Days, Fighting Days: Women in Manitoba History*, ed. Mary Kinnear (Regina: University of Regina, Canadian Plains Research Center, 1987), 120–33. For an older but still useful account see Christopher Headon, 'Women and Organized Religion in Mid and Late Nineteenth Century Canada,' *JCCHS* 20 (Mar.–Jun. 1978), 3–18.

9 See Gagan, *Sensitive Independence*, 5, 30ff.; Brouwer, *New Women for God*, 55ff.; Veronica Strong-Boag, 'Canada's Women Doctors: Feminism Constrained,' in *A Not Unreasonable Claim: Women and Reform in Canada, 1880s to 1920s*, ed. Linda Kealey (Toronto: Women's Educational Press 1979), 118–19.

10 R.D. Gidney and W.P.J. Millar, *Inventing Secondary Education: The Rise of the High School in Nineteenth-Century Ontario* (Montreal and Kingston: McGill-Queen's University Press 1990), 281–2

11 Elizabeth Smith, for example, already held a teaching certificate, and Clara Brett Martin a university degree. Both women, in other words, could have opted for a career in teaching rather than medicine or law. And the same is true of many church workers: see Brouwer, *New Women for God*, appendix B; Gagan, *Sensitive Independence*, 33–6; Thomas, 'Servants of the Church,' 381, 384.

12 Strong-Boag, 'Feminism Constrained,' 113

13 See for example Thomas, 'Servants of the Church,' 372–3; Lauretta A. Hazzard, 'Towards Professionalization: Ontario Nursing, 1874–1925' (MA, University of Western Ontario 1991), 9–14.

14 Backhouse, *Petticoats and Prejudice*, 305–6, 314

15 *CMJ* 6 (1870), 502

16 Announcement, CPSO, 1877–8, 10

17 Carlotta Hacker, *The Indomitable Lady Doctors* (1974; Halifax, NS: Federation of Medical Women of Canada 1984), 22

18 Backhouse, *Petticoats and Prejudice*, 301–3

19 There are two basic accounts here. See *'A Woman with a Purpose': The Diaries of Elizabeth Smith, 1872–1884*, ed. with an introduction by Veronica Strong-Boag (Toronto: University of Toronto Press 1980), esp. xxxvi ff. and ch. 10; Travill, *Medicine at Queen's*, ch. 7.

20 See *Diaries of Elizabeth Smith*, 280, 282–3; Travill, *Medicine at Queen's*, 129–36; *Globe*, 12 and 15 Dec. 1882.
21 There are several accounts of the two colleges, but for an introduction see Lykke de la Cour and Rose Sheinin, 'The Ontario Medical College for Women, 1883–1906: Lessons from Gender-Separatism in Medical Education,' in *Despite the Odds: Essays on Canadian Women and Science*, ed. M.G. Ainley (Montreal: Véhicule Press 1990), 112–20; reprinted in *Rethinking Canada: The Promise of Women's History*, 2d ed., ed. Veronica Strong-Boag and Anita Clair Fellman (Toronto: Copp Clark Pitman 1991), 206–14.
22 Backhouse, *Petticoats and Prejudice*, 306ff.
23 The phrase is Nancy F. Cott's, from her essay 'On Men's History and Women's History,' in *Meanings for Manhood: Constructions of Masculinity in Victorian America*, ed. Mark C. Carnes and Clyde Griffen (Chicago: University of Chicago Press 1990), 206. Throughout the rest of this chapter we use 'separate spheres' primarily in this sense, though there are also cases where it was literally 'geographical' as well.
24 Strong-Boag, 'Feminism Constrained,' 113
25 See for example *Globe*, 22 Apr. 1884, 4.
26 See for example ibid., 5 Nov. 1885, 4; *CG*, 10 Oct. 1883, 316, and 25 Jan. 1888, 56.
27 For an American comparison between medicine and law on this point see Michael Grossberg, 'Institutionalizing Masculinity: The Law as a Masculine Profession,' in *Meanings for Manhood*, ed. Carnes and Griffen, 133–51, esp. 149.
28 See for example *DC*, 14 Jun. 1883; *Cdn Chman*, 3 Nov. 1892, 660; *CG*, 25 Jan. 1888, 56; 4 Apr. 1894, 216; Thomas, 'Servants of the Church,' 371–95.
29 See for example Gagan, *A Sensitive Independence*, 183.
30 Ibid., 205
31 Ibid., 15–25; Brouwer, *New Women for God*, ch. 2 and 188–92
32 See for example Ruth Compton Brouwer, 'The Canadian Methodist Church and Ecclesiastical Suffrage for Women, 1902–1914,' *Canadian Methodist Historical Society Papers* 2 (1980), 1–21; John Webster Grant, *A Profusion of Spires: Religion in Nineteenth-Century Ontario* (Toronto: University of Toronto Press 1988), 192–3; *EC*, 19 Jun. 1884, 69; *Cdn Chman*, 17 Jul. 1890, 457–8; *Globe*, 10 Jun. 1898, 12.
33 *Lancet* 6 (Sep. 1873), 20ff.; 7 (May 1875), 260; 18 (Dec. 1885), 1201; 20 (Apr. 1888), 251
34 Hazzard, 'Towards Professionalization,' 9–10. Though the primary focus of Hazzard's work is Ontario, she also situates her study within a developing international literature: see esp. ch. 1. More generally see Veronica Strong-Boag's historiographical review, 'Making a Difference: The History of Canada's Nurses,' *CBMH* 8 (1991), 231–48.
35 Though we have altered the terminology somewhat, we have been influenced

here by the first sustained attempt to integrate feminist theory into the larger literature on the sociology of the professions. See Anne Witz, *Professions and Patriarchy* (London: Routledge 1992).
36 Linda K. Kerber, 'Separate Spheres, Female Worlds, Woman's Place: The Rhetoric of Women's History,' *Journal of American History* 75 (Jun. 1988), 28. There is now a very large international literature on this subject, but Kerber provides a fine overview and critique. For the best recent application to Ontario, see Barbara Maas, *Helpmates of Man: Middle-Class Women and Gender Ideology in Nineteenth-Century Ontario* (Bochum: Universitätsverlag Dr N Brockmeyer 1990). But see also Wendy Mitchinson, *The Nature of Their Bodies: Women and Their Doctors in Victorian Canada* (Toronto: University of Toronto Press 1991), ch. 1.
37 Quoted in Stieb, 'Women in Ontario Pharmacy,' 130
38 *QCJ*, 19 Oct. 1885, 3
39 *Globe*, 3 Dec. 1887, 4
40 *CG*, 19 Sep. 1883, 292
41 Backhouse, *Petticoats and Prejudice*, 315
42 *Canadian Magazine* I (Mar.–Oct. 1893), 467–70
43 Nor was it. See for example *DDJ* 9 (Jul. 1897), 345–6, and also the commentary on the effects of the school system generally in the following chapter.
44 Quoted in Backhouse, *Petticoats and Prejudice*, 311
45 Ibid., 313
46 J.L. Payne, 'The Displacement of Young Men,' *Canadian Magazine* I (Mar.–Oct. 1893), 469
47 *Globe*, 15 Mar. 1882, 8
48 Michael Roper and John Tosh, 'Introduction,' in *Manful Assertions: Masculinities in Britain since 1800*, ed. Michael Roper and John Tosh (London: Routledge 1991), 18
49 Ibid., 2. Italics in original
50 *CG*, 28 Feb. 1877, 68
51 Quoted in Ramsay Cook and Wendy Mitchinson, eds., *The Proper Sphere: Woman's Place in Canadian Society* (Toronto: University of Toronto Press 1976), 123–4
52 Quoted in Backhouse, *Petticoats and Prejudice*, 299
53 *Globe*, 23 Aug. 1886, 4
54 *CG*, 10 Oct. 1883, 316
55 *Globe*, 15 Jun. 1887, 6
56 See for example ibid., 2 Oct. 1885, 6; 3 Nov. 1885, 8; 7 Apr. 1898, 8. See also Keith Walden, 'Hazes, Hustles, Scraps, and Stunts: Initiations at the University of Toronto, 1880–1925,' in *Youth, University, and Canadian Society: Essays in the Social History of Higher Education*, ed. Paul Axelrod and John G. Reid (Montreal and Kingston: McGill-Queen's University Press 1989), 94–121.

57 *EC*, 2 Jul. 1891, 99
58 *Globe*, 2 Oct. 1883
59 *Diaries of Elizabeth Smith*, 274-5
60 Stieb, 'Women in Ontario Pharmacy,' 125
61 Quoted in Paula J.S. LaPierre, 'The First Generation: The Experience of Women University Students in Central Canada' (PhD diss., University of Toronto 1993), 108
62 See for example *Acts and Proceedings*, General Assembly, Presbyterian Church in Canada, 1882, cxlv; *EC*, 25 Oct. 1888, 294, and 15 Jun. 1899, 382; *Cdn Chman*, 15 Jun. 1899, 376; David MacLeod, 'A Live Vaccine: The YMCA and Male Adolescence in the United States and Canada, 1870-1920,' *Histoire sociale* 21 (May 1978), 5-11; M. Lucille Marr, 'Church Teen Clubs, Feminized Organizations? Tuxis Boys, Trail Rangers, and Canadian Girls in Training, 1919-1939,' *Historical Studies in Education/Revue d'histoire de l'éducation* 3 (Fall 1991), 249-51.
63 *EC*, 12 May 1892, 226. See also ibid., 6 Oct. 1892, 479; *CG*, 3 Jan. 1894, 8
64 *Cdn Chman*, 27 Sep. 1894, 460
65 Quoted in *EC*, 7 Feb. 1895, 66
66 See for example ibid., 28 Feb. 1895, 99-101; 7 Mar. 1895, 112-14; 28 Mar. 1895, 150-1.
67 *CG*, 19 Oct. 1898, 658
68 *EC*, 25 Oct. 1888, 294

CHAPTER 16   *Portents Bleak, and Promising*

1 *Lancet* 28 (Sep. 1895), 29
2 *CLJ* 31 (1 Nov. 1895), 553
3 Ibid., 29 (16 Jun. 1893), 386-7
4 *Lancet* 25 (Feb. 1893), 211-12
5 Ibid., 28 (Sep. 1895), 29-30. Similarly see ibid., 25 (Feb. 1893), 211-12.
6 *CLJ* 33 (2 Jan. 1897), 1
7 *OMJ* 2 (Oct. 1893), 52
8 *CP* 22 (Jun. 1897), 392
9 Beverly Boutilier, '"An Intelligent Handmaid and Not an Interfering Interloper": Gender, Medical Authority, and the Founding of the Victorian Order of Nurses for Canada,' unpublished paper presented to Canadian Historical Association annual meeting, 1991
10 *CP* 22 (Feb. 1897), 137
11 Ibid., 24 (Sep. 1899), 536. See also ibid., 24 (Jul. 1899), 418.
12 Ibid.
13 Ibid., 23 (Jul. 1898), 427-8

14 *DDJ* 11 (Aug. 1899), 257
15 Ibid., 7 (Oct. 1895), 284
16 See C. David Naylor, 'Rural Protest and Medical Professionalism in Turn-of-the-Century Ontario,' *Journal of Canadian Studies* 21 (Spring 1986), 17.
17 See *DMM* 8 (Jul. 1897), 584. The president of the Medical Council was reporting here on negotiations with Ross which had taken place over the previous year.
18 Ibid.
19 Elizabeth MacNab, *A Legal History of Health Professions in Ontario* (Toronto: Queen's Printer 1970), 30–1
20 Ibid., 70
21 Curtis J. Cole, '"A Learned and Honorable Body": The Professionalization of the Ontario Bar, 1867–1929' (PhD diss., University of Western Ontario 1987), 158–64
22 *CG*, 13 Oct. 1897, 642
23 See for example *Cdn Chman*, 23 Feb. 1899, 122; *CG*, 19 Oct. 1898, 658.
24 *EC*, 13 Jul. 1899, 442
25 See for example ibid., 6 Oct. 1892, 479; 3 Nov. 1892, 526.
26 The debate began following the Provincial Synod of 1898 and can be traced through successive issues of the *EC* (cf. 22 Sep. 1898, 609) and the *Cdn Chman* (cf. 17 Nov. 1898, 696–7; 1 Dec. 1898, 735; 29 Dec. 1898, 805–6).
27 *Cdn Chman*, 17 Nov. 1898, 696
28 *CG*, 19 Oct. 1898, 658
29 See ibid., 26 Oct. 1898, 680 (Burwash's rebuttal); 9 Nov. 1898, 706; 23 Nov. 1898, 738; 7 Dec. 1898, 770.
30 See for example *Canadian Methodist Magazine* XLII (Jul.–Dec. 1895), 141.
31 See John Webster Grant, *A Profusion of Spires: Religion in Nineteenth-Century Ontario* (Toronto: University of Toronto Press 1988), 175. For ministerial reaction see *Globe*, 21 Apr. 1891, 8.
32 There is now a substantial literature on these issues. For an introduction and review of the historiography see the first chapter of David B. Marshall, *Secularizing the Faith: Canadian Protestant Clergy and the Crisis of Belief, 1850–1940* (Toronto: University of Toronto Press 1992). But see also Marshall's 'Canadian Historians, Secularization, and the Problem of the Nineteenth Century,' *Canadian Catholic Historical Association Historical Studies* (1993).
33 *Presbyterian Review*, 13 Feb. 1896, 760
34 *EC*, 18 May 1899, 313
35 See for example *Proceedings* of the Ontario Association of Architects, in *CAB* 10 (Jan. 1897), 9–10, 19–20; 11 (Jan. 1898), 8ff.
36 For an introduction to the subject, see MacNab, *Health Professions*, 39–41; Boyde Beck, 'Imperialism and Professionalization, Dominion Registration and Canadian Physicians during the Boer War,' *Scientia Canadensis* 8 (Jun. 1984), 3–

19. For Ontario, however, both accounts need to be supplemented by a careful reading of the local medical journals, especially in the late 1890s and the early years of the twentieth century.
37. See MacNab, *Health Professions*, 70; D.W. Gullett, *A History of Dentistry in Canada* (Toronto: University of Toronto Press 1971), ch. 8.
38. See Mariana Valverde, *The Age of Light, Soap and Water: Moral Reform in English Canada, 1885-1925* (Toronto: McClelland and Stewart 1991), 47, and generally ch. 3. While Heather MacDougall's book touches on early developments in the public-health movement and the role of doctors in it, her dissertation is much richer. See *Activists and Advocates: Toronto's Health Department, 1883-1983* (Toronto, Dundurn Press 1990); '"Health Is Wealth": The Development of Public Health Activity in Toronto, 1834-1890' (PhD diss., University of Toronto 1982).
39. See for example *DDJ* 7 (Nov. 1895), 297; 9 (Aug. 1897), 276; *Constitution and Bylaws, Toronto Dental Society*, 5-6.
40. *DDJ* 10 (Aug. 1898), 285. Similarly see ibid., 8 (Mar. 1896), 80; 10 (Feb. 1898), 67-8; 10 (May 1898), 147-8; 10 (Aug. 1898), 295-300.
41. Ibid., 9 (May 1897), 166
42. See for example ibid., 167; 8 (Jul. 1896), 177-85.
43. *Lancet* 3 (Dec. 1870), 116
44. For an introduction to and analysis of the CMA Code, see C.D. Naylor, 'The CMA's First Code of Ethics: Medical Morality or Borrowed Ideology?' *Journal of Canadian Studies* 17 (Winter 1982-3), 20-32.
45. The modern Ontario Dental Association was known as the Ontario Dental Society until 1920. See James W. Shosenberg, *The Rise of the Ontario Dental Association* (n.p.: Ontario Dental Association 1992), 118; and generally ch. 6 for the early history of the association.
46. *Globe*, 3 Jun. 1886, 8
47. *DDJ* 3 (Sep. 1891), 152-5
48. *CP* 8 (Oct. 1883), 311. Similarly see *CJMS* 5 (Nov. 1880), 341.
49. *Lancet* 12 (May 1880), 286
50. See J.T.H. Connor, 'Minority Medicine in Ontario, 1795 to 1903: A Study of Medical Pluralism and Its Decline' (PhD diss., University of Waterloo 1989), 239.
51. Ibid.
52. *CP* 12 (Jul. 1887), 228-9
53. *Lancet* 24 (Jul. 1892), 333-4
54. *DDJ* 3 (Sep. 1891), 149-52
55. See the early chapters of John Ferguson, *The Ontario Medical Association, 1880-1930* (Toronto: Murray Printing Co. 1930). Ferguson's account gives a running review of each annual meeting.
56. *CLJ* 32 (1 Apr. 1896), 224

57 Generally on this see Cole, 'A Learned and Honorable Body,' 303ff.
58 'Over the long haul' is the critical phrase, however. In 1917 membership in the OMA was still about 900 despite the overall growth in the number of practitioners, and in the early 1930s it stood at 35 per cent of the total. See Ontario Commission on Medical Education, Transcripts, Minutes of Proceedings and Submissions, 16 Oct. 1915–30 Jun. 1917, 84; C. David Naylor, *Private Practice, Public Payment: Canadian Medicine and the Politics of Health Insurance, 1911–1966* (Montreal and Kingston: McGill-Queen's University Press 1986), 96.
59 N. Keith Clifford, *The Resistance to Church Union in Canada, 1904–1919* (Vancouver: University of British Columbia Press 1985), 3
60 See for example Michael Gauvreau, *The Evangelical Century: College and Creed in English Canada from the Great Revival to the Great Depression* (Montreal and Kingston: McGill-Queen's University Press 1991); Marguerite Van Die, *An Evangelical Mind: Nathanael Burwash and the Methodist Tradition in Canada, 1839–1918* (Montreal and Kingston: McGill-Queen's University Press 1989).
61 For example see *EC*, 21 Oct. 1886, 278; 8 Oct. 1891, 280 (Wycliffe); *QCJ*, 11 Mar. 1893, 132; Marguerite Van Die, 'Introduction,' in *From Heaven Down to Earth: A Centenary of Chancellor's Lectures at Queen's Theological College*, ed. M. Van Die (Kingston, ON: Queen's Theological College 1992), 7–22 (Queen's); *Globe*, 6 Feb. 1897, 36 (Knox); *Globe*, 26 Nov. 1895, 7 (Victoria).
62 Christopher Armstrong and H.V. Nelles, *Monopoly's Moment: The Organization and Regulation of Canadian Utilities, 1830–1930* (1986; Toronto: University of Toronto Press 1988), 93
63 Ibid., 63
64 Wendy Mitchinson, *The Nature of Their Bodies, Women and Their Doctors in Victorian Canada* (Toronto: University of Toronto Press 1991), 190
65 C. Lesley Biggs, 'The Case of the Missing Midwives,' *Ontario History* 75 (Mar. 1983), 29–30
66 There is nothing unique about Ontario in this respect. For the devastating impact of the depression of the 1890s on professional men in one Australian city, see Graeme Davison, *The Rise and Fall of Marvellous Melbourne* (Melbourne: Melbourne University Press 1978), 106ff.
67 Carol Wilton, 'Introduction,' in *Beyond the Law: Lawyers and Business in Canada, 1830 to 1930*, ed. Carol Wilton (Toronto: The Osgoode Society 1990), 14ff.
68 Elizabeth Bloomfield, 'Lawyers as Members of Urban Business Elites in Southern Ontario, 1860 to 1920,' in *Beyond the Law*, ed. Wilton, 121
69 Paul Starr, *The Social Transformation of American Medicine* (New York: Basic Books, 1982), 70
70 Some city dentists had instituted the appointment system as early as the late 1870s, though the few references to it suggest it may have remained unusual before the 1890s. See *CJDS* 4 (Aug. 1879), 89–91; *DDJ* 4 (Jul. 1892), 103–5.

71 Robert M. Pike, 'Kingston Adopts the Telephone,' *Urban History Review* 18 (Jun. 1989), 32–47
72 See Lykke de la Cour and Rose Sheinin, 'The Ontario Medical College for Women, 1883–1906: Lessons from Gender-Separatism in Medical Education,' in *Despite the Odds: Essays on Canadian Women and Science*, ed. M.G. Ainley (Montreal: Véhicule Press 1990), 112–20; Veronica Strong-Boag, 'Canada's Women Doctors: Feminism Constrained,' in *A Not Unreasonable Claim, Women and Reform in Canada, 1880s–1920s*, ed. Linda Kealey (Toronto: Women's Educational Press 1979), 128–9. Western would not admit a woman until 1919; Queen's not until 1943. See Murray L. Barr, *A Century of Medicine at Western* (London, ON: The University of Western Ontario 1977), 291; Strong-Boag, 'Feminism Constrained,' 118.
73 Constance Backhouse, *Petticoats and Prejudice: Women and Law in Nineteenth-Century Canada* (Toronto: The Osgoode Society, 1991), 337
74 Ernst W. Stieb, Gail C. Coulas, and Joyce A. Ferguson, assisted by Robert J. Clark and Roy W. Hornosty, 'Women in Ontario Pharmacy, 1867–1927,' in *Despite the Odds: Essays on Canadian Women and Science*, ed. M.G. Ainley (Montreal: Véhicule Press 1990), 127
75 University of Toronto, Faculty of Dentistry Library, 'Women Graduates'
76 At the moment we have only some suggestive hypotheses at best, and they tend to relate to the universities generally rather than the professions or the professional schools *per se*; but see for example Veronica Strong-Boag, *The New Day Recalled: Lives of Girls and Women in English Canada, 1919–1939* (Toronto: Copp Clark Pitman 1988), 23–4, and 'Feminism Constrained,' 127–9; Jo LaPierre, 'Women in Canadian Universities: The Admissions Debate,' unpublished paper presented to Canadian Historical Association annual meeting, 1991, 19.
77 The first argument of this sort we have located was applied in defence of the private sanatorium, which some doctors accused of taking patients away from the general practitioner. See *CP* 13 (Mar. 1888), 91–2.
78 The history of the Ontario general hospital remains to be written but in the interim see David Gagan, 'For "Patients of Moderate Means": The Transformation of Ontario's General Hospitals, 1880–1950,' *Canadian Historical Review* 70 (Jun. 1989), 151–79; and his '*A Necessity Among Us': The Owen Sound General and Marine Hospital, 1891–1985* (Toronto: University of Toronto Press, 1990). See also Mark W. Cortiula, 'Social Class and Health Care in a Community Institution: The Case of Hamilton City Hospital,' *CBMH* 6 (1989), 133–45; J.T.H. Connor, 'Hospital History in Canada and the United States,' *CBMH* 7 (1990), 93–104.
79 S.E.D. Shortt, '"Before the Age of Miracles": The Rise, Fall and Rebirth of General Practice in Canada, 1890–1940,' in *Health, Disease and Medicine: Essays in Canadian History*, ed. Charles G. Roland (Toronto: Hannah Institute for the History of Medicine 1984), 138–9

80 See J.T.H. Connor, 'The Adoption and Effects of X-Rays in Ontario,' *Ontario History* 79 (Mar. 1987), 92–107; 'Medical Technology in Victorian Canada,' *CBMH* 3 (Summer 1986), 97–123.
81 Toronto Academy of Medicine Archives, *Medical Tariff for the City of Ottawa, Ottawa, 1888*
82 *DDJ* 3 (Nov. 1891), 191
83 See M. Samuel Cannon, Evelyn D. Kapes, and Gabriel A. Palkuti, 'Dr. Black and the "Amalgam Question",' *JHM* 40 (Jul. 1985), 309–26.
84 Gullett, *History of Dentistry in Canada*, 92
85 John J. Mackenzie, 'Bacteria and Their Role in Nature,' *Canadian Magazine* 1 (Jun. 1893), 253
86 Generally here see John Harley Warner, *The Therapeutic Perspective: Medical Practice, Knowledge and Identity in America, 1820–1885* (Cambridge, MA: Harvard University Press 1985), esp. ch. 9; 'The Fall and Rise of Professional Mystery: Epistemology, Authority and the Rise of Laboratory Medicine in Nineteenth-Century America,' in *The Laboratory Revolution in Medicine*, ed. Andrew Cunningham and Perry Williams (Cambridge: Cambridge University Press 1992), 110–41.
87 Frank M. Turner, 'The Conflict between Science and Religion: A Professional Dimension,' *Isis* LXIX (1978), 358

CHAPTER 17 *The Universities and Professional Education*

1 For decades Knox maintained a 'preliminary programme' in the arts subjects required by Synod, for those students unable to complete them at University College or some other undergraduate institution.
2 Matriculation standards are set out in the annual announcements published by the CPSO. For dentistry see the summary in W.E. Willmott, 'History of Dentistry,' *DDJ* 39 (1927), 167. For the relationship between these standards and the length of the high-school course, see R.D. Gidney and W.P.J. Millar, *Inventing Secondary Education: The Rise of the High School in Nineteenth-Century Ontario* (Montreal and Kingston: McGill-Queen's University Press 1990), 309.
3 See for example *DDJ* 6 (Jan. 1894), 3–4; 6 (May 1894), 113; 6 (Aug. 1894), 187–9.
4 See Gidney and Millar, *Inventing Secondary Education*, esp. chs. 6 and 13.
5 See David Keane, 'Rediscovering Ontario University Students in the Mid–Nineteenth Century' (PhD diss., University of Toronto, 1982), 260ff. and 841ff.
6 In 1880 Edward Blake, having 'looked over the Law Society records for the last five years,' expressed disappointment that 'only about one-fourth were graduates of any university.' Despite his chagrin, that figure suggests that the legal profession probably had more highly educated members than any other occupations in Ontario except high-school teachers and the Anglican and Presbyterian clergy: *CEM* 2 (Sep. 1880), 402. A decade later the figure was about the same:

the editor of the *CLJ* reported in 1889 that 26 per cent of law students were graduates. The percentage may have risen rapidly in the 1890s however. The principal of the Law School claimed in 1899 that nearly half were graduates. See *CLJ* 25 (1 Feb. 1889), 52; C. Ian Kyer and Jerome E. Bickenbach, *The Fiercest Debate: Cecil A. Wright, the Benchers, and Legal Education in Ontario, 1923–1957* (Toronto: The Osgoode Society 1987), 34.

7 Of the more than 800 Queen's graduates who were awarded medical degrees between 1855 and 1900, only 8 per cent held a BA. Calculated from *Queen's University Faculty of Medicine, Annual Calendar, 1899–1900*, 47ff., Alphabetical List of Graduates

8 *QCJ*, 28 Oct. 1899, 12. See also *Lancet* 29 (Aug. 1897), 15–19.

9 For both the new matriculation standard and the marking scheme see *Annual Announcement of the Toronto School of Medicine for 1880–1* (Toronto 1880), 17–19.

10 See *Lancet* 13 (Mar. 1881), 217–18.

11 For one good example of the former bias see G.M. Grant's comment made during his inaugural address at Queen's in 1877: *QCJ*, 15 Dec. 1877, 3.

12 *CJMS* 5 (Jun. 1880): 176–7

13 See for example *Calendar, Queen's University, 1871–2* (Kingston 1871), 18.

14 *Queen's University and College. 36th Session. Report of the Trustees to the General Assembly of the Presbyterian Church in Canada* (Kingston 1877); QUA, Queen's University Board of Trustees Minutes, 26 Apr. 1877. For the numbers in the 1890s see QUA, Queen's University Senate Minutes. Each April there is a list of all graduands, and the number listed in theology is only two or three a year.

15 See for example *Globe*, 4 Jun. 1880, 4; 17 Sep. 1880, 6.

16 See William Osler's comment on the difference between Ontario and Britain in this respect: *Lancet* 18 (Nov. 1885), 66.

17 The best introduction here is Arthur Engel, 'The English Universities and Professional Education,' in *The Transformation of Higher Learning, 1860–1930*, ed. Konrad H. Jarausch (Chicago: University of Chicago Press 1983), 293–305.

18 See *DDJ* 1 (Jan. 1889), 29–32.

19 See Kelly Crossman, *Architecture in Transition: From Art to Practice, 1885–1906* (Montreal and Kingston: McGill-Queen's University Press 1987), 32–5.

20 *DDJ* 1 (Oct. 1889), 161

21 Ibid., 2 (Jan. 1890), 36

22 See D.W. Gullett, *A History of Dentistry in Canada* (Toronto: University of Toronto Press 1971), ch. 9.

23 See for example *DDJ* 1 (Oct. 1889), 163–7; 6 (Jan. 1894), 3–4; 6 (May 1894), 113, 115; 10 (Feb. 1898), 37.

24 *OMJ* 1 (Feb. 1893), 310

25 *DDJ* 6 (Apr. 1894), 88–9

26 For this passage generally see C.R. Young, *Early Engineering Education at*

Toronto, 1851–1919 (Toronto: University of Toronto Press 1958), chs. 3–5; *JLAO*, 1875–6, Sessional Papers, No. 27, SPS Supplementary Report (James Loudon); *JLAO*, Sessional Papers, 1880s and 1890s, Reports of the SPS.

27 See *JLAO*, Sessional Papers, 1880s, Reports of the SPS; Young, *Early Engineering Education*, 72.

28 See Natalie R. Neville, 'The School of Mining and Agriculture at Kingston: A Case Study in the Development of Canadian Engineering Education' (MA, Queen's University 1987); Hilda Neatby, *Queen's University, Volume I: 1841–1917* (Montreal and Kingston: McGill-Queen's University Press 1978), 217–22.

29 Though his figures are for Canada as a whole and not just Ontario, see the indicative table for the relative numbers of apprentices and university students in J. Rodney Millard, *The Master Spirit of the Age: Canadian Engineers and the Politics of Professionalism, 1887–1922* (Toronto: University of Toronto Press 1988), 152.

30 There is a fine account of the progress of negotiations and the outcome in A.A. Travill, *Medicine at Queen's, 1854–1920* (Kingston, ON: Faculty of Medicine, Queen's University, 1988), ch. 8.

31 For a detailed, though highly partisan, account see AO, Trinity Medical College, manuscript history of Trinity Medical College by Walter B. Geikie.

32 R.D. Gidney and W.P.J. Millar, 'The Reorientation of Medical Education in Late Nineteenth–Century Ontario: The Proprietary Medical Schools and the Founding of the Faculty of Medicine at the University of Toronto,' *JHM* 49/1 (1994), 52–78.

33 See 'The Research Ideal at the University of Toronto,' in A.B. McKillop, *Contours of Canadian Thought* (Toronto: University of Toronto Press 1987), 78–95.

34 For the general reader, the best introduction to these changes is Kenneth M. Ludmerer, *Learning to Heal: The Development of American Medical Education* (New York: Basic Books 1985), chs. 1 and 2. A more difficult but more rewarding account is John Harley Warner, *The Therapeutic Perspective: Medical Practice, Knowledge and Identity in America, 1820–1885* (Cambridge, MA: Harvard University Press 1986).

35 Sandra F. McRae, 'The "Scientific Spirit" in Medicine at the University of Toronto, 1880–1910' (PhD diss., University of Toronto 1987).

36 *Globe*, 4 Oct. 1887, 5; *CP* 12 (Nov. 1887), 347

37 *CP* 12 (Apr. 1887), 99–101

38 Ibid.

39 Ludmerer draws attention to this distinction as well, and points out that this was what differentiated Osler from some of his colleagues at Johns Hopkins: *Learning to Heal*, 133. For a broader introduction to this debate see John Harley Warner's 'The Fall and Rise of Professional Mystery: Epistemology, Authority and the Rise of Laboratory Medicine in Nineteenth-Century America,' in *The Laboratory*

Revolution in Medicine, ed. Andrew Cunningham and Perry Williams (Cambridge: Cambridge University Press 1992), 110–41.
40 *CP* 12 (Nov. 1887), 348
41 The phrase itself is not Ramsay Wright's but Caesar Wright's, when the latter was engaged in a rather similar debate over the future of the Osgoode Hall Law School. The distinction being drawn, however, is pertinent. See Clifford Ian Kyer, 'Caesar Wright and Ontario Legal Education, 1927–57,' *The Advocate* [Toronto] 14 (Apr. 1980), 20.
42 For a Canadian comment which reveals doubts among practitioners see *CJMS* 8 (Jan. 1882), 34. More generally see Warner, *Therapeutic Perspective*, ch. 9.
43 *CP* 12 (Apr. 1887), 101
44 Ibid., 99
45 *Lancet* 19 (May 1887), 282
46 See ibid., 22 (Feb. 1890), 185; *CP* 14 (Dec. 1889), 479.
47 *CP* 15 (16 Oct. 1890), 464
48 *Lancet* 22 (Feb. 1890), 185
49 Warner, *Therapeutic Perspective*, 260ff.
50 The phrase is Warner's: ibid., 245.
51 For a wide-ranging discussion of these issues see the latter half of John Harley Warner's essay, 'The History of Science and the Sciences of Medicine,' *Osiris* X (1994), ed. Arnold Thackray, *Critical Problems in the History of Science.*
52 For an introduction see A.B. McKillop, *Matters of Mind: The University in Ontario 1791–1951* (Toronto: University of Toronto Press 1994), ch. 13.
53 See Gidney and Millar, 'The Reorientation of Medical Education,' 67–8.
54 See Elizabeth MacNab, *A Legal History of Health Professions in Ontario* (Toronto: Queen's Printer 1970), 33, 44.
55 Though we disagree, at some points, with the interpretive biases involved, there are three good accounts of the background to this change. See the early chapters of C. Ian Kyer and Jerome E. Bickenbach, *The Fiercest Debate: Cecil A. Wright, the Benchers, and Legal Education in Ontario, 1923–1957* (Toronto: The Osgoode Society 1987); G. Blaine Baker, 'Legal Education in Upper Canada, 1785–1889: The Law Society as Educator,' in *Essays in the History of Canadian Law*, ed. David H. Flaherty (Toronto: University of Toronto Press 1983), II: 49–142; Curtis Cole, '"A Hand to Shake the Tree of Knowledge": Legal Education in Ontario, 1871–1889,' *Interchange* 17 (1986), 15–27.
56 *CLJ* 23 (1 Sep. 1887), 288
57 Ibid., 24 (16 Mar. 1888), 130–2
58 See ibid., 132; 24 (1 Aug. 1888), 393–8; 24 (1 Sep. 1888), 422.
59 There had been much interest expressed in these American exemplars. See for example ibid., 12 (Jul. 1876), 187–8; *Rose-Belford's Canadian Monthly* 4 (Feb. 1880), 122. For an extended introduction see the opening chapters of Robert

Stevens, *Law School: Legal Education in America from the 1850s to the 1980s* (Chapel Hill: University of North Carolina Press 1983).
60 *Globe*, 28 May 1888, 4
61 *CLJ* 24 (1 Sep. 1888), 422
62 Ibid., 25 (2 Jan. 1889), 5
63 Ibid., 24 (16 Mar. 1888), 153
64 Ibid., 24 (2 Apr. 1888), 173
65 Ibid., 24 (1 Aug. 1888), 397–8
66 Ibid., 25 (1 Feb. 1889), 51–3
67 Ibid., 24 (1 Aug. 1888), 395–6
68 Ibid.
69 *Globe*, 21 Dec. 1888, 8
70 *CLJ* 24 (16 Mar. 1888), 154
71 See ibid., 34 (15 Oct. 1898), 672–3
72 Ibid., 25 (1 Oct. 1889), 455.
73 For two examples see *Globe*, 13 Nov. 1877; *CLJ* 20 (15 Jan. 1884), 34.
74 See for example *CLJ* 22 (1 Sep. 1886), 273–5; *CG*, 19 Sep. 1888, 600.
75 *Globe*, 2 Jan. 1889, 5
76 *CLJ* 25 (1 Oct. 1889), 455
77 *Globe*, 3 Feb. 1899, 9
78 Kyer and Bickenbach, *Fiercest Debate*, take up the story of the Osgoode Hall Law School from the 1890s onwards and follow it through to the second major reorientation of legal education in Ontario, the transfer of responsibility to the university law schools in 1957.
79 For a more detailed account of what follows, see the pertinent sections of J.G. Althouse, *The Ontario Teacher: 1800–1910* (n.p.: Ontario Teachers' Federation 1967).

CHAPTER 18 *Retrospect*

1 See 'Featherstone Lake Osler,' *DCB* 12.
2 See W. Stewart Wallace, ed., *Macmillan Dictionary of Canadian Biography*, 3rd ed. rev. and enl. (Toronto: Bryant Press 1963), 566–7; Anne Wilkinson, *Lions in the Way* (Toronto: Macmillan Co. of Canada 1956).
3 See for example Wilkinson, *Lions*, 191.
4 Ian M. Drummond, 'Ontario's Industrial Revolution, 1867–1941,' *Canadian Historical Review* 69 (Sep. 1988), 297. See also Ian M. Drummond, *Progress without Planning: The Economic History of Ontario from Confederation to the Second World War* (Toronto: University of Toronto Press 1987), 23.
5 R.J. Clark, 'Professional Aspirations and the Limits of Occupational Autonomy: The Case of Pharmacy in Nineteenth-Century Ontario,' *CBMH* 8 (1991), 46

6 See for example *Globe*, 5 Dec. 1895, 10; 24 Apr. 1896, 10; *CP* 17 (16 Apr. 1892), 186.
7 Christopher Armstrong and H.V. Nelles, *Monopoly's Moment: The Organization and Regulation of Canadian Utilities, 1830–1930* (1986; Toronto: University of Toronto Press 1988), 63–5
8 *Globe*, 14 May 1890, 9
9 Ibid., 8 Jun. 1898, 6
10 For the origins of this frame of mind see Harold Perkin, *The Origins of Modern English Society* (London: Routledge and Kegan Paul 1969), 252–70. Since that book, he has extended the argument in *The Rise of Professional Society: England since 1880* (London: Routledge and Kegan Paul 1989): see esp. ch. 4.
11 *CG*, 16 Feb. 1887, 104
12 See for example Legislative Assembly of Ontario, Newspaper Hansard, 3 Mar. 1892 (estimates of the Education Department).
13 Compare Robert L. Fraser, 'Like Eden in Her Summer Dress: Gentry, Economy and Society, Upper Canada, 1812–1840' (PhD diss., University of Toronto 1979), 346.
14 Julius Isaac, 'Delos Rogest Davis, K.C.,' *Law Society Gazette* 24 (1990), 293–301; Constance Backhouse, *Petticoats and Prejudice: Women and Law in Nineteenth-Century Canada* (Toronto: The Osgoode Society 1991), 427n19; Ian Malcolm, 'Robert Sutherland: The First Black Lawyer in Canada?' *Law Society Gazette* 26 (1992), 183–6
15 Robin W. Winks, *The Blacks in Canada: A History* (New Haven, CT: Yale University Press 1971), 329
16 See *OMJ* 1 (Jul. 1893), 505–7; 'Oronhyatekha,' *DCB* 13.
17 Donald Maclean, *On the Medical Profession and Medical Education in Canada: Address delivered at his Installation as Professor of the Institutes of Medicine* (Kingston 1865), 21; *UCLJ* 9 (May 1863), 113.
18 There is a comprehensive bibliographical guide to the rich American literature on this subject in Bruce A. Kimball, *The 'True Professional Ideal' in America* (Cambridge, MA: Blackwell 1992), ch. 4.
19 Bruce Curtis, *Building the Educational State: Canada West, 1836–1871* (London, ON: The Althouse Press and Falmer Press 1988). See esp. his concluding chapter, 366ff. For a stimulating discussion of the linkages between professions and state formation, see Terry Johnson, 'The State and the Professions: Peculiarities of the British,' in *Social Class and the Division of Labour: Essays in Honour of Ilya Neustadt*, ed. Anthony Giddens and Gavin Mackenzie (Cambridge: Cambridge University Press 1982), 186–208. As Lykke de la Cour, Cecilia Morgan, and Mariana Valverde point out, the norms are themselves gender-biased, giving additional emphasis to the protection of male citadels. See their essay 'Gender Regulation and State Formation in Nineteenth-Century Canada,' in *Colonial*

Leviathan: State Formation in Mid-Nineteenth-Century Canada, ed. Allan Greer and Ian Radforth (Toronto: University of Toronto Press 1992), 163–91.
20 John Webster Grant, *A Profusion of Spires: Religion in Nineteenth-Century Ontario* (Toronto: University of Toronto Press 1988), 94
21 For our analysis here, see the appendix, section A and table 1. We have also developed this argument in some detail in *Inventing Secondary Education: The Rise of the High School in Nineteenth-Century Ontario* (Montreal and Kingston: McGill-Queen's University Press), 158–9.
22 See the biographical article by Hodgins and Careless's 'epilogue' in J.M.S. Careless, ed., *The Pre-Confederation Premiers: Ontario Government Leaders, 1841–1867* (Toronto: University of Toronto Press 1980), esp. 303 and 315.
23 For one recent example see ch. 2 of Bernard Blishen's otherwise admirable book, *Doctors in Canada* (Toronto: University of Toronto Press 1991). Entitled 'The Development of Medical Ascendancy,' it constitutes a 'historical overview' and draws on earlier work by several historians and sociologists but especially on Ronald Hamowy's blunt and constricted version of the march of medical progress in *Canadian Medicine: A Study in Restricted Entry* (Vancouver: Fraser Institute 1984).
24 See also Donald M. Scott, 'The Profession that Vanished: Public Lecturing in Mid-Nineteenth-Century America,' in *Professions and Professional Ideologies in America*, ed. Gerald L. Geison (Chapel Hill: University of North Carolina Press 1983), 12–28.
25 Andrew Abbott, *The System of Professions: An Essay on the Division of Expert Labor* (Chicago: University of Chicago Press 1988)
26 Christopher Armstrong and H.V. Nelles, *The Revenge of the Methodist Bicycle Company: Sunday Streetcars and Municipal Reform in Toronto, 1888–1897* (Toronto: Peter Martin Associates 1977), 5
27 See *The Week*, 12 Apr. 1895, 463–4, and following issues.
28 Two good examples are Koch's premature and mistaken announcement in 1890 of a cure for tuberculosis, which excited enormous hopes, sent several of Toronto's leading doctors and Ramsay Wright scurrying off to Berlin, and ended in a public *débâcle*; and inoculation against cholera. See *CP* 15 (1 Dec. 1890), 555; *The Week*, 2 Sep. 1892, 628, and 11 Nov. 1892, 788–9. See also ibid., 26 Apr. 1895, 510.
29 R.K. House, *Dentistry in Ontario*, A Study for the Committee on the Healing Arts (Ontario) (Toronto: Queen's Printer 1970), 20
30 Elizabeth MacNab, *A Legal History of Health Professions in Ontario* (Toronto: Queen's Printer 1970), 71–4
31 See for example C.S. Chittenden, 'Historical Reminiscences,' *Independent Practitioner* 7 (1886), 73; University of Toronto, Faculty of Dentistry Library, F.C. Van Duzer, notes on 'History of Canadian Dentistry,' Mar. 1953.

APPENDIX

1 See Michael Katz, *The People of Hamilton, Canada West* (Cambridge, MA: Harvard University Press 1975), appendix 2.
2 Gordon Darroch, 'Early Industrialization and Inequality in Toronto, 1861–1899,' *Labour/Le Travailleur* 11 (Spring 1983), 36; see also his 'Occupational Structure, Assessed Wealth and Homeowning during Toronto's Early Industrialization, 1861–1899,' *Histoire sociale* 16 (Nov. 1983), 384–8. Another excellent analysis, and of particular interest for this study, is in David G. Burley, 'The Businessmen of Brantford, Ontario: Self-Employment in a Mid-Nineteenth-Century Town' (PhD diss., McMaster University 1983), appendix II.
3 See the comments, for example, in *Globe*, 22 Jul. 1886, 4.
4 Ibid., 20 Jul. 1886, 4
5 *EC*, 18 Dec. 1890, 385; *Globe*, 18 Jul. 1892, 4. However, portions of clerical incomes remained exempt – for example, allowances such as 'horse keep' and church property such as manses or parsonages.
6 Because several historians have taken the figures published in the *Globe* at face value, it is worth noting that the whole point was to demonstrate how fallacious the assessment figures were, something the *Globe* did with great glee and much heavy-handed irony. Professional men were not the only ones under scrutiny, but they received their share of pointed commentary on how they were evading taxes. See for example *Globe*, 20 Jul. 1886, 4; 21 Jul. 1886, 4.
7 Darroch, 'Occupational Structure, Assessed Wealth,' 386.
8 Ian M. Drummond, *Progress Without Planning: The Economic History of Ontario from Confederation to the Second World War* (Toronto: University of Toronto Press 1987), 227
9 David Gagan and Rosemary Gagan, 'Working-Class Standards of Living in Late-Victorian Urban Ontario,' *Journal of the Canadian Historical Association* N.S. 1 (Victoria 1990), 192
10 Using probate records in addition to assessment rolls, Livio Di Matteo and Peter George have analysed wealth during the last thirty years of the nineteenth century in Wentworth County among a population that was probably better off, in general, than the norm. They conclude that 'the distribution of wealth ... was persistently unequal,' although 'there was some material improvement over time,' at least until the 1890s: 'Canadian Wealth Inequality in the Late Nineteenth Century: A Study of Wentworth County, Ontario, 1872–1902,' *Canadian Historical Review* 73 (Dec. 1992), 482–3.
11 Douglas McCalla, *Planting the Province: The Economic History of Upper Canada, 1784–1870* (Toronto: University of Toronto Press 1993), 115
12 Michael J. Piva, 'Getting Hired: The Civil Service Act of 1857,' *Journal of the Canadian Historical Association* N.S. 3 (1992), 118
13 Paul Craven and Tom Traves, 'Dimensions of Paternalism: Discipline and

Culture in Canadian Railway Operations in the 1850s,' in *On the Job: Confronting the Labour Process in Canada*, ed. Craig Heron and Robert Storey (Montreal and Kingston: McGill-Queen's University Press 1986), 56.
14 Darroch, 'Early Industrialization,' 40
15 Gagan and Gagan, 'Working-Class Standards,' 176, 184. See also Drummond, *Progress Without Planning*, Table 13.2.
16 Craven and Traves, 'Dimensions of Paternalism,' 56
17 Piva, 'Getting Hired,' 118
18 Graham S. Lowe, *Women in the Administrative Revolution* (Toronto: University of Toronto Press 1987), 145
19 Brantford City assessment rolls, 1891; Gagan and Gagan, 'Working-Class Standards,' 174 and 176
20 R.D. Gidney and W.P.J. Millar, *Inventing Secondary Education: The Rise of the High School in Nineteenth-Century Ontario* (Montreal and Kingston: McGill-Queen's University Press 1990), 302–3

Index

Abbott, Andrew, 233, 244, 389
Abbott, A.R., 382
Adams, W.C., 216
Adamson, Anthony, 127
Agnew, J.N., 93, 95
Aikins, William T., 89, 183, 217–18
Althouse, J.G., 241
Anatomy Act (1843), 156
Anglican clergy. *See* clergy
Anthony, Susan B., 239, 245
apothecaries. *See* pharmacists
apprenticeship. *See* professional education
architects, 304–5, 308, 316, 320, 359, 361
Armstrong, Christopher, 102, 280, 346
Association of Ontario Land Surveyors (AOLS), 227, 230–1, 361, 389; *see also* surveyors
attorneys. *See* lawyers
Attorneys' Admission Act (1857), 78–9

Baby, Charles, 74
Backhouse, Constance, 323, 328, 349
Baker, Blaine, 19, 74, 170, 177
Baldwin, Robert, 21–2, 49, 61–4, 74, 170, 173, 175, 209
Baldwin, Robert, Jr, 42, 44

Baldwin, W.W., 7, 19–20, 183
Balfour, William, 308–10, 312, 322
Barr, Robert, 240
barristers. *See* lawyers
Beaumont, W.R., 94
Becher, Henry, 142–3
Bell, Rev. William, 135
Benchers, 18, 32, 73–5, 80–4, 164, 170–1, 209, 288, 293, 295, 298, 311, 313–14, 338, 370–1, 373, 386; *see also* Law Society of Upper Canada; lawyers
Benson, Thomas M., 139, 183, 193
Bethune, A.N. (bishop), 34, 90, 111, 278
Bethune, Angus, 88
Bethune, Norman, 90, 94
Bidwell, Barnabus, 45
Biggs, Lesley, 347
birthplace, 196–7, 393–4; of clergy, 13; of doctors, 88–90; of women professionals, 323
Black, G.V., 352
Blake, Edward, 80, 82–3, 110, 148, 293
Blake, Samuel Hume, 110
Blake, William Hume, 74, 148, 166
Bland, Emma Flesher, 150
Bland, Henry Flesher, 125–6, 129, 131–2, 137

Bliss, Michael, 203, 307
Bloomfield, Elizabeth, 148, 182, 348, 398–9
Bok, Edward, 333
Bostwick, John, 223
botanics. *See* Thomsonians
Boulter, G.W., 217–18
Boulton, H.J., 10, 63
Bovell, James, 94
Bowlby, D.S., 183
Bowlby, W.H., 183
Boyle, David, 243
Brantford, professionals in, 128, 186–7, 189–91, 195–200, 277, 374, 400–2, 404
British influence on professions, 3, 6–7, 9–25, 39, 153, 172–3
Brouse, William, 88, 90
Brown, George, 50, 68, 73, 102, 123, 139, 218, 233, 431n26
Brown, Gordon, 94, 431n26
Bucke, Richard, 146–7, 251
Buell, William, 48, 58
Burley, David, 190, 198
Burwash, Nathanael, 125, 130–2, 134, 151, 182
Burwell, Mahlon, 223

Cameron, J.H., 63, 74, 143, 173, 209
Cameron, Matthew Crooks, 83, 92, 218
Campbell, Alexander, 74
Canadian Medical Association, 95–7, 342–4
Canadian Society of Civil Engineers (CSCE), 229–31, 305, 309, 311, 319; *see also* engineers
Canniff, William, 94, 99
careers: of clergy, 180–2, 270–5; of doctors, 182–6; of lawyers, 182–7
Careless, J.M.S., 388
Cattanach, Angus, 183, 186
chartered accountants, 304

Chittenden, C.S., 216, 219
Church Association, 110
Church of England: coping with disestablishment, 107–12, 114–15, 269–70; disestablishment, 27–8, 52, 65–7, 106; *see also* British influence on professions; clergy; Clergy Reserves
Church of Scotland: coping with disestablishment, 112–14, 268–70; disestablishment, 52, 65–7, 106; *see also* British influence on professions; clergy; Clergy Reserves
Church Society, 28–9, 111–12
Clark, R.J., 221–2
Clarke, William, 87–8, 90, 92–3, 95–6
clergy: in church government, 107–8, 112–13; commutation fund, 66–7, 114–15, 187, 269, 436nn.29, 30; crisis of confidence, 276–81; dissenters and respectability, 35–6, 119; income, 26–31, 35–6, 117–18, 187–9, 191–6, 275–7, 451n.39; late nineteenth-century opportunities, 345–6; late nineteenth-century problems, 338–40; overcrowding, 121, 259–61, 266–7; responses to overcrowding, 262–4, 268–70; vis-à-vis laity, 108–13, 118–19, 270–5; women in church work, 323, 325–6, 329; *see also* birthplace; Brantford, professionals in; careers; professional education; professional privileges; professional work; social origins and standing; wealth of professionals
Clergy Reserves, 16, 25–31, 46, 51–2, 65–6
Cochrane, Jennie, 150–1
Cochrane, William, 125–6, 129, 132–6, 150, 182, 195
Cocks, Raymond, 172
Cole, Curtis, 81, 253, 288, 398

College of Physicians and Surgeons of
  Ontario (CPSO), 90, 93, 95, 97–8,
  100, 293, 357–8; composition, 87–8,
  91, 296; discipline of members, 284,
  288–9, 315; divisions in, 296–7;
  education regulations, 155, 157–8,
  178, 296, 300–1, 324, 338, 354, 356,
  368; 1870–4, 93, 95, 97–8; enforcement of medical act, 290–2, 297–8,
  300–2, 315, 344; revolts against,
  299–300; women doctors, 322; *see
  also* doctors
College of Physicians and Surgeons of
  Upper Canada, 11, 23–4, 53
College of Preceptors, 242
Conner, Jennifer, 48
Conner, J.T.H., 48, 55, 98, 146
Connor, Skeffington, 60, 74
conveyancing. *See* lawyers, competition
  of laity
Convocation of Benchers. *See* Benchers
County Attorneys Act (1857), 71, 73
courts of law 17–22, 60–4, 70–1, 140–1,
  164
Craven, Paul, 403
Cronyn, Benjamin, 51, 271
Crooks, Adam, 82–3, 183, 235
Curtis, Bruce, 384

Darroch, Gordon, 400, 402, 404
Davidoff, Leonore, 149, 206
Davis, Delos Rogest, 382
Day, Barnabas, 215–17
dentists: late nineteenth-century
  opportunities, 341–3, 351–2; late
  nineteenth-century problems, 337–8;
  market for services, 253–4; nature of
  profession, 219–22; organization in
  1860s, 215–18; overcrowding and
  competition, 256, 266–7, 317; results
  of competition, 262–4; unprofessional
  conduct, 286–8, 290; women dentists,
  322, 349; *see also* Perth County,
  professionals in; professional
  education; professional work; Royal
  College of Dental Surgeons of
  Ontario; social origins and standing
Dewart, E.H., 120–1
Dickson, John R., 90
Division Courts Act (1880), 298–9, 313
doctors, 31; competition, 254–6, 297,
  317; and homeopaths and eclectics,
  53–8, 91–100, 296, 432n.43; and
  hospitals, 85, 168–90, 350; income,
  38–9, 189–95; late nineteenth-century
  opportunities, 341–5, 346–52; late
  nineteenth-century problems, 300–1,
  336–8; lay competition, 38–41;
  medical legislation (to 1874), 53–9,
  87–8, 91–8, 415n.85, 430n.7; numbers of, 55, 85, 96, 249–50, 395–9;
  overcrowding, 248–9, 266–7, 297,
  335–6; results of competition, 261–5;
  settling in countryside, 249–52, 399;
  therapeutics, 41–5, 101–4, 350–3;
  unprofessional conduct, 283–5, 288–
  90; women doctors, 322–5, 327, 330,
  349, 383; *see also* birthplace;
  Brantford, professionals in; careers;
  College of Physicians and Surgeons of
  Ontario; eclectics; homeopaths;
  midwives; Perth County, professionals
  in; professional education; professional work; professional privileges;
  religious affiliation; social origins and
  standing; Thomsonians; wealth of
  professionals
Douglas, William, 143
Draper, William, 21, 32, 61, 74, 110,
  142, 165–6
druggists. *See* pharmacists
Drummond, Ian, 378, 403
Duck, George, Jr, 126, 136, 139–40,
  143, 148, 182

Duck, Henry, 182
Duffin, Jacalyn, 128, 144–7, 192–3
Duncan, Sara Jeannette, 126, 137
Duncombe, Charles, 4
Dwight, T.W., 369

eclectics, 43, 59, 86–7; see also doctors
Elliott, William, 165–7
Elmsley, John, 13
Engel, Arthur, 6
engineers, 224–32, 246, 319, 380, 389; stationary, 305, 308; see also Canadian Society of Civil Engineers; professional education; professional work; social origins and standing; surveyors

Fahey, Curtis, 29
Fergusson, A.J., 74
Fraser, Robert, 6
Free Church, 30, 113, 259
Friedson, Eliot, xii
Fulton, John, 89, 96–7, 157, 218, 284–5, 343–4

Gagan, David, 403–4
Gagan, Rosemary, 403–4
Galbraith, John, 229, 361
Geikie, Walter, 364–5, 367
Geison, Gerald, xi
Gemmill, John, 183–4, 186
Gilmore, William, 52
Glasgow Colonial Society, 27, 29
Glazebrook, G.P. de T., 391
Godley, J.R., 33
Goheen, Peter, 128
Gooderham, Henry, 110
Gooderham, William, 110
Goodyear, Charles, 215
Gorham, Eli, 56
Gourlay, Robert, 11, 38
Graham, J.E., 366

Grant, G.M., 135, 177, 325
Grant, John Webster, 16, 281, 385
Gullett, D.W., 256
Gwynne, W.C., 23
Gzowski, Sir Casimir, 110

Hagerman, Christopher, 7, 20–1
Hagerty, Justice, 142
Hall, Catherine, 149, 206
Hall, C.B., 94
Hardy, A.S., 227
Hardy, Stewart, 240–1
Harrison, Robert A., 126, 134, 136, 139–40, 142–3, 149, 184
Harrison, S.B., 74
Haskell, Thomas, 104, 316
Hayes, Alan, 272
Hazzard, Lauretta, 326
Helliwell, John, 167
Henderson, J.L.H., 53
Hincks, Francis, 49
Hodder, Edward, 90, 93
Hodgins, Bruce, 388
Hodgins, J.G., 110
Hodgins, Thomas, 149, 208
homeopaths, 43, 45, 59, 86–7, 296, 431n.26; see also doctors

Inns of Court, 10, 13
Irving, Aemilius, 294

Johnson, Rev. C.C., 271–2
judges, 17–22, 41, 71, 77, 142; see also courts of law; lawyers
Jury, Alfred, 303–4

Katz, Michael, 190, 395
Kealey, Gregory, 104, 247
Keefer, T.C., 207
Kerber, Linda, 326
King's College, 15, 24–5, 153, 164, 170

Kingston Women's Medical College, 327, 324, 349
Kirk. *See* Church of Scotland
Kitson Clark, George, 206
Knights of Labor, 303
Knox College, 153, 159–62
Knox Missionary Society, 161–2

Langdell, C.C., 369
Langstaff, James, 128, 144–7, 189, 192–3, 251, 391
Langton, Anne, 39, 41
Law Society of Upper Canada, 7, 11, 25, 46; and discipline of members, 288–90; and education at end of century, 368–75; enforcement of legislation, 290–1; entry requirements, 4, 19–20, 31–2, 74–80, 83–4, 164–5, 170–1, 294–5, 354–5; establishment, 18–19; reorganization, 81–4, 295, 298; revolts against, 294–5, 298–9, 311; *see also* lawyers
lawyers: attorney versus barrister, 7, 31–2, 77–84; competition of laity, 37–8, 256–9, 286, 298–9, 313–14, 467n.35; consolidation of powers after mid-century, 70–84; income, 189–91, 193–5; numbers of, 36, 65, 75, 77, 80–1, 248–9, 253, 395–9; overcrowding, 76–80, 248–9, 266–7, 335–6; results of competition, 262–3; settling in countryside, 249, 252–3, 399; turn-of-the-century opportunities, 345, 348; turn-of-the-century problems, 336, 338; unprofessional conduct, 285–6, 289; women lawyers, 322–8, 349, 383; *see also* birthplace; Brantford, professionals in; careers; courts of law; judges; Perth County, professionals in; professional education; professional work; religious affiliation; social origins and standing; wealth of professionals
Leitch, William, 176–7
Lesslie, James, 58
Lewis, John Travers, 278
Loudon, Irvine, 55
Loudon, James, 228–9
Ludmerer, Kenneth, 101
Lundy, J.F., 125–6, 129–30, 137–8, 150, 195

McCalla, Douglas, 403
McCaughey, Dan, 300
McCaul, John, 207
Macaulay, Ann, 214
Macdonald, John A., 64, 71–4, 90, 149, 184, 209
Macdonald, John Sandfield, 21, 57, 64, 74, 141–2, 174, 209, 228, 386–7
Macdonald, Peter, 184
Macdougall, Alan, 229–30, 309–10, 379–80, 389
MacDougall, Heather, 342
McDougall, William, 49–50
McGill, William, 90, 93, 95, 217
Mackenzie, William Lyon, 46–7, 50, 61–6, 68, 70, 73
McKerracher, Donald, 125–6, 130, 150, 162–3, 181, 185
McKerracher, Mrs, 150
McLean, Archibald, 74, 142
McLellan, James, 238
MacNab, Sir Allan, 21, 61, 74, 142
MacRae, Marion, 127
McRae, Sandra, 363
Malloch, J.G., 135, 142
Martin, Charles A., 217
Martin, Clara Brett, 322–5, 328–32, 349
medical act: (1865), 87; (1869), 91–7, 103, 386, 430n.7
Medical Board of Upper Canada 7, 13, 22–5, 31, 53, 58, 86

Medical Council of Ontario. *See* College of Physicians and Surgeons of Ontario
Medical Defence Association, 300, 344
Merritt, W.H., 47, 57–8, 72
Methodist clergy. *See* clergy
Methodist Woman's Missionary Society, 326
midwives, 41, 54–5, 102–3, 146, 254, 310, 314–15, 317, 347; *see also* doctors; women
Mikel, W.C., 345
Mills, David, 116
Mitchinson, Wendy, 103, 146, 347
Moir, John, 30
Moodie, Susanna, 39, 147
Morrison, J.C., 61, 74
Mowat, Oliver, 74–5, 139, 209, 311–12, 318, 325, 327
Mulock, William, 364
Murney, Edward, 74
Murray, Robert, 232

Nelles, H.H., 216–17
Nelles, H.V., 102, 281, 346
Noble, David, 8
Notman, William, 63
nurses 326, 337, 376; *see also* doctors; women

O'Boyle, Lenore, 266
O'Brien, Henry, 141, 165, 167–8
O'Brien, Lucius, 23
O'Brien, Mary, 8
Ontario Association of Architects. *See* architects
Ontario Bar Association, 345
Ontario College of Pharmacy, 349
Ontario Dental Association, 215–18, 220
Ontario Dental Society, 344
Ontario Educational Society, 242
Ontario Land Surveyors. *See* surveyors

Ontario Medical Association, 337, 343–5
Ontario Medical Council. *See* College of Physicians and Surgeons of Ontario
Ontario Teachers' Association (OTA), 234–5, 240, 243–4
Ormiston, Rev. Dr, 234
Oronhyatekha, Dr, 382
Orton, Henry, 146, 186, 194
Osgoode, William, 13, 17
Osgoode Hall, 74–6, 127, 166, 298
Osgoode Hall Law School, 171, 371–3, 375, 381
Osler, Rev. Featherstone, 37, 40–1, 213, 377–8
Osler family, 76, 377–8

Palmer, Bryan, 247
patent medicines. *See* pharmacists
Patterson, James, 140, 149
Patton, Hon. James, 110
Patrons of Industry, 310–13, 315, 317–18
Payne, J.L., 328–9
Petch, Robert, 145–6
Perth County, professionals in, 249–50, 252, 259, 399
pharmacists, 221–2, 255–6, 262, 300, 315–16, 336, 349, 379; women pharmacists, 322, 324, 327, 349; *see also* professional education
physicians. *See* doctors
Piva, Michael, 403
Powell, Anne, 42
Powell, William Dummer, 13, 16
Powley, Eva Maude, 322, 349
Prentice, Alison, 238
Presbyterian clergy. *See* clergy
Prince, Colonel, 21
Pringle, J.F., 141
profession: changing meaning of,

203–11, 305–10, 320–1, 327, 329, 332, 377–91; Georgian meaning of, 3–13, 205, 377; definition of, xi–xii
professional education, 177–9, 199; in Britain, 3, 6–7, 13–14, 33–4, 88–9, 126, 172, 217, 264–5, 474n.52; British models, 153, 168–9, 233, 358; of clergy, 119–22, 153, 159–63, 170, 174–7, 209–11, 354, 357, 438n.69; of dentists, 216–17, 219–20, 354–5, 357, 359–60; of doctors, 86, 88–9, 153–9, 168–70, 176–7, 209–11, 301, 324–8, 330–2, 349, 354–9, 362–8, 418n.29; in early nineteenth century, 14–15, 32–4, 39–40; of lawyers, 75–80, 164–8, 170–5, 209–11, 294, 328, 330–2, 354–7, 368–75, 447nn.35, 44, 448n.57, 487n.6; of nurses, 326, 376; of pharmacists, 349; and research ideal, 362–8; of surveyors and engineers, 207, 210, 223–4, 228–9, 361–2; of teachers, 207, 235–6, 240–1, 306, 375–6; in United States, 39, 43, 88–9, 126, 216–17, 219, 369; *see also* clergy; dentists; doctors; engineers; lawyers; nurses; pharmacists; surveyors; teachers
professional privileges: attack on, 46–50; of clergy, 51–3; of doctors, 56–8; in later nineteenth century, 308–18; of lawyers, 60–6; mid-century compromise, 66–9; *see also* clergy; dentists; doctors; engineers; lawyers; pharmacists; surveyors
professional work, 127–8; of clergy, 129–38, 149–51; of dentists, 212–15; of doctors, 144–8; of lawyers, 138–44, 148–9; of surveyors and engineers, 223–5, 228; *see also* clergy; dentists; doctors; engineers; lawyers; pharmacists; surveyors

Proudfoot, William, 35
Provincial Land Surveyors. *See* surveyors

Queen's College. *See* Queen's University
Queen's Medical College, 265, 293, 355, 368
Queen's University, 15, 153, 159–60, 178, 263, 357, 361–2, 371
Quinn, Kevin, 160

Radcliff, Thomas, 11
Rankin, Arthur, 52
Rawlyk, George, 160
religious affiliations of professionals, 197
Richards, W.B., 57–8, 64, 74
Richardson, James Henry, 90, 94, 183, 218
Richardson, Ruth, 169
Riddell, William, 46
Risk, R.C.B., 68
Robertson, W.J., 339
Robinson, Henry, 217
Robinson, John Beverley, 6, 8, 19–20, 74, 142
Rogers, Fred, 258
Roland, Charles, 38, 193
Rolph, John, 4, 23, 89, 183, 218
Rolph, Rev. Romaine, 35
Romney, Paul, 46, 71, 127
Roper, Michael, 329
Rosebrugh (doctors), 94
Rosenberg, Charles, 102
Ross, George, 301, 338, 359
Ross, John, 74
Royal College of Dental Surgeons of Ontario (RCDSO), 218, 220, 342, 359; discipline of members, 288, 391; enforcement of legislation, 290–4,

296, 298, 301–2; revolt against, 299–300; women dentists, 323, *see also* dentists
Royal College of Physicians (London), 7, 23, 89
Royal College of Surgeons (London), 14, 24, 89
Rubashewsky, Bohodar, 38, 193
Russell, Peter, 7
Ryerson, Egerton, 15, 36, 117, 182, 232–5, 244

Salvation Army, 279–80; *see also* clergy
Sangster, J.H., 300, 310, 337
School of Practical Science, 229, 361
Scott, Donald, 10
Scott, J.S., 217, 220
Seaborn, Edwin, 40
Semple, Neil, 118–19
Sherwood, Henry, 22, 63–4
Sherwood, Reuben, 223
Shortt, S.E.D., 102–3, 350, 391
Simcoe, Lt-Gov. J.G., 17–18
Smaller, Harry, 243
Smellie, T.S.T., 185–6
Smith, Elizabeth, 324, 329, 332
Smith, Harmaunus, 38–9, 193–4
Smith, Henry, 64, 74
Smith, Larratt, 165–6
social origins and standing, 33, 196–200, 383, 393–5; of clergy, 34, 118–19; of dentists, 216–17; of doctors, 23, 38–9, 88–90, 104–5; of lawyers, 73–5, 82–4; of surveyors and engineers, 223, 228–9; of women professionals, 323; *see also* profession, meaning of
Society for the Propagation of the Gospel, 26–9
solicitors. *See* lawyers
Spelt, Jacob, 249, 252
Stark, Rev. Mark, 28, 44

Starr, Paul, 250–1
stenographic reporters, 304
Stowe, Emily Howard, 323–4
Strachan, John: and definition of ministry, 11–12; and maintenance of clergy, 16, 27–9, 52, 109; and professional education, 14–15, 153; and teaching, 232
Strong-Boag, Veronica, 323, 325
Sullivan, Michael, 90
surgeons. *See* doctors
surveyors, 222–7, 230–2, 246, 318–19, 389; *see also* Association of Ontario Land Surveyors; engineers; professional education; professional work; social origins and standing
Sutton, J.P., 216

Talman, J.J., 13
teachers, 232–46, 306, 378–9; income, 404; women teachers, 238–9, 322; *see also* Ontario Teachers' Association; professional education
Teskey, Luke, 216–17
Thompson, E.P., 46, 200
Thomsonians, 42–3, 48; *see also* doctors
Thorburn, David, 47, 72
Thornburn, James, 218
Toronto General Hospital, 157–9, 264
Toronto School of Medicine, 89, 156–9, 362, 364
Toronto Woman's Medical College, 331, 324, 349
Tosh, John, 329
Townley, Adam, 111
Traill, Catharine Parr, 42, 44
Traves, Tom, 403
Trinity College, 153, 164, 330, 371
Trinity Medical College 89, 154, 156–9, 265, 362, 364
Trout, Dr Jennie, 322–4
Turner, Frank M., 229
Turner, H.E., 110

Ulrich, Laurel, 54
undertakers, 303–4, 308–9
United States, professional education in. *See* professional education
University College, 158, 207, 363
university education. *See* professional education
University of Toronto, 164, 228–9, 356–7, 359–62, 369–71; Faculty of Applied Science and Engineering, 361; Faculty of Law, 371; Faculty of Medicine, 89, 265, 349, 362, 368, 381
Usher, James, 191

Van Die, Marguerite, 182
Vankoughnet, Philip M.M.S., 74
veterinary surgeons, 320
Victoria College, 15, 120, 158, 210, 216–17
Victorian Order of Nurses. *See* nurses
voluntarism and the clergy, 27–31, 36, 51–3, 269–76; *see also* clergy

Wallbridge, Lewis, 74
Walton, Thomas, 185
Warner, John Harley, 45, 55, 98–100, 367

wealth of professionals, 400–5; *see also* clergy; doctors; lawyers
Wells, Josephine, 322, 349
Westfall, William, 13, 118, 127, 281, 387
White, John, 13, 17–18
Widmer, Christopher, 23, 145, 184
Willis, Principal, 160
Willmott, J.B., 216–17
Wilson, Adam, 74, 143, 172, 175, 183,
Wilson, Daniel, 110, 112, 364
Wilson, James, 47–8
women: in clerical partnerships, 149–51; as competitors to men, 328–32; entry into professions, reasons for, 323; feminization of education, 238–9; feminization of religion, 333–4; and meaning of profession, 8, 327, 329, 332; in medical partnership, 444n.108; limits on women's professional work, 325–7, 329–30, 349; *see also* clergy; dentists; doctors; lawyers; midwives; nurses; pharmacists; social origins and standing; teachers
Wright, R. Ramsay, 363–5, 367
Wrong, George, 332

Young, George Paxton, 161, 236

THE ONTARIO HISTORICAL STUDIES SERIES

Peter Oliver, G. *Howard Ferguson: Ontario Tory* (1977)
J.M.S. Careless, ed., *The Pre-Confederation Premiers: Ontario Government Leaders, 1841–1867* (1980)
Charles W. Humphries, *'Honest Enough to Be Bold': The Life and Times of Sir James Pliny Whitney* (1985)
Charles M. Johnston, *E.C. Drury: Agrarian Idealist* (1986)
A.K. McDougall, *John P. Robarts: His Life and Government* (1986)
Roger Graham, *Old Man Ontario: Leslie M. Frost* (1990)
John T. Saywell, *'Just call me Mitch': The Life of Mitchell F. Hepburn* (1991)
A. Margaret Evans, *Sir Oliver Mowat* (1992)
Joseph Schull, *Ontario since 1867* (McClelland and Stewart 1978)
Joseph Schull, *L'Ontario depuis 1867* (McClelland and Stewart 1987)
Olga B. Bishop, Barbara I. Irwin, Clara G. Miller, eds., *Bibliography of Ontario History, 1867–1976: Cultural, Economic, Political, Social* 2 volumes (1980)
Christopher Armstrong, *The Politics of Federalism: Ontario's Relations with the Federal Government, 1867–1942* (1981)
David Gagan, *Hopeful Travellers: Families, Land and Social Change in Mid-Victorian Peel County, Canada West* (1981)
Robert M. Stamp, *The Schools of Ontario, 1876–1976* (1982)
R. Louis Gentilcore and C. Grant Head, *Ontario's History in Maps* (1984)
K.J. Rea, *The Prosperous Years: The Economic History of Ontario, 1939–1975* (1985)
Ian M. Drummond, *Progress without Planning: The Economic History of Ontario from Confederation to the Second World War* (1987)
John Webster Grant, *A Profusion of Spires: Religion in Nineteenth-Century Ontario* (1988)
Susan E. Houston and Alison Prentice, *Schooling and Scholars in Nineteenth-Century Ontario* (1988)
Ann Saddlemyer, ed., *Early Stages: Theatre in Ontario, 1800–1914* (1990)
W.J. Keith, *Literary Images of Ontario* (1992)
Douglas McCalla *Planting the Province: The Economic History of Upper Canada, 1784–1870* (1993)
A.B. McKillop, *Matters of Mind: The University in Ontario, 1791–1951*
R.D. Gidney and W.P.J. Millar, *Professional Gentlemen: The Professions in Nineteenth-Century Ontario*